Today's Moral Problems

3RD EDITION

Today's Moral Problems

EDITED BY

Richard A. Wasserstrom
University of California, Santa Cruz

MACMILLAN PUBLISHING COMPANY
New York
COLLIER MACMILLAN PUBLISHERS
London

Macmillan Publishing Company
866 Third Avenue, New York, New York 10022

Collier Macmillan Canada, Inc.

Library of Congress Cataloging in Publication Data

Main entry under title:

Today's moral problems.
   Includes bibliographies.
   1. United States—Moral conditions.   I. Wasserstrom,
Richard A.
HN90.M6T63 1985   306'.0973   84-5761
ISBN 0-02-424840-1

Printing: 1 2 3 4 5 6 7 8   Year: 5 6 7 8 9 0 1 2 3

ISBN 0-02-424840-1

Preface

The writings in this collection deal with moral issues that have been of special concern to people living in the United States in recent years. In addition, almost all of the selections were written during the past fifteen years. It is worth asking why this latter fact is so. Part of the explanation, of course, is the problems selected for inclusion. Because such issues as abortion, preferential treatment, and sexual morality have been among the particular worries of this generation, it is not surprising that contemporary moral philosophers have turned their attention to them.

But this is not the whole answer. The problems considered in this collection are hardly new problems, or even problems that have only acquired a particular urgency in our own time. Nor have philosophers just become aware of moral issues such as these; morality has been a concern of philosophers for as long as there has been philosophy. So, the recent vintage of most of these pieces does not reflect either a new-found philosophical concern for morality or the rise to prominence of new moral problems. What it does reflect, at least, is a change of sorts in Anglo-American academic philosophy.

For some time philosophers who were interested in moral philosophy were interested primarily in what have been called the problems of metaethics. They were concerned with such things as the analysis and examination of the way moral concepts and moral arguments worked and, sometimes, the development of general theories about the meaning and characteristics of fundamental moral ideas. Their philosophical inquiries were about ethical statements and judgments.

Many of the writings found in this collection are not metaethics but rather normative ethics. That is to say, they are philosophical attempts to elucidate and assess what is to be said for and against particular ways of behaving in respect to particular moral problems. The distinction between metaethics and normative ethics is anything but precise. And even if it were, no philosophical inquiry worthy of respect could help engaging in substantial metaethical activity. Nonetheless, what distinguishes these writings from the writings in moral philosophy of the recent past is this immersion in specific moral issues and this willingness to move to the presentation of more particular moral assessments.

The legal cases and philosophical writings reproduced in this book are arranged in accordance with the particular topics to which they are directly addressed. There is, however, a certain degree of arbitrariness to the organization by topics, and there are themes discussed in the writings that cut across the topics. For example, some of the issues dealt with in the final section, "Humans and the Nonhuman Environment," are also relevant to the subjects of abortion, war, and sexual morality. And the question of who is a person and why that question matters is a theme that runs through most, if not all, of the topics considered. For this reason, the readings can certainly be approached in ways different from that suggested by the arrangement presented here. The reader should, in any event, be prepared to integrate the ideas discussed under any of the headings wherever they are elsewhere relevant.

I think that the inquiries collected here are exciting both because of what they teach about the moral problems they examine and because of what they show about this additional aspect of philosophical activity. I hope that those who read these philosophical writings will find them exhilarating. I hope that they will serve to introduce people to some of the important, but less traditional, types of philosophical explorations that can take place in respect to morality. And I hope, as well, that these writings reveal to them some of the ways in which philosophy can make an important contribution to an adequate and informed understanding of serious, live moral issues.

R. A. W.

Contents

THREE

Sexual Morality

177

FOUR

Professional Responsibility

243

FIVE

War

327

SIX

Abortion 395

SEVEN

Humans and the Nonhuman Environment 459

ONE

Racism and Sexism

ON RACISM AND SEXISM

RICHARD A. WASSERSTROM

INTRODUCTION

Racism and sexism are two central issues that engage the attention of many persons living within the United States today. But while there is relatively little disagreement about their importance as topics, there is substantial, vehement, and apparently intractable disagreement about what individuals, practices, ideas, and institutions are either racist or sexist—and for what reasons. In dispute are a number of related questions concerning how individuals ought to regard and respond to matters relating to race or sex.

There are, I think, a number of important similarities between issues of racism and issues of sexism, but there are also some significant differences. More specifically, while the same general method of analysis can usefully be employed to examine a number of the issues that arise in respect to either, the particular topics of controversy often turn out to be rather different. What I want to do in this essay is first propose a general way of looking at issues of racism and sexism, then look at several of the respects in which racism and sexism are alike and different, and then, finally, examine one somewhat

EDITOR'S NOTE: This is a somewhat revised version of Parts I and II of "Racism, Sexism, and Preferential Treatment: An Approach to the Topics" published in *UCLA Law Review* Vol. 24, 581–622 (1977), copyright © 1977 by Richard A. Wasserstrom. Some footnotes have been deleted and the remaining ones renumbered.

neglected but fundamental issue; namely that of what a genuinely nonracist or nonsexist society might look like.

There are, I think, at least four questions that anyone interested in issues of racism and sexism ought to see as both distinct and worth asking. The first is what I call the question of the social realities. That question is concerned with rendering a correct description of the existing social arrangements, including the existing institutional structures, practices, attitudes and ideology. The second is devoted to the question of explanation. Given a correct understanding of what the existing social reality is, there can be a variety of theories to explain how things got that way and by what mechanisms they tend to be perpetuated. Much of the feminist literature, for example, is concerned with the problem of explanation. Complex and sophisticated accounts have been developed which utilize the theories of Freud, Levi-Strauss, and Marx to explain the oppression of women. Other, equally complex accounts have insisted on the non-reductionist character of the nature and causes of the present sexual arrangements. Although important in their own right, as well as for the solution of other problems, I will have virtually nothing else to say about these explanatory issues in this essay.

The third question, and one that I will concentrate upon, is what I term the question of ideals. I see it as concerned with asking: If we had the good society, if we could change the social reality so that it conformed to some vision of what a nonracist or nonsexist society would be like, what would that society's institutions, practices, and ideology be in respect to matters of racial or sexual differentiation? Here, what I find especially interesting, is the question of whether anything like the ideal that is commonly accepted as a very plausible one for a nonracist society can be as plausibly proposed for a conception of a nonsexist society.

The fourth and final question is that of instrumentalities. Once one has developed the correct account of the social realities, and the most defensible conception of what the good society would look like, and the most comprehensive theory of how the social realities came about and are maintained, then the remaining question is the instrumental one of social change: How, given all of this, does one most effectively and fairly move from the social realities to a closer approximation of the ideal. This, too, is a question with which I will not be concerned in what follows, although it is, for instance, within this context and this perspective that, it seems to me, all of the significant questions concerning the justifiability of programs of preferential treatment arise. That is to say, the way to decide whether such programs are justifiable is to determine whether they are appropriate means by which to bring about a particular, independently justifiable end.

These, then, are four central questions which any inquiry into sexism, racism or any other comparable phenomenon must distinguish and examine. I turn first to an examination of this question of the social realities and then to a consideration of ideals and the nature of a nonracist or a nonsexist society.

I. SOCIAL REALITIES

A. The Position of Blacks and Women

Methodologically, the first thing it is important to note is that to talk about social realities is to talk about a particular social and cultural context. And in our particular social and cultural context race and sex are socially very important categories. They are so in virtue of the fact that we live in a culture which has, throughout its existence, made race and sex extremely important characteristics of and for all the people living in the culture.[1]

It is surely possible to imagine a culture in which race would be an unimportant, insignificant characteristic of individuals. In such a culture race would be largely if not exclusively a matter of superficial physiology; a matter, we might say, simply of the way one looked. And if it were, then any analysis of race and racism would necessarily assume very different dimensions from what they do in our society. In such a culture, the meaning of the term "race" would itself have to change substantially. This can be seen by the fact that in such a culture it would literally make no sense to say of a person that he or she was "passing."[2] This is something that can be said and understood in our own culture and it shows at least that to talk of race is to talk of more than the way one looks.[3]

Sometimes when people talk about what is wrong with affirmative action programs, or programs of preferential hiring, they say that what is wrong with such programs is that they take a thing as superficial as an individual's

---

[1] In asserting the importance of one's race and sex in our culture I do not mean to deny the importance of other characteristics—in particular, socioeconomic class. I do think that in our culture race and sex are two very important facts about a person, and I am skeptical of theories which "reduce" the importance of these features to a single, more basic one, *e.g.,* class. But apart from this one bit of skepticism I think that all of what I have to say is compatible with several different theories concerning why race and sex are so important—including, for instance, most versions of Marxism. *See, e.g.,* the account provided in J. Mitchell, *Woman's Estate* (1971). The correct causal explanation for the social realities I describe is certainly an important question, both in its own right and for some of the issues I address. It is particularly significant for the issue of how to alter the social realities to bring them closer to the ideal. Nonetheless, I have limited the scope of my inquiry to exclude a consideration of this large, difficult topic.

[2] Passing is the phenomenon in which a person who in some sense knows himself or herself to be black "passes" as white because he or she looks white. A version of this is described in Sinclair Lewis' novel *Kingsblood Royal* (1947), where the protagonist discovers when he is an adult that he, his father, and his father's mother are black (or, in the idiom of the late 1940s, Negro) in virtue of the fact that his great grandfather was black. His grandmother knew this and was consciously passing. When he learns about his ancestry, one decision he has to make is whether to continue to pass, or to acknowledge to the world that he is in fact "Negro."

[3] That looking black is not in our culture a necessary condition for being black can be seen from the phenomenon of passing. That it is not a sufficient condition can be seen from the book *Black Like Me* (1960), by John Howard Griffin, where "looking black" is easily understood by the reader to be different from being black. I suspect that the concept of being black is, in our culture, one which combines both physiological and ancestral criteria in some moderately complex fashion.

race and turn it into something important.[4] They say that a person's race doesn't matter; other things do, such as qualifications. Whatever else may be said of statements such as these, as descriptions of the social realities they seem to be simply false. One complex but true empirical fact about our society is that the race of an individual is much more than a fact of superficial physiology. It is, instead, one of the dominant characteristics that affects both the way the individual looks at the world and the way the world looks at the individual. As I have said, that need not be the case. It may in fact be very important that we work toward a society in which that would not be the case, but it is the case now and it must be understood in any adequate and complete discussion of racism. That is why, too, it does not make much sense when people sometimes say, in talking about the fact that they are not racists, that they would not care if an individual were green and came from Mars, they would treat that individual the same way they treat people exactly like themselves. For part of *our* social and cultural history is to treat people of certain races in a certain way, and we do not have a social or cultural history of treating green people from Mars in any particular way. To put it simply, it is to misunderstand the social realities of race and racism to think of them simply as questions of how some people respond to other people whose skins are of different hues, irrespective of the social context.

I can put the point another way: Race does not function in our culture as does eye color. Eye color is an irrelevant category; nobody cares what color people's eyes are; it is not an important cultural fact; nothing turns on what eye color you have. It is important to see that race is not like that at all. And this truth affects what will and will not count as cases of racism. In our culture to be nonwhite—especially to be black[5]—is to be treated and seen to be a member of a group that is different from and inferior to the group of standard, fully developed persons, the adult white males. To be black is to be a member of what was a despised minority and what is still a disliked and oppressed one.[6] That is simply part of the awful truth of our cultural

---

[4] Mr. Justice Douglas suggests something like this in his dissent in *DeFunis:* "The consideration of race as a measure of an applicant's qualification normally introduces a capricious and irrelevant factor working an invidious discrimination." *DeFunis* v. *Odegaard,* 416 U.S. 312, 333 (1974).

[5] There are significant respects in which the important racial distinction is between being white and being nonwhite, and there are other significant respects in which the fact of being black has its own special meaning and importance. My analysis is conducted largely in terms of what is involved in being black. To a considerable extent, however, what I say directly applies to the more inclusive category of being nonwhite. To the extent to which what I say does not apply to the other nonwhite racial distinctions, the analysis of those distinctions should, of course, be undertaken separately.

[6] *See, e.g.,* J. Baldwin, *The Fire Next Time* (1963); W. E. B. DuBois, *The Souls of Black Folks* (1903); R. Ellison, *Invisible Man* (1952); J. Franklin, *From Slavery to Freedom* (3d ed. 1968); C. Hamilton and S. Carmichael, *Black Power* (1967); Report of the U.S. Commission on Civil Disorders (1968); M. Kilson, "Whither Integration?," 45, *Am Scholar* 360 (1976); and hundreds, if not thousands of other books and articles, both literary and empirical. These sources describe a great variety of features of the black experience in America: such things as the historical as well as the present day material realities, and the historical as well as present day

and social history, and a significant feature of the social reality of our culture today.

We can see fairly easily that the two sexual categories, like the racial ones, are themselves in important respects products of the society. Like one's race, one's sex is not merely or even primarily a matter of physiology. To see this we need only realize that we can understand the idea of a transsexual. A transsexual is someone who would describe himself or herself as a person who is essentially a female but through some accident of nature is trapped in a male body, or a person who is essentially a male but through some accident of nature is trapped in the body of a female. His (or her) description is some kind of a shorthand way of saying that he (or she) is more comfortable with the role allocated by the culture to people who are physiologically of the opposite sex. The fact that we regard this assertion of the transsexual as intelligible seems to me to show how deep the notion of sexual identity is in our culture and how little it has to do with physiological differences between males and females. Because people do pass in the context of race and because we can understand what passing means; because people are transsexuals and because we can understand what transsexuality means, we can see that the existing social categories of both race and sex are in this sense creations of the culture.

It is even clearer in the case of sex than in the case of race that one's sexual identity is a centrally important, crucially relevant category within our culture. I think, in fact, that it is more important and more fundamental than one's race. It is evident that there are substantially different role expectations and role assignments to persons in accordance with their sexual physiology, and that the positions of the two sexes in the culture are distinct. We do have a patriarchal society in which it matters enormously whether one is a male or a female.[7] By almost all important measures it is more advantageous to be a male rather than a female.

---

ideological realities, the way black people have been and are thought about within the culture. In *Kingsblood Royal, supra* note 2, Lewis provides a powerful account of what he calls the "American Credo" about the Negro, circa 1946. *Id*. at 194–97.

[7] The best general account I have read of the structure of patriarchy and of its major dimensions and attributes is that found in *Sexual Politics* in the chapter, "Theory of Sexual Politics." K. Millett, *Sexual Politics* 23–58 (1970). The essay seems to me to be truly a major contribution to an understanding of the subject. Something of the essence of the thesis is contained in the following:

"[A] disinterested examination of our system of sexual relationship must point out that the situation between the sexes now, and throughout history, is a case of that phenomenon Max Weber defined as *herrschaft,* a relationship of dominance and subordinance. What goes largely unexamined, often even unacknowledged (yet is institutionalized nonetheless) in our social order, is the birthright priority whereby males rule females. Through this system a most ingenious form of 'interior colonization' has been achieved. It is one which tends moreover to be sturdier than any form of segregation and more rigorous than class stratification, more uniform, certainly more enduring. However muted its present appearance may be, sexual dominion obtains nevertheless as perhaps the most pervasive ideology of our culture and provides its most fundamental concept of power.

"This is so because our society, like all other historical civilizations, is a patriarchy. The fact

Women and men are socialized differently. We learn very early and force-fully that we are either males or females and that much turns upon which sex we are. The evidence seems to be overwhelming and well-documented that sex roles play a fundamental role in the way persons think of themselves and the world—to say nothing of the way the world thinks of them.[8] Men and women are taught to see men as independent, capable, and powerful; men and women are taught to see women as dependent, limited in abilities, and passive. A woman's success or failure in life is defined largely in terms of her activities within the family. It is important for her that she marry, and when she does she is expected to take responsibility for the wifely tasks: the housework, the child care, and the general emotional welfare of the husband and children.[9] Her status in society is determined in substantial measure by the vocation and success of her husband.[10] Economically, women

---

is evident at once if one recalls that the military, industry, technology, universities, science, political office, and finance—in short, every avenue of power within the society, including the coercive force of the police, is entirely in male hands. . . ."

"Sexual politics obtains consent through the 'socialization' of both sexes to basic patriarchal politics with regard to temperament, role, and status. As to status, a pervasive assent to the prejudice of male superiority guarantees superior status in the male, inferior in the female. The first item, temperament, involves the formation of human personality along stereotyped lines of sex category ('masculine' and 'feminine'), based on the needs and values of the dominant group and dictated by what its members cherish in themselves and find convenient in subordinates: aggression, intelligence, force and efficacy in the male; passivity, ignorance, docility, 'virtue,' and ineffectuality in the female. This is complemented by a second factor, sex role, which decrees a consonant and highly elaborate code of conduct, gesture and attitude for each sex. In terms of activity, sex role assigns domestic service and attendance upon infants to the female, the rest of human achievement, interest and ambition to the male. . . . Were one to analyze the three categories one might designate status as the political component, role as the sociological, and temperament as the psychological—yet their interdependence is unquestionable and they form a chain."

Id. at 24–26 (footnotes omitted).

[8] *See, e.g.*, Hochschild, "A Review of Sex Role Research," 78 *Am. J. Soc.*, 1011 (1973), which reviews and very usefully categorizes the enormous volume of literature on this topic. *See also* Stewart, "Social Influences on Sex Differences in Behavior," in Sex Differences 138 (M. Teitelbaum, ed., 1976); Weitzman, "Sex Role Socialization," in *Women: A Feminist Perspective*, 105 (J. Freeman, ed., 1975). A number of the other pieces in *Women: A Feminist Perspective* also describe and analyze the role of women in the culture, including the way they are thought of by the culture.

[9] "For the married woman, her husband and children must always come first; her own needs and desires, last. When the children reach school age, they no longer require constant attention. The emotional-expressive function assigned to the woman is still required of her. Called the 'stroking function' by sociologist Jessie Bernard, it consists of showing solidarity, raising the status of others, giving help, rewarding, agreeing, concurring, complying, understanding, and passively accepting. The woman is expected to give emotional support and comfort to other family members, to make them feel like good and worthwhile human beings." B. Deckard, *The Women's Movement*, 59 (1975), *citing* J. Bernard, *Women and the Public Interest*, 88 (1971).

"Patriarchy's chief institution is the family. It is both a mirror of and a connection with the larger society: a patriarchal unit within a patriarchal whole. Mediating between the individual and the social structure, the family effects control and conformity where political and other authorities are insufficient."

K. Millett, *supra* note 7, at 33.

[10] "Even if the couple consciously try to attain an egalitarian marriage, so long as the traditional division of labor is maintained, the husband will be 'more equal.' He is the provider not only of money but of status. Especially if he is successful, society values what he does; she

are substantially worse off than men. They do not receive any pay for the work that is done in the home. As members of the labor force their wages are significantly lower than those paid to men, even when they are engaged in similar work and have similar educational backgrounds.[11] The higher the prestige or the salary of the job, the less present women are in the labor force. And, of course, women are conspicuously absent from most positions of authority and power in the major economic and political institutions of our society.

As is true for race, it is also a significant social fact that to be a female is to be an entity or creature viewed as different from the standard, fully developed person who is male as well as white. But to be female, as opposed to being black, is not to be conceived of as simply a creature of less worth. That is one important thing that differentiates sexism from racism: The ideology of sex, as opposed to the ideology of race, is a good deal more complex and confusing. Women are both put on a pedestal and deemed not fully developed persons. They are idealized; their approval and admiration is sought; and they are at the same time regarded as less competent than men and less able to live fully developed, fully human lives—for that is what men do.[12] At best, they are viewed and treated as having properties and attributes that are valuable and admirable for humans of this type. For example, they may be viewed as especially empathetic, intuitive, loving, and nurturing. At best, these qualities are viewed as good properties for women to have, and, provided they are properly muted, are sometimes valued within the more well-rounded male. Because the sexual ideology is complex, con-

---

is just a housewife. Their friends are likely to be his friends and co-workers; in their company, she is just his wife. Because his provider function is essential for the family's survival, major family decisions are made in terms of how they affect his career. He need not and usually does not act like the authoritarian paterfamilius [*sic*] of the Victorian age. His power and status are derived from his function in the family and are secure so long as the traditional division of labor is maintained."
B. Deckard, *supra* note 9, at 62.
[11] In 1970, women workers were, on the average, paid only 59 percent of men's wages. And when wages of persons with similar educational levels are compared, women still were paid over 40 percent less than men. *Id.* at 79–81.
[12] "It is generally accepted that Western patriarchy has been much softened by the concepts of courtly and romantic love. While this is certainly true, such influence has also been vastly overestimated. In comparison with the candor of 'machismo' or oriental behavior, one realizes how much of a concession traditional chivalrous behavior represents—a sporting kind of reparation to allow the subordinate female certain means of saving face. While a palliative to the injustice of woman's social position, chivalry is also a technique for disguising it. One must acknowledge that the chivalrous stance is a game the master group plays in elevating its subject to pedestal level. Historians of courtly love stress the fact that the raptures of the poets had no effect upon the legal or economic standing of women, and very little upon their social status. As the sociologist Hugo Biegel has observed, both the courtly and the romantic versions of love are 'grants' which the male concedes out of his total powers. Both have the effect of obscuring the patriarchal character of Western culture and in their general tendency to attribute impossible virtues to women, have ended by confining them in a narrow and often remarkably conscribing sphere of behavior. It was a Victorian habit, for example, to insist the female assume the function of serving as the male's conscience and living the life of goodness he found tedious but felt someone ought to do anyway."
K. Millett, *supra* note 7, at 36–37.

fusing, and variable, it does not unambiguously proclaim the lesser value attached to being female rather than being male, nor does it unambiguously correspond to the existing social realities. For these, among other reasons, sexism could plausibly be regarded as a deeper phenomenon than racism. It is more deeply embedded in the culture, and thus less visible. Being harder to detect, it is harder to eradicate. Moreover, it is less unequivocally regarded as unjust and unjustifiable. That is to say, there is less agreement within the dominant ideology that sexism even implies an unjustifiable practice or attitude. Hence, many persons announce, without regret or embarrassment, that they are sexists or male chauvinists; very few announce openly that they are racists.[13] For all of these reasons sexism may be a more insidious evil than racism, but there is little merit in trying to decide between two seriously objectionable practices which one is worse.

While I do not think that I have made very controversial claims about either our cultural history or our present-day culture, I am aware of the fact that they have been stated very imprecisely and that I have offered little evidence to substantiate them. In a crude way we ought to be able both to understand the claims and to see that they are correct if we reflect seriously and critically upon our own cultural institutions, attitudes, and practices. But in a more refined, theoretical way, I am imagining that a more precise and correct description of the social reality in respect to race and sex would be derivable from a composite, descriptive account of our society which utilized the relevant social sciences to examine such things as the society's institutions, practices, attitudes and ideology[14]—if the social sciences could be value-free and unaffected in outlook or approach by the fact that they, themselves, are largely composed of persons who are white and male.[15]

[13] Thus, even after his "joke" about black persons became known to the public, the former secretary of agriculture, Earl Butz, took great pains to insist that this in no way showed that he was a racist. This is understandable, given the strongly condemnatory feature of being described as a racist.

Equally illuminating was the behavior of Butz's associates and superiors. Then-President Ford, for example, critized Butz for the joke, but did not demand Butz's removal until there was a strong public outcry. It was as though Butz's problem was that he had been indiscreet; he had done something rude like belching in public. What Ford, Butz, and others apparently failed to grasp is that it is just as wrong to tell these jokes in private because to tell a joke of this sort is to have a view about what black people are like: that they can appropriately be· ridiculed as being creatures who care only about intercourse, shoes, and defecation. What these persons also failed to grasp is how implausible it is to believe that one can hold these views about black people and at the same time deal with them in a nonracist fashion.

[14] At a minimum, this account would include (1) a description of the economic, political, and social positions of blacks and whites, males and females in the culture; (2) a description of the sexual and racial roles, *i.e.,* the rules, conventions and expectations concerning how males and females, blacks and whites, should behave, and the attitudes and responses produced by these roles; and (3) a description of the de facto ideology of racial and sexual differences. This would include popular beliefs about how males and females, blacks and whites, differ, as well as the beliefs as to what accounts for these differences, roles, and economic, political and social realities.

[15] The problem of empirical objectivity is compounded by the fact that part of the dominant, white male ideology is that white males are the one group in society whose members are able to be genuinely detached and objective when it comes to things like an understanding of the

Viewed from the perspective of social reality it should be clear, too, that racism and sexism should not be thought of as phenomena that consist simply in taking a person's race or sex into account, or even simply in taking a person's race or sex into account in an arbitrary way. Instead, racism and sexism consist in taking race and sex into account in a certain way, in the context of a specific set of institutional arrangements and a specific ideology which together create and maintain a specific *system* of institutions, role assignments, beliefs and attitudes. That system is one, and has been one, in which political, economic, and social power and advantage is concentrated in the hands of those who are white and male.

The evils of such systems are, however, not all of a piece. For instance, sometimes people say that what was wrong with the system of racial discrimination in the South was that it took an irrelevant characteristic, namely race, and used it systematically to allocate social benefits and burdens of various sorts. The defect was the irrelevance of the characteristic used, i.e., race, for that meant that individuals ended up being treated in a manner that was arbitrary and capricious.

I do not think that was the central flaw at all—at least of much of the system. Take, for instance, the most hideous of the practices, human slavery. The primary thing that was wrong with the institution was not that the particular individuals who were assigned the place of slaves were assigned there arbitrarily because the assignment was made in virtue of an irrelevant characteristic, i.e., their race. Rather, it seems to me clear that the primary thing that was and is wrong with slavery is the practice itself—the fact of some individuals being able to own other individuals and all that goes with that practice. It would not matter by what criterion individuals were assigned; human slavery would still be wrong. And the same can be said for many of the other discrete practices and institutions that comprised the system of racial discrimination even after human slavery was abolished. The practices were unjustifiable—they were oppressive—and they would have been so no matter how the assignment of victims had been made. What made it worse, still, was that the institutions and ideology all interlocked to create a system of human oppression whose effects on those living under it were as devastating as they were unjustifiable.

Some features of the system of sexual oppression are like this and others are different. For example, if it is true that women are socialized to play the role of servers of men and if they are in general assigned that position in the

place of race and sex in the culture. Thus, for example, when a sex-discrimination suit was brought against a law firm and the case was assigned to Judge Constance Motley, the defendant filed a motion that she be disqualified partly because, as a woman judge, she would be biased in favor of the plaintiff. Judge Motley denied the motion. *Blank* v. *Sullivan & Cromwell,* 418 F. Supp. 1 (S.D.N.Y. 1975), *writ of mandamus denied sub nom. Sullivan & Cromwell* v. *Motley,* No. 75–3045 (2d Cir. Aug. 26, 1975). Explaining her decision, Judge Motley stated: "[I]f background or sex or race of each judge were, by *definition,* sufficient grounds for removal, no judge on this court could hear this case, or many others, by virtue of the fact that all of them were attorneys, of a sex, often with distinguished law firm or public service backgrounds." 418 F. Supp. at 4 (emphasis added).

society, what is objectionable about that practice is the practice itself. It is not that women are being arbitrarily or capriciously assigned the social role of server, but rather that such a role is at least *prima facie* unjustifiable as a role in a decent society. As a result, the assignment on any basis of individuals to such a role is objectionable.

The assignment of women to primary responsibility for child rearing and household maintenance may be different; it may be objectionable on grounds of unfairness of another sort. That is to say, if we assume that these are important but undesirable aspects of social existence—if we assume that they are, relatively speaking, unsatisfying and unfulfilling ways to spend one's time, then the objection is that women are unduly and unfairly allocated a disproportionate share of unpleasant, unrewarding work. Here the objection, if it is proper, is to the degree to which the necessary burden is placed to a greater degree than is fair on women, rather than shared equally by persons of both sexes.

Even here, though, it is important to see that the essential feature of both racism and sexism consists in the fact that race or sex is taken into account in the context of a specific set of arrangements and a specific ideology which is systemic and which treats and regards persons who are nonwhite or female in a comprehensive, systemic way. Whether it would be capricious to take either a person's race or a person's sex into account in the good society, because race and sex were genuinely irrelevant characteristics is a question that can only be answered after we have a clearer idea of what the good society would look like in respect either to race or sex.

Another way to bring this out, as well as to show another respect in which racism and sexism are different, concerns segregated bathrooms. We know, for instance, that it is wrong, clearly racist, to have racially segregated bathrooms. There is, however, no common conception that it is wrong, clearly sexist, to have sexually segregated ones. How is this to be accounted for? The answer to the question of why it was and is racist to have racially segregated bathrooms can be discovered through a consideration of the role that this practice played in that system of racial segregation we had in the United States—from, in other words, an examination of the social realities. For racially segregated bathrooms were an important part of that system. And that system had an ideology; it was complex and perhaps not even wholly internally consistent. A significant feature of the ideology was that blacks were not only less than fully developed humans, but that they were also dirty and impure. They were the sorts of creatures who could and would contaminate white persons if they came into certain kinds of contact with them— in the bathroom, at the dinner table, or in bed, although it was appropriate for blacks to prepare and handle food, and even to nurse white infants. This ideology was intimately related to a set of institutional arrangements and power relationships in which whites were politically, economically, and socially dominant. The ideology supported the institutional arrangements, and the institutional arrangements reinforced the ideology. The net effect was that racially segregated bathrooms were both a part of the institutional mechanism of oppression and an instantiation of this ideology of racial taint. The point of maintaining racially segregated bathrooms was not in any simple or direct sense to keep both whites and blacks from using each other's bathrooms; it was to make sure that blacks would not contaminate bathrooms used by whites. The practice also taught both whites and blacks that certain kinds of contacts were forbidden because whites would be degraded by the contact with the blacks.

The failure to understand the character of these institutions of racial oppression is what makes some of the judicial reasoning about racial discrimination against blacks so confusing and unsatisfactory. At times when the courts have tried to explain what is constitutionally wrong with racial segregation, they have said that the problem is that race is an inherently suspect category. What they have meant by this, or have been thought to mean, is that any differentiation among human beings on the basis of racial identity is inherently unjust, because arbitrary, and therefore any particular case of racial differentiation must be shown to be fully rational and justifiable.[16] But the primary evil of the various schemes of racial segregation against blacks that the courts were being called upon to assess was not that such schemes were a capricious and irrational way of allocating public benefits and burdens. That might well be the primary wrong with racial segregation if we lived in a society very different from the one we have. The primary evil of these schemes was instead that they designedly and effectively marked off all black persons as degraded, dirty, less than fully developed persons who were unfit for full membership in the political, social, and moral community.[17]

It is worth observing that the social reality of sexually segregated bathrooms appears to be different. The idea behind such sexual segregation seems to have more to do with the mutual undesirability of the use by both sexes of the same bathroom at the same time. There is no notion of the possibility of

---

[16] Thus, in *Bolling* v. *Sharpe*, 347 U.S. 497 (1953), the Supreme Court said that what was wrong with preventing black children from attending the all white schools of the District of Columbia was that "[s]egregation in public education is not reasonably related to any proper governmental objective, and thus it imposes on Negro children of the District of Columbia a burden that constitutes an arbitrary deprivation of their liberty in violation of the Due Process Clause." *Id.* at 500. I ignore those cases in which the courts decline to formulate a view about racial differentiation because the behavior involved is not the sort that the law thinks it appropriate to deal with, *e.g.*, "private" racial discrimination.

[17] Others have made this general point about the nature of the evil of racial segregation in the United States. *See, e.g.,* Fiss, "Groups and Equal Protection," 5 *Phil. & Pub. Aff.,* 107 (1976); Thalberg, "Reverse Discrimination and the Future," 5 *Phil. F.,* 268 (1973).

The failure fully to understand this general point seems to me to be one of the things wrong with Weschler's famous article, "Toward Neutral Principles of Constitutional Interpretation," 73 *Harv. L. Rev.,* 1 (1959). Near the very end of the piece Weschler reports, "In the days when I joined with Charles H. Houston [a well-known black lawyer] in a litigation in the Supreme Court, before the present building was constructed, he did not suffer more than I in knowing that we had to go to Union Station to lunch together during the recess." *Id.* at 34. If the stress in that sentence is wholly on the fact of *knowing,* no one can say for certain that Weschler is wrong. But what is certain is that Charles H. Houston suffered more than Weschler from *living* in a system in which he could only lunch at Union Station.

contamination; or even directly of inferiority and superiority. What seems to be involved—at least in part—is the importance of inculcating and preserving a sense of secrecy concerning the genitalia of the opposite sex. What seems to be at stake is the maintenance of that same sense of mystery or forbiddenness about the other sex's sexuality which is fostered by the general prohibition upon public nudity and the unashamed viewing of genitalia.

Sexually segregated bathrooms simply play a different role in our culture than did racially segregated ones. But that is not to say that the role they play is either benign or unobjectionable—only that it is different. Sexually segregated bathrooms may well be objectionable, but here too, the objection is not on the ground that they are prima facie capricious or arbitrary. Rather, the case against them now would rest on the ground that they are, perhaps, one small part of that scheme of sex-role differentiation which uses the mystery of sexual anatomy, among other things, to maintain the primacy of hetero-sexual sexual attraction central to that version of the patriarchal system of power relationships we have today.[18] Once again, whether sexually segregated bathrooms would be objectionable, because irrational, in the good society depends once again upon what the good society would look like in respect to sexual differentiation.

B. Types of Racism or Sexism

Another recurring question that can profitably be examined within the perspective of social realities is whether the legal system is racist or sexist. Indeed, it seems to me essential that the social realities of the relationships and ideologies concerning race and sex be kept in mind whenever one is trying to assess claims that are made about the racism or sexism of important institutions such as the legal system. It is also of considerable importance in assessing such claims to understand that even within the perspective of social reality, racism or sexism can manifest itself, or be understood, in different ways. That these are both important points can be seen through a brief examination of the different, distinctive ways in which our own legal system might plausibly be understood to be racist. The mode of analysis I propose serves as well, I believe, for an analogous analysis of the sexism of the legal system, although I do not undertake the latter analysis in this paper.

The first type of racism is the simplest and the least controversial. It is the case of overt racism, in which a law or a legal institution expressly takes into account the race of individuals in order to assign benefits and burdens in such a way as to bestow an unjustified benefit upon a member or members of the racially dominant group or an unjustified burden upon members of the racial groups that are oppressed. We no longer have many, if any, cases

---

[18] This conjecture about the role of sexually segregated bathrooms may well be inaccurate or incomplete. The sexual segregation of bathrooms may have more to do with privacy than with patriarchy. However, if so, it is at least odd that what the institution makes relevant is sex rather than merely the ability to perform the eliminatory acts in private.

of overt racism in our legal system today, although we certainly had a number in the past. Indeed, the historical system of formal, racial segregation was both buttressed by, and constituted of, a number of overtly racist laws and practices. At different times in our history, racism included laws and practices which dealt with such things as the exclusion of nonwhites from the franchise, from decent primary and secondary schools and most professional schools, and the prohibition against interracial marriages.

The second type of racism is very similar to overt racism. It is covert, but intentional, racism, in which a law or a legal institution has as its purpose the allocation of benefits and burdens in order to support the power of the dominant race, but does not use race specifically as a basis for allocating these benefits and burdens. One particularly good historical example involves the use of grandfather clauses which were inserted in statutes governing voter registration in a number of states after passage of the Fifteenth Amendment.[19]

Covert racism within the law is not entirely a thing of the past. Many instances of de facto school segregation in the North and West are cases of covert racism. At times certain school boards—virtually all of which are overwhelmingly white in composition—quite consciously try to maintain exclusively or predominantly white schools within a school district. The classifications such school boards use are not ostensibly racial, but are based upon the places of residence of the affected students. These categories provide the opportunity for covert racism in engineering the racial composition of individual schools within the board's jurisdiction.[20]

What has been said so far is surely neither novel nor controversial. What is interesting, however, is that a number of persons appear to believe that as long as the legal system is not overtly or covertly racist, there is nothing to the charge that it is racist. So, for example, Mr. Justice Powell said in a speech a few years ago:

> It is of course true that we have witnessed racial injustice in the past, as has every other country with significant racial diversity. But no one can fairly question the present national commitment to full equality and justice. Racial discrimination, by state action, is now proscribed by laws and court decisions which protect civil liberties more broadly than in any other country. But laws alone are not enough. Racial prejudice in the hearts of men cannot be legislated out of existence; it will

---

[19] *See, e.g., Guinn* v. *United States,* 238 U.S. 347 (1915). Such statutes provided that the grandchild of someone who had been registered to vote in the state was permitted to vote in that state; but the grandchild of somebody who had never been registered to vote in the state had to take a special test in order to become qualified to vote. It does not take much knowledge of history to know that in most of the southern states few if any black people had grandparents who before the Civil War were registered to vote. And the persons who enacted these laws knew it too. So even though race was not made a category by the described laws, they effectively divided people on grounds of race into those who were qualified to vote without more, and those who had to submit to substantially more rigorous tests before they could exercise the franchise. All of this was done, as is well known, so as to perpetuate the control of the franchise by whites.

[20] *See e.g., Crawford* v. *Board of Educ.,* 17 Cal. 3d 280 (1976); *Jackson* v. *Pasadena City School Dist.,* 59 Cal. 2d 876, 382 P.2d 878, 31 *Cal. Rptr.* 606 (1963).

pass only in time, and as human beings of all races learn in humility to respect each other—a process not furthered by recrimination or undue self-accusation.[21]

I believe it is a mistake to think about the problem of racism in terms of overt or covert racial discrimination by state action, which is now banished, and racial prejudice, which still lingers, but only in the hearts of persons. For there is another, more subtle kind of racism—unintentional, perhaps, but effective—which is as much a part of the legal system as are overt and covert racist laws and practices. It is what some critics of the legal system probably mean when they talk about the "institutional racism" of the legal system.[22]

There are at least two kinds of institutional racism. The first is the racism of sub-institutions within the legal system such as the jury, or the racism of practices built upon or countenanced by the law. These institutions and practices very often, if not always, reflect in important and serious ways a variety of dominant values in the operation of what is apparently a neutral legal mechanism. The result is the maintenance and reenforcement of a system in which whites dominate over nonwhites. One relatively uninteresting (because familiar) example is the case of de facto school segregation. As observed above, some cases of de facto segregation are examples of covert racism. But even in school districts where there is no intention to divide pupils on grounds of race so as to maintain existing power relationships along racial lines, school attendance zones are utilized which are based on the geographical location of the pupil. Because it is a fact in our culture that there is racial discrimination against black people in respect to housing, it is also a fact that any geographical allocation of pupils—unless one pays a lot of attention to housing patterns—will have the effect of continuing to segregate minority pupils very largely on grounds of race. It is perfectly appropriate to regard this effect as a case of racism in public education.[23]

A less familiar, and hence perhaps more instructive, example concerns the question of the importance of having blacks on juries, especially in cases in which blacks are criminal defendants. The orthodox view within the law is

---

[21] *New York Times,* August 31, 1972, § 1, at 33, col. 3.

[22] All of the laws, institutional arranagements, etc., that I analyze are, I think, cases of racism and not, for example, cases of prejudice. The latter concept I take to refer more specifically to the defective, incomplete or objectionable beliefs and attitudes of individuals. Prejudiced individuals often engage in racist acts, enact racist laws and participate in racist institutions. But they need not. Nor is it true that the only persons connected with racist acts, laws, or institutions need be prejudiced individuals.

A perceptive account of the differences between prejudice and racism, and of the different kinds of racism, including institutional racism of the sorts I discuss below, can be found in M. Jones, "Prejudice and Racism" (1972). *See especially id.* at 60–115 (ch. 4, "Perspectives on Prejudice"); *id.* at 116–67 (ch. 5, "Realities of Racism"). A somewhat analogous set of distinctions concerning sexism is made in Jaggar, "On Sexual Equality," 84 *Ethics,* 275, 276–77 (1974).

[23] One example of what may have been an instance of genuine de facto racism in a non-educational setting is found in *Gregory* v. *Litton Systems, Inc.,* 316 F. Supp. 401 (C.D. Cal. 1970), *modified,* 472 F.2d 631 (9th Cir. 1972). Litton Systems had a policy of refusing to employ persons who had been frequently arrested. The court found this to violate Title VII of the Civil Rights Act of 1964. 42 U.S.C. § 2000e (1970):

that it is unfair to try a black defendant before an all-white jury if blacks were overtly or covertly excluded from the jury rolls used to provide the jury panel, but not otherwise.[24] One reason that is often given is that the systematic exclusion of blacks increases too greatly the chance of racial prejudice operating against the black defendant.[25] The problem with this way of thinking about things is that it does not make much sense. If whites are apt to be prejudiced against blacks, then an all-white jury is just as apt to be prejudiced against a black defendant, irrespective of whether blacks were systematically excluded from the jury rolls. I suspect that the rule has developed in the way it has because the courts think that many, if not most, whites are not prejudiced against blacks, unless, perhaps, they happen to live in an area where there is systematic exclusion of blacks from the jury rolls. Hence prejudice is the chief worry, and a sectional, if not historical, one at that.

White prejudice against blacks is, I think, a problem, and not just a sectional one. However, the existence or nonexistence of prejudice against blacks does not go to the heart of the matter. It is a worry, but it is not the chief worry. A black person may not be able to get a fair trial from an all-white jury even though the jurors are disposed to be fair and impartial, because the whites may unknowingly bring into the jury box a view about a variety of matters which affects in very fundamental respects the way they will look at and assess the facts. Thus, for example, it is not, I suspect, part of the experience of most white persons who serve on juries that police often lie in their dealings with people and the courts. Indeed, it is probably not part of their experience that persons lie about serious matters except on rare occasions. And they themselves tend to take truth telling very seriously. As a result, white persons for whom these facts about police and lying are a part of their social reality will have very great difficulty taking seriously the possibility that the inculpatory testimony of a police witness is a deliberate untruth. However, it may also be a part of the social reality that many black persons, just because they are black, have had encounters with the police in which the police were at best indifferent to whether they, the police, were speaking the truth. And even more black persons may have known a friend or a relative who has had

---

"Negroes are arrested substantially more frequently than whites in proportion to their numbers. The evidence on this question was overwhelming and utterly convincing. For example, negroes nationally comprise some 11 percent of the population and account for 27 percent of reported arrests and 45 percent of arrests reported as 'suspicious arrests.' Thus, any policy that disqualifies prospective employees because of having been arrested once, or more than once, discriminates in fact against negro applicants. This discrimination exists even though such a policy is objectively and fairly applied as between applicants of various races. A substantial and disproportionately large number of negroes are excluded from employment opportunities by Defendant's policy." 316 F. Supp. at 403.

[24] *Whitus* v. *Georgia*, 385 U.S. 545 (1967), *Avery* v. *Georgia*, 345 U.Ss. 559 (1953), and *Strauder* v. *West Virginia*, 100 U.S. 303 (1880), are three of the many cases declaring it unconstitutional to exclude blacks systematically from the jury rolls when the defendant is black. *Swain* v. *Alabama*, 380 U.S. 202 (1965), is one of the many cases declaring that it is not unconstitutional that no blacks were in fact on the jury that tried the defendant.

[25] *See, e.g., Peters* v. *Kiff,* 407 U.S. 493, 508–509 (Burger C. J., dissenting).

such an experience. As a result, a black juror would be more likely than his or her white counterpart to approach skeptically the testimony of ostensibly neutral, reliable witnesses such as police officers. The point is not that all police officers lie; nor is the point that all whites always believe everything police say, and blacks never do. The point is that because the world we live in is the way it is, it is likely that whites and blacks will on the whole be disposed to view the credibility of police officers very differently. If so, the legal system's election to ignore this reality, and to regard as fair and above reproach the common occurrence of all-white juries (and white judges) passing on the guilt or innocence of black defendants is a decision in fact to permit and to perpetuate a kind of institutional racism within the law.[26]

The second type of institutional racism is what I will call "conceptual" institutional racism. We have a variety of ways of thinking about the legal system, and we have a variety of ways of thinking within the legal system about certain problems. We use concepts. Quite often without realizing it, the concepts used take for granted certain objectionable aspects of racist ideology without our being aware of it. The second *Brown* case *(Brown II)* provides an example.[27] There was a second *Brown* case because, having decided that the existing system of racially segregated public education was unconstitutional *(Brown I),*[28] the Supreme Court gave legitimacy to a second issue— the nature of the relief to be granted—by treating it as a distinct question to be considered and decided separately. That in itself was striking because in most cases, once the Supreme Court has found unconstitutionality, there has been no problem about relief (apart from questions of retroactivity): The unconstitutional practices and acts are to cease. As is well known, the Court in *Brown II* concluded that the desegregation of public education had to proceed "with all deliberate speed."[29] The Court said that there were "com-

---

[26] I discuss this particular situation in somewhat more detail in Wasserstrom, "The University and the Case for Preferential Treatment," 13 *Am. Phil. Q.,* 165, 169–70 (1976). Mr. Justice Marshall expresses a view that I take to be reasonably close to mine in *Peters* v. *Kiff,* 407 U.S. 493 (1972). The case involved the question of whether a white defendant could challenge the systematic exclusion of blacks from the jury rolls. Mr. Justice Marshall held that he could:

"[W]e are unwilling to make the assumption that the exclusion of Negroes has relevance only for issues involving race. When any large and identifiable segment of the community is excluded from jury service, the effect is to remove from the jury room qualities of human nature and varieties of human experience, the range of which is wide and perhaps unknowable. It is not necessary to assume that the excluded group will consistently vote as a class in order to conclude, as we do, that its exclusion deprives the jury of a perspective on human events that may have unsuspected importance in any case that may be presented."
Id. at 503–04 (footnote omitted).

Given my analysis, I think any defendant is disadvantaged by the absence of blacks from the jury, where, for instance, the testimony of a police officer is a significant part of the prosecution case. Because police are more apt to lie about black defendants, and because black jurors are more apt to be sensitive to this possibility, black defendants are, I think, especially likely to be tried unfairly by many all-white juries. What matters in terms of fairness is that blacks be represented on particular juries; nonexclusion from the jury rolls is certainly not obviously sufficient.

[27] *Brown* v. *Board of Educ.,* 349 U.S. 294 (1955).

[28] *Brown* v. *Board of Educ.,* 347 U.S. 483 (1954).

[29] 349 U.S. at 301.

plexities arising from the transition to a system of public education freed from racial discrimination."[30] More specifically, time might be necessary to carry out the ruling because of

> problems related to administration, arising from the physical condition of the school plant, the school transportation system personnel, revision of school districts and attendance areas into compact units to achieve a system of determining admission to the public school on a non-racial basis, and revision of local laws and regulations which may be necessary in solving the foregoing problems.[31]

Now, I do not know whether the Court believed what it said in this passage, but it is a fantastic bit of nonsense that is, for my purposes, most instructive. Why? Because there was nothing complicated about most of the dual school systems of the southern states. Many counties, especially the rural ones, had one high school, typically called either "Booker T. Washington High School" or "George Washington Carver High School," where all the black children in the county went; another school, often called "Sidney Lanier High School" or "Robert E. Lee High School," was attended by all the white children in the county. There was nothing difficult about deciding that—as of the day after the decision—half of the children in the county, say all those who lived in the southern part of the county, would go to Robert E. Lee High School, and all those who lived in the northern half would go to Booker T. Washington High School. *Brown I* could have been implemented the day after the Court reached its decision. But it was also true that the black schools throughout the South were utterly wretched when compared to the white schools. There never had been any system of separate but equal education. In almost every measurable respect, the black schools were inferior. One possibility is that, without being explicitly aware of it, the members of the Supreme Court made use of some assumptions that were a significant feature of the dominant racist ideology. If the assumptions had been made explicit, the reasoning would have gone something like this: Those black schools are wretched. We cannot order white children to go to those schools, especially when they have gone to better schools in the past. So while it is unfair to deprive blacks, to make them go to these awful, segregated schools, they will have to wait until the black schools either are eliminated or are sufficiently improved so that there are good schools for everybody to attend.

What seems to me to be most objectionable, and racist, about *Brown II* is the uncritical acceptance of the idea that during this process of change, black schoolchildren would have to suffer by continuing to attend inadequate schools. The Supreme Court's solution assumed that the correct way to deal with this problem was to continue to have the black children go to their schools until the black schools were brought up to par or eliminated. That is a kind of conceptual racism in which the legal system accepts the dominant racist ideology, which holds that the claims of black children are worth less

---

[30] *Id.* at 299.
[31] *Id.* at 300–01.

than the claims of white children in those cases in which conflict is inevitable.[32] It seems to me that any minimally fair solution would have required that during the interim process, if anybody had to go to an inadequate school, it would have been the white children, since they were the ones who had previously had the benefit of the good schools. But this is simply not the way racial matters are thought about within the dominant ideology.

A study of *Brown II* is instructive because it is a good illustration of conceptual racism within the legal system. It also reflects another kind of conceptual racism—conceptual racism about the system. *Brown I* and *II* typically are thought of by our culture, and especially by our educational institutions, as representing one of the high points in the legal system's fight against racism. The dominant way of thinking about the desegregation cases is that the legal system was functioning at its very best. Yet, as I have indicated, there are important respects in which the legal system's response to the then existing system of racially segregated education was defective and hence should hardly be taken as a model of the just, institutional way of dealing with this problem of racial oppression. But the fact that we have, as well as inculcate, these attitudes of effusive praise toward *Brown I* and *II* and its progeny reveals a kind of persistent conceptual racism in talk about the character of the legal system, and what constitutes the right way to have

---

[32] The unusual character of *Brown II* was recognized by Mr. Justice Goldberg in *Watson* v. *City of Memphis,* 373 U.S. 526 (1963):

Most importantly, of course, it must be recognized that even the delay countenanced by *Brown* was a necessary, albeit significant, adaptation of the usual principle that any deprivation of constitutional rights calls for prompt rectification. The rights here asserted are, like all such rights, *present* rights; they are not merely hopes to some *future* enjoyment of some formalistic constitutional promise. The basic guarantees of our Constitution are warrants for the here and now and, unless there is an overwhelmingly compelling reason, they are to be promptly fulfilled. The second *Brown* decision is but a narrowly drawn, and carefully limited, qualification upon usual precepts of constitutional adjudication. . . ."

Id. at 532–33 (emphasis in original; footnote omitted).

As I have indicated, the problem with *Brown II* is that there was no "overwhelmingly compelling reason" to delay. It might be argued though, that the Court deliberately opted for "all deliberate speed" and all that meant about the dreary pace of desegregation because it believed the country would not accept full, immediate implementation of *Brown I.* If this was the reasoning, it is equally pernicious. It is sound, only if the country is identified with white people; blacks were surely willing to accept the immediate elimination of the system of racial segregation.

But someone might still say that the Court was just dealing sensibly with the political realities. The white power structure would not have accepted anything more drastic. Arguments such as these are developed at considerable length by A. Bickel, *The Least Dangerous Branch,* 247–54 (1962). The problem with this is twofold. First, what is deemed a drastic solution has a lot to do with whether whites or blacks are being affected, and how. It was and is thought to be drastic for force and the criminal law to be used against whites to secure compliance with laws relating to segregation. It was and is thought to be much less drastic to use force and the criminal law against blacks who object vigorously and sometimes violently to the system of racial oppression. The simple truth is that when the executive branch, as well as the judiciary, thought about these issues it typically weighed the claims of whites very differently from the claims of blacks. The history of the enforcement of civil rights by the federal government in the 1950s and early 1960s is largely a history of the consistent overvaluation of the claims and concerns of whites vis-à-vis blacks. I have suggested some of the ways this was true of the Civil Rights Division of the Department of Justice. *See* Wasserstrom, Book review of B. Marshall, *Federalism and Civil Rights* (N.Y.: Columbia University Press, 1964), 33 *Chi. L. Rev.* 406, 409–413 (1966); Wasser-

dealt with the social reality of American racial oppression of black people.[33]

In theory, the foregoing analytic scheme can be applied as readily to the social realities of sexual oppression as to racism. Given an understanding of the social realities in respect to sex—the ways in which the system of patriarchy inequitably distributes important benefits and burdens for the benefit of males, and the idealogy which is a part of that patriarchal system and supportive of it—one can examine the different types of sexism that exist within the legal system. In practice the task is more difficult because we are inclined to take as appropriate even overt instances of sexist laws, *e.g.*, that it is appropriately a part of the definition of rape that a man cannot rape his wife.[34] The task is also more difficult because sexism is, as I have suggested, a "deeper" phenomenon than racism.[35] As a result, there is less awareness of the significance of much of the social reality, *e.g.*, that the language we use to talk about the world and ourselves has embedded within it ideological assumptions and preferences that support the existing patriarchal system.[36] Cases of institutional sexism will therefore be systematically harder to detect. But these difficulties to one side, the mode of analysis seems to me to be in principle equally applicable to sexism, although, as I indicate in the next section on ideals, a complete account of the sexism of the legal system necessarily awaits a determination of what is the correct picture of the good society in respect to sexual differences.

II. IDEALS

The second perspective, described at the outset, which is also important for an understanding and analysis of racism and sexism, is the perspective of the ideal. Just as we can and must ask what is involved today in our culture in

---

strom, "Postscript: Lawyers and Revolution," 30 *U. Pitt. L. Rev.*, 125, 131 (1968).

Second, whether the decision would have been "accepted" is in large measure a function of what the United States government would have been prepared to do to get the decision implemented. During this same era things that were viewed as absolutely unacceptable or as not feasible suddenly became acceptable and feasible without any substantial change in material circumstances, *e.g.*, the passage of the 1965 Voting Rights Act, 42 U.S.C. §§ 1973 *et. seq.* (1970). It mysteriously became acceptable to the Congress, enforceable by the government and accepted by the South when Reverend Reeb and Mrs. Liuzzo were murdered during the time of the Selma march, and former President Johnson declared his determination to see the law enacted and enforced.

[33] A discussion of some of these same kinds of issues concerning ideology can be found in Thalberg, "Justifications for Institutional Racism," 5 *Phil. F.*, 243 (1973).

[34] In California, rape is defined as "an act of sexual intercourse, accomplished with a female *not the wife of the perpetrator,* under either of the following circumstances. . . ." *Cal. Penal Code* § 261 (West Supp. 1976) (emphasis added).

[35] For an example of a kind of analysis that is beginning to show some of the ways in which the law builds upon and supports the patriarchal system of marriage, see Johnston, "Sex and Property: The Common Law Tradition, The Law School Curriculum, and Developments Toward Equality," 47 *N.Y.U. L. Rev.*, 1033, 1071–89 (1972). Another very rich source is the recent casebook on sex discrimination by B. Babcock, A. Freedman, E. Norton, and S. Ross, *Sex Discrimination and the Law—Causes and Remedies* (1975).

[36] *See, e.g.*, R. Lakoff, Language and Woman's Place (1975); Baker, " 'Pricks' and 'Chicks': A Plea for 'Persons,' " in *Philosophy and Sex*, 45 (R. Baker and F. Elliston, eds., 1975); Moulton, "Sex and Reference" in *id.*, at 34.

being of one race or of one sex rather than the other, and how individuals are in fact viewed and treated, we can also ask different questions: namely, what would the good or just society make of race and sex, and to what degree, if at all, would racial and sexual distinctions ever be taken into account? Indeed, it could plausibly be argued that we could not have an adequate idea of whether a society was racist or sexist unless we had some conception of what a thoroughly nonracist or nonsexist society would look like. This perspective is an extremely instructive as well as an often neglected one. Comparatively little theoretical literature that deals with either racism or sexism has concerned itself in a systematic way with this perspective.

In order to ask more precisely what some of the possible ideals are of desirable racial or sexual differentiation, it is necessary to see that we must ask: "In respect to what?" And one way to do this is to distinguish in a crude way among three levels or areas of social and political arrangements and activities. These correspond very roughly to the matters of status, role, and temperament identified earlier. First, there is the area of basic political rights and obligations, including the rights to vote and to travel, and the obligation to pay income taxes. Second, there is the area of important, non-governmental institutional benefits and burdens. Examples are access to and employment in the significant economic markets, the opportunity to acquire and enjoy housing in the setting of one's choice, the right of persons who want to marry each other to do so, and the duties (nonlegal as well as legal) that persons acquire in getting married. And third, there is the area of individual, social interaction, including such matters as whom one will have as friends, and what aesthetic preferences one will cultivate and enjoy.

As to each of these three areas we can ask, for example, whether in a nonracist society it would be thought appropriate ever to take the race of the individuals into account. Thus, one picture of a nonracist society is that which is captured by what I call the assimilationist ideal: a nonracist society would be one in which the race of an individual would be the functional equivalent of the eye color of individuals in our society today.[37] In our society no basic political rights and obligations are determined on the basis of eye color. No important institutional benefits and burdens are connected with eye color. Indeed, except for the mildest sort of aesthetic preferences, a person would be thought odd who even made private, social decisions by taking eye color into account. And for reasons that we could fairly readily state we could explain why it would be wrong to permit anything but the mildest, most trivial aesthetic preference to turn on eye color. The reasons would concern the irrelevance of eye color for any political or social institution, practice or arrangement. According to the assimilationist ideal, a nonracist society would

[37] There is a danger in calling this ideal the "assimilationist" ideal. That term suggests the idea of incorporating oneself, one's values, and the like into the dominant group and its practices and values. I want to make it clear that no part of that idea is meant to be captured by my use of this term. Mine is a stipulative definition.

be one in which an individual's race was of no more significance in any of these three areas than is eye color today.

The assimilationist ideal in respect to sex does not seem to be as readily plausible and obviously attractive here as it is in the case of race. In fact, many persons invoke the possible realization of the assimilationist ideal as a reason for rejecting the Equal Rights Amendment and indeed the idea of women's liberation itself. My own view is that the assimilationist ideal may be just as good and just as important an ideal in respect to sex as it is in respect to race. But many persons think there are good reasons why an assimilationist society in respect to sex would not be desirable.

To be sure, to make the assimilationist ideal a reality in respect to sex would involve more profound and fundamental revisions of our institutions and our attitudes than would be the case in respect to race. On the institutional level we would have to alter radically our practices concerning the family and marriage. If a nonsexist society is a society in which one's sex is no more significant than eye color in our society today, then laws that require the persons who are getting married to be of different sexes would clearly be sexist laws.

And on the attitudinal and conceptual level, the assimilationist ideal would require the eradication of all sex-role differentiation. It would never teach about the inevitable or essential attributes of masculinity or feminity; it would never encourage or discourage the ideas of sisterhood or brotherhood; and it would be unintelligible to talk about the virtues as well as disabilities of being a woman or a man. Were sex like eye color, these things would make no sense. Just as the normal, typical adult is virtually oblivious to the eye color of other persons for all major interpersonal relationships, so the normal, typical adult in this kind of nonsexist society would be indifferent to the sexual, physiological differences of other persons for all interpersonal relationships.

To acknowledge that things would be very different is, of course, hardly to concede that they would be undesirable. But still, perhaps the problem is with the assimilationist ideal. And the assimilationist ideal is certainly not the only possible, plausible ideal.

There are, for instance, two others that are closely related, but distinguishable. One I call the ideal of diversity; the other, the ideal of tolerance. Both can be understood by considering how religion, rather than eye color, tends to be thought about in our culture. According to the ideal of diversity, heterodoxy in respect to religious belief and practice is regarded as a positive good. On this view there would be a loss—it would be a worse society— were everyone to be a member of the same religion. According to the other view, the ideal of tolerance, heterodoxy in respect to religious belief and practice would be seen more as a necessary, lesser evil. On this view there is nothing intrinsically better about diversity in respect to religion, but the evils of achieving anything like homogeneity far outweigh the possible benefits.

Now, whatever differences there might be between the ideals of diversity and tolerance, the similarities are more striking. Under neither ideal would it be thought that the allocation of basic political rights and duties should take an individual's religion into account. And we would want equalitarianism even in respect to most important institutional benefits and burdens—for example, access to employment in the desirable vocations. Nonetheless, on both views it would be deemed appropriate to have some institutions (typically those that are connected in an intimate way with these religions) that do in a variety of ways take the religion of members of the society into account. For example, it might be thought permissible and appropriate for members of a religious group to join together in collective associations which have religious, educational and social dimensions. And on the individual, inter-personal level, it might be thought unobjectionable, or on the diversity view, even admirable, were persons to select their associates, friends, and mates on the basis of their religious orientation. So there are two possible and plausible ideals of what the good society would look like in respect to religion in which religious differences would be to some degree maintained because the diversity of religions was seen either as an admirable, valuable feature of the society, or as one to be tolerated. The picture is a more complex, less easily describable one than that of the assimilationist ideal.

It may be that in respect to sex (and conceivably, even in respect to race) something more like either of these ideals in respect to religion is the right one. But one problem then—and it is a very substantial one—is to specify with a good deal of precision and care what that ideal really comes to. Which legal, institutional and personal differentiations are permissible and which are not? Which attitudes and beliefs concerning sexual identification and differences are properly introduced and maintained and which are not? Part, but by no means all, of the attractiveness of the assimilationist ideal is its clarity and simplicity. In the good society of the assimilationist sort we would be able to tell easily and unequivocally whether any law, practice, or attitude was in any respect either racist or sexist. Part, but by no means all, of the unattractiveness of any pluralistic ideal is that it makes the question of what is racist or sexist a much more difficult and complicated one to answer. But although simplicity and lack of ambiguity may be virtues, they are not the only virtues to be taken into account in deciding among competing ideals. We quite appropriately take other considerations to be relevant to an as-sessment of the value and worth of alternative nonracist and nonsexist so-cieties.

Nor do I even mean to suggest that all persons who reject the assimilationist ideal in respect to sex would necessarily embrace either something like the ideal of tolerance or the ideal of diversity. Some persons might think the right ideal was one in which substantially greater sexual differentiation and sex-role identification was retained than would be the case under either of these conceptions. Thus, someone might believe that the good society was, perhaps, essentially like the one they think we now have in respect to sex:

equality of political rights, such as the right to vote, but all of the sexual differentiation in both legal and nonlegal institutions that is characteristic of the way in which our society has been and still is ordered. And someone might also believe that the usual ideological justifications for these arrangements are the correct and appropriate ones.

This could, of course, be regarded as a version of the ideal of diversity, with the emphasis upon the extensive character of the institutional and personal difference connected with sexual identity. Whether it is a kind of ideal of diversity or a different ideal altogether turns, I think, upon two things: First, however pervasive the sexual differentiation is, second, whether the ideal contains a conception of the appropriateness of significant institutional and interpersonal inequality, e.g., that the woman's job is in large measure to serve and be dominated by the male. The more this latter feature is present, the clearer the case for regarding this as ideal, distinctively different from any of those described by me so far.

The next question, of course, is that of how a choice is rationally to be made among these different, possible ideals. One place to begin is with the empirical world. For the question of whether something is a plausible and attractive ideal does turn in part on the nature of the empirical world. If it is true, for example, that any particular characteristic, such as sex, is not only a socially significant category in our culture but that it is largely a socially created one as well, then many ostensible objections to the assimilationist ideal appear immediately to disappear.

What I mean is this: It is obvious that we could formulate and use some sort of a crude, incredibly imprecise physiological concept of race. In this sense we could even say that race is a naturally occurring rather than a socially created feature of the world. There are diverse skin colors and related physiological characteristics distributed among human beings. But the fact is that except for skin hue and the related physiological characteristics, race is a socially created category. And skin hue, as I have shown, is neither a necessary nor a sufficient condition for being classified as black in our culture. Race as a naturally occurring characteristic is also a socially irrelevant category. There do not in fact appear to be any characteristics that are part of this natural concept of race and that are in any plausible way even relevant to the appropriate distribution of any political, institutional, or interpersonal concerns in the good society. Because in this sense race is like eye color, there is no plausible case to be made on this ground against the assimilationist ideal.[38]

There is, of course, the social reality of race. In creating and tolerating a

[38] This is not to deny that certain people believe that race is linked with characteristics that prima facie are relevant. Such beliefs persist. They are, however, unjustified by the evidence. *See, e.g.*, Block and Dworkin, "IQ, Heritability and Inequality" (pts. 1–2), 3 *Phil. & Pub. Aff.*, 331, 4 *id.* 40 (1974). More to the point, even if it were true that such a linkage existed, none of the characteristics suggested would require that political or social institutions, or interpersonal relationships, would have to be structured in a certain way.

society in which race matters, we must recognize that we have created a vastly more complex concept of race which includes what might be called the idea of ethnicity as well—a set of attitudes, traditions, beliefs, etc., which the society has made part of what it means to be of a race. It may be, therefore, that one could argue that a form of the pluralist ideal ought to be preserved in respect to race, in the socially created sense, for reasons similar to those that might be offered in support of the desirability of some version of the pluralist ideal in respect to religion. As I have indicated, I am skeptical, but for the purposes of this essay it can well be left an open question.

Despite appearances, the case of sex is more like that of race than is often thought. What opponents of assimilationism seize upon is that sexual difference appears to be a naturally occurring category of obvious and inevitable social relevance in a way, or to a degree, which race is not. The problems with this way of thinking are twofold. To begin with, an analysis of the social realities reveals that it is the socially created sexual differences which tend in fact to matter the most. It is sex-role differentiation, not gender per se,[39] that makes men and women as different as they are from each other, and it is sex-role differences which are invoked to justify most sexual differentiation at any of the levels of society.[40]

More importantly, even if naturally occurring sexual differences were of such a nature that they were of obvious prima facie social relevance, this would by no means settle the question of whether in the good society sex should or should not be as minimally significant as eye color. Even though there are biological differences between men and women in nature, this fact does not determine the question of what the good society can and should make of these differences. I have difficulty understanding why so many persons seem to think that it does settle the question adversely to anything like the assimilationist ideal. They might think it does settle the question for two different reasons. In the first place, they might think the differences are of such a character that they substantially affect what would be possible within a good society of human persons. Just as the fact that humans are mortal necessarily limits the features of any possible good society, so, they might argue, the fact that males and females are physiologically different limits the features of any possible good society.

In the second place, they might think the differences are of such a character that they are relevant to the question of what would be desirable in the good society. That is to say, they might not think that the differences *determine* to a substantial degree what is possible, but that the differences ought to be

[39] The term "gender" may be used in a number of different senses. I use it to refer to those anatomical, physiological, and other differences (if any) that are naturally occurring in the sense described above. Some persons refer to these differences as "sex differences," but that seems to me confusing. In any event, I am giving a stipulative definition to "gender."

[40] *See, e.g.,* authorities cited in note 8 *supra;* M. Mead, *Sex and Temperament in Three Primitive Societies* (1935):

"These three situations [the cultures of the Anapesh, the Mundugumor, and the Tchambuli] suggest, then, a very definite conclusion. If those temperamental attitudes which we have traditionally regarded as feminine—such as passivity, responsiveness, and a willingness to cherish

taken into account in any rational construction of an ideal social existence.

The second reason seems to me to be a good deal more plausible than the first. For there appear to be very few, if any, respects in which the ineradicable, naturally occurring differences between males and females *must* be taken into account. The industrial revolution has certainly made any of the general differences in strength between the sexes capable of being ignored by the good society in virtually all activities.[41] And it is sex-role acculturation, not biology, that mistakenly leads many persons to the view that women are both naturally and necessarily better suited than men to be assigned the primary responsibilities of child rearing. Indeed, the only fact that seems required to be taken

---

children—can so easily be set up as the masculine pattern in one tribe, and in another to be outlawed for the majority of women as well as for the majority of men, we no longer have any basis for regarding such aspects of behavior as sex-linked. . . .

". . . We are forced to conclude that human nature is almost unbelievably malleable, responding accurately and contrastingly to contrasting cultural conditions. . . . Standardized personality differences between the sexes are of this order, cultural creations to which each generation, male and female, is trained to conform."

Id. at 190–91.

A somewhat different view is expressed in J. Sherman. *On the Psychology of Women* (1971). There, the author suggests there are "natural" differences of a psychological sort between men and women, the chief ones being aggressiveness and strength of sex drive. *See id.* at 238. However, even if she is correct as to these biologically based differences, this does little to establish what the good society should look like.

Almost certainly the most complete discussion of this topic is E. Macoby and C. Jacklin, *The Psychology of Sex Differences* (1974). The authors conclude that the sex differences which are, in their words, "fairly well established," are: (1) that girls have greater verbal ability than boys; (2) that boys excel in visual-spacial ability; (3) that boys excel in mathematical ability; and (4) that males are more aggressive. *Id* at 351–52. They conclude, in respect to the etiology of these psychological sex differences, that there appears to be a biological component to the greater visual-spacial ability of males and to their greater aggressiveness. *Id.* at 360.

[41] As Sherman observes:

"Each sex has its own special physical assets and liabilities. The principal female liability of less muscular strength is not ordinarily a handicap in a civilized, mechanized, society. . . . There is nothing in the biological evidence to prevent women from taking a role of equality in a civilized society."

J. Sherman, *supra* note 40, at 11.

There are, of course, some activities that would be sexually differentiated in the assimilationist society; namely, those that were specifically directed toward, say, measuring unaided physical strength. Thus, I think it likely that even in this ideal society, weight lifting contests and boxing matches would in fact be dominated, perhaps exclusively so, by men. But it is hard to find any *significant* activities or institutions that are analogous. And it is not clear that such insignificant activities would be thought worth continuing, especially since sports function in existing patriarchal societies to help maintain the dominance of males. See K. Millett, *supra* note 7, at 48–49.

It is possible that there are some nontrivial activities or occupations that depend sufficiently directly upon unaided physical strength that most if not all women would be excluded. Perhaps being a lifeguard at the ocean is an example. Even here, though, it would be important to see whether the way lifeguarding had traditionally been done could be changed to render such physical strength unimportant. If it could be changed, then the question would simply be one of whether the increased cost (or loss of efficiency) was worth the gain in terms of equality and the avoidance of sex-role differentiation. In a nonpatriarchal society very different from ours, where sex was not a dominant social category, the argument from efficiency might well prevail. What is important, once again, is to see how infrequent and peripheral such occupational cases are.

into account is the fact that reproduction of the human species requires that the fetus develop *in utero* for a period of months. Sexual intercourse is not necessary, for artificial insemination is available. Neither marriage nor the family is required for conception or child rearing. Given the present state of medical knowledge and the natural realities of female pregnancy, it is difficult to see why any important institutional or interpersonal arrangements *must* take the existing gender difference of *in utero* pregnancy into account.

But, as I have said, this is still to leave it a wholly open question to what degree the good society *ought* to build upon any ineradicable gender differences to construct institutions which would maintain a substantial degree of sexual differentiation. The arguments are typically far less persuasive for doing so than appears upon the initial statement of this possibility. Someone might argue that the fact of menstruation, for instance, could be used as a premise upon which to predicate different social roles for females than for males. But this could only plausibly be proposed if two things were true: first, that menstruation would be debilitating to women and hence relevant to social role even in a culture which did not teach women to view menstruation as a sign of uncleanliness or as a curse;[42] and second, that the way in which menstruation necessarily affected some or all women was in fact related in an important way to the role in question. But even if both of these were true, it would still be an open question whether any sexual differentiation ought to be built upon these facts. The society could still elect to develop institutions that would nullify the effect of the natural differences. And suppose, for example, what seems implausible—that some or all women will not be able to perform a particular task while menstruating, *e.g.,* guard a border. It would be easy enough, if the society wanted to, to arrange for

---

[42] *See, e.g.,* Paige, "Women Learn to Sing the Menstrual Blues," in *The Female Experience,* 17 (C. Tavis, ed., 1973).

"I have come to believe that the 'raging hormones' theory of menstrual distress simply isn't adequate. All women have the raging hormones, but not all women have menstrual symptoms, nor do they have the same symptoms for the same reasons. Nor do I agree with the 'raging neurosis' theory, which argues that women who have menstrual symptoms are merely whining neurotics, who need only a kind pat on the head to cure their problems.

"We must instead consider the problem from the perspective of women's subordinate social position, and of the cultural ideology that so narrowly defines the behaviors and emotions that are appropriately 'feminine.' Women have perfectly good reasons to react emotionally to reproductive events. Menstruation, pregnancy and childbirth—so sacred, yet so unclean—are the woman's primary avenues of achievement and self-expression. Her reproductive abilities define her femininity; other routes to success are only second-best in this society. . . .

• • •

". . . My current research on a sample of 114 societies around the world indicates that ritual observances and taboos about menstruation are a method of controlling women and their fertility. Men apparently use such rituals, along with those surrounding pregnancy and childbirth, to assert their claims to women and their children.

". . . The hormone theory isn't giving us much mileage, and it's time to turn it in for a better model, one that looks to our beliefs about menstruation and women. It is no mere coincidence that women get the blue meanies along with an event they consider embarrassing, unclean— and a curse."

Id. at 21.

substitute guards for the women who were incapacitated. We know that persons are not good guards when they are sleepy, and we make arrangements so that persons alternate guard duty to avoid fatigue. The same could be done for menstruating women, even given these implausibly strong assumptions about menstruation. At the risk of belaboring the obvious, what I think it important to see is that the case against the assimilationist ideal—if it is to be a good one—must rest on arguments concerned to show why some other ideal would be preferable; it cannot plausibly rest on the claim that it is either necessary or inevitable.

There is, however, at least one more argument based upon nature, or at least the "natural," that is worth mentioning. Someone might argue that significant sex-role differentiation is natural not in the sense that it is biologically determined but only in the sense that it is a virtually universal phenomenon in human culture. By itself, this claim of virtual universality, even if accurate, does not directly establish anything about the desirability or undesirability of any particular ideal. But it can be made into an argument by the addition of the proposition that where there is a virtually universal social practice, there is probably some good or important purpose served by the practice. Hence, given the fact of sex-role differentiation in all, or almost all, cultures, we have some reson to think that substantial sex-role differentiation serves some important purpose for and in human society.

This is an argument, but I see no reason to be impressed by it. The premise which turns the fact of sex-role differentiation into any kind of a strong reason for sex-role differentiation is the premise of conservatism. And it is no more convincing here than elsewhere. There are any number of practices that are typical and yet upon reflection seem without significant social purpose. Slavery was once such a practice; war perhaps, still is.

More to the point, perhaps, the concept of "purpose" is ambiguous. It can mean in a descriptive sense "plays some role" or "is causally relevant." Or it can mean in a prescriptive sense "does something desirable" or "has some useful function." If "purpose" is used descriptively in the conservative premise, then the argument says nothing about the continued desirability of sex-role differentiation or the assimilationist ideal. If "purpose" is used prescriptively in the conservative premise, then there is no reason to think that premise is true.

To put it another way, the question is whether it is desirable to have a society in which sex-role differences are to be retained at all. The straightforward way to think about that question is to ask what would be good and what would be bad about a society in which sex functioned like eye color does in our society. We can imagine what such a society would look like and how it would work. It is hard to see how our thinking is substantially advanced by reference to what has typically or always been the case. If it is true, as I think it is, that the sex-role differentiated societies we have had so far have tended to concentrate power in the hands of males, have developed institutions and ideologies that have perpetuated that concentration and have restricted and prevented women from living the kinds of lives that persons ought to be able to live for themselves, then this says far more about what may be wrong with any nonassimilationist ideal than does the conservative premise say what may be right about any nonassimilationist ideal.

Nor is this all that can be said in favor of the assimilationist ideal. For it seems to me that the strongest affirmative moral argument on its behalf is that it provides for a kind of individual autonomy that a nonassimilationist society cannot attain. Any nonassimilationist society will have sex roles. Any nonassimilationist society will have some institutions that distinguish between individuals in virtue of their gender, and any such society will necessarily teach the desirability of doing so. Any substantially nonassimilationist society will make one's sexual identity an important characteristic, so that there are substantial psychological, role, and status differences between persons who are males and those who are females. Even if these could be attained without systemic dominance of one sex over the other, they would, I think, be objectionable on the ground that they necessarily impaired an individual's ability to develop his or her own characteristics, talents and capacities to the fullest extent to which he or she might desire. Sex roles, and all that accompany them, necessarily impose limits—restrictions on what one can do, be or become. As such, they are, I think, at least prima facie wrong.

To some degree, all role-differentiated living is restrictive in this sense. Perhaps, therefore, all role-differentiation in society is to some degree troublesome, and perhaps all strongly role-differentiated societies are objectionable. But the case against sexual differentiation need not rest upon this more controversial point. For one thing that distinguishes sex roles from many other roles is that they are wholly involuntarily assumed. One has no choice whatsoever about whether one shall be born a male or female. And if it is a consequence of one's being born a male or a female that one's subsequent emotional, intellectual, and material development will be substantially controlled by this fact, then substantial, permanent, and involuntarily assumed restraints have been imposed on the most central factors concerning the way one will shape and live one's life. The point to be emphasized is that this would necessarily be the case, even in the unlikely event that substantial sexual differentiation could be maintained without one sex or the other becoming dominant and developing institutions and an ideology to support that dominance.

I do not believe that all I have said in this section shows in any conclusive fashion the desirability of the assimilationist ideal in respect to sex. I have tried to show why some typical arguments against the assimilationist ideal are not persuasive,[43] and why some of the central ones in support of that ideal are persuasive. But I have not provided a complete account, or a complete analysis. At a minimum, what I have shown is how thinking about this topic

---

[43] Still other arguments against something like the assimilationist ideal and in favor of something like the idea of diversity are considered by Jaggar and shown by her to be unpersuasive. *See* Jaggar, *supra* note 20, at 281–91.

ought to proceed, and what kinds of arguments need to be marshalled and considered before a serious and informed discussion of alternative conceptions of a nonsexist society can even take place. Once assembled, these arguments need to be individually and carefully assessed before any final, reflective choice among the competing ideals can be made. There does, however, seem to me to be a strong presumptive case for something very close to, if not identical with, the assimilationist ideal.

SEXUAL BLINDNESS AND SEXUAL EQUALITY

BERNARD R. BOXILL

In a recent important essay, Richard Wasserstrom describes what he thinks the "good or just society" would make of racial and sexual differences.[1] The good or just society, he argues, would exemplify the "assimilationist ideal."[2] That is, it would make of racial and sexual differences what present society makes of differences in eye color. In present society, no "basic political rights and obligations are determined on the basis of eye-color;" no "institutional benefits and burdens are connected with eye color;" and "except for the mildest sort of aesthetic preferences, a person would be thought odd who even made private, social decisions by taking eye-color into account."[3] In the good or just society, Wasserstrom contends, race and sex would be of no greater significance.[4] And, he continues, just as the typical adult in present society is "virtually oblivious to the eye color of other persons for all major inter-personal relationships," so the typical adult in the assimilationist society would be "indifferent to the sexual, physiological differences of other persons for all inter-personal relationships."[5]

The assimilationist vision of the sexually and racially ideal society springs, no doubt, from the most humane sentiments. We are seemingly so drawn to invidious discrimination against those of a different race or sex that it must be few who have not yearned for a society where people are blind to both their racial and sexual differences. Yet I shall argue that the assimilationist ideal is defective. The problem it attempts but fails to solve is the old one

Reprinted from *Social Theory and Practice,* Vol. 6, No. 3 (Fall 1980), 281–298, with permission of the publisher and the author.

[1] Richard A. Wasserstrom, "Racism, Sexism and Preferential Treatment: An Approach to the Topics," *UCLA Law Review,* 24 (February 1977), 603.

[2] Ibid., p. 604.

[3] Ibid.

[4] Ibid., p. 605.

[5] Ibid., p. 606.

that has long troubled egalitarians: How are we to deal with the fact that, though we are undeniably equal, we are also undeniably different? In this essay I focus on the defects in the assimilationist argument that are due to the fact that though we are equal because we are human, we are also different because we are female and male. However, my arguments should apply as well to the assimilationist position on racial differences. My conclusion is that we cannot plan that the good and just society be either "sex-blind" or "color-blind."

1

As Wasserstrom allows, there can be no important sex-role differentiations in the assimilationist society. If women are better than men at certain significant activities, or if men are better than women at certain significant activities, people will not likely be oblivious to their sexual differences. The correlation of sexual differences with activities that are significant would tend to make sexual differences themselves appear significant. Accordingly he proposes to break down all sex-activity correlations by designing activities so that women and men can succeed and excel equally at every activity. To use his illustration, if lifeguarding at the ocean as now practiced puts a premium on the kind of strength that gives men an advantage over women, the sexually ideal society would change the way lifeguarding is now practiced so that this advantage is nullified.[6]

Two misunderstandings of the nature and purpose of this reform must be forestalled. First, its purpose is not to make *equality of opportunity* more perfect. Its purpose is to equalize the *chances* for success of men and women at every activity. Equality of opportunity between the sexes does not demand this. Equality of opportunity demands only the removal of all social and environmental barriers to available positions and to the means to becoming qualified for such positions. Thus two people can have equal opportunities but not equal chances. They would have equal chances only if they had equal abilities and interests.

The second misunderstanding of the reform is thinking that it is incompatible with equality of opportunity. Some strategies for equalizing the chances of women and men are incompatible with equality of opportunity. Placing social or environmental barriers in the path of the able so that the less able have an equal chance to attain the goal is an example. But this is not Wasserstrom's strategy. It places no social and environmental barriers in anybody's path to available jobs and positions. It simply eliminates some jobs and positions.

Wasserstrom is aware that his reform may have costs. But he seems to think that the only such cost is a possible loss in efficiency. The question

---

[6] Ibid., p. 611 n. 59.

whether to institute his reforms, he says, is simply "whether the increased cost (or loss of efficiency) was worth the gain in terms of equality and the avoidance of sex-role differentiation."[7] But I argue that he is mistaken. There are two major possible costs he does not consider: the loss of a whole province of our most significant activities, and a loss of opportunities to acquire self-esteem.

Significant Activities

"It is likely," Wasserstrom writes, "that even in this ideal society, weight-lifting contests and boxing matches would in fact be dominated, perhaps exclusively so, by men. But it is hard to find any *significant* activities or institutions that are analogous. And it is not clear that such insignificant activities would be worth continuing, especially since sports function in existing patriarchal societies to help maintain the dominance of males."[8] But surely this conclusion is hasty. Even if sports function in *existing* patriarchal societies to help maintain male dominance, it certainly does not follow that they will perform the same function in an *ideal* society. Consequently, the inference that they would not be "worth continuing" is invalid. But the deeper difficulties concern the claim that sports are *insignificant*.

What Wasserstrom may mean by this is suggested in the next paragraph where he allows that lifeguarding, which also requires considerable unaided strength, is "nontrivial."[9] Since lifeguarding is distinguished from say, weight-lifting, because it performs a service, the implication is that sports are "trivial" and "insignificant" because they do not perform a service and (by extension) have no product. It is true that sports need not perform a service or have a product. Though "spectator sports" may be said to perform the service of entertaining the spectators, and sports in general may produce health, people can engage in sport without entertaining spectators or improving their health. But it is false that sports are for that reason "insignificant" and not worth continuing. There are many activities that, like sports, need have no product and need perform no service. But these activities are not "insignificant" or "not worth continuing." On the contrary some of them are among our more significant activities and are well worth continuing. They are significant and well worth continuing because of what they are in themselves. These activities are unalienated activities. First I shall describe their nature. Then I shall show that sports are among them.

Alienated activity is not itself "the satisfaction of a need, but only a means to satisfy needs outside itself."[10] These needs are "outside" the activity in the sense that they can, at least conceivably, be satisfied "outside," that is, without

---

[7] Ibid.

[8] Ibid., italics in the original.

[9] Ibid.

[10] Karl Marx, "Alienated Labour." In David McLellan ed., *Karl Marx Selected Writings,* (Oxford: Oxford University Press, 1977), p. 80.

the activity that usually provides for their satisfaction. As I understand it, what is really essential about labor's being alienated is that it is not in this sense itself the satisfaction of a need. Consequently, though Marx may have believed otherwise, I describe alienated activity as not essentially, though perhaps usually, involving the other man or capitalist who owns the alienated activity.[11] Now the products and services that happen to be demanded by society, as, for example, shoes, ships, and safe swimming are needs "outside" activities because they all can at least conceivably be satisfied without the usual human activities of shoemaking, shipbuilding and lifeguarding. Since alienated labor is "only a means" to satisfy such needs, the overwhelming consideration in its design is that it satisfy these needs efficiently. Hence, except inadvertently, that design will not allow the worker room to express himself or to "develop freely his mental and physical energies."[12] Further, if there is a need to engage in such activity, alienated labor cannot satisfy that need. Since such a need is for a particular kind of activity, and so can be satisfied only by engaging in that activity, it does not meet the condition of being "outside" the activity that satisfies it.

But if alienated labor is of this nature, unalienated activity must be activity that the worker has a need to engage in, and in particular, activity that is designed specifically to provide him with room to express and develop himself freely. This does not mean that it is unprincipled or undisciplined. As Marx wrote, "Really free labor, the composing of music, for example, is at the same time damned serious and requires the greatest effort."[13] That is to say, activity which is truly a form of self-expression and self-development is necessarily governed by the discipline of laws and principles. We can express ourselves in writing, music, painting and so on, and exercise our literary, musical, and in general our creative talents, only because there are laws governing literary, musical and artistic composition, and only if we submit ourselves to the discipline of these laws. As Marx put it most generally, in his free activity man "constructs in accordance with the laws of beauty."[14]

My account of unalienated labor is independent of the controversy of whether, for Marx, unalienated activity includes economically productive activity.[15] Whether it does or not is irrelevant to the point I wish to make, which is that some activity that is not economically productive is unalienated. A second possible misunderstanding of my account is that painting, composing, and so on, have "products" and are significant, not in themselves but as a means to these "products." But this is a misunderstanding. Paintings and compositions are significant because of the activities they result from, *not* vice versa as in the usual case. As Marx noted, spiders or bees can do

[11] For further discussion of this, see Richard Schact, *Alienation* (Garden City, N.Y.: Anchor Books, 1971), pp. 100, 101.

[12] Karl Marx, "Alienated Labor" in *Karl Marx Selected Writings,* p. 80.

[13] Karl Marx, "Grundrisse" in *Karl Marx Selected Writings,* p. 368.

[14] Karl Marx, "Alienated Labor" in *Karl Marx Selected Writings,* p. 82.

[15] Karl Marx, *Capital,* Volume I in *Karl Marx Selected Writings,* p. 456.

certain things better than an architect. However, their activities are quite different because the architect, unlike the bee or spider, had the idea in his imagination.[16] Thus, part of the activity in question here is the working out of ideas.[17]

In elaborating his Aristotelian Principle, Rawls comes to relevantly similar conclusions. The Aristotelian Principle is a "principle of motivation" that "accounts for many of our major desires."[18] According to it "human beings enjoy the exercise of their realized capacities . . . and this enjoyment increases the more the capacity is realized, or the greater its complexity." Thus, "of two activities they do equally well [people] prefer the one calling on a larger repertoire of intricate and subtle discriminations."[19] Presumably such activities are more enjoyable because they "satisfy the desire for variety and novelty of experience" and permit or even require "individual style and personal expression."[20] This desire is, moreover, "relatively strong" and it must be reckoned with in the design of social institutions; for "otherwise human beings will find their culture and form of life dull and empty. Their vitality and zest will fail as their life becomes a tiresome routine."[21] Thus human beings have a need to engage in activities that call on the exercise of their abilities "simply for their own sakes."[22]

In sum, then, activities can be significant in themselves both in the sense that they are forms of self-expression in which excellence can be achieved, and in the sense that human beings have a profound need to engage in them. I now show that the assimilationist proposes to eliminate a considerable class of these activities.

Consider first, sport: We have seen that Wasserstrom proposes to eliminate it for the sake of sexual blindness. Now in practically all cultures and societies people engage in sport for its own sake. Assuming that people tend to recognise their own needs, it would seem that engaging in sport is in itself the satisfaction of an important human need.[23] To forestall objections that this may be a "false need," I can show that sports can also be forms of self-expression in which excellence is achieved. Sports are not merely undisciplined, unprincipled explosions of physical energy. Though they are exercises of human energy that are freely engaged in because they are engaged in for themselves, they are governed by the most exacting rules. Moreover, since sport is not subservient to satisfying needs "outside" itself, in accordance with the Aristotelian Principle, its rules can be, and usually are, constructed to require the utmost in "intricate and subtle discriminations" that the players are

[16] For a discussion of this see G. A. Cohen, "Marx's Dialectic of Labor," *Philosophy and Public Affairs,* **3** (1974), 235–61.

[17] See further Karl Marx, "Alienated Labor," in *Karl Marx Selected Writings,* p. 80.

[18] John Rawls, *A Theory of Justice* (Cambridge: Harvard University Press, 1971), p. 427.

[19] Ibid., p. 426.

[20] Ibid., p. 427.

[21] Ibid., p. 429.

[22] Ibid., p. 431.

[23] Jan Boxill develops this theme in "Sport as unalienated activity," unpublished manuscript.

capable of. Though Rawls allows that the Aristotelian Principle operates "even in games and pastimes,"[24] he unfortunately, but I think inadvertently, gives the notion of intricacy and subtlety involved an excessively intellectual interpretation. But anyone who has tried to describe a Dr. J stuff shot, or the fastidious shifts in balance and speed of the best high jumpers or shot-putters, and who also understands that what he or she would put into words is not the spontaneous perfection of the animal, but a deliberately acquired art, must acknowledge that sport, too, calls for "intricate and subtle discriminations." Further, as Rawls notes, since it is the very complexity of activities which makes them important avenues of self-expression—"for how could everyone do them in the same way?"[25]—being complex, sports too are important avenues of self-expression. And again, to prove this we need only take an educated look at the best practitioners of any sport. As infallibly as any maestro, they, too, put their personal stamp on their best performances. Finally, many sports are to a considerable extent art forms governed by the "laws of beauty." Few who have seen an accomplished performance of gymnastics or diving, or a perfect pole vault, or a well-run hurdles race, would care to deny this. In ancient Greece, Myron captured the beauty of the discus thrower in his famous discobolus.

An assimilationist might grant my argument that sports are significant, but deny my conclusion that assimilationism requires the suppression of sport. What he or she needs to show is that Wasserstrom allowed too easily that sports necessarily involve the sex-activity correlations that subvert sexual blindness. Thus, a philosopher once argued to me that, even granting the physical differences between women and men, we could avoid sex-activity correlations in sport by classing competitors according to the physical talent that the particular sport called on, be it height, weight, oxygenation rate, or testosterone level. And he pointed out that we already do this in a rudimentary way, when we put competitors in age or weight classes. But this is too ingenious. It fails to see the forest for the trees. If one of the sexes has generally higher levels of the physical characteristic relevant to a particular sport, the other sex will simply not be represented, or well represented, in the classes of the sport that achieve real excellence. And this will do little for the cause of sex-blindness.

Wasserstrom is correct, then, in saying that the assimilationist must eliminate sport. But it is not only sport he must eliminate. The sexes do not differ only in strength. They differ also in physical appearance, flexibility, grace, and texture of voice, for example. Further, the exercise of these differences is central to many of our most aesthetically appealing and culturally important activities. The exercise of man's greater natural strength and woman's greater natural flexibility and grace is of course obvious in many forms of dance. Similarly, the importance of woman's naturally higher, and man's naturally deeper, voice is obvious in practically all forms of singing. Anyone who thinks

[24] Rawls, *A Theory of Justice,* p. 429.
[25] Ibid., p. 427.

of questioning the importance of the aesthetic value of the mix of soprano and bass voices should recall the lengths to which—including in particular the castration of little boys—the medievals went to secure it.

Finally, these losses of the assimilationist society cannot be "made up." Sport and the other activities the assimilationist would suppress have their own peculiar standards of excellence and beauty, and exercise different and peculiar sets of our abilities. Hence given the human need to engage in, and express the self in, all-around activity, though we could, for example, engage in the unalienated activity of philosophizing in the assimilationist society, we could not *replace* sport with philosophizing.

Self-Esteem

Turning to the second cost of the assimilationist ideal, I now argue that in cutting off opportunities to engage in unalienated activity, the assimilationist society cuts off opportunities to acquire self-esteem.

Following Rawls, I take self-esteem as including "a person's sense of his own value, his secure conviction that his conception of his good, his plan of life, is worth carrying out." [26] As Rawls further notes, one of the two main sorts of circumstances that support a person's self-esteem is finding his "person and deeds appreciated and confirmed by others who are likewise esteemed and their association enjoyed . . . unless our endeavors are appreciated by our associates it is impossible for us to maintain the conviction that they are worthwhile." [27] This theory that a person's self-esteem depends on his associates' appreciation of his endeavors has long been recognized by social theorists. Without denying that appreciation of any of our endeavors is likely to support self-esteem, I argue that appreciation of our unalienated activity is especially important.

If alienated activity is activity one feels to be somehow not one's own activity, that is, not activity which expresses one's own ideas and aspirations, the fact that others appreciate it is unlikely to give much support to one's self-esteem. Support for one's self-esteem would seem to come more surely from others' appreciation of activity one feels to be an expression of one's own ideas and aspirations, that is, activity which is truly an expression of oneself. But such activity is unalienated activity. Further, since unalienated activity is done only for itself and for no ulterior motive, all other considerations can be set aside in order to achieve excellence and beauty. Consequently, there can be much for others to appreciate in one's unalienated activity. For these reasons, it would seem that an opportunity to engage in unalienated activity is also an important opportunity to acquire self-esteem. Hence in curtailing opportunities for unalienated activity, the assimilationists curtail opportunities to acquire self-esteem. And that is a serious cost.

However, it may seem that others' appreciation of one's endeavors, espe-

---

[26] Ibid., p. 440.
[27] Ibid., p. 441.

cially one's unalienated activity, is a chancy way to secure self-esteem. For what if one never achieves excellence or beauty? Must one lack self-esteem? This does not seem to be necessarily the case. If it is not, there must be another support for self-esteem that I have not mentioned. Further, if it flourishes in the assimilationist society, my present objection will seem less important.

What this other support for self-esteem could be may be suggested by Bernard Williams's distinction between regarding a person's life, and actions from a "technical point of view," and regarding them from "the human point of view."[28] It may be urged that what is important to persons' self-esteem is not so much that we appreciate their endeavors, which is only to see them from the technical point of view, but that we appreciate what it is for them to attempt what they attempted, which is to see them from the human point of view. I agree that because appreciation from the human point of view can be accorded irrespective of the success or importance of our endeavors—and is to that extent unconditional—it probably offers a far more secure support for self-esteem than the appreciation accorded from the technical point of view. The question is whether the human point of view is likely to flourish in the assimilationist society. Though it is possible, I think there is reason to doubt it. To regard persons from the "human point of view," we must consider their endeavors important just because they are important *to them.* Thus, as Williams notes, from the human point of view, we regard the failed inventor, "not merely as failed inventor, but as a man who wanted to be a successful inventor," that is, as one to whom inventing was important.[29] But, as we have seen, whatever its ultimate significance many people find sport important. Hence the assimilationist's proposal to eliminate it casts doubt on the assumption that he or she views the members of the ideal society from the human point of view.

Finally, the fact that the costs of the assimilationist society involve essentially unalienated activity shows how inadequate Wasserstrom's reassurance is that the "occupational cases" that would have to be phased out are "infrequent and peripheral."[30] It is inadequate because the important costs of his reforms are not the elimination of the few "occupational cases" that the industrial revolution would have eliminated anyway. They are the elimination of the unalienated activity that the industrial revolution, by increasing our leisure time, has simultaneously made more possible and more important. Thus, perhaps what is most paradoxical is the assimilationist's belief that the industrial and technological revolution will reduce the significance of the differences between the sexes. For if I am right the very *opposite* is the truth.

[28] Bernard Williams, "The Idea of Equality." In Joel Feinberg, ed. *Moral Concepts* (London: Oxford University Press, 1970), p. 159.
[29] Ibid.
[30] Wasserstrom, "Racism, Sexism and Preferential Treatment," p. 611, n. 59.

2

At this point, critics may grant that I have pointed to some hitherto unnoticed costs of the sexually blind society, but maintain that I have not shown that society to be unjustified because I have not shown that it is not *worth* the costs. In particular, they may argue that the assimilationist society is worth the costs I mention because it gains so much for sexual equality.

To forestall any unjustified egalitarian sympathy for the assimilationist society, I stress that the sexual equality allegedly gained by the assimilationist society is not equality of income between the sexes. That equality is not at issue. I can propose a distribution of income between the sexes which is as radically egalitarian as the assimilationists can propose.

My first objection is that it is not necessary to incur the costs of the assimilationist society in order to have equality of opportunity between the sexes. These costs are the loss of opportunities to engage in unalienated activities and to achieve self-esteem, which are incurred by the elimination of all sex-activity correlations. But it is not necessary to eliminate correlations between sex and activity in order to have equality of opportunity between the sexes. Sex roles do subvert that equality, and perhaps human beings do tend to change sex-activity correlations into sex roles. Thus, the bare existence of correlations between sex and activities may engender a societal expectation that the sexes tend to excel at different activities, and this in turn can lead to societal factors that actively discourage women and men from pursuing certain activities.[31] When this occurs, sex roles exist and equality of opportunity ceases to exist. The point, however, is that sex-activity correlations need not thus develop into sex roles.[32] There is no reason that people cannot learn to successfully resist the tendency to move from a perception of sex-activity correlations to instituting sex roles.

Wasserstrom fails to see that it is not necessary to eliminate sex-activity correlations to have sexual equality because he blurs the distinction between a sex-activity correlation and a sex role. Sex roles, he says, "necessarily impose limits—restrictions on what one can do, be or become." They impose "substantial, permanent, and involuntarily assumed restraints . . . on the most central factors concerning the way one will shape and live one's life. The point to be emphasized is that this would *necessarily* be the case even in the unlikely event that the substantial sexual differentiation could be maintained without one sex or the other becoming dominant. . . ."[33] I could not agree more with all this *if* by "sexual differentiation" Wasserstrom means "sex roles." But if this is what he means, his statement is irrelevant to the question

---

[31] On this point see Joyce Trebilcot, "Sex Roles: The Argument From Nature." In Jane English ed. *Sex Equality* (Englewood Cliffs, N.J.: Prentice-Hall, Inc., 1977), p. 125. From *Ethics,* (1975), 249–55.

[32] Ibid.

[33] Wasserstrom, "Racism, Sexism, and Preferential Treatment," p. 614.

whether it is necessary to abolish sex-activity correlations to secure sexual equality.

Some may object that it is too risky to rely on people to control the tendency to change sex-activity correlations into sex roles. But I do not recommend this. We can provide those liable to be discriminated against with a "special bill of rights" and educate them to stand up for their rights. This would, of course, mean the end of "sexual blindness," but "sexual blindness" was never defended as intrinsically valuable.

It could be said that though abolishing sex-activity correlations is not necessary for sexual equality, it makes that equality more secure: If we do not notice our sexual differences we can hardly discriminate against each other on their basis. Further, it could be argued that the alternative arrangement I propose would leave society with a built-in potential for conflict between the sexes, and that the more harmonious society that sexual blindness would secure would be infinitely superior. But even this considerably weakened case for sexual blindness collapses. Though sexual blindness may give us a safer enjoyment of sexual equality as equality of opportunity between the sexes, it does so at the expense of a more fundamental precept of egalitarianism, in terms of which equality of opportunity is itself justified.

That precept, which I refer to as equality of respect, is that each person has an equal right to the maximum opportunity, compatible with a like opportunity for others, to express himself or herself and to exercise and develop his or her talents as he or she sees fit.[34] It is clearly a stronger requirement than equality of opportunity. As I defined it, and as it is commonly understood, equality of opportunity is equality of opportunity to gain available positions or careers. Hence, since we can express ourselves and exercise and develop our talents *outside* our positions and careers, equality of respect makes broader and stronger demands than equality of opportunity. More importantly—for the egalitarian at least—it is the precept in terms of which equality of opportunity is justified. Thus one reason why equality of opportunity is so important is that although careers are not the only avenues of self-expression and self-realization, they are major avenues of self-expression and self-realization.

Now the assimilationists do propose to sacrifice equality of respect for equality of opportunity. As we have seen, they propose to eliminate a substantial portion of our unalienated activities for the sake of sexual blindness. These activities are an especially rich medium of self-expression and self-realization, and probably for some people more than others. Consequently, to eliminate such activities for the sake of sexual blindness is to sacrifice equality of respect for sexual blindness. But the purpose of sexual blindness is that it secures equality of opportunity between the sexes. Hence the assimilationists propose to sacrifice equality of respect for equality of opportunity.

[34] This conception is close, though not identical with Dworkin's "equality of respect and concern." See Ronald Dworkin, *Taking Rights Seriously* (Cambridge: Harvard University Press, 1977), pp. 272, 273.

Finally, since it is equality of respect which justifies equality of opportunity, their position is incoherent.

The immediate objection may be that I have been unfair in arguing that Wasserstrom pursues equality of opportunity at the expense of equality of respect. For, in arguing against sex roles, Wasserstrom appeals explicitly to an egalitarian ideal which is practically identical with what I have called "equality of respect." Sex roles are objectionable, he argues, because "they necessarily impair an individual's ability to develop his or her own characteristics, talents and capacities to the fullest extent to which he or she might desire." [35] Thus it may seem that if Wasserstrom focuses mainly on equality of opportunity for positions and careers, this is only because this equality is very important to equality of respect; so ultimately his proposal is intended to secure equality of respect.

But if this is indeed its purpose, it is very unlikely to secure it. His proposal will probably be bad for both men and women. Consider first the case for women. There are certainly activities at which women are better than men. These activities are not necessarily among the scorned "domestic" activities. Indeed, some are among those activities that the assimilationists want to eliminate: sports. Women's relative lack of success in sports is not written in the nature of things. It is merely a sign of our provincialism and lack of imagination. The very anatomical and physiological differences which place women at a disadvantage in some sports give them a decided advantage in other sports. As Jane English notes, "what is a physiological disadvantage in one activity may be an advantage in others: weight is an asset to a Sumo wrestler and a drawback for marathon running; height is an aid in basketball but not on the balance beam." Consequently, as she goes on to conclude, "in some sports, women have natural advantages over men. The hip structure that slows running gives a lower center of gravity" and this gives women an advantage on the balance beam. Similarly, "fat provides insulation and an energy source for running fifty mile races," and "the hormones that hinder development of heavy muscles promote flexibility," and give women an advantage over men in ballet. [36] The point I wish to stress here is that the pursuit of sexual blindness would require the elimination of all these activities. Let us see how unfair and unequal this is. Suppose there are women whose main talents are precisely those most strongly correlated to excellence in the above-mentioned activities. The assimilationists propose to eliminate these activities and to make the talents of these women "unimportant." But why is this fair? The men disadvantaged in these activities may already be richly and variously talented. And exactly parallel arguments apply to the case for eliminating activities for which men have natural advantages.

This argument is not decisive because it depends on assumptions which, though plausible, are clearly contingent. The decisive objection is that it is

---

[35] Wasserstrom, "Racism, Sexism and Preferential Treatment," p. 614.
[36] Jane English, "Sex Equality in Sports," *Philosophy and Public Affairs,* 7 (1978), 275.

mistaken in principle to eliminate activities for the reasons the assimilationist gives. This may seem a bit extreme. The assimilationist may point out that for a safe enjoyment of equality we already rule out activities that are of the very kind that I would protect. For example, we have laws against reckless driving and even some sports. These activities could conceivably be classified as unalienated activity, and quite obviously engaging in them seems to help many people's self-esteem. Yet it seems clear that we are justified in eliminating them. In a similar vein he or she may continue that on my own account economic inequalities can be eliminated or reduced if they threaten equality of respect. But if so, why can't sex-role correlations be eliminated for the same reason?

These arguments depend, however, on a very questionable assumption. That assumption is that the factors which militate against, say, reckless driving militate also against, say, weightlifting, but this is far from clear. The factors which militate against reckless driving are that it risks harming others because it risks maiming, disfiguring and killing them. On the assimilationist's account the factors which militate against weightlifting are that the sex-activity correlations it engenders risk harming others by being the occasion by which they may come to have *false beliefs.*

For similar reasons, any parallel between the effects of allowing all activities to flourish and the effects of allowing great economic inequalities to flourish is highly questionable. For example, Norman Daniels has urged that the economic inequalities allowed by Rawls's second principle of justice militate against the equal liberties demanded by his first principle of justice.[37] Similarly, Gerald Cohen has argued against the wide economic inequalities permitted in Nozick's system.[38] Whatever the force of these arguments, they are of little help to the assimilationist. For what they maintain is that economic inequalities harm the poor because they diminish the poor's objective opportunities, *not* that they harm the poor because in contemplating them the poor may come to have false beliefs which harm them.

But if we can eliminate reckless driving because it risks harming others, why can't we eliminate sex-activity correlations on the ground that they too risk harming others? Why should it matter that the harm involved in the latter case is false belief or stems from false belief? In Chapter II of *On Liberty,* Mill argues that it is wrong for a government to restrict acts of expression, though these acts may harm certain individuals by being the occasion by which these individuals come to have "false beliefs." Following Thomas Scanlon, I defend Mill's position on the ground that the autonomous person could not allow the state to protect him against false beliefs. If a person did allow the state to do this he or she would be surrendering to it

[37] Norman Daniels, "Equal Liberty and Unequal Worth of Liberty." In Norman Daniels ed. *Reading Rawls* (New York: Basic Books, 1975), pp. 253–83.

[38] Gerald Cohen, "Robert Nozick and Wilt Chamberlain." In John Arthur and William Shaw eds. *Justice and Economic Distribution* (Englewood Cliffs, N.J.: Prentice-Hall, Inc., 1978), pp. 246–62.

the authority to decide what he or she should believe. But in the relevant sense, an autonomous person is one who sees herself or himself as "sovereign in deciding what to believe and in weighing competing reasons for action."[39] Hence, autonomous persons could not allow the state to protect them against false beliefs by restricting activities. In particular, they could not allow the state to protect them against false beliefs about the sexes by restricting activities which generate sex-activity correlations.

Critics may feel that the sudden intrusion here of the notion of the state is unfair. But I do not see how it can really be avoided. The state seems the most likely agency to institute the reforms of the assimilationist society. But it may be argued that if that society were some sort of participatory democracy its members could freely decide to impose on themselves the restrictions in question. In this way the notion of an autocratic state, at odds with the autonomy of its members, could seem to be dispelled. That is, of course, a well-known and attractive solution to the old conflict between the individual and the state. It is, for example, Rousseau's solution. There is conceptually no difficulty in imagining people in their "cool moments" collectively deciding to outlaw actions which they know could lead them to have false beliefs. The difficulty is that this offers no help to the assimilationists. If, to break down sex-activity correlations, the autonomous members of a participatory democracy denied themselves the opportunity to engage in certain kinds of unalienated activity, then they could not be sexually blind. Remember the considerable costs of eliminating unalienated activity. Is it even intelligible to think that we could impose these costs on ourselves just to prevent correlations from arising between activities and persons different in a way we barely notice? Is it even intelligible to think that we could impose these costs on ourselves just to prevent correlations from arising between activities and persons different in ways to which we are "indifferent," or think have "no significance"? Can we imagine autonomous persons in present society eliminating *any* activity just to prevent correlations from arising between activities and persons who are different in eye-color?

3

So the pursuit of sexual blindness is the pursuit of a chimera. The sexually blind or assimilationist society is either unequal in the most fundamental sense and incompatible with the autonomy of its members, or else it is impossible. The assimilationists fail to see these paradoxes because they try to describe the sexually ideal society in terms of equality of opportunity in abstraction from other values. But this is sure to lead to lop-sided results. If we give due weight to all our values—in particular, to autonomy, to the

[39] Thomas Scanlon, "A Theory of Freedom of Expression," *Philosophy and Public Affairs,* 1 (1972), 215, 216.

uplifting use of our leisure time, to excellence and beauty in all its forms, as well as to equality of opportunity and equality of respect—we get a society that is saner, kinder, more equal, more familiar, and also more interesting and exciting than the bizarre and bleak world of the assimilationists.

For rather than requiring us to suppress opportunities, a true egalitarianism requires us to multiply and diversify them. For example, if men excel at firefighting and other activities requiring strength, we better use our ingenuity in the service of sex-equality to create activities women can excel at rather than to superannuate activities men excel at. Similarly, turning to activities we find valuable in themselves, if men dominate weightlifting, the way to sex equality is not to abolish weightlifting—that is only the way to a dreary sex-blind world—but to design activities women will dominate. As Jane English saw clearly, sexual equality does not require abolishing sports—indeed she never even considers that option—but rather inventing "alternative sports using women's distinctive abilities."[40]

Given that this is the right way to proceed, though I expect that individuals in a society that enjoys a genuine sexual equality will have a far wider appreciation of talents than we do, I do not expect that we shall no longer find that certain excellences are largely peculiar to one of the sexes or that the sex-activity correlations so dreaded by the assimilationist will have disappeared. On the contrary, I expect that they will be more numerous, more varied, and more striking.

In such a society, of course, there will be a danger of sex roles emerging. Just because sex-activity correlations exist we will tend to influence others to choose activities their sex excels at, and even to assign others to activities because of their sex. Consequently, we shall have to be on guard. We shall have to watch ourselves, and watch others. Further, organizations created and designed to protect women's rights (and men's rights too) will not disappear. Perhaps the law will have to mention sex (and color) explicitly, and perhaps there may have to be special bills of rights for women or any racial or other group that is liable to need them. Perhaps these are costs. On the other hand, they are not without usefulness. Vigilance builds character and self-respect, and I do not anticipate the end of morality. Also we must not exaggerate the danger of sex roles emerging. No doubt much of the tendency of sex-activity correlations to develop into sex roles is due to inequalities in income and power which traditionally have been correlated with activities. But as egalitarians we need not tolerate such inequalities. Finally, we should not exaggerate either the value of that "harmony" which sexual blindness promises to bestow on us. The pursuit of harmony has often subverted equality.

Once we see how little can be said for sex-blindness and how much can be said against it, it should be easier to see why its associated principle of "color-blindness" should be accepted only with circumspection. Insofar as

---

[40] English, "Sex Equality in Sports," p. 277.

that principle means that we should be "color-blind" in the sense that we should ignore racial differences and, except in order to make compensation, set them aside as irrelevant to what positions others can fill—then, of course, it is secure. But if it means that we should institute reforms to *make* us "color-blind" in a sense analogous to "sexual blindness" in the assimilationist society, then it should be viewed with the gravest suspicion. Even in the ideal society, we must not let "color-blindness" (or "sexual blindness") distract us from equality.[41]

[41] I thank Professor Wasserstrom, Jan Boxill, and the referees of *Social Theory and Practice* for helpful comments. My criticisms of Professor Wasserstrom do not depreciate the value of his work. No one has dealt with the subjects treated here with greater sensitivity and intelligence.

POLITICAL PHILOSOPHIES OF WOMEN'S LIBERATION

ALISON JAGGAR

Feminists are united by a belief that the unequal and inferior social status of women is unjust and needs to be changed. But they are deeply divided about what changes are required. The deepest divisions are not differences about strategy or the kinds of tactics that will best serve women's interests; instead, they are differences about what *are* women's interests, what constitutes women's liberation.

Within the women's liberation movement, several distinct ideologies can be discerned. All[1] believe that justice requires freedom and equality for women, but they differ on such basic philosophical questions as the proper account of freedom and equality, the functions of the state, and the notion of what constitutes human, and especially female, nature. In what follows, I shall outline the feminist ideologies which are currently most influential and show how these give rise to differences on some particular issues. Doing this will indicate why specific debates over feminist questions cannot be settled in isolation but can only be resolved in the context of a theoretical framework derived from reflection on the fundamental issues of social and political philosophy.

[1] All except one: as we shall see later, lesbian separatism is evasive on the question whether men should, even ultimately, be equal with women.

THE CONSERVATIVE VIEW

This is the position against which all feminists are in reaction. In brief, it is the view that differential treatment of women, as a group, is not unjust. Conservatives admit, of course, that some individual women do suffer hardships, but they do not see this suffering as part of the systematic social oppression of women. Instead, the clear differences between women's and men's social roles are rationalized in one of two ways. Conservatives either claim that the female role is not inferior to that of the male, or they argue that women are inherently better adapted than men to the traditional female sex role. The former claim advocates a kind of sexual apartheid, typically described by such phrases as "complementary but equal;" the latter postulates an inherent inequality between the sexes.[2]

All feminists reject the first claim, and most feminists, historically, have rejected the second. However, it is interesting to note that, as we shall see later, some modern feminists have revived the latter claim.

Conservative views come in different varieties, but they all have certain fundamentals in common. All claim that men and women should fulfill different social functions, that these differences should be enforced by law where opinion and custom are insufficient, and that such action may be justified by reference to innate differences between men and women. Thus all sexual conservatives presuppose that men and women are inherently unequal in abilities, that the alleged difference in ability implies a difference in social function and that one of the main tasks of the state is to ensure that the individual perform his or her proper social function. Thus, they argue, social differentiation between the sexes is not unjust, since justice not only allows but requires us to treat unequals unequally.

LIBERAL FEMINISM

In speaking of liberal feminism, I am referring to that tradition which received its classic expression in J. S. Mill's *The Subjection of Women* and which is alive today in various "moderate" groups, such as the National Organization for Women, which agitate for legal reform to improve the status of women.

The main thrust of the liberal feminist's argument is that an individual woman should be able to determine her social role with as great freedom as does a man. Though women now have the vote, the liberal sees that we are

---

[2] The inequalities between the sexes are said to be both physical and psychological. Alleged psychological differences between the sexes include women's emotional instability, greater tolerance for boring detail, incapacity for abstract thought, and less aggression. Writers who have made such claims range from Rousseau (*Émile, or Education* [1762; translation, London: J. M. Dent, 1911]; see especially Book 5 concerning the education of "Sophie, or Woman"), through Schopenhauer (*The World As Will and Idea* and his essay "On Women"), Fichte *(The Science of Rights),* Nietzsche *(Thus Spake Zarathustra),* and Freud down to, in our own times, Steven Goldberg with *The Inevitability of Patriarchy* (New York: William Morrow, 1973–74).

still subject to many constraints, legal as well as customary, which hinder us from success in the public worlds of politics, business and the professions. Consequently the liberal views women's liberation as the elimination of those constraints and the achievement of equal civil rights.

Underlying the liberal argument is the belief that justice requires that the criteria for allocating individuals to perform a particular social function should be grounded in the individual's ability to perform the tasks in question. The use of criteria such as "race, sex, religion, national origin or ancestry"[3] will normally not be directly relevant to most tasks. Moreover, in conformity with the traditional liberal stress on individual rights, the liberal feminist insists that each person should be considered separately in order than an outstanding individual should not be penalized for deficiencies that her sex as a whole might possess.[4]

This argument is buttressed by the classic liberal belief that there should be a minimum of state intervention in the affairs of the individual. Such a belief entails rejection of the paternalistic view that women's weakness requires that we be specially protected.[5] Even if relevant differences between women and men in general could be demonstrated, the existence of those differences still would not constitute a sufficient reason for allowing legal restrictions on women as a group. Even apart from the possibility of penalizing an outstanding individual, the liberal holds that women's own good sense or, in the last resort, our incapacity to do the job will render legal prohibitions unnecessary.[6]

From this sketch it is clear that the liberal feminist interprets equality to mean that each individual, regardless of sex, should have an equal opportunity to seek whatever social positions she or he wishes. Freedom is primarily the absence of legal constraints to hinder women in this enterprise. However, the modern liberal feminist recognizes that equality and freedom, construed in the liberal way, may not always be compatible. Hence, the modern liberal feminist differs from the traditional one in believing not only that laws should not discriminate against women, but that they should be used to make discrimination illegal. Thus she would outlaw unequal pay scales, prejudice in the admission of women to job-training programs and professional schools, and discrimination by employers in hiring practices. She would also outlaw such things as discrimination by finance companies in the granting of loans, mortgages, and insurance to women.

In certain areas, the modern liberal even appears to advocate laws which discriminate in favor of women. For instance, she may support the preferential hiring of women over men, or alimony for women unqualified to work outside the home. She is likely to justify her apparent inconsistency by claiming that such differential treatment is necessary to remedy past inequalities—but that

---

[3] This is the language used by Title VII of the Civil Rights Act with Executive Order 11246, 1965, and Title IX.

[4] J. S. Mill, *The Subjection of Women* (1869; reprint ed., London: J. M. Dent, 1965), p. 236.

[5] Ibid, p. 243.

[6] Ibid, p. 235.

it is only a temporary measure. With regard to (possibly paid) maternity leaves and the employer's obligation to reemploy a woman after such a leave, the liberal argues that the bearing of children has at least as good a claim to be regarded as a social service as does a man's military or jury obligation, and that childbearing should therefore carry corresponding rights to protection. The liberal also usually advocates the repeal of laws restricting contraception and abortion, and may demand measures to encourage the establishment of private day-care centers. However, she points out that none of these demands, nor the father's payment of child support, should really be regarded as discrimination in favor of women. It is only the customary assignment of responsibility for children to their mothers which it makes it possible to overlook the fact that fathers have an equal obligation to provide and care for their children. Women's traditional responsibility for child care is culturally determined, not biologically inevitable—except for breast-feeding, which is now optional. Thus the liberal argues that if women are to participate in the world outside the home on equal terms with men, not only must our reproductive capacity come under our own control but, if we have children, we must be able to share the responsibility for raising them. In return, as an extension of the same principle of equal responsibility, the modern liberal supports compulsory military service for women so long as it is obligatory for men.

Rather than assuming that every apparent difference in interests and abilities between the sexes is innate, the liberal recognizes that such differences, if they do not result entirely from our education, are at least greatly exaggerated by it. By giving both sexes the same education, whether it be cooking or carpentry, the liberal claims that she is providing the only environment in which individual potentialities (and, indeed, genuine sexual differences) can emerge. She gives little weight to the possible charge that in doing this she is not liberating women but only imposing a different kind of conditioning. At the root of the liberal tradition is a deep faith in the autonomy of the individual which is incapable of being challenged within that framework.

In summary, then, the liberal views liberation for women as the freedom to determine our own social role and to compete with men on terms that are as equal as possible. She sees every individual as being engaged in constant competition with every other in order to maximize her or his own self-interest, and she claims that the function of the state is to see that such competition is fair by enforcing "equality of opportunity." The liberal does not believe that it is necessary to change the whole existing social structure in order to achieve women's liberation. Nor does she see it as being achieved simultaneously for all women; she believes that individual women may liberate themselves long before their condition is attained by all. Finally, the liberal claims that her concept of women's liberation also involves liberation for men, since men are not only removed from a privileged position but they are also freed from having to accept the entire responsibility for such things as the support of their families and the defense of their country.

CLASSICAL MARXIST FEMINISM

On the classical Marxist view, the oppression of women is, historically and currently, a direct result of the institution of private property; therefore, it can only be ended by the abolition of that institution. Consequently, feminism must be seen as part of a broader struggle to achieve a communist society. Feminism is one reason for communism. The long-term interests of women are those of the working class.

For Marxists, everyone is oppressed by living in a society where a small class of individuals owns the means of production and hence is enabled to dominate the lives of the majority who are forced to sell their labor power in order to survive. Women have an equal interest with men in eliminating such a class society. However, Marxists also recognize that women suffer special forms of oppression to which men are *not* subject, and hence, insofar as this oppression is rooted in capitalism, women have additional reasons for the overthrow of that economic system.

Classical Marxists believe that the special oppression of women results primarily from our traditional position in the family. This excludes women from participation in "public" production and relegates us to domestic work in the "private" world of the home. From its inception right up to the present day, monogamous marriage was designed to perpetuate the consolidation of wealth in the hands of a few. Those few are men. Thus, for Marxists, an analysis of the family brings out the inseparability of class society from male supremacy. From the very beginning of surplus production, "the sole exclusive aims of monogamous marriage were to make the man supreme in the family, and to propagate, as the future heirs to his wealth, children indisputably his own."[7] Such marriage is "founded on the open or concealed domestic slavery of the wife,"[8] and is characterized by the familiar double standard which requires sexual fidelity from the woman but not from the man.

Marxists do not claim, of course, that women's oppression is a creation of capitalism. But they do argue that the advent of capitalism intensified the degradation of women and that the continuation of capitalism requires the perpetuation of this degradation. Capitalism and male supremacy each reinforce the other. Among the ways in which sexism benefits the capitalist system are: by providing a supply of cheap labor for industry and hence exerting a downward pressure on all wages; by increasing the demand for the consumption goods on which women are conditioned to depend; and by allocating to women, for no direct pay, the performance of such socially necessary but unprofitable tasks as food preparation, domestic maintenance and the care of the children, the sick and the old.[9]

---

[7] Friedrich Engels, *The Origin of the Family, Private Property and the State* (1884), reprint ed. (New York: International Publishers, 1942), pp. 57–58.

[8] Ibid., p. 65.

[9] This is, of course, very far from being a complete account of the ways in which Marxists believe that capitalism benefits from sexism.

This analysis indicates the directions in which classical Marxists believe that women must move. "The first condition for the liberation of the wife is to bring the whole female sex back into public industry."[10] Only then will a wife cease to be economically dependent on her husband. But for woman's entry into public industry to be possible, fundamental social changes are necessary: all the work which women presently do—food preparation, child care, nursing, etc.—must come within the sphere of public production. Thus, whereas the liberal feminist advocates an egalitarian marriage, with each spouse shouldering equal responsibility for domestic work and economic support, the classical Marxist feminist believes that the liberation of women requires a more radical change in the family. Primarily, women's liberation requires that the economic functions performed by the family should be undertaken by the state. Thus the state should provide child care centers, public eating places, hospital facilities, etc. But all this, of course, could happen only under socialism. Hence it is only under socialism that married women will be able to participate fully in public life and end the situation where "within the family [the husband] is the burgeois and the wife represents the proletariat."[11]

It should be noted that "the abolition of the monogamous family as the economic unit of society"[12] does not necessitate its disappearance as a social unit. Since "sexual love is by its nature exclusive,"[13] marriage will continue, but now it will no longer resemble an economic contract, as it has done hitherto in the property-owning classes. Instead, it will be based solely on "mutual inclination"[14] between a woman and a man who are now in reality, and not just formally, free and equal.

It is clear that classical Marxist feminism is based on very different philosophical presuppositions from those of liberal feminism. Freedom is viewed not just as the absence of discrimination against women but rather as freedom from the coercion of economic necessity. Similarly, equality demands not mere equality of opportunity to compete against other individuals but rather approximate equality in the satisfaction of material needs. Hence, the classical Marxist feminist's view of the function of the state is very different from the view of the liberal feminist. Ultimately, the Marxist pays at least lip service to the belief that the state is an instrument of class oppression which eventually will wither away. In the meantime, she believes that it should undertake far more than the minimal liberal function of setting up fair rules for the economic race. Instead, it should take over the means of production and also assume those economic responsibilities that capitalism assigned to the individual family and that placed that woman in a position of dependence on the man. This view of the state presupposes a very different account of human nature

[10] Engels, op. cit., p. 66.
[11] Ibid., pp. 65–66.
[12] Ibid., p. 66.
[13] Ibid., p. 72.
[14] Ibid.

from that held by the liberal. Instead of seeing the individual as fundamentally concerned with the maximization of her or his own self-interest, the classical Marxist feminist believes that the selfish and competitive aspects of our natures are the result of their systematic perversion in an acquisitive society. Viewing human nature as flexible and as reflecting the economic organization of society, she argues that it is necessary for women (indeed for everybody) to be comprehensively reeducated, and to learn that ultimately individuals have common rather than competing goals and interests.

Since she sees women's oppression as a function of the larger socioeconomic system, the classical Marxist feminist denies the possibility, envisaged by the liberal, of liberation for a few women on an individual level. However, she does agree with the liberal that women's liberation would bring liberation for men, too. Men's liberation would now be enlarged to include freedom from class oppression and from the man's traditional responsibility to "provide" for his family, a burden that under liberalism the man merely lightens by sharing it with his wife.

RADICAL FEMINISM

Radical feminism is a recent attempt to create a new conceptual model for understanding the many different forms of the social phenomenon of oppression in terms of the basic concept of sexual oppression. It is formulated by such writers as Ti-Grace Atkinson and Shulamith Firestone.[15]

Radical feminism denies the liberal claim that the basis of women's oppression consists in our lack of political or civil rights; similarly, it rejects the classical Marxist belief that basically women are oppressed because they live in a class society. Instead, in what seems to be a startling regression to conservatism, the radical feminist claims that the roots of women's oppression are biological. She believes that the origin of women's subjection lies in the fact that, as a result of the weakness caused by childbearing, we became dependent on men for physical survival. Thus she speaks of the origin of the family in apparently conservative terms as being primarily a biological rather than a social or economic organization.[16] The radical feminist believes that the physical subjection of women by men was historically the most basic form of oppression, prior rather than secondary to the institution of private property and its corollary, class oppression.[17] Moreover, she believes that the power

---

[15] Ti-Grace Atkinson, "Radical Feminism" and "The Institution of Sexual Intercourse" in *Notes from the Second Year: Major Writings of the Radical Feminists,* ed. S. Firestone (New York, 1970); and Shulamith Firestone, *The Dialectic of Sex: The Case for Feminist Revolution* (New York: Bantam Books; 1970).

[16] Engels recognizes that early forms of the family were based on what he calls "natural" conditions, which presumably included the biological, but he claims that monogamy "was the first form of the family to be based, not on natural, but on economic conditions—on the victory of private property over primitive, natural communal property." Engels, op. cit., p. 57.

[17] Atkinson and Firestone do talk of women as a "political class," but not in Marx's classic

relationships which develop within the biological family provide a model for understanding all other types of oppression such as racism and class society. Thus she reverses the emphasis of the classical Marxist feminist by explaining the development of class society in terms of the biological family rather than explaining the development of the family in terms of class society. She believes that the battles against capitalism and against racism are both subsidiary to the more fundamental struggle against sexism.

Since she believes that the oppression of women is basically biological, the radical feminist concludes that our liberation requires a biological revolution. She believes that only now, for the first time in history, is technology making it possible for women to be liberated from the "fundamental inequality of the bearing and raising of children." It is achieving this through the development of techniques of artificial reproduction and the consequent possibility of diffusing the childbearing and child-raising role throughout society as a whole. Such a biological revolution is basic to the achievement of those important but secondary changes in our political, social and economic systems which will make possible the other prerequisites for women's liberation. As the radical feminist sees them, those other prerequisites are: the full self-determination, including economic independence, of women (and children); the total integration of women (and children) into all aspects of the larger society; and the freedom of all women (and children) to do whatever they wish to do sexually.[18]

Not only will technology snap the link between sex and reproduction and thus liberate women from our childbearing and child-raising function; the radical feminist believes that ultimately technology will liberate both sexes from the necessity to work. Individual economic burdens and dependencies will thereby be eliminated, along with the justification for compelling children to attend school. So both the biological and economic bases of the family will be removed by technology. The family's consequent disappearance will abolish the prototype of the social "role system,"[19] the most basic form, both historically and conceptually, of oppressive and authoritarian relationships. Thus, the radical feminist does not claim that women should be free to determine their own social roles: she believes instead that the whole "role system" must be abolished, even in its biological aspects.

The end of the biological family will also eliminate the need for sexual repression. Male homosexuality, lesbianism, and extramarital sexual intercourse will no longer be viewed in the liberal way as alternative options, outside the range of state regulation, in which the individual may or may not choose to participate. Nor will they be viewed, in the classical Marxist

---

sense where the criterion of an individual's class membership is her/his relationship to the means of production. Atkinson defines a class more broadly as a group treated in some special manner by other groups: in the case of women, the radical feminists believe that women are defined as a "class" in virtue of our childbearing capacity. "Radical Feminism," op. cit., p. 24.

[18] These conditions are listed and explained in *The Dialectic of Sex*, pp. 206–9.

[19] "Radical Feminism," op. cit., p. 36.

way, as unnatural vices, perversions resulting from the degrading influence of capitalist society.[20] Instead, even the categories of homosexuality and heterosexuality will be abandoned; the very "institution of sexual intercourse," where male and female each play a well-defined role, will disappear.[21] "Humanity could finally revert to its natural 'polymorphously perverse' sexuality."[22]

For the radical feminist, as for other feminists, justice requires freedom and equality for women. But for the radical feminist "equality" means not just equality under the law nor even equality in satisfaction of basic needs; rather, it means that women, like men, should not have to bear children. Correspondingly, the radical feminist conception of freedom requires not just that women should be free to compete, nor even that we should be free from material want and economic dependence on men; rather, freedom for women means that any woman is free to have close relationships with children without having to give birth to them. Politically, the radical feminist envisions an eventual "communistic anarchy,"[23] an ultimate abolition of the state. This will be achieved gradually, through an intermediate state of "cybernetic socialism" with household licenses to raise children and a guaranteed income for all. Perhaps surprisingly, in view of Freud's reputation among many feminists, the radical feminist conception of human nature is neo-Freudian. Firestone believes, with Freud, that "the crucial problem of modern life [is] sexuality."[24] Individuals are psychologically formed through their experience in the family, a family whose power relationships reflect the underlying biological realities of female (and childhood) dependence. But technology will smash the universality of Freudian psychology. The destruction of the biological family, never envisioned by Freud, will allow the emergence of new women and men, different from any people who have previously existed.

The radical feminist theory contains many interesting claims. Some of these look almost factual in character: they include the belief that pregnancy and childbirth are painful and unpleasant experiences, that sexuality is not naturally genital and heterosexual, and that technology may be controlled by men and women without leading to totalitarianism. Other presuppositions are more clearly normative: among them are the beliefs that technology should be used to eliminate all kinds of pain, that hard work is not in itself a virtue, that sexuality ought not to be institutionalized and, perhaps most controversial of all, that children have the same rights to self-determination as adults.

Like the other theories we have considered, radical feminism believes that women's liberation will bring benefits for men. According to this concept of

---

[20] Engels often expresses an extreme sexual puritanism in *The Origin of the Family, Private Property and the State*. We have already seen his claim that "sexual love is by its nature exclusive." Elsewhere (p. 57) he talks about "the abominable practice of sodomy." Lenin is well known for the expression of similar views.

[21] "The Institution of Sexual Intercourse," op. cit.

[22] *The Dialectic of Sex,* p. 209.

[23] Ibid., final chart, pp. 244–45.

[24] Ibid., p. 43.

women's liberation, not only will men be freed from the role of provider, but they will also participate on a completely equal basis in childbearing as well as child-rearing. Radical feminism, however, is the only theory which argues explicitly that women's liberation also necessitates children's liberation. Firestone explains that this is because "The heart of woman's oppression is her childbearing and child-rearing roles. And in turn children are defined in relation to this role and are psychologically formed by it; what they become as adults and the sorts of relationships they are able to form determine the society they will ultimately build."[25]

NEW DIRECTIONS

Although the wave of excitement about women's liberation which arose in the late '60s has now subsided, the theoretical activity of feminists has continued. Since about 1970, it has advanced in two main directions: lesbian separatism and socialist feminism.

Lesbian separatism is less a coherent and developed ideology than an emerging movement, like the broader feminist movement, within which different ideological strains can be detected. All lesbian separatists believe that the present situation of male supremacy requires that women should refrain from heterosexual relationships. But for some lesbian separatists, this is just a temporary necessity, whereas for others, lesbianism will always be required.

Needless to say, all lesbian separatists reject the liberal and the classical Marxist beliefs about sexual preferences; but some accept the radical feminist contention that ultimately it is unimportant whether one's sexual partner be male or female.[26] However, in the immediate context of a male-supremacist society, the lesbian separatist believes that one's sexual choice attains tremendous political significance. Lesbianism becomes a way of combating the overwhelming heterosexual ideology that perpetuates male supremacy.

> Women ... become defined as appendages to men so that there is a coherent ideological framework which says it is natural for women to create the surplus to take care of men and that men will do other things. Reproduction itself did not have to determine that. The fact that male supremacy developed the way it has and was institutionalized is an ideological creation. The ideology of heterosexuality, not the simple act of intercourse, is the whole set of assumptions which maintains the ideological power of men over women.[27]

----

[25] Ibid., p. 72.

[26] "In a world devoid of male power and, therefore, sex roles, who you lived with, loved, slept with and were committed to would be irrelevant. All of us would be equal and have equal determination over the society and how it met our needs. Until this happens, how we use our sexuality and our bodies is just as relevant to our liberation as how we use our minds and time." Coletta Reid, "Coming Out in the Women's Movement." In Nancy Myron and Charlotte Buch, eds., *Lesbianism and the Women's Movement,* (Baltimore: Diana Press, 1975), p. 103.

[27] Margaret Small, "Lesbians and the Class Position of Women," in *Lesbianism and the Women's Movement,* p. 58.

Although this writer favors an ultimate de-institutionalization of sexual activity, her rejection of the claim that reproduction as such does not determine the inferior status of women clearly places her outside the radical feminist framework; indeed, she would identify her methodological approach as broadly Marxist. Some lesbian separatists are more radical, however. They argue explicitly for a matriarchal society which is "an affirmation of the power of female consciousness of the Mother."[28] Such matriarchists talk longingly about ancient matriarchal societies where women were supposed to have been physically strong, adept at self-defense, and the originators of such cultural advances as: the wheel, pottery, industry, leather working, metal working, fire, agriculture, animal husbandry, architecture, cities, decorative art, music, weaving, medicine, communal child care, dance, poetry, song, etc.[29] They claim that men were virtually excluded from these societies. Women's culture is compared favorably with later patriarchal cultures as being peaceful, egalitarian, vegetarian, and intellectually advanced. Matriarchal lesbian separatists would like to recreate a similar culture which would probably imitate the earlier ones in its exclusion of men as full members. Matriarchal lesbian separatists do not claim unequivocally that "men are genetically predisposed towards destruction and dominance,"[30] but, especially given the present research on the behavioral effects of the male hormone testosterone,[31] they think it is a possibility that lesbians must keep in mind.

Socialist feminists believe that classical Marxism and radical feminism each have both insights and deficiencies. The task of socialist feminism is to construct a theory that avoids the weaknesses of each but incorporates its (and other) insights. There is space here for only a brief account of some of the main points of this developing theory.

Socialist feminists reject the basic radical feminist contention that liberation for women requires the abolition of childbirth. Firestone's view is criticized as ahistorical, anti-dialectical, and utopian. Instead, socialist feminists accept the classical Marxist contention that socialism is the main precondition for women's liberation. But though socialism is necessary, socialist feminists do not believe that it is sufficient. Sexism can continue to exist despite public ownership of the means of production. The conclusion that socialist feminists draw is that it is necessary to resort to direct cultural action in order to develop a specifically feminist consciousness in addition to transforming the economic base. Thus their vision is totalistic, requiring "transformation of the entire fabric of social relationships."[32]

In rejecting the radical feminist view that the family is based on biological

---

[28] Jane Alpert, "Mother Right: A New Feminist Theory," *Ms* (August 1973), p. 94.

[29] Alice, Gordon, Debbie, and Mary, *Lesbian Separatism: An Amazon Analysis,* typescript, 1973, p. 5 (To be published by Diana Press, Baltimore.)

[30] Ibid., p. 23.

[31] It is interesting that this is the same research on which Steven Goldberg ground his thesis of "the inevitability of patriarchy"; see note 2.

[32] Barbara Ehrenreich, "Socialist/Feminism and Revolution" (unpublished paper presented to the National Socialist-Feminist Conference, Antioch College, Ohio, July 1975), p. 1.

conditions, socialist feminists turn toward the classical Marxist account of monogamy as being based "not on natural but on economic conditions." [33] But they view the classical Marxist account as inadequate, overly simple. Juliet Mitchell [34] argues that the family should be analyzed in a more detailed, sophisticated, and historically specific way in terms of the separate, though interrelated, functions that women perform within it: production, reproduction, sexuality, and the socialization of the young.

Socialist feminists agree with classical Marxists that women's liberation requires the entry of women into public production. But this in itself is not sufficient. It is also necessary that women have access to the more prestigious and less deadening jobs and to supervisory and administrative positions. There should be no "women's work" within public industry. [35]

In classical Marxist theory, "productive labor" is viewed as the production of goods and services within the market economy. Some socialist feminists believe that this account of productiveness obscures the socially vital character of the labor that women perform in the home. They argue that, since it is clearly impossible under capitalism to bring all women into public production, individuals (at least as an interim measure) should be paid a wage for domestic work. This reform would dignify the position of housewives, reduce their dependence on their husbands and make plain their objective position, minimized by classical Marxists, as an integral part of the working class. [36] Not all socialist feminists accept this position, however, and the issue is extremely controversial at the time of this writing.

One of the main insights of the feminist movement has been that "the personal is political." Socialist feminists are sensitive to the power relations involved in male/female interaction and believe that it is both possible and necessary to begin changing these, even before the occurrence of a revolution in the ownership of the means of production. Thus, socialist feminists recognize the importance of a "subjective factor" in revolutionary change and reject the rigid economic determinism that has characterized many classical Marxists. They are sympathetic to attempts by individuals to change their life styles and to share responsibility for each other's lives, even though they recognize that such attempts can never be entirely successful within a capitalist context. They also reject the sexual puritanism inherent in classical Marxism, moving closer to the radical feminist position in this regard.

Clearly there are sharp differences between socialist feminism and most forms of lesbian separatism. The two have been dealt with together in this section only because each is still a developing theory and because it is not

[33] Engels, op. cit., p. 57.

[34] Juliet Mitchell, *Woman's Estate* (New York: Random House, 1971). Lively discussion of Mitchell's work continues among socialist feminists.

[35] For one socialist feminist account of women's work in public industry see Sheila Rowbotham, *Woman's Consciousness, Man's World* (Baltimore: Penguin Books, 1973), chap. 6, "Sitting Next to Nellie."

[36] One influential exponent of wages for housework is Mariarosa Dalla Costa, *The Power of Women and the Subversion of Community* (Bristol, England: Falling Wall Press, 1973).

yet clear how far either represents the creation of a new ideology and how far it is simply an extension of an existing ideology. One suspects that at least the matriarchal version of lesbian separatism may be viewed as a new ideology: after all, the interpretation of "freedom" to mean "freedom from men" is certainly new, as is the suggestion that women are innately superior to men. Socialist feminism, however, should probably be seen as an extension of classical Marxism, using essentially similar notions of human nature, of freedom and equality, and of the role of the state, but attempting to show that women's situation and the sphere of personal relations in general need more careful analysis by Marxists.[37]

This sketch of some new directions in feminism completes my outline of the main contemporary positions on women's liberation. I hope that I have made clearer the ideological presuppositions at the root of many feminist claims and also shed some light on the philosophical problems that one needs to resolve in order to formulate one's own position and decide on a basis for action. Many of these philosophical questions, such as the nature of the just society, the proper account of freedom and equality, the functions of the state and the relation between the individual and society, are traditional problems which now arise in a new context; others, such as the role of technology in human liberation, are of more recent origin. In either case, feminism adds a fresh dimension to our discussion of the issues and points to the need for the so-called philosophy of man to be transformed into a comprehensive philosophy of women and men and their social relations.

[37] Since I wrote this section, I have learned of some recent work by socialist feminists which seems to provide an excitingly new theoretical underpinning for much socialist feminist practice. An excellent account of these ideas is given by Gayle Rubin in "The Traffic in Women: Notes on the 'Political Economy' of Sex." This paper appears in *Toward an Anthropology of Women,* ed. Rayna R. Reiter (New York: Monthly Review Press, 1975). If something like Rubin's account is accepted by socialist feminists, it will be a difficult and important question to work out just how far they have moved from traditional Marxism and how much they still share with it.

SELF-DETERMINATION AND AUTONOMY

SHARON BISHOP HILL

Some have spoken as if the sexual revolution amounts to greatly increased liberality about sex. Recently there is talk that it will not be accomplished until there is an end to sexual discrimination and women as well as men are

Reprinted with permission of the author.
AUTHOR'S NOTE: I wish to thank Thomas Hill, Jr., and Richard Wasserstrom who read earlier versions of this paper and made many helpful comments and suggestions.

liberated. Not a few are certain that they know what changes are required
to liberate women. Many are content with things as they are, and some are
merely complacent about this revolution. Others are perplexed though not
unwilling to change, for those they love seem unhappy. In winding a way
through an unreal but not unlikely dispute, I suggest a way of allaying these
perplexities and justifying some of these demands. If what I say about how
to set aside certain doubts about women's liberation is plausible, then I imagine
radical changes are in order, not just about how we view and treat women,
but also about how we view and treat men and children. What these changes
are is difficult to say. In any case, my interest here is primarily in principles
and arguments which might be used to explain and justify some of the demands
now being made in the name of women's liberation. But to begin with, the
dispute.

I. THE DISPUTE

Over the years, John and Harriet have had long arguments about women's
liberation. Both have come a long way. When Harriet first decided that she
could not find self-fulfillment without a paying job, John felt threatened and
protested that it would not be proper. But now he is reconciled and even
insists that women get equal pay for equal work. He supports the Equal
Rights Amendment and urges his company to give talented and well-trained
women an equal chance at job opportunities. He has given up as muddled
his old belief that women are naturally inferior to men in intelligence, objectivity, emotional stability and the like. He acknowledges that women have
often been treated in degrading ways, and like many liberals, he has tried
hard to purge his vocabulary of such words as "chick," "broad," and "piece."
He even tries, not always successfully, to avoid references like "the girls in
the office." Women, he says, have as much right to happiness as men, and
so he is ready to oppose any social scheme which makes them, relative to
men, systematically discontent or unhappy. But this is as far as he will go.

Harriet says that this is not far enough. And the dispute came to a head
when she protested to the school principal and finally to the school board
about their daughter's education. Harriet was distressed that girls were encouraged in numerous ways to accept the traditional feminine role. For
example, the practice at most school dances was for girls to wait to be asked
by boys. The school had well-developed and financed athletic programs for
boys, but few for girls, and very little staff to help girls to develop their skills.
The counselors were comparatively uninterested in advising girls about their
futures. When they did, they assumed that, for the most part, appropriate
careers for girls were as secretaries, decorators, teachers, nurses or medical
assistants. Students' programs were then tailored for these vocations. These,
in turn, were viewed as stop-gap or carry-over measures to enable girls to
get through any periods in which they were not married or supported by

someone. If they did marry, it was assumed that there would be children and a home to which the woman should devote herself.

Harriet gradually came to see that her objections to these practices arose as she faced her own feelings of resentment and betrayal at the kinds of opportunities and counseling she had early in life. Though she acknowledged the occasion of her objections, she also became convinced that her complaints were well founded. She was less clear how to support them, but her way of life seemed unnecessarily restrictive and she believed that she had interests and capacities which should have been developed but were not. She was irked, too, that she had never had a genuine opportunity to choose the way of life in which she and other women were so deeply involved. Whatever she might have chosen and whether or not she liked having a family and the feminine virtues, she felt that she had never really had any choice. She realized that part of the problem was that she herself had not regarded these as proper objects of her own choice. This failure she thought was the result of a complicated and overlapping set of teachings which had it that women were almost inevitably unfulfilled without having children, that normally they were better at raising children than men and men better suited for earning a living. Consequently, as the story went, the current division of labor is really most efficient, better for almost everyone and thus best. Both men and women were said to have duties associated with these roles. She now resents these teachings, justifiably she believes. She became especially anxious as she saw her daughter falling into the patterns of behavior and belief to which she now objects and so she complained to the school board.

John found Harriet less than convincing on these matters. It is important to oppose sex roles, he argued, if the roles function in a way which humiliates or degrades women or deprives them of political or economic rights. If these abuses could be avoided, he thinks the current standard division of labor and roles would not only be legitimate but quite a good way to arrange things. Someone, after all, needs to care for children and most women seem quite content. These arrangements seem natural to him. He suspects that women are naturally more sensitive and so make better parents for the very young; moreover, those he knows who have either not married or not had children seem to be weak and stunted characters or else hostile and aggressive. These observations suggest to him that most people, including women, are well off under something like the current division of labor and role. He acknowledges some, at least, of the difficulties about his belief that women are naturally suited for the domestic role. He does not, for example, rely on personality inventories of women versus men, because the traits they test for are bound to be influenced by the culture in which people grow up including, of course, some of the practices Harriet finds obnoxious. He does not appeal to the obvious physical differences between men and women, and he regards as irrelevant, at least in the modern world, appeals to differences in brute strength. Still he believes that some of the relevant differences are natural. He supports his suspicion by appeals to anthropological evidence about widely divergent groups in which women have almost invariably had the domestic role and quite often the traits which suit them for raising children and managing households. Were this not natural, he thinks it would not be so frequent. He has been known to remark that estrogen is associated with passive as opposed to aggressive personality traits, reminding Harriet that women maintain a higher level of this hormone than men. He suspects that the thwarted and hostile women he finds among the unmarried and childless result from frustration of the natural capacities of women for close emotional relations. There are, he admits, extraordinarily ambitious women who would be frustrated in following the traditional pattern; but a society which grants full political and economic rights to all adults can accommodate these exceptional people. Consequently, he resists the idea that there is something wrong with encouraging in young girls the feminine traits he so likes. He wants his daughter to be ladylike in figure and personality and hopes, for her sake, that she will never choose a career at the expense of having a family. He communicates this to her in innumerable, sometimes subtle, sometimes direct ways.

It is at this point that Harriet becomes most exasperated and even despairing. By all the conventional criteria, John seems liberal enough. He believes in equal pay for equal work and equal opportunities for those of equal achievement, motivation and talent. He acknowledges that women have been deprived of income, opportunities, power and their associated satisfactions by unfair social practices of various sorts. What he envisages is a world in which these injustices are eradicated but one in which women remain sensitive, understanding and charming, and in which most take up a domestic life while most men take up a paying vocation. Since he thinks it only efficient to prepare people for these likely different but quite natural futures, he thinks sound educational policy calls for certain subtle differences in the training of males and females. Harriet, on the other hand, believes that her resentment is justified, that she had been wronged in some way and would continue to be wronged if the world were magically transformed to match John's dreams. She becomes most desperate when she thinks of her daughter who is being similarly wronged.

The perplexed, like John, may say, "But where is the difficulty?" They understand complaints about violations of political and economic rights, like the right to vote, hold office and receive equal pay for equal work. They admit that a person would be wronged if gratuitously insulted or deliberately injured. But none of these seem to fit the case of Harriet or her daughter at least in the world John wants. There is no reason to believe they will be insulted, and it is difficult to pick out any political or economic right which we could confidently claim would be violated. Even if we think that Harriet and her daughter have been injured by the workings of the social system in this world, it is not clear that the harm was deliberate. No definite person designed the social system for the purpose of keeping women down, much less for the purpose of harming Harriet; it, like Topsy, just growed. If that is the case, whatever harm they may have suffered seems in important respects like a natural misfortune and not a deliberate wrong. If Harriet's objections to John's views can be defended, it must be on some other pattern of reasoning.

In the following, I shall try to isolate and explain some principles which could be used to justify Harriet's feelings about her own life and her protests of school practices. Roughly, I shall argue that if adults are viewed as having a right to self-determination, then Harriet and other adult women do nothing inappropriate in eschewing a traditional role nor do they have duties directly associated with such a role. Moreover, if as adults, we are to have a right of self-determination which is meaningful, we ought not be treated in ways which distort or prevent the development of the capacity for autonomous choice. I do not attempt to justify the claim that adults have a right of self-determination nor the claim that viewing adults as having such a right is better than any of a variety of other ways of regarding them, for example, as potential contributors to the general welfare or to some social or economic ideal. I hope that some of what I say will make respect for a right of self-determination attractive, but here I only set out to explain something about the right.

I try this line of argument, first, because I think it a promising one to explain the depth and kind of feeling generated in women who begin thinking seriously about their lives and their daughters' prospects. In the end, it may help explain why such pervasive changes are required and why some of them must be changes in attitude. Secondly, it seems possible with this reasoning to avoid some philosophical and empirical difficulties involved in more familiar arguments. For example, a number of people argue for sweeping changes in the treatment of women on the grounds that the resulting system will be more efficient in turning out happy individuals or in using the available pool of natual abilities. One problem here, of course, is to determine what is to count as being happy and so what is to count as evidence that some new system will be more efficient producing it than the present one. Others suggest that there has been a deliberate male conspiracy to keep women in the kitchen and out of the most lucrative and satisfying jobs. There are innumerable problems about what could be meant by "deliberate conspiracy" in this case; there does not seem to have been a conspiratorial meeting attended by anyone much less by most men or by representative men. It does not even seem plausible that some rather large number of men have consciously intended to keep women out of the mainstream of social and economic life at least in recent history. Even if some clear sense can be given to the notion, successful completion of the argument would require complicated empirical inquiries. Although it is true that a deliberate conspiracy to do wrong makes things rather worse, what seems important here is rather the wrong that has been done. If questions about the deliberateness of the wrongs are important at all, they seem to belong rather with attempts to decide to whom the burdens of change may legitimately fall. Finally, the line of reasoning I propose directly undercuts two of the kinds of arguments John suggested against Harriet. In the end, he claimed that his views about women and educational policy could be supported by appeals to efficient ways of arranging for child rearing as well as the natural suitability of current sex roles and the division of labor. Once a right of self-determination is granted, however, it does not matter whether the complex facts John appeals to are true or not, that is, it does not matter whether current sex roles are efficient means of rearing children or whether women, on the average, are better at domestic affairs than men. There are other considerations having to do with self-determination and autonomy which make these alleged facts irrelevant and which do justice to Harriet's response. She does not need to await empirical evidence about what is suitable for women and what makes women and children happy in order to know that something is wrong.

II. THE RIGHT OF SELF-DETERMINATION

To say that persons or states have a right of self-determination is to say minimally that they and only they have the authority to determine certain sorts of things. This does not necessarily mean that they have the power or capacity to determine these things, but rather that they have the title to. Sovereign states, for example, are widely regarded as having rather extensive authority to choose for themselves; they are said to have a right to determine how and who shall govern them, to have rights to determine for themselves what their ideals shall be, how they will allocate funds, what forms of culture they will support and devote themselves to, and the like. Having title to make these choices means that they have a right to expect others not to interfere with the legitimate exercise of their authority and a right to protect themselves from interference. It means, too, that they have a right to expect to carry on the processes of their government without foreign interest groups bribing their officials, and without being flooded with propaganda designed to influence the outcome of elections and the like. All this seems rather uncontroversial. More controversially, a small dependent state might claim that its right of self-determination was violated by threats of loss of essential support just because it failed to adopt the policies its larger, more affluent neighbor wanted. Withdrawal of such support makes it impossible to exercise its right of self-determination, consequently, threatening such withdrawal may be counted as incompatible with respecting the small nation's right. This may seem especially plausible where the support is well established, and where the threat is given for failure, say, to give up some local ritual or some trading policy mildly contrary to the interests of the affluent. Mature adults are often said to have a similar right, for example, to determine for themselves what their vocations shall be, whether to use their money for steaks or tennis balls, their leisure time for concerts or back-packing, and so on. Again, what is meant is that only they have the authority to make such choices, that others ought to refrain from interfering with the legitimate exercise of the title, and that they have the right to protect themselves from interference. Individuals may, if they wish, delegate parts of that authority. They give up some of it when they take a job, put themselves under the tutelage of an instructor or decide to let a friend choose the day's activities. Even in these cases, however, it is only they who may decide not to exercise the right.

Like other rights, this one is limited. Sovereign states do not have a right to make war on their neighbors for profit. Individuals do not have the right to harm or restrain one another simply for the fun of it however much they want to. The limitations on this right will be roughly what is prohibited by other moral principles. Although these limitations cannot be spelled out here, we could get agreement about a number of cases like injuring another for one's own pleasure. While this does not give us a satisfactory criterion for what morality forbids, it is enough to permit us to focus on the right of self-determination confident that it need not commit us to silly views about the rights of sadists.

Obviously the right is not in fact granted or guaranteed to everyone by the state or culture in which they live. Like the rights to life, liberty and security, it is a natural right, that is, it is thought of as belonging to everyone simply by virtue of their being human and so it is a right which everyone has equally. Society can and should protect us in exercising it in some ways, for example, in choosing a vocation. A state should not, however, enforce all the behavior and attitudes which might be appropriate in someone who believes in the right of self-determination. For example, I suspect that some committed to honoring the right of self-determination would regard themselves as bound not to influence those close to them by exploiting any emotional dependence they might have. If this is a reasonable attitude, it does not seem that it would be wise for a society to protect us from the influence of those on whom we are dependent emotionally. The right of self-determination does not, in general, determine a particular outcome as the just or only acceptable one. It rather outlines a range of considerations which should come into play whenever we are trying to adjust our behavior or attitudes to persons making permissible choices. I call it a right because it is thought of as a title and because the considerations it picks out as relevant mark off an area in which we do not allow conclusions about either the general good or an individual's good to be decisive. The point of the right of self-determination is to enable people to work out their own way of life in response to their own assessments of current conditions and their own interests, capacities and needs, rather than to secure the minimal conditions for living or to maximize a person's expectations for satisfaction. In respecting an individual's right of self-determination, one expresses a certain view about that person which is not a belief that one is acting for the good of that person (at least in some narrow sense of the person's good having to do with his or her welfare or happiness). The rough idea is that persons are, among other things, creatures who have title to select what they will do from among the permitted options. This establishes a presumption that other people should refrain from interfering with our selections whatever their content. They should refrain even if they do not like the particular choice or if they correctly believe that it is not in the chooser's or society's long-term interests.

Applying the right of self-determination to questions about the treatment of women, John and Harriet readily agree on a number of conclusions. First, bending the will of a woman by force is wrong. Conquering nations violate the right of self-determination and so does the man who keeps a woman or harem in servitude however nice he may make their lives. The man who prevents his wife from attending her therapy session or sky-diving lessons by force also violates this right. He does not allow her to do what she has a right to do. He violates the right whether he prevents her because he fears the changes in her personality, or is jealous of her handsome teacher, or because he correctly and sincerely believes the group is harming her or that sky-diving is dangerous. So long as we are talking about a mature woman who is choosing nothing prohibited by morality, it does not matter whether he acts in her own interests or not, he will still have violated her right to determine on her own what she will do.

The husband who achieves similar results by threatening to divorce his wife who has no other means of support may also violate her right to self-determination. This would be like a powerful state that threatens to cut off aid whenever a dependent state acts contrary to its wishes. Some may feel more certain that the threatening husband makes a mistake than that the powerful state violates the right of self-determination of the smaller state. Someone may note that it is quite accepted that relations among nations proceed by threat and counter threat. Things do not go all that well when carried on in this manner, but they go on. When husband, wife, parents or friends resort to such tactics, the relation of friendship or love is effectively off. Someone who is prepared to use such tactics displays special callousness toward the friendship. If they care about maintaining it at all, they will have made a grave blunder. They will also have indicated that they are indifferent to the feelings of the individual they threaten. They show a willingness to harm them, and this may be considered a moral fault for which there is no analogue in the threatening state. These observations can be accepted, I think, without weakening the original claim. We began by saying that states and persons have a right to make certain sorts of choices for themselves without interference by force or threat of force or withdrawal of essential support. This implies in both the case of states and individuals that there is a special wrong in threatening those who are making perfectly permissible policy, namely the violation of this right; that other wrongs and blunders may also be involved is beside the point.

Finally, if a group of men were to conspire together to discourage their wives from taking jobs or joining groups where women work through their problems together, they would violate the women's right of self-determination. These conclusions are not a problem for a liberal like John. He is not tempted to prevent his wife from going anywhere by force. Nor is he tempted to use the threat of loss of support in order to win a battle. He knows that would be to lose the war, and he wants her love and respect, not simply her presence and obedience. He knows, too, that his wife could find other means of support in this world. She is able, and this is not the nineteenth century where his support may well have been essential. Moreover, he has always been inclined to resist the temptation to adjust his relation to his wife in response to or in concert with others. So far the right of self-determination adds nothing startling to the list of legitimate complaints that women might have.

It does, however, add something to the reasons we may have for objecting to a variety of policies. For example, it means that some wrong is involved in the above cases apart from the objectionable techniques used to bring about the desired result. The wrong is not either simply that someone made a conscious attempt to interfere with someone's legitimate choice, but rather that someone's selections were blocked or interfered with. In addition, the right of self-determination takes us a good way toward directly undermining John's views about women. He seemed to think that it was perfectly all right to advise adult women to engage in and stick with traditional domestic life styles on the grounds that it was efficient and natural for women to have them. What appears to be the case now, is that, even if it is efficient and natural, enticing women to take this role for these reasons is likely to interfere with their right of self-determination. It is likely to do this because it encourages the false belief that these reasons are or should be decisive in determining an important lifetime commitment. Instead the right of self-determination establishes a presumption that within the range of permissible selections a person's uncoerced, unforced spontaneous responses to her own interests and circumstances are or should be decisive. It does not matter whether the interference is deliberate or non-deliberate or whether it is well-intended guidance. Once it is known that a practice, policy or teaching interferes, there is good reason to believe it should be revised. That is not to say that there is always sufficient reason, for this presumption like others can be rebutted. If the rebuttal is to work, however, it must give something like an equally important reason, for example, that revising the policy will cause perpetual or irremediable disaster, that it represents the only possible way for anyone to have a decent life, that some other natural right would be violated or that some particular person is not capable of exercising the right for some special reason. While this is not an adequate account of what will rebut the presumption established by the right of self-determination, it does suggest that John's arguments were simply beside the point if he was trying to justify policies which encourage a group of people to take up some lifetime role.

It is even difficult to see why the argument from efficiency should be effective in persuading a particular person like Harriet to exercise her right of self-determination by choosing a traditional domestic role. It seemed to be an argument that society in general will run more efficiently under the current role division, and it is not obvious that it is wise to make important lifetime commitments on the grounds that society in general is likely to run more efficiently. If the argument is rather that Harriet's life would work more smoothly and efficiently if she has a domestic role, then the right of self-determination says that it is up to her whether to take these facts (supposing them to be determinate) as decisive. If she does not want to struggle or if she does not fancy some other definite way of life, she may prefer the so-called efficient way. At the same time, it should be noted that it is a little difficult to determine what is meant by saying that her life would be more efficient, for surely that will depend to some very great extent on what her ends are. If her ends are to develop some talents she has or even to remain a lively and developing person, this may not be an efficient route at all. Nor is the evidence clear that this is the most efficient way for her to raise healthy children; that will depend to some extent on whom she thinks of raising them with, how that is likely to work, and so on.

The argument that the current division of labor and role is in some deep and important sense natural is also beside the point. If these roles are "natural," then persons who are taught that they have a right of self-determination will tend to choose them. There is, then, no need to worry about what it might mean to say that the sex roles are natural, nor to await the empirical evidence about whether they are before we decide whether it is justifiable to encourage them or not. Moreover, taking the perspective of someone committed to the right of self-determination accords nicely with a reasonable suspicion that what is natural for persons is not determinate. Sometimes when people talk about a person being a natural in a role, they have in mind that given the person's background, achievement and current interests, he or she would do well at it and flourish in it. Sometimes, however, they attempt to tie success and satisfaction with a role more closely to a person's genetic heritage. In this sense, a role is natural for persons if, because of their genetic endowment, they have certain special capacities which enable them to play the role well, the role does not frustrate some deep need and it provides opportunities for them to express their central interests. In the former sense, it is probably true that the domestic role is a natural for most women now, but it is the latter sense that plays a part in arguments that the current division of labor and role is natural and therefore justifiable. In a modern industrial community, however, there must be at the very least several life styles which could be natural in this sense for most any normal person. That is, there must be several ways of life in which their natural talents could be used and which would provide circumstances for the expression of a range of strong human interests without tending to frustrate deep needs. What the right of self-determination gives people is the title to let their own preferences put together a way of life. If these preferences are properly weighted by themselves and others, then the style they put together is very likely to be one which makes use of their special capacities, does not frustrate and provides opportunities for the expression of central interests.

Unfortunately, it is not clear that the right of self-determination will complete the job Harriet hoped it would; that is, adjudicate in her favor the dispute with John over their daughter's education. John, we may suppose, says that it will not do this because the right of self-determination is a right of adults and not of children. He says that it would be absurd if not impossible and immoral to treat young children as if they had the right to make major choices regarding their futures. Either we would give the children no guidance at all, in which case they may well feel lost and have too little discipline to gain what they will want as adults, or we would be required to use the techniques of rational persuasion that we use with adults. This, too, is likely to have disastrous consequences. At best it leads children to confuse the forms of reasoning with reasonable choosing and tends to make them overrate their capacities and status. Guidance must be given to children for their own sakes, and it will be guidance which inevitably will influence what they want later in life. The question is what kind of guidance to give. John wants to encourage in his daughter the feminine virtues. He wants her to be graceful in figure and movement, he is afraid that too much concentration on competitive athletic games will spoil her development. He thinks the modern dance and figure control programs the school has for girls are all that is important for them. He wants her to remain sweet and coy, affectionate and sensitive, and to develop feminine interests in cooking, sewing and children. Not only does he do what he can to encourage these traits in her, but he wants the school to. He thinks that Harriet and her friends have gone too far in complaining about the fact that only a few exceptionally talented or stubborn women are presented as professionals, and in demanding that the girls be taught the manual arts as well as home economics.

In the following section, I argue that even if the right of self-determination is reserved for adults, John's arguments about his daughter's education do not succeed. Even if the right of self-determination does not itself directly limit the kinds of guidance we may give our children, it does in an indirect way.

III. THE IMPORTANCE OF AUTONOMY

Let us say that parents have the authority to make certain decisions affecting the welfare of their offspring. They have this authority because children lack the know-how and the physical and psychological resources to make it on their own. Typically parents are supposed to exercise this authority in the interests of their children though sometimes they may exercise it for their own peace of mind, especially after nine and on weekends. Even given this picture of legitimate parental authority, there is something wrong with John's educational policies. There are, I think, two objections to teaching girls the traditional feminine virtues and role. First (A), such teaching interferes subtly with their exercise of the right of self-determination as mature women. Second (B), anyone committed to the right of self-determination and its importance has reasons for attaching special significance to the development of the capacity to exercise it autonomously.

(A) To begin with, when we say that mature persons have a right of self-determination, we mean that they are entitled to decide for themselves which career they will attempt, whether or whom to marry, whether to have children, how to spend their leisure time and the like. We all know that deciding for oneself is incompatible with being coerced at the time of choice, but there are subtle influences which may occur earlier and which interfere with the exercise of the right of self-determination.

Let us imagine that a school system has the following practices. First, the system leads girls to take up domestic activities and keeps them from others like competitive games and mechanics. Then, when women reach the age to choose how to spend their time, they have already developed the skills to enjoy cooking and sewing at a high level and discover, not surprisingly, that they like domestic tasks, and not car repair, carpentry or basketball. Surely the possibility that these latter might have been the objects of their choice is virtually extinguished. By hypothesis, home economics training for the girls has been successful, that is, many of them really have learned to manage themselves in the kitchen or sewing room so that they are creative and effective, and they have not made similar progress in the workroom. People tend to prefer doing what they are good at, and so women will tend to prefer cooking.

It might be said that at the age of reason, women have the right of self-determination, to choose, for example, to learn carpentry or mechanics, but the right to choose these things will not be worth much if at that time they do not have the possibility of getting satisfaction from these activities at some fairly advanced level because whatever original interest they might have had was never exposed. Not, of course, that everyone should be forced to take home economics, mechanics, and so on, but adults would have a reason to complain if they were systematically deprived of the opportunity to develop some legitimate interest; whereas, if the opportunity had been there and they failed to take it, they would not.

Secondly, the schools do not provide girls with information about women's capacities except for domestic affairs like mothering and cooking. If this occurs, then when the girls become women, they will be unlikely to imagine alternatives and choose intelligently between them. If this were to happen, then women could not even freely choose a domestic life, since they would be likely to see it as the only possibility instead of one among several. Alternatively, suppose that girls are presented with a few examples of women professionals, but these are always presented as rare, extraordinary persons who had to pay a high price for their aspirations. They either gave up the possibility of developing a marriage or they withstood criticism and ostracism for their strange ambitions or both. This makes the cost of choosing another way of life seem so high that most would be unwilling to select it.

Imagine next that girls are rewarded for being patient, sensitive, responsive and obedient, but that displays of ambition and curiosity are met with frowns or silence. The result is that the girls learn to be passive, understanding and sensitive, and not at the same time confident, interested and active. What has happened is that the pattern of traits they develop suit them for domestic life, and when they come to choose between being a housewife and a doctor, they may judge quite correctly that given their current wants and tempera-ment, housewifery is a better prospect for them. If, however, they had been rewarded for curiosity and ambition, the pattern of their personalities would have been different, and it might have been worthwhile for them to develop interests they have in, say, some science, and so to choose another style of life. The difficulty with the training they in fact had is that it has made such a choice unreasonable and done so without attending to the spontaneous and quite legitimate preferences of girls as they developed.

Finally, suppose that certain styles of dress and standards of etiquette are insisted upon for girls and that boys are encouraged to expect girls to meet these and admire those who meet them well. Anyone who deviates from the norm is made to feel uneasy or embarrassed. Imagine, too, that style of dress, while insignificant in itself, is associated with certain career roles and basic life styles. Dress in such a world serves to symbolize the career role and set up important expectations. When the time comes for a woman to choose what she will do, her expectations tend to be fixed not just with regard to the otherwise insignificant matter of dress, but also with regard to what role she will take up. When this happens, it is difficult for her to choose any unexpected role, for any deviation from expectations about her will produce stress and recall the uneasiness she felt upon breaking the dress code.

If the above practices in fact have the effects I envisage, they interfere with the right of self-determination of mature women. To believe that mature persons have a right of self-determination and that such practices are justifiable is rather like believing that Southern Blacks have a right to vote, but that Whites may legitimately ostracize those who exercise it. It would be like believing that Blacks have a right to eat where Whites do and that it would be merely impolite for Whites to stare as if they did not. In some important respects, it would be like a government maintaining that its citizens have a right to travel wherever they choose, but confiscating the passports of those who go to Cuba. If these analogies are acceptable, then even though the educational policies described above do not violate the right of self-deter-mination, they should be changed. Or rather they should be revised unless it can be argued reasonably that each proposed revision would cause disaster or violate some equally important right.

(B) So far Harriet's commitment to the right of self-determination inclines her to prevent and avoid violations and to minimize interferences like those described above. If, however, she is also committed to the importance of the right, she will want those she cares about to exercise it and to exercise it in a worthwhile way. It is not in general true that belief that one has a right means that one cares about having it or exercising it; for example, the right to travel or to marry do not seem to be rights that one need care about exercising or having. The right of self-determination, however, seems importantly different at least when it is accepted for the suggested rationale. The right was granted to persons to enable them to work out their own way of life in response to their own assessment of their situation, interests and capacities because it was thought appropriate and important that persons work out their own way of life believing that they have a right to. We may ask why this is important, but that is beyond the scope of the present inquiry. It would require explaining the advantages of regarding persons in part as creators of their own way of life rather than merely contributors to the general welfare or some other social ideal.

Assuming, then, that Harriet is also committed to the importance of the right of self-determination, she will want those she loves to exercise it and that its exercise be worthwhile for them. The right of self-determination tends to be worth less to mature persons the fewer opportunities and more interferences they are confronted with and the more they have been trained to have personality traits which make them suited for some definite life role. To say further what tends to make the right worth more, it helps to ask what one would want for persons one loves as they exercise the right of self-determination. Using this device, we are blocked from regarding ourselves as proper determiners of their life style. We do, however, want their good, but partly because we cannot properly determine it and partly because we do not know what will confront them, we do not know what in particular will be good or best for them. Still something can be said about what we want for them.

First, talking of our children and not knowing what they will face, we shall want them to develop the kind of personality which will enable them to respond well to their circumstances whatever they are. We shall want them to have what might be called broadly useful traits, that is, traits which will be helpful whatever their interests and circumstances, traits like confidence, intelligence and discipline. Self-confidence is, for example, a trait which it is good to have because it is useful in a wide variety of ways and inevitably satisfying. Broadly useful traits are the kinds which make a wider range of alternatives feasible for those who have them and so are important for exercising the right of self-determination. We should set about teaching these, then, rather than those associated with some culturally variable sex role.

Secondly, given that our children when mature will have a right of self-determination and given our ignorance of what they will face, it is not in general reasonable for us to aim for a particular outcome of our children's choices, but rather to develop their capacity to make choices in a certain way, namely, autonomously. That is, at least we want them to make the selections free from certain kinds of pressure. We do not want their selections to be coerced, threatened or bribed, and we do not want them to succumb easily to seductive advice or the bare weight of tradition. Neither do we want their preferences to be neurotic or self-destructive even though there are admittedly circumstances in which neurotic responses pay. In short, we want them to have certain psychological strengths which will enable them to make sensible use of the right of self-determination.

To want our children's choices to be autonomous is also to want their selections to express genuine interests of theirs which arise spontaneously under certain conditions. These are the circumstances in which they have the above psychological strengths and as they are making rational assessments of their capacities and situation. The selections should be spontaneous under these conditions because those are the choices we think of as expressive of us as individuals, and those in turn are the selections we tend to find most deeply satisfying and with which we feel most comfortable. Although we do not usually know what in particular these interests will be, we do know that there are certain basic human interests which anyone might have regardless of their sex or other peculiarities about them. Basic human interests are those taken in the kinds of activities which typically individuals find satisfying and which are potentially healthy. For example, people are capable of gaining satisfaction directly in their work or indirectly because it provides them with income, they find successful friendships and love relations satisfying, they enjoy play and developing their talents. The capacities to enjoy each of these interests, unlike other human capacities—for example, for self-destruction, enmity, hostility, envy and so on—are potentially healthy. They are potentially healthy in that they can be coordinated in one person to produce a satisfying way of life and styles of life in which these capacities are exploited (and the others minimized) are styles which can be coordinated together in a smooth way. What we can legitimately want and hope that our children have, then, are the satisfactions associated with each of these kinds of interests, and more rather than less. These are legitimate aspirations for us to have for our children because they are the kinds they would want to build their lives around if they were mature and reasonable and if the background conditions of life were decent. Given that these are legitimate aspirations, we should set about helping children understand these potential satisfactions vividly and not to suiting them for some particular lifetime role. Then when people are of an age to warrant saying they have a right of self-determination, ideally they will have psychological strengths and a vivid appreciation of the range of enjoyments possible for them so that they are able to work out a satisfying way of life which is an expression of their spontaneous preferences. This does not require that each be equally capable of fitting in anywhere, but only that there is for everyone some array of feasible options.

According to the preceding argument, young persons should be treated in whatever ways give them the strength and imagination to make use of their right of self-determination autonomously when they reach maturity. Treating them in ways which are believed to do this is a way of respecting the right they will have when they reach maturity. In addition, if one is to respect someone's right of self-determination fully, one must be willing to allow its exercise even when one believes it is being done badly. This suggests that some importance should be attached to the choices of people simply because they are attempts to arrive at the available alternative most in line with their autonomous preferences. For the most part, this will probably amount to keeping out of others' business. In those we care about and love, however, it will mean valuing and appreciating what they choose simply because it is their choice. This is, perhaps, one way of expressing our love. If so, then Harriet may have taken John's reticence about some of her projects as signs that he did not love her. Equally, of course, he may have believed that Harriet was a bit wacky and irresponsible, or he may not be committed to the right of self-determination or its importance. None of these is likely to sit well with Harriet, who we might imagine really has reached a vision about the moral life which is incompatible with John's view and with which she feels quite comfortable.

SERVILITY AND SELF-RESPECT

THOMAS E. HILL, JR.

Several motives underlie this paper.[1] In the first place, I am curious to see if there is a legitimate source for the increasingly common feeling that servility can be as much a vice as arrogance. There seems to be something morally defective about the Uncle Tom and the submissive housewife; and yet, on the other hand, if the only interests they sacrifice are their own, it seems that we should have no right to complain. Secondly, I have some sympathy for the now unfashionable view that each person has duties to himself as well as to others. It does seem absurd to say that a person could literally violate his own rights or owe himself a debt of gratitude, but I suspect that the classic defenders of duties to oneself had something different in mind. If there are duties to oneself, it is natural to expect that a duty to avoid being servile would have a prominent place among them. Thirdly, I am interested in making sense of Kant's puzzling, but suggestive, remarks about respect for persons and respect for the moral law. On the usual reading, these remarks seem

Reprinted from *The Monist,* Vol. 57, No. 1 (January 1973), 87–104, with the permission of the publisher and the author.

   [1] An earlier version of this paper was presented at the meetings of the American Philosophical Association, Pacific Division. A number of revisions have been made as a result of the helpful comments of others, especially Norman Dahl, Sharon Hill, Herbert Morris, and Mary Mothersill.

unduly moralistic; but, viewed in another way, they suggest an argument for a kind of self-respect which is incompatible with a servile attitude.

My procedure will not be to explicate Kant directly. Instead I shall try to isolate the defect of servility and sketch an argument to show why it is objectionable, noting only in passing how this relates to Kant and the controversy about duties to oneself. What I say about self-respect is far from the whole story. In particular, it is not concerned with esteem for one's special abilities and achievements or with the self-confidence which characterizes the especially autonomous person. Nor is my concern with the psychological antecedents and effects of self-respect. Nevertheless, my conclusions, if correct, should be of interest; for they imply that, given a common view of morality, there are nonutilitarian moral reasons for each person, regardless of his merits, to respect himself. To avoid servility to the extent that one can is not simply a right but a duty, not simply a duty to others but a duty to oneself.

I

Three examples may give a preliminary idea of what I mean by *servility*. Consider, first, an extremely deferential black, whom I shall call the *Uncle Tom*. He always steps aside for white men; he does not complain when less qualified whites take over his job; he gratefully accepts whatever benefits his all-white government and employers allot him, and he would not think of protesting its insufficiency. He displays the symbols of deference to whites, and of contempt towards blacks; he faces the former with bowed stance and a ready 'sir' and 'Ma'am'; he reserves his strongest obscenities for the latter. Imagine, too, that he is not playing a game. He is not the shrewdly prudent calculator, who knows how to make the best of a bad lot and mocks his masters behind their backs. He accepts without question the idea that, as a black, he is owed less than whites. He may believe that blacks are mentally inferior and of less social utility, but that is not the crucial point. The attitude which he displays is that what he values, aspires for, and can demand is of less importance than what whites value, aspire for, and can demand. He is far from the picture book's carefree, happy servant, but he does not feel that he has a right to expect anything better.

Another pattern of servility is illustrated by a person I shall call the *Self-Deprecator*. Like the Uncle Tom, he is reluctant to make demands. He says nothing when others take unfair advantage of him. When asked for his preferences or opinions, he tends to shrink away as if what he said should make no difference. His problem, however, is not a sense of racial inferiority but rather an acute awareness of his own inadequacies and failures as an individual. These defects are not imaginary: he has in fact done poorly by his own standards and others'. But, unlike many of us in the same situation, he acts as if his failings warrant quite unrelated maltreatment even by strangers. His sense of shame and self-contempt make him content to be the instrument of others. He feels that nothing is owed him until he has earned it and that he has earned very little. He is not simply playing a masochist's game of winning sympathy by disparaging himself. On the contrary, he assesses his individual merits with painful accuracy.

A rather different case is that of the *Deferential Wife*. This is a woman who is utterly devoted to serving her husband. She buys the clothes *he* prefers, invites the guests *he* wants to entertain, and makes love whenever *he* is in the mood. She willingly moves to a new city in order for him to have a more attractive job, counting her own friendships and geographical preferences insignificant by comparison. She loves her husband, but her conduct is not simply an expression of love. She is happy, but she does not subordinate herself as a means to happiness. She does not simply defer to her husband in certain spheres as a trade-off for his deference in other spheres. On the contrary, she tends not to form her own interests, values, and ideals; and, when she does, she counts them as less important than her husband's. She readily responds to appeals from Women's Liberation that she agrees that women are mentally and physically equal, if not superior, to men. She just believes that the proper role for a woman is to serve her family. As a matter of fact, much of her happiness derives from her belief that she fulfills this role very well. No one is trampling on her rights, she says; for she is quite glad, and proud, to serve her husband as she does.

Each one of these cases reflects the attitude which I call servility.[2] It betrays the absence of a certain kind of self-respect. What I take this attitude to be, more specifically, will become clearer later on. It is important at the outset, however, not to confuse the three cases sketched above with other, superficially similar cases. In particular, the cases I have sketched are not simply cases in which someone refuses to press his rights, speaks disparagingly of himself, or devotes himself to another. A black, for example, is not necessarily servile because he does not demand a just wage; for, seeing that such a demand would result in his being fired, he might forbear for the sake of his children. A self-critical person is not necessarily servile by virtue of bemoaning his faults in public; for his behavior may be merely a complex way of satisfying his own inner needs quite independent of a willingness to accept abuse from others. A woman need not be servile whenever she works to make her husband happy and prosperous; for she might freely and knowingly choose to do so from love or from a desire to share the rewards of his success. If the effort did not require her to submit to humiliation or maltreatment, her choice would not mark her as servile. There may, of course, be grounds for objecting

---

[2] Each of these cases is intended to represent only one possible pattern of servility. I make no claims about how often these patterns are exemplified, nor do I mean to imply that only these patterns could warrant the labels "Deferential Wife," "Uncle Tom," etc. All the more, I do not mean to imply any comparative judgments about the causes or relative magnitude of the problems of racial and sexual discrimination. One person, e.g., a self-contemptuous woman with a sense of racial inferiority, might exemplify features of several patterns at once; and, of course, a person might view her being a woman the way an Uncle Tom views his being black, etc.

to the attitudes in these cases; but the defect is not servility of the sort I want to consider. It should also be noted that my cases of servility are not simply instances of deference to superior knowledge or judgment. To defer to an expert's judgment on matters of fact is not to be servile; to defer to his every wish and whim is. Similarly, the belief that one's talents and achievements are comparatively low does not, by itself, make one servile. It is no vice to acknowledge the truth, and one may in fact have achieved less, and have less ability, than others. To be servile is not simply to hold certain empirical beliefs but to have a certain attitude concerning one's rightful place in a moral community.

II

Are there grounds for regarding the attitudes of the Uncle Tom, the Self-Deprecator, and the Deferential Wife as morally objectionable? Are there moral arguments we could give them to show that they ought to have more self-respect? None of the more obvious replies is entirely satisfactory.

One might, in the first place, adduce utilitarian considerations. Typically the servile person will be less happy than he might be. Moreover, he may be less prone to make the best of his own socially useful abilities. He may become a nuisance to others by being overly dependent. He will, in any case, lose the special contentment that comes from standing up for one's rights. A submissive attitude encourages exploitation, and exploitation spreads misery in a variety of ways. These considerations provide a prima facie case against the attitudes of the Uncle Tom, the Deferential Wife, and the Self-Deprecator, but they are hardly conclusive. Other utilities tend to counterbalance the ones just mentioned. When people refuse to press their rights, there are usually others who profit. There are undeniable pleasures in associating with those who are devoted, understanding, and grateful for whatever we see fit to give them—as our fondness for dogs attests. Even the servile person may find his attitude a source of happiness, as the case of the Deferential Wife illustrates. There may be comfort and security in thinking that the hard choices must be made by others, that what I would say has little to do with what ought to be done. Self-condemnation may bring relief from the pangs of guilt even if it is not deliberately used for that purpose. On balance, then, utilitarian considerations may turn out to favor servility as much as they oppose it.

For those who share my moral intuitions, there is another sort of reason for not trying to rest a case against servility on utilitarian considerations. Certain utilities seem irrelevant to the issue. The utilitarian must weight them along with others, but to do so seems morally inappropriate. Suppose, for example, that the submissive attitudes of the Uncle Tom and the Deferential Wife result in positive utilities for those who dominate and exploit them. Do we need to tabulate *these* utilities before conceding that servility is objectionable? The Uncle Tom, it seems, is making an error, a moral error, quite apart from consideration of how much others in fact profit from his attitude. The Deferential Wife may be quite happy; but if her happiness turns out to be contingent on her distorted view of her own rights and worth as a person, then it carries little moral weight against the contention that she ought to change that view. Suppose I could cause a woman to find her happiness in denying all her rights and serving my every wish. No doubt I could do so only by nonrational manipulative techniques, which I ought not to use. But is this the only objection? My efforts would be wrong, it seems, not only because of the techniques they require but also because the resultant attitude is itself objectionable. When a person's happiness stems from a morally objectionable attitude, it ought to be discounted. That a sadist gets pleasure from seeing others suffer should not count even as a partial justification for his attitude. That a servile person derives pleasure from denying her moral status, for similar reasons, cannot make her attitude acceptable. These brief intiutive remarks are not intended as a refutation of utilitarianism, with all its many varieties; but they do suggest that it is well to look elsewhere for adequate grounds for rejecting the attitudes of the Uncle Tom, the Self-Deprecator, and the Deferential Wife.

One might try to appeal to meritarian considerations. That is, one might argue that the servile person *deserves* more than he allows himself. This line of argument, however, is no more adequate than the utilitarian one. It may be wrong to deny others what they deserve, but it is not so obviously wrong to demand less for oneself than one deserves. In any case, the Self Deprecator's problem is not that he underestimates his merits. By hypothesis, he assesses his merits quite accurately. We cannot reasonably tell him to have more respect for himself because he *deserves* more respect; he knows that he has not *earned* better treatment. His problem, in fact, is that he thinks of his moral status with regard to others as entirely dependent upon his merits. His interests and choices are important, he feels, only if he has earned the right to make demands; or if he had rights by birth, they were forfeited by his subsequent failures and misdeeds. My Self-Deprecator is no doubt an atypical person, but nevertheless he illustrates an important point. Normally when we find a self-contemptuous person, we can plausibly argue that he is not so bad as he thinks, that his self-contempt is an overreaction prompted more by inner needs than by objective assessment of his merits. Because this argument cannot work with the Self-Deprecator, his case draws attention to a distinction, applicable in other cases as well, between saying that someone deserves respect for his merits and saying that he is owed respect as a person. On meritarian grounds we can only say 'You deserve better than this,' but the defect of the servile person is not merely failure to recognize his merits.

Other common arguments against the Uncle Tom, et al., may have some force but seem not to strike to the heart of the problem. For example, philosophers sometimes appeal to the value of human potentialities. As a human being, it is said, one at least has a capacity for rationality, morality, excellence, or autonomy, and this capacity is worthy of respect. Although such arguments have the merit of making respect independent of a person's actual deserts, they seem quite misplaced in some cases. There comes a time when we have sufficient evidence that a person is not ever going to *be* rational, moral, excellent, or autonomous even if he still has a capacity, in some sense, for being so. As a person approaches death with an atrocious record so far, the chances of his realizing his diminishing capacities become increasingly slim. To make these capacities the basis of his self-respect is to rest it on a shifting and unstable ground. We do, of course, respect persons for capacities which they are not exercising at the moment; for example, I might respect a person as a good philosopher even though he is just now blundering into gross confusion. In these cases, however, we respect the person for an active capacity, a ready disposition, which he has displayed on many occasions. On this analogy, a person should have respect for himself only when his capacities are developed and ready, needing only to be triggered by an appropriate occasion or the removal of some temporary obstacle. The Uncle Tom and the Deferential Wife, however, may in fact have quite limited capacities of this sort, and, since the Self-Deprecator is already overly concerned with his own inadequacies, drawing attention to his capacities seems a poor way to increase his self-respect. In any case, setting aside the Kantian nonempirical capacity for autonomy, the capacities of different persons vary widely; but what the servile person seems to overlook is something by virtue of which he is equal with every other person.

III

Why, then, is servility a moral defect? There is, I think, another sort of answer which is worth exploring. The first part of this answer must be an attempt to isolate the objectionable features of the servile person; later we can ask why these features are objectionable. As a step in this direction, let us examine again our three paradigm cases. The moral defect in each case, I suggest, is a failure to understand and acknowledge one's own moral rights. I assume, without argument here, that each person has moral rights.[3] Some of these rights may be basic human rights; that is, rights for which a person needs only to be human to qualify. Other rights will be derivative and contigent upon his special commitments, institutional affiliations, etc. Most rights will be prima facie ones; some may be absolute. Most can be waived under appropriate conditions; perhaps some cannot. Many rights can be forfeited; but some, presumably, cannot. The servile person does not, strictly speaking, violate his own rights. At least in our paradigm cases he fails to acknowledge

---

[3] As will become evident, I am also presupposing some form of cognitive or "naturalistic" interpretation of rights. If, to accommodate an emotivist or prescriptivist, we set aside talk of moral knowledge and ignorance, we might construct a somewhat analogous case against servility from the point of view of those who adopt principles ascribing rights to all; but the argument, I suspect, would be more complex and less persuasive.

fully his own moral status because he does not fully understand what his rights are, how they can be waived, and when they can be forfeited.

The defect of the Uncle Tom, for example, is that he displays an attitude that denies his moral equality with whites. He does not realize, or apprehend in an effective way, that he has as much right to a decent wage and a share of poltical power as any comparable white. His gratitude is misplaced; he accepts benefits which are his by right as if they were gifts. The Self-Deprecator is servile in a more complex way. He acts as if he has forfeited many important rights which in fact he has not. He does not understand, or fully realize in his own case, that certain rights to fair and decent treatment do not have to be earned. He sees his merits clearly enough, but he fails to see that what he can expect from others is not merely a function of his merits. The Deferential Wife *says* that she understands her rights vis-à-vis her husband, but what she fails to appreciate is that her consent to serve him is a valid waiver of her rights only under certain conditions. If her consent is coerced, say, by the lack of viable options for women in her society, then her consent is worth little. If socially fostered ignorance of her own talents and alternatives is responsible for her consent, then her consent should not count as a fully legitimate waiver of her right to equal consideration within the marriage. All the more, her consent to defer constantly to her husband is not a legitimate setting aside of her rights if it results from her mistaken belief that she has a moral duty to do so. (Recall: "the *proper* role for a woman is to serve her family.") If she believes that she has a *duty* to defer to her husband, then, whatever she may say, she cannot fully understand that she has a *right* not to defer to him. When she says that she freely gives up such a right, she is confused. Her confusion is rather like that of a person who has been persuaded by an unscrupulous lawyer that it is legally incumbent on him to refuse a jury trial but who nevertheless tells the judge that he understands that he has a right to a jury trial and freely waives it. He does not really understand what it is to have and freely give up the right if he thinks that it would be an offense for him to exercise it.

Insofar as servility results from moral ignorance or confusion, it need not be something for which a person is to blame. Even self-reproach may be inappropriate; for at the time a person is in ignorance he cannot feel guilty about his servility, and later he may conclude that his ignorance was unavoidable. In some cases, however, a person might reasonably believe that he should have known better. If, for example, the Deferential Wife's confusion about her rights resulted from a motivated resistance to drawing the implications of her own basic moral principles, then later she might find some ground for self-reproach. Whether blameworthy or not, servility could still be morally objectionable at least in the sense that it ought to be discouraged, that social conditions which nourish it should be reformed, and the like. Not all morally undesirable features of a person are ones for which he is responsible, but that does not mean that they are defects merely from an esthetic or prudential point of view.

In our paradigm cases, I have suggested, servility is a kind of deferential attitude towards others resulting from ignorance or misunderstanding of one's moral rights. A sufficient remedy, one might think, would be moral enlightenment. Suppose, however, that our servile persons come to know their rights but do not substantially alter their behavior. Are they not still servile in an objectionable way? One might even think that reproach is more appropriate now because they know what they are doing.

The problem, unfortunately, is not as simple as it may appear. Much depends on what they tolerate and why. Let us set aside cases in which a person merely refuses to *fight* for his rights, chooses not to exercise certain rights, or freely waives many rights which he might have insisted upon. Our problem concerns the previously servile person who continues to display the same marks of deference even after he fully knows his rights. Imagine, for example, that even after enlightenment our Uncle Tom persists in his old pattern of behavior, giving all the typical signs of believing that the injustices done to him are not really wrong. Suppose, too, that the newly enlightened Deferential Wife continues to defer to her husband, refusing to disturb the old way of life by introducing her new ideas. She acts as if she accepts the idea that she is merely doing her duty though actually she no longer believes it. Let us suppose, further, that the Uncle Tom and the Deferential Wife are not merely generous with their time and property; they also accept without protest, and even appear to sanction, treatment which is humiliating and degrading. That is, they do not simply consent to waive mutually acknowledged rights; they tolerate violations of their rights with apparent approval. They pretend to give their permission for subtle humiliations which they really believe no permission can make legitimate. Are such persons still servile despite their moral knowledge?

The answer, I think, should depend upon why the deferential role is played. If the motive is a morally commendable one, or a desire to avert dire consequences to oneself, or even an ambition to set an oppressor up for a later fall, then I would not count the role player as servile. The Uncle Tom, for instance, is not servile in my sense if he shuffles and bows to keep the Klan from killing his children, to save his own skin, or even to buy time while he plans the revolution. Similarly, the Deferential Wife is not servile if she tolerates an abusive husband because he is so ill that further strain would kill him, because protesting would deprive her of her only means of survival, or because she is collecting atrocity stories for her book against marriage. If there is fault in these situations, it seems inappropriate to call it *servility.* The story is quite different, however, if a person continues in his deferential role just from laziness, timidity, or a desire for some minor advantage. He shows too little concern for his moral status as a person, one is tempted to say, if he is willing to deny it for a small profit or simply because it requires some effort and courage to affirm it openly. A black who plays the Uncle Tom merely to gain an advantage over other blacks is harming them, of course; but he is also displaying disregard for his own moral position as an equal

among human beings. Similarly, a woman throws away her rights too lightly
if she continues to play the subservient role because she is used to it or is
too timid to risk a change. A Self-Deprecator who readily accepts what he
knows are violations of his rights may be indulging his peculiar need for
punishment at the expense of denying something more valuable. In these
cases, I suggest, we have a kind of servility independent of any ignorance or
confusion about one's rights. The person who has it may or may not be
blameworthy, depending on many factors; and the line between servile and
nonservile role playing will often be hard to draw. Nevertheless, the objectionable feature is perhaps clear enough for persent purposes: it is a willingness
to disavow one's moral status, publicly and systematically, in the absence of
any strong reason to do so.

My proposal, then, is that there are at least two types of servility: one
resulting from misunderstanding of one's rights and the other from placing
a comparatively low value on them. In either case, servility manifests the
absence of a certain kind of self-respect. The respect which is missing is not
respect for one's merits but respect for one's rights. The servile person displays
this absence of respect not directly by acting contrary to his own rights but
indirectly by acting as if his rights were nonexistent or insignificant. An
arrogant person ignores the rights of others, thereby arrogating for himself
a higher status than he is entitled to; a servile person denies his own rights,
thereby assuming a lower position than he is entitled to. Whether rooted in
ignorance or simply lack of concern for moral rights, the attitudes in both
cases may be incompatible with a proper regard for morality. That this is so
is obvious in the case of arrogance; but to see it in the case of servility requires
some further argument.

IV

The objectionable feature of the servile person, as I have described him, is
his tendency to disavow his own moral rights either because he misunderstands
them or because he cares little for them. The question remains: why should
anyone regard this as a moral defect? After all, the rights which he denies
are his own. He may be unfortunate, foolish, or even distasteful; but why
morally deficient? One sort of answer, quite different from those reviewed
earlier, is suggested by some of Kant's remarks. Kant held that servility is
contrary to a perfect nonjuridical duty to oneself.[4] To say that the duty is
perfect is roughly to say that it is stringent, never overridden by other considerations (e.g. beneficence). To say that the duty is nonjuridical is to say
that a person cannot legitimately be coerced to comply. Although Kant did

---

[4] See Immanuel Kant, *The Doctrine of Virtue,* Part II of *The Metaphysics of Morals,* M. J.
Gregor, ed. (New York: Harper and Row, 1964), pp. 99–103; Prussian Academy edition, Vol.
VI, pp. 434–37.

not develop an explicit argument for this view, an argument can easily be constructed from materials which reflect the spirit, if not the letter, of his moral theory. The argument which I have in mind is prompted by Kant's contention that respect for persons, strictly speaking, is respect for moral law.[5] If taken as a claim about all sorts of respect, this seems quite implausible. If it means that we respect persons only for their moral character, their capacity for moral conduct, or their status as "authors" of the moral law, then it seems unduly moralistic. My strategy is to construe the remark as saying that at least one sort of respect for persons is respect for the rights which the moral law accords them. If one respects the moral law, then one must respect one's own moral rights; and this amounts to having a kind of self-respect incompatible with servility.

The premises for the Kantian argument, which are all admittedly vague can be sketched as follows:

First, let us assume, as Kant did, that all human beings have equal basic human rights. Specific rights vary with different conditions, but all must be justified from a point of view under which all are equal. Not all rights need to be earned, and some cannot be forfeited. Many rights can be waived but only under certain conditions of knowledge and freedom. These conditions are complex and difficult to state; but they include something like the condition that a person's consent releases others from obligation only if it is autonomously given, and consent resulting from underestimation of one's moral status is not autonomously given. Rights can be objects of knowledge, but also of igorance, misunderstanding, deception, and the like.

Second, let us assume that my account of servility is correct; or, if one prefers, we can take it as a definition. That is, in brief, a servile person is one who tends to deny or disavow his own moral rights because he does not understand them or has little concern for the status they give him.

Third, We need one formal premise concerning moral duty, namely, that each person ought, as far as possible, to respect the moral law. In less Kantian language, the point is that everyone should approximate, to the extent that he can, the ideal of a person who fully adopts the moral point of view. Roughly, this means not only that each person ought to do what is morally required and refrain from what is morally wrong but also that each person should treat all the provisions of morality as valuable—worth preserving and prizing as well as obeying. One must, so to speak, take up the spirit of morality as well as meet the letter of its requirements. To keep one's promises, avoid hurting others, and the like, is not sufficient; one should also take an attitude of respect towards the principles, ideals, and goals of morality. A respectful attitude towards a system of rights and duties consists of more

[5] Immanuel Kant, *Groundwork of the Metaphysics of Morals,* H. J. Paton, ed. (New York: Harper and Row, 1964), p. 69; Prussian Academy edition, Vol. IV, p. 401; *The Critique of Practical Reason,* Lewis W. Beck, ed. (New York: Bobbs-Merrill, 1956), pp. 81, 84; Prussian Academy edition, Vol. V, pp. 78, 81. My purpose here is not to interpret what Kant meant but to give a sense to his remark.

than a disposition to conform to its definite rules of behavior; it also involves holding the system in esteem, being unwilling to ridicule it, and being reluctant to give up one's place in it. The essentially Kantian idea here is that morality, as a system of equal fundamental rights and duties, is worthy of respect and hence a completely moral person would respect it in word and manner as well as in deed. And what a completely moral person would do, in Kant's view, is our duty to do so far as we can.

The assumptions here are, of course, strong ones, and I make no attempt to justify them. They are, I suspect, widely held though rarely articulated. In any case, my present purpose is not to evaluate them but to see how, if granted, they constitute a case against servility. The objection to the servile person, given our premises, is that he does not satisfy the basic requirement to respect morality. A person who fully respected a system of moral rights would be disposed to learn his proper place in it, to affirm it proudly, and not to tolerate abuses of it lightly. This is just the sort of disposition that the servile person lacks. If he does not understand the system, he is in no position to respect it adequately. This lack of respect may be no fault of his own, but it is still a way in which he falls short of a moral ideal. If, on the other hand, the servile person knowingly disavows his moral rights by pretending to approve of violations of them, barring special explanations, he shows an indifference to whether the provisions of morality are honored and publicly acknowledged. This avoidable display of indifference, by our Kantian premises, is contrary to the duty to respect morality. The disrespect in this second case is somewhat like the disrespect a religious believer might show toward his religion if, to avoid embarrassment, he laughed congenially while non-believers were mocking the beliefs which he secretly held. In any case, the servile person, as such, does not express disrespect for the system of moral rights in the obvious way by violating the rights of others. His lack of respect is more subtly manifested by his acting before others as if he did not know or care about his position of equality under that system.

The central idea may be illustrated by an analogy. Imagine a club, say, an old German dueling fraternity. By the rules of the club, each member has certain rights and responsibilities. These are the same for each member regardless of what titles he may hold outside the club. Each has, for example, a right to be heard at meetings, a right not to be shouted down by the others. Some rights cannot be forfeited: for example, each may vote regardless of whether he has paid his dues and satisfied other rules. Some rights cannot be waived: for example, the right to be defended when attacked by several members of the rival fraternity. The members show respect for each other by respecting the status which the rules confer on each member. Now one new member is careful always to allow the others to speak at meetings; but when they shout him down, he does nothing. He just shrugs as if to say, 'Who am I to complain?' When he fails to stand up in defense of a fellow member, he feels ashamed and refuses to vote. He does not deserve to vote, he says. As the only commoner among illustrious barons, he feels that it is his place to serve them and defer to their decisions. When attackers from the rival fraternity come at him with swords drawn, he tells his companions to run and save themselves. When they defend him, he expresses immense gratitude—as if they had done him a gratuitous favor. Now one might argue that our new member fails to show respect for the fraternity and its rules. He does not actually violate any of the rules by refusing to vote, asking others not to defend him, and deferring to the barons, but he symbolically disavows the equal status which the rules confer on him. If he ought to have respect for the fraternity, he ought to change his attitude, Our servile person, then, is like the new member of the dueling fraternity in having insufficient respect for a system of rules and ideals. The difference is that everyone ought to respect morality whereas there is no comparable moral requirement to respect the fraternity.

The conclusion here is, of course, a limited one. Self-sacrifice is not always a sign of servility. It is not a duty always to press one's rights. Whether a given act is evidence of servility will depend not only on the attitude of the agent but also on the specific nature of his moral rights, a matter not considered here. Moreover, the extent to which a person is responsible, or blameworthy, for his defect remains an open question. Nevertheless, the conclusion should not be minimized. In order to avoid servility, a person who gives up his rights must do so with a full appreciation for what they are. A woman, for example, may devote herself to her husband if she is uncoerced, knows what she is doing, and does not pretend that she has no decent alternative. A self-contemptuous person may decide not to press various unforfeited rights but only if he does not take the attitude that he is too rotten to deserve them. A black may demand less than is due to him provided he is prepared to acknowledge that no one has a right to expect this of him. Sacrifices of this sort, I suspect, are extremely rare. Most people, if they fully acknowledged their rights, would not autonomously refuse to press them.

An even stronger conclusion would emerge if we could assume that some basic rights cannot be waived. This is, if there are some rights that others are bound to respect regardless of what we say, then, barring special explanation, we would be obliged not only to acknowledge these rights but also to avoid any appearance of consenting to give them up. To act as if we could release others from their obligation to grant these rights, apart from special circumstances, would be to fail to respect morality. Rousseau, held, for example, that at least a minimal right to liberty cannot be waived. A man who consents to be enslaved, giving up liberty without *quid pro quo,* thereby displays a conditioned slavish mentality that renders his consent worthless. Similarly, a Kantian might argue that a person cannot release others from the obligation to refrain from killing him: consent is no defense against the charge of murder. To accept principles of this sort is to hold that rights to life and liberty are, as Kant believed, rather like a trustee's rights to preserve something valuable entrusted to him: he has not only a right but a duty to preserve it.

Even if there are no specific rights which cannot be waived, there might be at least one formal right of this sort. This is the right to some minimum degree of respect from others. No matter how willing a person is to submit to humiliation by others, they ought to show him some respect as a person. By analogy with self-respect, as presented here, this respect owed by others would consist of a willingness to acknowledge fully, in word as well as action, the person's basically equal moral status as defined by his other rights. To the extent that a person gives even tacit consent to humiliations incompatible with this respect, he will be acting as if he waives a right which he cannot in fact give up. To do this, barring special explanations, would mark one as servile.

V

Kant held that the avoidance of servility is a duty to oneself rather than a duty to others. Recent philosophers, however, tend to discard the idea of a duty to oneself as a conceptual confusion. Although admittedly the analogy between a duty to oneself and a duty to others is not perfect, I suggest that something important is reflected in Kant's contention.

Let us consider briefly the function of saying that a duty is *to* someone. *First,* to say that a duty is *to* a given person sometimes merely indicates who is the object of that duty. That is, to tell us that the duty is concerned with how that person is to be treated, how his interests and wishes are to be taken into account, and the like. Here we might as well say that we have a duty *towards,* or *regarding* that person. Typically the person in question is the beneficiary of the fulfillment of the duty. For example, in this sense I have a duty to my children and even a duty to a distant stranger if I promised a third party that I would help that stranger. Clearly a duty to avoid servility would be a duty to oneself at least in this minimal sense, for it is a duty to avoid, so far as possible, the denial of one's own moral status. The duty is concerned with understanding and affirming one's rights, which are, at least as a rule, for one's own benefit.

Second, when we say that a duty is *to* a certain person, we often indicate thereby the person especially entitled to complain in case the duty is not fulfilled. For example, if I fail in my duty to my colleagues, then it is they who can most appropriately reproach me. Others may sometimes speak up on their behalf, but, for the most part, it is not the business of strangers to set me straight. Analogously, to say that the duty to avoid servility is a duty to oneself would indicate that, though sometimes a person may justifiably reproach himself for being servile, others are not generally in the appropriate position to complain. Outside encouragement is sometimes necessary, but, if any blame is called for, it is primarily self-recrimination and not the censure of others.

Third, mention of the person to whom a duty is owed often tells us something about the source of that duty. For example, to say that I have a duty to another person may indicate that the argument to show that I have such a duty turns upon a promise to that person, his authority over me, my having accepted special benefits from him, or, more generally, his rights. Accordingly, to say that the duty to avoid servility is a duty to oneself would at least imply that it is not entirely based upon promises to others, their authority, their beneficence, or an obligation to respect their rights. More positively the assertion might serve to indicate that the source of the duty is one's own rights rather than the rights of others, etc. That is, one ought not to be servile because, in some broad sense, one ought to respect one's own rights as a person. There is, to be sure, an asymmetry: one has certain duties to others because one ought not to violate their rights, and one has a duty to oneself because one ought to affirm one's own rights. Nevertheless, to dismiss duties to oneself out of hand is to overlook significant similarities.

Some familiar objections to duties to oneself, moreover, seem irrelevant in the case of servility. For example, some place much stock in the idea that a person would have no duties if alone on a desert island. This can be doubted, but in any case is irrelevant here. The duty to avoid servility is a duty to take a certain stance towards others and hence would be inapplicable if one were isolated on a desert island. Again, some suggest that if there were duties to oneself then one could make promises to oneself or owe oneself a debt of gratitude. Their paradigms are familiar ones. Someone remarks, 'I promised myself a vacation this year' or 'I have been such a good boy I owe myself a treat'. Concentration on these facetious cases tends to confuse the issue. In any case the duty to avoid servility, as presented here, does not presuppose promises to oneself or debts of gratitude to oneself. Other objections stem from the intuition that a person has no duty to promote his own happiness. A duty to oneself, it is sometimes assumed, must be a duty to promote one's own happiness. From a utilitarian point of view, in fact, this is what a duty to oneself would most likely be. The problems with such alleged duties, however, are irrelevant to the duty to avoid servility. This is a duty to understand and affirm one's rights, not to promote one's own welfare. While it is usually in the interest of a person to affirm his rights, our Kantian argument against servility was not based upon this premise. Finally, a more subtle line of objection turns on the idea that, given that rights and duties are correlative, a person who acted contrary to a duty to oneself would have to be violating his own rights, which seems absurd.[6] This objection raises issues too complex to examine here. One should note, however, that I have tried to give a sense to saying that servility is contrary to a duty to oneself

---

[6] This, I take it, is part of M. G. Singer's objection to duties to oneself in *Generalization in Ethics* (New York: Alfred A. Knopf, 1961), pp. 311–18. I have attempted to examine Singer's arguments in detail elsewhere.

without presupposing that the servile person violates his own rights. If acts contrary to duties to others are always violations of their rights, then duties to oneself are not parallel with duties to others to that extent. But this does not mean that it is empty or pointless to say that a duty is to oneself.

My argument against servility may prompt some to say that the duty is "to morality" rather than "to oneself." All this means, however, is that the duty is derived from a basic requirement to respect the provisions of morality; and in this sense every duty is a duty "to morality". My duties to my children are also derivative from a general requirement to respect moral principles, but they are still duties *to* them.

Kant suggests that duties to oneself are a precondition of duties to others. On our acount of servility, there is at least one sense in which this is so. Insofar as the servile person is ignorant of his own rights, he is not in an adequate position to appreciate the rights of others. Misunderstanding the moral basis for his equal status with others, he is necessarily liable to underestimate the rights of those with whom he classifies himself. On the other hand, if he plays the servile role knowingly, then, barring special explanation, he displays a lack of concern to see the principles of morality acknowledged and respected and thus the absence of one motive which can move a moral person to respect the rights of others. In either case, the servile person's lack of self-respect necessarily puts him in a less than ideal position to respect others. Failure to fulfill one duty to oneself, then, renders a person liable to violate duties to others. This, however, is a consequence of our argument against servility, not a presupposition of it.

SELECTED BIBLIOGRAPHY: RACISM AND SEXISM

Bishop, Sharon, and **Marjorie Weinzweig** (eds.). *Philosophy and Women.* Belmont, Calif.: Wadsworth Publishing Co., 1979.

Boxill, Bernard. "Self-Respect and Protest." *Philosophy & Public Affairs,* 6: (1976), 58.

————. *Blacks and Social Justice.* Totowa, N.J.: Rowman and Allanheld, 1984.

Carmichael, Stokely, and **Charles Hamilton.** *Black Power.* New York: Random House, Inc., 1967.

English, Jane (ed.). *Sex Equality.* Englewood Cliffs, N.J.: Prentice-Hall, Inc., 1977.

Gould, Carol C., and **Marx W. Wartofsky** (eds.). *Women and Philosophy.* New York: G. P. Putnam's Sons, 1976.

Harding, Sandra, and **Merrill B. Hintikka (eds.).** *Discovery Reality: Feminist Perspectives on Epistemology, Metaphysics, Methodology, and Philosophy of Science.* Dordrecht, Holland: D. Reidel Publishing Company, 1983.

Jaggar, Alison M., and **Paula Rothenberg Struhl** (eds.). *Feminist Frameworks.* New York: McGraw-Hill Book Company, 1978.

Jaggar, Alison. *Feminist Politics and Human Nature.* Totowa, N.J.: Rowman and Allanheld, 1983.

McMillan, Carol. *Women, Reason and Nature.* Princeton, N.J.: Princeton University Press, 1982.

Melden, A. I. (ed.). *Human Rights.* Belmont, Calif.: Wadsworth Publishing Co., 1970.

Mill, John Stuart. *The Subjection of Women.* London: Longman's, 1869.

Okin, Susan Moller. "Women and the Making of the Sentimental Family." *Philosophy & Public Affairs,* 11:1 (1982), 65.

Philosophia, 8:1–2 (1978). (Philosophical Essays on Racism.)

Thalberg, Irving. "Justifications of Institutional Racism." *The Philosophical Forum,* III:2 (1972), 243.

————. "Visceral Racism." *The Monist,* **56:**4 (1972), 43.

Vetterling-Braggin, Mary (ed.). *"Femininity," "Masculinity," and "Androgyny."* Totowa, N.J.: Rowman and Allanheld, 1982.

————, **Frederick A. Elliston,** and **Jane English** (eds.). *Feminism and Philosophy.* Totowa, N.J.: Littlefield, Adams & Co., 1977.

Wolgast, Elizabeth. *Equality and the Rights of Women.* Ithaca, N.Y.: Cornell University Press, 1980.

TWO

Preferential Treatment

REGENTS OF THE UNIVERSITY OF CALIFORNIA v. ALLAN BAKKE

438 U.S. 265, 98 S.CT. 2733, 46 L.W. 4896 (1978)

MR. JUSTICE POWELL announced the judgment of the Court.

This case presents a challenge to the special admissions program of the petitioner, the Medical School of the University of California at Davis, which is designed to assure the admission of a specified number of students from certain minority groups. The Superior Court of California sustained respondent's challenge, holding that petitioner's program violated the California Constitution, Title VI of the Civil Rights Act of 1964, 42 U.S.C. § 2000d, and the Equal Protection Clause of the Fourteenth Amendment. The court enjoined petitioner from considering respondent's race or the race of any other applicant in making admissions decisions. It refused, however, to order respondent's admission to the Medical School, holding that he had not carried his burden of proving that he would have been admitted but for the constitutional and statutory violations. The Supreme Court of California affirmed those portions of the trial court's judgment declaring the special admissions program unlawful and enjoining petitioner from considering the race of any

EDITOR'S NOTE: Six of the nine justices of the Supreme Court wrote opinions in the Bakke case. The opinions of Justices White and Stevens have been omitted. The opinions of Justices Powell, Brennan, Marshall, and Blackmun have been edited. Page references to *The Record* have been deleted, as have most of the citations to prior Supreme Court opinions. A number of footnotes have been deleted from the opinions and those that remain have been renumbered.

applicant. It modified that portion of the judgment denying respondent's requested injunction and directed the trial court to order his admission.

For the reasons stated in the following opinion, I believe that so much of the judgment of the California court as holds petitioner's special admissions program unlawful and directs that respondent be admitted to the Medical School must be affirmed. For the reasons expressed in a separate opinion, my Brothers THE CHIEF JUSTICE, MR. JUSTICE STEWART, MR. JUSTICE REHNQUIST, and MR. JUSTICE STEVENS concur in this judgment.

I also conclude for the reasons stated in the following opinion that the portion of the court's judgment enjoining petitioner from according any consideration to race in its admissions process must be reversed. For reasons expressed in separate opinions, my Brothers MR. JUSTICE BRENNAN, MR. JUSTICE WHITE, MR. JUSTICE MARSHALL, and MR. JUSTICE BLACKMUN concur in this judgment.

Affirmed in part and reversed in part.

I

The Medical School of the University of California at Davis opened in 1968 with an entering class of 50 students. In 1971, the size of the entering class was increased to 100 students, a level at which it remains. No admissions program for disadvantaged or minority students existed when the school opened, and the first class contained three Asians but no blacks, no Mexican-Americans, and no American Indians. Over the next two years, the faculty devised a special admissions program to increase the representation of "disadvantaged" students in each medical school class. The special program consisted of a separate admissions system operating in coordination with the regular admissions process.

Under the regular admissions procedure, a candidate could submit his application to the medical school beginning in July of the year preceding the academic year for which admission was sought. Because of the large number of applications,[1] the admissions committee screened each one to select candidates for further consideration. Candidates whose overall undergraduate grade point averages fell below 2.5 on a scale of 4.00 were summarily rejected. About one out of six applicants was invited for a personal interview. Following the interviews, each candidate was rated on a scale of 1 to 100 by his interviewers and four other members of the admissions committee. The rating embraced the interviewers' summaries, the candidate's overall grade point average, grade point average in science courses, and scores on the Medical College Admissions Test (MCAT), letters of recommendation, extracurricular activities, and other biographical data. The ratings were added together to arrive at each candidate's "benchmark" score. Since five committee members

---

[1] For the 1973 entering class of 100 seats, the Davis medical school received 2,464 applications. For the 1974 entering class, 3,737 applications were submitted.

rated each candidate in 1973, a perfect score was 500; in 1974, six members rated each candidate, so that a perfect score was 600. The full committee then reviewed the file and scores of each applicant and made offers of admission on a "rolling" basis. The chairman was responsible for placing names on the waiting list. They were not placed in strict numerical order; instead, the chairman had discretion to include persons with "special skills."

The special admissions program operated with a separate committee, a majority of whom were members of minority groups. On the 1973 application form, candidates were asked to indicate whether they wished to be considered as "economically and/or educationally disadvantaged" applicants; on the 1974 form the question was whether they wished to be considered as members of a "minority group," which the medical school apparently viewed as "Blacks," "Chicanos," "Asians," and "American Indians." If these questions were answered affirmatively, the application was forwarded to the special admissions committee. No formal definition of "disadvantaged" was ever produced, but the chairman of the special committee screened each application to see whether it reflected economic or educational deprivation. Having passed this initial hurdle, the applications then were rated by the special committee in a fashion similar to that used by the general admissions committee, except that special candidates did not have to meet the 2.5 grade point average cutoff applied to regular applicants. About one-fifth of the total number of special applicants were invited for interviews in 1973 and 1974.[2] Following each interview, the special committee assigned each special applicant a benchmark score. The special committee then presented its top choices to the general admissions committee. The latter did not rate or compare the special candidates against the general applicants but could reject recommended special candidates for failure to meet course requirements or other specific deficiencies. The special committee continued to recommend special applicants until a number prescribed by faculty vote were admitted. While the overall class size was still 50, the prescribed number was eight; in 1973 and 1974, when the class size had doubled to 100, the prescribed number of special admissions also doubled, to 16.

From the year of the increase in class size—1971—through 1974, the special program resulted in the admission of 21 black students, 30 Mexican-Americans, and 12 Asians, for a total of 63 minority students. Over the same period, the regular admissions program produced one black, six Mexican-Americans, and 37 Asians, for a total of 44 minority students.[3] Although disadvantaged whites applied to the special program in large numbers, none received an offer of admission through that process. Indeed, in 1974, at least, the special committee explicitly considered only "disadvantaged" special applicants who were members of one of the designated minority groups.

---

[2] For the class entering in 1973, the total number of special applicants was 297, of whom 73 were white. In 1974, 628 persons applied to the special committee, of whom 172 were white.

[3] The following table provides a year-by-year comparison of minority admissions at the Davis Medical School:

Allan Bakke is a white male who applied to the Davis Medical School in both 1973 and 1974. In both years Bakke's application was considered by the general admissions program, and he received an interview. His 1973 interview was with Dr. Theodore H. West, who considered Bakke "a very desirable applicant to [the] medical school." Despite a strong benchmark score of 468 out of 500, Bakke was rejected. His application had come late in the year, and no applicants in the general admissions process with scores below 470 were accepted after Bakke's application was completed. There were four special admissions slots unfilled at that time, however, for which Bakke was not considered. After his 1973 rejection, Bakke wrote to Dr. George H. Lowrey, Associate Dean and Chairman of the Admissions Committee, protesting that the special admissions program operated as a racial and ethnic quota.

Bakke's 1974 application was completed early in the year. His student interviewer gave him an overall rating of 94, finding him "friendly, well tempered, conscientious and delightful to speak with." His faculty interviewer was, by coincidence, the same Dr. Lowrey to whom he had written in protest of the special admissions program. Dr. Lowrey found Bakke "rather limited in his approach" to the problems of the medical profession and found disturbing Bakke's "very definite opinions which were based more on his personal viewpoints than upon a study of the total problem." *Id.,* at 226. Dr. Lowrey gave Bakke the lowest of his six ratings, an 86; his total was 549 out of 600. Again, Bakke's application was rejected. In neither year did the chairman of the admissions committee, Dr. Lowrey, exercise his discretion to place Bakke on the waiting list. In both years, applicants were admitted under the special program with grade point averages, MCAT scores, and benchmark scores significantly lower than Bakke's.[4]

After the second rejection, Bakke filed the instant suit in the Superior Court of California.[5] He sought mandatory, injunctive, and declaratory relief compelling his admission to the Medical School. He alleged that the Medical

	Special Admissions Program				General Admissions				
	Blacks	Chi-canos	Asians	Total	Blacks	Chi-canos	Asians	Total	Total
1970	5	3	0	8	0	0	4	4	12
1971	4	9	2	15	1	0	8	9	24
1972	5	6	5	16	0	0	11	11	27
1973	6	8	2	16	0	2	13	15	31
1974	6	7	3	16	0	4	5	9	25

Sixteen persons were admitted under the special program in 1974, but one Asian withdrew before the start of classes, and the vacancy was filled by a candidate from the general admissions waiting list.

[4] The following table compares Bakke's science grade point average, overall grade point average, and MCAT Scores with the average scores of regular admittees and of special admittees in both 1973 and 1974.

School's special admissions program operated to exclude him from the school on the basis of his race, in violation of his rights under the Equal Protection Clause of the Fourteenth Amendment,[6] Art. I, § 21 of the California Constitution,[7] and § 601 of Title VI of the Civil Rights Act of 1964, 42 U.S.C. § 2000d.[8] The University cross-complained for a declaration that its special admissions program was lawful. The trial court found that the special program operated as a racial quota, because minority applicants in the special program were rated only against one another, Record 388, and 16 places in the class of 100 were reserved for them. Declaring that the University could not take race into account in making admissions decisions, the trial court held the challenged program violative of the Federal Constitution, the state con-

Class Entering in 1973					
			MCAT (Percentiles)		
	SGPA	*OGPA*	*Verbal*	*Quanti-* *tative*	*Science*	*General* *Information*
Bakke	3.44	3.51	96	94	97	72
Average of regular admittees	3.51	3.49	81	76	83	69
Average of special admittees	2.62	2.88	46	24	35	33

Class Entering in 1974					
			MCAT (Percentiles)		
	SGPA	*OGPA*	*Verbal*	*Quanti-* *tative*	*Science*	*General* *Information*
Bakke	3.44	3.51	96	94	97	72
Average of regular admittees	3.36	3.29	69	67	82	72
Average of special admittees	2.42	2.62	34	30	37	18

Applicants admitted under the special program also had benchmark scores significantly lower than many students, including Bakke, rejected under the general admissions program, even though the special rating system apparently gave credit for overcoming "disadvantage."

[5] Prior to the actual filing of the suit, Bakke discussed his intentions with Peter C. Storandt, Assistant to the Dean of Admissions at the Davis Medical School. Storandt expressed sympathy for Bakke's position and offered advice on litigation strategy. Several *amici* imply that these discussions render Bakke's suit "collusive." There is no indication, however, that Storandt's views were those of the medical school or that anyone else at the school even was aware of Storandt's correspondence and conversations with Bakke. Storandt is no longer with the University.

[6] ". . . [N]or shall any state . . . deny to any person within its jurisdiction the equal protection of the laws."

[7] "No special privileges or immunities shall ever be granted which may not be altered, revoked, or repealed by the Legislature; nor shall any citizen, or class of citizens, be granted privileges, or immunities which, upon the same terms, shall not be granted to all citizens."

This section was recently repealed and its provisions added to Art. § 7 of the state constitution.

[8] Section 601 of Title VI provides as follows:

"No person in the United States shall, on the ground of race, color, or national origin, be excluded from participation in, be denied the benefits of, or be subjected to discrimination under any program or activity receiving Federal financial assistance."

stitution and Title VI. The court refused to order Bakke's admission, however, holding that he had failed to carry his burden of proving that he would have been admitted but for the existence of the special program.

Bakke appealed from the portion of the trial court judgment denying him admission, and the University appealed from the decision that it special admissions program was unlawful and the order enjoining it from considering race in the processing of applications. The Supreme Court of California transferred the case directly from the trial court, "because of the importance of the issues involved." 18 Cal. 3d 34, 39, 553 P. 2d 1152, 1156 (1976). The California court accepted the findings of the trial court with respect to the University's program.[9] Because the special admissions program involved a racial classification, the supreme court held itself bound to apply strict scrutiny. *Id.,* at 49, 553 P. 2d, at 1162–1163. It then turned to the goals the University presented as justifying the special program. Although the court agreed that the goals of integrating the medical profession and increasing the number of physicians willing to serve members of minority groups were compelling state interests, *id.,* at 53, 553 P. 2d, at 1165, it concluded that the special admissions program was not the least intrusive means of achieving those goals. Without passing on the state constitutional or the federal statutory grounds cited in the trial court's judgment, the California court held that the Equal Protection Clause of the Fourteenth Amendment required that "no applicant may be rejected because of his race, in favor of another who is less qualified, as measured by standards applied without regard to race." *Id.,* at 55, 553 P. 2d, at 1166.

Turning to Bakke's appeal, the court ruled that since Bakke had established that the University had discriminated against him on the basis of his race, the burden of proof shifted to the University to demonstrate that he would not have been admitted even in the absence of the special admissions program. *Id.,* at 63–64, 553 P. 2d, at 1172. The court analogized Bakke's situation to that of a plaintiff under Title VII to the Civil Rights Act of 1964, 42 U.S.C. §§ 200e–17. . . . On this basis, the court initially ordered a remand for the purpose of determining whether, under the newly allocated burden of proof, Bakke would have been admitted to either the 1973 or the 1974 entering class in the absence of the special admissions program. In its petition for rehearing below, however, the University conceded its inability to carry that burden. The California court thereupon amended its opinion to direct that the trial court enter judgment ordering Bakke's admission to the medical school. 18 Cal. 3d, at 64, 553 P. 2d, at 1172. That order was stayed pending review in this Court. . . . We granted certiorari to consider the important constitutional issue. . . .

•   •   •

---

[9] Indeed, the University did not challenge the finding that applicants who were not members of a minority group were excluded from consideration in the special admissions process. 18 Cal. 3d, at 44, 553 P. 2d, at 1159.

III

A

Petitioner does not deny that decisions based on race or ethnic origin by faculties and administrations of state universities are reviewable under the Fourteenth Amendment. . . . For his part, respondent does not argue that all racial or ethnic classifications are *per se* invalid. . . . The parties do disagree as to the level of judicial scrutiny to be applied to the special admissions program. Petitioner argues that the court below erred in applying strict scrutiny, as this inexact term has been applied in our cases. That level of review, petitioner asserts, should be reserved for classifications that disadvantage "discrete and insular minorities." See *United States* v. *Carolene Products Co.,* 304 U.S. 144, 152 n. 4 (1938). Respondent, on the other hand, contends that the California court correctly rejected the notion that the degree of judicial scrutiny accorded a particular racial or ethnic classification hinges upon membership in a discrete and insular minority and duly recognized that the "rights established [by the Fourteenth Amendment] are personal rights." *Shelley* v. *Kraemer,* 334 U.S. 1, 22 (1948).

En route to this crucial battle over the scope of judicial review,[10] the parties fight a sharp preliminary action over the proper characterization of the special admissions program. Petitioner prefers to view it as establishing a "goal" of minority representation in the medical school. Respondent, echoing the courts below, labels it a racial quota.[11]

This semantic distinction is beside the point: the special admissions program is undeniably a classification based on race and ethnic background. To the extent that there existed a pool of at least minimally qualified minority

[10] That issue has generated a considerable amount of scholarly controversy. See, *e.g.,* Ely, "The Constitutionality of Reverse Racial Discrimination," 41 *U. Chi. L. Rev.* 723 (1974); Greenawalt, "Judicial Scrutiny of 'Benign' Racial Preferences in Law School Admissions," 75 *Colum. L. Rev.,* 559 (1975); Kaplan, "Equal Justice in an Unequal World: Equality for the Negro," 61 *Nw. U. L. Rev.,* 363 (1966); Karst and Horowitz, "Affirmative Action and Equal Protection," 60 *Va. L. Rev.,* 955 (1974); O'Neil, "Racial Preference and Higher Education: The Larger Context," 60 *Va. L. Rev.,* 925 (1974); Posner, "The DeFunis Case and the Constitutionality of Preferential Treatment of Racial Minorities," *1974 Sup. Ct. Rev.,* 1; Redish, "Preferential Law School Admissions and the Equal Protection Clause: An Analysis of the Competing Arguments," 22 *UCLA L. Rev.,* 343 (1974); Sandalow, "Racial Preferences in Higher Education: Political Responsibility and the Judicial Role," 42 *U. Chi. L. Rev.,* 536, (1975); Sedler, "Racial Preference, Reality and the Constitution: *Bakke* v. *Regents of the University of California,*" 17 *Santa Clara L. Rev.,* 329 (1977); Seeburger, A Heuristic Argument Against Preferential Admissions," 39 *U. Pitt. L. Rev.,* 285 (1977).

[11] Petitioner defines "quota" as a requirement which must be met but can never be exceeded, regardless of the quality of the minority applicants. Petitioner declares that there is no "floor" under the total number of minority students admitted; completely unqualified students will not be admitted simply to meet a "quota." Neither is there a "ceiling," since an unlimited number could be admitted through the general admissions process. On this basis the special admissions program does not meet petitioner's definition of a quota.

The court below found—and petitioner does not deny—that white applicants could not compete for the 16 places reserved solely for the special admissions program. 18 Cal. 3d, at 44, 553 P. 2d, at 1159. Both courts below characterized this as a "quota" system.

applicants to fill the 16 special admissions seats, white applicants could compete only for 84 seats in the entering class, rather than the 100 open to minority applicants. Whether this limitation is described as a quota or a goal, it is a line drawn on the basis of race and ethnic status.[12]

The guarantees of the Fourteenth Amendment extend to persons. Its language is explicit: "No state shall . . . deny to any person within its jurisdiction the equal protection of the laws." It is settled beyond question that the "rights created by the first section of the Fourteenth Amendment are, by its terms, guaranteed to the individual. They are personal rights," *Shelley* v. *Kraemer, supra,* at 22. . . . The guarantee of equal protection cannot mean one thing when applied to one individual and something else when applied to a person of another color. If both are not accorded the same protection, then it is not equal.

Nevertheless, petitioner argues that the court below erred in applying strict scrutiny to the special admissions programs because white males, such as respondent, are not a "discrete and insular minority" requiring extraordinary protection from the majoritarian political process. . . . This rationale, however, has never been invoked in our decisions as prerequisite to subjecting racial or ethnic distinctions to strict scrutiny. Nor has this Court held that discreteness and insularity constitute necessary preconditions to a holding that a particular classification is invidious.[13] . . . These characteristics may be relevant in deciding whether or not to add new types of classifications to the list of "suspect" categories or whether a particular classification survives close examination. See, *e.g., Massachusetts Bd. of Retirement* v. *Murgia,* 427 U.S. 307, 313 (1976) (age); *San Antonio Indep. School Dist.* v. *Rodriquez,* 411 U.S. 1, 28 (1973) (wealth); *Graham* v. *Richardson,* 403 U.S. 365, 372 (1971) (aliens). Racial and ethnic classifications, however, are subject to stringent examination without regard to these additional characteristics. We declared as much in the first cases explicitly to recognize racial distinctions as suspect:

> Distinctions between citizens solely because of their ancestry are by their very nature odious to a free people whose institutions are founded upon the doctrine of equality. *Hirabayashi,* 320 U.S., at 100.

> . . . [A]ll legal restrictions which curtail the rights of a single racial group are immediately suspect. That is not to say that all such restrictions are unconstitutional. It is to say that courts must subject them to the most rigid scrutiny. *Korematsu,* 323 U.S., at 216.

---

[12] Moreover, the University's special admissions program involves a purposeful, acknowledged use of racial criteria. This is not a situation in which the classification on its face is racially neutral, but has a disproportionate racial impact. In that situation, plaintiff must establish an intent to discriminate. . . .

[13] After *Carolene Products,* the first specific reference in our decisions to the elements of "discreteness and insularity" appears in *Minersville School District* v. *Gobitis,* 310 U.S. 586, 606 (1940) (Stone, J., dissenting). The next does not appear until 1970. *Oregon* v. *Mitchell,* 400 U.S. 112, 295 n. 14 (1970) (STEWART, J., concurring in part and dissenting in part). These elements have been relied upon in recognizing a suspect class in only one group of cases, those involving aliens. *E.g., Graham* v. *Richardson,* 403 U.S. 365, 372 (1971).

The Court has never questioned the validity of those pronouncements. Racial and ethnic distinctions of any sort are inherently suspect and thus call for the most exacting judicial examination.

B

This perception of racial and ethnic distinctions is rooted in our Nation's constitutional and demographic history. The Court's initial view of the Fourteenth Amendment was that its "one pervading purpose" was "the freedom of the slave race, the security and firm establishment of that freedom, and the protection of the newly made freeman and citizen from the oppressions of those who had formerly exercised dominion over him." *Slaughter-House Cases,* 16 Wall. 36, 71 (1873). The Equal Protection Clause, however, was "[v]irtually strangled in its infancy by post-civil-war judicial reactionism."[14] It was relegated to decades of relative desuetude while the Due Process Clause of the Fourteenth Amendment, after a short germinal period, flourished as a cornerstone in the Court's defense of property and liberty of contract. . . . In that cause, the Fourteenth Amendment's "one pervading purpose" was displaced. See, *e.g., Plessy* v. *Ferguson,* 163 U.S. 537 (1896). It was only as the era of substantive due process came to a close, see, *e.g., Nebbia* v. *New York,* 291 U.S. 502 (1934); *West Coast Hotel* v. *Parrish,* 300 U.S. 379 (1937), that the Equal Protection Clause began to attain a genuine measure of vitality. . . .

By that time it was no longer possible to peg the guarantees of the Fourteenth Amendment to the struggle for equality of one racial minority. During the dormancy of the Equal Protection Clause, the United States had become a nation of minorities.[15] Each had to struggle[16]—and to some extent struggle still[17]—to overcome the prejudices not of a monolithic majority, but of a "majority" composed of various minority groups of whom it was said— perhaps unfairly in many cases—that a shared characteristic was a willingness to disadvantage other groups.[18] As the Nation filled with the stock of many lands, the reach of the Clause was gradually extended to all ethnic groups seeking protection from official discrimination. See *Strauder* v. *West Virginia,* 100 U.S. 303, 308 (1880). (Celtic Irishmen) (dictum); *Yick Wo* v. *Hopkins,*

[14] Tussman and tenBroek, "The Equal Protection of the Laws," 37 *Calif. L. Rev.,* 341, 381 (1949).

[15] M. Jones, *American Immigration,* 177–246 (1960).

[16] J. Higham, *Strangers in the Land* (1955); G. Abbott, *The Immigrant and the Community* (1917); P. Roberts, *The New Immigration,* 66–73, 86–91, 248–61 (1912). See also E. Fenton, *Immigrants and Unions: A Case Study,* 561–62 (1975).

[17] "Members of various religious and ethnic groups, primarily but not exclusively of eastern, and middle and southern European ancestry, such as Jews, Catholics, Italians, Greeks and Slavic groups [continue] to be excluded from executive, middle-management and other job levels because of discrimination based upon their religion and/or national origin." 41 CFR § 60–50.1 (b) (1977).

[18] *E.g.,* P. Roberts, *The New Immigration,* 75 (1912); G. Abbott, *The Immigrant and the Community,* 270–71 (1971).

118 U.S. 356 (1886) (Chinese); *Truax* v. *Raich,* 239 U.S. 33, 41 (1915) (Austrian resident aliens); *Korematsu, supra* (Japanese); *Hernandez* v. *Texas,* 347 U.S. 475 (1954) (Mexican-Americans). The guarantees of equal protection, said the Court in *Yick Wo,* "are universal in their application, to all persons within the territorial jurisdiction, without regard to any differences of race, of color, or of nationality; and the equal protection of the laws is a pledge of the protection of equal laws." 118 U.S., at 369.

• • •

Over the past 30 years, this Court has embarked upon the crucial mission of interpreting the Equal Protection Clause with the view of assuring to all persons "the protection of equal laws," *Yick Wo, supra,* at 369, in a Nation confronting a legacy of slavery and racial discrimination. . . . Because the landmark decisions in this area arose in response to the continued exclusion of Negroes from the mainstream of American society, they could be characterized as involving discrimination by the "majority" white race against the Negro minority. But they need not be read as depending upon that characterization for their results. It suffices to say that "[o]ver the years, this Court consistently repudiated '[d]istinctions between citizens solely because of their ancestry' as being 'odious to a free people whose institutions are founded upon the doctrine of equality.' " *Loving* v. *Virginia,* 388 U.S. 1, 11 (1967), quoting *Hirabayashi,* 320 U.S., at 100.

Petitioner urges us to adopt for the first time a more restrictive view of the Equal Protection Clause and hold that discrimination against members of the white "majority" cannot be suspect if its purpose can be characterized as "benign." [19] The clock of our liberties, however, cannot be turned back to 1868. *Brown* v. *Board of Education, supra,* at 492; accord, *Loving* v. *Virginia, supra,* at 9. It is far too late to argue that the guarantee of equal protection to *all* persons permits the recognition of special wards entitled to a degree

---

[19] In the view of MR. JUSTICE BRENNAN, MR. JUSTICE WHITE, MR. JUSTICE MARSHALL, and MR. JUSTICE BLACKMUN, the pliable notion of "stigma" is the crucial element in analyzing racial classifications. The Equal Protection Clause is not framed in terms of "stigma." Certainly the word has no clearly defined constitutional meaning. It reflects a subjective judgment that is standardless. *All* state-imposed classifications that rearrange burdens and benefits on the basis of race are likely to be viewed with deep resentment by the individuals burdened. The denial to innocent persons of equal rights and opportunities may outrage those so deprived and therefore may be perceived as invidious. These individuals are likely to find little comfort in the notion that the deprivation they are asked to endure is merely the price of membership in the dominant majority and that its imposition is inspired by the supposedly benign purpose of aiding others. One should not lightly dismiss the inherent unfairness of, and the perception of mistreatment that accompanies, a system of allocating benefits and privileges on the basis of skin color and ethnic origin. Moreover, MR. JUSTICE BRENNAN, MR. JUSTICE WHITE, MR. JUSTICE MARSHALL, and MR. JUSTICE BLACKMUN offer no principle for deciding whether preferential classification reflect a benign remedial purpose or a malevolent stigmatic classification, since they are willing in this case to accept mere *post hoc* declarations by an isolated state entity—a medical school faculty—unadorned by particularized findings of past discrimination, to establish such a remedial purpose.

of protection greater than that accorded others.[20] "The Fourteenth Amendment is not directed solely against discrimination due to a 'two-class theory'—that is, based upon differences between 'white' and Negro." *Hernandez, supra,* at 478.

Once the artificial line of a "two-class theory" of the Fourteenth Amendment is put aside, the difficulties entailed in varying the level of judicial review according to a perceived "preferred" status of a particular racial or ethnic minority are intractable. The concepts of "majority" and "minority" necessarily reflect temporary arrangements and political judgments. As observed above, the white "majority" itself is composed of various minority groups, most of which can lay claim to a history of prior discrimination at the hands of the state and private individuals. Not all of these groups can receive preferential treatment and corresponding judicial tolerance of distinctions drawn in terms of race and nationality, for then the only "majority" left would be a new minority of White Anglo-Saxon Protestants. There is no principled basis for deciding which groups would merit "heightened judicial solicitude" and which would not.[21] Courts would be asked to evaluate the extent of the prejudice and consequent harm suffered by various minority

---

[20] Professor Bickel noted the self-contradiction of that view:

"The lesson of the great decisions of the Supreme Court and the lesson of contemporary history have been the same for at least a generation: discrimination on the basis of race is illegal, immoral, unconstitutional, inherently wrong, and destructive of democratic society. Now this is to be unlearned and we are told that this is not a matter of fundamental principle but only a matter of whose ox is gored. Those for whom racial equality was demanded are to be more equal than others. Having found support in the Constitution for equality, they now claim support for inequality under the same Constitution." A. Bickel, *The Morality of Consent,* 133 (1975).

[21] As I am in agreement with the view that race may be taken into account as a factor in an admissions program, I agree with my Brothers BRENNAN, WHITE, MARSHALL, and BLACKMUN that the portion of the judgment that would prescribe all consideration of race must be reversed. See Part V, *infra.* But I disagree with much that is said in their opinion.

They would require as a justification for a program such as petitioner's, only two findings: (i) that there has been some form of discrimination against the preferred minority groups "by society at large," (it being conceded that petitioner had no history of discrimination), and (ii) that "there is reason to believe" that the disparate impact sought to be rectified by the program is the "product" of such discrimination:

"If it was reasonable to conclude—as we hold that it was—that the failure of Negroes to qualify for admission at Davis under regular procedures was due principally to the effects of past discrimination, then there is a reasonable likelihood that, but for pervasive racial discrimination, respondent would have failed to qualify for admission even in the absence of Davis's special admission program."

The breadth of this hypothesis is unprecedented in our constitutional system. The first step is easily taken. No one denies the regrettable fact that there has been societal discrimination in this country against various racial and ethnic groups. The second step, however, involves a speculative leap: but for this discrimination by society at large, Bakke "would have failed to qualify for admission" because Negro applicants—nothing is said about Asians, would have made better scores. Not one word in the record supports this conclusion, and the plurality offers no standard for courts to use in applying such a presumption of causation to other racial or ethnic classifications. This failure is a grave one, since if it may be concluded *on this record* that each of the minority groups preferred by the petitioner's special program is entitled to the benefit of the presumption, it would seem difficult to determine that any of the dozens of minority groups that have suffered "societal discrimination" cannot also claim it, in any area of social intercourse. See Part IV-B, *infra.*

groups. Those whose societal injury is thought to exceed some arbitrary level of tolerability then would be entitled to preferential classifications at the expense of individuals belonging to other groups. Those classifications would be free from exacting judicial scrutiny. As these preferences began to have their desired effect, and the consequences of past discrimination were undone, new judicial rankings would be necessary. The kind of variable sociological and political analysis necessary to produce such rankings simply does not lie within the judicial competence—even if they otherwise were politically feasible and socially desirable.[22]

Moreover, there are serious problems of justice connected with the idea of preference itself. First, it may not always be clear that a so-called preference is in fact benign. Courts may be asked to validate burdens imposed upon individual members of particular groups in order to advance the group's general interest. . . . Nothing in the Constitution supports the notion that individuals may be asked to suffer otherwise impermissible burdens in order to enhance the societal standing of their ethnic groups. Second, preferential programs may only reinforce common stereotypes holding that certain groups are unable to achieve success without special protection based on a factor having no relationship to individual worth. . . . Third, there is a measure of inequity in forcing innocent persons in respondent's position to bear the burdens of redressing grievances not of their making.

By hitching the meaning of the Equal Protection Clause to these transitory

---

[22] MR. JUSTICE DOUGLAS has noted the problems associated with such inquiries:

"The reservation of a proportion of the law school class for members of selected minority groups is fraught with . . . dangers, for one must immediately determine which groups are to receive such favored treatment and which are to be excluded, the proportions of the class that are to be allocated to each, and even the criteria by which to determine whether an individual is a member of a favored group. [Cf. *Plessy* v. *Ferguson,* 163 U.S. 537, 549, 552 (1896).] There is no assurance that a common agreement can be reached, and first the schools, and then the courts, will be buffeted with the competing claims. The University of Washington included Filipinos, but excluded Chinese and Japanese; another school may limit its program to blacks, or to blacks and Chicanos. Once the Court sanctioned racial preferences such as these, it could not then wash its hands of the matter, leaving it entirely in the discretion of the school, for then we would have effectively overruled *Sweatt* v. *Painer,* 339 U.S. 629, and allowed imposition of a "zero" allocation. But what standard is the Court to apply when a rejected applicant of Japanese ancestry brings suit to require the University of Washington to extend the same privileges to his group? The Committee might conclude that the population of Washington is now 2 percent Japanese, and that Japanese also constitute 2 percent of the Bar, but that had they not been handicapped by a history of discrimination, Japanese would now constitute 5 percent of the Bar, or 20 percent. Or, alternatively, the Court could attempt to assess how grievously each group has suffered from discrimination, and allocate proportions accordingly; if that were the standard the current University of Washington policy would almost surely fall, for there is no Western state which can claim that it has always treated Japanese and Chinese in a fair and evenhanded manner. See, *e.g., Yick Wo* v. *Hopkins,* 118 U.S. 356; *Terrace* v. *Thompson,* 263 U.S. 197; *Oyama* v. *California,* 332 U.S. 633. This Court has not sustained a racial classification since the wartime cases of *Korematsu* v. *United States,* 323 U.S. 214, and *Hirabayashi* v. *United States,* 320 U.S. 81, involving curfews and relocations imposed upon Japanese-Americans.

"Nor obviously will the problem be solved if next year the Law School included only Japanese and Chinese, for then Norwegians and Swedes, Poles and Italians, Puerto Ricans and Hungarians, and all other groups which form this diverse Nation would have just complaints." *DeFunis* v. *Odegaard,* 416 U.S. 312, 337–40 (1974) (Douglas, J., dissenting) (footnotes omitted).

considerations, we would be holding, as a constitutional principle, that judicial scrutiny of classifications touching on racial and ethnic background may vary with the ebb and flow of political forces. Disparate constitutional tolerance of such classifications well may serve to exacerbate racial and ethnic antagonisms rather than alleviate them. . . . Also, the mutability of a constitutional principle, based upon shifting political and social judgments, undermines the chances for consistent application of the Constitution from one generation to the next, a critical feature of its coherent interpretation. . . . In expounding the Constitution, the Court's role is to discern "principles sufficiently absolute to give them roots throughout the community and continuity over significant periods of time, and to lift them above the level of the pragmatic political judgments of a particular time and place." A. Cox, The Role of the Supreme Court in American Government 114 (1976).

If it is the individual who is entitled to judicial protection against classifications based upon his racial or ethnic background because such distinctions impinge upon personal rights, rather than the individual only because of his membership in a particular group, then constitutional standards may be applied consistently. Political judgments regarding the necessity for the particular classfication may be weighed in the constitutional balance, *Korematsu* v. *United States,* 323 U.S. 214 (1944), but the standard of justification will remain constant. This is as it should be, since those political judgments are the product of rough compromise struck by contending groups within the democratic process.[23] When they touch upon an individual's race or ethnic background, he is entitled to a judicial determination that the burden he is asked to bear on that basis is precisely tailored to serve a compelling governmental interest. The Constitution guarantees that right to every person regardless of his background. . . .

• • •

IV

We have held that in "order to justify the use of a suspect classification, a State must show that its purpose or interest is both constitutionally permissible and substantial, and that its use of the classification is 'necessary . . . to the accomplishment' of its purpose or the safeguarding of its interest." *In re Griffiths,* 413 U.S. 717, 722–723 (1973) (footnotes omitted); *Loving* v. *Virginia,* 388 U.S. 1, 11 (1967); *McLaughlin* v. *Florida,* 379 U.S. 184, 196 (1964). The special admissions program purports to serve the purposes of: (i) "reducing the historic deficit of traditionally disfavored minorities in medical schools

---

[23] R. Dahl, *A Preface to Democratic Theory* (1956); Posner, "The DeFunis Case and the the Constitutionality of Preferential Treatment of Minorities," 1974 Sup. Ct. Rev. 1, 27; cf. Stewart, The Reformation of American Administrative Law, 88, *Harv. L. Rev.,* 1683–1685, and nn. 64–67 (1975) and sources cited therein.

and the medical professions," Brief for Petitioner 32; (ii) countering the effects of societal discrimination;[24] (iii) increasing the number of physicians who will practice in communities currently underserved; and (iv) obtaining the educational benefits that flow from an ethnically diverse student body. It is necessary to decide which, if any, of these purposes is substantial enough to support the use of a suspect classification.

A

If petitioner's purpose is to assure within its student body some specified percentage of a particular group merely because of its race or ethnic origin, such a preferential purpose must be rejected not as insubstantial but as facially invalid. Preferring members of any one group for no reason other than race or ethnic origin is discrimination for its own sake. This the Constitution forbids. . . .

B

The State certainly has a legitimate and substantial interest in ameliorating, or eliminating where feasible, the disabling effects of identified discrimination. The line of school desegregation cases, commencing with *Brown,* attests to the importance of this state goal and the commitment of the judiciary to affirm all lawful means towards its attainment. In the school cases, the States were required by court order to redress the wrongs worked by specific instances of racial discrimination. That goal was far more focused than the remedying of the effects of "societal discrimination," an amorphous concept of injury that may be ageless in its reach into the past.

----

[24] A number of distinct sub-goals have been advanced as falling under the rubric of "compensation for past discrimination." For example, it is said that preferences for Negro applicants may compensate for harm done them personally, or serve to place them at economic levels they might have attained but for discrimination against their forebears. Greenawalt, *supra,* n. 1, at 581–86. Another view of the "compensation" goal is that it serves as a form of reparation by the "majority" to a victimized group as a whole. B. Bittker, *The Case for Black Reparations* (1973). That justification for racial or ethnic preference has been subjected to much criticism. . . . Finally it has been argued that ethnic preferences "compensate" the group by providing examples of success whom other members of the group will emulate, thereby advancing the group's interest and society's interest in encouraging new generations to overcome the barriers and frustrations of the past. . . . For purposes of analysis these sub-goals need not be considered separately.

Racial classifications in admissions conceivably could serve a fifth purpose, one which petitioner does not articulate: fair appraisal of each individual's academic promise in the light of some cultural bias in grading or testing procedures. To the extent that race and ethnic background were considered only to the extent of curing established inaccuracies in predicting academic performance, it might be argued that there is no "preference" at all. Nothing in this record, however, suggests either that any of the quantitative factors considered by the Medical School were culturally biased or that petitioner's special admissions program was formulated to correct for any such biases. Furthermore, if race or ethnic background were used solely to arrive at an unbiased prediction of academic success, the reservation of fixed numbers of seats would be inexplicable.

We have never approved a classification that aids persons perceived as members of relatively victimized groups at the expense of other innocent individuals in the absence of judicial, legislative or administrative findings of constitutional or statutory violations. . . . After such findings have been made, the governmental interest in preferring members of the injured groups at the expense of others is substantial, since the legal rights of the victims must be vindicated. In such a case, the extent of the injury and the consequent remedy will have been judicially, legislatively, or administratively defined. Also, the remedial action usually remains subject to continuing oversight to assure that it will work the least harm possible to other innocent persons competing for the benefit. Without such findings of constitutional or statutory violations, it cannot be said that the government has any greater interest in helping one individual than in refraining from harming another. Thus, the government has no compelling justification for inflicting such harm.

Petitioner does not purport to have made, and is in no position to make, such findings. Its broad mission is education, not the formulation of any legislative policy or the adjudication of particular claims of illegality. . . .

Hence, the purpose of helping certain groups whom the faculty of the Davis Medical School perceived as victims of "societal discrimination" does not justify a classification that imposes disadvantages upon persons like respondent, who bear no responsibility for whatever harm the beneficiaries of the special admissions program are thought to have suffered. To hold otherwise would be to convert a remedy heretofore reserved for violations of legal rights into a privilege that all institutions throughout the Nation could grant at their pleasure to whatever groups are perceived as victims of societal discrimination. That is a step we have never approved. . . .

C

Petitioner identifies, as another purpose of its program, improving the delivery of health care services to communities currently underserved. It may be assumed that in some situations a State's interest in facilitating the health care of its citizens is sufficiently compelling to support the use of a suspect classification. But there is virtually no evidence in the record indicating that petitioner's special admissions program is either needed or geared to promote that goal.[25] The court below addressed this failure of proof:

> The University concedes it cannot assure that minority doctors who entered under the program, all of whom express an 'interest' in participating in a disadvantaged community, will actually do so. It may be correct to assume that some of them will carry out this intention, and that it is more likely they will practice in minority communities than the average white doctor. (See Sandalow, "Racial Preferences in Higher Education: Political Responsibility and the Judicial Role" (1975), 42 *U. Chi. L. Rev.* 653, 688). Nevertheless, there are more precise and reliable ways to

---

[25] The only evidence in the record with respect to such underservice is a newspaper article.

identify applicants who are genuinely interested in the medical problems of minorities than by race. An applicant of whatever race who has demonstrated his concern for disadvantaged minorities in the past and who declares that practice in such a community is his primary professional goal would be more likely to contribute to alleviation of the medical shortage than one who is chosen entirely on the basis of race and disadvantage. In short, there is [sic] no empirical data to demonstrate that any one race is more selflessly socially oriented or by contrast that another is more selfishly acquisitive. 18 Cal. 3d, at 56, 553 P. 2d, at 1167.

Petitioner simply has not carried its burden of demonstrating that it must prefer members of particular ethnic groups over all other individuals in order to promote better health care delivery to deprived citizens. Indeed, petitioner has not shown that its preferential classification is likely to have any significant effect on the problem.[26]

D

The fourth goal asserted by petitioner is the attainment of a diverse student body. This clearly is a constitutionally permissible goal for an institution of higher education. Academic freedom, though not a specifically enumerated constitutional right, long has been viewed as a special concern of the First Amendment. The freedom of a university to make its own judgments as to education includes the selection of its student body. MR. JUSTICE FRANK-FURTER summarized the "four essential freedoms" that comprise academic freedom:

> . . . It is the business of a university to provide that atmosphere which is most conducive to speculation, experiment and creation. It is an atmosphere, in which there prevail "the four essential freedoms" of a university—to determine for itself on academic grounds who may teach, what may be taught, how it shall be taught, and who may be admitted to study. *Sweezy* v. *New Hampshire,* 354 U.S. 234, 263 (1957) (FRANKFURTER, J., concurring).

Our national commitment to the safeguarding of these freedoms with university communities was emphasized in *Keyishian* v. *Board of Regents,* 385 U.S. 589, 693 (1967):

> Our Nation is deeply committed to safeguarding academic freedom which is of transcendent value to all of us and not merely to the teachers concerned. That freedom is therefore a special concern of the First Amendment. . . . The Nation's future depends upon leaders trained through wide exposure to that robust exchange

---

[26] It is not clear that petitioner's two-track system, even if adopted throughout the country, would substantially increase representation of blacks in the medical profession. That is the finding of a recent study by Sleeth and Mishell, "Black Under-Representation in United States Medical Schools," *N. Engl. J. Med.,* 1146 (Nov. 24, 1977). Those authors maintain that the cause of black underrepresentation lies in the small size of the national pool of qualified black applicants. In their view, this problem is traceable to the poor premedical experiences of black undergraduates, and can be remedied effectively only by developing remedial programs for black students before they enter college.

of ideas which discovers truth "out of a multitude of tongues, rather than through any kind of authoritative selection." *United States* v. *Associated Press,* 52 F. Supp. 362, 372.

The atmosphere of "speculation, experiment and creation"—so essential to the quality of a higher education—is widely believed to be promoted by a diverse student body.[27] As the Court noted in *Keyishian,* it is not too much to say that the "nation's future depends upon leaders trained through wide exposure" to the ideas and mores of students as diverse as this Nation of many peoples.

Thus, in arguing that its universities must be accorded the right to select those students who will contribute the most to the "robust exchange of ideas," petitioner invokes a countervailing constitutional interest, that of the First Amendment. In this light, petitioner must be viewed as seeking to achieve a goal that is of paramount importance in the fulfillment of its mission.

It may be argued that there is greater force to these views at the undergraduate level than in a medical school where the training is centered primarily on professional competency. But even at the graduate level, our tradition and experience lend support to the view that the contribution of diversity is substantial. In *Sweatt* v. *Painter,* 339 U.S. 629, 634 (1950), the Court made a similar point with specific reference to legal education:

> The law school, the proving ground for legal learning and practice, cannot be effective in isolation from the individuals and institutions with which the law interacts. Few students and no one who has practiced law would choose to study in an academic vacuum, removed from the interplay of ideas and the exchange of views with which the law is concerned.

Physicians serve a heterogeneous population. An otherwise qualified medical student with a particular background—whether it be ethnic, geographic, culturally advantaged or disadvantaged— may bring to a professional school of medicine experiences, outlooks and ideas that enrich the training of its

---

[27] The president of Princeton University has described some of the benefits derived from a diverse student body:

". . . [A] great deal of learning occurs informally. It occurs through interactions among students of both sexes; of different races, religions, and backgrounds; who come from cities and rural areas, from various states and countries; who have a wide variety of interests and perspectives; and who are able, directly or indirectly, to learn from their differences and to stimulate one another to reexamine even their most deeply held assumptions about themselves and their world. As a wise graduate of ours once observed in commenting on this aspect of the educational process, 'People do not learn very much when they are surrounded only by the likes of themselves.'

                                   . . .

"In the nature of things, it is hard to know how, and when, and even if, this informal 'learning through diversity' actually occurs. It does not occur for everyone. For many, however, the unplanned, casual encounters with roommates, fellow sufferers in an organic chemistry class, student workers in the library, teammates on a basketball squad, or other participants in class affairs or student government can be subtle and yet powerful sources of improved understanding and personal growth." Bowen, "Admissions and the Relevance of Race," *Princeton Alumni Weekly,* 7, 9 (Sept. 26, 1977).

student body and better equip its graduates to render with understanding their vital service to humanity.[28]

Ethnic diversity, however, is only one element in a range of factors a university properly may consider in attaining the goal of a heterogeneous student body. Although a university must have wide discretion in making the sensitive judgments as to who should be admitted, constitutional limitations protecting individual rights may not be disregarded. Respondent urges—and the courts below have held—that petitioner's dual admissions program is a racial classification that impermissibly infringes his rights under the Fourteenth Amendment. As the interest of diversity is compelling in the context of a university's admissions program, the question remains whether the program's racial classification is necessary to promote this interest. . . .

V

A

It may be assumed that the reservation of a specified number of seats in each class for individuals from the preferred ethnic groups would contribute to the attainment of considerable ethnic diversity in the student body. But petitioner's argument that this is the only effective means of serving the interest of diversity is seriously flawed. In a most fundamental sense the argument misconceives the nature of the state interest that would justify consideration of race or ethnic background. It is not an interest in simple ethnic diversity, in which a specific percentage of the student body is in effect guaranteed to be members of selected ethnic groups, with the remaining percentage an undifferentiated aggregation of students. The diversity that furthers a compelling state interest encompasses a far broader array of qualifications and characteristics of which racial or ethnic origin is but a single though important element. Petitioner's special admissions program, focused *solely* on ethnic diversity, would hinder rather than further attainment of genuine diversity.[29]

Nor would the state interest in genuine diversity be served by expanding petitioner's two-track system into a multitrack program with a prescribed number of seats set aside for each identifiable category of applicants. Indeed, it is inconceivable that a university would thus pursue the logic of petitioner's

---

[28] Graduate admissions decisions, like those at the undergraduate level, are concerned with "assessing the potential contributions to the society of each individual candidate following his or her graduation—contributions defined in the broadest way to include the doctor and the poet, the most active participant in business or government affairs and the keenest critic of all things organized, the solitary scholar and the concerned parent." Bowen, *supra,* n. 27, at 10.

[29] See Manning, "The Pursuit of Fairness in Admissions to Higher Education," in *Carnegie Council on Policy Studies in Higher Education, Selective Admissions in Higher Education,* 19, 57–59 (1977).

two-track program to the illogical end of insulating each category of applicants with certain desired qualifications from competition with all other applicants.

The experience of other university admissions programs, which take race into account in achieving the educational diversity valued by the First Amendment, demonstrates that the assignment of a fixed number of places to a minority group is not a necessary means toward that end. An illuminating example is found in the Harvard College program:

> In recent years Harvard College has expanded the concept of diversity to include students from disadvantaged economic, racial and ethnic groups. Harvard College now recruits not only Californians or Louisianans but also blacks and Chicanos and other minority students.

> • • •

> In practice, this new definition of diversity has meant that race has been a factor in some admission decisions. When the Committee on Admissions reviews the large middle group of applicants who are 'admissible' and deemed capable of doing good work in their courses, the race of an applicant may tip the balance in his favor just as geographic origin or a life spent on a farm may tip the balance in other candidates' cases. A farm boy from Idaho can bring something to Harvard College that a Bostonian cannot offer. Similarly, a black student can usually bring something that a white person cannot offer. . . .

> • • •

> In Harvard college admissions the Committee has not set target-quotas for the number of blacks, or of musicians, football players, physicists or Californians to be admitted in a given year. . . . But that awareness [of the necessity of including more than a token number of black students] does not mean that the Committee sets the minimum number of blacks or of people from west of the Mississippi who are to be admitted. It means only that in choosing among thousands of applicants who are not only 'admissible' academically but have other strong qualities, the Committee, with a number of criteria in mind, pays some attention to distribution among many types and categories of students. (Brief for Columbia University, Harvard University, Stanford University, and the University of Pennsylvania, as *Amici Curiae,* App. 2, 3.)

In such an admissions program,[30] race or ethnic background may be deemed a "plus" in a particular applicant's file, yet it does not insulate the individual

---

[30] The admissions program at Princeton has been described in similar terms:
"While race is not in and of itself a consideration in determining basic qualifications, and while there are obviously significant differences in background and experience among applicants of every race, in some situations race can be helpful information in enabling the admissions office to understand more fully what a particular candidate has accomplished—and against what odds. Similarly, such factors as family circumstances and previous educational opportunities may be relevant, either in conjunction with race or ethnic background (with which they may be associated) or on their own." Bowen *supra,* n. 27, at 8–9.
For an illuminating discussion of such flexible admissions systems, see Manning, *supra,* n. 29, at 57–59.

from comparison with all other candidates for the available seats. The file of a particular black applicant may be examined for his potential contribution to diversity without the factor of race being decisive when compared, for example, with that of an applicant identified as an Italian-American if the latter is thought to exhibit qualities more likely to promote beneficial educational pluralism. Such qualities could include exceptional personal talents, unique work or service experience, leadership potential, maturity, demonstrated compassion, a history of overcoming disadvantage, ability to communicate with the poor, or other qualifications deemed important. In short, an admissions program operated in this way is flexible enough to consider all pertinent elements of diversity in light of the particular qualifications of each applicant, and to place them on the same footing for consideration, although not necessarily according them the same weight. Indeed, the weight attributed to a particular quality may vary from year to year depending upon the "mix" both of the student body and the applicants for the incoming class.

The kind of program treats each applicant as an individual in the admissions process. The applicant who loses out on the last available seat to another candidate receiving a "plus" on the basis of ethnic background will not have been foreclosed from all consideration for that seat simply because he was not the right color or had the wrong surname. It would mean only that his combined qualifications, which may have included similar nonobjective factors, did not outweigh those of the other applicant. His qualifications would have been weighed fairly and competitively, and he would have no basis to complain of unequal treatment under the Fourteenth Amendment.[31]

It has been suggested that an admissions program which considers race only as one factor is simply a subtle and more sophisticated—but no less effective—means of according racial preference than the Davis program. A facial intent to discriminate, however, is evident in petitioner's preference program and not denied in this case. No such facial infirmity exists in an admissions program where race or ethnic background is simply one element— to be weighed fairly against other elements—in the selection process. "A boundary line," as Mr. Justice Frankfurter remarked in another connection, "is none the worse for being narrow." *McLeod* v. *Dilworth,* 322 U.S. 327, 329 (1944). And a Court would not assume that a university, professing to employ a racially nondiscriminatory admissions policy, would operate it as a cover for the functional equivalent of a quota system. In short, good faith would be presumed in the absence of a showing to the contrary in the manner permitted by our cases. See, *e.g., Arlington Heights* v. *Metropolitan Housing*

---

[31] The denial to respondent of this right to individualized consideration without regard to his race is the principal evil of petitioner's special admissions program. Nowhere in the opinion of Mr. JUSTICE BRENNAN, MR. JUSTICE WHITE, MR. JUSTICE MARSHALL, and MR. JUSTICE BLACKMUN is this denial even addressed.

Development Corp., 429 U.S. 252 (1977); *Washington* v. *Davis,* 426 U.S. 229 (1976); *Swain* v. *Alabama,* 380 U.S. 202 (1965).[32]

B

In summary, it is evident that the Davis special admission program involves the use of an explicit racial classification never before countenanced by this Court. It tells applicants who are not Negro, Asian, or "Chicano" that they are totally excluded from a specific percentage of the seats in an entering class. No matter how strong their qualifications, quantitative and extracurricular, including their own potential for contribution to educational diversity, they are never afforded the chance to compete with applicants from the preferred groups for the special admission seats. At the same time, the preferred applicants have the opportunity to compete for every seat in the class.

The fatal flaw in petitioner's preferential program is its disregard of individual rights as guaranteed by the Fourteenth Amendment. . . . Such rights are not absolute. But when a State's distribution of benefits or imposition of burdens hinges on the color of a person's skin or ancestry, that individual is entitled to a demonstration that the challenged classification is necessary to promote a substantial state interest. Petitioner has failed to carry this burden. For this reason, that portion of the California court's judgment holding petitioner's special admissions program invalid under the Fourteenth Amendment must be affirmed.

C

In enjoining petitioner from ever considering the race of any applicant, however, the courts below failed to recognize that the State has a substantial interest that legitimately may be served by a properly devised admissions program involving the competitive consideration of race and ethnic origin. For this reason, so much of the California court's judgment as enjoins petitioner from any consideration of the race of any applicant must be reversed.

VI

With respect to respondent's entitlement to an injunction directing his admission to the Medical School, petitioner has conceded that it could not carry

[32] Universities, like the prosecutor in *Swain,* may make individualized decisions, in which ethnic background plays a part, under a presumption of legality and legitimate educational purpose. So long as the university proceeds on an individualized, case-by-case basis, there is no warrant for judicial interference in the academic process. If an applicant can establish that the institution does not adhere to a policy of individual comparisons, or can show that a systematic exclusion of certain groups results, the presumption of legality might be overcome, creating the necessity of proving legitimate educational purpose.

There also are strong policy reasons that correspond to the constitutional distinction between petitioner's preference program and one that assures a measure of competition among all applicants. Petitioner's program will be viewed as inherently unfair by the public generally as well

its burden of proving that, but for the existence of its unlawful special admissions program, respondent still would not have been admitted. Hence, respondent is entitled to the injunction, and that portion of the judgment must be affirmed.

• • •

Opinion of MR. JUSTICE BRENNAN, MR. JUSTICE WHITE, MR. JUSTICE MARSHALL, and MR. JUSTICE BLACKMUN, concurring in the judgment in part and dissenting.

The Court today, in reversing in part the judgment of the Supreme Court of California, affirms the constitutional power of Federal and State Government to act affirmatively to achieve equal opportunity for all. The difficulty of the issue presented—whether Government may use race conscious programs to redress the continuing effects of past discrimination—and the mature consideration which each of our Brethren has brought to it have resulted in many opinions, no single one speaking for the Court. But this should not and must not mask the central meaning of today's opinions: Government may take race into account when it acts not to demean or insult any racial group, but to remedy disadvantages cast on minorities by past racial prejudice, at least when appropriate findings have been made by judicial, legislative, or administrative bodies with competence to act in this area.

• • •

We agree with MR. JUSTICE POWELL that, as applied to the case before us, Title VI goes no further in prohibiting the use of race than the Equal Protection Clause of the Fourteenth Amendment itself. We also agree that the effect of the California Supreme Court's affirmance of the judgment of the Superior Court of California would be to prohibit the University from establishing in the future affirmative action programs that take race into account. Since we conclude that the affirmative admissions program at the Davis Medical School is constitutional, we would reverse the judgment below in all respects. MR. JUSTICE POWELL agrees that some uses of race in university admissions are permissible and, therefore, he joins with us to make five votes reversing the judgment below insofar as it prohibits the University from establishing race-conscious programs in the future.[1]

---

as by applicants for admission to state universities. Fairness in individual competition for opportunities, especially those provided by the State, is a widely cherished American ethic. Indeed, in a broader sense, an underlying assumption of the rule of law is the worthiness of a system of justice based on fairness to the individual. As MR. JUSTICE FRANKFURTER declared in another connection, "[j]ustice must satisfy the appearance of justice." *Offut* v. *United States,* 348 U.S. 11, 14 (1954).

[1] We also agree with MR. JUSTICE POWELL that a plan like the "Harvard" plan is constitutional under our approach, at least so long as the use of race to achieve an integrated student body is necessitated by the lingering effects of past discrimination.

I

Our Nation was founded on the principle that "all men are created equal." Yet candor requires acknowledgment that the Framers of our Constitution, to forge the Thirteen Colonies into one Nation, openly compromised this principle of equality with its antithesis: slavery. The consequences of this compromise are well known and have aptly been called our "American Dilemma." Still, it is well to recount how recent the time has been, if it has yet come, when the promise of our principles has flowered into the actuality of equal opportunity for all regardless of race or color.

The Fourteenth Amendment, the embodiment in the Constitution of our abiding belief in human equality, has been the law of our land for only slightly more than half of its 200 years. And for half of that half, the Equal Protection Clause of the Amendment was largely moribund so that, as late as 1927, Mr. Justice Holmes could sum up the importance of that Clause by remarking that it was "the last resort of constitutional arguments." *Buck* v. *Bell,* 274 U.S. 200, 208 (1927). Worse than desuetude, the Clause was early turned against those whom it was intended to set free, condemning them to a "separate but equal" status before the law, a status always separate but seldom equal. Not until 1954—only 24 years ago—was this odious doctrine interred by our decision in *Brown* v. *Board of Education,* 347 U.S. 483 (1954) (*Brown I*), and its progeny, which proclaimed that separate schools and public facilities of all sorts were inherently unequal and forbidden under our Constitution. Even then inequality was not eliminated with "all deliberate speed." *Brown* v. *Board of Education,* 349 U.S. 294, 301 (1955). In 1968 and again in 1971, for example, we were forced to remind school boards of their obligation to eliminate racial discrimination root and branch. And a glance at our docket and at those of lower courts will show that even today officially sanctioned discrimination is not a thing of the past.

Against this background, claims that law must be "colorblind" or that the datum of race is no longer relevant to public policy must be seen as aspiration rather than as description of reality. This is not to denigrate aspiration; for reality rebukes us that race has too often been used by those who would stigmatize and oppress minorities. Yet we cannot—and as we shall demonstrate, need not under our Constitution or Title VI, which merely extends the constraints of the Fourteenth Amendment to private parties who receive federal funds—let color blindness become myopia which marks the reality that many "created equal" have been treated within our lifetimes as inferior both by law and by their fellow citizens.

• • •

III

A

The assertion of human equality is closely associated with the proposition that differences in color or creed, birth or status, are neither significant nor relevant to the way in which persons should be treated. Nonetheless, the position that such factors must be "[c]onstitutionally an irrelevance," *Edwards* v. *California,* 314 U.S. 160, 185 (1941) (JACKSON, J., concurring), summed up by the shorthand phrase "[o]ur Constitution is color-blind," *Plessy* v. *Ferguson,* 162 U.S. 537, 559 (1896) (HARLAN, J., dissenting), has never been adopted by this Court as the proper meaning of the Equal Protection Clause. Indeed, we have expressly rejected this proposition on a number of occasions.

• • •

B

Respondent argues that racial classifications are always suspect and, consequently, that this Court should weigh the importance of the objectives served by Davis' special admissions program to see if they are compelling. In addition, he asserts that this Court must inquire whether, in its judgment, there are alternatives to racial classifications which would suit Davis' purposes. Petitioner, on the other hand, states that our proper role is simply to accept petitioner's determination that the racial classifications used by its program are reasonably related to what it tells us are its benign purposes. We reject petitioner's view, but because our prior cases are in many respects inapposite to that before us now, we find it necessary to define with precision the meaning of that inexact term, "strict scrutiny."

Unquestionably we have held that a government practice or statute which restricts "fundamental rights" or which contains "suspect classifications" is to be subjected to "strict scrutiny" and can be justified only if it furthers a compelling government purpose and, even then, only if no less restrictive alternative is available.[2] . . . But no fundamental right is involved here. . . . Nor do whites as a class have any of the "traditional indicia of suspectness: the class is not saddled with such disabilities, or subjected to such a history of purposeful unequal treatment, or relegated to such a position of political powerlessness as to command extraordinary protection from the majoritarian political process." *Id.,* at 28; see *United States* v. *Carolene Products Co.,* 304 U.S. 144, 152 n. 4 (1938).[3]

---

[2] We do not pause to debate whether our cases establish a "two-tier" analysis, a "sliding scale" analysis, or something else altogether. It is enough for present purposes that strict scrutiny is applied at least in some cases.

[3] Of course, the fact that whites constitute a political majority in our Nation does not necessarily mean that active judicial scrutiny of racial classifications that disadvantage whites is inappropriate. Cf. *Castaneda* v. *Partida,* 430 U.S. 482, 499–500 (1977); *id.,* at 501 (MARSHALL, J., concurring).

Moreover, if the University's representations are credited, this is not a case where racial classifications are "irrelevant and therefore prohibited." *Hirabayashi,* 320 U.S., at 100. Nor has anyone suggested that the University's purposes contravene the cardinal principle that racial classifications that stigmatize—because they are drawn on the presumption that one race is inferior to another or because they put the weight of government behind racial hatred and separatism—are invalid without more. . . .

On the other hand, the fact that this case does not fit neatly into our prior analytic framework for race cases does not mean that it should be analyzed by applying the very loose rational basis standard of review that is the very least that is always applied in equal protection cases.[4] " '[T]he mere recitation of a benign, compensatory purpose is not an automatic shield which protects against any inquiry into the actual purposes underlying a statutory scheme.' " *California* v. *Webster,* 430 U.S. 313, 317 (1977), quoting *Weinberger* v. *Weisenfeld,* 420 U.S. 636, 648 (1975). Instead, a number of considerations— developed in gender discrimination cases but which carry even more force when applied to racial classifications—lead us to conclude that racial classifications designed to further remedial purposes " 'must serve important governmental objectives and must be substantially related to achievement of those objectives.' " *Califano* v. *Webster, supra,* at 316, quoting *Craig* v. *Boren,* 429 U.S. 190, 197 (1976).[5]

---

[4] Paradoxically, petitioner's argument is supported by the cases generally thought to establish the "strict scrutiny" standard in race cases, *Hirabayashi* v. *United States,* 320 U.S. 81 (1943), and *Korematsu* v. *United States,* 323 U.S. 214 (1944). In *Hirabayashi,* for example, the Court, responding to a claim that a racial classification was rational, sustained a racial classification solely on the basis of a conclusion in the double-negative that it could not say that facts which might have been available "could afford no ground for differentiating citizens of Japanese ancestry from other groups in the United States." *Id.,* at 101. A similar mode of analysis was followed in *Korematsu,* see 323 U.S., at 224, even though the Court stated there that racial classifications were "immediately suspect" and should be subject to "the most rigid scrutiny." *Id.,* at 216.

[5] We disagree with our Brother POWELL's suggestion that the presence of "rival groups who can claim that they, too, are entitled to preferential treatment," distinguishes the gender cases or is relevant to the question of scope of judicial review of race classifications. We are not asked to determine whether groups other than those favored by the Davis program should similarly be favored. All we are asked to do is to pronounce the constitutionality of what Davis has done. But, were we asked to decide whether any given rival group—German-Americans for example—must constitutionally be accorded preferential treatment, we do have a "principled basis," for deciding this question, one that is well-established in our cases: The Davis program expressly sets out four classes which receive preferred status. The program clearly distinguishes whites, but one cannot reason from this to a conclusion that German-Americans, as a national group, are singled out for invidious treatment. And even if the Davis program had a differential impact on German-Americans, they would have no constitutional claim unless they could prove that Davis intended invidiously to discriminate against German-Americans. If this could not be shown, then "the principle that calls for the closest scrutiny of distinctions in laws denying fundamental rights . . . is inapplicable," *Katzenbach* v. *Morgan,* 384 U.S. 641, 657 (1967), and the only question is whether it was rational for Davis to conclude that the groups it preferred had a greater claim to compensation than the groups it excluded. See *ibid.; San Antonio Indep.*

First, race, like, "gender-based classifications too often [has] been inexcusably utilized to stereotype and stigmatize politically powerless segments of society." *Kahn* v. *Shevin,* 416 U.S. 351, 357 (1974) (dissenting opinion). While a carefully tailored statute designed to remedy past discrimination could avoid these vices, . . . we nonetheless have recognized that the line between honest and thoughtful appraisal of the effects of past discrimination and paternalistic stereotyping is not so clear and that a statute based on the latter is patiently capable of stigmatizing all women with a badge of inferiority. . . . State programs designed ostensibly to ameliorate the effects of past racial discrimination obviously create the same hazard of stigma, since they may promote racial separatism and reinforce the views of those who believe that members of racial minorities are inherently incapable of succeeding on their own. . . .

Second, race, like gender and illegitimacy, . . . is an immutable characteristic which its possessors are powerless to escape or set aside. While a classification is not *per se* invalid because it divides classes on the basis of an immutable characteristic, see *supra,* pp. 31–32, it is nevertheless true that such divisions are contrary to our deep belief that "legal burdens should bear some relationship to individual responsibility or wrongdoing," *Weber, supra,* at 175; *Frontiero* v. *Richardson,* 411 U.S. 667, 686 (1973) (opinion of BRENNAN, WHITE, and MARSHALL, JJ.), and that advancement sanctioned, sponsored, or approved by the State should ideally be based on individual merit or achievement, or at the least on factors within the control of an individual. . . .

Because this principle is so deeply rooted it might be supposed that it would be considered in the legislative process and weighed against the benefits of programs preferring individuals because of their race. But this is not necessarily so: The "natural consequence of our governing process [may well be] that the most 'discrete and insular' of whites . . . will be called upon to bear the immediate, direct costs of benign discrimination." *UJO,* 430 U.S., at 174 (concurring opinion). Moreover, it is clear from our cases that there are limits beyond which majorities may not go when they classify on the basis of immutable characteristics. See, *e.g., Weber, supra.* Thus, even if the concern for individualism is weighed by the political process, that weighing cannot waive the personal rights of individuals under the Fourteenth Amendment. . . .

In sum, because of the significant risk that racial classifications established for ostensibly benign purposes can be misused, causing effects not unlike those created by invidious classifications, it is inappropriate to inquire only whether

---

School Dist. v. *Rodriguez,* 411 U.S. 1, 38–39 (1973) (applying *Katzenbach* test to state action intended to remove discrimination in educational opportunity). Thus, claims of rival groups, although they may create thorny political problems, create relatively simple problems for the courts.

there is any conceivable basis that might sustain such a classification. Instead, to justify such a classification an important and articulated purpose for its use must be shown. In addition, any statute must be stricken that stigmatizes any group or that singles out those least well represented in the political process to bear the brunt of a benign program. Thus our review under the Fourteenth Amendment should be strict—not " 'strict' in theory and fatal in fact,"[6] because it is stigma that causes fatality—but strict and searching nonetheless.

IV

Davis' articulated purpose of remedying the effects of past societal discrimination is, under our cases, sufficiently important to justify the use of race-conscious admissions programs where there is a sound basis for concluding that minority underrepresentation is substantial and chronic, and that the handicap of past discrimination is impeding access of minorities to the medical school.

• • •

B

Properly construed, therefore, our prior cases unequivocally show that a state government may adopt race-conscious programs if the purpose of such programs is to remove the disparate racial impact its actions might otherwise have and if there is reason to believe that the disparate impact is itself the product of past discrimination, whether its own or that of society at large. There is no question that Davis' program is valid under this test.

Certainly, on the basis of the undisputed factual submissions before this Court, Davis had a sound basis for believing that the problem of underrepresentation of minorities was substantial and chronic and that the problem was attributable to handicaps imposed on minority applicants by past and present racial discrimination. Until at least 1973, the practice of medicine in this country was, in fact, if not in law, largely the prerogative of whites.[7] In 1950, for example, while Negroes comprised 10 percent of the total population,

---

[6] Gunther, "The Supreme Court, 1971 Term—Foreword: In Search of Evolving Doctrine on a Changing Court: A Model for a Newer Equal Protection," 86 *Harv. L. Rev.,* 1, 8 (1972).

[7] According to 89 schools responding to a questionnaire sent to 112 medical schools (all of the then-accredited medical schools in the United States except Howard and Meharry), substantial efforts to admit minority students did not begin until 1968. That year was the earliest year of involvement for 34 percent of the schools; an additional 66 percent became involved during the years 1969 to 1973. See C. Odegaard, *Minorities in Medicine: From Receptive Passivity to Positive Action, 1966–1976,* at 19 (1977) (hereinafter Odegaard). These efforts were reflected in a significant increase in the percentage of minority MD graduates. The number of American Negro graduates increased from 2.2 percent in 1970 to 3.3 percent in 1973 and 5.0 percent in 1975.

Negro physicians constituted only 2.2 percent of the total number of physicians.[8] The overwhelming majority of these, moreover, were educated in two predominantly Negro medical schools, Howard and Meharry.[9] By 1970, the gap between the proportion of Negroes in medicine and their proportion in the population had widened. The number of Negroes employed in medicine remained frozen at 2.2 percent[10] while the Negro population had increased to 11.1 percent.[11] The number of Negro admittees to predominantly white medical schools, moreover, had declined in absolute numbers during the years 1955 to 1964. (Odegaard 19)

Moreover, Davis had very good reason to believe that the national pattern of underrepresentation of minorities in medicine would be perpetuated if it retained a single admissions standard. For example, the entering classes in 1968 and 1969, the years in which such a standard was used, included only one Chicano and two Negroes out of 100 admittees. Nor is there any relief from this pattern of underrepresentation in the statistics for the regular admissions program in later years.

Davis clearly could conclude that the serious and persistent underrepresentation of minorities in medicine depicted by these statistics is the result of handicaps under which minority applicants labor as a consequence of a background of deliberate, purposeful discrimination against minorities in education and in society generally, as well as in the medical profession. From the inception of our national life, Negroes have been subjected to unique legal disabilities impairing access to equal educational opportunity. Under slavery, penal sanctions were imposed upon anyone attempting to educate Negroes.[12] After enactment of the Fourteenth Amendment the States continued to deny Negroes equal educational opportunity, enforcing a strict policy of segregation that itself stamped Negroes as inferior, *Brown, supra,* which relegated minorities to inferior educational institutions,[13] and which denied them intercourse in the mainstream of professional life necessary to advancement. . . . Segregation was not limited to public facilities, moreover, but was enforced by criminal penalties against private action as well. Thus, as

---

Significant percentage increases in the number of Mexican-American, American-Indian, and Mainland Puerto Rican graduates were also recorded during those years.

    The statistical information cited in this and the following notes was compiled by government officials or medical educators, and has been brought to our attention in many of the briefs. Neither the parties nor the *amici* challenge the validity of the statistics alluded to in our discussion.

    [8] D. Reitzes, *Negroes and Medicine,* XXVII, 3 (1958).

    [9] Between 1955 and 1964, for example, the percentage of Negro physicians graduated in the United States who were trained at these schools ranged from 69.0 percent to 75.8 percent. See Odegaard, at 19.

    [10] "Minorities and Women in Health Fields," United States Dept. of Health, Education, and Welfare Pub. No. (HRA) 75–22, at 7 (May 1974).

    [11] U.S. Bureau of the Census, 1970, Census, Vol. 1, "Characteristics of the Population," Pt. 1, "United States Summary," sec. 1, "General Population Characteristics," 1–293 (Table 60) (1973).

    [12] See, *e.g.,* R. Wade, *Slavery in the Cities,* 90–91 (1964).

    [13] For an example of unequal facilities in California schools, see *Soria* v. *Oxnard School Dist.,* 386 F. Supp. 539, 542 (C. D. Cal. 1974). See also R. Kluger, *Simple Justice* (1976).

late as 1908, this Court enforced a state criminal conviction against a private college for teaching Negroes together with whites. . . .

Green v. *County School Board, supra,* gave explicit recognition to the fact that the habit of discrimination and the cultural tradition of race prejudice cultivated by centuries of legal slavery and segregation were not immediately dissipated when *Brown I, supra,* announced the constitutional principle that equal educational opportunity and participation in all aspects of American life could not be denied on the basis of race. Rather, massive official and private resistance prevented, and to a lesser extent still prevents, attainment of equal opportunity in education at all levels and in the professions. The generation of minority students applying to Davis Medical School since it opened in 1968—most of whom were born before or about the time *Brown I* was decided—clearly have been victims of this discrimination. Judicial decrees recognizing discrimination in public education in California testify to the fact of widespread discrimination suffered by California-born minority applicants;[14] many minority group members living in California, moreover, were born and reared in school districts in southern States segregated by law.[15] Since separation of school children by race "generates a feeling of inferiority as to their status in the community that may affect their hearts and minds in a way unlikely ever to be undone," *Brown I,* 347 U.S., at 494, the conclusion is inescapable that applicants to medical school must be few indeed who endured the effects of *de jure* segregation, the resistance to *Brown I,* or the equally debilitating pervasive private discrimination fostered by our long history of official discrimination, cf. *Reitman* v. *Mulkey, supra,* and yet come to the starting line with an education equal to whites.[16]

• • •

C

The second prong of our test—whether the Davis program stigmatizes any discrete group or individual and whether race is reasonably used in light of the program's objectives—is clearly satisfied by the Davis program.

It is not even claimed that Davis' program in any way operates to stigmatize or single out any discrete and insular, or even any identifiable, nonminority group. Nor will harm comparable to that imposed upon racial minorities by

[14] See, *e.g., Crawford* v. *Board of Educ.,* 17 Cal 3d 280, 130 *Cal. Rptr.* 724, 551 P.2d 28 (1976); *Soria* v. *Oxnard School District,* 386 F. Supp. 539 (CD Cal. 1974); *Spangler* v. *Pasadena City Board of Educ.,* 311 F. Supp. 501 (CD Cal. 1970); C. Wollenberg, *All Deliberate Speed: Segregation and Exclusion in California's Schools, 1855–1975,* at 136–177 (1976).

[15] For example, over 40 percent of American-born Negro males aged 20 to 24 residing in California in 1970 were born in the South, and the same statistic for females was over 48 percent. These statistics were computed from data contained in Census, *supra,* n. 49, pt. 6, California, sec. 2, "Detailed Characteristics," 6–1146 (table 139), 6–1149 (table 140).

[16] See, *e.g.,* O'Neil, "Preferential Admissions: Equalizing the Access of Minority Groups to Higher Education," 80 *Yale L. J.,* 699, 729–31 (1971).

exclusion or separation on grounds of race be the likely result of the program. It does not, for example, establish an exclusive preserve for minority students apart from and exclusive of whites. Rather, its purpose is to overcome the effects of segregation by bringing the races together. True, whites are excluded from participation in the special admissions program, but this fact only operates to reduce the number of whites to be admitted in the regular admissions program in order to permit admission of a reasonable percentage— less than their proportion of the California population[17]—of otherwise underrepresented qualified minority applicants.[18]

Nor was Bakke in any sense stamped as inferior by the Medical School's rejection of him. Indeed, it is conceded by all that he satisfied those criteria regarded by the School as generally relevant to academic performance better than most of the minority members who were admitted. Moreover, there is absolutely no basis for concluding that Bakke's rejection as a result of Davis' use of racial preference will affect him throughout his life in the same way as the segregation of the Negro school children in *Brown I* would have affected them. Unlike discrimination against racial minorities, the use of racial preferences for remedial purposes does not inflict a pervasive injury upon individual whites in the sense that wherever they go or whatever they do there is a significant likelihood that they will be treated as second-class citizens because of their color. This distinction does not mean that the exclusion of a white resulting from the preferential use of race is not sufficiently serious to require justification; but it does mean that the injury inflicted by such a policy is not distinguishable from disadvantages caused by a wide range of government actions, none of which has ever been thought impermissible for that reason alone.

In addition, there is simply no evidence that the Davis program discriminates intentionally or unintentionally against any minority group which it purports to benefit. The program does not establish a quota in the invidious sense of a ceiling on the number of minority applicants to be admitted. Nor

[17] Negroes and Chicanos alone comprise approximately 22 percent of California's population. This percentage was computed from data contained in Census, *supra*, n. 49, pt. 6, California, sec. 1, 6–4, and *id.*, sec. 2, 6–1146 to 6–1147 (Table 139).

[18] The constitutionality of the special admissions program is buttressed by its restriction to only 16 percent of the positions in the Medical School, a percentage less than that of the minority population in California, see *id.*, and to those minority applicants deemed qualified for admission and deemed likely to contribute to the medical school and the medical profession. *Record* 67.This is consistent with the goal of putting minority applicants in the position they would have been in if not for the evil of racial discrimination. Accordingly, the case does not raise the question whether even a remedial use of race would be unconstitutional if it admitted unqualified minority applicants in preference to qualified applicants or admitted, as a result of preferential consideration, racial minorities in numbers significantly in excess of their proportional representation in the relevant population. Such programs might well be inadequately justified by the legitimate remedial objectives. Our allusion to the proportional percentage of minorities in the population of the State administering the program is not intended to establish either that figure or that population universe as a constitutional benchmark. In this case, even respondent, as we understand him, does not argue that, if the special admissions program is otherwise constitutional, the allotment of 16 places in each entering class for special admittees is unconstitutionally high.

can the program reasonably be regarded as stigmatizing the program's beneficiaries or their race as inferior. The Davis program does not simply advance less qualified applicants; rather, it compensates applicants, whom it is uncontested are fully qualified to study medicine, for educational disadvantage which it was reasonable to conclude was a product of state-fostered discrimination. Once admitted, these students must satisfy the same degree requirements as regularly admitted students; they are taught by the same faculty in the same classes; and their performance is evaluated by the same standards by which regularly admitted students are judged. Under these circumstances, their performance and degrees must be regarded equally with the regularly admitted students with whom they compete for standing. Since minority graduates cannot justifiably be regarded as less well qualified than nonminority graduates by virtue of the special admissions program, there is no reasonable basis to conclude that minority graduates at schools using such programs would be stigmatized as inferior by the existence of such programs.

D

We disagree with the lower courts' conclusion that the Davis program's use of race was unreasonable in light of its objectives. First, as petitioner argues, there are no practical means by which it could achieve its ends in the foreseeable future without the use of race-conscious measures. With respect to any factor (such as poverty or family educational background) that may be used as a substitute for race as an indicator of past discrimination, whites greatly outnumber racial minorities simply because whites make up a far larger percentage of the total population and therefore far outnumber minorities in absolute terms at every socioeconomic level.[19] For example, of a class of recent medical school applicants from families with less than $10,000 income, at least 71% were white.[20] Of all 1970 families headed by a person *not* a high school graduate which included related children under 18, 80% were white and 20% were racial minorities.[21] Moreover, while race is positively correlated with differences in GPA and MCAT scores, economic disadvantage is not. Thus, it appears that economically disadvantaged whites do not score less well than economically advantages whites, while economically advantaged blacks score less well than do disadvantaged whites.[22] These statistics graphically illustrate that the University's purpose to integrate its classes by compensating for past discrimination could not be achieved by a general preference

---

[19] See Census, *supra,* n. 16, "Sources and Structure of Family Income," 1–12.

[20] This percentage was computed from data presented in B. Waldman, *Economic and Racial Disadvantage as Reflected in Traditional Medical School Selection Factors: A Study of 1976 Applicants to U.S. Medical Schools,* 34 (Table A–15), 42 (Table A–12), Association of American Medical Colleges.

[21] This figure was computed from data contained in Census, *supra,* 16, pt. 1, "United States Summary," sec. 2, 1–666 (Table 209).

[22] See Waldman, *supra,* n. 20, 10–14 (Figures 1–5).

for the economically disadvantaged or the children of parents of limited education unless such groups were to make up the entire class.

Second, the Davis admissions program does not simply equate minority status with disadvantage. Rather, Davis considers on an individual basis each applicant's personal history to determine whether he or she has likely been disadvantaged by racial discrimination. The record makes clear that only minority applicants likely to have been isolated from the mainstream of American life are considered in the special program; other minority applicants are eligible only through the regular admissions program. True, the procedure by which disadvantage is detected is informal, but we have never insisted that educators conduct their affairs through adjudicatory proceedings, and such insistence here is misplaced. A case-by-case inquiry into the extent to which each individual applicant has been affected, either directly or indirectly, by racial discrimination, would seem to be, as a practical matter, virtually impossible, despite the fact that there are excellent reasons for concluding that such effects generally exist. When individual measurement is impossible or extremely impractical, there is nothing to prevent a State from using categorical means to achieve its ends, at least where the category is closely related to the goal. . . . And it is clear from our cases that specific proof that a person has been victimized by discrimination is not a necessary predicate to offering him relief where the probability of victimization is great. . . .

E

Finally, Davis' special admissions program cannot be said to violate the Constitution simply because it has set aside a predetermined number of places for qualified minority applicants rather than using minority status as a positive factor to be considered in evaluating the applications of disadvantaged minority applicants. For purposes of constitutional adjudication, there is no difference between the two approaches. In any admissions program which accords special consideration to disadvantaged racial minorities, a determination of the degree of preference to be given is unavoidable, and any given preference that results in the exclusion of a white candidate is no more or less constitutionally acceptable than a program such as that at Davis. Furthermore, the extent of the preference inevitably depends on how many minority applicants the particular school is seeking to admit in any particular year so long as the number of qualified minority applicants exceeds that number. There is no sensible, and certainly no constitutional, distinction between, for example, adding a set number of points to the admissions rating of disadvantaged minority applicants as an expression of the preference with the expectation that this will result in the admission of an approximately determined number of qualified minority applicants and setting a fixed number of places for such applicants as was done here.[23]

[23] The excluded white applicant, despite MR. JUSTICE POWELL'S contention to the contrary, receives no more or less "individualized consideration" under our approach than under his.

The "Harvard" program, as those employing it readily concede, openly and successfully employs a racial criterion for the purpose of ensuring that some of the scarce places in institutions of higher education are allocated to disadvantaged minority students. That the Harvard approach does not also make public the extent of the preference and the precise workings of the system while the Davis program employs a specific, openly stated number, does not condemn the latter plan for purposes of Fourteenth Amendment adjudication. It may be that the Harvard plan is more acceptable to the public than is the Davis "quota." If it is, any State, including California, is free to adopt it in preference to a less acceptable alternative, just as it is generally free, as far as the Constitution is concerned, to abjure granting any racial preferences in its admissions program. But there is no basis for preferring a particular preference program simply because in achieving the same goals that the Davis Medical School is pursuing, it proceeds in a manner that is not immediately apparent to the public.

IV

Accordingly, we would reverse the judgment of the Supreme Court of California holding the Medical School's special admissions program unconstitutional and directing respondent's admission, as well as that portion of the judgment enjoining the Medical School from according any consideration to race in the admissions process.

• • •

MR. JUSTICE MARSHALL.

I agree with the judgment of the Court only insofar as it permits a university to consider the race of an applicant in making admissions decisions. I do not agree that petitioner's admissions program violates the Constitution. For it must be remembered that, during most of the past 200 years, the Constitution as interpreted by this Court did not prohibit the most ingenious and pervasive forms of discrimination against the Negro. Now, when a State acts to remedy the effects of that legacy of discrimination, I cannot believe that this same Constitution stands as a barrier.

I

A

Three hundred and fifty years ago, the Negro was dragged to this country in chains to be sold into slavery. Uprooted from his homeland and thrust into bondage for forced labor, the slave was deprived of all legal rights. It was unlawful to teach him to read; he could be sold away from his family and friends at the whim of his master; and killing or maiming him was not a crime. The system of slavery brutalized and dehumanized both master and slave.[1]

The denial of human rights was etched into the American colonies' first attempts at establishing self-government. When the colonists determined to seek their independence from England, they drafted a unique document cataloguing their grievances against the King and proclaiming as "self-evident" that "all men are created equal" and are endowed "with certain unalienable Rights," including those to "Life, Liberty and the pursuit of Happiness." The self-evident truths and the unalienable rights were intended, however, to apply only to white men. An earlier draft of the Declaration of Independence, submitted by Thomas Jefferson to the Continental Congress, had included among the charges against the King that

> [h]e has waged cruel war against human nature itself, violating its most sacred rights of life and liberty in the persons of a distant people who never offended him, captivating and carrying them into slavery in another hemisphere, or to incur miserable death in their transportation thither. (Franklin 88)

The Southern delegation insisted that the charge be deleted; the colonists themselves were implicated in the slave trade, and inclusion of this claim might have made it more difficult to justify the continuation of slavery once the ties to England were severed. Thus, even as the colonists embarked on a course to secure their own freedom and equality, they ensured perpetuation of the system that deprived a whole race of those rights.

The implicit protection of slavery embodied in the Declaration of Independence was made explicit in the Constitution, which treated a slave as being equivalent to three-fifths of a person for purposes of apportioning representatives and taxes among the States. Art. I, § 2. The Constitution also contained a clause ensuring that the "migration or importation" of slaves into the existing States would be legal until at least 1808, Art. I, § 9, and a fugitive slave clause requiring that when a slave escaped to another State, he must be returned on the claim of the master. Art. IV, § 2. In their declaration of the principles that were to provide the cornerstone of the new Nation, therefore, the Framers made it plain that "we the people," for whose protection the Constitution was designed, did not include those whose skins were the wrong color. As Professor John Hope Franklin has observed, Americans "proudly accepted the challenge and responsibility of their new political freedom by establishing the machinery and safeguards that insured the continued enslavement of blacks." (Franklin 100)

---

[1] The history recounted here is perhaps too well known to require documentation. But I must acknowledge the authorities on which I rely in retelling it. J. H. Franklin, *From Slavery to Freedom* (4th ed., 1974) (hereinafter Franklin): R. Kluger, *Simple Justice* (1975) (hereinafter Kluger); C. V. Woodward, *The Strange Career of Jim Crow* (3rd ed., 1974) (hereinafter Woodward).

The individual States likewise established the machinery to protect the system of slavery through the promulgation of the Slave Codes, which were designed primarily to defend the property interest of the owner in his slave. The position of the Negro slave as mere property was confirmed by this Court in *Dred Scott* v. *Sandford,* 19 How. 393 (1857), holding that the Missouri Compromise—which prohibited slavery in the portion of the Louisiana Purchase Territory north of Missouri—was unconstitutional because it deprived slave owners of their property without due process. The Court declared that under the Constitution a slave was property, and "[t]he right to traffic in it, like an ordinary article of merchandise and property, was guaranteed to the citizens of the United States. . . ." *Id.*, at 451. The Court further concluded that Negroes were not intended to be included as citizens under the Constitution but were "regarded as beings of an inferior order . . . altogether unfit to associate with the white race, either in social or political relations; and so far inferior, that they had no rights which the white man was bound to respect. . . ." *Id.,* at 407.

B

The status of the Negro as property was officially erased by his emancipation at the end of the Civil War. But the long awaited emancipation, while freeing the Negro from slavery, did not bring him citizenship or equality in any meaningful way. Slavery was replaced by a system of "laws which imposed upon the colored race onerous disabilities and burdens, and curtailed their rights in the pursuit of life, liberty, and property to such an extent that their freedom was of little value." *Slaughter-House Cases,* 16 Wall. 36, 70 (1873). Despite the passage of the Thirteenth, Fourteenth, and Fifteenth Amendments, the Negro was systematically denied the rights those amendments were supposed to secure. The combined actions and inactions of the State and Federal Government maintained Negroes in a position of legal inferiority for another century after the Civil War.

The Southern States took the first steps to re-enslave the Negroes. Immediately following the end of the Civil War, many of the provisional legislatures passed Black Codes, similar to the Slave Codes, which among other things, limited the rights of Negroes to own or rent property and permitted imprisonment for breach of employment contracts. Over the next several decades, the South managed to disenfranchise the Negroes in spite of the Fifteenth Amendment by various techniques, including poll taxes, deliberately complicated balloting processes, property and literacy qualifications, and finally the white primary.

Congress responded to the legal disabilities being imposed in the Southern States by passing the Reconstruction Acts and the Civil Rights Acts. Congress also responded to the needs of the Negroes at the end of the Civil War by establishing the Bureau of Refugees, Freedmen, and Abandoned Lands, better known as the Freedmen's Bureau, to supply food, hospitals, land and education to the newly freed slaves. Thus for a time it seemed as if the Negro might be protected from the continued denial of his civil rights and might be relieved of the disabilities that prevented him from taking his place as a free and equal citizen.

That time, however, was short-lived. Reconstruction came to a close, and, with the assistance of this Court, the Negro was rapidly stripped of his new civil rights. In the words of C. Vann Woodward: "By narrow and ingenious interpretation [the Supreme Court's] decisions over a period of years had whittled away a great part of the authority presumably given the government for protection of civil rights." (Woodward 139)

The Court began by interpreting the Civil War Amendments in a manner that sharply curtailed their substantive protections. . . . Then in the notorious *Civil Rights Cases,* 109 U.S. 3 (1883), the Court strangled Congress' efforts to use its power to promote racial equality. In those cases the Court invalidated sections of the Civil Rights Act of 1875 that made it a crime to deny equal access to "inns, public conveyances . . . , theatres, and other places of public amusement." According to the Court, the Fourteenth Amendment gave Congress the power to proscribe only discriminatory action by the State. The Court ruled that the Negroes who were excluded from public places suffered only an invasion of their social rights at the hands of private individuals, and Congress had no power to remedy that. *Id.,* at 24–25. "When a man has emerged from slavery, and by the aid of beneficient legislation has shaken off the inseparable concomitants of that state," the Court concluded, "there must be some stage in the progress of his elevation when he takes the rank of a mere citizen, and ceases to be the special favorite of the laws . . . ." *Id.,* at 25. As JUSTICE HARLAN noted in dissent, however, the Civil War Amendments and Civil Rights Acts did not make the Negroes the "special favorite" of the laws but instead "sought to accomplish in reference to that race . . .—what had already been done in every State of the Union for the white race—to secure and protect rights beglonging to them as freemen and citizens; nothing more." *Id.,* at 61.

The Court's ultimate blow to the Civil War Amendments and to the equality of Negroes came in *Plessy* v. *Ferguson,* 163 U.S. 537 (1896). In upholding a Louisiana law that required railway companies to provide "equal but separate" accommodations for whites and Negroes, the Court held that the Fourteenth Amendment was not intended "to abolish distinctions based upon color, or to enforce social, as distinguished from political equality, or a commingling of the two races upon terms unsatisfactory to either." *Id.,* at 544. Ignoring totally the realities of the positions of the two races, the Court remarked:

> We consider the underlying fallacy of the plaintiff's argument to consist in the assumption that the enforced separation of the two races stamps the colored race with a badge of inferiority. If this be so, it is not by reason of anything found in the act, but solely because the colored race chooses to put that construction upon it. (*Id.,* at 551)

MR. JUSTICE HARLAN's dissenting opinion recognized the bankruptcy of the Court's reasoning. He noted that the "real meaning" of the legislation was "that colored citizens are so inferior and degraded that they cannot be allowed to sit in public coaches occupied by white citizens." *Id.,* at 560. He expressed his fear that if like laws were enacted in other States, "the effect would be in the highest degree mischievous." *Id.,* at 563. Although slavery would have disappeared, the States would retain the power "to interfere with the full enjoyment of the blessings of freedom; to regulate civil rights, common to all citizens, upon the basis of race; and to place in a condition of legal inferiority a large body of American citizens . . . ." *Id.,* at 563.

The fears of MR. JUSTICE HARLAN were soon to be realized. In the wake of *Plessy,* many States expanded their Jim Crow laws, which had up until that time been limited primarily to passenger trains and schools. The segregation of the races was extended to residential areas, parks, hospitals, theaters, waiting rooms and bathrooms. There were even statutes and ordinances which authorized separate phone booths for Negroes and whites, which required that textbooks used by children of one race be kept separate from those used by the other, and which required that Negro and white prostitutes be kept in separate districts. In 1898, after *Plessy,* the Charlestown News and Courier printed a parody of Jim Crow laws:

> If there must be Jim Crow cars on the railroads, there should be Jim Crow cars on the street railways. Also on all passenger boats. . . . If there are to be Jim Crow cars, moreover, there should be Jim Crow waiting saloons at all stations, and Jim Crow eating houses. . . . There should be Jim Crow sections of the jury box, and a separate Jim Crow dock and witness stand in every court—and a Jim Crow Bible for colored witnesses to kiss. (Woodward 68)

The irony is that before many years had passed, with the exception of the Jim Crow witness stand, "all the improbable applications of the principle suggested by the editor in derision had been put into practice—down to and including the Jim Crow Bible." (Woodward 69)

Nor were the laws restricting the rights of Negroes limited solely to the Southern States. In many of the Northern States, the Negro was denied the right to vote, prevented from serving on juries and excluded from theaters, restaurants, hotels, and inns. Under President Wilson, the Federal Government began to require segregation in Government buildings; desks of Negro employees were curtained off; separate bathrooms and separate tables in the cafeteria were provided; and even the galleries of the Congress were segregated. When his segregationist policies were attacked, President Wilson responded that segregation was "not humiliating but a benefit" and that he was "rendering [the Negroes] more safe in their possession of office and less likely to be discriminated against." (Kluger 91)

The enforced segregation of the races continued into the middle of the 20th century. In both World Wars, Negroes were for the most part confined to separate military units; it was not until 1948 that an end to segregation in the military was ordered by President Truman. And the history of the exclusion of Negro children from white public schools is too well known and recent to require repeating here. That Negroes were deliberately excluded from public graduate and professional schools—and thereby denied the opportunity to become doctors, lawyers, engineers, and the like—is also well established. It is of course true that some of the Jim Crow laws (which the decisions of this Court had helped to foster) were struck down by this Court in a series of decisions leading up to *Brown* v. *Board of Education of Topeka,* 347 U.S. 483 (1954). . . . Those decisions, however, did not automatically end segregation, nor did they move Negroes from a position of legal inferiority to one of equality. The legacy of years of slavery and of years of second-class citizenship in the wake of emancipation could not be so easily eliminated.

II

The position of the Negro today in America is the tragic but inevitable consequence of centuries of unequal treatment. Measured by any benchmark of conduct or achievement, meaningful equality remains a distant dream for the Negro.

A Negro child today has a life-expectancy which is shorter by more than five years than that of a white child.[2] The Negro child's mother is over three times more likely to die of complications in childbirth,[3] and the infant mortality rate for Negroes is nearly twice that for whites.[4] The median income of the Negro family is only 60% that of the median of a white family,[5] and the percentage of Negroes who live in families with incomes below the poverty line in nearly four times greater than that of whites.[6]

When the Negro child reaches working age, he finds that America offers him significantly less than it offers for his white counterpart. For Negro adults, the unemployment rate is twice that of whites,[7] and the unemployment rate for Negro teenagers is nearly three times that of white teenagers.[8] A Negro male who completes four years of college can expect a median annual income of merely $110 more than a white male who has only a high school diploma.[9] Although Negroes represent 11.5% of the population,[10] they are only 1.2% of the lawyers and judges, 2% of the physicians, 2.3% of the dentists, 1.1% of the engineers and 2.6% of the college and university professors.[11]

[2] U.S. Dept. of Commerce, Bureau of the Census, *Statistical Abstract of the United States,* 65 (1977) (table 94).
[3] *Id.,* at 70 (table 102).
[4] *Ibid.*
[5] U.S. Dept. of Commerce, Bureau of the Census, *Current Population Reports,* Series P-60. No. 107, at 7 (1977) (table 1).
[6] *Id.,* at 20 (table 14).
[7] U.S. Dept. of Labor, Bureau of Labor Statistics, *Employment and Earnings,* January 1978, at 170 (table 44).
[8] *Ibid.*
[9] U.S. Dept. of Commerce, Bureau of the Census, *Current Population Reports,* Series P-60. No. 105, at 198 (1977) (table 47).
[10] U.S. Dept. of Commerce, Bureau of the Census, *Statistical Abstract of the United States,* 25 (table 24).
[11] *Id.,* at 407–408 (table 662) (based on 1970 census).

The relationship between those figures and the history of unequal treatment afforded to the Negro cannot be denied. At every point from birth to death the impact of the past is reflected in the still disfavored position of the Negro.

In light of the sorry history of discrimination and its devastating impact on the lives of Negroes, bringing the Negro into the mainstream of American life should be a state interest of the highest order. To fail to do so is to ensure that America will forever remain a divided society.

III

I do not believe that the Fourteenth Amendment requires us to accept that fate. Neither its history nor our past cases lend any support to the conclusion that a University may not remedy the cumulative effects of society's discrimination by giving consideration to race in an effort to increase the number and percentage of Negro doctors.

A

This Court long ago remarked that

> in any fair and just construction of any section or phrase of these [Civil War] amendments, it is necessary to look to the purpose which we have said was the pervading spirit of them all, the evil which they were designed to remedy. . . . (*Slaughter-House Cases,* 16 Wall., at 72)

It is plain that the Fourteenth Amendment was not intended to prohibit measures designed to remedy the effects of the Nation's past treatment of Negroes. The Congress that passed the Fourteenth Amendment is the same Congress that passed the 1866 Freedman's Bureau Act, an act that provided many of its benefits only to Negroes. Act of July 16, 1866, ch. 200, 14 Stat. 173; . . .

• • •

Despite the objection to the special treatment the bill would provide for Negroes, it was passed by Congress. *Id.,* at 421, 688. President Johnson vetoed this bill and also a subsequent bill that contained some modifications; one of his principal objections to both bills was that they gave special benefits to Negroes. VIII Messages and Papers of the Presidents 3596, 3599, 3620, 3623 (1866). Rejecting the concerns of the President and the bill's opponents, Congress overrode the President's second veto. Cong. Globe, at 3842, 3850.

Since the Congress that considered and rejected the objections to the 1866 Freedman's Bureau Act concerning special relief to Negroes also proposed the Fourteenth Amendment, it is inconceivable that the Fourteenth Amendment was intended to prohibit all race-conscious relief measures. It "would be a distortion of the policy manifested in that amendment, which was adopted to prevent state legislation designed to perpetuate discrimination on the basis of race or color," *Railway Mail Association* v. *Corsi,* 326 U.S. 88, 94 (1945), to hold that it barred state action to remedy the effects of that discrimination. Such a result would pervert the intent of the framers by substituting abstract equality for the genuine equality the amendment was intended to achieve.

• • •

IV

While I applaud the judgment of the Court that a university may consider race in its admissions process, it is more than a little ironic that, after several hundred years of class-based discrimination against Negroes, the Court is unwilling to hold that a class-based remedy for that discrimination is permissible. In declining to so hold, today's judgment ignores the fact that for several hundred years Negroes have been discriminated against, not as individuals, but rather solely because of the color of their skins. It is unnecessary in 20th century America to have individual Negroes demonstrate that they have been victims of racial discrimination; the racism of our society has been so pervasive that none, regardless of wealth or position, has managed to escape its impact. The experience of Negroes in America has been different in kind, not just in degree, from that of other ethnic groups. It is not merely the history of slavery alone but also that a whole people were marked as inferior by the law. And that mark has endured. The dream of America as the great melting pot has not been realized for the Negro; because of his skin color he never even made it into the pot.

These differences in the experience of the Negro make it difficult for me to accept that Negroes cannot be afforded greater protection under the Fourteenth Amendment where it is necessary to remedy the effects of past discrimination. In the *Civil Rights Cases, supra,* the Court wrote that the Negro emerging from slavery must cease "to be the special favorite of the laws." 109 U.S., at 25; see p. 5, *supra.* We cannot in light of the history of the last century yield to that view. Had the Court in that case and others been willing to "do for human liberty and the fundamental rights of American citizenship, what it did . . . for the protection of slavery and the rights of the masters of fugitive slaves," *id.,* at 53 (HARLAN J., dissenting), we would not need now to permit the recognition of any "special wards."

Most importantly, had the Court been willing in 1896, in *Plessy* v. *Ferguson,* to hold that the Equal Protection Clause forbids differences in treatment based on race, we would not be faced with this dilemma in 1978. We must remember, however, that the principle that the "Constitution is colorblind" appeared only in the opinion of the lone dissenter. 163 U.S., at 559. The majority of the Court rejected the principle of color blindness, and for the next 60 years, from *Plessy* to *Brown* v. *Board of Education,* ours was a Nation where, *by law,* an individual could be given "special" treatment based on the color of his skin.

It is because of a legacy of unequal treatment that we now must permit the institutions of this society to give consideration to race in making decisions about who will hold the positions of influence, affluence and prestige in America. For far too long, the doors to those positions have been shut to Negroes. If we are ever to become a fully integrated society, one in which the color of a person's skin will not determine the opportunities available to him or her, we must be willing to take steps to open those doors. I do not believe that anyone can truly look into America's past and still find that a remedy for the effects of that past is impermissible.

It has been said that this case involves only the individual, Bakke, and this University. I doubt, however, that there is a computer capable of determining the number of persons and institutions that may be affected by the decision in this case. For example, we are told by the Attorney General of the United States that at least 27 federal agencies have adopted regulations requiring recipients of federal funds to take "*affirmative action* to overcome the effects of conditions which resulted in limiting participation . . . by persons of a particular race, color, or national origin." Supplemental Brief for the United States as *Amicus Curiae* 16 (emphasis added). I cannot even guess the number of state and local governments that have set up affirmative action programs, which may be affected by today's decision.

I fear that we have come full circle. After the Civil War our government started several "affirmative action" programs. This Court in the *Civil Rights Cases* and *Plessy* v. *Ferguson* destroyed the movement toward complete equality. For almost a century no action was taken, and this nonaction was with the tacit approval of the courts. Then we had *Brown* v. *Board of Education* and the Civil Rights Acts of Congress, followed by numerous affirmative action programs. *Now,* we have this Court again stepping in, this time to stop affirmative action programs of the type used by the University of California.

MR. JUSTICE BLACKMUN.

I participate fully, of course, in the opinion that bears the names of my Brothers BRENNAN, WHITE, MARSHALL, and myself. I add only some general observations that hold particular significance for me, and then a few comments on equal protection.

I

At least until the early 1970s, apparently only a very small number, less than 2% of the physicians, attorneys, and medical and law students in the United States were members of what we now refer to as minority groups. In addition, approximately three-fourths of our Negro physicians were trained at only two medical schools. If ways are not found to remedy that situation, the country can never achieve its professed goal of a society that is not race conscious.

I yield to no one in my earnest hope that the time will come when an "affirmative action" program is unnecessary and is, in truth, only a relic of the past. I would hope that we could reach this stage within a decade at the most. But the story of *Brown* v. *Board of Education,* 347 U.S. 483 (1954), decided almost a quarter of a century ago, suggests that that hope is a slim one. At some time, however, beyond any period of what some would claim is only transitional inequality, the United States must and will reach a stage of maturity where action along this line is no longer necessary. Then persons will be regarded as persons, and discrimination of the type we address today will be an ugly feature of history that is instructive but that is behind us.

The number of qualified, indeed highly qualified, applicants for admissions to existing medical schools in the United States far exceeds the number of places available. Wholly apart from racial and ethnic considerations, therefore, the selection process inevitably results in the denial of admission to many *qualified* persons, indeed, to far more than the number of those who are granted admission. Obviously, it is a denial to the deserving. This inescapable fact is brought into sharp focus here because Allan Bakke is not himself charged with discrimination and yet is the one who is disadvantaged, and because the Medical School of the University of California at Davis itself is not charged with historical discrimination.

One theoretical solution to the need for more minority members in higher education would be to enlarge our graduate schools. Then all who desired and were qualified could enter, and talk of discrimination would vanish. Unfortunately, this is neither feasible nor realistic. The vast resources that apparently would be required simply are not available. And the need for more professional graduates, in the strict numerical sense, perhaps has not been demonstrated at all.

There is no particular or real significance in the 84–16 division at Davis. The same theoretical, philosophical, social, legal, and constitutional considerations would necessarily apply to the case if Davis' special admissions program had focused on any lesser number, that is, on 12 or 8 or 4 places or, indeed, on only 1.

It is somewhat ironic to have us so deeply disturbed over a program where race is an element of consciousness, and yet to be aware of the fact, as we are, that institutions of higher learning, albeit more on the undergraduate than the graduate level, have given conceded preferences up to a point to those possessed of athletic skills, to the children of alumni, to the affluent who may bestow their largess on the institutions, and to those having connections with celebrities, the famous, and the powerful.

Programs of admission to institutions of higher learning are basically a responsibility for academicians and for administrators and the specialists they employ. The judiciary, in contrast, is ill-equipped and poorly trained for this. The administration and management of educational institutions are beyond the competence of judges and are within the special competence of educators, provided always that the educators perform within legal and constitutional bounds. For me, therefore, interference by the judiciary must be the rare exception and not the rule.

II

I, of course, accept the propositions that (a) Fourteenth Amendment rights are personal; (b) racial and ethnic distinctions where they are stereotypes are inherently suspect and call for exacting judicial scrutiny; (c) academic freedom is a special concern of the First Amendment; and (d) the Fourteenth Amendment has expanded beyond its original 1868 conception and now is recognized to have reached a point where as MR. JUSTICE POWELL states, quoting from the Court's opinion in *McDonald* v. *Santa Fe Trail Transp. Co.,* 427 U.S. 273, 296 (1976), it embraces a "broader principle."

This enlargement does not mean for me, however, that the Fourteenth Amendment has broken away from its moorings and its original intended purposes. Those original aims persist. And that, in a distinct sense, is what "affirmative action," in the face of proper facts, is all about. If this conflicts with idealistic equality, that tension is original Fourteenth Amendment tension, constitutionally conceived and constitutionally imposed, and it is part of the Amendment's very nature until complete equality is achieved in the area. In this sense, constitutional equal protection is a shield.

• • •

I am not convinced, as MR. JUSTICE POWELL seems to be, that the difference between the Davis program and the one employed by Harvard is very profound or constitutionally significant. The line between the two is a thin and indistinct one. In each, subjective application is at work. Because of my conviction that admission programs are primarily for the educators, I am willing to accept the representation that the Harvard program is one where good faith in its administration is practiced as well as professed. I agree that such a program, where race or ethnic background is only one of many factors, is a program better formulated than Davis' two-track system. The cynical, of course, may say that under a program such as Harvard's one may accomplish covertly what Davis concedes it does openly. I need not go that far, for despite its two-track aspect, the Davis program, for me, is within constitutional bounds, though perhaps barely so. It is surely free of sitgma, and, as in *United Jewish Organizations,* I am not willing to infer a constitutional violation.

It is worth noting, perhaps, that governmental preference has not been a stranger to our legal life. We see it in veterans' preferences. We see it in the aid-to-the-handicapped programs. We see it in the progressive income tax.

We see it in the Indian programs. We may excuse some of these on the ground that they have specific constitutional protection or, as with Indians, that those benefited are awards of the Government. Nevertheless, these preferences exist and may not be ignored. And in the admissions field, as I have indicated, educational institutions have always used geography, athletic ability, anticipated financial largess, alumni pressure, and other factors of that kind.

I add these only as additional components on the edges of the central question as to which I join my Brothers BRENNAN, WHITE, and MARSHALL in our more general approach. It is gratifying to know that the Court at least finds it constitutional for an academic institution to take race and ethnic background into consideration as one factor, among many, in the administration of its admissions program. I presume that that factor always has been there, though perhaps not conceded or even admitted. It is a fact of life, however, and a part of the real world of which we are all a part. The sooner we get down the road toward accepting and being a part of the real world, and not shutting it out and away from us, the sooner will these difficulties vanish from the scene.

I suspect that it would be impossible to arrange an affirmative action program in a racially neutral way and have it succeesful. To ask that this be so is to demand the impossible. In order to get beyond racism, we must first take account of race. There is no other way. And in order to treat some persons equally, we must treat them differently. We cannot—we dare not— let the Equal Protection Clause perpetuate racial supremacy.

So the ultimate question, as it was at the beginning of this litigation, is: Among the qualified, how does one choose?

A long time ago, as time is measured for this Nation, a Chief Justice, both wise and far-sighted, said:

> In considering this question, then, we must never forget, that it is *a constitution* we are expounding. [Emphasis in original.] (*M'Culloch* v. *Maryland,* 4 Wheat. 316, 407 [1819])

In the same opinion, the Great Chief Justice further observed:

> Let the end be legitimate, let it be within the scope of the constitution, and all means which are appropriate, which are plainly adapted to that end, which are not prohibited but consist with the letter and spirit of the constitution, are constitutional. (*Id.,* at 421)

More recently, one destined to become a Justice of this Court observed:

> The great generalities of the constitution have a content and a significance that vary from age to age. (B. Cardozo, *The Nature of the Judicial Process* 17 [1921])

And an educator who became a President of the United States said:

> But the Constitution of the United States is not a mere lawyers' document: it is a vehicle of life, and its spirit is always the spirit of the age. (W. Wilson, *Constitutional Government in the United States,* 69 [1911])

These precepts of breadth and flexibility and ever-present modernity are basic to our constitutional law. Today, again, we are expounding a *Constitution*. The same principles that governed M'Culloch's case in 1819 govern Bakke's case in 1978. There can be no other answer.

WHO ARE EQUALS?

CARL COHEN

Equals ought to have equality. But there still remains a question: equality or inequality of what?

—ARISTOTLE, *Politics,* Bk. III, chap. 12

The Fourteenth Amendment to the U.S. Constitution reads in part: "No State shall . . . deny to any person within its jurisdiction the equal protection of the laws." What is the point of this passage? What would a law be like that did not apply equally to those to whom it applied at all? Imagine the law: "All citizens eighteen years of age and over shall have the right to vote." Under it, the seventeen-year-old and the nineteen-year-old are treated very differently; but all nineteen-year-old citizens are treated in one way (if the law is obeyed) and all seventeen-year-old citizens in another—neither group is denied the equal protection of the law. Suppose, when I went to register to vote, the county clerk responded to my request with an embarrassed smile, saying: "Ah yes, Mr. Cohen, but, you see, your're Jewish, so—I'm afraid— we can't register you." Well—we'd make short work of him.

Now suppose the law were different. Suppose it read: "All citizens eighteen years of age and over—except Jews—shall have the right to vote." The clerk will not smile when he is handed my application in this case. "I'm sorry, Mr. Cohen," one can hear the mechanical voice of that bureaucrat, "but the law prescribes that Jews may not vote." I am stunned as I read the printed act of Congress he puts before me; but there it is; non-Jews (over eighteen) vote, Jews don't. Suppose the clerk is efficient and incorruptible—all Jews are treated alike with utmost scrupulosity. Then it would appear that all were treated justly under that law, receiving its equal protection.

Surely we never supposed that the equal protection of the law entails identical treatment for everyone. We know that would be absurd. Employers have legal obligations that employees have not. Students have legal rights (and duties) that teachers have not. Rich people must pay taxes that poor people need not. Our legal codes are replete with distinctions—hundreds and

Reprinted from *National Forum: The Phi Kappa Phi Journal,* Vol. LVIII, No. 1 (Winter 1978) 10–14, with permission of the publisher and the author.

thousands of distinctions determining the applicability of the laws. I may be angered by a distinction drawn—yet I will reluctantly agree that if that is the law, and since I am in a specific category, it is fair for me to be obliged under that law, as others are who are in the same class.

We argue about these distinctions—but in three very different ways. We may argue (lawyers are constantly arguing) about who are and who are not in the same class. When you defend a contested deduction on your income tax against the IRS, or I insist that as a college professor I am not a "public official" in the sense that would require public disclosure of my finances, we are disputing over the application of the legal categories drawn, not over the categories themselves.

We may argue—as students of political science, or as legislators—that it is wise (or unwise) to introduce certain categorial distinctions. For example, should the law distinguish between large and small entrepreneurs in the application of industrial safety regulations? Should the law distinguish between different categories of employment in establishing minimum wage requirements? (And so on.)

We may argue about whether categories of a particular kind should be permitted in the law at all. Some legislation duly enacted, or administrative regulations duly authorized, may distinguish categories of persons we think ought not be distinguished. Some discriminations are worse than unwise; they are unjust.

Return now to the Fourteenth Amendment and its "equal protection clause." The prohibition in that clause bears chiefly on arguments of the third sort. It does not bar legislatures from categorizing, but is interpreted so as to require categories used in laws to have a rational foundation. Some categorial distinctions will by that clause be prohibited altogether. Under Hitler's Nuremberg Laws all Jews were treated alike, but justice in America does not permit that sort of equal protection. The central thrust of the Fourteenth Amendment was, and is, to forbid the use—in law, or by administrators under color of law—of categories intrinsically unfair.

But which categories are unfair? The Amendment itself was clearly designed to insure that blacks, former slaves, were to be as free as whites. The laws were to protect all races equally. Now, more than a century later, seeking to give redress for long-standing racial injustice, we encounter the problem of fairness from the other side. May we, in the honest effort to achieve real equality among the races, distinguish between black and white (and yellow and brown, etc.) giving preference to some over others? Does our commitment to the equal protection of the laws permit it?

When the courts, and especially the United States Supreme Court, speak to such questions, they decide not simply what the U.S. Constitution requires, but what (in their view) justice requires. High courts must frame principles to guide the resolution of disputes between real parties, in the case before them and in future cases, Judicial reasoning is often profoundly moral reasoning. Actual cases, faced and decided, are the grist upon which the mill of American justice grinds. We do well to philosophize with the courts, and as they do, in living contexts.

The context now forcing a deeper understanding of "the equal protection of the laws" is that of racially preferential admissions to law schools and medical schools. Some call the problem that of "reverse discrimination," others "benign quotas." Let the name not prejudice the issue. What is *not* before us, or the courts, is the appropriateness of affirmative action. None of the participants in this dispute question the pressing need to take vigorous action, affirmative action, to correct long-standing racial injustice. What is at issue is *what* we may justly do to advance this objective—what categories we may (or must not) use, how we may (or must not) apply them.

The case of *The Regents of the University of California* v. *Allen Bakke,* now before the Supreme Court of the United States, puts this problem in sharp focus. Allan Bakke was twice rejected (in 1973 and 1974) by the medical school of the University of California at Davis. His undergraduate performance was fine, his test scores excellent, his character and interview performance admirable; he ranked very high among the more than 3,000 applicants for 100 seats. But 16 of those seats were reserved for minority-group applicants, who faced admission standards deliberately and markedly lower than did majority-group students like Bakke. The University of California (like many of its sister universities) was determined to enroll a representative proportion of blacks and members of other minority groups in its medical school—however distasteful the double standard believed necessary to accomplish that end.

The Davis medical school established a special committee to fill the reserved slots, and the committee evaluated the minority-group candidates, who competed only against one another. Officially, any disadvantaged person could seek admission under the special program; in fact, all persons admitted under that program, from its inception in 1969, were minority-group members. Officially, that committee reported to the admissions committee; in fact, the applicants chosen by the special committee were invariably admitted. In each of the years Bakke was rejected, some minority-group admittees had grade-point averages so low (2.11 in 1973, 2.21 in 1974) that, if they had been white, they would have been summarily rejected.

The University of California does not deny that the overall ranking of many of the minority-group applicants who were accepted—after interviews, and with character, interests, test scores, and averages all considered—was substantially below that of many majority applicants who were rejected. Bakke contends that had his skin been of a darker color he would certainly have been admitted. He argues that, refused admission solely because of his race, he was denied "the equal protection of the laws" guaranteed him by the Fourteenth Amendment to the U.S. Constitution.

All sides in this litigation agree that professional schools may properly use, in screening for admission, a host of factors other than test scores and grade-point averages: dedication or dexterity, compassion or professional aims. All sides agree that persons unfairly injured are entitled to full, appropriate, and timely redress. What remains at issue in this case is one thing only: *preference by race.*

The advocates of racially preferential systems reason as follows: Equal protection of the laws requires different treatment for people in different circumstances. Minority-group members are in very special circumstances. Preference by race is here a reasonable instrument to achieve, for members of minority groups, objectives both just and compelling.

Such preference (not denied by the medical school) is thus defended by two central arguments. The first is grounded in alleged demands of justice: Only by deliberately preferring minority applicants can we give adequate compensation for generations of oppressive maltreatment. The second is grounded in the alleged needs of society: If we do not continue to give deliberate racial preference, our medical and law schools will again become what they long were—white enclaves. *Conpensation* is the heart of the first argument, *integration* of the second. Both arguments are profoundly mistaken.

Redress is rightly given for injury—not for being black or brown. Members of minority groups have been cruelly damaged, but whatever damage is rightly compensated for (cultural or economic deprivation, inferior schooling, or other), *any* applicant so unfairly damaged is fully entitled to the same special consideration, regardless of his race or ethnic group. The prohibition of special favor by race—any race—is the central thrust of a constitutional guarantee that all will receive the protection of the laws equally. Classification by race for the distribution of goods or opportunities is intrinsically odious, always invidious, and morally impermissible, no matter how laudable the goals in view.

What of the school-desegregation cases in which the U.S. Supreme Court has approved the use of racial categories to insure racial integration? Don't these show that racial preference is permissible if the aim is good? Certainly not. In these cases attention to race was allowed in order to ascertain whether school boards that had been discriminating wrongfully by race had really ceased to do so. Racial identification was there permitted—but only to insure that all students, of whatever race, received absolutely equal treatment. The distinction between that use of racial counting, and the use of racial categories to reintroduce special preference, is sharp and profound.

Can the University of California be defended on the ground that its system of racial preference is not injurious but benign? No. Results, not intentions, determine benignity. All racial quotas have injurious results and therefore cannot be benign. When the goods being distributed are in short supply, and some get more of those goods because of their race, then others get less because of their race. There is no escaping that cold logic. Bakke and others like him are seriously penalized for no other reason than their race. Such a system, as even the Washington State Supreme Court in the *DeFunis* case agreed, "is certainly not benign with respect to non-minority students who are displaced by it."

All this says not an iota against compensation. If redress is due, let us give it, and give it fully. If compensation is to be offered through special favor in professional-school admissions—a questionable mode of payment but a possible one—then let us be certain we look in every case to the injury for which we give redress, and not to the race of the applicant.

If the requirements of justice cannot support racial preference, perhaps the society's interest in integration can. The Supreme Court of California, while upholding Bakke's claim, allowed, *arguendo,* that integration is a compelling interest. "Integration" has different meanings, of course. That ambiguity invites the university's most appealing complaint. "You have told us to integrate," the university has said, in effect, "and when we devise admissions systems designed to do just that, you tell us we may not use racial preference. But the problem is a racial one. We cannot achieve racial balance unless we give special preference to racial minorities. Do not ask the impossible of us. And do not ask us to do in indirect ways what you will not permit us to do directly."

That argument by the University of California is not sound. A considered reply to it (here much compressed) is fourfold.

First, some of the ends in view are important, some are questionable. That the entire package is "compelling" is very doubtful.

(a) Better medical and legal services for minorities is a pressing need, but it is far from obvious that minority professionals reared in city slums will return to practice there. And it is patently unfair to burden them with this restrictive expectation. If the intention to give service to particular segments of the community is to be a consideration in admission to professional school, let that be known, and let all persons, of whatever race, make their case for establishing such intentions, if they claim them.

(b) Some defend preferential admission on the ground that many persons seeking professional help will be "more comfortable" with a lawyer or a doctor of their own race or religion. Possibly true. But the argument based upon this interest, now to serve as a justification of institutionalized racial preference, has long been used to exclude blacks from white hospitals and Jews from gentile law firms. It is an argument in which bigots of every color will take satisfaction.

(c) Diversity of cultural background in the professional schools, and in the professions themselves, will increase the richness of education and of service, and will provide role-models for youngsters from cultural groups long oppressed. These are genuine and worthy interests, but are they compelling in the requisite sense? What *is* compelling is integration in the classical sense: the removal of every obstruction to genuinely equal opportunity, the elimination of every racial qualification. Integration in the now fashionable sense— entailing some *de facto* mix of races approaching proportionality—may be desirable in some contexts and undesirable in others, but is in any case certainly not compelling.

Second, the Supreme Court of California emphasized that no party has shown preference by race in admissions (which all agree is objectionable) to be necessary to achieve appropriate social goals. Even if arbitrary numerical ratios are established as the only acceptable standard of success, that cannot be shown. But from whence comes that standard? The entire history of our nation has been one of ethnic layering, in which different interests and activities tend to be pursued by different cultural and ethnic groups. That is not unwholesome. The effort to homogenize society in spite of this natural tendency is already proving to be divisive, frustrating, and unworkable. Substantial increases of diversity in some professions are reasonably sought. With non-preferential forms of affirmative action pursued vigorously, and admissions criteria enlarged and enriched and applied evenhandedly to all applicants, diversity and *de facto* integration may be much advanced. Still more might be accomplished if various compensatory schemes were introduced, but they must be applied in a racially neutral way. Some majority applicants who deserve compensatory preference will also benefit under such programs, but this is entirely fitting.

There is nothing crafty about this reply. The claim that these are but devious ways to reach the same ends is simply false, and betrays an inclination to introduce racial preference somehow, "through the back door" if necessary. That would be ugly. There is no reason to fear or to be ashamed of an honest admissions program, or of an honest compensatory program, honestly applied. The racial count that results may not be the same as that when racial preference is used, but perhaps it ought not be. Even if the count were the same, the individuals (admitted using principles, not race) would be different, and that makes all the difference. It is certain that substantial progress in diversifying and integrating professional school classes can be achieved without racial preference.

Third, we must see that granting favor on the basis of race alone is a nasty business, however honorable the goal. The moral issue comes in classic form: Terribly pressing objectives (integrated professions, adequate legal and medical service for members of minority groups) appear to require impermissible means. Might we not wink at the Constitution, this once, in view of the importance and decency of our objectives?

Such winking is precisely the hope of every party having aims that are, to that party's profound conviction, of absolutely overriding importance. Constitutional short-cuts have been and will be urged for the sake of national security (e.g., the internment of Japanese-Americans during World War II), for the enforcement of criminal laws (e.g., admission of illegally seized evidence), and in other spheres. But wink we must not! Each party in its turn must abide the restrictions of constitutional process. The single most important feature of a constitution, if it is more than paper, is its preclusion of unjust means. Hence the preciousness and power of the guarantee of equality before the law. When good process and laudable objectives conflict, long experience teaches the priority of process. Means that are corrupt will infect the result and (with societies as with individuals) will corrupt the user in the end. So it is with wire-tapping, with censorship, and with every short-cut taken knowingly at the expense of the rights of individuals. So it is also with racial preference, even when well-intended.

The fourth response to the integration argument is as compelling as the first three, but adds bitter irony. Hating the taste of racial preference in admissions, the advocates of these programs swallow them only because of a conviction that they are so good for us. Bitter but (they think) medicinal. In this, too, they are mistaken. Racial preference is good for nobody, black or white, majority or minority. It will not integrate the races but will *dis*-integrate them, forcing attention to race, creating anxiety and agitation about race in all the wrong contexts, exciting envy, ill-will, and widespread resentment of unfair penalties and undeserved rewards.

It will not serve the minority well if it becomes clear that minority-group students admitted preferentially are less qualified to pursue their studies and to practice their professions. A black psychiatrist at Case Western Reserve University Hospital, Dr. Charles DeLeon, told the *New York Times* in 1974: "I wouldn't hit a dog with some of the minority students I've seen, and I have an idea that you honkies are taking in these dummies so that eight years from now you'll be able to turn around and say, 'Look how bad they all turned out.'"

Above all, racial preference clouds the accomplishments and undermines the reputations of those superbly qualified minority-group professionals who neither need nor get special favor. When, in the minds of everyone, black and white, a physician's dark skin is automatically linked to charity and payoff, who among members of minority groups is served? It is a cruel result.

Racial preference is dynamite. Many who play with such preference are now blinded by honest zeal and hide from themselves the explosions in the sequel. Justice John Marshall Harlan, dissenting in 1896 from the Supreme Court ruling that established the "separate but equal" doctrine, insisted that the U.S. Constitution was and must be color-blind. Some would have the law be color-conscious now so that it can indeed become color-blind in the future. That cannot be. One is reminded of political leaders who "suspend" constitutions to "build a firmer base for democracy." Once established as constitutionally acceptable grounds for discriminatory distribution, racial categories will wax, not wane, in importance. No prescription for racial disharmony can be surer of success.

Official favoritism by race or national origin is poison in society. In American society, built of manifold racial and ethnic layers, it is deadly poison. How gravely mistaken it will be to take new doses of the same stuff, while still suffering the pains of recovery from the old.

WHY BAKKE HAS NO CASE

RONALD DWORKIN

On October 12, 1977 the Supreme Court heard oral argument in the case of *The Regents of the University of California* v. *Allan Bakke.* No lawsuit has ever been more widely watched or more thoroughly debated in the national and international press before the Court's decision. Still, some of the most pertinent facts set before the Court have not been clearly summarized.

The medical school of the University of California at Davis has an affirmative action program (called the "task force program") designed to admit more black and other minority students. It sets sixteen places aside for which only members of "educationally and economically disadvantaged minorities" compete. Allan Bakke, white, applied for one of the remaining eighty-four places; he was rejected but, since his test scores were relatively high, the medical school has conceded that it could not prove that he would have been rejected if the sixteen places reserved had been open to him. Bakke sued, arguing that the task force program deprived him of his constitutional rights. The California Supreme Court agreed, and ordered the medical school to admit him. The university appealed to the Supreme Court.

The Davis program for minorities is in certain respects more forthright (some would say cruder) than similar plans now in force in many other American universities and professional schools. Such programs aim to increase the enrollment of black and other minority students by allowing the fact of their race to count affirmatively as part of the case for admitting them. Some schools set a "target" of a particular number of minority places instead of setting aside a flat number of places. But Davis would not fill the number of places set aside unless there were sixteen minority candidates it considered clearly qualified for medical education. The difference is therefore one of administrative strategy and not of principle.

So the constitutional question raised by *Bakke* is of capital importance for higher education in America, and a large number of universities and schools have entered briefs *amicus curiae* urging the Court to reverse the California decision. They believe that if the decision is affirmed then they will no longer be free to use explicit racial criteria in any part of their admissions programs, and that they will therefore be unable to fulfill what they take to be their responsibilities to the nation.

It is often said that affirmative action programs aim to achieve a racially conscious society divided into racial and ethnic groups, each entitled, as a group, to some proportionable share of resources, careers, or opportunities. That is a perverse description. American society is currently a racially conscious society; this is the inevitable and evident consequence of a history of

Reprinted from *The New York Review of Books,* Nov. 10, 1977, pp. 11–15, with permission of the publisher and the author.

slavery, repression, and prejudice. Black men and women, boys and girls, are not free to choose for themselves in what roles—or as members of which social groups—others will characterize them. They are black, and no other feature of personality or allegiance or ambition will so thoroughly influence how they will be perceived and treated by others, and the range and character of the lives that will be open to them.

The tiny number of black doctors and professionals is both a consequence and a continuing cause of American racial consciousness, one link in a long and self-fueling chain reaction. Affirmative action programs use racially explicit criteria because their immediate goal is to increase the number of members of certain races in these professions. But their long-term goal is to *reduce* the degree to which American society is overall a racially conscious society.

The programs rest on two judgments. The first is a judgment of social theory: that America will continue to be pervaded by racial divisions as long as the most lucrative, satisfying, and important careers remain mainly the prerogative of members of the white race, while others feel themselves systematically excluded from a professional and social elite. The second is a calculation of strategy: that increasing the number of blacks who are at work in the professions will, in the long run, reduce the sense of frustration and injustice and racial self-consciousness in the black community to the point at which blacks may begin to think of themselves as individuals who can succeed like others through talent and initiative. At that future point the consequences of nonracial admissions programs, whatever these consequences might be, could be accepted with no sense of racial barriers or injustice.

It is therefore the worst possible misunderstanding to suppose that affirmative action programs are designed to produce a balkanized America, divided into racial and ethnic subnations. They use strong measures because weaker ones will fail; but their ultimate goal is to lessen not to increase the importance of race in American social and professional life.

According to the 1970 census, only 2.1 percent of US doctors were black. Affirmative action programs aim to provide more black doctors to serve black patients. This is not because it is desirable that blacks treat blacks and whites treat whites, but because blacks, for no fault of their own, are now unlikely to be well served by whites, and because a failure to provide the doctors they trust will exacerbate rather than reduce the resentment that now leads them to trust only their own. Affirmative action tries to provide more blacks as classmates for white doctors, not because it is desirable that a medical school class reflect the racial makeup of the community as a whole, but because professional association between blacks and whites will decrease the degree to which whites think of blacks as a race rather than as people, and thus the degree to which blacks think of themselves that way. It tries to provide "role models" for future black doctors, not because it is desirable for a black boy or girl to find adult models only among blacks, but because our history has made them so conscious of their race that the success of whites, for now, is likely to mean little or nothing for them.

The history of the campaign against racial injustice since 1954, when the Supreme Court decided *Brown* v. *Board of Education,* is a history in large part of failure. We have not succeeded in reforming the racial consciousness of our society by racially neutral means. We are therefore obliged to look upon the arguments for affirmative action with sympathy and an open mind. Of course, if Bakke is right that such programs, no matter how effective they may be, violate his constitutional rights then they cannot be permitted to continue. But we must not forbid them in the name of some mindless maxim, like the maxim that it cannot be right to fight fire with fire, or that the end cannot justify the means. If the strategic claims for affirmative action are cogent, they cannot be dismissed simply on the ground that racially explicit tests are distasteful. If such tests are distasteful it can only be for reasons that make the underlying social realities the programs attack more distasteful still.

The New Republic, in a recent editorial opposing affirmative action, missed that point. "It is critical to the success of a liberal pluralism," it said, "that group membership itself is not among the permissible criteria of inclusion and exclusion." But group membership is in fact, as a matter of social reality rather than formal admissions standards, part of what determines inclusion or exclusion for us now. If we must choose between a society that is in fact liberal and an illiberal society that scrupulously avoids formal racial criteria, we can hardly appeal to the ideals of liberal pluralism to prefer the latter.

Professor Archibald Cox of Harvard Law School, speaking for the University of California in oral argument, told the Supreme Court that this is the choice the United States must make. As things stand, he said, affirmative action progrms are the only effective means of increasing the absurdly small number of black doctors. The California Supreme Court, in approving Bakke's claim, had urged the university to pursue that goal by methods that do not explicitly take race into account. But that is unrealistic. We must distinguish, as Cox said, between two interpretations of what the California court's recommendation means. It might mean that the university should aim at the same immediate goal, of increasing the proportion of black and other minority students in the medical school, by an admissions procedure that on the surface is not racially conscious.

That is a recommendation of hypocrisy. If those who administer the admissions standards, however these are phrased, understand that their immediate goal is to increase the number of blacks in the school, then they will use race as a criterion in making the various subjective judgments the explicit criteria will require, because that will be, given the goal, the only right way to make those judgments. The recommendation might mean, on the other hand, that the school should adopt some nonracially conscious goal, like increasing the number of disadvantaged students of all races, and then hope that that goal will produce an increase in the number of blacks as a by-product. But even if that strategy is less hypocritical (which is far from plain), it will almost certainly fail because no different goal, scrupulously administered in a nonracially conscious way, will in fact significantly increase the number of black medical students.

Cox offered powerful evidence for that conclusion, and it is supported by the recent and comprehensive report of the Carnegie Council on Policy Studies in Higher Education. Suppose, for example, that the medical school sets aside separate places for applicants "disadvantaged" on some racially neutral test, like poverty, allowing only those disadvantaged in that way to compete for these places. If the school selects these from that group who scored best on standard medical school aptitude tests, then it will take almost no blacks, because blacks score relatively low evern among the economically disadvantaged. But if the school chooses among the disadvantaged on some basis other than test scores, just so that more blacks will succeed, then it will not be administering the special procedure in a nonracially conscious way.

So Cox was able to put his case in the form of two simple propositions. A racially conscious test for admission, even one that sets aside certain places for qualified minority applicants exclusively, serves goals that are in themselves unobjectionable and even urgent. Such programs are, moreover, the only means that offer any significant promise of achieving these goals. If these programs are halted, then no more than a trickle of black students will enter medical or other professional schools for another generation at least.

If these propositions are sound, then on what ground can it be thought that such programs are either wrong or unconstitutional? We must notice an important distinction between two different sorts of objections that might be made. These programs are intended, as I said, to decrease the importance of race in the United States in the long run. It may be objected, first, that the programs will in fact harm that goal more than they will advance it. There is no way now to prove that that is so. Cox conceded, in his argument, that there are costs and risks in these programs.

Affirmative action programs seem to encourage, for example, a popular misunderstanding, which is that they assume that racial or ethnic groups are entitled to proportionate shares of opportunities, so that Italian or Polish ethnic minorities are, in theory, as entitled to their proportionate shares as blacks or Chicanos or American Indians are entitled to the shares the present programs give them. That is a plain mistake: the programs are not based on the idea that those who are aided are entitled to aid, but only on the strategic hypothesis that helping them is now an effective way of attacking a national problem. Some medical schools may well make that judgment, under certain circumstances, about a white ethnic minority. Indeed it seems likely that some medical schools are even now attempting to help white Appalachian applicants, for example, under programs of regional distribution.

So the popular understanding is wrong, but so long as it persists it is a cost of the program because the attitudes it encourages tend to a degree to make people more rather than less conscious of race. There are other possible costs. It is said, for example, that some blacks find affirmative action degrading; they find that it makes them more rather than less conscious of prejudice against their race as such. This attitude is also based on a misperception, I think, but for a small minority of blacks at least it is a genuine cost.

In the view of the many important universities who have such programs, however, the gains will very probably exceed the losses in reducing racial consciousness over-all. This view is hardly so implausible that it is wrong for these universities to seek to acquire the experience that will allow us to judge whether they are right. It would be particularly silly to forbid these experiments if we know that the failure to try will mean, as the evidence shows, that the status quo will almost certainly continue. In any case, this first objection could provide no argument that would justify a decision by the Supreme Court holding the programs unconstitutional. The Court has no business substituting its speculative judgment about the probable consequences of educational policies for the judgment of professional educators.

So the acknowledged uncertainties about the long-term results of such programs could not justify a Supreme Court decision making them illegal. But there is a second and very different form of objection. It may be argued that even if the programs *are* effective in making our society less a society dominated by race, they are nevertheless unconstitutional because they violate the individual constitutional rights of those, like Allan Bakke, who lose places in consequence. In the oral argument Reynold H. Colvin of San Francisco, who is Bakke's lawyer, made plain that his objection takes this second form. Mr. Justice White asked him whether he accepted that the goals affirmative action programs seek are important goals. Mr. Colvin acknowledged that they were. Suppose, Justice White continued, that affirmative action programs are, as Cox had argued, the only effective means of seeking such goals. Would Mr. Colvin nevertheless maintain that the programs are unconstitutional? Yes, he insisted, they would be, because his client has a constitutional right that the programs be abandoned, no matter what the consequences.

Mr. Colvin was wise to put his objections on this second ground; he was wise to claim that his client has rights that do not depend on any judgment about the likely consequences of affirmative action for society as a whole, because if he makes out that claim then the Court must give him the relief he seeks.

But can he be right? If Allan Bakke has a constitutional right so important that the urgent goals of affirmative action must yield, then this must be because affirmative action violates some fundamental principle of political morality. This is not a case in which what might be called formal or technical law requires a decision one way or the other. There is no language in the Constitution whose plain meaning forbids affirmative action. Only the most naïve theories of statutory construction could argue that such a result is required by the language of any earlier Supreme Court decision or of the Civil Rights Act of 1964 or of any other congressional enactment. If Mr. Colvin is right it must be because Allan Bakke has not simply some technical legal right but an important moral right as well.

What could that right be? The popular argument frequently made on editorial pages is that Bakke has a right to be judged on his merit. Or that he has a right to be judged as an individual rather than as a member of a social group. Or that he has a right, as much as any black man, not to be sacrificed or excluded from any opportunity because of his race alone. But these catch phrases are deceptive here, because, as reflection demonstrates, the only genuine principle they describe is the principle that no one should suffer from the prejudice or contempt of others. And that principle is not at stake in this case at all. In spite of popular opinion, the idea that the *Bakke* case presents a conflict between a desirable social goal and important individual rights is a piece of intellectual confusion.

Consider, for example, the claim that individuals applying for places in medical school should be judged on merit, and merit alone. If that slogan means that admissions committees should take nothing into account but scores on some particular intelligence test, then it is arbitrary and, in any case, contradicted by the long-standing practice of every medical school. If it means, on the other hand, that a medical school should choose candidates that it supposes will make the most useful doctors, then everything turns on the judgment of what factors make different doctors useful. The Davis medical school assigned to each regular applicant, as well as to each minority applicant, what it called a "benchmark score." This reflected not only the results of aptitude tests and college grade averages, but a subjective evaluation of the applicant's chances of functioning as an effective doctor, in view of society's present needs for medical service. Presumably the qualities deemed important were different from the qualities that a law school or engineering school or business school would seek, just as the intelligence tests a medical school might use would be different from the tests these other schools would find appropriate.

There is no combination of abilities and skills and traits that constitutes "merit" in the abstract; if quick hands count as "merit" in the case of a prospective surgeon, this is because quick hands will enable him to serve the public better and for no other reason. If a black skin will, as a matter of regrettable fact, enable another doctor to do a different medical job better, then that black skin is by the same token "merit" as well. That argument may strike some as dangerous; but only because they confuse its conclusion— that black skin may be a socially useful trait in particular circumstances— with the very different and despicable idea that one race may be inherently more worthy than another.

Consider the second of the catch phrases I have mentioned. It is said that Bakke has a right to be judged as an "individual," in deciding whether he is to be admitted to medical school and thus to the medical profession, and not as a member of some group that is being judged as a whole. What can that mean? Any admissions procedure must rely on generalizations about groups that are justified only statistically. The regular admissions process at Davis, for example, set a cutoff figure for college grade-point averages. Applicants whose averages fell below that figure were not invited to any interview, and therefore rejected out of hand.

An applicant whose average fell one point below the cutoff might well have had personal qualities of dedication or sympathy that would have been revealed at an interview, and that would have made him or her a better doctor than some applicant whose average rose one point above the line. But the former is excluded from the process on the basis of a decision taken for administrative convenience and grounded in the generalization, unlikely to hold true for every individual, that those with grade averages below the cutoff will not have other qualities sufficiently persuasive. Indeed, even the use of standard Medical College Aptitude Tests (MCAT) as part of the admissions procedure requires judging people as part of groups because it assumes that test scores are a guide to medical intelligence which is in turn a guide to medical ability. Though this judgment is no doubt true statistically, it hardly holds true for every individual.

Allan Bakke was himself refused admission to two other medical schools, not because of his race but because of his age: these schools thought that a student entering medical school at the age of thirty-three was likely to make less of a contribution to medical care over his career than someone entering at the standard age of twenty-one. Suppose these schools relied, not on any detailed investigation of whether Bakke himself had abilities that would contradict the generalization in his specific case, but on a rule of thumb that allowed only the most cursory look at applicants over (say) the age of thirty. Did these two medical schools violate his right to be judged as an individual rather than as a member of a group?

The Davis Medical School permitted whites to apply for the sixteen places reserved for members of "educationally or economically disadvantaged minorities," a phrase whose meaning might well include white ethnic minorities. In fact several whites have applied, though none has been accepted, and the California Court found that the special committee charged with administering the program had decided, in advance, against admitting any. Suppose that decision had been based on the following administrative theory: it is so unlikely that any white doctor can do as much to counteract racial imbalance in the medical professions as a well-qualified and trained black doctor can do that the committee should for reasons of convenience proceed on the presumption no white doctor could. That presumption is, as a matter of fact, more plausible than the corresponding presumption about medical students over the age of thirty, or even the presumption about applicants whose grade-point averages fall below the cutoff line. If the latter presumptions do not deny the alleged right of individuals to be judged as individuals in an admissions procedure, then neither can the former.

Mr. Colvin, in oral argument, argued the third of the catch phrases I mentioned. He said that his client had a right not to be excluded from medical school because of his race alone, and this as a statement of constitutional right sounds more plausible than claims about the right to be judged on merit or as an individual. It sounds plausible, however, because it suggests the following more complex principle. Every citizen has a constitutional right that he not suffer disadvantage, at least in the competition for any public benefit, because the race or religion or sect or region or other natural or artificial group to which he belongs is the object of prejudice or contempt.

That is a fundamentally important constitutional right, and it is that right that was systematically violated for many years by racist exclusions and anti-Semitic quotas. Color bars and Jewish quotas were not unfair just because they made race or religion relevant or because they fixed on qualities beyond individual control. It is true that blacks or Jews do not choose to be blacks or Jews. But it is also true that those who score low in aptitude or admissions tests do not choose their levels of intelligence. Nor do those denied admission because they are too old, or because they do not come from a part of the country underrepresented in the school, or because they cannot play basketball well, choose not to have the qualities that made the difference.

Race seems different because exclusions based on race have historically been motivated not by some instrumental calculation, as in the case of intelligence or age or regional distribution or athletic ability, but because of contempt for the excluded race or religion as such. Exclusion by race was in itself an insult, because it was generated by and signaled contempt.

Bakke's claim, therefore, must be made more specific than it is. He says he was kept out of medical school because of his race. Does he mean that he was kept out because his race is the object of prejudice or contempt? That suggestion is absurd. A very high proportion of those who were accepted (and, presumably, of those who run the admissions program) were members of the same race. He therefore means simply that if he had been black he would have been accepted, with no suggestion that this would have been so because blacks are thought more worthy or honorable than whites.

That is true: no doubt he would have been accepted if he were black. But it is also true, and in exactly the same sense, that he would have been accepted if he had been more intelligent, or made a better impression in his interview, or, in the case of other schools, if he had been younger when he decided to become a doctor. Race is not, in *his* case, a different matter from these other factors equally beyond his control. It is not a different matter because in his case race is not distinguished by the special character of public insult. On the contrary the program presupposes that his race is still widely if wrongly thought to be superior to others.

In the past, it made sense to say that an excluded black or Jewish student was being sacrificed because of his race or religion; that meant that his or her exclusion was treated as desirable in itself, not because it contributed to any goal in which he as well as the rest of society might take pride. Allan Bakke is being "sacrificed" because of his race only in a very artificial sense of the word. He is being "sacrificed" in the same artificial sense because of his level of intelligence, since he would have been accepted if he were more clever than he is. In both cases he is being excluded not by prejudice but because of a rational calculation about the socially most beneficial use of limited resources for medical education.

It may now be said that this distinction is too subtle, and that if racial classifications have been and may still be used for malign purposes, then everyone has a flat right that racial classifications not be used at all. This is the familiar appeal to the lazy virtue of simplicity. It supposes that if a line is difficult to draw, or might be difficult to administer if drawn, then there is wisdom in not making the attempt to draw it. There may be cases in which that is wise, but those would be cases in which nothing of great value would as a consequence be lost. If racially conscious admissions policies now offer the only substantial hope for bringing more qualified black and other minority doctors into the profession, then a great loss is suffered if medical schools are not allowed voluntarily to pursue such programs. We should then be trading away a chance to attack certain and present injustice in order to gain protection we may not need against speculative abuses we have other means to prevent. And such abuses cannot, in any case, be worse than the injustice to which we would then surrender.

We have now considered three familiar slogans, each widely thought to name a constitutional right that enables Allan Bakke to stop programs of affirmative action no matter how effective or necessary these might be. When we inspect these slogans, we find that they can stand for no genuine principle except one. This is the important principle that no one in our society should suffer because he is a member of a group thought less worthy of respect, as a group, then other groups. We have different aspects of that principle in mind when we say that individuals should be judged on merit, that they should be judged as individuals, and that they should not suffer disadvantages because of their race. The spirit of that fundamental principle is the spirit of the goal that affirmative action is intended to serve. The principle furnishes no support for those who find, as Bakke does, that their own interests conflict with that goal.

It is of course regrettable when any citizen's expectations are defeated by new programs serving some more general concern. It is regrettable, for example, when established small businesses fail because new and superior roads are built; in that case people have invested more than Bakke has. And they have more reason to believe their businesses will continue than Bakke had to suppose he could have entered the Davis medical school at thirty-three even without a task force program.

There is, of course, no suggestion in that program that Bakke shares in any collective or individual guilt for racial injustice in America; or that he is any less entitled to concern or respect than any black student accepted in the program. He has been disappointed, and he must have the sympathy due that disappointment, just as any other disappointed applicant—even one with much worse test scores who would not have been accepted in any event—must have sympathy. Each is disappointed because places in medical schools are scarce resources and must be used to provide what the more general society most needs. It is hardly Bakke's fault that racial justice is now a special need—but he has no right to prevent the most effective measures of securing that justice from being used.

ON PREFERENTIAL HIRING

ROBERT K. FULLINWIDER

I

Is it justified, as a matter of social policy, to give general preference in employment to blacks and women? What considerations favor such a policy? Defenders of preferential hiring of blacks and women have offered a number of different grounds for its justification. I subject the three most important justifications to examination in this essay. I shall briefly consider the argument from social utility and the argument from distributive justice, and I shall take up at greater length the argument from compensatory justice.

Defenders of preferential hiring[1] of blacks and women can point to many social goals that such a policy would likely serve. It would increase the well-being of many persons, provide additional role-models for young women and blacks, undermine racial and sexual stereotypes, and make available better services to women and blacks. These gains, of course, will be bought at a certain cost, but perhaps it plausibly can be argued that the long-run gains outweigh the costs.[2]

Such a defense of preferential hiring of women and blacks does not fully explain, however, why preferential treatment should be accorded to *blacks* and *women.* It is probable that the enumerated goals, and others, could be accomplished by a policy of preferring in employment some blacks, some women, and some non-black males; and that the net gains from such a policy would be greater than the net gains from preferring *all and only women and blacks.* A similar problem besets a second ground for justifying preferential hiring. The argument in this case is that distributive justice requires society

Reprinted from Mary Vetterling Braggin, Frederick A. Elliston, and Jane English (eds.), *Feminism and Philosophy* (Totowa, N.J.: Littlefield, Adams and Co., 1981) 210–224, with the permission of the author and the publisher.

[1] I mean by preferential hiring the deliberate preferring of blacks or women over equally or better qualified candidates.

[2] For an analysis of costs and gains which comes to the opposite conclusion, see Virginia Black, "The Erosion of Legal Principles in the Creation of Legal Policies," *Ethics* 84 (January 1974).

to channel resources (including jobs) so as to increase the opportunities and well-being of those who "are toward the bottom of the socio-economic-political pecking order, and unlikely to rise as things are presently arranged."[3] By such means as preferential hiring policies deficiencies in opportunity can be ameliorated.[4]

A policy of preferring blacks and women would make little sense on this ground. The class of blacks and women fails by a wide margin to fit the class of persons eligible to be preferred on the distributive-justice criterion. Thus, appeal to considerations of distributive justice does not explain why a policy of preferring blacks and women is justified.[5] Since both the utilitarian argument and the distributive-justice argument seem unable to explain this, I am inclined to think that the strongest defense for preferential hiring of women and blacks lies elsewhere.

There is yet another more troubling difficulty with the two foregoing defenses of preferential hiring. The utilitarian argument requires social policy that channels resources so as to create the most social good. The distributive-justice argument requires social policy that channels resources to the bottom sector of society. What these simplified utilitarian and distributive-justice arguments fail to do is to take into account the existing rights of individuals to some or all of the resources to be channeled. These defenses of preferential hiring leave out of account the existing rights of persons—rights that may be violated by a policy of preferential hiring. How can a social policy preferring some in employment because of their race or sex be consistent with the Constitutional right to equal protection of the laws? How can we concede to all citizens the right to equal consideration or equal access to any position or job and at the same time support a policy of preferential hiring? Were it not for individuals' rights, social policy might be able more efficiently to achieve many social goals by re-allocating the various holdings and opportunities of persons; we might more efficiently realize the pattern of oppor-

---

[3] Irving Thalberg, "Reverse Discrimination and the Future," *Philosophical Forum,* 5 (Fall-Winter 1973–74), 300. See also Bernard Boxill, "The Morality of Reparations," *Social Theory and Practice,* 2 (1972).

[4] See Marlene Fried, "In Defense of Preferential Hiring," *Philosophical Forum,* 5 (Fall-Winter 1973–74), 309, 310.

[5] Considering the following (extremely rough) estimates and calculations will show this. In adopting a policy of distributing resources to lower sectors, and using employment preference as a tool, let us suppose that those who are members of families making less than $5,000 a year are eligible for preference. In 1970, 45 percent of black families and 20 percent of white families were below this line. In order to simplify calculations, consider a population of 20 million blacks and 180 million whites; and assume 5 members per family, and 1.5 job-seeking members of each family. Then in 1970, 2,700,000 blacks and 10,800,000 whites would have been eligible for preference, constituting an eligibility class of 13,500,000. A policy which preferred blacks and women who were below the cutoff point would prefer 8,100,000 (assuming half the whites are women), fully 39 percent *less* than all those entitled. A policy which preferred all and only blacks and women *regardless of their income* would fall far short of preferring all those who were entitled, and would prefer fully 50 percent not entitled to preference by the distributive-justice criterion and the cutoff point. Altering the assumptions or the cutoff point will not affect the ratios involved in this analysis. Figures on family income levels are taken from *The World Almanac 1971* (New York: Newspaper Enterprise Association, 1970), p. 45.

tunities and advantages that pleases us most. But people's rights stand in the way of our treating social problems as if they required managerial decisions regarding efficient utilization and allocation of resources and goods. For many, at any rate, a social policy stands condemned if it is shown to violate or sacrifice persons' important rights.[6]

If preferential hiring of blacks and women is to be fully justified, it must deal with the fact of people's preexisting rights. It needs to be shown that where preferential hiring appears to conflict with some individual's rights there is a valid basis for setting aside the putative right; or that the individual actually does not have the apparent right. How can this be shown? A natural recourse lies in the appeal to compensatory justice. It is arguments from this ground that seem to promise a more adequate defense of preferential hiring of blacks and women, and it is to arguments of this kind that I now turn.

II

I have a right (liberty or privilege)[7] not to give anyone a sum of money. That is to say, I am at liberty to do as I please in this respect, to give or not to give anyone money. But suppose, in exchange for a service, I promise another person a certain sum, S. Now the situation is altered; I no longer am completely at liberty to dispose of my money as I will. I have incurred an obligation to yield S to the promisee, and he has a right (claim-right) to have S from me. By my act of promising S, I have *waived* a portion of my liberty; I have given another a rightful claim to a portion of my money.

The same effect occurs when I wrongfully injure or harm someone. *By being at fault I incur an obligation* to repair the damage I have done, and to do so with my money if necessary. Whereas previous to my action I was completely at liberty to spend or not spend my money, now, by my action, I have *forfeited* a portion of my liberty. I *owe* the wronged party whatever I have that will make good the harm I caused.

It would seem that a promising defense for preferential hiring lies in seeing it as a form of reparation or compensation[8] for harms or injustices. This mode of defense would seem to promise avoidance of the two difficulties of the utilitarian and distributive-justice defenses. In the first place, we would seem

---

[6] Consider: ". . . there is no moral outweighing of one of our lives by others so as to lead to a greater overall *social* good. There is no justified sacrifice of some of us for others" (Robert Nozick, *Anarchy, State, and Utopia* [New York: Basic Books, 1974], p. 33). It is possession of basic rights which reflects this fact of individual worth and inviolability; and violating a person's rights to attain a worthy social goal or to benefit others (or even to gain others *their* rights) amounts to sacrificing the person for others.

[7] See Wesley N. Hohfeld, *Fundamental Legal Conceptions* (New Haven: Yale University Press, 1964), pp. 36, 38ff, 42–43, 47; and Joel Feinberg, *Social Philosophy* (Englewood Cliffs, N.J.: Prentice-Hall, Inc., 1973), pp. 55–59.

[8] I use "compensation" throughout synonymously with "reparation." It need not be used this way; for example, see the role it plays in Bernard Boxill's argument in "The Morality of Reparations," loc. cit.

to have at hand an account of individual cases of preferential treatment which showed that no one's rights were being violated, because it was evident that the relevant rights had been forfeited. And, moreover, we could apparently account for the justification for preferring blacks and women. For unlike any other major group,[9] both blacks and women have been subjected to legally enforced denial of their basic rights. Blacks were subjected to legal slavery and then to legally sanctioned discrimination, the latter circumstance persisting into the middle of this century. They have been severely deprived of opportunities for advancement; and, though the legal apparatus of discrimination has been dismantled, residual discrimination still persists. There are many living blacks who have suffered from the legal or the residual discrimination or both. Perhaps most have suffered from the general effects of discrimination.

Women were not admitted to full legal citizenship in this country until the early twentieth century, and even thereafter they have labored under legal restrictions that have greatly narrowed the range of opportunities open to them. Many living women can establish a plausible case for having suffered under arrangements and policies now recognized as unjust. A larger number have experienced the general effects of discrimination. Of course, not only women and blacks but other social groups have suffered from informal social discrimination. Women and blacks, however, having suffered under the weight of unjust state action, would seem to have legitimate ground for advancing a claim for state compensation; and preferential hiring might be seen as a form of reparation or compensation warranted by this claim.

There are two problems facing this justification of preferential hiring of blacks and women as a social policy. The first has to do with who receives the benefits of compensation, and the second, with who bears the costs of compensation. In discussing a policy of preferential hiring we are not talking about individual women or blacks bringing legal action for damages against identifiable individuals who have deprived them of their rights, nor are we talking about bringing such action against governmental bodies. What we are talking about is a general policy favoring blacks and women in employment. The policy will therefore favor individual blacks and women who have actually suffered under legal racism and legal sexism and, in addition, it will favor blacks and women who have not so suffered.[10] Moreover, those who will bear the costs of this policy, primarily young white male job seekers, are least likely to be those with any fault or having any responsibility for the wrongs now requiring compensation.

The problem of who receives the benefits I believe to be comparatively minor; if it is the only objection to preferential hiring, it can be overcome or

[9] American Indians excepted.

[10] Certainly, some women have benefited from sexism. Consider merely the well-endowed starlet who makes $100,000 a year entirely because of her possession of attributes valued as a consequence of the special attitudes toward women and sexuality promulgated by the regnant form of sexism. It is less the case that many blacks have benefited from racism.

tolerated. This problem with the compensatory-justice defense of preferential hiring is not like the parallel problem of the utilitarian and distributive-justice defenses. In their cases, the policy of preferential hiring grossly failed to include individuals who should have been included, given the justifications of the policy. In a policy of bestowing benefits, this is a far graver fault than the fault of not excluding some who ought to be excluded.

Much more serious is the problem of who bears the costs of compensation in preferential hiring. If those who are (involuntarily) paying the costs are not at fault for the wrongs being compensated, then we can no longer be assured that a compensatory program does not violate anyone's rights. And this was precisely the assurance that we were looking for with respect to preferential hiring. Is there a way around this difficulty?

Let us consider two job applicants, X, a white male, and Y, a black or a woman. Both X and Y are minimally qualified for the job. Let us further assume that X and Y (and all job applicants) have the basic right to equal consideration. I mean by this that they have the right that the successful applicant be chosen on the basis of job-related qualifications.[11] (In the present case, by hypothesis, neither color nor sex are job-related qualifications.) A policy of preferring blacks and women would prefer Y over X on account of features of Y that are not job-related. How has X's right not been violated?

Consider the following argument:

1. The community owes compensation to women and blacks.
2. In order to pay its debt, it may deny X his right.
3. Thus, assuming that the community may repay its debt by paying Y (and other individual blacks and women), then the community may adopt a policy of preferential hiring.

I attribute an argument like this to Judith Thomson, whose important paper, "Preferential Hiring,"[12] attempts to justify such a policy by appeal to compensatory justice. The puzzle in this argument is premise (2). Why may the community deny X his right? X is not at fault. But Thomson declares that it is "wrongheaded" to ask whether X has harmed Y or any other black or woman.[13]

This is surely mistaken. Thomson asks us to consider "those debts which are incurred by one who wrongs another. It is here [she continues] that we find what seems to me the most powerful argument for the conclusion that preferential hiring . . . is not unjust."[14] This "powerful argument" relies on *those debts that are incurred by one who wrongs another*. The debt is incurred by the one who wrongs and is incurred as a consequence of his fault. How,

[11] Many assume such right (see fn. 12). I don't defend the assumption here, although it carries most of the weight of the following argument.

[12] Judith Thomson, "Preferential Hiring," *Philosophy and Public Affairs*, 2 (Summer 1973). I have examined this argument in detail in my "Preferential Hiring and Compensation," *Social Theory and Practice*, 3 (Spring 1975). Some of what follows parallels arguments therein.

[13] Thomson, pp. 380–81.

[14] Ibid., p. 380.

then, can it be wrongheaded to ask about X's fault? If X has fault in the situation, then he has a debt to Y. If the community subsequently exacts an appropriate sacrifice from him to pay Y, X has no right that is being denied or violated; the community is simply requiring X to discharge *his* obligation to Y.

But if X has no fault, then he has no debt (not directly, and not to Y). He has not forfeited or otherwise lost any of his rights. If the community denies X his right to equal consideration, does it not violate his right? Perhaps it will be contended that the morally relevant debt in this case is the community's, so that the question of X's fault need not arise. This brings us back to premise (2). Does the mere fact that the community owes something justify it in taking any action it pleases to discharge its debt? Does it justify the community in taking something from X? Specifically, in the present case does it justify the community in denying X one of his fundamental rights, the right to equal consideration in employment? Thomson offers remarks that might be taken as defenses or explanations of (2).[15] She says that the community is justified in having preferential hiring because it is the *best* form of compensation for blacks and women. And she says that debts of compensation provide a ground for overriding rights. I look at both of these claims in turn in the following section.

III

Thomson seems to be addressing the problem of the defensibility of premise (2) when she says:

> Still, the community does impose a burden upon him [X, the white male applicant]: it is able to make amends for its wrongs only by taking something away from him, something which, after all, we are supposing he has a right to. And why should *he* pay the cost of the community's amends-making?
>
> If there were some appropriate way in which the community could make amends to its blacks and women, some way which did not require depriving anyone of anything he has a right to, then that would be the best course of action to take. Or if there were anyway some way in which the costs could be shared by everyone, and not imposed entirely on the young white male applicants, then that would be, if not the best, then anyway better than opting for a policy of preferential hiring. *But in fact the nature of the wrongs done is such as to make jobs the best and most suitable form of compensation.*[16]

[15] Since Thomson never explicitly states premise (2), there is no explicit argument for it. However, the premise seems necessary to her position, and there are remarks throughout her paper that can be seen as relevant to the justification of (2). It is from these that I reconstruct the argument for (2). For more detail, see "Preferential Hiring and Compensation," pp. 307–10.

[16] Thomson, p. 383. Emphasis added.

The last line of this passage appears to contain the defense of the community's paying its debt in a way that deprives X of his right. The "defense" rests on a confusion and will not withstand scrutiny.

Consider the following example.[17] Suppose you have stolen from me a rare ancient musket, the centerpiece of my gun collection. Before you can be made to return it, it is somehow irretrievably lost or destroyed. Suppose further that, by coincidence, there is one other such gun in existence in the world, and it is possessed by your brother. Unquestionably, from my point of view, the "best and most suitable form of compensation" I can have from you, since I cannot have my gun back, is to have a gun exactly like the one you have stolen. Neither any other kind of gun nor money can fully make up my loss. You can pay me the "best and most suitable form of compensation" by giving me your brother's gun. Are you thereby under an obligation to give me your brother's gun? Obviously not. Do you have the right to give me your brother's gun? You do not. If you take the gun and give it to me, you pay your debt to me with what is not yours to pay. You steal from your brother; and your act, though done to discharge your debt to me, is no different from your original act of stealing from me.

Alter the example in this way: imagine that the owner of the first musket is a French citizen. The musket is destroyed wrongfully by a United States customs agent. The French citizen demands compensation from the United States government. It so happens that the second musket is owned by a United States citizen. Is the United States government obligated to expropriate its citizen's musket to compensate the Frenchman, on the grounds that this constitutes the "best and most suitable" compensation? Obviously not. Does the United States government have the right to expropriate the musket? It does not.

Of the optional means of compensating me/Frenchman morally open to you/United States government, giving me/Frenchman the musket is not one of them. Its being the best form of compensation is irrelevant to its justifiability. The question of the best form of compensation becomes relevant only after we have settled the moral justifiability of exacting something from someone and settled on what the debtor has that he can pay. With reference to the community's paying Y (and other blacks and women) by taking something from X that X has a right to, it *first* must be established that this is a morally legitimate option of the community before the "suitability" of this payment to Y becomes a relevant question. By arguing that preferential hiring is the best and most suitable form of compensation to women and blacks, Thomson has not succeeded in establishing the defensibility of premise (2).

Thomson's other defense of premise (2) is more complicated. In the usual case of compensation, the person who pays the compensation has no right not to pay it. Thus, no right of that person is violated (or denied) by making

---

[17] Borrowed from "Preferential Hiring and Compensation," pp. 314–15.

him or her pay. In our present case, however, X's right to not pay compensation to Y has not been shown to have been forfeited or waived, and thus it still exists. The community, in establishing preferential hiring, simply *overrides* X's right not to pay (that is, his right to equal consideration).[18] I have been taking such overriding as a violating of X's right. But Thomson believes that sometimes a person's rights may be overridden without this being a violation. Thomson relies on the use of examples to persuade us that this is so. One example involves an eating club that gives a seating preference to one of its members over others because the club owes him a debt of gratitude. Another example is this:

> Suppose two candidates for a civil service job have equally good test scores, but that there is only one job available. We could decide between them by coin-tossing. But in fact we do allow for declaring for A straightway, where A is a veteran, and B is not. It may be that B is a nonveteran through no fault of his own. . . . Yet the fact is that B is not a veteran and A is. On the assumption that the veteran has served his country, the country owes him something. And it seems plain that giving him preference is a not unjust way in which part of that debt of gratitude can be paid.[19]

But, contrary to Thomson's confident claim in the last sentence, it is not plain that veterans' preference is just, although it is embodied in law. Veterans' preference can be objected to on the same grounds that preferential hiring of blacks and women can be objected to: the community acts unfairly in discharging its debt by imposing the cost not on all its members but only upon a few of its (nonculpable or nonresponsible) members.[20] It certainly is not plain that this charge of unfairness is ill-founded, if it is in fact ill-founded. It is not plain that overriding B's right to equal consideration is not simply a violation of his right. Thomson's example is insufficient to show us how X's right can be overridden without being violated.[21]

---

[18] My argument in "Preferential Hiring and Compensation" is obscured by my not distinguishing between the situation where a person forfeits or loses a right (and thus it is no longer in force) and where a person still retains a right (it is still in force) but the right is simply ignored or denied (overridden). Thus, I do not give sufficient attention there to the parts of Thomson's argument that I discuss at this point.

[19] Thomson, pp. 379–80.

[20] Such, in fact, was the argument in the legal challenge to veterans' preference in *McNamara* v. *Director of Civil Service,* 330 Mass. 22, 22–26, 110 N.E. 2d 840, 842–43 (1952). See James Nickel, "Preferential Policies in Hiring and Admissions: A Jurisprudential Approach," *Columbia Law Review,* 75 (April 1975), 546: "Thus, it might be argued that putting the burden of helping to compensate and meet the needs of veterans on those who are excluded from government jobs by policies which prefer veterans is an unfair way of distributing the cost of a legitimate goal. A well-qualified nonveteran who hoped to get a government job but who was denied it because of a policy which gives veterans an advantage may feel that too much of the cost of helping veterans was placed on him. This person may feel that providing benefits from taxes—where the cost can be spread among many taxpayers—is preferable as a means of helping veterans to programs which impose the burden on a few people whose opportunities are reduced by preferential policies."

[21] The eating-club example is no more persuasive, and is less apt. In this example, one member of an eating club is voted, out of gratitude, preference in being seated. Thomson sees no impropriety in this and views any member who complains as insensitive (pp. 378–79). Even if

Thomson remarks that

> it is . . . widely believed that we may, without injustice, refuse to grant a man what
> he has a right to only if *either* someone else has a conflicting and more stringent
> right, *or* there is some very great benefit to be obtained by doing so—perhaps that
> a disaster of some kind is thereby averted. If so, then there is really trouble for
> preferential hiring.

She goes on to claim that "there are other ways in which a right may be overridden."[22] But the other ways turn out to be the way B's right is denied in the veteran's case. Insofar as we have no confidence that B's right is overridden without injustice in this case, we can have no confidence that X's right is overridden without injustice in the case of preferring women and blacks. Thus, we have no reason to believe that preferential hiring has surmounted the major objection against it: that it violates some persons' fundamental rights.

IV

Suppose it is argued that there is a basis for overriding X's right after all, and it lies in the existence of a conflict of rights (a conflict of rights being one of the grounds listed by Thomson above). The argument might go like this: X has a right to equal consideration, but Y has right to compensation. In the present case the two rights conflict—to adopt preferential hiring is to override X's right, while to refuse to adopt it is to deny Y's right. My argument against preferential hiring rests on the fact that such a policy overrides someone's rights; but, in fact, someone's rights will be overridden both by the adoption of a policy of preferential hiring and by the nonadoption of such a policy. So my argument fails. It rests on a covert and undefended assumption that X's right is more important than Y's right.

This line of reasoning is mistaken. In the first place, preferential hiring is not the only way Y can be compensated. To fail to prefer Y in employment is not necessarily to fail to compensate Y at all. But even if preferential hiring were the only possible mode of compensation, the situation is still not as represented by the above argument. There is no conflict of rights.

If Y's having a right to compensation were his having a right from anyone to anything and everything that would make up for his loss, then perhaps there would be a conflict between Y's right and X's right. But Y's right to compensation is not to be understood this way at all, as our gun example above should have made clear. In the first place, Y's right is against a specific

---

we were all to agree that there is no impropriety here, this intuition is too tenuous a base upon
which to rest an argument for preferential hiring. For one thing, the eating-club example lacks
precisely the factors—the overriding of a basic right, and a potentially serious harm—so crucial
to our appraisal of preferential hiring.

[22] Thomson, p. 378.

agent, the community. X does not owe Y. Secondly, Y's right is to whatever resources necessary for compensation that are legitimately available to the community to give him. X's right to equal consideration is not among the eligible items that the community may yield to Y as compensation. Whatever the scope of Y's right to compensation, it does not encompass X's right to equal consideration. Thus, there is no conflict of rights between X and Y. It cannot be argued that X's right to equal consideration may be justly put aside on grounds of a conflict of rights.[23]

It is worth considering here one other attempt to undercut my criticism of preferential hiring. I have conceded that the community owes Y but I have claimed that X does not. Yet X is part of the community. If the community owes Y, must not X owe Y? If so, then the major premise of my criticism collapses. However, I deny that because the community owes Y it follows *from this alone* that X owes Y.

If the community owes Y, then its members *collectively* owe Y. But the debt does not *distribute* through the members. The community is a corporate agent. If General Motors owes damages to the unlucky owner of a defective Corvair, it does not follow that a General Motors employee in Flint owes the Corvair owner anything. If the United States owes Japanese companies damages because it has imposed an illegal surcharge on imports, it does not follow that, say, Judith Thomson, a United States citizen, owes anything to any Japanese. If the community seeks through taxation to raise resources for paying Y (and other blacks and women), then X, as a member of the community, *owes his share of taxes* to support the community's discharge of its legitimate obligation. But this is not to say that X owes Y.

V

A justified program to remedy past wrongs cannot itself create new wrongs. Though the wrongs done blacks and women provide a plausible ground for supporting their claims to compensation by the community, their legitimate claims seem to provide no justification for a policy of preferential hiring. Such a program will invariably violate the basic rights of some persons,

---

[23] Suppose that the loss of my gun (see section III above) is such that nothing except having one like it could conceivably count as compensating for my loss. Even so, I don't have a right to your brother's gun; and there is no conflict between my right to compensation and your brother's right to his gun. *A conflict of rights would exist only where your brother has a right to the gun and I have a right to it as well, and both rights cannot be honored.*

The following kind of situation may be confused with a conflict of rights: I have a right to do something (or have something), but I cannot do (have) what I have a right to do (have) so long as we honor other's rights. For example, each man has a right to marry; but suppose all the females of age marry other men, there being more males than females. Then, I cannot marry though I have a right to. This is unfortunate, but it is not the case that my right to marry has been denied me, or overridden; nor is there a conflict between my right to marry and anyone else's right.

primarily young white male applicants.[24] It will do so because the applicants who will be discriminated against by preferential hiring have not lost their rights due to any culpability in wrongdoing.[25] And we have found no valid basis for overriding their rights.[26] The compensation argument may justify individual cases of preferential hiring of blacks and women but not a general policy.[27] The utilitarian argument and the distributive-justice argument seem even less likely to justify a policy of preferring blacks and women in employment. Unless it is shown that valid, in-force fundamental rights of individuals may be overridden for *weaker* reasons than conflict of rights or to avoid disaster, then a policy of preferential hiring of women and blacks must be deemed unjust.

That we have failed to find in the claims to compensation a justification for preferential hiring does not mean, however, that we thus dismiss the claims to compensation themselves as illegitimate. Preferential hiring is not the only way, nor is it indisputably the best way (Judith Thomson to the contrary notwithstanding) to compensate most blacks and women for the wrongs done them, or for the effects of wrongs done their predecessors. In principle, any program that distributes its costs fairly and does not violate anyone's rights is open to consideration. Many programs for increasing representation of blacks and women in industry, business, education, and so on are thus not ruled out. Practical problems of implementation and political problems of adoption may, of course, diminish the likelihood of any particular program, or any program at all, coming into being. It may be that entrenched interests are strong enough to prevent any effective compensatory program.[28] In this unfortunate event, no general governmental program will be available, and compensatory remedies, if any, will have to come through individual actions for judicial relief.[29]

---

[24] Assuming, of course, that we grant that everyone has the right to equal consideration for jobs and offices.

[25] Even though Thomson claims it is "wrongheaded" to ask about the fault of white male applicants, she seems to recognize the implausibility of her position when, in the end, she tries to persuade us that they are not so innocent after all: ". . . it is not entirely inappropriate that these applicants [white males] should pay the cost. No doubt few, if any, have themselves individually, done any wrongs to blacks and women. But they have profited from the wrongs the community did" (p. 383). This will not do. In order to become an "accessory" to a wrong, and thereby less than innocent, one must benefit *knowingly* and *voluntarily* from the wrong. See "Preferential Hiring and Compensation," pp. 316–18, for a more detailed discussion of this point.

[26] There is no conflict of rights; there is no catastrophe to be averted; and, contrary to Thomson's claim, debts of gratitude and compensation do not standardly legitimize overriding anyone's fundamental rights.

[27] Suppose X has wronged Y, and in such a way as to undercut Y's job opportunities. Then, if Y and X are again in competition for the same job it might be legitimate remedy here to prefer Y for the job (even if X is more qualified).

[28] Or it may be that they will yield *only* to a program of preferential hiring. For one who thinks *this* justifies preferential hiring see Marlene Fried, op. cit. (above, n. 4), pp. 317–18.

[29] For the limited possibilities in individual action see Boris Bittker, *The Case for Black Reparations* (New York: Random House, 1973).

THE MORALITY OF PREFERENTIAL HIRING

BERNARD R. BOXILL

Many philosophers have held that preferential hiring is morally objectionable. They do not object to the compensation of those who have suffered from various forms of discrimination, but hold, rather, that preferential hiring is not, for a number of reasons, an appropriate method of compensation.[1] In this essay I rebut two of the principal arguments raised against preferential hiring, namely (1) that preferential hiring benefits just those from among the groups that have suffered discrimination who do not deserve compensation, and (2) that preferential hiring is unfair to young white men.

I

The most common version of the first argument, always dragged out with an air of having played a trump, is that since those of discriminated groups who benefit from preferential hiring must be minimally qualified, they are not those of the group who deserve compensation. Alan Goldman, for example, argues this way: "Since hiring within the preferred group still depends upon relative qualifications and hence upon past opportunities for acquiring qualifications, there is in fact a reverse ratio established between past discriminations and present benefits, so that those who most benefit from the program, those who actually get jobs, are those who least deserve to."[2] But surely to argue from the above to the conclusion that preferential hiring is unjustified is a non sequitur. Let us grant, that qualified blacks, for example, are less deserving of compensation than unqualified blacks, that those who most deserve compensation should be compensated first, and finally that preferential hiring of qualified blacks is unjustified? Surely, the assumption that unqualified blacks are more deserving of compensation than qualified blacks does not require us to conclude that qualified blacks deserve no compensation. Because I have lost only one leg, I may be less deserving of compensation than another who has lost two legs, but it does not follow that I deserve no compensation at all.

Reprinted from *Philosophy & Public Affairs*, Vol. 7, No. 3 (1978) 246–268, with permission of the author and the publisher, Princeton University Press.

[1] See for example, Alan H. Goldman, "Reparations to Individuals or Groups?" *Reverse Discrimination*, ed. Barry Gross (New York: Prometheus Books, 1977); Goldman, "Justice and Hiring by Competence," *American Philosophical Quarterly*, 14, No. 1 (1977); Goldman "Affirmative Action," *Equality and Preferential Treatment*, ed. Marshall Cohen, Thomas Nagel, and Thomas Scanlon (Princeton: Princeton University Press, 1977), pp. 192–209; Robert Simon, "Preferential Hiring: A Reply to Judith Jarvis Thomson," *Equality and Preferential Treatment*.

[2] Goldman, "Reparations to Individuals or Groups?" p. 322.

Much the same can be said of Simon's somewhat less contentious argument that "preferential hiring policies award compensation to . . . those who have the ability and qualifications to be seriously considered for the jobs available. Surely it is far more plausible to think that collective compensation ought to be equally available to all group members."[3] But again, from the fact that preferential hiring does not award compensation to "all group members" how does it follow that preferential hiring is unjustified compensation to those of the group who "have the ability and qualifications"? It is easy to turn Simon's argument against him. If "all group members" should be compensated, then why insinuate that the qualified ones should be left out? And, if they should not be left out, why not compensate them in the manner best suited to their situation and aspirations — with good jobs — and compensate the unqualified in the manner best suited to their situation — cash settlements, remedial training, and so on.

The premise which would make the above argument less objectionable and which these critics of preferential hiring have not appeared to notice is that compensation can be made to only one section of the group — either the qualified or the unqualified, but not both. Given that the unqualified are most deserving of compensation, then a case should be mounted for claiming that, in the circumstances, preferential hiring should not be instituted because it takes from those who are most deserving of compensation (the unqualified) to give to those who are less deserving (the qualified). But it should be noted that even with the above premise, the argument does not quite yield what the critics want. For they want to show that preferential hiring of qualified minorities is unjustified *tout court*. And that is much more than showing that it is impracticable.

Now suppose the critics say that they meant that qualified blacks, for example, are not simply less deserving of compensation than unqualified blacks but that they deserve no compensation at all, just because they are qualified. The previous argument was that the ground for compensation is wrongful injury, so that if qualified blacks are generally less wronged they are therefore less deserving of compensation than unqualified blacks. The present argument is that the ground for compensation is not wrongful injury but, rather, lack of qualifications. In other words, though qualified blacks are discriminated against or suffer wrongful injury, their qualifications exclude them from consideration for compensation. Thus, James W. Nickel, who is one of the very few to have noticed the complication that discriminated persons can overcome the handicap of discrimination, adopts this last view. Allowing that it is perhaps only the least "problematic approach," he determines that "the ones who have a right to compensation are those who have personally been injured by discrimination and who have not been able to overcome this injury."[4]

---

[3] Simon, "Preferential Hiring: A Reply," p. 43.
[4] Nickel, "Preferential Policies in Hiring and Admissions," *Reverse Discrimination,* p. 329.

But why should this be so? I am not questioning that on practical grounds we may be unable to compensate the qualified members of a general discriminated group. I am questioning that just because a person has overcome his injury, he no longer has a right to compensation. Nickel himself gives no argument, but it may be that he mistakenly narrows the grounds for compensation.

Certainly the unqualified person is hurt and probably harmed. He is hurt in the sense that he will lose out to the qualified in the competition for jobs. And he is harmed too, if his lack of qualification involves a stunting of his intellectual and moral development. But though these are grounds for saying that he deserves compensation, they are not the only ones. For, as I have argued in an earlier essay, there are at least two very different grounds for compensation or reparation.[5] One ground looks forward; it evaluates present harms and, disregarding whether or not they are due to wrong, seeks to remedy them to secure some future good. The other looks backward; it seeks to rectify past injustices and can ignore whether or not the victims are *now* in a sorry state. Thus, I do not dispute that the unqualified have a claim to compensation — whether or not they have been wronged. What I do dispute is that just because they have overcome their injuries the qualified have no claim to compensation. For if they have overcome their injuries, they have borne the costs of compensation that should be borne by those who inflicted the injuries. If I am swindled and by time and effort retrieve my money, shouldn't I be compensated for my time and effort? Or if I have plenty of money and hire a good lawyer, shouldn't I also claim from my swindlers the money I paid the lawyer?

The costs, in time and effort, of overcoming an injury have results other than overcoming the injury. A person who has worked hard and long to overcome an injury is not what he would have been had he never been injured. He may be better, or he may be worse. Adversity can strengthen or it can merely harden. Thus middle-class blacks are alternately praised for their toughness and deprecated for their insensitivity. But these side-effects of the cost of overcoming wrongful injury are not the main issue. In particular, though I may be a better person for prevailing over unfair obstacles, this does not absolve my injurers from the obligation to compensate me.

Consequently, being harmed is not the only ground for deserving compensation. There is also the ground of simply having been wronged. Goldman, for example, has overlooked this, Repeatedly he stresses that qualified blacks are the least harmed of blacks, while ignoring that this does not entail they have not been wronged. "Do we want a policy which inverts the ratio of past harm to present benefit . . . ?" he asks, pointing to the "inconsistency of compensating past harm with benefits to those harmed least . . ." and to the fact that "the beneficiaries of affirmative action, with the exception of certain

[5] Boxill, "The Morality of Reparations," *Reverse Discrimination,* pp. 270-78.

blue collar workers, are generally not economically depressed." [6] But this view overlooks that being unqualified and economically depressed are not the only grounds for compensation.

This does not affect the proposition that unqualified blacks are more deserving of compensation than qualified blacks. Irving Thalberg, for example, asks us to consider two groups of persons K' and K''. K' consists of persons who, despite "dreadful persecution," now manage to hold their own in the larger society, and K'' consists of persons who, though "never oppressed," now are at the "bottom of the socioeconomic-political pecking order." [7] Which of these groups, he asks us, "most deserve special treatment?" It is clear that, though they are admittedly not at all the victims of injustice, he is himself inclined to choose K''. But though Thalberg takes this position, he does not at all commit himself to the claim that K' deserves nothing. On the contrary, by stressing that "our resources are enough for one group only" he clearly implies that he would allow that K' has a claim too, though K'' has a stronger claim. Now as it happens, I agree with Thalberg, though the case I have in mind is easier than his. My case is that when we have one group, say K, whose members are equally oppressed because they are K's, those K's who nevertheless manage to qualify themselves are less deserving of compensation than those K's who fail to qualify themselves. This case is easier than Thalberg's because the people to whom he would give preference are not victims but only unqualified, while the people to whom I would give preference are both victims and unqualified.

So far I have agreed that qualified blacks are less deserving of compensation than unqualified blacks. And I have agreed that this is because they may be less harmed and perhaps less wronged than unqualified blacks. What I reject is the facile assumption that this in any way implies or suggests that preferential hiring is unjustified. My premise — which at first seemed to be allowed by critics of preferential hiring — is that qualified blacks, though perhaps less harmed or wronged than unqualified blacks, are still harmed and wronged or, at least, still wronged. But it is just this premise that now seems to be denied. Thus Goldman first makes the claim (which I can allow) that in the preferential hiring of qualified minority candidates, there is "an inverse ratio established between past discrimination and present benefits." But then, on the next page, he makes the very much stronger claim — which does not at all follow from the first — that preferential hiring "singles out for benefits within a generally unjustly treated minority just that minority that has not been unjustly treated." [8]

[6] Goldman, "Affirmative Action," pp. 206, 207.

[7] Thalberg, "Reverse Discrimination and the Future," *Women and Philosophy,* ed. Carol Gould and Marx Wartofsky (New York: G. P. Putnam's Sons, Capricorn Books, 1976), pp. 300, 301.

[8] Goldman, "Reparations to Individuals or Groups?" pp. 322, 323. I am not saying that Goldman tries to draw the second proposition from the first. My point is that the second—that the qualified of an otherwise generally mistreated minority are not unjustly treated—does not

This confusion between being the *least* wronged and harmed of a group and being only *slightly,* or not at all, harmed or wronged is essential to the present objection to preferential hiring. Thus, since preferential hiring has been proposed as giving the edge to persons characterized by some group quality — for example, being black — the question has been raised about how high the correlation is between being black and being harmed or wronged. We may agree, I trust, that it must be very high. Goldman, for example, does not deny this. It is only perfect correlation, that "every member of the group has suffered from unjust denial of a job or of a decent education" that he labels a "drastic claim."[9] But if so, then the serious objection to preferential hiring as a practice cannot be that a tiny fraction of qualified blacks will get breaks they do not deserve. Surely, if this is the only practical way to help a group, the vast majority of which fully deserves compensation, that objection would be only grudging.[10] But I contend that it is not the serious objection. The serious objection is that no qualified blacks deserve compensation. And that, I submit, can seem plausible only if we confuse being less harmed and wronged than others of their group with being only slightly, or not at all, harmed and wronged.

Suppose, however, that there is not a high correlation between being harmed or wronged and being black. This is an important possibility for, if true, it undoes the argument in the preceding paragraph. Blackstone, for example, after noting the unexceptional proposition that there is "no invariable connection between a person's being black or female and suffering from past invidious discrimination," leaps to the conclusion that there are lots of blacks who have suffered from no invidious discrimination. Thus, he writes, "there are many blacks ... who are highly advantaged, who are the sons and daughters of well educated and affluent lawyers, doctors and industrialists. A policy of reverse discrimination would mean that such highly advantaged individuals would receive preferential treatment over the sons and daughters of disadvantaged whites ... I submit that such a situation is not social justice."[11] Now this may seem like a commendable effort to define the groups deserving compensation in socioeconomic, rather than racial, terms. But it raises troubling questions. Why does Blackstone assume so easily, for example, that "reverse discrimination" would mean that the "highly advantaged" blacks he speaks of would be getting preferred treatment over disadvantaged

---

follow from the first—that the qualified of such a minority are the least unjustly treated. Further, no justification is given or attempted for the second proposition. In "Affirmative Action," Goldman claims that minority members with "Ph.Ds or other professional qualifications who will benefit from the policy ..." have not been "appreciably harmed." But it does not at all follow that because they have such qualifications, they have not been harmed or "appreciably harmed." If among a group of amputees who all have lost two legs, I have lost only one, I may be the least harmed, but I am still appreciably harmed.

[9] Goldman, "Limits to the Justification of Reverse Discrimination," *Social Theory and Practice,* 3, No. 3 (1975): 294.

[10] By "group" here I mean the group of qualified blacks, not the group of blacks in general.

[11] Blackstone, "Reverse Discrimination and Compensatory Justice," *Social Theory and Practice,* 3, No. 3 (1975), 268.

whites? I would have thought that being so advantaged they would likely be vying with their peers — the highly advantaged sons and daughters of white doctors, lawyers, and industrialists — leaving the sons and daughters of disadvantaged blacks to get preferential treatment over the children of disadvantaged whites. If, with all their advantages, the black people Blackstone describes are still reduced to competing against disadvantaged whites then all the more would it seem that they have been harmed most deeply and grievously.

Taken at its best, Blackstone's objection may be that preferential hiring gives an unfair edge to advantaged blacks who have lost out in the competition for jobs and places. Unquestionably, preferential hiring gives such blacks an edge over disadvantaged blacks. Since, however, this is the edge the middle-class has over the lower class, to make his objection stick, Blackstone should recommend sweeping changes in the class structure. But Blackstone makes no such recommendation. Preferential hiring would give an unfair edge to advantaged blacks over disadvantaged whites, if the positions and places it serves them would otherwise go to disadvantaged whites. But this would be so only if the competition they have "lost out" in were fair. Since the small number of blacks gaining desirable positions and places shows the competition is not fair, the edge advantaged blacks gain is over advantaged whites.

In arriving at the above claim, I have left several assumptions unstated. The most obvious is that the black and white groups are roughly equal in native talent and intelligence. If they are not, then unless differences in native ability between the groups are remediable and justice requires that they be removed, it is not at all clear that the lower qualifications of blacks are any indication that they had been wronged. Fortunately, this difficulty can be avoided. The weight of informed opinion is against Jensen, but even if it is ultimately shown to have some merit, his theory that as a group blacks have less native intellectual talent than whites is, for now, extremely controversial. Jensen himself, though regrettably not chary enough in proposing policies based on this theory, is tentative enough in stating it.[12] Consequently, given its present uncertainty and the great injustice that would be wreaked on a people if it proved false and educational policies were based on it, I submit that we are not warranted now in basing any policies on it.

A more serious attempt to explain the group differences in qualifications between blacks and whites is to attribute them to cultural differences. This is a complex issue. Though controversial, it cannot be swept aside in the manner of the last objection. For it has several different versions which must be considered separately. The first, with which we are all by now familiar, is that the tests administered for admission to colleges and professional schools are culturally biased, giving an unfair advantage to white applicants. This version is irrelevant. It explains, perhaps, why blacks are underrepresented

---

[12] Jensen, "How much can we boost IQ and Scholastic Achievement?" *Environment, Heredity and Intelligence* (Cambridge: Harvard University Press), p. 117.

in positions of responsibility and wealth, but it does not purport to show that underrepresentation is just. The second version, more to the point, is that blacks simply are not as interested as whites in society's positions of affluence and prestige. Barry Gross suggests this line in his argument that underrepresentation is no clear indication of discrimination: "The members of a group might simply lack interest in certain jobs (for example, Italians in the public school system are in short supply)."[13] But this analogy fails, though Gross does not appear to notice it, when applied to the case of blacks. For it isn't as if blacks are underrepresented in the public school system or in law or in banking or in the professions. It is that they are underrepresented in all of these. Consequently, though Gross may be right that "sociologically, groups are simply not represented in various jobs and at various levels in percentages closely approximating their percentage of the population," he fails to see that the case of blacks presents a matter of an altogether different order.[14] Lack of interest in this or in that area — presumably culturally determined — may explain away underrepresentation of a cultural group in this or in that area. Unless, however, we assume that some cultures have no interest in any of the traditional areas, we cannot explain a group's general underrepresentation in all desirable positions in society by citing cultural differences.

The more common version of the argument that cultural differences explain black underrepresentation in desirable positions is not that blacks lack an interest in these positions but that they lack the discipline for them. This argument is a non sequitur. Even if the traits which inhibit the success of blacks are cultural traits — supposedly a lack of appropriate work habits and discipline — it does not follow that they are not wrongful injuries. In order to survive and retain their sanity and equilibrium in impossibly unjust situations, people may have to resort to patterns of behavior and consequently may develop habits or cultural traits which are debilitating and unproductive in a more humane environment. I see no reason why these cultural traits — which may be deeply ingrained and extremely difficult to eradicate — should not be classed as unjust injuries.[15] It is admittedly unusual to think of cultural traits as injuries because we think of cultures as, in an important sense, self-imposed. This is true of most cultures in the traditional sense of national and ethnic cultures. Such cultures come with built-in philosophical self-justifications. In the sense that participants in them necessarily have elaborate resources with which to justify themselves, they may be viewed as self-imposed. Consequently, though such cultures may encourage development of traits which inhibit advancement in modern society, it would be hazardous to call the traits injuries.[16] At most, they would be self-imposed injuries. But

---

[13] Gross, "Is Turn About Fair Play?" in *Reverse Discrimination,* p. 381.

[14] Ibid., p. 380. Gross here incisively makes the point that the two questions—Who fails to do well? and Who is discriminated against?—are quite different and can yield different answers. Goldman implies the answers are the same when he assumes that qualified blacks (presumably because they are qualified) are not unjustly treated.

[15] For example, chronic tardiness.

[16] For examples of such cultural traits, see P. T. Bauer, *Dissent on Development* (London: Weidenfeld & Nicolson, 1976), p. 201.

not all cultures are, in that important sense, self-imposed. Certain cultures contain none of the elaborate philosophical self-justification of ordinary cultures. Thus, in describing what he called the "culture of poverty" for example, Oscar Lewis notes that though it is a genuine culture in the traditional anthropological sense, in that it provides human beings with a "design for living" it "does not provide much support ... poverty of culture is one of the crucial traits of the culture of poverty." [17]

But the idea that blacks form a cultural group is not notably advantageous for the critics of preferential hiring. For it can be argued that since blacks have been discriminated against as a group, they deserve compensation as a group. Further, individual blacks — in particular qualified ones — should not have to prove specific cases of discrimination against them in order to qualify for preferential treatment. But the critics claim that blacks do not comprise a group in the sense required by the argument. Goldman, for example, objects to treating blacks as a legitimate group eligible for compensatory treatment because they "do not qualify as genuine groups or social organizations in the sense in which sociologists generally use these terms." He goes on to point out that in genuine groups there is "actual interaction among members, each of whom occupies a certain position or plays a certain role in the group reciprocal to other roles, roles being reciprocal when their performances are mutually dependent." [18] But I submit, on that very account, that cultural groups do qualify as genuine groups. There is, for example, "actual interaction" among the members of a cultural group. That interaction is, of course, not specifically economic or political. Members of a cultural group do not, for example, necessarily buy from each other or employ each other or rule each other. Still they *do* interact and that interaction is just as important as the activities already mentioned.

Members of a cultural group share basic values and ideals—that is what we mean by calling them members of the same cultural group—and they interact intellectually by exchanging ideas about these values and ideals, by clarifying, criticizing, and extending them and by severing and drawing connections between them. In this way they come better to understand themselves. All prosperous and progressive peoples engage in this bustling process of self-clarification. Some call it the cause of all progress, others the reward of progress. In either case, it is a great good. If then it is objected that blacks are underrepresented in positions of wealth and prestige because of cultural differences, then if they have been wronged as a group, preferential hiring of qualified blacks is justified as a way of compensating the group. For it needs no argument to show that the intellectually most active and advanced of a cultural group play a crucial role in the above-mentioned process of self-clarification. [19] If then, as seems likely, they will be among those qualified,

---

[17] Lewis, "The Culture of Poverty," *Scientific American,* 215, No. 4 (Oct. 1966), 25.

[18] Goldman, "Limits to the Justification of Reverse Discrimination," p. 292.

[19] W. E. B. Dubois makes this point about the talented tenth of every group. See W. E. B. Dubois, "The Talented Tenth," *Negro Social and Political Thought 1880–1920,* ed. Howard Brotz (New York: Basic Books, 1966), p. 518.

and preferential hiring will give them the opportunity to play their crucial role in the group, then it is a way of compensating the group. And it will not do to object that if blacks form a cultural group, then the qualified among them should seek employment within that group. Though cultural groups may have originally been economic units, this is no longer the case in today's world of mass migrations. There is no reason why distinct cultural groups cannot be economically integrated.

But even if blacks do not form a cultural group, then preferential hiring is still justified. For if blacks have the same basic goals, aspirations, dreams, and hopes as whites and would, if given real opportunities, work assiduously to realize them, then—given the unjustness of assuming at this stage that blacks as a group have less native intelligence than whites and given the existence of independent evidence of widespread and pervasive discrimination against blacks—it is a reasonable assumption that the lesser merit of qualified blacks relative to qualified whites is due to injustice. What other explanation is there?

Goldman, for example, opposes Thalberg's example of a group K which, though never the victim of oppression, is now at the bottom of society or, as we may say here, underrepresented in positions of wealth and influence.[20] He stresses the "historical unlikelihood" of such a group and claims that it is either a "statistical accident" or "impossible." Of course he does not conclude—and neither, it should be emphasized, have I—that therefore the only reasonable assumption is, *contra hypothesis,* that group K'' was oppressed. It could, after all, be accidental. For example, if the class of left-handed redheads were thus underrepresented, it would be unreasonable to infer unjust discrimination. Independent evidence of discrimination is necessary in order to attribute their position to discrimination. No one, I imagine, would be willing to deny such evidence in the case of blacks. Consequently, we are again forced back to the conclusion that even qualified blacks have been wronged and harmed and deserve compensation.

But it may be objected that my easy passage from "pervasive discrimination" against blacks to "even qualified blacks have been wronged and harmed" is unwarranted. Thus many critics of preferential hiring, while admitting that discrimination against blacks exists, maintain that if it affects mainly lower-class unqualified blacks, then middle-class and qualified blacks suffer only vicariously and indirectly. Before showing the spurious nature of this theory of vicarious and indirect suffering, I want to stress the ambiguity in the claim that middle-class blacks escape discrimination. On the one hand, it could mean that by talent, tenacity, effort, the use of scarce resources and a tough hide, the middle-class blacks overcome or avoid the more obvious effects of discrimination. But if this is what is meant, then as I have argued, it does not at all follow that they have not been wronged or harmed and are un-

---

[20] Goldman, "Reverse Discrimination and the Future: A Reply to Irving Thalberg," *The Philosophical Forum,* 11, Nos. 2–3, 322.

deserving of compensation. On the other hand, the claim that middle-class blacks escape discrimination may mean literally that certain blacks are simply never, or almost never, discriminated against in any way. They are never — just because they are black — refused jobs and housing, compelled to spend extra money to send their children to adequate schools, harassed by police, and so on.

I shall not take time to argue that this other meaning is unlikely. There is another answer. Even if some blacks escape discrimination altogether, it must be admitted that there is a pervasive prejudice against blacks as a group and a tendency to discriminate against them. Consequently, even those who escape discrimination are witnesses to the discrimination against other blacks. This takes us to the argument proposed by Judith Jarvis Thomson — "even those who were not themselves down-graded for being black or female have suffered the consequences of the down-grading of other blacks and women: lack of self confidence and lack of self respect."[21] Certain authors have taken this as argument for a kind of "indirect," "vicarious" wrong. In responding to it, Goldman, for example, has objected that we should reserve "vicarious compensation to those who suffer psychologically or vicariously from injustice toward others" and that we should "draw the line at indirect psychological pressures."[22] I shall show, however, that Goldman's response completely misses the point, which has nothing to do with "vicarious suffering."

It may seem to be relevant to the question only because it conflates two distinct cases. Consider, for example, Goldman's argument that a traumatized witness does not "suffer the harm of the real victim. Similarly a Jewish millionaire in Scarsdale, no matter how much he suffered vicariously or psychologically from hearing of the German concentration camps, is not owed the reparations due a former inmate."[23] But it seems clear that two very different cases are indiscriminately mixed together here. On the one hand, a witness might identify with the victim and suffer vicariously and indirectly; on the other hand, the transgressors might identify the witness with their victim and say that there is as much reason for persecuting the witness as the victim. But the witness who suffers vicariously may not be in imminent danger, and the witness who is in imminent danger need not suffer vicariously.

It would, however, be an egregious error to conclude that the latter witness does not suffer at all. He could certainly suffer at the realization that he too was under sentence and could be next. There are, therefore, two completely different sufferings that a witness to the persecution of others might endure. The first stems from sympathy for the victims; it is vicarious and could be called indirect. The second stems from the witness' self-interested realization that he is under sentence too and could be next. But, though it may be

[21] Thomson, "Preferential Hiring," p. 36.
[22] Goldman, "Reverse Discrimination and the Future: A Reply," p. 324; Goldman, "Limits to the Justification of Reverse Discrimination," p. 296.
[23] Goldman, "Affirmative Action," p. 206.

"psychological," it is not vicarious and there is nothing indirect about it. The example of the Scarsdale Jew—that he is a millionaire is irrelevant—obscures this. Safely ensconced in Scarsdale, any Jew, millionaire or not, was safe from Hitler. That example insinuates that the Jew who was not himself victimized could feel only vicarious suffering. To bring back balance, I suggest pondering the plight of a Jewish multimillionaire in Berlin.

Failure to distinguish these two kinds of "suffering" is responsible for the idea that vicarious suffering is relevant to the undermining of the self-confidence and self-respect that Judith Jarvis Thomson was presumably referring to. For while the realization that, like the actual victim, one is also under sentence and could be next has everything to do with this undermining of self-confidence and self-respect, vicarious suffering has nothing to do with it. Clearly, it is the realization that one is perpetually under suspicious scrutiny, that one is under sentence, that one is only tolerated, that one's life and prospects may suddenly change for the worse in a way one cannot control which undermines self-confidence. Thus, vicarious suffering is irrelevant. As I have shown, I can suffer vicariously for others and not at all feel threatened. In fact, it is not implausible that a feeling of security is in many cases a condition for vicarious suffering; for it may be, as some psychologists say, that to sympathize with others, a person must be secure. In other words, if I feel myself threatened, I may be too worried about my own prospects to be able to sympathize with and suffer for others. Consequently, the vicarious suffering of middle-class blacks for lower-class blacks, if it exists to any appreciable degree, is completely irrelevant to the question of the undermining of their self-confidence and self-respect. What is relevant is the uncertainty and ambiguity of their own lives.

But the red herring of vicarious suffering is misleading in yet another way: It suggests that the undermining of self-confidence and self-respect under discussion is a consequence of "injustice toward others." Of course, vicarious suffering is not indication of injustice to oneself. Though, for example, a white person may suffer vicariously at the thought of discrimination against lower-class blacks, the injustice is to them and not to him. When, however, black persons feel threatened and insulted when other black persons are discriminated against because they are black, the injustice is both to those actually discriminated against and to those who are spared. Because the blacks discriminated against are discriminated against because they are black, all black people are warned that they too deserve the same treatment. The injustice toward them is twofold. First, they suffer the "judgmental injustice" that because they are black they deserve less consideration than others.[24] Second, they suffer the uncertainty to which judgmental injustice condemns them and the possible loss of self-confidence and self-respect resulting from that uncertainty.

[24] See Joel Feinberg, "Non-Comparative Justice," *The Philosophical Review,* 83 (July 1974), 300.

Accordingly, even if we assume that certain black people are not actually discriminated against, it does not follow that they are not unjustly treated, or that the losses they endure are due to "vicarious suffering." Consequently, the argument for excluding them from compensation fails. Here, that even the blacks who are spared actual discrimination are treated unjustly by the discrimination against other blacks because they are black is essential. For if the spared blacks were not themselves treated unjustly but only suffered vicariously because of injustice to others, then even if in some conceivable way this should cost them their self-confidence and self-respect, they would deserve no compensation. The objection that vicarious suffering for injustice to others does not deserve compensation is thus well taken. The point is that the case we are considering is not a case of vicarious suffering for injustice to others.

II

Even if the force of all the preceding arguments is acknowledged, however, the case for preferential hiring is still not established at this point. For, while I have shown that the qualified members of groups which have been generally discriminated against deserve some compensation, I have not shown that the compensation they deserve is preferential hiring.

This issue raises two different questions. First, given that qualified minorities do deserve some compensation, why is preferential hiring the best form of compensation for them? Second, even if preferential hiring of qualified minorities is best for them, is it best or even justifiable overall? What, for example, about the costs to general productivity? Or to excellence? Most of all, perhaps, what about the costs to the young white males who will be displaced in favor of minorities? Why should the burden of compensation be placed on their shoulders alone?

Professor Thomson has already given, I think, the main answer to the first difficulty. She argues persuasively that "what blacks and women were denied was full membership in the community; and nothing can more appropriately make amends for that wrong than precisely what will make them feel they now finally have it. And that means jobs. Financial compensation . . . slips through the fingers; having a job, and discovering you do it well, yield— perhaps better than anything else—that very self-respect which blacks and women have had to do without."[25] It is only necessary to add perhaps that particularly in the case of the qualified is it appropriate that their compensation be jobs. For by the very fact that they have taken the trouble to become qualified they show that what they want is jobs, or at least, that they are fully prepared and anxious to get jobs. Though it may be generally true that jobs will make those previously excluded finally feel that they are "part of

[25] Thomson, "Preferential Hiring," p. 38.

it," it need not be generally true, that all those previously excluded will want jobs. Some may prefer "financial compensation."

But, even though it may be admitted that getting and keeping a job is an excellent thing for the self-respect and self-esteem of qualified members of minority groups—for having a job helps a person to feel he is contributing his "fair share" and, if he discovers that he does it well, also helps him to recognize and appreciate his powers—the question has been raised whether getting and keeping a job *because of preferential hiring* may not undermine self-respect. Thus Barry Gross writes that the beneficiary of preferential hiring "may come to feel himself inferior." Thomas Nagel warns that preferential hiring "cannot do much for the self-esteem of those who know they have benefited from it, and it may threaten the self-esteem of those in the favored group who would in fact have gained their positions even in the absence of the discriminatory policy, but who cannot be sure that they are not among its beneficiaries." Thomas Sowell cautions that though "here and there, this program has undoubtedly caused some individuals to be hired who would otherwise not have been hired . . . even that is a doubtful gain in the larger context of attaining self-respect and the respect of others."[26]

Though evidently closely related, these objections are not all quite the same. Gross' objection, for example, seems to be that a person preferentially hired for a job for which he is incompetent or who is outclassed by his colleagues will come to feel inferior. This is true but irrelevant, for preferential hiring does not require that incompetents be hired or that a candidate be hired who will be outclassed by his colleagues. The points made by Nagel and Sowell overlap but raise two distinct difficulties. On the one hand, the difficulty may be that the beneficiary of preferential hiring may lose self-respect because he may fear that he is getting what he does not deserve. I admit that a person who accepts what he knows he does not deserve (or have a right to) and knows he is taking away from someone more deserving acts in opposition to his self-respect and in trying to rationalize his act, may come to compromise and lose his self-respect. But I deny that this is relevant here. For the major conclusion of all the preceding arguments is that though the preferred candidate may be less excellently qualified than another candidate, he must still overall be the most deserving. Given this, the present difficulty does not arise. On the other hand, the difficulty may be that though the preferred candidate knows that he is overall the most deserving, he may still feel uneasy and compromised because he knows he is not the most qualified or, at least, he does not know that he is the most qualified. This difficulty is quite different from the previous one. Here, the preferred candidate knows his deserts and that he is the most deserving. What he would like to be reassured about are his qualifications. This does not, however, argue against preferential hiring.

---

[26] See Gross, "Is Turn About Fair Play?" p. 383; Nagel, "Equal Treatment and Compensatory Discrimination," *Equality and Preferential Treatment,* p. 17; Sowell, "Affirmative Action Reconsidered," *Reverse Discrimination,* p. 130.

For suppose preferential hiring is not instituted and that as a result more qualified but perhaps less deserving candidates are routinely hired. What about their self-respect and self-esteem? Shouldn't *they* feel their self-respect jeopardized for filling jobs others deserve more? Since this is evidently a more serious worry than the more deserving person's worry, on this point too, preferential hiring is not unjustified.

Having shown that there is every reason to believe that preferential hiring is the best form of compensatory treatment for qualified minorities and that they would suffer no severe penalties to self-respect and self-esteem from it, I turn to the question whether it is best or justifiable overall. But I shall not spend much time on the question of its costs to efficiency or excellence.[27] I shall concentrate instead on the objection that preferential hiring is unjustified because it puts all the burden of compensation on the white male applicant.

Here again I think that Professor Thomson has proceeded in the right way. She admits first that there is no reason why the young white male applicants should bear the major costs of compensating, but then argues that though few of these have "themselves individually, done any wrongs to blacks and women . . . ," because "they have profited from the wrongs the community did" there is reason why they should bear some of the costs of compensation. In opposing the second part of her argument, Simon objects to her "assumption that if someone gains from an unjust practice for which he is not responsible and even opposes, the gain is not his and can be taken from him without injustice."[28] What he fails to notice, however, is that if his objection stands, it just may turn out that no one should have to bear the costs of compensation and thus no compensation should be given. For though it is probably not true of actual societies, it is quite possible to conceive of a society some of whose members have gained at the expense of others because of earlier unjust practices, but none of whose members now have any responsibility for these practices. In such a society all of the beneficiaries of injustice would be analogous to the young white male applicants, and if Simon is right, those who have suffered losses because of the earlier injustice have no claim to compensation. It is important therefore to consider carefully the claim that the innocent beneficiaries of injustice owe no obligation of compensation to those from whose unfair losses they have profited.

Few of its proponents, however, have offered a sustained argument for it. Blackstone, for example, says simply that the fact that the white male applicant has profited from past injustice is "inadequate" ground to exact compensation from him, and Simon seems to argue mainly for the minor point that if the white male applicant has himself suffered from some unjust social practice then it is "questionable" whether he owes anyone compensation.[29] Fullinwider,

[27] On this question see, for example, Richard Wasserstrom, "The University and the Case for Preferential Treatment," *American Philosophical Quarterly,* 13, No. 2 (April 1976), 165.

[28] Thomson, "Preferential Hiring," p. 38; Simon, "Preferential Hiring: A Reply," p. 46.

[29] Blackstone, "Reverse Discrimination and Compensatory Justice," p. 269; Simon, "Preferential Hiring: A Reply," p. 46.

however, has attempted a more thorough treatment. Conceding first what he calls the compensation principle—"he who wrongs another shall pay for the wrong"—he accuses Professor Thomson of confusing it with the "suspect" principle—"he who benefits from a wrong shall pay for the wrong." To clinch the point, Fullinwider asks us to consider the followng ingenious example. A neighbor pays a construction company to pave his driveway, but someone maliciously directs the workmen to pave Fullinwider's driveway instead. Fullinwider admits that his neighbor has been "wronged and damaged" and that he himself has "benefited from the wrong." However, since he is not responsible for the wrong, he denies that he is "morally required to compensate" his neighbor by "paying" him for it.[30]

This example makes us see that not all cases where compensation may be due are straightforward, though one kind of case clearly is. If John steals Jeff's bicycle and "gives" it to me, however innocent I may be, I have no right to it and must return it to Jeff as soon as I discover the theft. Given that this kind of example is unproblematic, in what way does it differ from Fullinwider's, which is problematic?

One difference is that whereas I can simply hand over Jeff's bicycle to him, Fullinwider cannot simply hand over the pavement in his driveway. It will be objected that the proposal was not that Fullinwider should hand over the pavement, but that he should pay his neighbor for it. But now the case has been changed. I did not say that I had a duty to pay Jeff the cost of his bicycle. I said that I had a duty to return the bicycle to Jeff. If Jeff told me to keep the bicycle but pay him for it, I do not admit that I would have a duty to do so. I could fairly object that when I accepted the bicycle I did not believe that I would have to pay for it, and if I had thought that I would have to, I might not have accepted it. Paying for the bicycle now would impose a cost on me because I might have preferred to spend my money in a different way and, being innocent of any wrongdoing, I see no reason why I should be penalized. The point is that though the beneficiary of an injustice has no right to his advantage, if he is innocent of the injustice, he does not deserve to be penalized. Thus, where compensation is concerned, the obligations of the innocent beneficiary of injustice and of the person responsible for the injustice are quite different. Though the former has no right to his benefits, the obligation of compensation cannot impose any losses on him over and above the loss of his unfair benefits. If compensation is impossible without such loss, it is unjustified. On the other hand, in the case of the person responsible for injustice, even if compensation requires him to give up more than he has unfairly gained, it is still justified.

But though Fullinwider's example is cogent as far as it goes, it is irrelevant as an argument against preferential hiring. It is cogent as far as it goes because, as the above analysis shows, requiring young white males to pay women and minorities all the unfair advantages they enjoyed would indeed be unfair. The

---

[30] Fullinwider, "Preferential Hiring and Compensation," *Social Theory and Practice,* 3 (1975), 316, 317.

advantages cannot simply be transferred from their hands into those of the preferred group as in my example of the bicycle. Compensation of this form would impose on young white males costs in time and effort over and above the costs of the unfair advantages they are required to return. They could with justice protest that they are being penalized becaue they might not have accepted the advantages had they known what it would cost them—now they are "out" both the advantages plus their time and effort. But though cogent, this argument is irrelevant to preferential hiring. Preferential hiring does not require young white males to pay over, at additional costs to themselves, the price of their advantages. It proposes instead to compensate the injured with goods no one yet has established a right to and in a way, therefore, which imposes no unfair losses on anyone. And these goods are, of course, jobs.

To that it may be objected that although a white male applicant may not have established a right to this or that job, he has a right to a fair competition for it, and preferential hiring violates that right. But on the contrary, by refusing to allow him to get the job because of an unfair advantage, preferential hiring makes the competition fairer. The white male applicant can still complain, of course, that had he known that preferential hiring would be instituted, he would not have accepted his advantages in the first place. Since, if he knew that preferential hiring would be instituted, he would necessarily also have known that his advantages were unfair, his complaint amounts to his saying that had he known his advantages were unfair, he would not have accepted them. But then, if he is so concerned with fairness, and if preferential hiring makes the competition fairer, he should have no objections to it. Or somewhat less contentiously, preferential hiring imposes no unfair losses on him.

Thus, a fairer application of Fullinwider's example of the driveway to preferential hiring would go as follows: Suppose an "improve your neighborhood group" offered a valuable prize for the best driveway on the block. Would Fullinwider, though he is totally innocent of his unfair advantage, be justified in insisting that he deserves to get the prize over his neighbor who has, at further cost to himself, built another somewhat inferior driveway? If someone objects that jobs are not analogous to prizes, suppose a visitor wants to rent a driveway on the block to park his car, would Fullinwider be justified in insisting that he most *deserves* to have his driveway chosen? Of course, Fullinwider can still truly point out that his driveway is the best, and perhaps if efficiency alone were the consideration, it ought to be chosen. But laying aside efficiency as I have, it is clear that it is the neighbor who most deserves that his driveway be chosen.

III

In Part I, I considered one set of objections to preferential hiring: that it compensates those who do not deserve it. At bottom these objections failed, because those who proposed them focused their attentions too exclusively on how much more fortunately placed the black middle class is than the black lower class. This made it seem as if members of the black middle class were absolutely advantaged. From being least harmed of blacks, it came to seem as if they were not appreciably harmed or not harmed at all. For balance, why not compare the black middle class with the white middle class?

Why shouldn't the black community have a vigorous and prosperous middle class as does the white community? Certainly it is a great tradition in western political philosophy that the stability and progress of a community depends on its having such a class. On the other hand, it may be, of course, as another tradition in western political philosophy has it, that there should be no classes at all. But that is another debate.[31]

In Part II, I took up the objections against preferential hiring as a form of compensation, the most troubling of which was that young white men are compelled to bear the major costs of compensation. I admitted this point but argued that preferential hiring does not require it. What preferential hiring requires is that young white males bear some of the costs of compensation. Here I showed that though they may be innocent of wrongdoing against women and blacks, because they have had the advantage of such wrongdoing, it is not unjustified that they bear some of the costs. I conclude that no telling argument has been raised against preferential hiring.

AUTHOR'S NOTE: I am indebted to Gregory Kavka, Thomas Hill, Sidney Trivus, and Jan Boxill for comments on an earlier draft of this paper.

---

[31] On this see Thomas Nagel, "Equal Treatment and Compensatory Discrimination"; and Richard Wasserstrom, "Racism, Sexism and Preferential Treatment: An Approach to the Topics," *UCLA Law Review,* 24, No. 2 (Feb. 1977), 581–622.

SELECTED BIBLIOGRAPHY: PREFERENTIAL TREATMENT

Bayles, Michael. "Compensatory Reverse Discrimination in Hiring." *Social Theory and Practice,* 2:3 (1973), 301.

Black, Virginia. "The Erosion of Legal Principles in the Creation of Legal Policies." *Ethics,* 84:2 (1974), 93.

Blackstone, William T., and Robert D. Heslep (eds.). *Social Justice and Preferential Treatment.* Athens, Georgia: University of Georgia Press, 1977.

Cohen, Marshall, Thomas Nagel, and Thomas Scanlon (eds.). *Equality and Preferential Treatment.* Princeton, N.J.: Princeton University Press, 1977.

Davis, Michael. "Racial Quotas, Weights, and Real Possibilities: A Moral for Moral Theory." *Social Theory and Practice,* 7:1 (1981), 49.

Fullinwider, Robert K. *The Reverse Discrimination Controversy: A Moral and Legal Analysis.* Totowa, N.J.: Rowman and Littlefield, 1980.

Goldman, Alan H. *Justice and Reverse Discrimination.* Princeton, N.J.: Princeton University Press, 1979.

Gross, Barry (ed.). *Reverse Discrimination.* Buffalo, N.Y.: Prometheus Press, 1977.

Held, Virginia. "Reasonable Progress and Self-Respect." *The Monist,* 57 (1973), 12.

Massey, Stephen J. "Rethinking Affirmative Action." *Social Theory and Practice,* 7:1 (1981), 21.

Newton, Lisa H. "Reverse Discrimination As Unjustified." *Ethics,* 83:4 (1973), 308.

Sher, George. "Reverse Discrimination, the Future and the Past." *Ethics,* 90 (1979), 81.

Thalberg, Irving. "Reverse Discrimination and the Future." *Philosophical Forum,* 5:1–2 (1973–74), 263.

Wasserstrom, Richard A. "Preferential Treatment." In Richard A. Wasserstrom, *Philosophy and Social Issues: Five Studies.* Notre Dame, Ind.: University of Notre Dame Press, 1980.

THREE

Sexual Morality

PETTIT v. STATE BOARD OF EDUCATION
10 C.3D 29; 109 CAL.RPTR. 665, 513 P.2D 889 (1973)

BURKE, J. In this case we are asked to review a judgment denying plaintiff mandate to vacate an order of the State Board of Education revoking her elementary school life diploma on the ground that she engaged in certain acts of sexual misconduct evidencing her unfitness to teach. We have concluded that the conduct complained of furnished ample ground to support the order of revocation.

Plaintiff is an elementary school teacher, having held a California teaching credential since 1957. According to the record, in November 1967 plaintiff (then 48 years old) and her husband applied for membership in "The Swingers," a private club in Los Angeles evidently devoted primarily to promoting diverse sexual activities between members at club parties. Sergeant Berk, an undercover officer working for the Los Angeles Police Department, investigated the club, was accepted for membership, and, on December 2, 1967, attended a party at a private residence during which he observed the incidents in question. According to Berk, he entered the residence where the party was held and immediately observed a man and woman (not plaintiff) engaged in sexual intercourse in an open bedroom. Throughout the evening Sergeant Berk saw various other couples similarly engaged. Berk estimated that there were 20 persons at the party, some of whom were "walking around the residence observing people engaged in these [sexual] acts." In a one-hour period, Berk observed plaintiff commit three separate acts of oral copulation with three different men at the party. When these acts took place, the participants were undressed, and there were other persons looking on.

Plaintiff was subsequently arrested and charged with violating Penal Code Section 288a (oral copulation). Evidently a plea bargain was arranged and plaintiff pleaded guilty to Penal Code section 650½ (outraging public decency), a misdemeanor. Plaintiff was fined and placed on probation; upon payment of the fine probation was terminated and the criminal proceedings dismissed.

Subsequently, in February 1970, the disciplinary proceedings now before us were initiated to revoke plaintiff's teaching credential on the grounds (among others) that her conduct involved moral turpitude and demonstrated her unfitness to teach. At the board hearing, Sergeant Berk testified as summarized above. In addition, three elementary school superintendents testified that in their opinion plaintiff's conduct disclosed her unfitness to teach.[1] Plaintiff did not testify at the hearing. However, her husband testified, among other things, that plaintiff realized in advance that sexual activities would occur at the Swingers Club party, and that with her consent he had observed plaintiff engage in sexual intercourse and oral copulation with other men in the past. Mr. Pettit also testified that he and plaintiff had, in 1966, appeared on the Joe Pyne television show and also another similar show a few weeks later, and had on both occasions discussed "nonconventional sexual life styles." Mr. Pettit recalled that the subjects of adultery and "wife swapping" were discussed and that "probably" the Pettits expressed a "philosophic" attitude on those subjects since they were not "uptight" about them. Although plaintiff and her husband wore a mask and false beard respectively on these shows, Superintendent Calton testified that one of plaintiff's fellow teachers had discussed plaintiff's televised statements with him and with other teachers.

Dr. William Hartman testified on plaintiff's behalf. Dr. Hartman is a licensed clinical psychologist, a professor of sociology, and a director of center for marital and sexual studies. He had also known plaintiff socially for several years prior to the hearing. According to Hartman, plaintiff was well-adjusted, and in view of the trauma and emotional turmoil caused by her suspension, was not likely to repeat the prior offenses. Hartman disputed the testimony of the board's witnesses that the nature of the sexual misconduct involved herein would render plaintiff unfit to teach.

Plaintiff introduced an evaluation by her school principal finding her teaching to be satisfactory and commenting upon her classes' progress and improvement. Plaintiff also introduced a contract of employment with her school district offering to rehire her for the 1968–1969 school year. The record is

---

[1] William B. Calton, superintendent of the Cypress School District which employed plaintiff, testified that a person who committed the sexual acts performed by plaintiff would be unfit to teach in an elementary school. In Calton's opinion, a teacher has the responsibility to practice as well as teach moral values; one who failed to practice morality would have difficulty teaching it. Since pupils look to their teacher for moral guidance, plaintiff would lose her effectiveness and ability as a teacher and might even inject her ideas regarding sexual morals into the classroom.

Sylvester A. Moffett, superintendent of the Huntington Beach City Schools, testified that in his opinion plaintiff was unfit to teach, that every teacher should possess high morals, and that it would be difficult to teach morality without practicing it.

Archie J. Haskins, assistant superintendent of the Magnolia School District, testified that one who engaged in the sexual conduct performed by plaintiff would be unfit to instruct elementary school children. According to Haskins, a teacher must set a good moral example for her pupils, for she spends much time with them and has a strong influence over them.

unclear, however, as to when her employer first learned of her Swingers Club activities.

At the conclusion of the hearing, the hearing examiner found that plaintiff had engaged in acts of sexual intercourse and oral copulation with men other than her husband; that plaintiff appeared on television programs while facially disguised and discussed nonconventional sexual behavior, including wife swapping; that although plaintiff's services as a teacher have been "satisfactory," and although she is unlikely to repeat the sexual misconduct, nevertheless she has engaged in immoral and unprofessional conduct, in acts involving moral turpitude, and in acts evidencing her unfitness for service. Accordingly, the hearing examiner concluded that cause exists for the revocation of her life diploma. The board adopted the findings and conclusions of its hearing officer in toto.

Thereafter, plaintiff sought a writ of mandate from the superior court to review and set aside the board's order. (Code Civ. Proc., § 1094.5.) The court, exercising its independent judgment of the evidence,[2] likewise concluded that proper cause existed to revoke plaintiff's teaching credentials and denied mandate.[3] Plaintiff appeals.

The Education Code contains the provisions governing revocation of a teacher's life diploma or credential. Section 13202 provides in pertinent part that the board "shall revoke or suspend for immoral or unprofessional conduct . . . or for any cause which would have warranted the denial of an application for a certification document or the renewal thereof, or for evident unfitness for service, ..." Among the various statutory grounds for denial of an application for a credential or life diploma, or renewal thereof, are the commission of an act involving moral turpitude and the failure to furnish reasonable evidence of good moral character. (Former § 13129, subds. (e) and (h), now § 13174, subds. (e) and (h).) Finally, *conviction* of various penal offenses, including Penal Code section 288a, is likewise ground for revocation

---

[2] See *Morrison* v. *State Board of Education,* 1 Cal.3d 214, 240, and footnote 51 [82 *Cal.Rptr.* 175, 461 P.2d 375].

[3] The trial court noted that the acts "undeniably committed" by plaintiff were criminal in nature, and were committed in a place where 16 to 20 persons were present. The court also referred to plaintiff's television appearance and the fact that teachers and others on the school staff had learned of them. The court believed that although the opinions of the three school superintendents may not be entitled to great weight, nevertheless they are some evidence of plaintiff's unfitness. In concluding, the court explained the primary basis for its ruling as follows: "The intimate and delicate relationships between teachers and students require that teachers be held to standards of morality in their private lives that may not be required of others. Parents have the right to demand high standards of conduct in the personal lives of the teachers of their children, and should have the right to expect that the teachers' concepts of morals and sexual relationships not be at substantial variance with concepts that are generally accepted and approved in the community, and that they not engage in conduct which is proscribed by the criminal laws of this state. It should not be necessary for such unacceptable conduct to manifest itself in the classroom before the Board may, in the best interests of the educational system and of the students, revoke the teaching credentials of one who has evidenced such a disregard of the accepted standards of moral conduct and of the criminal statutes."

of a life diploma or credential (§ 13206; see also § 13207 [conviction of sex offenses]; § 12912 [definition of sex offenses]; *DiGenova* v. *State Board of Education,* 45 Cal.2d 255 [288 P.2d 862].)

As stated above, plaintiff was not convicted of the offense of oral copulation but of the misdemeanor offense of outraging public decency, an offense not specified in the foregoing sections as sufficient per se to justify revocation. Therefore, revocation of plaintiff's life diploma cannot be upheld solely by reason of conviction entered against her.[4] On the other hand, plaintiff has never denied that the acts of oral copulation took place. Accordingly, we must determine whether the trial court properly concluded that plaintiff's conduct constituted "immoral or unprofessional conduct," "evident unfitness to teach," "acts involving moral turpitude," or acts evidencing a lack of "good moral character" within the meaning of the code sections set forth above.

In *Morrison* v. *State Board of Education, supra,* 1 Cal.3d 214, this court was faced with the problem whether certain homosexual conduct by a public school teacher justified revocation under the above statutory language. A majority of the court concluded that, in order to save the statute from attack on vagueness grounds, a teacher's actions could not constitute "immoral or unprofessional conduct" or "moral turpitude" unless that conduct indicated an unfitness to teach. In view of the total lack of evidence in the record demonstrating Morrison's unfitness to teach, the court reversed the superior court's judgment denying mandate. We made it clear, however, that in future cases revocation will be upheld if the evidence discloses that the teacher's retention within the school system "poses a significant danger of harm to either students, school employees, or others who might be affected by his actions as a teacher." (P. 235.) The court suggested that a showing of significant "harm" could be based upon adverse inferences drawn from the teacher's past conduct as to his probable future teaching ability, as well as upon the likelihood that the publicity surrounding the past conduct "may in and of itself substantially impair his function as a teacher." (*Id.,* see *Comings* v. *State Bd. of Education,* 23 Cal.App.3d 94, 104 [100 *Cal.Rptr.* 73, 47 A.L.R.3d 742]; *Board of Trustees* v. *Stubblefield,* 16 Cal.App.3d 820, 826–827 [94 *Cal.Rptr.* 318].)

---

[4] Plaintiff and amici suggest that plaintiff's conviction under Penal Code section 650½ is invalid, because of the vagueness of that statute and its reference to "public decency" (see *In re Davis,* 242 Cal.App.2d 645 [51 *Cal.Rptr.* 702]), the assertedly "private" nature of the offenses in the instant case, or the "ruse" committed by Sergeant Berk in obtaining admission to the club. However, neither the board nor the trial court relied upon plaintiff's conviction itself as grounds for revocation, but upon her underlying *conduct* apart from the conviction.

Amici also call into question the validity of Penal Code section 288a, asserting that oral copulation is an activity protected by the constitutional rights of association and privacy. (But see *People* v. *Drolet,* 30 Cal.App.3d 207 [105 *Cal.Rptr.* 824]; *People* v. *Hurd,* 5 Cal.App.3d 865 [85 *Cal.Rptr.* 718]; *People* v. *Roberts,* 256 Cal.App.2d 488 [64 *Cal.Rptr.* 70].) Without deciding whether section 288a is valid in all of its various applications, we point out that plaintiff is not here seeking any relief from criminal prosecution for her sexual conduct, and accordingly the validity of section 288a is not before us. Instead, the sole question presented herein is whether the record contains sufficient evidence to sustain the trial court's determination that plaintiff's conduct rendered her unfit to teach.

Plaintiff contends that *Morrison* controls here and that the record contains no substantial evidence of her unfitness to teach. We disagree. Initially, we note several important factors which would distinguish *Morrison* from the instant case. In *Morrison,* the unspecified conduct at issue was noncriminal in nature, and the court was careful to point out that oral copulation was not involved. (1 Cal.3d at p. 218, fn. 4.) We further explained that under the Education Code a distinction was made between certain sex crimes (such as oral copulation) which require automatic revocation, and lesser sex offenses which result in "discipline only if it is 'immoral,' 'unprofessional' or involves 'moral turpitude.'" (*Id.* see *Purifoy* v. *State Board of Education,* 30 Cal.App.3d 187, 197 [106 *Cal.Rptr.* 201].)

A second distinguishing feature between *Morrison* and the instant case is, of course, that in *Morrison* the conduct at issue occurred entirely *in private* and involved only two persons, whereas plaintiff's indiscretions involved three different "partners," were witnessed by several strangers, and took place in the semi-public atmosphere of a club party.[5] Plaintiff's performance certainly reflected a total lack of concern for privacy, decorum or preservation of her dignity and reputation. Even without expert testimony, the board was entitled to conclude that plaintiff's flagrant display indicated a serious defect of moral character, normal prudence and good common sense. A further indication that plaintiff lacked that minimum degree of discretion and regard for propriety expected of a public school teacher is disclosed by her television appearances, giving notoriety to her unorthodox views regarding sexual morals. As noted above, apparently plaintiff's disguise was not wholly effective for she was recognized by at least one teacher at plaintiff's school.

Finally, in *Morrison* the board acted without sufficient evidence of unfitness to teach. In the instant case, in addition to the evidence of plaintiff's misconduct itself and its criminal and semi-public nature, the board heard expert testimony asserting plaintiff's unfitness to teach. Unlike *Morrison,* wherein we noted that "The board produced no testimony from school officials or others to indicate whether a man such as petitioner might publicly advocate improper conduct" (1 Cal.3d at p. 236), in the instant case three school administrators gave their opinion that plaintiff is unfit to teach (see fn. 1, *ante*). In general, these witnesses expressed concern that plaintiff might attempt to inject her views regarding sexual morality into the classroom or into her private discussions with her pupils, and that plaintiff would be unable effectively to act as a moral example for the children she taught. Plaintiff attacks this testimony as reflecting only the personal opinions of the witnesses regarding unorthodox sexual mores,[6] yet the testimony goes further and calls

[5] Various cases have emphasized the significance of the public nature of a teacher's misconduct, or the notoriety and publicity accorded it. (See *Moser* v. *State Bd. of Education,* 22 Cal.App.3d 988, 990–991 [101 *Cal.Rptr.* 86]; *Watson* v. *State Bd. of Education,* 22 Cal.App.3d 559, 564 [99 *Cal.Rptr.* 468]; *Comings* v. *State Bd. of Education, supra,* 23 Cal.App.3d 94, 105–106; *Board of Trustees* v. *Stubblefield, supra,* 16 Cal.App.3d 820, 826.)

[6] As noted above (fn. 3), the trial court found that, the superintendents' testimony, although not entitled to "great weight," did constitute some evidence of unfitness to teach.

into question plaintiff's fitness to teach moral principles. Expert testimony is necessarily based to an extent upon the personal opinion of the witness, supported by his special education and experience. (1) We see no reason for discrediting the opinion of a school superintendent regarding the fitness of teachers to teach merely because that opinion is based in part upon personal moral views. Many courts have recognized that testimony by other teachers or school administrators may furnish the necessary evidence of unfitness to teach required by *Morrison.* (See *Board of Trustees* v. *Metzger,* 8 Cal.3d 206, 210 [104 *Cal.Rptr.* 452, 501 P.2d 1172]; *Governing Board* v. *Brennan,* 18 Cal.App.3d 396, 402 [95 *Cal.Rptr.* 712]; *Comings* v. *State Bd. of Education, supra,* 23 Cal.App.3d 94, 105–106.)

As noted above, the board's witnesses testified that in their opinion it was likely that plaintiff would be unable to set a proper example for her pupils or to teach moral principles to them. Yet it is the statutory duty of a teacher to "endeavor to impress upon the minds of the pupils the principles of morality . . . and to instruct them in manners and morals. . . . " (Ed. Code, § 13556.5.) Accordingly, several cases have held that the inability of a teacher to obey the laws of this state or otherwise to act in accordance with traditional moral principles may constitute sufficient ground for revocation or dismissal. (See *Watson* v. *State Bd. of Education, supra,* 22 Cal.App.3d 559, 564–565 [alcoholic teacher with record of drunken driving]; *Governing Board* v. *Brennan, supra,* 18 Cal.App.3d 396, 402 [teacher advocated illegal marijuana use]; *Board of Trustees* v. *Stubblefield, supra,* 16 Cal.App.3d 820, 824–826 [teacher was found in compromising position with student, assaulted police officer and resisted arrest]; *Sarac* v. *State Bd. of Education,* 249 Cal.App.2d 58, 63–64 [57 *Cal.Rptr.* 69] [disapproved on other grounds in *Morrison* v. *State Board of Education, supra,* 1 Cal.3d 214, 238; teacher made homosexual advance toward police officer at public beach]; *Vogulkin* v. *State Board of Education,* 194 Cal.App.2d 424, 429–430 [15 *Cal.Rptr.* 335] [teacher convicted of unspecified sex offense].)

As this court stated in *Board of Education* v. *Swan,* 41 Cal.2d 546, 552 [261 P.2d 261], "A teacher . . . in the public school system is regarded by the public and pupils in the light of an exemplar, whose words and actions are likely to be followed by the children coming under her care and protection." (2) In the instant case, the board and the trial court were entitled to conclude, on the basis of the expert testimony set forth above and the very nature of the misconduct involved, that Mrs. Pettit's illicit and indiscreet actions disclosed her unfitness to teach in public elementary schools.[7]

The judgment is affirmed.

---

[7] Plaintiff points to the finding of the board that she is unlikely to repeat the misconduct which led to her suspension. Yet the "risk of harm" which justified revocation of plaintiff's license in this case is not the likelihood that plaintiff will perform additional sexual offenses but instead that she will be unable to teach moral principles, to act as an exemplar for her pupils, or to offer them suitable moral guidance.

WRIGHT, C. J., McCOMB, J., SULLIVAN, J., and CLARK, J., concurred.

TOBRINER, J. For the past 13 years plaintiff has taught mentally retarded elementary school children, a task requiring exceptional skill and patience. Throughout her career her competence has been unquestioned; not a scintilla of evidence suggests that she has ever failed properly to perform her professional responsibilities. One can ask for no better proof of fitness to teach than this record of consistent, capable performance.

Yet in the face of this record, the State Board of Education, branding plaintiff "unfit," revokes her elementary school life diploma—a ruling that will not only force her discharge from her present employment, but, regardless of the need for a teacher of her experience and qualifications, will also bar any school district in California from hiring her. Looking only to the loss of future earnings, we must recognize that the board inflicts a penalty of well over $100,000; the ruling, moreover, entails immeasurably greater psychological damage. Equally immeasurable is the loss to school districts that are denied the right to employ a skilled and dedicated teacher.

One would expect that before inflicting such injury, the board would insist upon solid and credible evidence that clearly established plaintiff's lack of fitness to teach. Instead, as I shall show, the board has acted on the basis of questionable conjecture.[1]

Our analysis of the issues in this case must begin with *Morrison* v. *State Board of Education* (1969) 1 Cal.3d. 214 [82 *Cal.Rptr.* 175, 461 P.2d 375], an opinion of this court that defines the showing required for a revocation of teaching credentials. That decision recognized the general proposition that no person may be barred from a profession upon grounds unrelated to his fitness to perform his professional obligations. (See *Board of Trustees* v. *Metzger* (1972) 8 Cal.3d 206, 210 [104 *Cal.Rptr.* 452, 501 P.2d 1172]; *Nightingale* v. *State Personnel Board* (1972) 7 Cal.3d 507, 512 [102 *Cal.Rptr.* 758, 498 P.2d 1006]; *Monroe* v. *Trustees of the California State Colleges* (1971) 6 Cal.3d 399, 412 [99 *Cal.Rptr.* 129, 491 P.2d 1105]; *Perrine* v. *Municipal Court* (1971) 5 Cal.3d 656, 663 [97 *Cal.Rptr.* 320, 488 P.2d 648].)

Morrison had engaged in a single incident of homosexual activity involving another teacher. Concluding that this activity constituted "immoral conduct," "unprofessional conduct," and "acts involving moral turpitude" under Education Code section 13202, the State Board of Education revoked his life diploma. On appeal, Morrison contended that the vagueness of the standards for revocation set out in section 13202 would permit the board to discipline a teacher merely because his private, personal conduct affronted the moral views of the board members.

---

[1] In proceedings for the disbarment of attorneys or for the revocation of real estate licenses, the courts have held that "guilt must be established to a reasonable certainty . . . and cannot be based on surmise or conjecture, suspicion or theoretical conclusions, or uncorroborated hearsay." (*Small* v. *Smith* (1971) 16 Cal.App.3d 450, 457 [94 *Cal.Rptr.* 136].) The same degree of proof should be required for the revocation of a teaching certificate.

To avoid finding section 13202 unconstitutional, we adopted a limited construction of that statute, holding that its "terms denote immoral or un-professional conduct or moral turpitude of the teacher which indicates un-fitness to teach." (1 Cal.3d at p. 225.) Specifically, we held that "an individual can be removed from the teaching profession only upon a showing that his retention in the profession poses a significant danger of harm to either students, school employees, or others who might be affected by his action as a teacher." (1 Cal.3d at p. 235.)

We then turned to the question whether proof of Morrison's homosexual conduct in itself constituted evidence of unfitness to teach. We stated: "Before the board can conclude that a teacher's continued retention in the profession presents a significant danger of harm to students or fellow teachers, essential factual premises in its reasoning should be supported by evidence or official notice. In this case, despite the quantity and quality of information available about human sexual behavior, the record contains no such evidence as to the significance and implications of the . . . incident. Neither this court nor the superior court is authorized to rectify this failure by uninformed speculation or conjecture as to petitioner's future conduct." (1 Cal.3d at p. 237). Concluding that no competent, credible evidence supported any inference of Morrison's unfitness to teach, we reversed the judgment of the superior court.

The majority opinion maintains that in the present case, unlike *Morrison,* substantial evidence supports the superior court's finding of unfitness to teach. They base this conclusion on three asserted differences between *Morrison* and the present case: that plaintiff's conduct was criminal in nature; that the acts occurred in a "semi-public atmosphere," and that the board presented expert opinion that she was unfit to teach. None of these distinctions will stand analysis.

Although the majority's whole case rests upon the proposition that one who engages in oral copulation commits a criminal act that constitutes "immoral or unprofessional conduct," the record does not show any such conviction for such offense by plaintiff. The majority likewise frankly concede that the "revocation of plaintiff's life diploma cannot be upheld solely by reason of the conviction [of outraging public decency] entered against her." (Majority opn., *ante,* p. 33.)[2] The record of that conviction, moreover, has been cleared from the books; it is no longer extant; those criminal proceedings have been dismissed. (See Pen. Code, § 1203.4.)

The board in the instant case has been driven to exhume an old and admitted indiscretion in order to lay the basis for the revocation of plaintiff's teaching credential. The challenged act was committed on December 2, 1967; the criminal proceedings were thereafter dismissed; subsequently, in February 1970—years later—the disciplinary proceedings were initiated. I am hard-

---

[2] I note that Penal Code section 650½, which declares the misdemeanor of outraging public decency, was held unconstitutional in *In re Davis* (1966) 242 Cal.App.2d 645 [51 *Cal.Rptr.* 702]. In any event plaintiff's conduct, which occurred in a private home rather than in "public," and offended no one present, could not fall within the terms of this statute.

put to understand the motivation of the board in bringing charges on a matter which plaintiff now recognizes as an indiscretion and for which she has paid the penalty—charges brought despite the fact that plaintiff has devoted 13 years to the exemplary and humane teaching of retarded elementary school children—charges designed to bar her permanently from teaching.

The kind of wastefulness of needed human resources that this procedure threatens becomes the more dangerous when we examine it in the context of other professions. If a highly proficient attorney commits an unorthodox sex act and thereafter suffers a misdemeanor conviction that is subsequently dismissed, may he then, years later, be disbarred because he admittedly committed the act and hence was guilty of "immoral" and "unprofessional" conduct? Should the skilled surgeon involved in a parallel situation suffer the same tragedy? The university professor? The danger of the majority's doctrine becomes especially onerous when we know that a large proportion of the younger generation do engage in unorthodox sexual activities deemed anathema by some members of the older generation. To what extent will we frustrate highly productive careers of younger persons in order to castigate conduct that is widely practiced by some but regarded by others as abominable? Is the legal standard to be no more definite or precise than that the involved practice is regarded as "immoral" or "unprofessional" or "tasteless" by judges?

The majority opinion does, indeed, proceed on the premise that plaintiff's failure to deny the act of oral copulation suffices to make her a confessed criminal and hence subject to cancellation of her certificate. On this ground the majority would distinguish *Morrison* because there the teacher's conduct infringed no penal statute. Yet in *Morrison* we expressly stated that "[i]n determining whether discipline is authorized and reasonable, a criminal conviction has no talismanic significance." (1 Cal.3d at p. 219, fn. 4.) This principle was recently reaffirmed by the Court of Appeal in *Comings* v. *State Bd. of Education* (1972) 23 Cal.App.3d 94 [100 *Cal.Rptr.* 73, 47 A.L.R.3d 742], which held that proof that a teacher had been convicted of possession of marijuana was not evidence of his unfitness to teach, and thus insufficient to sustain the revocation of a credential.

The principle that a criminal conviction is not ipso facto the basis for revocation of a certificate on the grounds of immoral or unprofessional conduct becomes clear when tested against specific acts of unlawful conduct. Obviously the commission of a misdemeanor, such as a traffic offense, could not seriously be urged as an automatic ground for revocation of a certificate. Convictions of other technical and legal offenses common in the society do not intrinsically constitute "immoral" or "unprofessional" conduct. Hence, in order to resolve the issue, we must examine the nature of the conduct and its relation, if any, to the role and functions of the teacher.

In the instant case the conduct involved consensual sexual behavior which deviated from traditional norms. Yet recognized authority tells us the practice pursued here is, indeed, quite common. An estimated "95 percent of adult

American men and a large percentage of American women have experienced orgasm in an illegal manner." (McCary, Human Sexuality (2d ed. 1973) p. 460.)[3] The 1953 Kinsey report, Sexual Behavior in the Human Female, at page 399 indicates that 62 percent of the adult women of plaintiff's educational level and age range engage in oral copulation; more recently, the report's co-authors have stated that newer studies suggest the figure now lies around 75 to 80 percent.[4]

The consensual and, as I shall explain, private act did not affect, and could not have affected, plaintiff's teaching ability. The whole matter would have been forgotten and lost in the limbo of the privacy of its occurrence if it had not been clandestinely observed by means of a surreptitious intrusion which reminds one of the surveillance of restrooms which this court has condemned. (*People* v. *Triggs* (1973) 8 Cal.3d 884 [106 *Cal.Rptr.* 408, 506 P.2d 232].) The commission of a sex act, surreptitiously observed, not disclosed to fellow teachers or to pupils, not remotely adversely affecting plaintiff's teaching ability, must fail to support revocation of the certificate even though the act is labelled "criminal" on the books.

I am at somewhat of a loss to understand the majority's second ground for distinguishing *Morrison:* that plaintiff's acts in the instant case took place in the "semi-public atmosphere of a club party." (Majority opn., *ante,* p. 35.) Recognizing that many sexual acts incur no disapprobation when done in private, yet are properly punishable when forced upon an unwilling and disapproving viewer, statutes and decisions distinguish between private acts and those which occur in a public place or are open to public observation. For this purpose, the defining characteristic of a public place (Pen. Code, § 647) is "annoyance to or the possibility of annoyance to members of the public present on premises where such acts are committed." (*In re Steinke* (1969) 2 Cal.App.3d 569, 576–577 [82 *Cal.Rptr.* 789].)

Plaintiff's acts occurred in the bedroom of a private home. The only persons witnessing the conduct were members of "The Swingers," a private club limited to persons who expressly attested their desire to view or engage in diverse sexual activity. Consequently, I conclude that plaintiff's acts occurred in a private place, not a public one or one open to public view.

By engaging in sexual activity in the presence of other "swingers," plaintiff, the majority assert, demonstrated "a serious defect of moral character, normal prudence and good common sense." (Majority opn., *ante,* p. 35.)[5] Yet plaintiff

---

[3] The Kinsey Reports (Kinsey, Pomeroy, and Martin, *Sexual Behavior in the Human Male* (1948); Kinsey, Pomeroy, Martin, and Gebhard, *Sexual Behavior in the Human Female* (1953)) remain the only large-scale studies.

[4] Testimony of Dr. William Hartman, professor of sociology at California State College, Long Beach, before the State Board of Education in the present proceeding.

[5] The majority's argument is analogous to that presented by the school board in *Fisher* v. *Snyder* (D.Neb. 1972) 346 F.Supp. 396, in which a teacher who permitted men to stay overnight in her apartment was discharged for "conduct unbecoming a teacher." Finding the discharge a violation of the teacher's constitutional right to freedom of association (see 346 F.Supp. at p. 400), the court stated that the evidence supplied "no proof of impropriety in Mrs. Fisher's conduct which affected her classroom performance, . . ." (346 F.Supp. at p. 398.) The court

took reasonable precautions to assure that she was viewed only by persons who would not be offended by her conduct; many would argue that under such circumstances her behavior was neither imprudent nor immoral. In essence, the majority are saying that even though her fellow "swingers" were not offended, they—the majority—find plaintiff's behavior shocking and embarrassing. Yet this important issue of plaintiff's right to teach should not turn on the personal distaste of judges, the test, as this court has announced in the cases, is the rational one of the effect of the conduct, if any, on the teacher's fitness to teach.

I turn now to an examination of the underlying expert testimony presented to establish plaintiff's unfitness to teach. The first witness, William B. Calton, opined that plaintiff would be unable to teach "moral and spiritual principles." On cross-examination he limited this opinion to asserting that she would be unable to teach principles of sexual morality. But petitioner teaches retarded elementary school children, and, as Calton affirmed, her teaching duties do not encompass instruction on sexual morality. To sum up Calton's testimony: he states that plaintiff is unable to teach principles of sexual morality but that her teaching duties do not include the teaching of sexual morality.[6]

The second expert, Sylvester A. Moffet, testified with a broader brush. He stated that any teacher who ever engaged in sexual relations with anyone other than his lawful spouse was lacking in "clean morals," and thus could not instruct his students in "clean morals." In *Morrison* we stated that "[s]urely incidents of extramarital heterosexual conduct against a background of years of satisfactory teaching would not constitute 'immoral conduct' sufficient to justify revocation of a life diploma without any showing of an adverse effect on fitness to teach." (1 Cal.3d at pp. 225–26.) Moffet obviously disagrees, and would raise a standard that would furnish grounds for dismissal of innumerable teachers of this state.

The final expert, Archie Haskins, advanced an idiosyncratic definition of a "dishonest marriage;" honesty, to him, is not a matter of truthfulness and open dealing, but of sexual fidelity. Reasoning from this personal premise, he concludes that petitioner's marriage is a dishonest one. On cross-examination Haskins added the interesting note that "possibly sixty or seventy

---

added that the evidence, at most, raised a question of her good judgment in her personal affairs, but that issue was not sufficient to indicate unfitness to teach.

[6] The majority opinion cites Education Code section 13556.5, which requires teachers to "endeavor to impress upon the minds of the pupils the principles of morality," and assumes this statute refers to orthodox sexual practices. The State Board of Education, however, has adopted regulations implementing this statute. Those regulations, which are too lengthy to quote here, make no mention of sexual practices, but define morality in terms of truthfulness, respect for the opinion of others, freedom of conscience, respect for personal and group differences, and appreciation of the contribution of religious heritage. This administrative interpretation of the statute "is entitled to great weight, and courts generally will not depart from such construction unless it is clearly erroneous or unauthorized." (*Coca-Cola Co.* v. *State Bd. of Equalization* (1945) 25 Cal.2d 918, 921 [156 P.2d 1]; *Meyer* v. *Board of Trustees* (1961) 195 Cal.App. 2d 420, 431 [15 *Cal.Rptr.* 717].) No evidence appears to suggest that plaintiff is unable to teach principles of honesty and respect for others.

percent of me would feel that she was unfit and thirty percent of me would feel that I would need to give her some latitude personally." Haskins, however, is willing to subordinate his personal doubts to that which he believes would be the desires of his school board; as he testified "I may have private opinions as a school administrator, but I have five people on the Board of Education that I report to, and again, depending on what you know about that board; how they feel . . . I would probably designate her as unfit."

As we said in *People* v. *Bassett* (1968) 69 Cal.2d 122, 141 [70 *Cal.Rptr.* 193, 443 P.2d 777]: " 'Expert evidence is really an argument of an expert to the court, and is valuable only in regard to the proof of the *facts* and the validity of the *reasons* advanced for the conclusions.' " (Quoting, with added italics, from *People* v. *Martin* (1948) 87 Cal.App.2d 581, 584 [197 P.2d 379].) The only "fact" mentioned by the experts was the incident at the "swingers' " party; this fact was already in the record; we have submitted that in itself, it is not proof of unfitness to teach. The experts present no *reasons* for their conclusions. None of them know plaintiff; none considered her 13-year record of competent teaching; none could point to a single instance of past misconduct with students, nor articulate the nature of any possible future misconduct.

It is not surprising that the trial court concluded that the experts' opinions were not entitled to "great weight." JUSTICE COBEY of the Court of Appeal put it even more accurately, holding that this expert opinion "does not reasonably inspire confidence nor is it of solid value."

The unproven premise of both the expert testimony and the majority opinion is that the fact of plaintiff's sexual acts at the "swingers' " party in itself demonstrates that she would be unable to set a proper example for her pupils or to teach them moral principles; this inability in turn demonstrates her unfitness to teach. This reasoning rests on factual assumptions concerning the relationship of consensual adult sexual behavior to classroom teaching which have absolutely no support in the evidence. If "immoral conduct" ipso facto shows inability to model or teach morals, and this in turn shows unfitness to teach, then we are left with the proposition that proof of "immoral conduct," whatever it may be, will always justify revocation of a teaching credential.

But in traveling this road the majority overlook constitutional predicates. Under the majority's interpretation of Education Code section 13202, the opinion of a superintendent that a teacher has committed an "immoral" act is sufficient to bar that teacher permanently from the profession; so interpreted, section 13202 would be unconstitutionally vague and overbroad. The concept of "immoral" conduct as enunciated by the majority roams without restraint. Undoubtedly some school superintendents believe the drinking of alcohol, the smoking of tobacco, or the playing of cards is immoral; others believe it immoral to serve in the military forces, and still others believe it immoral to refuse to serve. As the present case illustrates, there is a wide divergence of views on sexual morality; plaintiff did not believe her conduct immoral, and many would agree.[7] Since the statute, so interpreted, presents a vortex of vagueness, provides no warning of the kind of conduct that will lead to discipline, and establishes no standard by which the decision of the board can be measured, it is unconstitutionally vague.[8] These are the reasons why this court in *Morrison* concluded that the only viable test was the fitness of the teacher to teach.

In conclusion, I submit that the majority opinion is blind to the reality of sexual behavior. Its view that teachers in their private lives should exemplify Victorian principles of sexual morality, and in the classroom should subliminally indoctrinate the pupils in such principles, is hopelessly unrealistic and atavistic. The children of California are entitled to competent and dedicated teachers; when, as in this case, such a teacher is forced to abandon her lifetime profession, the children are the losers.

MOSK, J.   I dissent for the reasons thoughtfully and persuasively discussed by Justice Tobriner. I am also impressed with the cogent amici curiae argument presented, significantly, by two respected professional organizations: the National Education Association and the California Teachers' Association. And I note that a similar considered conclusion was reached by Justices Cobey and Schweitzer for the Court of Appeal.

In my opinion this court is conclusively bound by two unequivocal factual findings of the State Board of Education: that petitioner's "services as a teacher have been satisfactory and she was invited back to teach by the tender of a contract from her employer for the school year 1968–69" (*subsequent* to the incident involved herein); and that petitioner "is unlikely to repeat" the activities charged in the accusation.

In view of those controlling factual determinations the majority opinion is unsupportable.

---

[7] As JUSTICE SIMS observed in his concurring opinion in *Oakland Unified Sch. Dist.* v. *Olicker* (1972) 25 Cal.App.3d 1098, 1112 [102 *Cal.Rptr.* 421]: "[I]n this world there are many cultures and many concepts of what is acceptable sexual conduct, . . . It may be impossible to impose one strict moral code on all of society, and we may have to acquaint ourselves with, and accept, without puritanical prudery, as natural to them, the standards of others."

[8] I note that the United States District Court for the District of Oregon, in a recent decision, held an Oregon statute permitting the dismissal of teachers for "immorality" to be unconstitutionally vague. (*Burton* v. *Cascade School Dist.* (D.Ore. 1973) (353 F.Supp. 254.)

BETTER SEX

SARA L. RUDDICK

It might be argued that there is no specifically sexual morality. We have, of course, become accustomed to speaking of sexual morality, but the "morality" of which we speak has a good deal to do with property, the division of labor, and male power, and little to do with our sexual lives. Sexual experiences, like experiences in driving automobiles, render us liable to specific moral situations. As drivers we must guard against infantile desires for revenge and excitement. As lovers we must guard against cruelty and betrayal, for we know sexual experiences provide special opportunities for each. We drive soberly because, before we get into a car, we believe that it is wrong to be careless of life. We resist temptations to adultery because we believe it wrong to betray trust, whether it be a parent, a sexual partner, or a political colleague who is betrayed. As lovers and drivers we act on principles that are particular applications of general moral principles. Moreover, given the superstitions from which sexual experience has suffered, it is wise to free ourselves, as lovers, from any moral concerns, other than those we have as human beings. There is no specifically sexual morality, and none should be invented. Or so it might be argued.

When we examine our moral "intuitions," however, the analogy with driving fails us. Unburdened of *sexual* morality, we do not find it easy to apply general moral principles to our sexual lives. The "morally average" lover can be cruel, violate trust, and neglect social duties with less opprobrium precisely *because* he is a lover. Only political passions and psychological or physical deprivation serve as well as sexual desire to excuse what would otherwise be seriously and clearly immoral acts. (Occasionally, sexual desire is itself conceived of as a deprivation, an involuntary lust. And there is, of course, a tradition that sees sexual morality as a way of controlling those unable to be sexless: "It is better to marry than to burn.") Often, in our sexual lives, we neither flout nor simply apply general moral principles. Rather, the values of sexual experience themselves figure in the construction of moral dilemmas. The conflict between better sex (more complete, natural, and pleasurable sex acts) and, say, social duty is not seen as a conflict between the immoral and compulsive, on one hand, and the morally good, on the other, but as a conflict between alternative moral acts.

Our intuitions vary but at least they suggest we can use "good" sex as a positive weight on some moral balance. What is that weight? Why do we put

Reprinted with permission of the author. Copyright © 1975 by Sara L. Ruddick. The postscript has not been previously published.

AUTHOR'S NOTE: An earlier version of this paper was published in *Moral Problems,* edited by James Rachels (New York: Harper & Row, 1971). I am grateful to many friends and students for their comments on the earlier version, especially to Bernard Gert, Evelyn Fox Keller, and James Rachels.

it there? How do we, in the first place, evaluate sexual experiences? On reflection, should we endorse these evaluations? These are the questions whose answers should constitute a specifically sexual morality.

In answering them, I will first consider three characteristics that have been used to distinguish some sex acts as better than others—greater pleasure, completeness, and naturalness. Other characteristics may be relevant to evaluating sex acts, but these three are central. If they have *moral* significance, then the sex acts characterized by them will be better than others not so characterized.

After considering those characteristics in virtue of which some sex acts are allegedly better than others, I will ask whether the presence of those characteristics renders the acts *morally* superior. I will not consider here the unclear and overused distinction between the moral and the amoral, nor the illegitimate but familiar distinction between the moral and the prudent. I hope it is sufficient to set out dogmatically and schematically the moral notions I will use. I am confident that better sex is morally preferable to other sex, but I am not at all happy with my characterization of its moral significance. Ultimately, sexual morality cannot be considered apart from a "prudential" morality in which it is shown that what is good is good for us and what is good for us makes us good. In such a morality, not only sex, but art, fantasy, love, and a host of other intellectual and emotional enterprises will regain old moral significances and acquire new ones. My remarks here, then, are partial and provisional.

A characteristic renders a sex act morally preferable to one without that characteristic if it gives, increases, or is instrumental in increasing the "benefit" of the act for the person engaging in it. Benefits can be classified as peremptory or optional. Peremptory benefits are experiences, relations, or objects that anyone who is neither irrational nor anhedonic will want so long as s/he wants anything at all. Optional benefits are experiences, relations, or objects that anyone, neither irrational nor anhedonic, will want so long as s/he will not thereby lose a peremptory benefit. There is widespread disagreement about which benefits are peremptory. Self-respect, love, and health are common examples of peremptory benefits. Arms, legs, and hands are probably optional benefits. A person still wanting a great deal might give up limbs, just as s/he would give up life, when mutilation or death is required by self-respect. As adults we are largely responsible for procuring our own benefits and greatly dependent on good fortune for success in doing so. However, the moral significance of benefits is most clearly seen not from the standpoint of the person procuring and enjoying them but from the standpoint of another *caring* person, for example, a lover, parent, or political leader responsible for procuring benefits for specific others. A benefit may then be described as an experience, relation, or object that anyone who properly cares for another is obliged to attempt to secure for him/her. Criteria for the virtue of care and for benefit are reciprocally determined, the virtue consisting in part in recognizing and attempting to secure benefits for the person cared for, the identification of benefit depending on its recognition by those already seen to be properly caring.

In talking of benefits I shall be looking at our sexual lives from the vantage point of hope, not of fear. The principal interlocutor may be considered to be a child asking what s/he should rightly and reasonably hope for in living, rather than a potential criminal questioning conventional restraints. The specific question the child may be imagined to ask can now be put: In what way is better sex beneficial or conducive to experiences or relations or objects that are beneficial?

A characteristic renders a sex act morally preferable to one without that characteristic if either the act is thereby more just or the act is thereby likely to make the person engaging in it more just. Justice includes giving others what is due them, taking no more than what is one's own, and giving and taking according to prevailing principles of fairness.

A characteristic renders a sex act morally preferable to one without that characteristic if because of the characteristic the act is more virtuous or more likely to lead to virtue. A virtue is a disposition to attempt, and an ability to succeed in, good acts—acts of justice, acts that express or produce excellence, and acts that yield benefits to oneself or others.

SEXUAL PLEASURE

Sensual experiences give rise to sensations and experiences that are paradigms of what is pleasant. Hedonism, in both its psychological and ethical forms, has blinded us to the nature and to the benefits of sensual pleasure by overextending the word "pleasure" to cover anything enjoyable or even agreeable.[1] The paradigmatic type of pleasure is sensual. Pleasure is a temporally extended, more or less intense quality of particular experiences. Pleasure is enjoyable independent of any function pleasurable activity fulfills. The infant who continues to suck well after s/he is nourished, expressing evident pleasure in doing so, gives us a demonstration of the nature of pleasure.[2]

As we learn more about pleasant experiences we not only apply but also extend and attenuate the primary notion of "pleasure." But if pleasure is to have any nonsophistical psychological or moral interest, it must retain its connections with those paradigm instances of sensual pleasure that gives rise to it. We may, for example, extend the notion of pleasure so that particular episodes in the care of children give great pleasure; but the long-term caring

---

[1] This may be a consequence of the tepidness of the English "pleasant." It would be better to speak of lust and its satisfaction if our suspicion of pleasure had not been written into that part of our language.

[2] The example is from Sigmund Freud. *Three Essays on Sexuality,* standard ed., vol. 7 (London: Hogarth, 1963), p. 182. The concept of pleasure I urge here is narrower but also, I think, more useful than the popular one. It is a concept that, to paraphrase Wittgenstein, we (could) learn when we learn the language. The idea of paradigmatic uses and subsequent more-or-less-divergent, more-or-less-"normal" uses also is derived from Wittgenstein.

for children, however intrinsically rewarding, is not an experience of pleasure or unpleasure.

Sexual pleasure is a species of sensual pleasure with its own conditions of arousal and satisfaction. Sexual acts vary considerably in pleasure, the limiting case being a sexual act where no one experiences pleasure even though someone may experience affection or "relief of tension" through orgasm. Sexual pleasure can be considered either in a context of deprivation and its relief or in a context of satisfaction. Psychological theories have tended to emphasize the frustrated state of sexual desire and to construe sexual pleasure as a relief from that state. There are, however, alternative accounts of sexual pleasure that correspond more closely with our experience. Sexual pleasure is "a primary distinctively poignant pleasure experience that manifests itself from early infancy on. . . . Once experienced it continues to be savored. . . ."[3] Sexual desire is not experienced as frustration but as part of sexual pleasure. Normally, sexual desire transforms itself gradually into the pleasure that appears, misleadingly, to be an aim extrinsic to it. The natural structure of desire, not an inherent quality of frustration, accounts for the pain of an aroused but unsatisfied desire.

Sexual pleasure, like addictive pleasure generally, does not, except very temporarily, result in satiety. Rather, it increases the demand for more of the same while sharply limiting the possibility of substitutes. The experience of sensual pleasures, and particularly of sexual pleasures, has a pervasive effect on our perceptions of the world. We find bodies inviting, social encounters alluring, and smells, tastes, and sights resonant because our perception of them includes their sexual significance. Merleau-Ponty has written of a patient for whom "perception had lost its erotic structure, both temporally and physically."[4] As the result of a brain injury the patient's capacity for sexual desire and pleasure (though not his capacity for performing sexual acts) was impaired. He no longer sought sexual intercourse of his own accord, was left indifferent by the sights and smells of available bodies, and if in the midst of sexual intercourse his partner turned away, he showed no signs of displeasure. The capacity for sexual pleasure, upon which the erotic structure of perception depends, can be accidentally damaged. The question that this case raises is whether it would be desirable to interfere with this capacity in a more systematic way than we now do. With greater biochemical and psychiatric knowledge we shall presumably be able to manipulate it at will.[5] And if that becomes possible, toward what end should we interfere? I shall return

[3] George Klein, "Freud's Two Theories of Sexuality," in L. Berger, ed., *Clinical-Cognitive Psychology, Models and Integrations* (Englewood Cliffs, N.J.: Prentice-Hall, 1969), pp. 131–81. This essay gives a clear idea of alternative psychological accounts of sexual pleasure.

[4] Maurice Merleau-Ponty, *Phenomenology of Perception,* trans. Colin Smith (London: Routledge & Kegan Paul, 1962), p. 156.

[5] See Kurt Vonnegut, Jr., "Welcome to the Monkey House," in *Welcome to the Monkey House* (New York: Dell, 1968), which concerns both the manipulation and the benefit of sexual pleasure.

to this question after describing the other two characteristics of better sex—
completeness and naturalness.

COMPLETE SEX ACTS

The completeness of a sexual act depends upon the *relation* of the participants
to their own and each other's *desire*. A sex act is complete if each partner
allows him/herself to be "taken over" by an active desire, which is desire
not merely for the other's body but also for her/his active desire. Completeness is hard to characterize, though complete sex acts are at least as natural
as any others—especially, it seems, among those people who take them
casually and for granted. The notion of "completeness" (as I shall call it)
has figured under various guises in the work of Sartre, Merleau-Ponty, and
more recently Thomas Nagel. "The being which desires is consciousness
making itself body."[6] "What we try to possess, then, is not just a body, but
a body brought to life by consciousness."[7] "It is important that the partner
be aroused, and not merely aroused, but aroused by the awareness of one's
desire."[8]

The precondition of complete sex acts is the "embodiment" of the participants. Each participant submits to sexual desires that take over consciousness
and direct action. It is sexual desire and not a separable satisfaction of it (for
example, orgasm) that is important here. Indeed, Sartre finds pleasure external
to the essence of desire, and Nagel gives an example of embodiment in which
the partners do not touch each other. Desire is pervasive and "overwhelming,"
but it does not make its subject its involuntary victim (as it did the Boston
Strangler, we are told), nor does it, except at its climax, alter capacities for
ordinary perceptions, memories, and inferences. Nagel's embodied partners
can presumably get themselves from bar stools to bed while their consciousness
is "clogged" with desire. With what, then, is embodiment contrasted?

Philosophers make statements that when intended literally are evidence of
pathology: "Human beings are automata"; "I never really see physical objects"; "I can never know what another person is feeling." The clearest
statement of disembodiment that I know of is W. T. Stace's claim: "I become
aware of my body in the end chiefly because it insists on accompanying me
wherever I go."[9] What "just accompanies me" can also stay away. "When
my body leaves me/I'm lonesome for it./. . .body/goes away I don't know

[6] Jean-Paul Sartre, *Being and Nothingness*, trans. Hazel E. Barnes (New York: Philosophical
Library, 1956), p. 389.
[7] Merleau-Ponty, *Phenomenology of Perception*, p. 167.
[8] Thomas Nagel, "Sexual Perversion," *The Journal of Philosophy*, 66, no. 1 (January 16,
1969): 13. . . . My original discussion of completeness was both greatly indebted to and confused
by Nagel's. I have tried here to dispel some of the confusion.
[9] W. T. Stace, "Solipsism," from *The Theory of Knowledge and Existence;* reprinted in Tillman,
Berofsky, and O'Connor, eds. *Introductory Philosophy* (New York: Harper and Row, 1967),
p. 113.

where/and it's lonesome to drift/above the space it/fills when it's here." [10]
If "the body is felt more as one object among other objects in the world than
as the core of the individual's own being," [11] then what appears to be bodily
can be dissociated from the "real self." Both a generalized separation of "self"
from body and particular disembodied experiences have had their advocates.
The attempt at disembodiment has also been seen as conceptually confused
and psychologically disastrous.

We may often experience ourselves as relatively disembodied, observing or
"using" our bodies to fulfill our intentions. On some occasions, however,
such as in physical combat, sport, physical suffering, or danger, we "become"
our bodies; our consciousness becomes bodily experience of bodily activity. [12]
Sexual acts are occasions for such embodiment; they may, however, fail for
a variety of reasons, for example, because of pretense or an excessive need
for self-control. If someone is embodied by sexual desire, s/he submits to its
direction. Spontaneous impulses of desire become her/his movements—some
involuntary, like gestures of "courting behavior" or physical expressions of
intense pleasure, and some deliberate. Her/his consciousness, or "mind," is
taken over by desire and the pursuit of its object, in the way that at other
times it may be taken over by an intellectual problem or by obsessive fantasies.
But unlike the latter takeovers, this one is bodily. A desiring consciousness
is flooded with specifically sexual feelings that eroticize all perception and
movement. Consciousness "becomes flesh."

Granted the precondition of embodiment, complete sex acts occur when
each partner's embodying desire is active and actively responsive to the other's.
This second aspect of complete sex constitutes a "reflexive mutual recognition" of desire by desire. [13]

The partner *actively* desires another person's desire. Active desiring includes
more than embodiment, which might be achieved in objectless masturbation.
It is more, also, than merely being aroused by and then taken over by desire,
though it may come about as a result of deliberate arousal. It commits the
actively desiring person to her/his desire and requires her/him to identify
with it—that is, to recognize him/herself as a sexual agent as well as respondent. (Active desiring is less encouraged in women, and probably more
women than men feel threatened by it.)

The other recognizes and responds to the partner's desire. Merely to recognize the desire as desire, not to reduce it to an itch or to depersonalize it
as a "demand," may be threatening. Imperviousness to desire is the deepest

---

[10] Denise Levertov, "Gone Away," in *O Taste and See* (New York: New Directions, 1962),
p. 59. Copyright by Denise Levertov Goodman, New Directions Publishing Corporation, New
York.

[11] R. D. Laing, *The Divided Self* (Baltimore: Pelican Books, 1965), p. 69.

[12] We need not become our bodies on such occasions. Pains, muscular feelings, and emotions
can be reduced to mere "sensations" that may impinge on "me" but that I attempt to keep at
a distance. Laing describes the case of a man who when beaten up felt that any damage to his
body could not really hurt *him*. See *The Divided Self,* p. 68.

[13] Nagel, "Sexual Perversion," p. 254.

defense against it. We have learned from research on families whose members tend to become schizophrenic that such imperviousness, the refusal to recognize a feeling for what it is, can force a vulnerable person to deny or to obscure the real nature of her/his feelings. Imperviousness tends to deprive even a relatively invulnerable person of her/his efficacy. The demand that our feelings elicit a response appropriate to them is part of a general demand that *we* be recognized, that our feelings be allowed to make a difference.

There are many ways in which sexual desire may be recognized, countless forms of submission and resistance. In complete sex, desire is recognized by a responding and active desire that commits the other, as it committed the partner. Given responding desire, both people identify themselves as sexually desiring the other. They are neither seducer nor seduced, neither suppliant nor benefactress, neither sadist nor victim, but sexual agents acting sexually out of their recognized desire. Indeed, in complete sex one not only welcomes and recognizes active desire, one desires it. Returned and endorsed desire becomes one of the features of an erotically structured perception. Desiring becomes desirable. (Men are less encouraged to desire the other's active and demanding desire, and such desiring is probably threatening to more men than women.)

In sum, in complete sex two persons embodied by sexual desire actively desire and respond to each other's active desire. Although it is difficult to write of complete sex without suggesting that one of the partners is the initiator, while the other responds, complete sex is reciprocal sex. The partners, whatever the circumstances of their coming together, are equal in activity and responsiveness of desire.

Sexual acts can be partly incomplete. A necrophiliac may be taken over by desire, and one may respond to a partner's desire without being embodied by one's own. Partners whose sexual activities are accompanied by private fantasies engage in an incomplete sex act. Consciousness is used by desire but remains apart from it, providing it with stimulants and controls. Neither partner responds to the other's desire, though each may appear to. Sartre's "dishonest masturbator," for whom masturbation is the sex act of choice, engages in a paradigmatically incomplete sex act: "He asks only to be slightly distanced from his own body, only for there to be a light coating of otherness over his flesh and over his thoughts. His personae are melting sweets. . . . The masturbator is enchanted at never being able to feel himself sufficiently another, and at producing for himself alone the diabolic appearance of a couple that fades away when one touches it. . . . Masturbation is the derealisation of the world and of the masturbator himself."[14]

Completeness is more difficult to describe than incompleteness, for it turns on precise but subtle ways of responding to a particular person's desire with specific expressions of impulse that are both spontaneous and responsive.

---

[14] Jean-Paul Sartre, *Saint Genet* (New York: Braziller, 1963), p. 398; cited and translated by R. D. Laing, *Self and Others* (New York: Pantheon, 1969), pp. 39–40.

There are many possible sex acts that are pleasurable but not complete. Sartre, Nagel, and Merleau-Ponty each suggest that the desire for the responsive desire of one's partner is the "central impulse" of sexual desire.[15] The desire for a sleeping woman, for example, is possible only "in so far as this sleep appears on the ground of consciousness."[16] This seems much too strong. Some lovers desire that their partners resist, others like them coolly controlled, others prefer them asleep. We would not say that there was anything abnormal or less fully sexual about desire. Whether or not complete sex is preferable to incomplete sex (the question to which I shall turn shortly), incompleteness does not disqualify a sex act from being fully sexual.

SEXUAL PERVERSION

The final characteristic of allegedly better sex acts is that they are "natural" rather than "perverted." The ground for classifying sexual acts as either natural or unnatural is that the former type serve or could serve the evolutionary and biological function of sexuality—namely, reproduction. "Natural" sexual desire has as its "object" living persons of the opposite sex, and in particular their postpuberial genitals. The "aim" of natural sexual desire— that is, the act that "naturally" completes it—is genital intercourse. Perverse sex acts are deviations from the natural object (for example, homosexuality, fetishism) or from the standard aim (for example, voyeurism, sadism). Among the variety of objects and aims of sexual desire, I can see no other ground for selecting some as natural, except that they are of the type that can lead to reproduction.[17]

The connection of sexual desire with reproduction gives us the criterion but not the motive of the classification. The concept of perversion depends on a disjointedness between our experience of sexual desire from infancy on and the function of sexual desire—reproduction. In our collective experience of sexuality, perverse desires are as natural as nonperverse ones. The sexual desire of the polymorphously perverse child has many objects—for example, breasts, anus, mouth, genitals—and many aims—for example, autoerotic or other-directed looking, smelling, touching, hurting. From the social and developmental point of view, natural sex is an achievement, partly biological, partly conventional, consisting in a dominant organization of sexual desires in which perverted aims or objects are subordinate to natural ones. The concept of perversion reflects the vulnerability as much as the evolutionary warrant of this organization.

The connection of sexual desire with reproduction is not sufficient to yield the concept of perversion, but it is surely necessary. Nagel, however, thinks

---

[15] Ibid., p. 13.

[16] Sartre, *Being and Nothingness*, p. 386.

[17] See, in support of this point, Sigmund Freud, *Introductory Lectures on Psychoanalysis*, standard ed., vol. 26 (London: Hogarth, 1963), chaps. 20, 21.

otherwise. There are, he points out, many sexual acts that do not lead to reproduction but that we are not even inclined to call perverse—for example, sexual acts between partners who are sterile. Perversion, according to him, is a psychological concept while reproduction is (only?) a physiological one. (Incidentally, this view of reproduction seems to me the clearest instance of male bias in Nagel's paper.)

Nagel is right about our judgments of particular acts, but he draws the wrong conclusions from those judgments. The perversity of sex acts does not depend upon whether they are intended to achieve reproduction. "Natural" sexual desire is for heterosexual genital activity, not for reproduction. The ground for classifying that desire as natural is that it is so organized that it *could* lead to reproduction in normal physiological circumstances. The reproductive organization of sexual desires gives us a *criterion* of naturalness, but the *virtue* of which it is a criterion is the "naturalness" itself, not reproduction. Our vacillating attitude toward the apparently perverse acts of animals reflects our shifting from criterion to virtue. If, when confronted with a perverse act of animals, we withdraw the label "perverted" from our own similar acts rather than extend it to theirs, we are relinquishing the reproductive criterion of naturalness, while retaining the virtue. Animals cannot be "unnatural." If, on the other hand, we "discover" that animals can be perverts too, we are maintaining our criterion, but giving a somewhat altered sense to the "naturalness" of which it is a criterion.

Nagel's alternative attempt to classify acts as natural or perverted on the basis of their completeness fails. "Perverted" and "complete" are evaluations of an entirely different order. The completeness of a sex act depends upon qualities of the participants' experience and upon qualities of their relation— qualities of which they are the best judge. To say a sex act is perverted is to pass a conventional judgment about characteristics of the act, which could be evident to any observer. As one can pretend to be angry but not to shout, one can pretend to a complete, but not to a natural, sex act (though one may, of course, conceal desires for perverse sex acts or shout in order to mask one's feelings). As Nagel himself sees, judgments about particular sex acts clearly differentiate between perversion and completeness. Unadorned heterosexual intercourse where each partner has private fantasies is clearly "natural" and clearly "incomplete," but there is nothing prima facie incomplete about exclusive oral-genital intercourse or homosexual acts. If many perverse acts are incomplete, as Nagel claims, this is an important fact *about* perversion, but it is not the basis upon which we judge its occurrence.

IS BETTER SEX REALLY BETTER?

Some sex acts are, allegedly, better than others insofar as they are more pleasurable, complete, and natural. What is the moral significance of this evaluation? In answering this question, official sexual morality sometimes appeals to the social consequences of particular types of better sex acts. For example, since dominantly perverse organizations of sexual impulses limit reproduction, the merits of perversion depend upon the need to limit or increase population. Experience of sexual pleasure may be desirable if it promotes relaxation and communication in an acquisitive society, undesirable if it limits the desire to work or, in armies, to kill. The social consequences of complete sex have not received particular attention, because the quality of sexual experience has been of little interest to moralists. It might be found that those who had complete sexual relations were more cooperative, less amenable to political revolt. If so, complete sexual acts would be desirable in just and peaceable societies, undesirable in unjust societies requiring revolution.

The social desirability of types of sexual acts depends on particular social conditions and independent criteria of social desirability. It may be interesting and important to assess particular claims about the social desirability of sex acts, but this is not my concern. What is my concern is the extent to which we will allow our judgments of sexual worth to be influenced by social considerations. But this issue cannot even be raised until we have a better sense of sexual worth.

THE BENEFIT OF SEXUAL PLEASURE

To say that an experience is pleasant is to give a self-evident, terminal reason for seeking it. We can sometimes "see" that an experience is pleasant. When, for example, we observe someone's sensual delight in eating, her/his behavior can expressively characterize pleasure. We can only question the benefit of such an experience by referring to other goods with which it might conflict. Though sensual pleasures may not be sufficient to warrant giving birth or to deter suicide, so long as we live they are self-evidently benefits to us.

The most eloquent detractors of sexual experience have admitted that it provides sensual pleasures so poignant that once experienced they are repeatedly, almost addictively, sought. Yet, unlike other appetites, such as hunger, sexual desire can be permanently resisted, and resistance has been advocated. How can the prima facie benefits of sexual pleasure appear deceptive?

There are several grounds for complaint. Sexual pleasure is ineradicably mixed, frustration being part of every sexual life. The capacity for sexual pleasure is unevenly distributed, cannot be voluntarily acquired, and diminishes through no fault of its subject. If such a pleasure were an intrinsic benefit, benefit would in this case be independent of moral effort. Then again, sexual pleasures are not serious. Enjoyment of them is one of life's greatest recreations, but none of its business. And finally, sexual desire has the defects of its strengths. Before satisfaction, it is, at the least, distracting; in satisfaction, it "makes one little roome, an everywhere." Like psychosis, sexual desire turns us from "reality"—whether the real be God, social justice, children, or intellectual endeavor. This turning away is more than a social consequence of desire, though it is that. Lovers themselves feel that their sexual desires are separate from their "real" political, domestic, ambitious, social selves.

If the plaintiff is taken to argue that sensual pleasures are not peremptory benefits, s/he is probably right. We can still want a good deal and forego sexual pleasures. We often forego pleasure just because we want something incompatible with it, for example, a continuing marriage. We must distinguish between giving up some occasions for sexual pleasure and giving up sexual pleasure itself. If all circumstances of sexual pleasure . . . threaten a peremptory benefit, such as self-respect, then the hope and the possibility of sexual pleasure may be relinquished. Since sexual pleasure is such a great, though optional, benefit, its loss is a sad one.

In emphasizing the unsocial, private nature of sexual experiences, the plaintiff is emphasizing a morally important characteristic of them. But her/his case against desire, as I have sketched it, is surely overstated. The mixed, partly frustrated character of any desire is not particularly pronounced for sexual desire, which is in fact especially plastic, or adaptable to changes (provided perverse sex acts have not been ruled out). Inhibition, social deprivation, or disease make our sexual lives unpleasant, but that is because they interfere with sexual desire, not because the desire is by its nature frustrating. More than other well-known desires (for example, desire for knowledge, success, or power), sexual desire is simply and completely satisfied upon attaining its object. Partly for this reason, even if we are overtaken by desire during sexual experience, our sexual experiences do not overtake us. Lovers turn away from the world while loving, but return—sometimes all too easily—when loving is done. The moralist rightly perceives sexual pleasure as a recreation, and those who upon realizing its benefits make a business of its pursuit appear ludicrous. The capacity for recreation, however, is surely a benefit that any human being rightly hopes for who hopes for anything. Indeed, in present social and economic conditions we are more likely to lay waste our powers in work than in play. Thus, though priest, revolutionary, and parent are alike in fearing sexual pleasure, this fear should inspire us to psychological and sociological investigation of the fearing rather than to moral doubt about the benefit of sexual pleasure.

THE MORAL SIGNIFICANCE OF PERVERSION

What is the moral significance of the perversity of a sexual act? Next to none, so far as I can see. Though perverted sex may be "unnatural" both from an evolutionary and developmental perspective, there is no connection, inverse or correlative, between what is natural and what is good. Perverted sex is sometimes said to be less pleasurable than natural sex. We have little reason to believe that this claim is true and no clear idea of the kind of evidence on which it would be based. In any case, to condemn perverse acts for lack of pleasure is to recognize the worth of pleasure, not of naturalness.

There are many other claims about the nature and consequences of perversion. Some merely restate "scientific" facts in morally tinged terminology. Perverse acts are, by definition and according to psychiatric theory, "immature" and "abnormal," since natural sex acts are selected by criteria of "normal" sexual function and "normal" and "mature" psychological development. But there is no greater connection of virtue with maturity and normality than there is of virtue with nature. The elimination of a village by an invading army would be no less evil if it were the expression of controlled, normal, natural, and mature aggression.

Nagel claims that many perverted sex acts are incomplete, and in making his point, gives the most specific arguments that I have read for the inferiority of perverted sex. But as he points out, there is no reason to think an act consisting solely of oral-genital intercourse is incomplete; it is doubtful whether homosexual acts and acts of buggery are especially liable to be incomplete; and the incompleteness of sexual intercourse with animals is a relative matter depending upon their limited consciousness. And again, the alleged inferiority is not a consequence of perversion but of incompleteness, which can afflict natural sex as well.

Perverted acts might be thought to be inferior because they cannot result in children. Whatever the benefits and moral significance of the procreation and care of children (and I believe they are extensive and complicated), the virtue of proper care for children neither requires nor follows from biological parenthood. Even if it did, only a sexual life consisting solely of perverse acts rules out conception.

If perverted sex acts did rule out normal sex acts, if one were *either* perverted *or* natural, then certain kinds of sexual relations would be denied some perverts—relations that are benefits to those who enjoy them. It seems that sexual relations with the living and the human would be of greater benefit than those with the dead or with animals. But there is no reason to think that heterosexual relations are of greater benefit than homosexual ones. It might be thought that children can only be raised by heterosexual couples who perform an abundance of natural sex acts. If true (though truth seems highly unlikely), perverts will be denied the happiness of parenthood. This deprivation would be an *indirect* consequence of perverted sex and might yield a moral dilemma: How is one to choose between the benefits of children and the benefits of more pleasurable, more complex sex acts?

Some perversions are immoral on independent grounds. Sadism is the obvious example, though sadism practiced with a consenting masochist is far less evil than other, more familiar forms of aggression. Voyeurism may seem immoral because, since it must be secret to be satisfying, it violates others' rights to privacy.[18] Various kinds of rape can constitute perversion if rape,

---

[18] I am indebted to Dr. Leo Goldberger for this example.

rather than genital intercourse, is the aim of desire. Rape is always seriously immoral, a vivid violation of respect for persons. Sometimes doubly perverse rape is doubly evil (the rape of a child), but in other cases (the rape of a pig) its evil is halved. In any case, though rape is always *wrong*, it is only perverse when raping becomes the aim and not the means of desire.

Someone can be dissuaded from acting on her/his perverse desires either from moral qualms or from social fears. Although there may be ample basis for the latter, I can find none for the former except the possible indirect loss of the benefits of child care. I am puzzled about this since reflective people who do not usually attempt to legislate the preferences of others think differently. There is no doubt that beliefs in these matters involve deep emotions that should be respected. But for those who do in fact have perverted desires, the first concern will be to satisfy them, not to divert or to understand them. For sexual pleasure is intrinsically a benefit, and complete sex acts, which depend upon expressing the desires one in fact has, are both beneficial and conducive to virtue. Therefore, barring extrinsic moral or social considerations, perverted sex acts are preferable to natural ones if the latter are less pleasurable or less complete.

THE MORAL SIGNIFICANCE OF COMPLETENESS

Complete sex consists in mutually embodied, mutually active, responsive desire. Embodiment, activity, and mutual responsiveness are instrumentally beneficial because they are conducive to our psychological well-being, which is an intrinsic benefit. The alleged pathological consequences of disembodiment are more specific and better documented than those of perversity.[19] To dissociate oneself from one's actual body, either by creating a delusory body or by rejecting the bodily, is to court a variety of ill effects, ranging from self-disgust to diseases of the will, to faulty mental development, to the destruction of a recognizable "self," and finally to madness. It is difficult to assess psychiatric claims outside their theoretical contexts, but in this case I believe that they are justified. Relative embodiment is a stable, *normal* condition that is not confined to cases of complete embodiment. But psychiatrists tell us that exceptional physical occasions of embodiment seem to be required in order to balance tendencies to reject or to falsify the body. Sexual acts are

---

[19] See, for example, R. D. Laing, *The Divided Self;* D. W. Winnicott, "Transitional Objects and Transitional Phenomena," *International Journal of Psychoanalysis,* 34 (1953), 89–97; Paul Federn, *Ego Psychology and the Psychoses* (New York: Basic Books, 1952); Phyllis Greenacre, *Trauma, Growth, and Personality* (New York: International Universities Press, 1969); Paul Schilder, *The Image and Appearance of the Human Body* (New York: International Universities Press, 1950); Moses Laufer, "Body Image and Masturbation in Adolescence," *The Psychoanalytic Study of the Child,* 23 (1968), 114–46. Laing's work is most specific about both the nature and consequences of disembodiment, but the works cited, and others similar to them, give the clinical evidence upon which much of Laing's work depends.

not the only such occasions, but they do provide an immersion of consciousness in the bodily, which is pleasurable and especially conducive to correcting
experiences of shame and disgust that work toward disembodiment.

The mutual responsiveness of complete sex is also instrumentally beneficial.   *uh'.*
It satisfies a general desire to be recognized as a particular "real" person and
to make a difference to other particular "real" people. The satisfaction of
this desire in sexual experience is especially rewarding, its thwarting especially
cruel. Vulnerability is increased in complete sex by the active desiring of the
partners. When betrayal, or for that matter, tenderness or ecstasy, ensues,
one cannot dissociate oneself from the desire with which one identified and
out of which one acted. The psychic danger is real, as people who attempt
to achieve a distance from their desires could tell us. But the cost of distance
is as evident as its gains. Passivity in respect to one's own sexual desire not
only limits sexual pleasure but, more seriously, limits the extent to which the
experience of sexual pleasure can be included as an experience of a coherent
person. With passivity comes a kind of irresponsibility in which one can hide
from one's desire, even from one's pleasure, "playing" seducer or victim,
tease or savior. Active sexual desiring in complete sex acts affords an especially
threatening but also especially happy occasion to relinquish these and similar
roles. To the extent that the roles confuse and confound our intimate relations,
the benefit from relinquishing them in our sexual acts, or the loss from
adhering to them then, is especially poignant.

In addition to being beneficial, complete sex acts are morally superior for
three reasons. They tend to resolve tensions fundamental to moral life; they
are conducive to emotions that, if they become stable and dominant, are in
turn conducive to the virtue of loving; and they involve a preeminently moral
virtue—respect for persons.

In one of its aspects, morality is opposed to the private and untamed.
Morality is "civilization," social and regulating; desire is "discontent," resisting the regulation. Obligation, rather than benefit, is the notion central
to morality so conceived, and the virtues required of a moral person are
directed to preserving right relations and social order. Both the insistence on
natural sex and the encouragement of complete sex can be looked upon as
attempts to make sexual desire more amenable to regulation. But whereas
the regulation of perverted desires is extrinsic to them, those of completeness
modify the desires themselves. The desiring sensual body that in our social
lives we may laugh away or disown becomes our "self" and enters into a
social relation. Narcissism and altruism are satisfied in complete sex acts in
which one gives what one receives by receiving it. Social and private "selves"
are unified in an act in which impersonal, spontaneous impulses govern an
action that is responsive to a particular person. For this to be true we must
surmount our social "roles" as well as our sexual "techniques," though we
incorporate rather than surmount our social selves. We must also surmount
regulations imposed in the name of naturalness if our desires are to be

spontaneously expressed. Honestly spontaneous first love gives us back our private desiring selves while allowing us to see the desiring self of another. Mutually responding partners confirm each other's desires and declare them good. Such occasions, when we are "moral" without cost, help reconcile us to our moral being and to the usual mutual exclusion between our social and private lives.

The connection between sex and certain emotions—particularly love, jealousy, fear, and anger—is as evident as it is obscure. Complete sex acts seem more likely than incomplete pleasurable ones to lead toward affection and away from fear and anger, since any guilt and shame will be extrinsic to the act and meliorated by it. It is clear that we need not feel for someone any affection beyond that required (if any is) simply to participate with him/her in a complete sex act. However, it is equally clear that sexual pleasure, especially as experienced in complete sex acts, is conducive to many feelings— gratitude, tenderness, pride, appreciation, dependency, and others. These feelings magnify their object who occasioned them. When these magnifying feelings become stable and habitual they are conducive to love—not universal love, of course, but love of a particular sexual partner. However, even "selfish" love is a virtue, a disposition to care for someone as her/his interests and demands would dictate. Neither the best sex nor the best love require each other, but they go together more often than reason would expect—often enough to count the virtue of loving as one of the rewards of the capacity for sexual pleasure exercised in complete sex acts.

It might be argued that the coincidence of sex acts and several valued emotions is a cultural matter. It is notoriously difficult to make judgments about the emotional and, particularly, the sexual lives of others, especially culturally alien others. There is, however, some anthropological evidence that at first glance relativizes the connection between good sex and valued emotion. For example, among the Manus of New Guinea, it seems that relations of affection and love are encouraged primarily among brother and sister, while easy familiarity, joking, and superficial sexual play is expected only between cross-cousins. Sexual intercourse is, however, forbidden between siblings and cross-cousins but required of married men and women, who are as apt to hate as to care for each other and often seem to consider each other strangers. It seems, however, that the Manus do not value or experience complete or even pleasurable sex. Both men and women are described as puritanical, and the sexual life of women seems blatantly unrewarding. Moreover, their emotional life is generally impoverished. This impoverishment, in conjunction with an unappreciated and unrewarding sexual life dissociated from love or affection, would argue for a *connection* between better sex and valued emotions. If, as Peter Winch suggests, cultures provide their members with particular possibilities of making sense of their lives, and thereby with possibilities of good and evil, the Manus might be said to deny themselves one possibility both of sense and of good—namely the coincidence of good sex and of affection and love. Other cultures, including our own, allow this possibility, whose realization is encouraged in varying degrees by particular groups and members of the culture.[20]

Finally, as Sartre has suggested, complete sex acts preserve a respect for persons. Each person remains conscious and responsible, a "subject" rather than a depersonalized, will-less, or manipulated "object." Each actively desires that the other likewise remain a "subject." Respect for persons is a central virtue when matters of justice and obligation are at issue. Insofar as we can speak of respect for persons in complete sex acts, there are different, often contrary requirements of respect. Respect for persons, typically and in sex acts, requires that *actual present* partners participate, partners whose desires are recognized and endorsed. Respect for persons typically requires taking a distance from both one's own demands and those of others. But in sex acts the demands of desire take over, and equal distance is replaced by mutual responsiveness. Respect typically requires refusing to treat another person merely as a means to fulfilling demands. In sex acts, another person is so clearly a means to satisfaction that s/he is always on the verge of becoming merely a means ("intercourse counterfeits masturbation"). In complete sex acts, instrumentality vanishes only because it is mutual and mutually desired. Respect requires encouraging, or at least protecting, the autonomy of another. In complete sex, autonomy of will is recruited by desire, and freedom from others is replaced by frank dependence on another person's desire. Again the respect consists in the reciprocity of desiring dependence, which bypasses rather than violates autonomy.

Despite the radical differences between respect for persons in the usual moral contexts and respect for persons in sex acts, it is not, I think, a mere play on words to talk of respect in the latter case. When, in any sort of intercourse, persons are respected, their desires are not only, in fair measure, *fulfilled.* In addition, their desires are *active* and determine, in fair measure, the form of intercourse and the *manner* and *condition* of desire's satisfaction. These conditions are not only met in sexual intercourse when it is characterized by completeness; they come close to defining completeness.

Sartre is not alone in believing that just because the condition of completeness involves respect for persons, complete sex is impossible. Completeness is surely threatened by pervasive tendencies to fantasy, to possessiveness, and to varieties of a sadomasochistic desire. But a complete sex act, as I see it, does not involve an heroic restraint on our sexual interpulses. Rather, a complete sex act is a normal mode of sexual activity expressing the natural structure and impulses of sexual desire.

While complete sex is morally superior because it involves respect for persons, incomplete sex acts do not necessarily involve immoral disrespect for persons. Depending upon the desires and expectations of the partners,

---

[20] The evidence about the life of the Manus comes from Margaret Mead, *Growing Up in New Guinea* (Harmondsworth, England: Penguin Books, 1942). Peter Winch's discussion can be found in his "Understanding a Primitive Society," *American Philosophical Quarterly,* 1 (1964), 307–34.

incompleteness may involve neither respect nor disrespect. Masturbation, for example, allows only the limited completeness of embodiment and often fails of that. But masturbation only rarely involves disrespect to anyone. Even the respect of Sartre's allegedly desirable sleeping woman may not be violated if she is unknowingly involved in a sex act. Disrespect, though probable, may in some cases be obviated by her sensibilities and expectations that she has previously expressed and her partner has understood. Sex acts provide one context in which respect for persons can be expressed. That context is important both because our sexual lives are of such importance to us and because they are so liable to injury because of the experience and the fear of the experience of disrespect. But many complete sex acts in which respect is maintained make other casual and incomplete sex acts unthreatening. In this case a goodly number of swallows can make a summer.

In sum, then, complete sex acts are superior to incomplete ones. First, they are, whatever their effects, better than various kinds of incomplete sex acts because they involve a kind of "respect for persons" in acts that are otherwise prone to violation of respect for, and often to violence to, persons. Second, complete sex acts are good because they are good for us. They are conducive to some fairly clearly defined kinds of psychological well-being that are beneficial. They are conducive to moral well-being because they relieve tensions that arise in our attempts to be moral and because they encourage the development of particular virtues.

To say that complete sex acts are preferable to incomplete ones is not to court a new puritanism. There are many kinds and degrees of incompleteness. Incomplete sex acts may not involve a disrespect for persons. Complete sex acts only *tend* to be good for us, and the realization of these tendencies depends upon individual lives and circumstances of sexual activity. The proper object of sexual desire is sexual pleasure. It would be a foolish ambition indeed to limit one's sexual acts to those in which completeness was likely. Any sexual act that is pleasurable is prima facie good, though the more incomplete it is—the more private, essentially autoerotic, unresponsive, unembodied, passive, or imposed—the more likely it is to be harmful to someone.

ON SEXUAL MORALITY: CONCLUDING REMARKS

There are many questions we have neglected to consider because we have not been sufficiently attentive to the quality of sexual lives. For example, we know little about the ways of achieving better sex. When we must choose between inferior sex and abstinence, how and when will our choice of inferior sex damage our capacity for better sex? Does, for example, the repeated experience of controlled sexual disembodiment ("desire which takes over will take you too far") that we urge (or used to urge) on adolescents damage their capacity for complete sex? The answers to this and similar questions are not obvious, though unfounded opinions are always ready at hand.

Some of the traditional sexual vices might be condemned on the ground that they are inimical to better sex. Obscenity, or repeated public exposure to sexual acts, might impair our capacity for pleasure or for response to desire. Promiscuity might undercut the tendency of complete sex acts to promote emotions that magnify their object. Other of the traditional sexual vices are neither inimical nor conducive to better sex, but are condemned because of conflicting nonsexual benefits and obligations. For example, infidelity qua infidelity neither secures nor prevents better sex. The obligations of fidelity have many sources, one of which may be a past history of shared complete sex acts, a history that included promises of exclusive intimacy. Such past promises are as apt to conflict with as to accord with a current demand for better sex. I have said nothing about how such a conflict would be settled. I hope I have shown that where the possibility of better sex conflicts with obligations and other benefits, we have a *moral dilemma,* not just an occasion for moral self-discipline.

The pursuit of more pleasurable and more complete sex acts is, among many moral activities, distinguished not for its exigencies but for its rewards. Since our sexual lives are so important to us, and since, whatever our history and our hopes, we are sexual beings, this pursuit rightly engages our moral reflection. It should not be relegated to the immoral, nor to the "merely" prudent.

POSTSCRIPT

I wrote this essay fourteen years ago. Since that time my ideas about thinking and writing, as well as about sexual morality, have been transformed by feminist and anti-militarist politics. The tone and language of the essay, as well as certain basic presuppositions of its arguments, now ring strangely in my ears. Nonetheless, what has been made public belongs to the public and I am pleased if this early paper still proves useful. In one respect, however, the essay seems seriously insensitive and limited. In 1970 I was largely unaware of the deep and extensive pain suffered by those whose sexuality is labeled "abnormal," "perverted," or "immature." On a more theoretical level, since 1970 we have learned to see the connections between misogyny, homophobia, militarism, and racism. I would like here to acknowledge my debt to the work of the feminist and gay liberation movements, which has made these theoretical connections while fighting ignorant and arrogant sexual politics. As a result many people now lead more complete and pleasurable sexual lives.

IS ADULTERY IMMORAL?

RICHARD A. WASSERSTROM

Many discussions of the enforcement of morality by the law take as illustrative of the problem under consideration the regulation of various types of sexual behavior by the criminal law. It was, for example, the Wolfenden Report's recommendations concerning homosexuality and prostitution that led Lord Devlin to compose his now famous lecture, "The Enforcement of Morals." And that lecture in turn provoked important philosophical responses from H. L. A. Hart, Ronald Dworkin, and others.

Much, if not all, of the recent philosophical literature on the enforcement of morals appears to take for granted the immorality of the sexual behavior in question. The focus of discussion, at least, is whether such things as homosexuality, prostitution, and adultery ought to be made illegal even if they are immoral, and not whether they are immoral.

I propose in this paper to think about the latter, more neglected topic, that of sexual morality, and to do so in the following fashion. I shall consider just one kind of behavior that is often taken to be a case of sexual immorality— adultery. I am interested in pursuing at least two questions. First, I want to explore the question of in what respects adulterous behavior falls within the domain of morality at all: For this surely is one of the puzzles one encounters when considering the topic of sexual morality. It is often hard to see on what grounds much of the behavior is deemed to be either moral or immoral, for example, private homosexual behavior between consenting adults. I have purposely selected adultery because it seems a more plausible candidate for moral assessment than many other kinds of sexual behavior.

The second question I want to examine is that of what is to be said about adultery, without being especially concerned to stay within the area of morality. I shall endeavor, in other words, to identify and to assess a number of the major arguments that might be advanced against adultery. I believe that they are the chief arguments that would be given in support of the view that adultery is immoral, but I think they are worth considering even if some of them turn out to be nonmoral arguments and considerations.

A number of the issues involved seem to me to be complicated and difficult. In a number of places I have at best indicated where further philosophical exploration is required without having successfully conducted the exploration myself. The paper may very well be more useful as an illustration of how one might begin to think about the subject of sexual morality than as an elucidation of important truths about the topic.

Before I turn to the arguments themselves there are two preliminary points that require some clarification. Throughout the paper I shall refer to the immorality of such things as breaking a promise, deceiving someone, etc. In a very rough way, I mean by this that there is something morally wrong that is done in doing the action in question. I mean that the action is, in a strong sense, of *"prima facie"* prima facie wrong or unjustified. I do not mean that it may never be right or justifiable to do the action; just that the fact that it is an action of this description always does count against the rightness of the action. I leave entirely open the question of what it is that makes actions of this kind immoral in this sense of "immoral."

The second preliminary point concerns what is meant or implied by the concept of adultery. I mean by "adultery" any case of extramarital sex, and I want to explore the arguments for and against extramarital sex, undertaken in a variety of morally relevant situations. Someone might claim that the concept of adultery is conceptually connected with the concept of immorality, and that to characterize behavior as adulterous is already to characterize it as immoral or unjustified in the sense described above. There may be something to this. Hence the importance of making it clear that I want to talk about extramarital sexual relations. If they are always immoral, this is something that must be shown by argument. If the concept of adultery does in some sense entail or imply immorality, I want to ask whether that connection is a rationally based one. If not all cases of extramarital sex are immoral (again, in the sense described above), then the concept of adultery should either be weakened accordingly or restricted to those classes of extramarital sex for which the predication of immorality is warranted.

One argument for the immorality of adultery might go something like this: what makes adultery immoral is that it involves the breaking of a promise, and what makes adultery seriously wrong is that it involves the breaking of an important promise. For, so the argument might continue, one of the things the two parties promise each other when they get married is that they will abstain from sexual relationships with third persons. Because of this promise both spouses quite reasonably entertain the expectation that the other will behave in conformity with it. Hence, when one of the parties has sexual intercourse with a third person he or she breaks that promise about sexual relationships which was made when the marriage was entered into, and defeats the reasonable expectations of exclusivity entertained by the spouse.

In many cases the immorality involved in breaching the promise relating to extramarital sex may be a good deal more serious than that involved in the breach of other promises. This is so because adherence to this promise may be of much greater importance to the parties than is adherence to many of the other promises given or received by them in their lifetime. The breaking of this promise may be much more hurtful and painful than is typically the case.

Why is this so? To begin with, it may have been difficult for the non-adulterous spouse to have kept the promise. Hence that spouse may feel the unfairness of having restrained himself or herself in the absence of reciprocal restraint having been exercised by the adulterous spouse. In addition, the spouse may perceive the breaking of the promise as an indication of a kind of indifference on the part of the adulterous spouse. If you really cared about me and my feelings—the spouse might say—you would not have done this to me. And third, and related to the above, the spouse may see the act of sexual intercourse with another as a sign of affection for the other person and as an additional rejection of the nonadulterous spouse as the one who is loved by the adulterous spouse. It is not just that the adulterous spouse does not take the feelings of the spouse sufficiently into account, the adulterous spouse also indicates through the act of adultery affection for someone other than the spouse. I will return to these points later. For the present, it is sufficient to note that a set of arguments can be developed in support of the proposition that certain kinds of adultery are wrong just because they involve that breach of a serious promise which, among other things, leads to the intentional infliction of substantial pain by one spouse upon the other.

Another argument for the immorality of adultery focuses not on the existence of a promise of sexual exclusivity but on the connection between adultery and deception. According to this argument, adultery involves deception. And because deception is wrong, so is adultery.

Although it is certainly not obviously so, I shall simply assume in this paper that deception is always immoral. Thus the crucial issue for my purposes is the asserted connection between extramarital sex and deception. Is it plausible to maintain, as this argument does, that adultery always does involve deception and is on that basis to be condemned?

The most obvious person on whom deceptions might be practiced is the nonparticipating spouse; and the most obvious thing about which the nonparticipating spouse can be deceived is the existence of the adulterous act. One clear case of deception is that of lying. Instead of saying that the afternoon was spent in bed with *A,* the adulterous spouse asserts that it was spent in the library with *B,* or on the golf course with *C.*

There can also be deception even when no lies are told. Suppose, for instance, that a person has sexual intercourse with someone other than his or her spouse and just does not tell the spouse about it. Is that deception? It may not be a case of lying if, for example, the spouse is never asked by the other about the situation. Still, we might say, it is surely deceptive because of the promises that were exchanged at marriage. As we saw earlier, these promises provide a foundation for the reasonable belief that neither spouse will engage in sexual relationships with any other persons. Hence the failure to bring the fact of extramarital sex to the attention of the other spouse deceives that spouse about the present state of the marital relationship.

Adultery, in other words, can involve both active and passive deception. An adulterous spouse may just keep silent or, as is often the fact, the spouse may engage in an increasingly complex way of life devoted to the concealment of the facts from the nonparticipating spouse. Lies, half-truths, clandestine meetings, and the like may become a central feature of the adulterous spouse's existence. These are things that can and do happen, and when they do they make the case against adultery an easy one. Still neither active nor passive deception is inevitably a feature of an extramarital relationship.

It is possible, though, that a more subtle but pervasive kind of deceptiveness is a feature of adultery. It comes about because of the connection in our culture between sexual intimacy and certain feelings of love and affection. The point can be made indirectly at first by seeing that one way in which we can, in our culture, mark off our close friends from our mere acquaintances is through the kinds of intimacies that we are prepared to share with them. I may, for instance, be willing to reveal my very private thoughts and emotions to my closest friends or to my wife, but to no one else. My sharing of these intimate facts about myself is from one perspective a way of making a gift to those who mean the most to me. Revealing these things and sharing them with those who mean the most to me is one means by which I create, maintain, and confirm those interpersonal relationships that are of most importance to me.

Now in our culture, it might be claimed, sexual intimacy is one of the chief currencies through which gifts of this sort are exchanged. One way to tell someone—particularly someone of the opposite sex—that you have feelings of affection and love for them is by allowing to them or sharing with them sexual behaviors that one doesn't share with the rest of the world. This way of measuring affection was certainly very much a part of the culture in which I matured. It worked something like this. If you were a girl, you showed how much you liked someone by the degree of sexual intimacy you would allow. If you liked a boy only a little, you never did more than kiss—and even the kiss was not very passionate. If you liked the boy a lot and if your feelings was reciprocated, necking, and possibly petting, was permissible. If the attachment was still stronger and you thought it might even become a permanent relationship, the sexual activity was correspondingly more intense and more intimate, although whether it would ever lead to sexual intercourse depended on whether the parties (and particularly the girl) accepted fully the prohibition on nonmarital sex. The situation for the boy was related, but not exactly the same. The assumption was that males did not naturally link sex with affection in the way in which females did. However, since women did, males had to take this into account. That is to say, because a woman would permit sexual intimacies only if she had feelings of affection for the male and only if those feelings were reciprocated, the male had to have and express those feelings, too, before sexual intimacies of any sort would occur.

The result was that the importance of a correlation between sexual intimacy and feelings of love and affection was taught by the culture and assimilated by those growing up in the culture. The scale of possible positive feelings toward persons of the other sex ran from casual liking at the one end to the love that was deemed essential to and characteristic of marriage at the other. The scale of possible sexual behavior ran from brief, passionless kissing or hand-holding at the one end to sexual intercourse at the other. And the correlation between the two scales was quite precise. As a result, any act of sexual intimacy carried substantial meaning with it, and no act of sexual intimacy was simply a pleasurable set of bodily sensations. Many such acts were, of course, more pleasurable to the participants because they were a way of saying what the participants feelings were. And sometimes they were less pleasurable for the same reason. The point is, however, that in any event sexual activity was much more than mere bodily enjoyment. It was not like eating a good meal, listening to good music, lying in the sun, or getting a pleasant back rub. It was behavior that meant a great deal concerning one's feelings for persons of the opposite sex in whom one was most interested and with whom one was most involved. It was among the most authoritative ways in which one could communicate to another the nature and degree of one's affection.

If this sketch is even roughly right, then several things become somewhat clearer. To begin with, a possible rationale for many of the rules of conventional sexual morality can be developed. If, for example, sexual intercourse is associated with the kind of affection and commitment to another that is regarded as characteristic of the marriage relationship, then it is natural that sexual intercourse should be thought properly to take place between persons who are married to each other. And if it is thought that this kind of affection and commitment is only to be found within the marriage relationship, then it is not surprising that sexual intercourse should only be thought to be proper within marriage.

Related to what has just been said is the idea that sexual intercourse ought to be restricted to those who are married to each other as a means by which to confirm the very special feelings that the spouses have for each other. Because the culture teaches that sexual intercourse means that the strongest of all feelings for each other are shared by the lovers, it is natural that persons who are married to each other should be able to say this to each other in this way. Revealing and confirming verbally that these feelings are present is one thing that helps to sustain the relationship; engaging in sexual intercourse is another.

In addition, this account would help to provide a framework within which to make sense of the notion that some sex is better than other sex. As I indicated earlier, the fact that sexual intimacy can be meaningful in the sense described tends to make it also the case that sexual intercourse can sometimes be more enjoyable than at other times. On this view, sexual intercourse will typically be more enjoyable where the strong feelings of affection are present than it will be where it is merely "mechanical." This is so in part because people enjoy being loved, especially by those whom they love. Just as we like to hear words of affection, so we like to receive affectionate behavior. And the meaning enhances the independently pleasurable behavior.

More to the point, moreover, an additional rationale for the prohibition on extramarital sex can now be developed. For given this way of viewing the sexual world, extramarital sex will almost always involve deception of a deeper sort. If the adulterous spouse does not in fact have the appropriate feelings of affection for the extramarital partner, then the adulterous spouse is deceiving that person about the presence of such feelings. If, on the other hand, the adulterous spouse does have the corresponding feelings for the extramarital partner but not toward the nonparticipating spouse, the adulterous spouse is very probably deceiving the nonparticipating spouse about the presence of such feelings toward that spouse. Indeed, it might be argued, whenever there is no longer love between the two persons who are married to each other, there is deception just because being married implies both to the participants and to the world that such a bond exists. Deception is inevitable, the argument might conclude, because the feelings of affection that ought to accompany any act of sexual intercourse can only be held toward one other person at any given time in one's life. And if this is so, then the adulterous spouse always deceives either the partner in adultery or the nonparticipating spouse about the existence of such feelings. Thus extramarital sex involves deception of this sort and is for this reason immoral even if no deception vis-à-vis the occurrence of the act of adultery takes place.

What might be said in response to the foregoing arguments? The first thing that might be said is that the account of the connection between sexual intimacy and feelings of affection is inaccurate. Not inaccurate in the sense that no one thinks of things that way, but in the sense that there is substantially more divergence of opinion than that account suggests. For example, the view I have delineated may describe reasonably accurately the concept of the sexual world in which I grew up, but it does not capture the sexual *weltanschauung* of today's youth at all. Thus, whether or not adultery implies deception in respect to feelings depends very much on the persons who are involved and the way they look at the "meaning" of sexual intimacy.

Second, the argument leaves to be answered the question of whether it is desirable for sexual intimacy to carry the sorts of messages described above. For those persons for whom sex does have these implications, there are special feelings and sensibilities that must be taken into account. But it is another question entirely whether any valuable end—moral or otherwise—is served by investing sexual behavior with such significance. That is something that must be shown and not just assumed. It might, for instance, be the case that substantially more good than harm would come from a kind of demystification of sexual behavior: one that would encourage the enjoyment of sex more for its own sake and one that would reject the centrality both of the association of sex with love and of love with only one other person.

I regard these as two of the more difficult, unresolved issues that our culture faces today in respect to thinking sensibly about the attitudes toward sex and love that we should try to develop in ourselves and in our children. Much of the contemporary literature that advocates sexual liberation of one sort or another embraces one or the other of two different views about the relationship between sex and love.

One view holds that sex should be separated from love and affection. To be sure sex is probably better when the partners genuinely like and enjoy each other. But sex is basically an intensive, exciting sensuous activity that can be enjoyed in a variety of suitable settings with a variety of suitable partners. The situation in respect to sexual pleasure is no different from that of the person who knows and appreciates fine food and who can have a very satisfying meal in any number of good restaurants with any number of congenial companions. One question that must be settled here is whether sex can be so demystified; another, more important question is whether it would be desirable to do so. What would we gain and what might we lose if we all lived in a world in which an act of sexual intercourse was no more or less significant or enjoyable than having a delicious meal in a nice setting with a good friend? The answer to this question lies beyond the scope of this paper.

The second view seeks to drive the wedge in a different place. It is not the link between sex and love that needs to be broken; rather, on this view, it is the connection between love and exclusivity that ought to be severed. For a number of the reasons already given, it is desirable, so this argument goes, that sexual intimacy continue to be reserved to and shared with only those for whom one has very great affection. The mistake lies in thinking that any "normal" adult will only have those feelings toward one other adult during his or her lifetime—or even at any time in his or her life. It is the concept of adult love, not ideas about sex, that, on this view, needs demystification. What are thought to be both unrealistic and unfortunate are the notions of exclusivity and possessiveness that attach to the dominant conception of love between adults in our and other cultures. Parents of four, five, six, or even ten children can certainly claim and sometimes claim correctly that they love all of their children, that they love them all equally, and that it is simply untrue to their feelings to insist that the numbers involved diminish either the quantity or the quality of their love. If this is an idea that is readily understandable in the case of parents and children, there is no necessary reason why it is an impossible or undesirable ideal in the case of adults. To be sure, there is probably a limit to the number of intimate "primary" relationships that any person can maintain at any given time without the quality of the relationship being affected. But one adult ought surely be able to love two, three, or even six other adults at any one time without that love being different in kind or degree from that of the traditional, monogamous, lifetime marriage. And as between the individuals in these relationships, whether within a marriage or without, sexual intimacy is fitting and good.

The issues raised by a position such as this one are also surely worth exploring in detail and with care. Is there something to be called "sexual love" which is different from parental love or the nonsexual love of close friends? Is there something about love in general that links it naturally and appropriately with feelings of exclusivity and possession? Or is there something about sexual love, whatever that may be, that makes these feelings especially fitting here? Once again the issues are conceptual, empirical, and normative all at once: What is love? How could it be different? Would it be a good thing or a bad thing if it were different.

Suppose, though, that having delineated these problems we were now to pass them by. Suppose, moreover, we were to be persuaded of the possibility and the desirability of weakening substantially either the links between sex and love or the links between sexual love and exclusivity. Would it not then be the case that adultery could be free from all of the morally objectionable features described so far? To be more specific, let us imagine that a husband and wife have what is today sometimes characterized as an "open marriage." Suppose, that is, that they have agreed in advance that extramarital sex is— under certain circumstances—acceptable behavior for each to engage in. Suppose, that as a result there is no impulse to deceive each other about the occurrence or nature of any such relationships, and that no deception in fact occurs. Suppose, too, that there is no deception in respect to the feelings involved between the adulterous spouse and the extramarital partner. And suppose, finally, that one or the other or both of the spouses then have sexual intercourse in circumstances consistent with these understandings. Under this description, so the argument might conclude, adultery is simply not immoral. At a minimum, adultery cannot very plausibly be condemned either on the ground that it involves deception or on the ground that it requires the breaking of a promise.

At least two responses are worth considering. One calls attention to the connection between marriage and adultery; the other looks to more instrumental arguments for the immorality of adultery. Both issues deserve further exploration.

One way to deal with the case of the "open marriage" is to question whether the two persons involved are still properly to be described as being married to each other. Part of the meaning of what it is for two persons to be married to each other, so this argument would go, is to have committed oneself to have sexual relationships only with one's spouse. Of course, it would be added, we know that that commitment is not always honored. We know that persons who are married to each other often do commit adultery. But there is a difference between being willing to make a commitment to marital fidelity, even though one may fail to honor that commitment, and not making the commitment at all. Whatever the relationship may be between the two individuals in the case described above, the absence of any commitment to sexual exclusivity requires the conclusion that their relationship is not a marital one. For a commitment to sexual exclusivity is a necessary although not a sufficient condition for the existence of a marriage.

Although there may be something to this suggestion, as it is stated it is too strong to be acceptable. To begin with, I think it is very doubtful that there are many, if any, *necessary* conditions for marriage; but even if there are, a commitment to sexual exclusivity is not such a condition.

To see that this is so, consider what might be taken to be some of the essential characteristics of a marriage. We might be tempted to propose that the concept of marriage requires the following: a formal ceremony of some sort in which mutual obligations are undertaken between two persons of the opposite sex; the capacity on the part of the persons involved to have sexual intercourse with each other; the willingness to have sexual intercourse only with each other; and feelings of love and affection between the two persons. The problem is that we can imagine relationships that are clearly marital and yet lack one or more of these features. For example, in our own society, it is possible for two persons to be married without going through a formal ceremony, as in the commonlaw marriages recognized in some jurisdictions. It is also possible for two persons to get married even though one or both lacks the capacity to engage in sexual intercourse. Thus, two very elderly persons who have neither the desire nor the ability to have intercourse can, nonetheless, get married, as can persons whose sexual organs have been injured so that intercourse is not possible. And we certainly know of marriages in which love was not present at the time of the marriage, as, for instance, in marriages of state and marriages of convenience.

Counterexamples not satisfying the condition relating to the abstention from extramarital sex are even more easily produced. We certainly know of societies and cultures in which polygamy and polyandry are practiced, and we have no difficulty in recognizing these relationships as cases of marriages. It might be objected, though, that these are not counterexamples because they are plural marriages rather than marriages in which sex is permitted with someone other than with one of the persons to whom one is married. But we also know of societies in which it is permissible for married persons to have sexual relationships with persons to whom they were not married; for example, temple prostitutes, concubines, and homosexual lovers. And even if we knew of no such societies, the conceptual claim would still, I submit, not be well taken. For suppose all of the other indicia of marriage were present: suppose the two persons were of the opposite sex, suppose they participated in a formal ceremony in which they understood themselves voluntarily to be entering into a relationship with each other in which substantial mutual commitments were assumed. If all these conditions were satisfied, we would not be in any doubt about whether or not the two persons were married even though they had not taken on a commitment of sexual exclusivity and even though they had expressly agreed that extramarital sexual intercourse was a permissible behavior for each to engage in.

A commitment to sexual exclusivity is neither a necessary nor a sufficient condition for the existence of a marriage. It does, nonetheless, have this much to do with the nature of marriage: like the other indicia enumerated above, its presence tends to establish the existence of a marriage. Thus, in the absence of a formal ceremony of any sort, an explicit commitment to sexual exclusivity would count in favor of regarding the two persons as married. The conceptual role of the commitment to sexual exclusivity can, perhaps, be brought out through the following example. Suppose we found a tribe which had a practice in which all the other indicia of marriage were present but in which the two parties were *prohibited* ever from having sexual intercourse with each other. Moreover, suppose that sexual intercourse with others was clearly permitted.

In such a case we would, I think, reject the idea that the two were married to each other and we would describe their relationship in other terms, for example, as some kind of formalized, special friendship relation—a kind of heterosexual "blood-brother" bond.

Compare that case with the following. Suppose again that the tribe had a practice in which all of the other indicia of marriage were present, but instead of a prohibition on sexual intercourse between the persons in the relationship there was no rule at all. Sexual intercourse was permissible with the person with whom one had this ceremonial relationship, but it was no more or less permissible than with a number of other persons to whom one was not so related (for instance, all consenting adults of the opposite sex). Although we might be in doubt as to whether we ought to describe the persons as married to each other, we would probably conclude that they were married and that they simply were members of a tribe whose views about sex were quite different from our own.

What all of this shows is that *a prohibition* on sexual intercourse between the two persons involved in a relationship is conceptually incompatible with the claim that the two of them are married. The *permissibility* of intramarital sex is a necessary part of the idea of marriage. But no such incompatibility follows simply from the added permissibility of extramarital sex.

These arguments do not, of course, exhaust the arguments for the prohibition on extramarital sexual relations. The remaining argument that I wish to consider—as I indicated earlier—is a more instrumental one. It seeks to justify the prohibition by virtue of the role that it plays in the development and maintenance of nuclear families. The argument, or set of arguments, might, I believe, go something like this.

Consider first a farfetched nonsexual example. Suppose a society were organized so that after some suitable age—say, 18, 19, or 20—persons were forbidden to eat anything but bread and water with anyone but their spouse. Persons might still choose in such a society not to get married. Good food just might not be very important to them because they have underdeveloped taste buds. Or good food might be bad for them because there is something wrong with their digestive system. Or good food might be important to them, but they might decide that the enjoyment of good food would get in the way of the attainment of other things that were more important. But most persons would, I think, be led to favor marriage in part because they preferred a richer, more varied, diet to one of bread and water. And they might remain married because the family was the only legitimate setting within which good food was obtainable. If it is important to have society organized so that persons will both get married and stay married, such an arrangement would be well suited to the preservation of the family, and the prohibitions relating to food consumption could be understood as fulfilling that function.

It is obvious that one of the more powerful human desires is the desire for sexual gratification. The desire is a natural one, like hunger and thirst, in the sense that it need not be learned in order to be present within us and operative upon us. But there is in addition much that we do learn about what the act of sexual intercourse is like. Once we experience sexual intercourse ourselves—and in particular once we experience orgasm—we discover that it is among the most intensive, short-term pleasures of the body.

Because this is so, it is easy to see how the prohibition upon extramarital sex helps to hold marriage together. At least during that period of life when the enjoyment of sexual intercourse is one of the desirable bodily pleasures, persons will wish to enjoy those pleasures. If one consequence of being married is that one is prohibited from having sexual intercourse with anyone but one's spouse, then the spouses in a marriage are in a position to provide an important source of pleasure for each other that is unavailable to them elsewhere in the society.

The point emerges still more clearly if this rule of sexual morality is seen as of a piece with the other rules of sexual morality. When this prohibition is coupled, for example, with the prohibition on nonmarital sexual intercourse, we are presented with the inducement both to get married and to stay married. For if sexual intercourse is only legitimate within marriage, then persons seeking that gratification which is a feature of sexual intercourse are furnished explicit social directions for its attainment; namely marriage.

Nor, to continue the argument, is it necessary to focus exclusively on the bodily enjoyment that is involved. Orgasm may be a significant part of what there is to sexual intercourse, but it is not the whole of it. We need only recall the earlier discussion of the meaning that sexual intimacy has in our own culture to begin to see some of the more intricate ways in which sexual exclusivity may be connected with the establishment and maintenance of marriage as the primary heterosexual, love relationship. Adultery is wrong, in other words, because a prohibition on extramarital sex is a way to help maintain the institutions of marriage and the nuclear family.

Now I am frankly not sure what we are to say about an argument such as this one. What I am convinced of is that, like the arguments discussed earlier, this one also reveals something of the difficulty and complexity of the issues that are involved. So, what I want now to do—in the brief and final portion of this paper—is to try to delineate with reasonable precision what I take several of the fundamental, unresolved issues to be.

The first is whether this last argument is an argument for the *immorality* of extramarital sexual intercourse. What does seem clear is that there are differences between this argument and the ones considered earlier. The earlier arguments condemned adulterous behavior because it was behavior that involved breaking of a promise, taking unfair advantage, or deceiving another. To the degree to which the prohibition on extramarital sex can be supported by arguments which invoke considerations such as these, there is little question but that violations of the prohibition are properly regarded as immoral. And such a claim could be defended on one or both of two distinct grounds. The first is that things like promise-breaking and deception are just wrong. The second is that adultery involving promise-breaking or deception is wrong because it involves the straightforward infliction of harm on another human being—typically the nonadulterous spouse—who has a strong claim not to have that harm so inflicted.

The argument that connects the prohibition on extramarital sex with the maintenance and preservation of the institution of marriage is an argument for the instrumental value of the prohibition. To some degree this counts, I think, against regarding all violations of the prohibition as obvious cases of immorality. This is so partly because hypothetical imperatives are less clearly within the domain of morality than are categorical ones, and even more because instrumental prohibitions are within the domain of morality only if the end they serve or the way they serve it is itself within the domain of morality.

What this should help us see, I think, is the fact that the argument that connects the prohibition on adultery with the preservation of marriage is at best seriously incomplete. Before we ought to be convinced by it, we ought to have reasons for believing that marriage is a morally desirable and just social institution. And this is not quite as easy or obvious a task as it may seem to be. For the concept of marriage is, as we have seen, both a loosely structured and a complicated one. There may be all sorts of intimate, inter-personal relationships which will resemble but not be identical with the typical marriage relationship presupposed by the traditional sexual morality. There may be a number of distinguishable sexual and loving arrangements which can all legitimately claim to be called *marriages.* The prohibitions of the traditional sexual morality may be effective ways to maintain some marriages and ineffective ways to promote and preserve others. The prohibitions of the traditional sexual morality may make good psychological sense if certain psychological theories are true, and they may be purveyors of immense psychological mischief if other psychological theories are true. The prohibitions of the traditional sexual morality may seem obviously correct if sexual intimacy carries the meaning that the dominant culture has often ascribed to it, and they may seem equally bizarre when sex is viewed through the perspective of the counterculture. Irrespective of whether instrumental arguments of this sort are properly deemed moral arguments, they ought not to fully convince anyone until questions like these are answered.

WHAT IS WRONG WITH INCEST?

JEROME NEU

A friend wanted to have an affair with her cousin. She asked me if I could think of any reason why she should not. I could not (on just that basis) think of any. But then, are there any grounds other than affection that are admissible in limiting the choice of sexual objects (especially in those cases where affection is presumably most natural)? Are all possible relations open? Are taboos silly? Is everything (in the sphere of sexuality) permissible? If we cannot think of good reasons for existing institutions or practices, does that mean that the institutions or practices are dismissible? What is a "good reason"? ... I thought some more:

I

What is "incest"? I shall take it to cover prohibited sexual relations where it is the identity of the persons involved rather than the nature of their acts that is essential, and where the relevant features of the parties are defined in terms of social roles or positions. Social roles or positions may or may not in turn be defined (within a particular society) in terms of biological relationships. This notion is broad enough to include prohibited sexual activities other than male-female genital intercourse (e.g. homosexual relations between fathers and sons), so long as the objection depends on the persons rather than the activity. The notion is narrow enough to exclude sexual prohibitions, say against homosexuality or particular perversions (e.g. shoe fetishism or bestiality), which do not include essential reference to particular parties (specified by social position) to whom the activities are prohibited. If an activity is prohibited to all in relation to all, the prohibition is not an "incest taboo." Thus, "incest" is meant to pick out a particular type of objection to sexual activities: objection based on *who* people are in relation to each other, on social position, that is, on nonsexual relationships.

What is wrong with incest? As I am using the term, incestuous relations are by nature objectionable, and the problem is what in their nature makes them so. Posed in this way, I doubt that the question admits of an informative general answer. The answer will vary from society to society, with the types of social relationships leading to prohibitions, and the basis for drawing distinctions among social positions and relationships. Some more general insight may perhaps be obtained if we narrow our conception of incest to objections to sexual relations on the basis of social closeness rather than distance. So rules of exogamy (where these cover sexual relations—whatever

Reprinted from *Inquiry*, Vol. 19, No. 1 (1976), 27–39, with the permission of the author and the publisher, Universitetsforlaget, Oslo, Norway.

else may or may not be included in "marriage" relations) would be included, but rules of endogamy would not. (Of course there are restrictions on sexual relations within endogamous societies, the question is whether it is helpful to treat the restrictions on sexual relations with outsiders, the rules of endogamy, as themselves cases of "incest" prohibitions.) And the fact that a woman may be prohibited in a certain society from marrying a man of lesser wealth does not necessarily reveal much about that society's view of the interdependence of class and sexuality. Such a prohibition might serve a vast range of functions and be based on a wide variety of beliefs. The same would be true were the prohibition to make reference to the man being of equal or greater wealth or even being "too close" in wealth. This suggests a further narrowing of the conception of incestuous relationships so that specifications of social role having to do only with "family," and not (say) "class," would be relevant. But this sort of distinction is very difficult and would require elaborate discussion, and we would risk losing the generality I had hoped to obtain by not taking "incest" as simply sexual relations between blood relatives. So I will try to take some first steps towards the problem by discussing a particular conception of incest, ours, and a particular incestuous relationship, father-daughter, bearing in mind their connection with the broader concept we started with.

II

What is wrong with father-daughter incest in the eyes of the West? Or rather, what reasons might there be for prohibiting father-daughter incest in our society if a prohibition did not already exist?

1. An easy, but inadequate, answer is that it leads to genetic disaster. That discovery (if the claim is true) may well have come long after the prohibitions it is meant to explain, and in relation to the present, modern contraceptive technology makes it irrelevant. And the truth is that under certain conditions, as animal breeders can tell us, inbreeding can actually help maintain desirable traits. In any case, since sexual relations need no longer carry with them the danger of procreation, one need neither calculate nor fear the genetic consequences of incest.

2. The next answer is far more significant: mother will not like it. This difficulty is real and serious. A person who has a right to consideration and affection is sure to be hurt. The Oedipal triangle exists (and conceived broadly enough may exist in every society),[1] and so the suffering comes inevitably (though allowing special exceptions) with the incest. This difficulty is structural and rather different from (say) the problem that daughters may not

---

[1] This point is elaborated in my "Genetic Explanation in *Totem and Taboo,*" in Richard Wollheim (ed.), *Freud: A Collection of Critical Essays* (Garden City, N.Y.: Anchor Modern Studies in Philosophy, Doubleday & Co., 1974), pp. 366–93.

happen to find their fathers sexually attractive: lack of physical attraction may arise as an objection to any sexual partner, but the suffering of an important third party, while not peculiar to incestuous relationships, is inherent in them. Other affairs in other circumstances may, it is true, leave third parties unhappy (the usual case with adultery). But, outside of incestuous situations, there is nothing to guarantee that any third parties who might be involved will be significant to *both* participants in an affair. Mothers are bound to their daughters as well as to their husbands. Societal structure ensures that they are significant figures to both, and entitled to the concern of both. And the impact may be reciprocal: from harm to the mother's feelings there may follow danger to the daughter's developmental needs. That is, if the mother has even the fantasy that she is raising her daughter to be a sexual object for the father (and it is significant that humans can have such fantasies and that there is no reason to believe that animals can), she may be less willing and able to provide the needed mothering. The taboo is a barrier to certain thoughts (including fantasies) as well as to action.

3. A third answer is one that attracted Freud's interest in *Civilization and Its Discontents:* it is difficult enough to break out of the family as it is, with the addition of sexual relations and dependence it becomes virtually impossible. Incest is (literally) anti-social. Dependence comes with the relations. Sexual urges (in the context of incest prohibitions) are among the leading forces for breaking out of the family and forming complex social structures and relationships; necessary conditions for civilization. It may also be true, as Freud suggests, that sex (even non-incestuous sex) is by its nature anti-social. The parties may become sufficient unto themselves. But where they are part of the same family, society is more likely to break up into little divided family enclaves, perhaps cooperating where they must but never forming a community.[2] If we add a further assumption about limited psychic energy, so that what is given over to sexuality is not available for social purposes, the difficulties for society are obvious. (We should note, of course, that this added assumption makes matters no worse in the case of incestuous sexual relations than for other kinds.) From the point of view of the individual, in addition to the loss of the advantages of larger society and civilization, if the family encroaches on sexual as well as all other needs, she becomes so much the more the prisoner of the family. And, of course, should the affair fail she may have to go on living in the midst of a ruined prison. (And even if she need not stay, the family may be ruined—though that involves a different sort of loss.)

4. This relation of dependence brings us to a fourth objectionable feature of incestuous relations, or at least the form we have been focusing on. And it is perhaps the feature that contributes most to making incest seem worse

---

[2] Lévi-Strauss develops this idea (though perhaps confusing sex and marriage—incest and exogamy—in the process) in terms of women as tokens for exchange in his *The Elementary Structures of Kinship.* See Edmund Leach, *Lévi-Strauss,* Fontana Modern Masters (Glasgow and London: Collins Publishers, 1970), ch. VI.

than merely odd or disagreeable. The power structure, the structure of dependency, is such that the propositioned daughter is put in an unfair position. (This way of putting it assumes that the father makes the initial overt move, even if in response to a seductively active daughter. But the point holds in any case.) Too much is at stake. The situation may be compared to that of the boss who insists on sexual relations with his secretary. She may fear for her job. Her refusal is not a simple refusal of sexual relations, for she remains involved and dependent in other ways. The situation is even more extreme in the case of the father who propositions his daughter. Even if there is no direct threat of breaking the many other ties, a refusal of sexual relations may be experienced (by both parties) as a rejection on more levels than that of the original approach. Society's disapproval takes the burden off the daughter (and father) by helping ensure that the question does not arise. Teacher-student affairs may also provide an analogy, perhaps a better one than bosses and secretaries, for here the age-gap, custodial obligations, and societal disapproval are clearer. Some taboos are irrational. Some, when understood, have a variety of virtues.

III

Now, where do these points take us? Some way, to be sure; but, unfortunately, not terribly far nor terribly deep. If we were a daughter wondering whether to have an affair with our father (or vice versa), we would now have some general reasons not to. These reasons are independent of whether or not a taboo against this form of incest happens to exist in our society. But precisely because the reasons are independent reasons for a prohibition, they do not explain why the prohibition should take the form of a taboo (we have only "rationalized" the taboo). Taboos allow no questioning. Reasons, precisely because they are reasons, leave room for questioning. The reasons we have brought forward depend on features (admittedly, broad structural features) of our society; and so, in a given case, may not apply. What if (looking to our second point) mother does not mind, or, what if she is dead? The inevitable suffering of a significant third party may no longer seem so inevitable. And who would be the aggrieved third party in brother-sister incest? To explain the taboo here one might have to consider that a father who cannot have his daughter may nonetheless be jealous of her and so place her off limits for his son as well. (Of course, he might wish to stop all rivals, but he can most readily enforce his jealousy against the rival who is in his home. In any case, there is a question about whether the jealousy is justifiable.) Clearly, not all of the four factors we have brought out underlie all incest taboos in all cultures, nor are they the only factors even in our own. And certainly more must be done to distinguish factors connected with incest from factors that may apply to more general sexual prohibitions. For example, what makes father-daughter incest more than just a special case of prohibitions on adult-child sexual relations? For one thing, incest taboos, as we have said, are a matter of closeness and adult-child (as opposed to parent-child) prohibitions are a matter of distance. For another thing, objections to father-daughter incest presumably hold even when the daughter has become an adult. But (thinking back) are the objections to incest really the same or as strong when the child has become an adult as when she (or he) is an adolescent or pre-pubescent? (In this connection, it might be useful to consider the different applications and consequences of laws against statutory rape and incest laws.) So far we have only a beginning or a fragment of an analysis; a hint at the character of some of the non-sexual objections to sexual relations involved in "incest" (understood in the broad sense we started with). It should be noted, however, that the points made already extend beyond a narrowly biological conception of incest: we rejected the objection to father-daughter incest that depended on genealogy and genetics, and the other points made would all (in our society) be as applicable to step-fathers as to fathers. (Lawyers speak of "consanguinity" and "affinity".)

Though the points we have so far brought forward may justify certain incest prohibitions, they neither justify nor explain incest taboos—even within our society and even restricting our view to father-daughter incest. They may provide reasons for obeying an incest prohibition for someone who does not accept the prohibition as a taboo. But there may be good reasons why the prohibition takes the form of a taboo—a form which puts the demand for reasons out of place, and which imposes strict liability and so puts the offering of excuses out of place as well. Moreover, every society, every way of life, has its taboos, and these taboos always include (so the anthropologists tell us) incest taboos. No society allows all forms of sexual activity among all of its members. Every society prohibits absolutely (that is, unconditionally) certain sexual relations between certain persons on the basis of their social closeness. Why should this be so?

IV

Let us look at a famous case of parent-child incest. What is the tragedy of Oedipus? Why is Oedipus so upset? As far as is in his power he does no wrong, at every point he makes what (in his culture) would be the right choice, and yet, despite his best intentions and efforts, he kills his father and sleeps with his mother. In reality, he has no choice. When he comes to know of what he has done, he recognizes that his actions, though they fulfill his fate and are not his fault (he did not know what he was doing, indeed he did what he did precisely in order to avoid his predicted fate—and so, by the standards of post-Kantian morality and perhaps by those of Sophocles' own later play, *Oedipus at Colonus,* he is not responsible), nevertheless constitute a misfortune. As far as the four factors brought out in relation to father-daughter incest go, it is not even clear what the misfortune in his case is. Ignorance, and the other circumstances in his case, would seem to make his actions unobjectionable. But surely something is wrong. We may wish Oedipus had not blinded himself—the punishment may seem extreme—but what would we think if he had merely chuckled and said "Oh well, too bad, I tried to avoid it but fate seems to have won through"? Part of the point of tragedy, like the point of taboo, is that it allows no excuse. It was *his* fate and *his* misfortune. Despite circumstances, certain losses cannot be cancelled and certain hands cannot be made clean. Ancient morality leaves important room for the actual, for what in fact happens (detached from one's will and intentions), and it may still have a place in modern morality marked, perhaps, by taboo, by strict prohibitions.

What stands on the surface of ancient morality may perhaps be understood with the help of the depth vision of modern psychology. Though Oedipus knew not what he did at the time he did it, he nonetheless *meant* to do it. It was his unconscious wish. And that it was his unconscious wish, that it included a sexual desire, that that desire was the object of an incest taboo, that incest taboos (of one form or another) are universal, and that the particular form of incest taboos is patterned on features of a given society's social structure—none of these things are accidents. I mentioned earlier that the Oedipal triangle, if conceived broadly enough, may exist in every society. Let me sketch briefly what I mean and why it is a consequence of the conditions (biological and social) for human development that such a constellation of desires and emotions should exist, and be the object of prohibitions.

Born a helpless mammal into the world, if the human infant is to survive there must be a supporting figure (or figures)—typically, in our society and in most (here consider the facts of lactation), the mother. A dependency relation is formed, and this early attachment is a primary form of love. But with the supporting figure there always comes a rival. And it is not a mere accident that there is a rival, that there is another party that takes the child's "mother" as a love object. That there was at one point, at least, a third party is a biological necessity, a matter of the conditions for procreation. That there continues to be a third party (or parties) after the child's birth—though it need not be the child's biological father—also has a biological basis. The mother is herself a mammal with needs and desires of her own, needs and desires that cannot be met by her infant, and that impel her to establish and maintain relations with other adult mammals. And these others come to be seen, by the child, as rivals for the love, affection, time and concern of the mother. Hence the Oedipal triangle is complete, and the essential emotional constellation established on the basis of the biologically prolonged dependency of the mammalian child and the biological needs and relations of the supporting mammalian adults. Breaking out of the triangle of dependent love and concomitant jealousy involves a long and complex process of growth. The conflicts themselves become most acute at a particular stage in the child's growth and development, a stage determined by biological conditions and the conditions for socialization. The shape of a particular society will help determine who the loved supporting figures and who the hated rivals and socializing authority figures will be. In the end, according to psychoanalytic theory, a superego is formed as the result of identification and introjection of the figures who restrain one's Oedipal wishes: moral prohibitions arise out of fear of punishment by or fear of the loss of love of an authority figure on whom one is dependent. In telling his complex story (and the story is doubtless more complex for women), Freud employs (in *Totem and Taboo*) the myth of the brothers who band together and slay and eat (and so literally incorporate) the primal father. The incest taboo emerges because their (ambivalent) love for the father comes to the fore after his slaying. The sons then identify with his prohibitions (incorporated in their superegos). What is prohibited is what father would not have liked. The taboo emerges also because the liberated brothers might otherwise renew among themselves the conflict over the women that led to their revolt against their father in the first place—without the taboo they might all continue their strife for their father's role. (Note that these two points have important connections with the second and third points in our discussion of father-daughter incest, points about mother not liking it and breaking out of the family for social cooperation.) It may be a condition for the maintenance of each society that it be true to its origins. The superego and its requirements, the strict liability that it imposes on us all, may be conditions for the formation of mature object relations and societal order. That every society must feel those prohibitions (in one form or another) may follow (perhaps not simply, but nonetheless may follow) from the conditions for its existence as a society.[3]

V

More has to be done, I think, to show how taboos may connect with the conditions of a moral consciousness and how, in the light of their universality, they connect with the conditions for any society. Taboos, particularly incest taboos, may be essential to the development of character, to the development of the superego and to full object relations, to the shape of a way of life. Unless we were able to feel guilt at incest, perhaps we could not feel guilt at anything, or be fit for social relations. A person undisturbed by incest might be undisturbable by any social prohibition. In my too brief sketch, it can be seen that we get our superego from precisely those whose love we fear to lose. Granted that we do not want their disapproval, however, why should they disapprove incest in particular? I hope that discussion of the nature of incest, of the nature of incest prohibitions, and of the place of drives towards

---

[3] What the role of the performance of plays such as *Oedipus Rex* and related rituals (e.g., the totemic feasts discussed by Freud) may be raises interesting questions. It may be that they provide occasions both for violating the taboo and for reaffirming its force (by repeating the feelings that led to its original institution).

incest in the development of individuals and societies may help us to see how the pieces fit together.

I cannot carry that discussion much further here, but perhaps I can at least suggest that the (or a) key may be in the notions of identity and identification. Each generation must win its identity, partly through struggle with the older generation and partly through something like mourning for its loss. The "something like mourning" amounts to identification. But the identification makes sense only through difference, as a culmination of the effort to overcome infantile dependence and achieve autonomy. Incest destroys difference: categories collapse, people cease to have clear and distinct sexual and social places (consider the scene in the film *Chinatown* where the confusion bursts out in the anguished "sister/daughter, sister/daughter . . ." confrontation); and with the destruction of difference people cease to have the possibility of shifting from one place to another as they develop. Perhaps that might make incest seem attractive to some. But I suspect that violation of incest taboos would not itself be an effective revolutionary act. While destroying difference and confusing roles and perhaps undermining authority, it would not overcome dependence—which, as I have said, I think is a biological and social necessity. Violation of incest taboos or their abolition would not, I think, allow the establishment of a stable, mature, independent identity.

If one turns to the clinical literature to confirm one's suspicions about the effects of incest on development, one encounters a number of problems. First, there is not much data. Secondly, the paucity is apparently systematic, i.e. in our society father-daughter incest is the form most commonly reported, but there is reason to believe sibling incest is the most common in occurrence. Mother-son incest is extremely rare in published accounts and homosexual incest is hardly ever even mentioned. Perhaps sibling incest is not usually reported precisely because its effects are not particularly deleterious, or perhaps precisely because it is so common. There are also questions about *who* would report it—is there a victim? an aggrieved third party?—and what exactly is the line between childish or adolescent sex play and incest? (If we understand sexuality in the broad way suggested by Freud in his *Three Essays on the Theory of Sexuality* then incestuous desires and acts need not involve genital intercourse.) Thirdly, the data are clinical (or even less helpful, criminal) and therefore of course reveal (if they reveal anything) severe psychological disruption. It is extremely difficult to get data on cases where consummated incest is not harmful. (Louis Malle's film, *Souffle au Coeur*, plays on the assumption, or wish, that such cases are possible.) Fourthly and finally, it is difficult to distinguish, in those cases where there is harm, how much of it is attributable to the existence of the prohibition rather than the incest itself. That is, is the harm a product of the prohibition or an independent reason for having a prohibition? The prohibition itself may cause problems, or given the prohibition perhaps only people who are already otherwise disturbed engage in incest. All this makes it difficult to isolate its consequences.

VI

But perhaps this sort of calculation of consequences is wrongheaded (or really only illuminates one special aspect of our question). For the prohibition is a taboo. It is unconditional. That is, in one sense of unconditional, it is not a means to an independently valued end, but a necessary part of a way of life and ideal of human relationship. And these notions of a "way of life" and an "ideal of relationship" may be more central than the conditions for development of the superego in understanding the role of fixed boundaries or prohibitions in morality. The simple calculation of psychological consequences may miss the importance of "identity," where the identity of the individual is intimately connected with the coherence of a way of life distinguished by the characteristic virtues and vices and patterns of relationship recognized within it. When one says taboos are absolute and unconditional but may not be irrational one should compare them with something like ideals of justice which are also not simply assimilable to utilitarian calculations. There are in fact a number of ideals in various spheres which make for absolute prohibitions. One must not betray friends, not simply because they might become angry, but because they would no longer be "friends," indeed, the betrayal might reveal that they never were. Certain sorts of loyalty may be necessary to certain sorts of friendship. And those sorts of friendship are valuable. One must beware too narrow notions of what counts as a reason here. Certain sorts of love demand certain sorts of trust. And certain sorts of trust may rule out certain sorts of reasons. To trust because one has weighed the evidence (where one is willing to waver if the evidence does) may be as bad as not trusting at all. One's love may then be of the wrong kind. A certain ideal of love lies behind unquestioning trust. And the value of that ideal, its place in a way of life, may count as a reason for valuing that sort of trust and excluding certain sorts of doubts. Unquestioning attitudes are needed for certain kinds or qualities of relationship. The role of faith in religion might provide another way to get a handle on this difficult set of issues. (We should remember that "taboo" is itself originally a religious notion.) I am inclined to think that these sorts of cases, and especially the restrictions placed on action by ideals of justice (which make certain actions "unthinkable" or "unconscionable"), provide the most useful parallels for understanding the restrictions that incest taboos place on sexual relations.

There may be prohibitions which are necessary (to morality, to society, to humanity) even though they may not be justifiable within a narrower conception (e.g., utilitarian) of morality and justification.[4] It is not an accident that every society has incest taboos, that every society prohibits some sexual

---

[4] On the place of absolute prohibitions in morality and ways of life, see Stuart Hampshire, "Morality and Pessimism," *New York Review of Books,* Vol. XIX, Nos. 11–12 (January 25, 1973), pp. 26–33.

relations on grounds independent of the intrinsic character of the activity involved (which is, in other circumstances, approved) but based rather on social relations. It may be that it is a condition of social relations that members of a society be able to feel the force of (if not obey) such prohibitions. The pattern of the prohibitions may vary from society to society and with the structure of social relations, but there could be no society without some such prohibitions and the possibility of respect for them. And the fact that the prohibitions are sexual may have to do with the conditions for psychosocial development of the individual, and so have a biological basis. (Restrictions on impulses to murder, on aggression, may similarly be universal, and necessary, and absolute, and also have a biological basis.) Prohibitions which are absolute within a particular society (even if they are different in different societies) even though they cannot be fully understood or justified (in a narrow sense) may be essential to morality (in a broader sense) and to society and so to humanity (insofar as man is a social animal). The key to understanding taboos, as opposed to other sorts of social prohibitions (legal, utilitarian, etc.), may lie in those very features of taboos that are most puzzling to modern moral consciousness: taboos are universal (every society has some, including, in particular, taboos on murder and incest), and absolute (are unconditional and allow no questioning), and impose strict liability (allow no excuse). These features may not be irrational. But while we must consider this possibility, we should also be aware of how paradoxical it is to reach this sort of conclusion, which calls a halt to questioning, after the sort of questioning or as the result of the sort of questioning we have just ourselves engaged in. The taboo is, of course, meant to extend to thought and not just action. Some things (incest, betrayal of a friend . . .) are supposed to be unthinkable. Is there a line between "thinking" and "thinking about"?

VII

In summary: Incest taboos should be seen as involving non-sexual objections to sexual relations, that is, objections based on who people are in relation to each other, rather than their activities. What is at stake is brought out by considering certain objections to father-daughter incest and certain features of taboos. The objections that matter do not depend on social ties and distinctions having a biological basis, but there is nonetheless a biological element in incest taboos. To see it, one must look to the nature of the Oedipus complex, and to the conditions for the development of the individual and of society. There may be prohibitions which are necessary (to morality, to society, to humanity) even though they may not be justifiable within a narrower conception (e.g., utilitarian) of morality and justification. And so taboos which are universal (occur, in one form or another, in every society), and absolute (allow no questioning), and impose strict liability (allow no excuse), may not be irrational: they may mark the boundaries that shape a way of life.[5]

[5] A version of this paper was presented at the Pacific Division Meeting of the American Philosophical Association in March 1975. It has benefited from the comments of a number of people, but I am especially indebted to Robert Meister for criticism of an earlier draft. What is best in the paper is due to him.

THE QUESTION OF HOMOSEXUALITY

JOSEPH P. MARGOLIS

The psychiatric discussion of homosexuality is at the present time pretty much in a shambles. The reasons happen to be largely conceptual, and expose, more effectively than any mere polemic, the extent to which our moral prejudices masquerade as medicine. Needless to say, the earnest quackery focused on one putative medical category is bound to manifest itself in others.

Early in December 1973 the board of trustees of the American Psychiatric Association voted to discontinue listing "homosexuality per se" as a "psychiatric disorder," defining it instead as a "sexual orientation disturbance."[1] The board did not by its action alter the classification of homosexuality in the American Psychiatric Association's *Diagnostic and Statistical Manual of Mental Disorders (DSM-2).*[2] There it is classified as a distinct mental disorder. It has been so classified by the profession for about one hundred years. The second edition of the manual introduced a good number of diagnostic changes in the original 1952 publication *(DSM-1),* but none affect the declassification of sexual disorders,[3] in spite of the fact that other professional bodies have been actively advocating the removal of homosexuality as an illness for some time—notably, the National Association for Mental Health and the Group for the Advancement of Psychiatry.[4] Furthermore, the nomenclature of the manual is intended to adhere as closely as possible to the classification provided in the World Health Organization's *International Classification of Dis-*

Reprinted from Robert Baker and Frederick Elliston (eds.), *Philosophy and Sex* (Buffalo, New York: Prometheus Books, 1975) pp. 288–302, with the permission of the author and the publisher.

[1] "Ideas and Trends," *New York Times,* December 23, 1973, p. E5. In April 1974 the membership of the American Psychiatric Association voted, in a referendum, to support the board's vote: 5,854 in favor, 3,810 against, out of 17,910 eligible voters. That vote has now been challenged on the grounds of having been improperly influenced by a letter signed by Association leaders but "conceived and paid for by the National Gay Task Force"! The matter is pending. Cf. *New York Times.* May 26, 1974, p. 39.

[2] Third edition (Washington, D.C.: American Psychiatric Association, 1968). The third edition appears to be identical with the second.

[3] Cf. Robert L. Spitzer and Paul T. Wilson, "A Guide to the New Nomenclature," *DSM-2,* sec. 7.

[4] Cf. *APA Monitor,* vol. 5, no. 2 (February 1974): 1, 9.

eases (ICD).[5] This, in effect, means that the manual's use of the terms "disorder," "mental disorders," and "nonpsychotic mental disorders" is intended to designate medically significant syndromes properly falling under the *ICD's* generic classification of disease (though not all the categories there provided designate diseases). In fact, the manual adheres to the *ICD-8's* diagnostic code numbers, with certain designated exceptions; and the efforts of Dr. Henry Brill, who was active in the preparation of *DSM-2,* seem to have influenced as well the final form of *ICD-8,* with regard to the classification of mental disorders.[6]

The relevant *DSM* category 302, headed "sexual deviations," includes the following: homosexuality (302.0); fetishism (302.1); pedophilia (302.2); transvestitism (302.3); exhibitionism (302.4); voyeurism (302.5); sadism (302.6); masochism (302.7); other sexual deviation (302.8); and unspecified sexual deviation (302.9).[7] Voyeurism, sadism, and masochism are categories added to *ICD-8* "for use in the United States only"; that is to say, the restriction represents a lack of international agreement on their classification as mental disorders. Unspecified sexual deviation is, apparently, an *ICD-8* category, "to be avoided in the United States or used by record librarians only."[8] The entire category 302 is listed, together with personality disorders, alcoholism, and drug dependence, as "personality disorders and certain other nonpsychotic mental disorders"; they were, apparently, linked as personality disorders in *DSM-1.* The subcategories are not described in the manual; the only description rendered is as follows:

> This category is for individuals whose sexual interests are directed primarily toward other than people of the opposite sex, toward sexual acts not usually associated with coitus, or toward coitus performed under bizarre circumstances as in necrophilia, pedophilia, sexual sadism, and fetishism. Even though many find their practices distasteful, they remain unable to substitute normal sexual behavior for them. This diagnosis is not appropriate for individuals who perform deviant sexual acts because normal sexual objects are not available to them.

Needless to say, the description is extremely slim, loose, unsystematic, and tendentious.

Prominent in the American Psychiatric Association's recent reversal regarding the classification of homosexuality was Dr. Robert L. Spitzer, who seems to have played an important role both in the preparation of *DSM-2* and in the APA's reasoned reversal (Spitzer served as head of the APA Task Force on Nomenclature and Statistics). Defending that action, Spitzer held that: "By removing homosexuality from the nomenclature we are not saying it is abnormal but we are not saying it is normal. And I also believe that

---

[5] *Eighth Revision International Classification of Diseases Adapted for Use in the United States,* Public Health Service Publication No. 1693 (Washington, D.C.: U.S. Government Printing Office, 1968).

[6] Cf. Morton Kramer, "The Historical Background of *ICD-8," DSM-2.* Intro.

[7] *DSM-2,* p. 44.

[8] *DSM-2,* p. 1.

normal and abnormal are, strictly speaking, not psychiatric terms."[9] The obvious difficulty that Spitzer's remark exposes is this: If "normal" and "abnormal" are not technical psychiatric terms, how can any mental disorders—in particular those classified together with sexual deviations—be properly so designated? And if "normal" and "abnormal" do designate objectively determined psychiatric distinctions, how are they actually to be discerned? On what grounds was homosexuality formerly classified as a mental disorder, as a form of sexual deviation, as not normal, and on what grounds is it now to be removed from the nomenclature? Clearly, the attempt of the APA to accommodate prevailing changes in personal convictions threatens to undermine the entire foundation of the manual. Spitzer apparently has admitted the pressure of the gay-liberation movement, but insists that the new category is psychiatrically sound.[10]

There seems to be considerable uncertainty in psychiatric circles as to whether so-called sexual deviations are, as disorders, to be classified as illnesses. The manual clearly subsumes mental diseases under mental disorders—"disease" regularly signifies a well-articulated syndrome in which physical causes are decisive; the reliable application of the term trails off as the etiology is linked, as in schizophrenia, to thought and mood disorders. The term "illness" never occurs in the manual except in certain titles of disorders—the varieties of so-called manic-depressive illness, for instance, where there is some reason to think the term "disease" is resisted, even though the syndromes are highly articulated, precisely because physical causes cannot be reliably assigned.[11]

On the other hand, "disorder" is nowhere defined in the manual and occurs in the major disease categories of *ICD-8* only in the major heading "mental disorders" (which corresponds, broadly, to the distinction of the *DSM*. In the *ICD-8*, clearly, "disease" does not actually cover all so-called "major disease categories," since other categories include "neoplasms," "complications" (as of pregnancy, childbirth, and the puerperium), "congenital anomalies," "certain causes of perinatal morbidity and mortality" (which may or may not include diseases), "symptoms and ill-defined conditions" (which may or may not include diseases), "accidents, poisonings, and violence." Nevertheless, nearly all informal discussions of mental disorders—whether by psychiatrists or others—tend to treat well-articulated disorders, particularly those in the manual, as illnesses. "Illness" seems to serve either as a substitute for "disease," wherever the etiology is not known to be definitely physical or is taken to be primarily concerned with affective processes or processes of mood or thought, or as a general term signifying a clinically significant departure from norms of health, whether or not the etiology is clear.

---

[9] "Ideas and Trends."

[10] *APA Monitor*, vol. 5, no. 2.

[11] This is undoubtedly related to Thomas Szasz's well-known attack on the concept of mental illness. Cf. *The Myth of Mental Illness* (New York: Harper & Row, 1961).

In an instructive exchange between Dr. Spitzer and Dr. Irving Bieber (professor of clinical psychiatry, New York Medical College) published by the *New York Times,*[12] the term "disease" never occurs, and Spitzer and Bieber do not use "disorder" and "illness" in the same sense: Spitzer (expressing the intentions of the APA) appears to regard "mental disorder" and "mental illness" as synonymous; and Bieber expressly wishes to use these terms as nonequivalent. The upshot is that Spitzer, claiming that it "does not meet the criteria for psychiatric disorder," denies that homosexuality is a mental illness; and Bieber, agreeing that it is not a mental illness, nevertheless regards it as a "psychiatric disorder." Usefully, Bieber also observes that voyeurism, fetishism, asexuality (celibacy), and frigidity are not, on his view, psychiatric illnesses; furthermore, he claims, they are not mental disorders, even if they appear (as do voyeurism and fetishism, for instance) in the *DSM*.

The difference between Spitzer and Bieber bears quite decisively on the medical controversy about homosexuality (and other sexual deviations). For Bieber expressly says the following:

> I say homosexuality is a psychiatric injury to function and belongs in any psychiatric manual. Now that doesn't mean I consider it an illness any more than I consider frigidity an illness. As long as something like frigidity will be in the manual, disorders of sexual functioning and homosexuality belong there. And to differentiate two types, to take what is really the most injured homosexual and say he shouldn't be in the *DSM,* and that the least injured, the one who has the potential left for restoring his heterosexuality, should be diagnosed as a sexual orientation disorder, to me seems wild.[13]

The point is fairly made, because Spitzer says:

> If homosexuality does not meet the criteria for psychiatric disorder, what is it? Descriptively, we can say that it is one form of sexual behavior. However, in no longer considering it a psychiatric disorder, we are not saying that it is normal or that it is as valuable as heterosexuality. We must recognize that for those homosexuals who are troubled, or dissatisfied with their homosexual feelings, that we are then dealing with a psychiatric disorder because we then have subjective distress.[14]

What the disagreement comes to is this: Bieber regards homosexuality as a psychiatric disorder (but not an illness) because it is an "injury to function," that is, to natural or normal function; and Spitzer admits that homosexuality may produce "subjective distress" in terms of the functioning preferred by those who happen to be homosexually inclined, although "normal" and "abnormal" are not psychiatric distinctions. Bieber holds heterosexual functioning to be injured by homosexuality: "in all homosexuals," he says, "there has been a disturbance of normal heterosexual development" (though he does *not*

---

[12] "Ideas and Trends"; also, in criticism of Szasz, see Joseph Margolis, *Psychotherapy and Morality* (New York: Random House, 1966).
[13] "Ideas and Trends."
[14] Ibid.

claim that such a disturbance is always behaviorally manifested or even felt as "subjective distress"—on the contrary, he seems to regard the "satisfied" homosexual as even more disturbed than the homosexual upset with his own condition). But though Spitzer resists the view that homosexuality is an injury (in a sense analogous to that in which the crippled are injured), he admits that it may contribute to psychiatric disorders. He faces, therefore, two sorts of difficulty. First, he offers no criterion for determining what is and what is not a psychiatric disorder—to which homosexuality could contribute (he has, it will be remembered, denied that psychiatric distinctions depend on the normal and abnormal). Second, he (and the board of trustees of the American Psychiatric Association) is disinclined to treat homosexuality and heterosexuality as fully equal and acceptable alternatives on any relevant psychiatric scale (after all, he and they construe homosexuality as a "sexual orientation disturbance"—though only for those homosexuals actually in conflict about their sexual orientation, only for those who may wish to change it or learn to live with it better).

So there is an obvious lacuna in the new APA ruling. Why did not the recommendation of Spitzer's committee consider *heterosexuality* as a "sexual orientation disturbance"—though *only,* of course, for those heterosexuals actually in conflict about their sexual orientation, only for those who wish to change it or learn to live with it better? It is obvious that the APA considers heterosexuality preferable in some (suppressed) psychiatrically significant way. Spitzer himself favorably cites Freud's remark, in a letter, in 1955, to the effect that homosexuality "cannot be classified as an illness. We consider it to be a variation of the sexual function produced by a certain arrest of sexual development." [15] Freud's view, however, for good or bad, squarely rests on a model of sexual normality; but Spitzer (and presumably the APA) has rejected this view in construing homosexuality as a disturbance *in terms of the "subjective distress" of particular homosexuals.* "Subjective distress" argues that homosexuality and heterosexuality should be treated symmetrically; but in that case there would be no sense—as Bieber quite rightly points out— in including homosexuality as a distinct category of mental disorder (or at least in including it without adding a complementary category regarding heterosexuality). Beyond this it should be noted that the classification "sexual orientation disturbance" designates a novel category not hitherto employed, explicated solely in terms of subjective distress. Consequently it is a parasitic category of a peculiar sort: it characterizes homosexuality (a form of "sexual orientation") as a "disturbance" if and only if it is causally responsible for some form of regularized "subjective distress" or "generalized impairment in social effectiveness or functioning"! But of course *any orientation* can and does so function for some population. There is only one possible explanation for the new category: it is premised on an at least attenuated commitment to Freudian notions of sexual normality, but formulated in terms of an official

[15] Ibid.

refusal to designate heterosexuality and homosexuality, as such, as normatively ordered psychiatric preferences.

Bieber's view is more orthodox and more plausible, in terms of the *DSM-2*. But it is also more directly vulnerable in just those terms in which Spitzer's committee was responding to newer social tendencies: an enormous number of homosexuals seek no clinical help for their homosexual "condition," are as comfortable and as "functional" socially as the ordinary run of heterosexuals, and view their own therapeutic problems as etiologically neutral to their "sexual orientation." Bieber's thesis that homosexuality *as such* is an injury to (heterosexual) function—more clinically poignant in the instance of a satisfied homosexual than in the instance of a troubled one (a sort of "crippling")—cannot possibly be understood except in terms of a general Freudian model, no matter how attenuated or modified.

But in that connection, it is extremely interesting that neither Bieber nor Spitzer ever considers the widespread phenomenon of bisexuality. Clinical psychologists not already committed to a Freudian model and attentive to actual consultations report that bisexual practice is a distinct phenomenon, that so-called homosexuals are very often bisexual, that bisexuality exhibits an extremely wide range of alternative forms of sexual "orientation," including, prominently, the rejection of fixed sexual roles. Further, bisexuality need not and characteristically does not entail an "injury" to heterosexual functioning, regardless of whether such functioning is viewed as normal and natural on any manageable scale whatsoever.[16] Bisexuals tend to be classified as homosexuals rather in the same spirit in which racially mixed people in the United States are classified as blacks. In any case, Bieber's thesis forces us to consider the notion of normal or natural (sexual) functioning. For one thing, bisexuality does not (by definition) interfere with heterosexual functioning—and yet, undoubtedly, it would be regarded as a form of sexual deviation (perhaps even a more alarming form than homosexuality), might even be thought to "cripple" or "injure" heterosexuality (which apparently must be exclusive, on the orthodox view), and might well be expected to produce a significant amount of "subjective distress" (even in the absence of confirming evidence). Further, it is by no means clear how to defend any exclusive norm of nondeviant sexual functioning on psychiatric or scientific grounds without resting one's case on shifting views of social preference and tolerance—which undercuts the presumption of the therapeutic community.

Broadly speaking, homosexuality (and other forms of so-called sexual de-

[16] There has been very little published on this issue as yet. The information regarding bisexuality has been collected, informally, from private communications among psychologists, and some psychiatrists, practicing in the Philadelphia area. The point is somewhat surprising since Freud himself definitely held the view that all human beings are bisexual by nature—though, in contemporary terms, he seems to have been particularly ignorant of lesbianism and construed male homosexuality in terms of a limitation of sexual maturity. Cf. *Three Essays on the Theory of Sexuality,* trans. James Strachey (standard ed., 1953). Cf. also, Charlotte Wolff, *Love Between Women* (New York: St. Martin's Press, 1971), chaps, 2, 3; and Kate Millett, *Sexual Politics* (New York: Doubleday, 1969).

viation) is viewed pejoratively in one of three distinct ways—either it is said to be a form of illness, or a form of criminal behavior, or a behavioral perversion.[17] There are systematic difficulties with each strategy, but they are, it should be noted, dialectically linked with one another. A full analysis of each category would take us too far afield.[18] Let it suffice to acknowledge that crime and illness represent institutionalizations, along somewhat different lines, of the dominant prudential interests of given societies. We have already noted the conceptual embarrassment to psychiatry of construing homosexuality as a form of illness: to speak of illness presupposes norms of bodily and mental and emotional functioning that can be independently validated. But however reasonable it may be to postulate certain syndromes as disorders—assuming the most limited and nontendentious level of functioning relative to prudential objectives, for instance, preserving life, minimizing pain, maintaining the movement of limbs, and the like—it can hardly be denied (on the empirical evidence) that homosexuality per se cannot be characterized as interfering with such prudential objectives. It is fair to say that to classify homosexuality as an illness or disorder as such is effectively to intrude moral or moral-like preferences in the guise of medicine.[19]

Rather little needs to be said about the complaint that homosexuality is a criminal activity. First of all, the complaint is likely to depend on contingent and irrelevant considerations—for example, that a particular episode (otherwise not so classifiable) was not an act between consenting adults; in the same spirit, and equally irrelevantly, voyeurism might be construed as an invasion of privacy. Secondly, there is a strong movement to decriminalize homosexuality precisely on the grounds that it forms one of those anomalous "crimes without victims," *unless* one supposes (analogously with the practice of medicine) that homosexuality violates in some sense certain inalienable prudential or overriding goods proper to human life itself—*regardless* of the apparent preferences of otherwise competent adults. Crime entails harm or the threat of harm to another. This is why, assuming the prevailing prudential concerns of given communities (for instance, preserving life, avoiding maiming and bodily injury, securing property, and the like), it is relatively easy to specify crimes without invoking norms of personal development or morally tendentious values of just that sort—with the important exceptions of political crimes and so-called crimes without victims. But crimes against the self are impossible to detail without reference to some conception of the normatively moral development of human beings. This is not to say that criminal law is independent of the moral preferences of particular societies—that is impossible.[20] It is to say only that criminal law may be relatively free from an

---

[17] It could, of course, also be said to be a form of insanity. But the charge is too preposterous to have had any significant historical support. Cf. Phyllis Chesler, *Women and Madness* (New York: Doubleday, 1972).

[18] An account is provided in Joseph Margolis, *Negativities: The Limits of Life and Death* (Columbus, Ohio: Charles Merrill, 1975). Cf. also, *Psychotherapy and Morality;* and "Illness and Medical Values," *The Philosophical Forum* (1969): 252–60.

[19] Compare Philip Rieff, *Freud: The Mind of a Moralist* (New York: Viking Press, 1959).

[20] Cf. Margolis, *Negativities,* chap. 5.

explicit dependence on "public morality," publicly approved standards of personal conduct that cannot be said to impinge, except tendentiously, on the minimal prudential interests of the community.[21] Hence, arguments against construing homosexuality as an illness may be readily complemented, and with at least as much force, by arguments against construing it as a criminal activity.

There remains the question of perversion. To construe homosexuality as a perversion is to construe it as a sexual deviation—not primarily of a statistical sort—that fails in some significant respect to conform with "appropriate" norms of sexual behavior and desire. Emphasis should be placed on the deliberate vagueness of the qualification "appropriate." The appropriate norms might be said to be medical or legal—in which case the provisions already considered would be called into play. On that interpretation the category of perversion is directly linked to the prevailing prudential interests of a society, and constraints are plausibly justified in terms of therapeutic and criminal considerations. "Functional" norms, however, may be elaborated along different lines. For instance, prudential values of a sort larger than the merely medical or legal may be claimed to be affected: homosexuality and other so-called sexual perversions may be said to threaten the survival of a people in deflecting sexual practice away from the reproductive function. Or, moral values, which prudential values serve merely instrumentally, may be claimed to be affected: homosexuality and other so-called perversions may be said to threaten the correct obligations and the like that bind human beings in their most intimate personal relations by attracting them appetitively into incompatible practices. Or, values regarding personal development and personal relationships that are neither clearly moral nor prudential—possibly, in some serious sense, aesthetic values regarding the quality of life—may be claimed to be affected: homosexuality and other so-called perversions may be said to threaten the "richness" or "fullness" or "style" or "quality" of life by diverting our tastes into narrower, more restricted, or less than fully "human" options. It is plain that condemnatory strategies of all these sorts have actually been pursued—some elaborated in functional terms, some not.

There are large difficulties confronting any claims about discovering the natural or normal functions or relations proper to human beings. There is no point in detailing these difficulties here.[22] It is enough to note that they are all related to the fact that, biologically, human beings may be classified as such without intruding any normative considerations whatsoever, and to the fact that human persons (sentient creatures having the capacity to use

---

[21] Cf. H. L. A. Hart, *Law, Liberty, and Morality* (Stanford, Calif.: Stanford University Press, 1963) on the relationship between law and morality; also, the argument of Lord Devlin, *The Enforcement of Morals* (Oxford: Oxford University Press, 1959). Cf. also, "Report on the Committee on Homosexual Offenses and Prostitution," London, H.M.S.O. Cmd. 247, September 1957, para. 13, cited in Norman St. John-Stevas, *Life, Death and the Law* (Bloomington: Indiana University Press, 1961). The essential issue concerns the concept of law as "the enforcement of morality as such."

[22] Cf. Joseph Margolis, *Values and Conduct* (New York: Clarendon; and Oxford: Oxford University Press, 1971); *Psychotherapy and Morality; Negativities.*

language and the power of self-reference) are culturally emergent entities whose values cannot be separated from the doctrines, ideologies, and ideals of the societies in which they develop. But the weakness of the usual functional and nonfunctional complaints against homosexuality (as a perversion) is fairly straightforward and hardly requires demonstrating the large conclusions sketched.

The functional complaint may be fairly represented (acknowledging the need for doctrinal adjustments here and there) by the following comment of the liberal Catholic theorist Norman St. John-Stevas, speaking of homosexuality as a distinct perversion (as opposed to "transient homosexuality" in children and adolescents):

> The Catholic natural law tradition accepts as self-evident that the primary purpose of sexual intercourse is procreation, and relegates as secondary such ends as fostering the mutual love of the spouses and allaying concupiscence. This conclusion is based on two propositions, that man by the use of his reason can discover God's purpose in the Universe, and that God makes known His purpose by certain "given" physical arrangements. Thus, man can deduce that the purpose of sexual activity is procreation, the continuation of the human race; and the physical arrangements God has provided may not be supplanted at man's will. We now know that not every act of *coitus* is conceptual and relational, and others relational only. But to recognize this fact is not to conclude that acts may be rendered conceptual or non-conceptual at man's will. Man is free to act only within the pattern imposed by nature.[23]

But St. John-Stevas also acknowledges Pius XII's *Humani Generis,* to the effect that "divine revelation must be called morally necessary," since though natural law is not beyond the power of human reason, it cannot be known "with ease, with unwavering certitude, and without any admixture of error," due to "the present condition of the human race."[24] St. John-Stevas himself says that "in many controverted moral problems ... the natural law does not provide a certain guide," but he treats this as "a practical difficulty"(*sic*).[25] The simple point remains that in the oldest and most persistent tradition of the West concerned with the specification of perversions, an absolutely critical methodological weakness is freely admitted. Apart from the fiat of the Church there seems to be no reliable way in which to discount otherwise coherent views about the "purpose" of sexual intercourse and sexual relations. Certainly, it seems that the "given" physical arrangements accommodate homosexuality every bit as well as heterosexuality; that the societal "purpose" of procreation is entirely compatible with the mixed personal "purposes" of homosexual, heterosexual, and bisexual behavior (or even of the other so-called sexual perversions); and that on the empirical evidence the reproduction of the species is hardly a sexual concern at the present time (as we approach an unheard-of population of about seven billion by the year 2000). It is even possible that deviant and perverted sexual practice may contribute to procreation, to mutual love, and the allaying of concupiscence.

[23] St. John-Stevas, pp. 83–84.
[24] Ibid., pp. 29–30.
[25] St. John-Stevas.

The nonfunctional complaint may be fairly represented by an essay of Thomas Nagel's.[26] Nagel's view is particularly interesting in that he denies that the concept of sexual perversion depends on a connection between sex and reproduction; he even holds that "social disapprobation or custom . . . has no bearing on the concept of sexual perversion."[27] On this extreme view, *if* homosexuality were to be construed as a perversion, it would have to be judged to violate, inherently, some natural or appropriate relationship (in terms either of inclinations or practices or both) between persons. What is essential, Nagel holds, is that "sexual desire has as its characteristic object a certain relation with something in the external world . . . usually a person."[28] The relation, adjusting Nagel's own remarks, must not be "unnatural," "incomplete," "unhealthy," "subhuman," "unsatisfactory," or "imperfect."

As it turns out, Nagel does *not* view homosexuality as a perversion—or at any rate as a perversion like shoe fetishism. Still, in spite of the fact that he avoids the tendentiousness of insisting on the "natural function" of intercourse and sexual relations, he does "exonerate" homosexuality on the basis of an alternative view of some normatively natural relationship between persons—what amounts to a sort of natural justice or natural respect between persons, not to be viewed as a moral matter, though involving evaluations of persons. The point is that Nagel's criterion of perversion *is* designed to justify characterizing certain acts as perverted, and his example may well encourage other critics to postulate alternative criteria on the strength of which his arguments would be overturned. We must, therefore, consider the defensibility of his criterion.

The key to Nagel's view is reciprocity, "the recognition by the sexual object of the subject's desire as the source of his (the object's) sexual self-awareness"; "physical possession must eventuate in creation of the sexual object in the image of one's desire, and not merely in the object's recognition of that desire, or in his or her own private arousal"; natural sexual relations permit "the full range of interpersonal perceptions" or "reflexive mutual recognition."[29] Sara Ruddick has rather conveniently paraphrased this thesis, which may not unfairly be regarded as drawn from an analogue of H. P. Grice's (which Nagel acknowledges[30]) and the contractarian theme of John Rawls's well-known theory,[31] read as a gloss on Sartre's notion of a "double reciprocal incarnation" (which Nagel mentions[32]). On Ruddick's interpretation, sexual completeness obtains "if each partner (1) allows himself to be 'taken over' by desire, which (2) is desire not merely for the other's body but also for his desire, and (3) where each desire is occasioned by a response to the partner's

---

[26] Thomas Nagel, "Sexual Perversion," in Baker and Elliston, *Philosophy and Sex,* pp. 247–60.

[27] Ibid.

[28] Ibid.

[29] Ibid.

[30] Cf. H. P. Grice, "Meaning," *The Philosophical Review,* 66 (1957): 377–88.

[31] Cf. John Rawls, *A Theory of Justice* (Cambridge, Mass.: Harvard University Press, 1971).

[32] Cf. Jean-Paul Sartre, *Being and Nothingness,* trans. Hazel E. Barnes (New York: Philosophical Library, 1956), part 3.

desire."[33] The principal difficulty with this view is that condition 3 seems idiosyncratic, certainly not compellingly linked to judgments of perversion—unless in accord with personal tastes. For one thing, sexual relations that are not "complete" in the respect required by condition 3, or even by condition 2, may be eminently pleasurable and congruent with successful reproduction. For another, failure to be complete, as in seduction or in unsatisfactory but conventional relations, need not—on any familiar view—be seen as a manifestation of perversion. As it turns out, homosexuality, oral-genital intercourse, anal intercourse, bisexuality, and group intercourse need not, on Nagel's view, be perverted; but shoe fetishism and, perhaps, masturbation, sadism and masochism, coprophilia and necrophilia, pedophilia, voyeurism, and exhibitionism would be viewed as perversions.

The most important objection, then, to Nagel's proposal is that it depends ultimately on a moral or quasi-moral criticism of sexual practice and desire, in spite of Nagel's own disclaimer. Though sexually viable, it appears to be relatively remote from common sexual practice—of any variety—and not significantly congruent with sexual pleasure and satisfaction. It supposes, therefore, some overriding consideration bearing on the "natural" development of one's desires and on the "requirement," in sexual matters, as in others, that in treating oneself and another as a "means" one signifies, by reciprocity, that in reality one is treating oneself and another as an "end." That this is a fair reading is supported in part by Nagel's remark that "narcissistic practices and intercourse with animals, infants, and inanimate objects seem to be stuck at some *primitive version* of the first [as sketched above]"; also, that "sadism concentrates on the evocation of passive self-awareness in others, but the sadist's engagement is itself active and requires a retention of deliberate control that impedes awareness of himself as a bodily subject of passion *in the required sense.*"[34] Nagel regards both sadism and masochism as "disorders" of the second stage.

Nagel does not, however, offer this thesis as entirely certain or entirely adequate. He recognizes that if homosexuality is a perversion, it must be one on grounds quite different from those that would apply, say, to shoe fetishism; he also recognizes that fantasy involving other persons is a familiar ingredient in "natural" sexual relations—one that would appear to be precluded (wrongly, he thinks) by his own criterion. Nevertheless, though he has suggested what may be regarded as "requirements" of (personal) sexual style, his account is curiously indifferent to the element not only of moral condemnation but also of abhorrence associated with standard judgments of perversion.

By a small adjustment we can accommodate the latter in a way that would

---

[33] "On Sexual Morality," in James Rachels, ed., *Moral Problems* (New York: Harper & Row, 1971).

[34] Nagel, "Sexual Perversion." Italics added. Compare the Freudian orientation of Charlotte Wolff, *Love Between Women:* "What is perversion? I think that it is a fixation of the libido on one organic system only, which may be the sexual organs or other parts of the body. Any fixation of this kind, whether it be in homosexual or heterosexual people, is obsessional. It is a form of fetishism which leads into the blind alley of destructive habits" chap. 1.

apply as readily to homosexuality as to the other perversions. Merely assume that a relatively homogeneous society accepts some doctrine about "appropriate" or "admissible" sexual practices, usually incorporated into moral convictions. Then admit that, subscribing to that doctrine, the habits of mind and the tastes and feelings of the members of that society are sensitized and trained congruently. Deviations from the admitted norms will, then, be noted, and relatively extreme departures will be viewed as perverted—in the strong sense that representative members of the society will be disposed to find such extreme practices and inclinations abhorrent. The corollary is obvious: In order to reduce the sense of abhorrence, a society must extend its tolerance from its own normative preference, via intermediary practices, toward the perverted; as it does so, it will inevitably alter its conception of "natural" practices. What the limits of its tolerance may be is difficult to say, but without doubt, they will be substantially in accord with the moral and prudential values prevailing in sectors of community life other than the sexual.[35] There simply is no sense of the perverted without the distasteful, the disgusting, the abhorrent—either morally or "aesthetically" articulated. And there is no way in which the relevant emotions could develop independently of a society's prevailing tastes. It is, therefore, just as tendentious to attempt to specify the perverted in terms of some normative notion of the "proper" sexual relationships that should hold between persons as it is to attempt it in terms of some normative notion of the "proper" function of sexual intercourse and sexual relations. Nagel's tentative approval of homosexuality, then, is just as dubious as the Catholic Church's condemnation. Nagel must be wrong in supposing that "social disapprobation or custom . . . has no bearing on the concept of sexual perversion." It is, in a sense, all there is to the concept of perversion.

The curious thing is that, contrary to widespread belief, homosexuality is almost unknown in the animal world—appearing only under conditions of extreme stress, never consummated in intercourse, and regularly confused with aggressive play.[36] In that sense, fully developed and rationalized among human beings, homosexuality bids fair to being as natural as any other sexual practice. Furthermore, in our own time—possibly as a result of the relative density of human populations, ideological convictions about population growth, and the gradual elimination of fixed differences between male and female social roles—homosexuality (and bisexuality) is clearly being accorded a more hospitable place in the public array of "natural" sexual practices. It is the concept of the perverted that clarifies the natural, and the natural includes, by extended practice and inclination, whatever, we no longer find abhorrent or distasteful.[37]

[35] Cf. Margolis, *Negativities.*

[36] Cf. Arno Karlen, *Sexuality and Homosexuality* (New York: W. W. Norton, 1971).

[37] *Deviation* is possible in nature, so the "unnatural" occurs in nature. This goes against an argument by Michael Slote in "Inapplicable Concepts and Sexual Perversion," in Baker and Elliston, *Philosophy and Sex,* pp. 261–67. Slote argues that whatever has a biologically determinate nature has "a place in nature"; hence the "unnatural" has no application in our world— a fortiori, the perverted.

SELECTED BIBLIOGRAPHY: SEXUAL MORALITY

Atkinson, Ronald. *Sexual Morality.* New York: Harcourt Brace and World, 1965.

Baker, Robert, and Frederick Elliston (eds.). *Philosophy and Sex.* Buffalo, NY: Prometheus Books, 1975.

Bertocci, Peter A. *Sex, Love and the Person.* New York: Sheed and Ward, Inc., 1967.

Goldman, Alan H. "Plain Sex." *Philosophy & Public Affairs,* 6:3 (1977), 267.

Jaggar, Alison M., and Paula Rothenberg Struhl (eds.). *Feminist Frameworks.* New York: McGraw-Hill Book Company, 1978.

Leiser, Burton. *Liberty, Justice and Morals.* New York: Macmillan Publishing Co., Inc., 1973, Chaps. 1, 2, 3, 4, and 6.

Morrison, Eleanor S., and Vera Borosage (eds.). *Human Sexuality: Contemporary Perspectives* (2d ed.). Palo Alto, Calif.: Mayfield Publishing Co., 1977.

Nagel, Thomas. "Sexual Perversion." *The Journal of Philosophy,* 66 (1969), 5.

Russell, Bertrand. *Marriage and Morals.* New York: Liveright, 1929.

Soble, Alan (ed.). *Philosophy of Sex.* Totowa, N.J.: Littlefield, Adams and Co., 1980.

Solomon, Robert. "Sexual Paradigms." *The Journal of Philosophy,* 71:11 (1974), 336.

Taylor, Richard, *Having Love Affairs.* Buffalo, N.Y.: Prometheus Books, 1982.

Tripp, C. A. *The Homosexual Matrix.* New York: McGraw-Hill Book Company, 1975.

Vannoy, Russell. *Sex Without Love: A Philosophical Investigation.* Buffalo, N.Y.: Prometheus Books, 1980.

Whitely, C. H., and W. M. Whitely. *Sex and Morals.* London: Batsford, 1967.

Wilson, John. *Logic and Sexual Morality.* Harmondsworth, England: Penguin Books, 1965.

FOUR

Professional Responsibility

TARASOFF v. THE REGENTS OF THE UNIVERSITY OF CALIFORNIA ET AL.
17 CAL. 3d 425, 131 CAL.RPTR. 14,551 P.2d 334 (1976)

TOBRINER, Justice.

On October 27, 1969, Prosenjit Poddar killed Tatiana Tarasoff. Plaintiffs, Tatiana's parents, allege that two months earlier Poddar confided his intention to kill Tatiana to Dr. Lawrence Moore, a psychologist employed by the Cowell Memorial Hospital at the University of California at Berkeley. They allege that on Moore's request, the campus police briefly detained Poddar, but released him when he appeared rational. They further claim that Dr. Harvey Powelson, Moore's superior, then directed that no further action be taken to detain Poddar. No one warned plaintiffs of Tatiana's peril.

Concluding that these facts set forth causes of action against neither therapists and policemen involved, nor against the Regents of the University of California as their employer, the superior court sustained defendants' demurrers to plaintiffs' second amended complaints without leave to amend. This appeal ensued.

Plaintiffs' complaints predicate liability on two grounds: defendants' failure to warn plaintiffs of the impending danger and their failure to bring about

EDITOR'S NOTE: Parts of Justice Tobriner's and Justice Clark's opinions have been omitted, and some of the citations to prior cases have been deleted from those opinions as well as from the opinion of Justice Mosk. A number of footnotes have been omitted and those that remain have been renumbered.

243

Poddar's confinement pursuant to the Lanterman-Petris-Short Act (Welf. & Inst.Code, § 5000ff.) Defendants, in turn, assert that they owed no duty of reasonable care to Tatiana and that they are immune from suit under the California Tort Claims Act of 1963 (Gov.Code, § 810ff.).

[1]   We shall explain that defendant therapists cannot escape liability merely because Tatiana herself was not their patient. When a therapist determines, or pursuant to the standards of his profession should determine, that his patient presents a serious danger of violence to another, he incurs an obligation to use reasonable care to protect the intended victim against such danger. The discharge of this duty may require the therapist to take one or more of various steps, depending upon the nature of the case. Thus it may call for him to warn the intended victim or others likely to apprise the victim of the danger, to notify the police, or to take whatever other steps are reasonably necessary under the circumstances.

In the case at bar, plaintiffs admit that defendant therapists notified the police, but argue on appeal that the therapists failed to exercise reasonable care to protect Tatiana in that they did not confine Poddar and did not warn Tatiana or others likely to apprise her of the danger. Defendant therapists, however, are public employees. Consequently, to the extent that plaintiffs seek to predicate liability upon the therapists' failure to bring about Poddar's confinement, the therapists can claim immunity under Government Code section 856. No specific statutory provision, however, shields them from liability based upon failure to warn Tatiana or others likely to apprise her of the danger, and Government Code section 820.2 does not protect such failure as an exercise of discretion.

[2]   Plaintiffs therefore can amend their complaints to allege that, regardless of the therapists' unsuccessful attempt to confine Poddar, since they knew that Poddar was at large and dangerous, their failure to warn Tatiana or others likely to apprise her of the danger constituted a breach of the therapists' duty to exercise reasonable care to protect Tatiana.

Plaintiffs, however, plead no relationship between Poddar and the police defendants which would impose upon them any duty to Tatiana, and plaintiffs suggest no other basis for such a duty. Plaintiffs have, therefore, failed to show that the trial court erred in sustaining the demurrer of the police defendants without leave to amend.

1. PLAINTIFFS' COMPLAINTS

[3]   Plaintiffs, Tatiana's mother and father, filed separate but virtually identical second amended complaints. The issue before us on this appeal is whether those complaints now state, or can be amended to state, causes of action against defendants. We therefore begin by setting forth the pertinent allegations of the complaints.

Plaintiffs' first cause of action, entitled "Failure to Detain a Dangerous Patient," alleges that on August 20, 1969, Poddar was a voluntary outpatient receiving therapy at Cowell Memorial Hospital. Poddar informed Moore, his therapist, that he was going to kill an unnamed girl, readily identifiable as Tatiana, when she returned home from spending the summer in Brazil. Moore, with the concurrence of Dr. Gold, who had initially examined Poddar, and Dr. Yandell, assistant to the director of the department of psychiatry, decided that Poddar should be committed for observation in a mental hospital. Moore orally notified Officers Atkinson and Teel of the campus police that he would request commitment. He then sent a letter to Police Chief William Beall requesting the assistance of the police department in securing Poddar's confinement.

Officers Atkinson, Brownrigg, and Halleran took Poddar into custody, but, satisfied that Poddar was rational, released him on his promise to stay away from Tatiana. Powelson, director of the department of psychiatry at Cowell Memorial Hospital, then asked the police to return Moore's letter, directed that all copies of the letter and notes that Moore had taken as therapist be destroyed, and "ordered no action to place Prosenjit Poddar in 72-hour treatment and evaluation facility."

Plaintiffs' second cause of action, entitled "Failure to Warn On a Dangerous Patient," incorporates the allegations of the first cause of action, but adds the assertion that defendants negligently permitted Poddar to be released from police custody without "notifying the parents of Tatiana Tarasoff that their daughter was in grave danger from Posenjit Poddar." Poddar persuaded Tatiana's brother to share an apartment with him near Tatiana's residence; shortly after her return from Brazil, Poddar went to her residence and killed her.

Plaintiffs' third cause of action, entitled "Abandonment of a Dangerous Patient," seeks $10,000 punitive damages against defendant Powelson. Incorporating the crucial allegations of the first cause of action, plaintiffs charge that Powelson "did the things herein alleged with intent to abandon a dangerous patient, and said acts were done maliciously and oppressively."

Plaintiffs' fourth cause of action, for "Breach of Primary Duty to Patient and the Public," states essentially the same allegations as the first cause of action, but seeks to characterize defendants' conduct as a breach of duty to safeguard their patient and the public. Since such conclusory labels add nothing to the factual allegations of the complaint, the first and fourth causes of action are legally indistinguishable.

As we explain in part 4 of this opinion, plaintiffs' first and fourth causes of action, which seek to predicate liability upon the defendants' failure to bring about Poddar's confinement, are barred by governmental immunity. Plaintiffs' third cause of action succumbs to the decisions precluding exemplary damages in a wrongful death action. . . . We direct our attention, therefore, to the issue of whether plaintiffs' second cause of action can be amended to state a basis for recovery.

2. PLAINTIFFS CAN STATE A CAUSE OF ACTION AGAINST DEFENDANT THERAPISTS FOR NEGLIGENT FAILURE TO PROTECT TATIANA

The second cause of action can be amended to allege that Tatiana's death proximately resulted from defendants' negligent failure to warn Tatiana or others likely to apprise her of her danger. Plaintiffs contend that as amended, such allegations of negligence and proximate causation, with resulting damages, establish a cause of action. Defendants, however, contend that in the circumstances of the present case they owed no duty of care to Tatiana or her parents and that, in the absence of such duty, they were free to act in careless disregard of Tatiana's life and safety.

[4]   In analyzing this issue, we bear in mind that legal duties are not discoverable facts of nature, but merely conclusory expressions that, in cases of a particular type, liability should be imposed for damage done. As stated in *Dillon* v. *Legg* (1968) 68 Cal.2d 728, 734, 69 Cal.Rptr. 72, 76, 441 P.2d 912, 916: "The assertion that liability must . . . be denied because defendant bears no 'duty' to plaintiff 'begs the essential question—whether the plaintiff's interests are entitled to legal protection against the defendant's conduct . . . [Duty] is not sacrosanct in itself, but only an expression of the sum total of those considerations of policy which lead the law to say that the particular plaintiff is entitled to protection.' (Prosser, Law of Torts [3d ed. 1964] at pp. 332–333.)"

In the landmark case of *Rowland* v. *Christian* (1968) 69 Cal.2d 108, 70 Cal.Rptr. 97, 443 P.2d 561, Justice Peters recognized that liability should be imposed "for an injury occasioned to another by his want of ordinary care or skill" as expressed in section 1714 of the Civil Code. Thus, Justice Peters, quoting from *Heaven* v. *Pender* (1883) 11 Q.B.D. 503, 509 stated: " 'whenever one person is by circumstances placed in such a position with regard to another . . . that if he did not use ordinary care and skill in his own conduct . . . he would cause danger of injury to the person or property of the other, a duty arises to use ordinary care and skill to avoid such danger.' "

[5–7]   We depart from "this fundamental principle" only upon the "balancing of a number of considerations"; major ones "are the foreseeability of harm to the plaintiff, the degree of certainty that the plaintiff suffered injury, the closeness of the connection between the defendant's conduct and the injury suffered, the moral blame attached to the defendant's conduct, the policy of preventing future harm, the extent of the burden to the defendant and consequences to the community of imposing a duty to exercise care with resulting liability for breach, and the availability, cost and prevalence of insurance for the risk involved."

The most important of these considerations in establishing duty is foreseeability. As a general principle, a "defendant owes a duty of care to all persons who are foreseeably endangered by his conduct, with respect to all risks which make the conduct unreasonably dangerous." (*Rodriguez* v. *Bethlehem Steel Corp.* (1974) 12 Cal.3d 382, 399, 115 Cal.Rptr. 765, 776, 525 P.2d 669, 680; . . .) As we shall explain, however, when the avoidance of foreseeable harm requires a defendant to control the conduct of another person, or to warn of such conduct, the common law has traditionally imposed liability only if the defendant bears some special relationship to the dangerous person or to the potential victim. Since the relationship between a therapist and his patient satisfies this requirement, we need not here decide whether foreseeability alone is sufficient to create a duty to exercise reasonably care to protect a potential victim of another's conduct.

[8–10] Although, as we have stated above, under the common law, as a general rule, one person owed no duty to control the conduct of another.[1] . . . nor to warn those endangered by such conduct (Rest. 2d Torts, *supra,* § 314, com. c; Prosser, Law of Torts (4th ed. 1971) § 56, p. 341), the courts have carved out an exception to this rule in cases in which the defendant stands in some special relationship to either the person whose conduct needs to be controlled or in a relationship to the foreseeable victim of that conduct (see Rest. 2d Torts, *supra,* §§ 315–320). Applying this exception to the present case, we note that a relationship of defendant therapists to either Tatiana or Poddar will suffice to establish a duty of care; as explained in section 315 of the Restatement Second of Torts, a duty of care may arise from either "(a) a special relation . . . between the actor and the third person which imposes a duty upon the actor to control the third person's conduct, or (b) a special relation . . . between the actor and the other which gives to the other a right of protection."

[11, 12] Although Plaintiffs' pleadings assert no special relation between Tatiana and defendant therapists, they establish as between Poddar and defendant therapists the special relation that arises between a patient and his doctor or psychotherapist.[2] Such a relationship may support affirmative duties

---

[1] This rule derives from the common law's distinction between misfeasance and nonfeasance, and its reluctance to impose liability for the latter. (See Harper & Kime, *The Duty to Control the Conduct of Another* (1934) 43 Yale L.J. 886, 887.) Morally questionable, the rule owes its survival to "the difficulties of setting any standards of unselfish service to fellow men, and of making any workable rule to cover possible situations where fifty people might fail to rescue. . . " (Prosser, Torts (4th ed. 1971) § 56, p. 341.) Because of these practical difficulties, the courts have increased the number of instances in which affirmative duties are imposed not by direct rejection of the common law rule, but by expanding the list of special relationships which will justify departure from that rule. (See Prosser, *supra,* § 56, at pp. 348–350.)

[2] The pleadings establish the requisite relationship between Poddar and both Dr. Moore, the therapist who treated Poddar, and Dr. Powelson, who supervised that treatment. Plaintiffs also allege that Dr. Gold personally examined Poddar, and that Dr. Yandell, as Powelson's assistant, approved the decision to arrange Poddar's commitment. These allegations are sufficient to raise the issue whether a doctor-patient or therapist-patient relationship, giving rise to a possible duty by the doctor or therapist to exercise reasonable care to protect a threatened person of danger arising from the patient's mental illness, existed between Gold or Yandell and Poddar. (See Harney, Medical Malpractice (1973) p. 7.)

for the benefit of third persons. Thus, for example, a hospital must exercise reasonable care to control the behavior of a patient which may endanger other persons.[3] A doctor must also warn a patient if the patient's condition or medication renders certain conduct, such as driving a car, dangerous to others.

[13]   Although the California decisions that recognize this duty have involved cases in which the defendant stood in a special relationship *both* to the victim and to the person whose conduct created the danger,[4] we do not think that the duty should logically be constricted to such situations. Decisions of other jurisdictions hold that the single relationship of a doctor to his patient is sufficient to support the duty to exercise reasonable care to protect others against dangers emanating from the patient's illness. The courts hold that a doctor is liable to persons infected by his patient if he negligently fails to diagnose a contagious disease (*Hofmann* v. *Blackmon* (Fla.App.1970) 241 So.2d 752), or, having diagnosed the illness, fails to warn members of the patient's family . . . .

Since it involved a dangerous mental patient, the decision in *Merchants Nat. Bank & Trust Co. of Fargo* v. *United States* (D.N.D.1967) 272 F.Supp. 409 comes closer to the issue. The Veterans Administration arranged for the patient to work on a local farm, but did not inform the farmer of the man's background. The farmer consequently permitted the patient to come and go freely during nonworking hours; the patient borrowed a car, drove to his wife's residence and killed her. Notwithstanding the lack of any "special relationship" between the Veterans Administration and the wife, the court found the Veterans Administration liable for the wrongful death of the wife.

In their summary of the relevant rulings Fleming and Maximov conclude that the "case law should dispel any notion that to impose on the therapists a duty to take precautions for the safety of persons threatened by a patient, where due care so requires, is in any way opposed to contemporary ground rules on the duty relationship. On the contrary, there now seems to be sufficient authority to support the conclusion that by entering into a doctor-

---

[3] When a "hospital has notice or knowledge of facts from which it might reasonably be concluded that a patient would be likely to harm himself *or others* unless preclusive measures were taken, then the hospital must use reasonable care in the circumstances to prevent such harm." (*Vistica* v. *Presbyterian Hospital* (1967) 67 Cal.2d 465, 469, 62 Cal.Rptr. 577, 580, 432 P.2d 193, 196.) (Emphasis added.) A mental hospital may be liable if it negligently permits the escape or release of a dangerous patient (*Semler* v. *Psychiatric Institute of Washington, D. C.* (4th Cir. 1976) 44 U.S.L.Week 2439; *Underwood* v. *United States* (5th Cir. 1966) 356 F.2d 92; *Fair* v. *United States* (5th Cir. 1956) 234 F.2d 288). *Greenberg* v. *Barbour* (E.D.Pa. 1971) 322 F.Supp. 745, upheld a cause of action against a hospital staff doctor whose negligent failure to admit a mental patient resulted in that patient assaulting the plaintiff.

[4] *Ellis* v. *D'Angelo* (1953) 116 Cal.App.2d 310, 253 P.2d 675, upheld a cause of action against parents who failed to warn a babysitter of the violent proclivities of their child; *Johnson* v. *State of California* (1968) 69 Cal.2d 782, 73 Cal.Rptr. 240, 447 P.2d 352, upheld a suit against the state for failure to warn foster parents of the dangerous tendencies of their ward; *Morgan* v. *City of Yuba* (1964) 230 Cal.App.2d 938, 41 Cal. Rptr. 508, sustained a cause of action against a sheriff who had promised to warn decedent before releasing a dangerous prisoner, but failed to do so.

patient relationship the therapist becomes sufficiently involved to assume some responsibility for the safety, not only of the patient himself, but also of any third person whom the doctor knows to be threatened by the patient." (Fleming & Maximov, *The Patient or His Victim: The Therapist's Dilemma* (1974) 62 Cal.L.Rev. 1025, 1030.)

Defendants contend, however, that imposition of a duty to exercise reasonable care to protect third persons is unworkable because therapists cannot accurately predict whether or not a patient will resort to violence. In support of this argument amicus representing the American Psychiatric Association and other professional societies cites numerous articles which indicate that therpists, in the present state of the art, are unable reliably to predict violent acts; their forecasts, amicus claims, tend consistently to overpredict violence, and indeed are more often wrong than right.[5] Since predictions of violence are often erroneous, amicus concludes, the courts should not render rulings that predicate the liability of therapists upon the validity of such predictions.

The role of the psychiatrist, who is indeed a practitioner of medicine, and that of the psychologist who performs an allied function, are like that of the physician who must conform to the standards of the profession and who must often make diagnoses and predictions based upon such evaluations. Thus the judgment of the therapist in diagnosing emotional disorders and in predicting whether a patient presents a serious danger of violence is comparable to the judgment which doctors and professionals must regularly render under accepted rules of responsibility.

[14] We recognize the difficulty that a therapist encounters in attempting to forecast whether a patient presents a serious danger of violence. Obviously we do not require that the therapist, in making that determination, render a perfect performance; the therapist need only exercise "that reasonable degree of skill, knowledge, and care ordinarily possessed and exercised by members of [that professional specialty] under similar circumstances." (*Bardessono* v. *Michels* (1970) 3 Cal.3d 780, 788, 91 Cal.Rptr. 760, 764, 478 P.2d 480, 484; *Quintal* v. *Laurel Grove Hospital* (1964) 62 Cal.2d 154, 159–160, 41 Cal.Rptr. 577, 397 P.2d 161; see 4 Witkin, Summary of Cal.Law (8th ed. 1974) Torts, § 514 and cases cited.) Within the broad range of reasonable practice and treatment in which professional opinion and judgment may differ, the therapist is free to exercise his or her own best judgment without liability; proof, aided by hindsight, that he or she judged wrongly is insufficient to establish negligence.

In the instant case, however, the pleadings do not raise any question as to failure of defendant therapists to predict that Poddar presented a serious danger of violence. On the contrary, the present complaints allege that de-

---

[5] See, e. g., *People* v. *Burnick* (1975) 14 Cal.3d 306, 325–328, 121 Cal.Rptr. 488, 535 P.2d 352; Monahan, *The Prevention of Violence,* in Community Mental Health in the Criminal Justice System (Monahan ed. 1975); Diamond, *The Psychiatric Prediction of Dangerousness* (1975) 123 U.Pa.L.Rev. 439; Ennis & Litwack, *Psychiatry and the Presumption of Expertise: Flipping Coins in the Courtroom* (1974) 62 Cal.L.Rev. 693.

fendant therapists did in fact predict that Poddar would kill, but were negligent in failing to warn.

[15, 16]   Amicus contends, however, that even when a therpist does in fact predict that a patient poses a serious danger of violence to others, the therapist should be absolved of any responsibility for failing to act to protect the potential victim. In our view, however, once a therapist does in fact determine, or under applicable professional standards reasonably should have determined, that a patient poses a serious danger of violence to others, he bears a duty to exercise reasonable care to protect the foreseeable victim of that danger. While the discharge of this duty of due care will necessarily vary with the facts of each case,[6] in each instance the adequacy of the therapist's conduct must be measured against the traditional negligence standard of the rendition of reasonable care under the circumstances. (Accord *Cobbs* v. *Grant* (1972) 8 Cal.3d 229, 243, 104 Cal.Rptr. 505, 502 P.2d 1.) As explained in Fleming and Maximov, *The Patient or His Victim: The Therapist's Dilemma* (1974) 62 Cal.L.Rev. 1025, 1067: " . . . the ultimate question of resolving the tension between the conflicting interests of patient and potential victim is one of social policy, not professional expertise. . . . In sum, the therapist owes a legal duty not only to his patient, but also to his patient's would-be victim and is subject in both respects to scrutiny by judge and jury."

[17]   Contrary to the assertion of amicus, this conclusion is not inconsistent with our recent decision in *People* v. *Burnick, supra,* 14 Cal.3d 306, 121 Cal.Rptr. 488, 535 P.2d 352. Taking note of the uncertain character of therapeutic prediction, we held in *Burnick* that a person cannot be committed as a mentally disordered sex offender unless found to be such by proof beyond a reasonable doubt. (14 Cal.3d at p. 328, 121 Cal.Rptr. 488, 535 P.2d 352). The issue in the present context, however, is not whether the patient should be incarcerated, but whether the therapist should take any steps at all to protect the threatened victim; some of the alternatives open to the therapist, such as warning the victim, will not result in the drastic consequences of depriving the patient of his liberty. Weighing the uncertain and conjectural character of the alleged damage done the patient by such a warning against the peril to the victim's life, we conclude that professional inaccuracy in predicting violence cannot negate the therapist's duty to protect the threatened victim.

The risk that unnecessary warnings may be given is a reasonable price to pay for the lives of possible victims that may be saved. We would hesitate to hold that the therapist who is aware that his patient expects to attempt

---

[6] Defendant therapists and amicus also argue that warnings must be given only in those cases in which the therapist knows the identity of the victim. We recognize that in some cases it would be unreasonable to require the therapist to interrogate his patient to discover the victim's identity, or to conduct an independent investigation. But there may also be cases in which a moment's reflection will reveal the victim's identity. The matter thus is one which depends upon the circumstances of each case, and should not be governed by any hard and fast rule.

to assassinate the President of the United States would not be obligated to warn the authorities because the therapist cannot predict with accuracy that his patient will commit the crime.

Defendants further argue that free and open communication is essential to psychotherapy (see *In re Lifschutz* (1970) 2 Cal.3d 415, 431–434, 85 Cal.Rptr. 829, 467 P.2d 557); that "Unless a patient . . . is assured that . . . information [revealed by him] can and will be held in utmost confidence, he will be reluctant to make the full disclosure upon which diagnosis and treatment . . . depends." (Sen.Com. on Judiciary, comment on Evid.Code, § 1014.) The giving of a warning, defendants contend, constitutes a breach of trust which entails the revelation of confidential communications.[7]

[18]   We recognize the public interest in supporting effective treatment of mental illness and in protecting the rights of patients to privacy (see *In re Liftschutz, supra,* 2 Cal.3d at p. 432, 85 Cal.Rptr. 829, 467 P.2d 557), and the consequent public importance of safeguarding the confidential character of psychotherapeutic communication. Against this interest, however, we must weigh the public interest in safety from violent assault. The Legislature has undertaken the difficult task of balancing the countervailing concerns. In Evidence Code section 1014, it established a broad rule of privilege to protect confidential communications between patient and psychotherapist. In Evidence Code section 1024, the Legislature created a specific and limited exception to the psychotherapist-patient privilege: "There is no privilege . . . if the psychotherapist has reasonable cause to believe that the patient is in such mental or emotional condition as to be dangerous to himself or to the person or property of another and that disclosure of the communication is necessary to prevent the threatened danger."[8]

---

[7] Counsel for defendant Regents and amicus American Psychiatric Association predict that a decision of this court holding that a therapist may bear a duty to warn a potential victimi will deter violence-prone persons from seeking therapy, and hamper the treatment of other patients. This contention was examined in Fleming and Maximov. *The Patient or His Victim: The Therapist's Dilemma* (1974) 62 Cal.L.Rev. 1025, 1038–1044; they conclude that such predictions are entirely speculative. In *In re Lifschutz, supra,* 2 Cal. 3d 415, 85 Cal.Rptr. 829, 467 P.2d 557, counsel for the psychiatrist argued that if the state could compel disclosure of some psychotherapeutic communications, psychotherapy could no longer be practiced successfully. (2 Cal.3d at p. 426, 85 Cal.Rptr. 829, 467 P.2d 557.) We rejected that argument, and it does not appear that our decision in fact adversely affected the practice of psychotherapy in California. Counsel's forecast of harm in the present case strikes us as equally dubious.

We note, moreover, that Evidence Code section 1024, enacted in 1965, established that psychotherapeutic communication is not privileged when disclosure is necessary to prevent threatened danger. We cannot accept without question counsels' implicit assumption that effective therapy for potentially violent patients depends upon either the patient's lack of awareness that a therapist can disclose confidential communications to avert impending danger, or upon the therapist's advance promise never to reveal nonprivileged threats of violence.

[8] Fleming and Maximov note that "While [section 1024] supports the therapist's less controversial *right* to make a disclosure, it admittedly does not impose on him a *duty* to do so. But the argument does not have to be pressed that far. For if it is once conceded . . . that a duty in favor of the patient's foreseeable victims would accord with general principles of tort liability, we need no longer look to the statute for a source of duty. It is sufficient if the statute can be relied upon . . . for the purposes of countering the claim that the needs of confidentiality are

[19, 20]   We realize that the open and confidential character of psycho-therapeutic dialogue encourages patients to express threats of violence, few of which are ever executed. Certainly a therapist should not be encouraged routinely to reveal such threats; such disclosures could seriously disrupt the patient's relationship with his therapist and with the persons threatened. To the contrary, the therapist's obligations to his patient require that he not disclose a confidence unless such disclosure is necessary to avert danger to others, and even then that he do so discreetly, and in a fashion that would preserve the privacy of his patient to the fullest extent compatible with the prevention of the threatened danger. (See Fleming & Maximov, *The Patient or His Victim: The Therapist's Dilemma* (1974) 62 Cal.L.Rev. 1025, 1065–1066.)[9]

The revelation of a communication under the above circumstances is not a breach of trust or a violation of professional ethics; as stated in the Principles of Medical Ethics of the American Medical Association (1957), section 9: "A physician may not reveal the confidence entrusted to him in the course of medical attendance . . . *unless he is required to do so by law or unless it becomes necessary in order to protect the welfare of the individual or of the community.*"[10] (Emphasis added.) We conclude that the public policy favoring protection of the confidential character of patient-psychotherapist communications must yield to the extent to which disclosure is essential to avert danger to others. The protective privilege ends where the public peril begins.

[21]   Our current crowded and computerized society compels the inter-dependence of its members. In this risk-infested society we can hardly tolerate the further exposure to danger that would result from a concealed knowledge of the therapist that his patient was lethal. If the exercise of reasonable care to protect the threatened victim requires the therapist to warn the endangered party or those who can reasonably be expected to notify him, we see no sufficient societal interest that would protect and justify concealment. The containment of such risks lies in the public interest. For the foregoing reasons, we find that plaintiffs' complaints can be amended to state a cause of action against defendants Moore, Powelson, Gold, and Yandell and against the

---

paramount and must therefore defeat any such hypothetical duty. In this more modest perspective, the Evidence Code's 'dangerous patient' exception may be invoked with some confidence as a clear expression of legislative policy concerning the balance between the confidentiality values of the patient and the safety values of his foreseeable victims." (Emphasis in original.) Fleming & Maximov, *The Patient or His Victim: The Therapist's Dilemma* (1974) 62 Cal.L.Rev. 1025, 1063.

[9]   Amicus suggests that a therapist who concludes that his patient is dangerous should not warn the potential victim, but institute proceedings for involuntary detention of the patient. The giving of a warning, however, would in many cases represent a far lesser inroad upon the patient's privacy than would involuntary commitment.

[10]   See also Summary Report of the Task Force on Confidentiality of the Council on Professions and Associations of the American Psychiatric Association (1975).

Regents as their employer, for breach of a duty to exercise reasonable care to protect Tatiana.[11]

• • •

[24]   Turning now to the police defendants, we conclude that they do not have any such special relationship to either Tatiana or to Poddar sufficient to impose upon such defendants a duty to warn respecting Poddar's violent intentions. . . . Plaintiffs suggest no theory,[12] and plead no facts that give rise to any duty to warn on the part of the police defendants absent such a special relationship. They have thus failed to demonstrate that the trial court erred in denying leave to amend as to the police defendants. . . .

3. DEFENDANT THERAPISTS ARE NOT IMMUNE FROM LIABILITY FOR FAILURE TO WARN

We address the issue of whether defendant therapists are protected by governmental immunity for having failed to warn Tatiana or those who reasonably could have been expected to notify her of her peril. We postulate our analysis on section 820.2 of the Government Code.[13] That provision declares, with exceptions not applicable here, that "a public employee is not liable for an injury resulting from his act or omission where the act or omission was the result of the exercise of the discretion vested in him, whether or not such discretion [was] abused."[14]

[11] Moore argues that after Powelson countermanded the decision to seek commitment for Poddar, Moore was obliged to obey the decision of his superior and that therefore he should not be held liable for any dereliction arising from his obedience to superior orders. Plaintiffs in response contend that Moore's duty to members of the public endangered by Poddar should take precedence over his duty to obey Powelson. Since plaintiffs' complaints do not set out the date of Powelson's order, the specific terms of that order, or Powelson's authority to overrule Moore's decisions respecting patients under Moore's care, we need not adjudicate this conflict; we pass only upon the pleadings at this stage and decide if the complaints can be amended to state a cause of action.

[12] We have considered *sua sponte* whether plaintiffs' complaints could be amended to assert a cause of action against the police defendants under the principles of Restatement Second of Torts (1965), section 321, which provides that "If the actor does an act, and subsequently realizes or should realize that it has created an unreasonable risk of causing physical harm to another, he is under a duty to exercise reasonable care to prevent the risk from taking effect." (See *Hartzler* v. *City of San Jose, supra,* 46 Cal.App.3d 6, 10, 120 Cal.Rptr. 5.) The record, however, suggests no facts which, if inserted into the complaints, might form the foundation for such cause of action. The assertion of a cause of action against the police defendants under this theory would raise difficult problems of causation and of public policy, which should not be resolved on the basis of conjectural facts not averred in the pleadings or in any proposed amendment to those pleadings.

[13] No more specific immunity provision of the Government Code appears to address the issue.

[14] Section 815.2 of the Government Code declares that "[a] public entity is liable for injury proximity caused by an act or omission of an employee of the public entity within the scope of his employment if the act or emission would, apart from this section, have given rise to a cause

[25]   Noting that virtually every public act admits of some element of discretion, we drew the line in *Johnson* v. *State of California* (1968) 69 Cal.2d 782, 73 Cal.Rptr. 240, 447 P.2d 352, between discretionary policy decisions which enjoy statutory immunity and ministerial administrative acts which do not. We concluded that section 820.2 affords immunity only for "*basic* policy decisions." (Emphasis added.) . . .

[26]   We also observed that if courts did not respect this statutory immunity, they would find themselves "in the unseemly position of determining the propriety of decisions expressly entrusted to a coordinate branch of government." (*Johnson* v. *State of California, supra,* 69 Cal.2d at p. 793, 73 Cal.Rptr. at p. 248, 447 P.2d at p. 360.) It therefore is necessary, we concluded, to "isolate those areas of quasilegislative policy-making which are sufficiently sensitive to justify a blanket rule that courts will not entertain a tort action alleging that careless conduct contributed to the governmental decision." (*Johnson* v. *State of California, supra,* at p. 794, 73 Cal.Rptr., at p. 248, 447 P.2d, at p. 360.) After careful analysis we rejected, in *Johnson,* other rationales commonly advanced to support governmental immunity[15] and concluded that the immunity's scope should be no greater than is required to give legislative and executive policymakers sufficient breathing space in which to perform their vital policymaking functions.

[27, 28]   Relying on *Johnson,* we conclude that defendant therapists in the present case are not immune from liability for their failure to warn of Tatiana's peril. *Johnson* held that a parole officer's determination whether to warn an adult couple that their prospective foster child had a background of violence "present[ed] no . . . reasons for immunity" (*Johnson* v. *State of California, supra,* at p. 795, 73 Cal.Rptr. 240, 447 P.2d 352), was "at the lowest, ministerial rung of official action" (*id.,* at p. 796, 73 Cal.Rptr., at p. 250, 447 P.2d, at p. 362), and indeed constituted "a classic case for the imposition of tort liability." (*Id.,* p. 797, 73 Cal.Rptr., p. 251, 447 P.2d, p. 363; cf. *Morgan* v. *County of Yuba, supra,* 230 Cal.App.2d 938, 942–943, 41

---

of action against that employee or his personal representative." The section further provides, with exceptions not applicable here, that "a public entity is not liable for an injury resulting from an act or omission of an employee of the public entity where the employee is immune from liability." The Regents, therefore, are immune from liability only if all individual defendants are similarly immune.

[15] We dismissed, in *Johnson,* the view that immunity continues to be necessary in order to insure that public employees will be sufficiently zealous in the performance of their official duties. The California Tort Claims Act of 1963 provides for indemnification of public employees against liability, absent bad faith, and also permits such employees to insist that their defenses be conducted at public expense. (See Gov.Code, §§ 825–825.6, 995–995.2.) Public employees thus no longer have a significant reason to fear liability as they go about their official tasks. We also, in *Johnson,* rejected the argument that a public employee's concern over the potential liability of his or her employer serves as a basis for immunity. (*Johnson* v. *State of California, supra,* at pp. 790–793, 73 Cal. Rptr. 240, 447 P.2d 352.)

Cal.Rptr. 508.) Although defendants in *Johnson* argued that the decision whether to inform the foster parents of the child's background required the exercise of considerable judgmental skills, we concluded that the state was not immune from liability for the parole officer's failure to warn because such a decision did not rise to the level of a "basic policy decision."

We also noted in *Johnson* that federal courts have consistently categorized failures to warn of latent dangers as falling outside the scope of discretionary omissions immunized by the Federal Tort Claims Act.[16]

• • •

We conclude, therefore, that the therapist defendants' failure to warn Tatiana or those who reasonably could have been expected to notify her of her peril does not fall within the absolute protection afforded by section 820.2 of the Government Code. We emphasize that our conclusion does not raise the specter of therapists employed by the government indiscriminately being held liable for damage despite their exercise of sound professional judgment. We require of publicly employed therapists only that quantum of care which the common law requires of private therapists. The imposition of liability in those rare cases in which a public employee falls short of this standard does not contravene the language or purpose of Government Code section 820.2.

• • •

6. PLAINTIFF'S COMPLAINTS STATE NO CAUSE OF ACTION FOR EXEMPLARY DAMAGES

[35] Plaintiff's third cause of action seeks punitive damages against defendant Powelson. The California statutes and decisions, however, have been interpreted to bar the recovery of punitive damages in a wrongful death action. (See *Pease* v. *Beech Aircraft Corp.* (1974) 38 Cal.App.3d 450, 460–462, 113 Cal.Rptr. 416, and authorities there cited.)

---

[16] By analogy, section 830.8 of the Government Code furnishes additional support for our conclusion that a failure to warn does not fall within the zone of immunity created by section 820.2. Section 830.8 provides: "Neither a public entity nor a public employee is liable ... for an injury caused by the failure to provide traffic or warning signals, signs, markings or devices described in the Vehicle Code. Nothing in this section exonerates a public entity or public employee from liability for injury proximately caused by such failure if a signal, sign, marking or device ... was necessary to warn of a dangerous condition which endangered the safe movement of traffic and which would not be reasonably apparent to, and would not have been anticipated by, a person exercising due care." The Legislature thus concluded at least in another context that the failure to warn of a latent danger is not an immunized discretionary omission. (See *Hilts* v. *County of Solano* (1968) 265 Cal.App.2d 161, 174, 71 Cal.Rptr. 275.)

7. CONCLUSION

For the reasons stated, we conclude that plaintiffs can amend their complaints to state a cause of action against defendant therapists by asserting that the therapists in fact determined that Poddar presented a serious danger of violence to Tatiana, or pursuant to the standards of their profession should have so determined, but nevertheless failed to exercise reasonable care to protect her from that danger. To the extent, however, that plaintiffs base their claim that defendant therapists breached that duty because they failed to procure Poddar's confinement, the therapists find immunity in Government Code section 856. Further, as to the police defendants we conclude that plaintiffs have failed to show that the trial court erred in sustaining their demurrer without leave to amend.

The judgment of the superior court in favor of defendants Atkinson, Beall, Brownrigg, Hallernan, and Teel is affirmed. The judgment of the superior court in favor of defendants Gold, Moore, Powelson, Yandell, and the Regents of the University of California is reversed, and the cause remanded for further proceedings consistent with the views expressed herein.

WRIGHT, C. J., and SULLIVAN and RICHARDSON, J. J., concur.

MOSK, Justice (concurring and dissenting).

I concur in the result in this instance only because the complaints allege that defendant therapists did in fact predict that Poddar would kill and were therefore negligent in failing to warn of that danger. Thus the issue here is very narrow: we are not concerned with whether the therapists, pursuant to the standards of their profession, "should have" predicted potential violence; they allegedly did so in actuality. Under these limited circumstances I agree that a cause of action can be stated.

Whether plaintiffs can ultimately prevail is problematical at best. As the complaints admit, the therapists *did* notify the police that Poddar was planning to kill a girl identifiable as Tatiana. While I doubt that more should be required, this issue may be raised in defense and its determination is a question of fact.

I cannot concur, however, in the majority's rule that a therapist may be held liable for failing to predict his patient's tendency to violence if other practitioners, pursuant to the "standards of the profession," would have done so. The question is, what standards? Defendants and a responsible amicus curiae, supported by an impressive body of literature discussed at length in our recent opinion in *People* v. *Burnick* (1975) 14 Cal.3d 306, 121 Cal.Rptr. 488, 535 P.2d 352, demonstrate that psychiatric predictions of violence are inherently unreliable.

In *Burnick,* at pages 325–326, 121 Cal. Rptr. at page 501, 535 P.2d at page 365, we observed: "In the light of recent studies it is no longer heresy to question the reliability of psychiatric predictions. Psychiatrists themselves would be the first to admit that however desirable an infallible crystal ball might be, it is not among the tools of their profession. It must be conceded that psychiatrists still experience considerable difficulty in confidently and accurately *diagnosing* mental illness. Yet those difficulties are multiplied manyfold when psychiatrists venture from diagnosis to prognosis and undertake to predict the consequences of such illness: 'A diagnosis of mental illness tells us nothing about whether the person so diagnosed is or is not dangerous. Some mental patients are dangerous, some are not. Perhaps the psychiatrist is an expert at deciding whether a person is mentally ill, but is he an expert at predicting which of the persons so diagnosed are dangerous? Sane people, too, are dangerous, and it may legitimately be inquired whether there is anything in the education, training or experience of psychiatrists which renders them particularly adept at predicting dangerous behavior. Predictions of dangerous behavior, no matter who makes them, are incredibly inaccurate, and there is a growing consensus that psychiatrists are not uniquely qualified to predict dangerous behavior and are, in fact, less accurate in their predictions than other professionals.' (*Murel* v. *Baltimore City Criminal Court* (1972) . . . 407 U.S. 355, 364–365, fn. 2, 92 S.Ct. 2091, 32 L.Ed.2d 791, 796–797 (DOUGLAS, J., dissenting from dismissal of certiorari).)" (Fns. omitted.) . . .

The majority confidently claim their opinion is not offensive to *Burnick,* on the stated ground that *Burnick* involved proceedings to commit an alleged mentally disordered sex offender and this case does not. I am not so sanguine about the distinction. Obviously the two cases are not factually identical, but the similarity in issues is striking: in *Burnick* we were likewise called upon to appraise the ability of psychiatrists to predict dangerousness, and while we declined to bar all such testimony (*id.* at pp. 327–328, 121 Cal.Rptr. 488, 535 P.2d 352) we found it so inherently untrustworthy that we would permit confinement even in a so-called civil proceeding only upon proof beyond a reasonable doubt.

I would restructure the rule designed by the majority to eliminate all reference to conformity to standards of the profession in predicting violence. If a psychiatrist does in fact predict violence, then a duty to warn arises. The majority's expansion of that rule will take us from the world of reality into the wonderland of clairvoyance.

CLARK, Justice (dissenting).

Until today's majority opinion, both legal and medical authorities have agreed that confidentiality is essential to effectively treat the mentally ill, and that imposing a duty on doctors to disclose patient threats to potential victims would greatly impair treatment. . . .

•   •   •

COMMON LAW ANALYSIS

• • •

Generally, a person owes no duty to control the conduct of another. . . .
Exceptions are recognized only in limited situations where (1) a special relationship exists between the defendant and injured party, or (2) a special
relationship exists between defendant and the active wrongdoer, imposing a
duty on defendant to control the wrongdoer's conduct. The majority does
not contend the first exception is appropriate to this case.

Policy generally determines duty. . . . Principal policy considerations include foreseeability of harm, certainty of the plaintiff's injury, proximity of
the defendant's conduct to the plaintiff's injury, moral blame attributable to
defendant's conduct, prevention of future harm, burden on the defendant,
and consequences to the community. . . .

Overwhelming policy considerations weigh against imposing a duty on
psychotherapists to warn a potential victim against harm. While offering
virtually no benefit to society, such a duty will frustrate psychiatric treatment,
invade fundamental patient rights and increase violence.

The importance of psychiatric treatment and its need for confidentiality
have been recognized by this court. (*In re Lifschutz* (1970) 2 Cal.3d 415,
421–422, 85 Cal.Rptr. 829, 467 P.2d 557.) "It is clearly recognized that the
very practice of psychiatry vitally depends upon the reputation in the community that the psychiatrist will not tell." (Slovenko, *Psychiatry and a Second
Look at the Medical Privilege* (1960) 6 Wayne L.Rev. 175, 188.)

Assurance of confidentiality is important for three reasons.

Deterrence From Treatment

First, without substantial assurance of confidentiality, those requiring treatment will be deterred from seeking assistance. (See Sen. Judiciary Com.
comment accompanying § 1014 of Evid.Code; Slovenko, *supra,* 6 Wayne
L.Rev. 175, 187–188; Goldstein & Katz, *Psychiatrist–Patient Privilege: The
GAP Proposal and the Connecticut Statute* (1962) 36 Conn.Bar J. 175, 178.)
It remains an unfortunate fact in our society that people seeking psychiatric
guidance tend to become stigmatized. Apprehension of such stigma—apparently increased by the propensity of people considering treatment to see
themselves in the worst possible light—creates a well-recognized reluctance
to seek aid. (Fisher, *The Psychotherapeutic Professions and the Law of Privileged Communications* (1964) 10 Wayne L.Rev. 609, 617; Slovenko, *supra,*
6 Wayne L.Rev. 175, 188; see also Rappeport, *Psychiatrist–Patient Privilege*
(1963) 23 Md.L.J. 39, 46–47.) This reluctance is alleviated by the psychiatrist's
assurance of confidentiality.

Full Disclosure

Second, the guarantee of confidentiality is essential in eliciting the full disclosure necessary for effective treatment. . . . Heller, *Some Comments to Lawyers on the Practice of Psychiatry* (1957) 30 Temp.L.Q. 401; Guttmacher & Weihofen, *Privileged Communications Between Psychiatrist and Patient* (1952) 28 Ind.L.J. 32, 34).[1] The psychiatric patient approaches treatment with conscious and unconscious inhibitions against revealing his innermost thoughts. "Every person, however well-motivated, has to overcome resistances to therapeutic exploration. These resistances seek support from every possible source and the possibility of disclosure would easily be employed in the service of resistance." (Goldstein & Katz, *supra,* 36 Conn.Bar J. 175, 179; see also, 118 Am.J.Psych. 734, 735.) Until a patient can trust his psychiatrist not to violate their confidential relationship, "the unconscious psychological control mechanism of repression will prevent the recall of past experiences." (Butler, *Psychotherapy and Griswold: Is Confidentiality a Privilege or a Right?* (1971) 3 Conn.L.Rev. 599, 604.)

Successful Treatment

Third, even if the patient fully discloses his thoughts, assurance that the confidential relationship will not be breached is necessary to maintain his trust in his psychiatrist—the very means by which treatment is effected. "[T]he essence of much psychotherapy is the contribution of trust in the external world and ultimately in the self, modelled upon the trusting relationship established during therapy." (Dawidoff, *The Malpractice of Psychiatrists,* 1966 Duke L.J. 696, 704.) Patients will be helped only if they can form a trusting relationship with the psychiatrist. (*Id.* at p. 704, fn. 34; Burham, *Separation Anxiety* (1965) 13 Arch.Gen. Psychiatry 346, 356; Heller, *supra,* 30 Temp.L.Q. 401, 406.) All authorities appear to agree that if the trust relationship cannot be developed because of collusive communication between the psychiatrist and others, treatment will be frustrated. (See, e.g., Slovenko (1973) Psychiatry and Law, p. 61; Cross, *Privileged Communications Between Participants in Group Psychotherapy* (1970) Law and the Social Order, 191, 199; Hollender, *The Psychiatrist and the Release of Patient Information* (1960) 116 Am.J. Psychiatry 828, 829.)

Given the importance of confidentiality to the practice of psychiatry, it becomes clear the duty to warn imposed by the majority will cripple the use and effectiveness of psychiatry. Many people, potentially violent—yet susceptible to treatment—will be deterred from seeking it; those seeking it will be inhibited from making revelations necessary to effective treatment; and,

---

[1] One survey indicated that five of every seven people interviewed said they would be less likely to make full disclosure to a psychiatrist in the absence of assurance of confidentiality. (See, Comment, *Functional Overlap Between the Lawyer and Other Professionals: Its Implications for the Doctrine of Privileged Communications* (1962) 71 Yale L.J. 1226, 1255.)

forcing the psychiatrist to violate the patient's trust will destroy the inter-personal relationship by which treatment is effected.

Violence and Civil Commitment

By imposing a duty to warn, the majority contributes to the danger to society of violence by the mentally ill and greatly increases the risk of civil commitment—the total deprivation of liberty—of those who should not be confined.[2] The impairment of treatment and risk of improper commitment resulting from the new duty to warn will not be limited to a few patients but will extend to a large number of the mentally ill. Although under existing psychiatric procedures only a relatively few receiving treatment will ever present a risk of violence, the number making threats is huge, and it is the latter group—not just the former—whose treatment will be impaired and whose risk of commitment will be increased.

Both the legal and psychiatric communities recognize that the process of determining potential violence in a patient is far from exact, being fraught with complexity and uncertainty. . . . Ennis & Litwack, *Psychiatry and the Presumption of Expertise: Flipping Coins in the Courtroom,* 62 Cal.L.Rev. 693, 711–716; Rector, *Who Are the Dangerous?* (July 1973) Bull. of Amer.Acad. of Psych. & L. 186; Kozol, Boucher & Garofalo, *The Diagnosis and Treatment of Dangerousness* (1972) 18 Crime & Delinquency 371; Justice & Birkman, *An Effort to Distinguish the Violent From the Nonviolent* (1972) 65 So.Med.J. 703.)[3] In fact precision has not even been attained in predicting who of those having already committed violent acts will again become violent, a task recognized to be of much simpler proportions. (Kozol, Boucher & Garofalo, *supra,* 18 Crime & Delinquency 371, 384.)

This predictive uncertainty means that the number of disclosures will necessarily be large. As noted above, psychiatric patients are encouraged to

[2] The burden placed by the majority on psychiatrists may also result in the improper deprivation of two other constitutionally protected rights. First, the patient's constitutional right of privacy (*In re Lifschutz, supra,* 2 Cal.3d 415, 85 Cal.Rptr. 829, 467 P.2d 557) is obviously encroached upon by requiring the psychotherapist to disclose confidential communications. Secondly, because confidentiality is essential to effective treatment, the majority's decision also threatens the constitutionally recognized right to receive treatment. . . .

[3] A shocking illustration of psychotherapists' inability to predict dangerousness . . . is cited and discussed in Ennis, Prisoners of Psychiatry: Mental Patients, Psychiatrists, and the Law (1972): "In a well-known study, psychiatrists predicted that 989 persons were so dangerous that they could not be kept even in civil mental hospitals, but would have to be kept in maximum security hospitals run by the Department of Corrections. Then, because of a United States Supreme Court decision, those persons were transferred to civil hospitals. After a year, the Department of Mental Hygiene reported that one-fifth of them had been discharged to the community, and over half had agreed to remain as voluntary patients. During the year, only 7 of the 989 committed or threatened any act that was sufficiently dangerous to require retransfer to the maximum security hospital. Seven correct predictions out of almost a thousand is not a very impressive record. [¶] Other studies, and there are many, have reached the same conclusion: psychiatrists simply cannot predict dangerous behavior." (*Id.* at p. 227.) Equally illustrative studies are collected in Rosenhan, *On Being Sane in Insane Places* (1973) 13 Santa Clara Law. 379, 384; Ennis & Litwack, *Psychiatry and the Presumption of Expertise: Flipping Coins in the Courtroom, supra,* 62 Cal.L.Rev. 693, 750–751.)

discuss all thoughts of violence, and they often express such thoughts. However, unlike this court, the psychiatrist does not enjoy the benefit of overwhelming hindsight in seeing which few, if any, of his patients will ultimately become violent. Now, confronted by the majority's new duty, the psychiatrist must instantaneously calculate potential violence from each patient on each visit. The difficulties researchers have encountered in accurately predicting violence will be heightened for the practicing psychiatrist dealing for brief periods in his office with heretofore nonviolent patients. And, given the decision not to warn or commit must always be made at the psychiatrist's civil peril, one can expect most doubts will be resolved in favor of the psychiatrist protecting himself.

Neither alternative open to the psychiatrist seeking to protect himself is in the public interest. The warning itself is an impairment of the psychiatrist's ability to treat, depriving many patients of adequate treatment. It is to be expected that after disclosing their threats, a significant number of patients, who would not become violent if treated according to existing practices, will engage in violent conduct as a result of unsuccessful treatment. In short, the majority's duty to warn will not only impair treatment of many who would never become violent but worse, will result in a net increase in violence.[4]

The second alternative open to the psychiatrist is to commit his patient rather than to warn. Even in the absence of threat of civil liability, the doubts of psychiatrists as to the seriousness of patient threats have led psychiatrists

---

[4] The majority concedes that psychotherapeutic dialogue often results in the patient expressing threats of violence that are rarely executed. . . . The practical problem, of course, lies in ascertaining which threats from which patients will be carried out. As to this problem, the majority is silent. They do, however, caution that a therapist certainly "should not be encouraged routinely to reveal such threats; such disclosures could seriously disrupt the patient's relationships with his therapist and with the persons threatened.". . .

Thus, in effect, the majority informs the therapists that they must accurately predict dangerousness—a task recognized as extremely difficult—or face crushing civil liability. The majority's reliance on the traditional standard of care for professionals that "therapist need only exercise 'that reasonable degree of skill, knowledge, and care ordinarily possessed and exercised by members of [that professional specialty] under similar circumstances' " . . . is seriously misplaced. This standard of care assumes that, to a large extent, the subject matter of the specialty is ascertainable. One clearly ascertainable element in the psychiatric field is that the therapist cannot accurately predict dangerousness, which, in turn, means that the standard is inappropriate for lack of a relevant criterion by which to judge the therapist's decision. The inappropriateness of the standard the majority would have us use is made patent when consideration is given to studies, by several eminent authorities, indicating that "[t]he chances of a second psychiatrist agreeing with the diagnosis of a first psychiatrist 'are barely better than 50–50; or stated differently, there is about as much chance that a different expert would come to some different conclusion as there is that the other would agree.' " (Ennis & Litwack, *Psychiatry and the Presumption of Expertise: Flipping Coins in the Courtroom, supra,* 62 Cal.L.Rev. 693, 701, quoting, Ziskin, Coping With Psychiatric and Psychological Testimony, 126.) The majority's attempt to apply a normative scheme to a profession which must be concerned with problems that balk at standardization is clearly erroneous.

In any event, an ascertainable standard would not serve to limit psychiatrist disclosure of threats with the resulting impairment of treatment. However compassionate, the psychiatrist hearing the threat remains faced with potential crushing civil liability for a mistaken evaluation of his patient and will be forced to resolve even the slightest doubt in favor of disclosure or commitment.

to overcommit to mental institutions. This overcommitment has been authoritatively documented in both legal and psychiatric studies. (Ennis & Litwack, *Psychiatry and the Presumption of Expertise: Flipping Coins in the Courtroom, supra,* 62 Cal.L.Rev. 693, 711 et seq.; Fleming & Maximov, *The Patient or His Victim: The Therapist's Dilemma,* 62 Cal.L.Rev. 1025, 1044–1046; Am. Psychiatric Assn. Task Force Rep. 8 (July 1974) Clinical Aspects of the Violent Individual, pp. 23–24; see Livermore, Malmquist & Meehl, *On the Justifications for Civil Commitment,* 117 U.Pa.L.Rev. 75, 84.) This practice is so prevalent that it has been estimated that "as many as twenty harmless persons are incarcerated for every one who will commit a violent act." (Steadman & Cocozza, *Stimulus/Response: We Can't Predict Who is Dangerous* (Jan. 1975) 8 Psych. Today 32, 35.)

Given the incentive to commit created by the majority's duty, this already serious situation will be worsened, contrary to CHIEF JUSTICE WRIGHT's admonition "that liberty is no less precious because forfeited in a civil proceeding than when taken as a consequence of a criminal conviction." (*In re W.* (1971) 5 Cal.3d 296, 307, 96 Cal.Rptr. 1, 9, 486 P.2d 1201, 1209.)

• • •

McCOMB, J., concurs.

PROFESSIONAL RESPONSIBILITY OF THE CRIMINAL DEFENSE LAWYER: THE THREE HARDEST QUESTIONS

MONROE H. FREEDMAN

In almost any area of legal counseling and advocacy, the lawyer may be faced with the dilemma of either betraying the confidential communications of his client or participating to some extent in the purposeful deception of the court. This problem is nowhere more acute than in the practice of criminal law, particularly in the representation of the indigent accused. The purpose of this article is to analyze and attempt to resolve three of the most difficult issues in this general area:

1. Is it proper to cross-examine for the purpose of discrediting the reliability

Reprinted from the *Michigan Law Review,* Vol. 64 (1966), 1469–1482, with permission of the publisher and the author. Professor Freedman has further developed the analysis in this article, in his book, *Lawyers' Ethics in an Adversary System* (Indianapolis, Ind.: The Bobbs-Merrill Company, 1975).

or credibility of an adverse witness whom you know to be telling the truth?

2. Is it proper to put a witness on the stand when you know he will commit perjury?
3. Is it proper to give your client legal advice when you have reason to believe that the knowledge you give him will tempt him to commit perjury?

These questions present serious difficulties with respect to a lawyer's ethical responsibilities. Moreover, if one admits the possibility of an affirmative answer, it is difficult even to discuss them without appearing to some to be unethical.[1] It is not surprising, therefore, that reasonable, rational discussion of these issues has been uncommon and that the problems have for so long remained unresolved. In this regard it should be recognized that the Canons of Ethics, which were promulgated in 1908 "as a general guide,"[2] are both inadequate and self-contradictory.

I. THE ADVERSARY SYSTEM AND THE NECESSITY FOR CONFIDENTIALITY

At the outset, we should dispose of some common question-begging responses. The attorney is indeed an officer of the court, and he does participate in a search for truth. These two propositions, however, merely serve to state the problem in different words: As an officer of the court, participating in a search for truth, what is the attorney's special responsibility, and how does that responsibility affect his resolution of the questions posed above?

The attorney functions in an adversary system based upon the presupposition that the most effective means of determining truth is to present to a judge and jury a clash between proponents of conflicting views. It is essential to the effective functioning of this system that each adversary have, in the words of Canon 15, "entire devotion to the interest of the client, warm zeal in the maintenance and defense of his rights and the exertion of his utmost learning and ability." It is also essential to maintain the fullest uninhibited communication between the client and his attorney, so that the attorney can most effectively counsel his client and advocate the latter's cause. This policy is safeguarded by the requirement that the lawyer must, in the words of Canon 37, "preserve his client's confidences." Canon 15 does, of course,

---

[1] The substance of this paper was recently presented to a Criminal Trial Institute attended by forty-five members of the District of Columbia Bar. As a consequence, several judges (none of whom had either heard the lecture or read it) complained to the Committee on Admissions and Grievances of the District Court for the District of Columbia, urging the author's disbarment or suspension. Only after four months of proceedings, including a hearing, two meetings, and a *de novo* review by eleven federal district court judges, did the Committee announce its decision to "proceed no further in the matter."

[2] American Bar Association, *Canons of Professional Ethics,* Preamble (1908).

qualify these obligations by stating that "the office of attorney does not permit, much less does it demand of him for any client, violations of law or any manner of fraud or chicane." In addition, Canon 22 requires candor toward the court.

The problem presented by these salutary generalities of the Canons in the context of particular litigation is illustrated by the personal experience of Samuel Williston, which was related in his autobiography.[3] Because of his examination of a client's correspondence file, Williston learned of a fact extremely damaging to his client's case. When the judge announced his decision, it was apparent that a critical factor in the favorable judgment for Williston's client was the judge's ignorance of this fact. Williston remained silent and did not thereafter inform the judge of what he knew. He was convinced, and Charles Curtis[4] agrees with him, that it was his duty to remain silent.

In an opinion by the American Bar Association Committee on Professional Ethics and Grievances, an eminent panel headed by Henry Drinker held that a lawyer should remain silent when his client lies to the judge by saying that he has no prior record, despite the attorney's knowledge to the contrary.[5] The majority of the panel distinguished the situation in which the attorney has learned of the client's prior record from a source other than the client himself. William B. Jones, a distinguished trial lawyer and now a judge in the United States District Court for the District of Columbia, wrote a separate opinion in which he asserted that in neither event should the lawyer expose his client's lie. If these two cases do not constitute "fraud or chicane" or lack of candor within the meaning of the Canons (and I agree with the authorities cited that they do not), it is clear that the meaning of the canons is ambiguous.

The adversary system has further ramifications in a criminal case. The defendant is presumed to be innocent. The burden is on the prosecution to prove beyond a reasonable doubt that the defendant is guilty. The plea of not guilty does not necessarily mean "not guilty in fact," for the defendant may mean "not legally guilty." Even the accused who knows that he committed the crime is entitled to put the government to its proof. Indeed, the accused who knows that he is guilty has an absolute constitutional right to remain silent.[6] The moralist might quite reasonably understand this to mean that, under these circumstances, the defendant and his lawyer are privileged to "lie" to the court in pleading not guilty. In my judgment, the moralist is right. However, our adversary system and related notions of the proper administration of criminal justice sanction the lie.

---

[3] Williston, *Life and Law* 271 (1940).

[4] Curtis, *It's Your Law*, 17–21 (1954). See also Curtis, "The Ethics of Advocacy," 4 *Stan. L. Rev.*, 3, 9–10 (1951); Drinker, "Some Remarks on Mr. Curtis' 'The Ethics of Advocacy,'" 4, *Stan. L. Rev.*, 349, 350–51 (1952).

[5] Opinion 287, Committee on Professional Ethics and Grievances of the American Bar Association (1953).

[6] *Escobedo* v. *Illinois,* 378 U.S. 478, 485, 491 (1964).

Some derive solace from the sophistry of calling the lie a "legal fiction," but this is hardly an adequate answer to the moralist. Moreover, this answer has no particular appeal for the practicing attorney, who knows that the plea of not guilty commits him to the most effective advocacy of which he is capable. Criminal defense lawyers do not win their cases by arguing reasonable doubt. Effective trial advocacy requires that the attorney's every word, action, and attitude be consistent with the conclusion that his client is innocent. As every trial lawyer knows, the jury is certain that the defense attorney knows whether his client is guilty. The jury is therefore alert to, and will be enormously affected by, any indication by the attorney that he believes the defendant to be guilty. Thus, the plea of not guilty commits the advocate to a trial, including a closing argument, in which he must argue that "not guilty" means "not guilty in fact."[7]

There is, of course, a simple way to evade the dilemma raised by the not guilty plea. Some attorneys rationalize the problem by insisting that a lawyer never knows for sure whether his client is guilty. The client who insists upon his guilt may in fact be protecting his wife, or may know that he pulled the trigger and that the victim was killed, but not that his gun was loaded with blanks and that the fatal shot was fired from across the street. For anyone who finds this reasoning satisfactory, there is, of course, no need to think further about the issue.

It is also argued that a defense attorney can remain selectively ignorant. He can insist in his first interview with his client that, if his client is guilty, he simply does not want to know. It is inconceivable, however, that an attorney could give adequate counsel under such circumstances. How is the client to know, for example, precisely which relevant circumstances his lawyer does not want to be told? The lawyer might ask whether his client has a prior record. The client, assuming that this is the kind of knowledge that might present ethical problems for his lawyer, might respond that he has no record. The lawyer would then put the defendant on the stand and, on cross-examination, be appalled to learn that his client has two prior convictions for offenses identical to that for which he is being tried.

Of course, an attorney can guard against this specific problem by telling his client that he must know about the client's past record. However, a lawyer can never anticipate all of the innumerable and potentially critical factors that his client, once cautioned, may decide not to reveal. In one instance, for example, the defendant assumed that his lawyer would prefer to be ignorant

---

[7] "The failure to argue the case before the jury, while ordinarily only a trial tactic not subject to review, manifestly enters the field of incompetency when the reason assigned is the attorney's conscience. It is as improper as though the attorney had told the jury that his client had uttered a falsehood in making the statement. The right to an attorney embraces effective representation throughout all stages of the trial, and where the representation is of such low caliber as to amount to no representation, the guarantee of due process has been violated." *Johns* v. *Smyth*, 176 F. Supp. 949, 953 (E.D. Va. 1959); Schwartz, *Cases on Professional Responsibility and the Administration of Criminal Justice*, 79 (1962).

of the fact that the client had been having sexual relations with the chief defense witness. The client was innocent of the robbery with which he was charged, but was found guilty by the jury—probably because he was guilty of fornication, a far less serious offense for which he had not even been charged.

The problem is compounded by the practice of plea bargaining. It is considered improper for a defendant to plead guilty to a lesser offense unless he is in fact guilty. Nevertheless, it is common knowledge that plea bargaining frequently results in improper guilty pleas by innocent people. For example, a defendant falsely accused of robbery may plead guilty to simple assault, rather than risk a robbery conviction and a substantial prison term. If an attorney is to be scrupulous in bargaining pleas, however, he must know in advance that his client is guilty, since the guilty plea is improper if the defendant is innocent. Of course, if the attempt to bargain for a lesser offense should fail, the lawyer would know the truth and thereafter be unable to rationalize that he was uncertain of his client's guilt.

If one recognizes that professional responsibility requires that an advocate have full knowledge of every pertinent fact, it follows that he must seek the truth from his client, not shun it.[8] This means that he will have to dig and pry and cajole, and, even then, he will not be successful unless he can convince the client that full and confidential disclosure to his lawyer will never result in prejudice to the client by any word or action of the lawyer. This is, perhaps, particularly true in the case of the indigent defendant, who meets his lawyer for the first time in the cell block or the rotunda. He did not choose the lawyer, nor does he know him. The lawyer has been sent by the judge and is part of the system that is attempting to punish the defendant. It is no easy task to persuade this client that he can talk freely without fear of prejudice. However, the inclination to mislead one's lawyer is not restricted to the indigent or even to the criminal defendant. Randolph Paul has observed a similar phenomenon among a wealthier class in a far more congenial atmosphere:

> The tax adviser will sometimes have to dynamite the facts of his case out of the unwilling witnesses on his own side—witnesses who are nervous, witnesses who are confused about their own interest, witnesses who try to be too smart for their own good, and witnesses who subconsciously do not want to understand what has happened despite the fact that they must if they are to testify coherently.[9]

Paul goes on to explain that the truth can be obtained only by persuading the client that it would be a violation of a sacred obligation for the lawyer ever to reveal a client's confidence. Beyond any question, once a lawyer has persuaded his client of the obligation of confidentiality, he must respect that obligation scrupulously.

---

[8] "[C]ounsel cannot properly perform their duties without knowing the truth." Opinion 23, Committee on Professional Ethics and Grievances of the American Bar Association (1930).

[9] Paul, "The Responsibilities of the Tax Adviser," 63 *Harv. L. Rev.*, 377, 383 (1950).

II. THE SPECIFIC QUESTIONS

The first of the difficult problems posed above will now be considered: Is it proper to cross-examine for the purpose of discrediting the reliability or the credibility of a witness whom you know to be telling the truth? Assume the following situation. Your client has been falsely accused of a robbery committed at 16th and P Streets at 11:00 P.M. He tells you at first that at no time on the evening of the crime was he within six blocks of that location. However, you are able to persuade him that he must tell you the truth and that doing so will in no way prejudice him. He then reveals to you that he was at 15th and P Streets at 10:55 that evening, but that he was walking east, away from the scene of the crime, and that, by 11:00 P.M., he was six blocks away. At the trial, there are two prosecution witnesses. The first mistakenly, but with some degree of persuasion, identifies your client as the criminal. At that point, the prosecution's case depends on this single witness, who might or might not be believed. Since your client has a prior record, you do not want to put him on the stand, but you feel that there is at least a chance for acquittal. The second prosecution witness is an elderly woman who is somewhat nervous and who wears glasses. She testifies truthfully and accurately that she saw your client at 15th and P Streets at 10:55 P.M. She has corroborated the erroneous testimony of the first witness and made conviction virtually certain. However, if you destroy her reliability through cross-examination designed to show that she is easily confused and has poor eyesight, you may not only eliminate the corroboration, but also cast doubt in the jury's mind on the prosecution's entire case. On the other hand, if you should refuse to cross-examine her because she is telling the truth, your client may well feel betrayed, since you knew of the witness's veracity only because your client confided in you, under your assurance that his truthfulness would not prejudice him.

The client would be right. Viewed strictly, the attorney's failure to cross-examine would not be violative of the client's confidence because it would not constitute a disclosure. However, the same policy that supports the obligation of confidentiality precludes the attorney from prejudicing his client's interest in any other way because of knowledge gained in his professional capacity. When a lawyer fails to cross-examine only because his client, placing confidence in the lawyer, has been candid with him, the basis for such confidence and candor collapses. Our legal system cannot tolerate such a result.

> The purposes and necessities of the relation between a client and his attorney require, in many cases, on the part of the client, the fullest and freest disclosures to the attorney of the client's objects, motives and acts. . . . To permit the attorney to reveal to others what is so disclosed, would be not only a gross violation of a sacred trust upon his part, but it would utterly destroy and prevent the usefulness and benefits to be derived from professional assistance.[10]

[10] 2 Mechem, Agency § 2297 (2d ed. 1914).

The client's confidences must "upon all occasions be inviolable," to avoid the "greater mischiefs" that would probably result if a client could not feel free "to repose [confidence] in the attorney to whom he resorts for legal advice and assistance."[11] Destroy that confidence, and "a man would not venture to consult any skillful person, or would only dare to tell his counsellor half his case."[12]

Therefore, one must conclude that the attorney is obligated to attack, if he can, the reliability or credibility of an opposing witness whom he knows to be truthful. The contrary result would inevitably impair the "perfect freedom of consultation by client with attorney," which is "essential to the administration of justice."[13]

The second question is generally considered to be the hardest of all: Is it proper to put a witness on the stand when you know he will commit perjury? Assume, for example, that the witness in question is the accused himself, and that he has admitted to you, in response to your assurances of confidentiality, that he is guilty. However, he insists upon taking the stand to protest his innocence. There is a clear consensus among prosecutors and defense attorneys that the likelihood of conviction is increased enormously when the defendant does not take the stand. Consequently, the attorney who prevents his client from testifying only because the client has confided his guilt to him is violating that confidence by acting upon the information in a way that will seriously prejudice his client's interests.

Perhaps the most common method for avoiding the ethical problem just posed is for the lawyer to withdraw from the case, at least if there is sufficient time before trial for the client to retain another attorney.[14] The client will then go to the nearest law office, realizing that the obligation of confidentiality is not what it has been represented to be, and withhold incriminating information or the fact of his guilt from his new attorney. On ethical grounds, the practice of withdrawing from a case under such circumstances is indefensible, since the identical perjured testimony will ultimately be presented. More important, perhaps, is the practical consideration that the new attorney will be ignorant of the perjury and therefore will be in no position to attempt to discourage the client from presenting it. Only the original attorney, who

---

[11] Opinion 150, Committee on Professional Ethics and Grievances of the American Bar Association (1936), quoting Thornton, Attorneys at Law § 94 (1914). See also Opinion 23, *supra* note 8.

[12] *Greenough* v. *Gaskell,* 1 Myl. & K. 98, 103, 39 Eng. Rep. 618, 621 (Ch. 1833) (Lord Chancellor Brougham).

[13] Opinion 91, Committee on Professional Ethics and Grievances of the American Bar Association (1933).

[14] See Orkin, "Defense of One Known To Be Guilty," 1 *Crim. L.Q.,* 170, 174 (1958). Unless the lawyer has told the client at the outset that he will withdraw if he learns that the client is guilty, "it is plain enough as a matter of good morals and professional ethics" that the lawyer should not withdraw on this ground. Opinion 90, Committee on Professional Ethics and Grievances of the American Bar Association (1932). As to the difficulties inherent in the lawyer's telling the client that he wants to remain ignorant of crucial facts, see note 8 *supra* and accompanying text.

knows the truth, has that opportunity, but he loses it in the very act of evading the ethical problem.

The problem is all the more difficult when the client is indigent. He cannot retain other counsel, and in many jurisdictions, including the District of Columbia, it is impossible for appointed counsel to withdraw from a case except for extraordinary reasons. Thus, appointed counsel, unless he lies to the judge, can successfully withdraw only by revealing to the judge that the attorney has received knowledge of his client's guilt. Such a revelation in itself would seem to be a sufficiently serious violation of the obligation of confidentiality to merit severe condemnation. In fact, however, the situation is far worse, since it is entirely possible that the same judge who permits the attorney to withdraw will subsequently hear the case and sentence the defendant. When he does so, of course, he will have had personal knowledge of the defendant's guilt before the trial began.[15] Moreover, this will be knowledge of which the newly appointed counsel for the defendant will probably be ignorant.

The difficulty is further aggravated when the client informs the lawyer for the first time during trial that he intends to take the stand and commit perjury. The perjury in question may not necessarily be a protestation of innocence by a guilty man. Referring to the earlier hypothetical of the defendant wrongly accused of a robbery at 16th and P, the only perjury may be his denial of the truthful, but highly damaging, testimony of the corroborating witness who placed him one block away from the intersection five minutes prior to the crime. Of course, if he tells the truth and thus verifies the corroborating witness, the jury will be far more inclined to accept the inaccurate testimony of the principal witness, who specifically identified him as the criminal.[16]

If a lawyer has discovered his client's intent to perjure himself, one possible solution to this problem is for the lawyer to approach the bench, explain his ethical difficulty to the judge, and ask to be relieved, thereby causing a mistrial. This request is certain to be denied, if only because it would empower the defendant to cause a series of mistrials in the same fashion. At this point, some feel that the lawyer has avoided the ethical problem and can put the defendant on the stand. However, one objection to this solution, apart from the violation of confidentiality, is that the lawyer's ethical problem has not

[15] The judge may infer that the situation is worse than it is in fact. In the case related in note 23 *infra,* the attorney's actual difficulty was that he did not want to permit a plea of guilty by a client who was maintaining his innocence. However, as is commonly done, he told the judge only that he had to withdraw because of "an ethical problem." The judge reasonably inferred that the defendant had admitted his guilt and wanted to offer a perjured alibi.

[16] One lawyer, who considers it clearly unethical for the attorney to present the alibi in this hypothetical case, found no ethical difficulty himself in the following case. His client was prosecuted for robbery. The prosecution witness testified that the robbery had taken place at 10:15, and identified the defendant as the criminal. However, the defendant had a convincing alibi for 10:00 to 10:30. The attorney presented the alibi, and the client was acquitted. The alibi was truthful, but the attorney knew that the prosecution witness had been confused about the time, and that his client had in fact committed the crime at 10:45.

been solved, but has only been transferred to the judge. Moreover, the client in such a case might well have grounds for appeal on the basis of deprivation of due process and denial of the right to counsel, since he will have been tried before, and sentenced by, a judge who has been informed of the client's guilt by his own attorney.

A solution even less satisfactory than informing the judge of the defendant's guilt would be to let the client take the stand without the attorney's participation and to omit reference to the client's testimony in closing argument. The latter solution, of course, would be as damaging as to fail entirely to argue the case to the jury, and failing to argue the case is "as improper as though the attorney had told the jury that his client had uttered a falsehood in making the statement."[17]

Therefore, the obligation of confidentiality, in the context of our adversary system, apparently allows the attorney no alternative to putting a perjurious witness on the stand without explicit or implicit disclosure of the attorney's knowledge to either the judge or the jury. Canon 37 does not proscribe this conclusion; the canon recognizes only two exceptions to the obligation of confidentiality. The first relates to the lawyer who is accused by his client and may disclose the truth to defend himself. The other exception relates to the "announced intention of a client to commit a crime." On the basis of the ethical and practical considerations discussed above, the Canon's exception to the obligation of confidentiality cannot logically be understood to include the crime of perjury committed during the specific case in which the lawyer is serving. Moreover, even when the intention is to commit a crime in the future, Canon 37 does not require disclosure, but only permits it. Furthermore, Canon 15, which does proscribe "violation of law" by the attorney for his client, does not apply to the lawyer who unwillingly puts a perjurious client on the stand after having made every effort to dissuade him from committing perjury. Such an act by the attorney cannot properly be found to be subornation—corrupt inducement—of perjury. Canon 29 requires counsel to inform the prosecuting authorities of perjury committed in a case in which he has been involved, but this can only refer to perjury by opposing witnesses. For an attorney to disclose his client's perjury "would involve a direct violation of Canon 37."[18] Despite Canon 29, therefore, the attorney should not reveal his client's perjury "to the court or to the authorities."[19]

Of course, before the client testifies perjuriously, the lawyer has a duty to attempt to dissuade him on grounds of both law and morality. In addition, the client should be impressed with the fact that his untruthful alibi is tactically dangerous. There is always a strong possibility that the prosecutor will expose the perjury on cross-examination. However, for the reasons already given, the final decision must necessarily be the client's. The lawyer's best course

---

[17] See note 7 *supra*.

[18] Opinion 287, Committee on Professional Ethics and Grievances of the American Bar Association (1953).

[19] *Ibid.*

thereafter would be to avoid any further professional relationship with a client whom he knew to have perjured himself.

The third question is whether it is proper to give your client legal advice when you have reason to believe that the knowledge you give him will tempt him to commit perjury. This may indeed be the most difficult problem of all, because giving such advice creates the appearance that the attorney is encouraging and condoning perjury.

If the lawyer is not certain what the facts are when he gives the advice, the problem is substantially minimized, if not eliminated. It is not the lawyer's function to prejudge his client as a perjurer. He cannot presume that the client will make unlawful use of his advice. Apart from this, there is a natural predisposition in most people to recollect facts, entirely honestly, in a way most favorable to their own interest. As Randolph Paul has observed, some witnesses are nervous, some are confused about their own interests, some try to be too smart for their own good, and some subconsciously do not want to understand what has happened to them.[20] Before he begins to remember essential facts, the client is entitled to know what his own interests are.

The above argument does not apply merely to factual questions such as whether a particular event occurred at 10:15 or at 10:45.[21] One of the most critical problems in a criminal case, as in many others, is intention. A German writer, considering the question of intention as a test of legal consequences, suggests the following situation.[22] A young man and a young woman decide to get married. Each has a thousand dollars. They decide to begin a business with these funds, and the young lady gives her money to the young man for this purpose. Was the intention to form a joint venture or a partnership? Did they intend that the young man be an agent or a trustee? Was the transaction a gift or a loan? If the couple should subsequently visit a tax attorney and discover that it is in their interest that the transaction be viewed as a gift, it is submitted that they could, with complete honesty, so remember it. On the other hand, should their engagement be broken and the young woman consult an attorney for the purpose of recovering her money, she could with equal honesty remember that her intention was to make a loan.

Assume that your client, on trial for his life in a first-degree murder case, has killed another man with a penknife but insists that the killing was in self-defense. You ask him, "Do you customarily carry the penknife in your pocket, do you carry it frequently or infrequently, or did you take it with you only on this occasion?" It is entirely appropriate to inform him that his carrying the knife only on this occasion, or infrequently, supports an inference of premeditation, while if he carried the knife constantly, or frequently, the inference of premeditation would be negated. Thus, your client's life may depend upon his recollection as to whether he carried the knife frequently

---

[20] See Paul, *supra* note 9.

[21] Even this kind of "objective fact" is subject to honest error. See note 16 *supra*.

[22] Wurzel, Das Juristische Denken," 82 (1904), translated in Fuller, *Basic Contract Law,* 67 (1964).

or infrequently. Despite the possibility that the client or a third party might infer that the lawyer was prompting the client to lie, the lawyer must apprise the defendant of the significance of his answer. There is no conceivable ethical requirement that the lawyer trap his client into a hasty and ill-considered answer before telling him the significance of the question.

A similar problem is created if the client has given the lawyer incriminating information before being fully aware of its significance. For example, assume that a man consults a tax lawyer and says, "I am fifty years old. Nobody in my immediate family has lived past fifty. Therefore, I would like to put my affairs in order. Specifically, I understand that I can avoid substantial estate taxes by setting up a trust. Can I do it?" The lawyer informs the client that he can successfully avoid the estate taxes only if he lives at least three years after establishing the trust or, should he die within three years, if the trust is found not to have been created in contemplation of death. The client then might ask who decides whether the trust is in contemplation of death. After learning that the determination is made by the court, the client might inquire about the factors on which such a decision would be based.

At this point, the lawyer can do one of two things. He can refuse to answer the question, or he can inform the client that the court will consider the wording of the trust instrument and will hear evidence about any conversations which he may have or any letters he may write expressing motives other than avoidance of estate taxes. It is likely that virtually every tax attorney in the country would answer the client's question, and that no one would consider the answer unethical. However, the lawyer might well appear to have prompted his client to deceive the Internal Revenue Service and the courts, and this appearance would remain regardless of the lawyer's explicit disclaimer to the client of any intent so to prompt him. Nevertheless, it should not be unethical for the lawyer to give the advice.

In a criminal case, a lawyer may be representing a client who protests his innocence, and whom the lawyer believes to be innocent. Assume, for example, that the charge is assault with intent to kill, that the prosecution has erroneous but credible eyewitness testimony against the defendant, and that the defendant's truthful alibi witness is impeachable on the basis of several felony convictions. The prosecutor, perhaps having doubts about the case, offers to permit the defendant to plead guilty to simple assault. If the defendant should go to trial and be convicted, he might well be sent to jail for fifteen years; on a plea of simple assault, the maximum penalty would be one year, and sentence might well be suspended.

The common practice of conveying the prosecutor's offer to the defendant should not be considered unethical, even if the defense lawyer is convinced of this client's innocence. Yet the lawyer is clearly in the position of prompting his client to lie, since the defendant cannot make the plea without saying to the judge that he is pleading guilty because he is guilty. Furthermore, if the client does decide to plead guilty, it would be improper for the lawyer to inform the court that his client is innocent, thereby compelling the defendant to stand trial and take the substantial risk of fifteen years' imprisonment.[23]

Essentially no different from the problem discussed above, but apparently more difficult, is the so-called *Anatomy of a Murder* situation.[24] The lawyer, who has received from his client an incriminating story of murder in the first degree, says, "If the facts are as you have stated them so far, you have no defense, and you will probably be electrocuted. On the other hand, if you acted in a blind rage, there is a possibility of saving your life. Think it over, and we will talk about it tomorrow." As in the tax case, and as in the case of the plea of guilty to a lesser offense, the lawyer has given his client a legal opinion that might induce the client to lie. This is information which the lawyer himself would have, without advice, were he in the client's position. It is submitted that the client is entitled to have this information about the law and to make his own decision as to whether to act upon it. To decide otherwise would not only penalize the less well-educated defendant, but would also prejudice the client because of his initial truthfulness in telling his story in confidence to the attorney.

III. CONCLUSION

The lawyer is an officer of the court, participating in a search for truth. Yet no lawyer would consider that he had acted unethically in pleading the statute of frauds or the statute of limitations as a bar to a just claim. Similarly, no lawyer would consider it unethical to prevent the introduction of evidence such as a murder weapon seized in violation of the fourth amendment or a truthful but involuntary confession, or to defend a guilty man on grounds of denial of a speedy trial.[25] Such actions are permissible because there are policy

[23] In a recent case, the defendant was accused of unauthorized use of an automobile, for which the maximum penalty is five years. He told his court-appointed attorney that he had borrowed the car from a man known to him only as "Junior," that he had not known the car was stolen, and that he had an alibi for the time of the theft. The defendant had three prior convictions for larceny, and the alibi was weak. The prosecutor offered to accept a guilty plea to two misdemeanors (taking property without right and petty larceny) carrying a combined maximum sentence of eighteen months. The defendant was willing to plead guilty to the lesser offenses, but the attorney felt that, because of his client's alibi, he could not permit him to do so. The lawyer therefore informed the judge that he had an ethical problem and asked to be relieved. The attorney who was appointed in his place permitted the client to plead guilty to the two lesser offenses, and the defendant was sentenced to nine months. The alternative would have been five or six months in jail while the defendant waited for his jury trial, and a very substantial risk of conviction and a much heavier sentence. Neither the client nor justice would have been well served by compelling the defendant to go to trial against his will under these circumstances.

[24] See Traver, *Anatomy of a Murder* (1958).

[25] *Cf.* Kamisar, "Equal Justice in the Gatehouses and Mansions of American Criminal Procedure," in *Criminal Justice in Our Time* 77–78 (Howard ed. 1965):

Yes, the presence of counsel in the police station may result in the suppression of truth, just

considerations that at times justify frustrating the search for truth and the prosecution of a just claim. Similarly, there are policies that justify an affirmative answer to the three questions that have been posed in this article. These policies include the maintenance of an adversary system, the presumption of innocence, the prosecution's burden to prove guilt beyond a reasonable doubt, the right to counsel, and the obligation of confidentiality between lawyer and client.

---

as the presence of counsel at the trial may, when a client is advised not to take the stand, or when an objection is made to the admissibility of trustworthy, but illegally seized, "real" evidence.

If the subject of police interrogation not only cannot be "coerced" into making a statement, but need not volunteer one, why shouldn't he be so advised? And why shouldn't court-appointed counsel, as well as retained counsel, so advise him?

LAWYERS AS PROFESSIONALS: SOME MORAL ISSUES

RICHARD A. WASSERSTROM

In this paper I examine two moral criticisms of lawyers which, if well-founded, are fundamental. Neither is new but each appears to apply with particular force today. Both tend to be made by those not in the mainstream of the legal profession and to be rejected by those who are in it. Both in some sense concern the lawyer-client relationship.

The first criticism centers around the lawyer's stance toward the world at large. The accusation is that the lawyer-client relationship renders the lawyer at best systematically amoral and at worst more than occasionally immoral in his or her dealings with the rest of mankind.

The second criticism focuses upon the relationship between the lawyer and the client. Here the charge is that it is the lawyer-client relationship which is morally objectionable because it is a relationship in which the lawyer dominates and in which the lawyer typically, and perhaps inevitably, treats the client in both an impersonal and paternalistic fashion.

To a considerable degree these two criticisms of lawyers derive, I believe, from the fact that the lawyer is a professional. And to the extent to which this is the case, the more generic problems I will be exploring are those of professionalism generally. But in some respects, the lawyer's situation is different from that of other professionals. The lawyer is vulnerable to some

Reprinted from *Human Rights,* Vol. 5, No. 1 (1975), 1–24, with permission of the American Bar Association, Section of Individual Rights and Responsibilities, and Southern Methodist University. Copyright © 1975, American Bar Association.

moral criticism that does not as readily or as easily attach to any other professional. And this, too, is an issue that I shall be examining.[1]

Although I am undecided about the ultimate merits of either criticism, I am convinced that each is deserving of careful articulation and assessment, and that each contains insights that deserve more acknowledgment than they often receive. My ambition is, therefore, more to exhibit the relevant considerations and to stimulate additional reflection, than it is to provide any very definite conclusions.

I

As I have indicated, the first issue I propose to examine concerns the ways the professional-client relationship affects the professional's stance toward the world at large. The primary question that is presented is whether there is adequate justification for the kind of moral universe that comes to be inhabited by the lawyer as he or she goes through professional life. For at best the lawyer's world is a simplified moral world; often it is an amoral one; and more than occasionally, perhaps, an overtly immoral one.

To many persons. Watergate was simply a recent and dramatic illustration

---

[1] Because of the significance for my analysis of the closely related concepts of a profession and a professional, it will be helpful to indicate at the outset what I take to be the central features of a profession.

But first there is an ambiguity that must be noted so that it can be dismissed. There is one sense of "professional" and hence of "profession" with which I am not concerned. That is the sense in which there are in our culture, professional athletes, professional actors, and professional beauticians. In this sense, a person who possesses sufficient skill to engage in an activity for money and who elects to do so is a professional rather than, say, an amateur or a volunteer. This is, as I have said, not the sense of "profession" in which I am interested.

I am interested, instead, in the characteristics of professions such as law, or medicine. There are, I think, at least six that are worth noting.

(1) The professions require a substantial period of formal education—at least as much if not more than that required by any other occupation.

(2) The professions require the comprehension of a substantial amount of theoretical knowledge and the utilization of a substantial amount of intellectual ability. Neither manual nor creative ability is typically demanded. This is one thing that distinguishes the professions both from highly skilled crafts—like glassblowing—and from the arts.

(3) The professions are both an economic monopoly and largely self-regulating. Not only is the practice of the profession restricted to those who are certified as possessing the requisite competencies, but the questions of what competencies are required and who possesses them are questions that are left to the members of the profession to decide for themselves.

(4) The professions are clearly among the occupations that possess the greatest social prestige in the society. They also typically provide a degree of material affluence substantially greater than that enjoyed by most working persons.

(5) The professions are almost always involved with matters which from time to time are among the greatest personal concerns that humans have: physical health, psychic well-being, liberty, and the like. As a result, persons who seek the services of a professional are often in a state of appreciable concern, if not vulnerability, when they do so.

(6) The professions almost always involve at their core a significant interpersonal relationship between the professional, on the one hand, and the person who is thought to require the professional's services: the patient or the client.

of this fact. When John Dean testified before the Select Senate Committee inquiring into the Watergate affair in the Spring of 1973, he was asked about one of the documents that he had provided to the Committee. The document was a piece of paper which contained a list of a number of the persons who had been involved in the cover-up. Next to a number of the names an asterisk appeared. What, Dean was asked, was the meaning of the asterisk? Did it signify membership in some further conspiracy? Did it mark off those who were decision makers from those who were not? There did not seem to be any obvious pattern: Ehrlichman was starred, but Haldeman was not; Mitchell was starred, but Magruder was not. Oh, Dean answered, the asterisk really didn't mean anything. One day when he had been looking at the list of participants, he had been struck by the fact that so many of them were lawyers. So, he marked the name of each lawyer with an asterisk to see just how many there were. He had wondered, he told the Committee, when he saw that so many were attorneys, whether that had had anything to do with it; whether there was some reason why lawyers might have been more inclined than other persons to have been so willing to do the things that were done in respect to Watergate and the cover-up. But he had not pursued the matter; he had merely mused about it one afternoon.

It is, I think, at least a plausible hypothesis that the predominance of lawyers was not accidental—that the fact that they were lawyers made it easier rather than harder for them both to look at things the way they did and to do the things that were done. The theory that I want to examine in support of this hypothesis connects this activity with a feature of the lawyer's professionalism.

As I have already noted, one central feature of the professions in general and of law in particular is that there is a special, complicated relationship between the professional, and the client or patient. For each of the parties in this relationship, but especially for the professional, the behavior that is involved is, to a very significant degree, what I call role-differentiated behavior. And this is significant because it is the nature of role-differentiated behavior that it often makes it both appropriate and desirable for the person in a particular role to put to one side considerations of various sorts—and especially various moral considerations—that would otherwise be relevant if not decisive. Some illustrations will help to make clear what I mean both by role-differentiated behavior and by the way role-differentiated behavior often alters, if not eliminates, the significance of those moral considerations that would obtain, were it not for the presence of the role.

Being a parent is, in probably every human culture, to be involved in role-differentiated behavior. In our own culture, and once again in most, if not all, human cultures, as a parent one is entitled, if not obligated, to prefer the interests of one's own children over those of children generally. That is to say, it is regarded as appropriate for a parent to allocate excessive goods to his or her own children, even though other children may have substantially more pressing and genuine needs for these same items. If one were trying to decide what the right way was to distribute assets among a group of children all of whom were strangers to oneself, the relevant moral considerations would be very different from those that would be thought to obtain once one's own children were in the picture. In the role of a parent, the claims of other children vis-à-vis one's own are, if not rendered morally irrelevant, certainly rendered less morally significant. In short, the role-differentiated character of the situation alters the relevant moral point of view enormously.

A similar situation is presented by the case of the scientist. For a number of years there has been debate and controversy within the scientific community over the question of whether scientists should participate in the development and elaboration of atomic theory, especially as those theoretical advances could then be translated into development of atomic weapons that would become a part of the arsenal of existing nation states. The dominant view, although it was not the unanimous one, in the scientific community was that the role of the scientist was to expand the limits of human knowledge. Atomic power was a force which had previously not been utilizable by human beings. The job of the scientist was, among other things, to develop ways and means by which that could now be done. And it was simply no part of one's role as a scientist to forego inquiry, or divert one's scientific explorations because of the fact that the fruits of the investigation could be or would be put to improper, immoral, or even catastrophic uses. The moral issues concerning whether and when to develop and use nuclear weapons were to be decided by others; by citizens and statesmen; they were not the concern of the scientist *qua* scientist.

In both of these cases it is, of course, conceivable that plausible and even thoroughly convincing arguments exist for the desirability of the role-differentiated behavior and its attendant neglect of what would otherwise be morally relevant considerations. Nonetheless, it is, I believe, also the case that the burden of proof, so to speak, is always upon the proponent of the desirability of this kind of role-differentiated behavior. For in the absence of special reasons why parents ought to prefer the interests of their children over those of children in general, the moral point of view surely requires that the claims and needs of all children receive equal consideration. But we take the rightness of parental preference so for granted, that we often neglect, I think, the fact that it is anything but self-evidently morally appropriate. My own view, for example, is that careful reflection shows that the *degree* of parental preference systematically encouraged in our own culture is far too extensive to be morally justified.

All of this is significant just because to be a professional is to be enmeshed in role-differentiated behavior of precisely this sort. One's role as a doctor, psychiatrist, or lawyer, alters one's moral universe in a fashion analogous to that described above. Of special significance here is the fact that the professional *qua* professional has a client or patient whose interests must be represented, attended to, or looked after by the professional. And that means that the role of the professional (like that of the parent) is to prefer in a variety of ways the interests of the client or patient over those of individuals generally.

Consider, more specifically, the role-differentiated behavior of the lawyer. Conventional wisdom has it that where the attorney-client relationship exists, the point of view of the attorney is properly different—and appreciably so—from that which would be appropriate in the absence of the attorney-client relationship. For where the attorney-client relationship exists, it is often appropriate and many times even obligatory for the attorney to do things that, all other things being equal, an ordinary person need not, and should not do. What is characteristic of this role of a lawyer is the lawyer's required indifference to a wide variety of ends and consequences that in other contexts would be of undeniable moral significance. Once a lawyer represents a client, the lawyer has a duty to make his or her expertise fully available in the realization of the end sought by the client, irrespective, for the most part, of the moral worth to which the end will be put or the character of the client who seeks to utilize it. Provided that the end sought is not illegal, the lawyer is, in essence, an amoral technician whose peculiar skills and knowledge in respect to the law are available to those with whom the relationship of client is established. The question, as I have indicated, is whether this particular and pervasive feature of professionalism is itself justifiable. At a minimum, I do not think any of the typical, simple answers will suffice.

One such answer focuses upon and generalizes from the criminal defense lawyer. For what is probably the most familiar aspect of this role-differentiated character of the lawyer's activity is that of the defense of a client charged with a crime. The received view within the profession (and to a lesser degree within the society at large) is that having once agreed to represent the client, the lawyer is under an obligation to do his or her best to defend that person at trial, irrespective, for instance, even of the lawyer's belief in the client's innocence. There are limits, of course, to what constitutes a defense: a lawyer cannot bribe or intimidate witnesses to increase the likelihood of securing an acquittal. And there are legitimate questions, in close cases, about how those limits are to be delineated. But, however these matters get resolved, it is at least clear that it is thought both appropriate and obligatory for the attorney to put on as vigorous and persuasive a defense of a client believed to be guilty as would have been mounted by the lawyer thoroughly convinced of the client's innocence. I suspect that many persons find this an attractive and admirable feature of the life of a legal professional. I know that often I do. The justifications are varied and, as I shall argue below, probably convincing.

But part of the difficulty is that the irrelevance of the guilt or innocence of an accused client by no means exhausts the altered perspective of the lawyer's conscience, even in criminal cases. For in the course of defending an accused, an attorney may have, as a part of his or her duty of representation, the obligation to invoke procedures and practices which are themselves morally objectionable and of which the lawyer in other contexts might thoroughly disapprove. And these situations, I think, are somewhat less comfortable to confront. For example, in California, the case law permits a defendant in a rape case to secure in some circumstances an order from the court requiring the complaining witness, that is the rape victim, to submit to a psychiatric examination before trial.[2] For no other crime is such a pretrial remedy available. In no other case can the victim of a crime be required to undergo psychiatric examination at the request of the defendant on the ground that the results of the examination may help the defendant prove that the offense did not take place. I think such a rule is wrong and is reflective of the sexist bias of the law in respect to rape. I certainly do not think it right that rape victims should be singled out by the law for this kind of special pretrial treatment, and I am skeptical about the morality of any involuntary psychiatric examination of witnesses. Nonetheless, it appears to be part of the role-differentiated obligation of a lawyer for a defendant charged with rape to seek to take advantage of this particular rule of law—irrespective of the independent moral view he or she may have of the rightness or wrongness of such a rule.

Nor, it is important to point out, is this peculiar, strikingly amoral behavior limited to the lawyer involved with the workings of the criminal law. Most clients come to lawyers to get the lawyers to help them do things that they could not easily do without the assistance provided by the lawyer's special competence. They wish, for instance, to dispose of their property in a certain way at death. They wish to contract for the purchase or sale of a house or a business. They wish to set up a corporation which will manufacture and market a new product. They wish to minimize their income taxes. And so on. In each case, they need the assistance of the professional, the lawyer, for he or she alone has the special skill which will make it possible for the client to achieve the desired result.

And in each case, the role-differentiated character of the lawyer's way of being tends to render irrelevant what would otherwise be morally relevant considerations. Suppose that a client desires to make a will disinheriting her children because they opposed the war in Vietnam. Should the lawyer refuse to draft the will because the lawyer thinks this a bad reason to disinherit one's children? Suppose a client can avoid the payment of taxes through a loophole only available to a few wealthy taxpayers. Should the lawyer refuse to tell the client of a loophole because the lawyer thinks it an unfair advantage for the rich? Suppose a client wants to start a corporation that will manufacture, distribute and promote a harmful but not illegal substance, *e.g.,* cigarettes. Should the lawyer refuse to prepare the articles of incorporation for the corporation? In each case, the accepted view within the profession is that these matters are just of no concern to the lawyer *qua* lawyer. The lawyer need not of course agree to represent the client (and that is equally true for the unpopular client accused of a heinous crime), but there is nothing wrong with representing a client whose aims and purposes are quite immoral. And

[2] *Ballard* v. *Superior Court,* 64 Cal. 2d 159, 410 P.2d 838, 49 *Cal. Rptr.* 302 (1966).

having agreed to do so, the lawyer is required to provide the best possible assistance, without regard to his or her disapproval of the objective that is sought.

The lesson, on this view, is clear. The job of the lawyer, so the argument typically concludes, is not to approve or disapprove of the character of his or her client, the cause for which the client seeks the lawyer's assistance, or the avenues provided by the law to achieve that which the client wants to accomplish. The lawyer's task is, instead, to provide that competence which the client lacks and the lawyer, as professional, possesses. In this way, the lawyer as professional comes to inhabit a simplified universe which is strikingly amoral—which regards as morally irrelevant any number of factors which nonprofessional citizens might take to be important, if not decisive, in their everyday lives. And the difficulty I have with all of this is that the arguments for such a way of life seem to be not quite so convincing to me as they do to many lawyers. I am, that is, at best uncertain that it is a good thing for lawyers to be so professional—for them to embrace so completely this role-differentiated way of approaching matters.

More specifically, if it is correct that this is the perspective of lawyers in particular and professionals in general, is it right that this should be their perspective? Is it right that the lawyer should be able so easily to put to one side otherwise difficult problems with the answer: but these are not and cannot be my concern as a lawyer? What do we gain and what do we lose from having a social universe in which there are professionals such as lawyers, who, as such, inhabit a universe of the sort I have been trying to describe?

One difficulty in even thinking about all of this is that lawyers may not be very objective or detached in their attempts to work the problem through. For one feature of this simplified, intellectual world is that it is often a very comfortable one to inhabit.

To be sure, on occasion, a lawyer may find it uncomfortable to represent an extremely unpopular client. On occasion, too, a lawyer may feel ill at ease invoking a rule of law or practice which he or she thinks to be an unfair or undesirable one. Nonetheless, for most lawyers, most of the time, pursuing the interests of one's clients is an attractive and satisfying way to live in part just because the moral world of the lawyer is a simpler, less complicated, and less ambiguous world than the moral world of ordinary life. There is, I think, something quite seductive about being able to turn aside so many ostensibly difficult moral dilemmas and decisions with the reply: but that is not my concern; my job as a lawyer is not to judge the rights and wrong of the client or the cause; it is to defend as best I can my client's interests. For the ethical problems that can arise within this constricted point of view are, to say the least, typically neither momentous nor terribly vexing. Role-differentiated behavior is enticing and reassuring precisely because it does constrain and delimit an otherwise often intractable and confusing moral world.

But there is, of course, also an argument which seeks to demonstrate that it is good and not merely comfortable for lawyers to behave this way.

It is good, so the argument goes, that the lawyer's behavior and concomitant point of view are role-differentiated because the lawyer *qua* lawyer participates in a complex institution which functions well only if the individuals adhere to their institutional roles.

For example, when there is a conflict between individuals, or between the state and an individual, there is a well-established institutional mechanism by which to get that dispute resolved. That mechanism is the trial in which each side is represented by a lawyer whose job it is both to present his or her client's case in the most attractive, forceful light and to seek to expose the weaknesses and defects in the case of the opponent.

When an individual is charged with having committed a crime, the trial is the mechanism by which we determine in our society whether or not the person is in fact guilty. Just imagine what would happen if lawyers were to refuse, for instance, to represent persons whom they thought to be guilty. In a case where the guilt of a person seemed clear, it might turn out that some individuals would be deprived completely of the opportunity to have the system determine whether or not they are in fact guilty. The private judgment of individual lawyers would in effect be substituted for the public, institutional judgment of the judge and jury. The amorality of lawyers helps to guarantee that every criminal defendant will have his or her day in court.

In addition, of course, appearances can be deceiving. Persons who appear before trial to be clearly guilty do sometimes turn out to be innocent. Even persons who confess their guilt to their attorney occasionally turn out to have lied or to have been mistaken. The adversary system, so this argument continues, is simply a better method than any other that has been established by which to determine the legally relevant facts in any given case. It is certainly a better method than the exercise of private judgment by any particular individual. And the adversary system only works if each party to the controversy has a lawyer, a person whose institutional role it is to argue, plead and present the merits of his or her case and the demerits of the opponent's. Thus if the adversary system is to work, it is necessary that there be lawyers who will play their appropriate, professional, institutional role of representative of the client's cause.

Nor is the amorality of the institutional role of the lawyer restricted to the defense of those accused of crimes. As was indicated earlier, when the lawyer functions in his most usual role, he or she functions as a counselor, as a professional whose task it is to help people realize those objectives and ends that the law permits them to obtain and which cannot be obtained without the attorney's special competence in the law. The attorney may think it wrong to disinherit one's children because of their views about the Vietnam war, but the attorney's complaint is really with the laws of inheritance and not with his or her client. The attorney may think the tax provision an unfair, unjustifiable loophole, but once more the complaint is really with the Internal Revenue Code and not with the client who seeks to take advantage of it. And these matters, too, lie beyond the ambit of the lawyer's moral point of view as institutional counselor and facilitator. If lawyers were to substitute their own private views of what ought to be legally permissible and impermissible for those of the legislature, this would constitute a surreptitious and undesirable shift from a democracy to an oligarchy of lawyers. For given the fact that lawyers are needed to effectuate the wishes of clients, the lawyer ought to make his or her skills available to those who seek them without regard for the particular objectives of the client.

Now, all of this certainly makes some sense. These arguments are neither specious nor without force. Nonetheless, it seems to me that one dilemma which emerges is that if this line of argument is sound, it also appears to follow that the behavior of the lawyers involved in Watergate was simply another less happy illustration of lawyers playing their accustomed institutional role. If we are to approve on institutional grounds of the lawyer's zealous defense of the apparently guilty client and the lawyer's effective assistance of the immoral cheat, does it not follow that we must also approve of the Watergate lawyer's zealous defense of the interests of Richard Nixon?

As I have indicated, I do not think there is any easy answer to this question. For I am not, let me hasten to make clear, talking about the easy cases—about the behavior of the lawyers that was manifestly illegal. For someone quite properly might reply that it was no more appropriate for the lawyer who worked in the White House to obstruct justice or otherwise violate the criminal law than it would be for a criminal defense lawyer to shoot the prosecution witness to prevent adverse testimony or bribe a defense witness in order to procure favorable testimony. What I am interested in is all of the Watergate behavior engaged in by the Watergate lawyers that was not illegal, but that was, nonetheless, behavior of which we quite properly disapprove. I mean lying to the public; dissembling; stonewalling; tape-recording conversations; playing dirty tricks. Were not these just effective lawyer-like activities pursued by lawyers who viewed Richard Nixon as they would a client and who sought, therefore, the advancement and protection of his interests—personal and political?

It might immediately be responded that the analogy is not apt. For the lawyers who were involved in Watergate were hardly participants in an adversary proceeding. They were certainly not participants in that institutional setting, litigation, in which the amorality of the lawyer makes the most sense. It might even be objected that the amorality of the lawyer *qua counselor* is clearly distinguishable from the behavior of the Watergate lawyers. Nixon as President was not a client; they, as officials in the executive branch, were functioning as governmental officials and not as lawyers at all.

While not wholly convinced by a response such as the above, I am prepared to accept it because the issue at hand seems to me to be a deeper one. Even if the involvement of so many lawyers in Watergate was adventitious (or, if not adventitious, explicable in terms of some more benign explanation) there still seems to me to be costs, if not problems, with the amorality of the lawyer that derives from his or her role-differentiated professionalism.

As I indicated earlier, I do believe that the amoral behavior of the *criminal* defense lawyer is justifiable. But I think that justification depends at least as much upon the special needs of an accused as upon any more general defense of a lawyer's role-differentiated behavior. As a matter of fact I think it likely that many persons such as myself have been misled by the special features of the criminal case. Because a deprivation of liberty is so serious, because the prosecutorial resources of the state are so vast, and because, perhaps, of a serious skepticism about the rightness of punishment even where wrongdoing has occurred, it is easy to accept the view that it makes sense to charge the defense counsel with the job of making the best possible case for the accused— without regard, so to speak, for the merits. This coupled with the fact that it is an adversarial proceeding succeeds, I think, in justifying the amorality of the criminal defense counsel. But this does not, however, justify a comparable perspective on the part of lawyers generally. Once we leave the peculiar situation of the criminal defense lawyer, I think it quite likely that the role-differentiated amorality of the lawyer is almost certainly excessive and at times inappropriate. That is to say, this special case to one side, I am inclined to think that we might all be better served if lawyers were to see themselves less as subject to role-differentiated behavior and more as subject to the demands of the moral point of view. In this sense it may be that we need a good deal less rather than more professionalism in our society generally and among lawyers in particular.

Moreover, even if I am wrong about all this, four things do seem to me to be true and important.

First, all of the arguments that support the role-differentiated amorality of the lawyer on institutional grounds can succeed only if the enormous degree of trust and confidence in the institutions themselves is itself justified. If the institutions work well and fairly, there may be good sense to deferring important moral concerns and criticisms to another time and place, to the level of institutional criticism and assessment. But the less certain we are entitled to be of either the rightness or the self-corrective nature of the larger institutions of which the professional is a part, the less apparent it is that we should encourage the professional to avoid direct engagement with the moral issues as they arise. And we are, today, I believe, certainly entitled to be quite skeptical both of the fairness and of the capacity for self-correction of our larger institutional mechanisms, including the legal system. To the degree to which the institutional rules and practices are unjust, unwise or undesirable, to that same degree is the case for the role-differentiated behavior of the lawyer weakened if not destroyed.

Second, it is clear that there are definite character traits that the professional such as the lawyer must take on if the system is to work. What is less clear is that they are admirable ones. Even if the role-differentiated amorality of the professional lawyer is justified by the virtues of the adversary system, this also means that the lawyer *qua* lawyer will be encouraged to be competitive rather than cooperative; aggressive rather than accommodating; ruthless rather than compassionate; and pragmatic rather than principled. This is, I think, part of the logic of the role-differentiated behavior of lawyers in particular, and to a lesser degree of professionals in general. It is surely neither accidental nor unimportant that these are the same character traits that are emphasized and valued by the capitalist ethic—and on precisely analogous grounds. Because the ideals of professionalism and capitalism are the dominant ones within our culture, it is harder than most of us suspect even to take seriously the suggestion that radically different styles of living, kinds of occupational outlooks, and types of social institutions might be possible, let alone preferable.

Third, there is a special feature of the role-differentiated behavior of the lawyer that distinguishes it from the comparable behavior of other professionals. What I have in mind can be brought out through the following question: Why is it that it seems far less plausible to talk critically about the amorality of the doctor, for instance, who treats all patients irrespective of their moral character than it does to talk critically about the comparable amorality of the lawyer? Why is it that it seems so obviously sensible, simple and right for the doctor's behavior to be narrowly and rigidly role-differentiated, *i.e.,* just to try to cure those who are ill? And why is it that at the very least it seems so complicated, uncertain, and troublesome to decide whether it is right for the lawyer's behavior to be similarly role-differentiated?

The answer, I think, is twofold. To begin with (and this I think is the less interesting point) it is, so to speak, intrinsically good to try to cure disease, but in no comparable way is it intrinsically good to try to win every lawsuit or help every client realize his or her objective. In addition (and this I take to be the truly interesting point), the lawyer's behavior is different in kind from the doctor's. The lawyer—and especially the lawyer as advocate— directly says and affirms things. The lawyer makes the case for the client. He or she tries to explain, persuade and convince others that the client's cause should prevail. The lawyer lives with and within a dilemma that is not shared by other professionals. If the lawyer actually believes everything that he or she asserts on behalf of the client, then it appears to be proper to regard the lawyer as in fact embracing and endorsing the points of view that he or she articulates. If the lawyer does not in fact believe what is urged by way of argument, if the lawyer is only playing a role, then it appears to be proper to tax the lawyer with hypocrisy and insincerity. To be sure, actors in a play take on roles and say things that the characters, not the actors, believe. But we know it is a play and that they are actors. The law courts are not, however, theaters, and the lawyers both talk about justice and they genuinely seek to persuade. The fact that the lawyer's words, thoughts, and convictions are, apparently, for sale and at the service of the client helps us, I think, to understand the peculiar hostility which is more than occasionally uniquely directed by lay persons toward lawyers. The verbal, role-differentiated behavior of the lawyer *qua* advocate puts the lawyer's integrity into question in a way that distinguishes the lawyer from the other professionals.[3]

---

[3] I owe this insight, which I think is an important and seldom appreciated one, to my colleague, Leon Letwin.

Fourth, and related closely to the three points just discussed, even if on balance the role-differentiated character of the lawyer's way of thinking and acting is ultimately deemed to be justifiable within the system on systemic instrumental grounds, it still remains the case that we do pay a social price for that way of thought and action. For to become and to be a professional, such as a lawyer, is to incorporate within oneself ways of behaving and ways of thinking that shape the whole person. It is especially hard, if not impossible, because of the nature of the professions, for one's professional way of thinking not to dominate one's entire adult life. Thus, even if the lawyers who were involved in Watergate were not, strictly speaking, then and there functioning as lawyers, their behavior was, I believe, the likely if not inevitable consequence of their legal acculturation. Having been taught to embrace and practice the lawyer's institutional role, it was natural, if not unavoidable, that they would continue to play that role even when they were somewhat removed from the specific institutional milieu in which that way of thinking and acting is arguably fitting and appropriate. The nature of the professions—the lengthy educational preparation, the prestige and economic rewards, and the con-comitant enhanced sense of self—makes the role of professional a difficult one to shed even in those obvious situations in which that role is neither required nor appropriate. In important respects, one's professional role be-comes and is one's dominant role, so that for many persons at least they become their professional being. This is at a minimum a heavy price to pay for the professions as we know them in our culture, and especially so for lawyers. Whether it is an inevitable price is, I think, an open question, largely because the problem has not begun to be fully perceived as such by the professionals in general, the legal profession in particular, or by the educa-tional institutions that train professionals.

II

The role-differentiated behavior of the professional also lies at the heart of the second of the two moral issues I want to discuss, namely, the character of the interpersonal relationship that exists between the lawyer and the client. As I indicated at the outset, the charge that I want to examine here is that the relationship between the lawyer and the client is typically, if not inevitably, a morally defective one in which the client is not treated with the respect and dignity that he or she deserves.

There is the suggestion of paradox here. The discussion so far has con-centrated upon defects that flow from what might be regarded as the lawyer's excessive preoccupation with and concern for the client. How then can it also be the case that the lawyer *qua* professional can at the same time be taxed with promoting and maintaining a relationship of dominance and in-difference vis-à-vis his or her client? The paradox is apparent, not real. Not only are the two accusations compatible; the problem of the interpersonal relationship between the lawyer and the client is itself another feature or manifestation of the underlying issue just examined—the role-differentiated life of the professional. For the lawyer can both be overly concerned with the interest of the client and at the same time fail to view the client as a whole person, entitled to be treated in certain ways.

One way to begin to explore the problem is to see that one pervasive, and I think necessary, feature of the relationship between any professional and the client or patient is that it is in some sense a relationship of inequality. This relationship of inequality is intrinsic to the existence of professionalism. For the professional is, in some respects at least, always in a position of dominance vis-à-vis the client, and the client in a position of dependence vis-à-vis the professional. To be sure, the client can often decide whether or not to enter into a relationship with a professional. And often, too, the client has the power to decide whether to terminate the relationship. But the significant thing I want to focus upon is that while the relationship exists, there are important respects in which the relationship cannot be a relationship between equals and must be one in which it is the professional who is in control. As I have said, I believe this is a necessary and not merely a familiar characteristic of the relationship between professionals and those they serve. Its existence is brought about by the following features.

To begin with, there is the fact that one characteristic of professions is that the professional is the possessor of expert knowledge of a sort not readily or easily attainable by members of the community at large. Hence, in the most straightforward of all senses the client, typically, is dependent upon the professional's skill or knowledge because the client does not possess the same knowledge.

Moreover, virtually every profession has its own technical language, a private terminology which can only be fully understood by the members of the profession. The presence of such a language plays the dual role of creating and affirming the membership of the professionals within the profession and of preventing the client from fully discussing or understanding his or her concerns in the language of the profession.

These circumstances, together with others, produce the added consequence that the client is in a poor position effectively to evaluate how well or badly the professional performs. In the professions, the professional does not look primarily to the client to evaluate the professional's work. The assessment of ongoing professional competence is something that is largely a matter of self-assessment conducted by the practising professional. Where external assessment does occur, it is carried out not by clients or patients but by other members of the profession, themselves. It is significant, and surely surprising to the outsider, to discover to what degree the professions are self-regulating. They control who shall be admitted to the professions and they determine (typically only if there has been a serious complaint) whether the members of the profession are performing in a minimally satisfactory way. This leads professionals to have a powerful motive to be far more concerned with the way they are viewed by their colleagues than with the way they are viewed by their clients. This means, too, that clients will necessarily lack the power to make effective evaluations and criticisms of the way the professional is responding to the client's needs.

In addition, because the matters for which professional assistance is sought usually involve things of great personal concern to the client, it is the received wisdom within the professions that the client lacks the perspective necessary to pursue in a satisfactory way his or her own best interests, and that the client requires a detached, disinterested representative to look after his or her interests. That is to say, even if the client had the same knowledge or competence that the professional had, the client would be thought to lack the objectivity required to utilize that competency effectively on his or her own behalf.

Finally, as I have indicated, to be a professional is to have been acculturated in a certain way. It is to have satisfactorily passed through a lengthy and allegedly difficult period of study and training. It is to have done something hard. Something that not everyone can do. Almost all professions encourage this way of viewing oneself; as having joined an elect group by virtue of hard work and mastery of the mysteries of the profession. In addition, the society at large treats members of a profession as members of an elite by paying them more than most people for the work they do with their heads rather than their hands, and by according them a substantial amount of social prestige and power by virtue of their membership in a profession. It is hard, I think, if not impossible, for a person to emerge from professional training and participate in a profession without the belief that he or she is a special kind of person, both different from and somewhat better than those nonprofessional members of the social order. It is equally hard for the other members of society not to hold an analogous view of the professionals. And these beliefs surely contribute, too, to the dominant role played by a professional in any professional-client relationship.

If the foregoing analysis is correct, then one question that is raised is whether it is a proper and serious criticism of the professions that the relationship between the professional and the client is an inherently unequal one in this sense.

One possible response would be to reject the view that all relationships of inequality (in this sense of inequality) are in fact undesirable. Such a response might claim, for example, that there is nothing at all wrong with inequality in relationships as long as the inequality is consensually imposed. Or, it may be argued, this kind of inequality is wholly unobjectionable because it is fitting, desired, or necessary in the circumstances. And, finally, it may be urged, whatever undesirability does attach to relationships by virtue of their lack of equality is outweighed by the benefits of role-differentiated relationships.

Another possible response would be to maintain that all human relationships of inequality (again in this sense of inequality) are for that reason alone objectionable on moral grounds—any time two or more persons are in a relationship in which power is not shared equally, the relationship is on that ground appropriately to be condemned. This criticism would solve the problem by abolishing the professions.

A third possible response, and the one that I want to consider in some detail, is a more sophisticated variant of the second response. It might begin by conceding, at least for purposes of argument, that some inequality may be inevitable in any professional-client relationship. It might concede, too, that a measure of this kind of inequality may even on occasion be desirable. But it sees the relationship between the professional and the client as typically flawed in a more fundamental way, as involving far more than the kind of relatively benign inequality delineated above. This criticism focuses upon the fact that the professional often, if not systematically, interacts with the client in both a manipulative and a paternalistic fashion. The point is not that the professional is merely dominant within the relationship. Rather, it is that from the professional's point of view the client is seen and responded to more like an object than a human being, and more like a child than an adult. The professional does not, in short, treat the client like a person; the professional does not accord the client the respect that he or she deserves. And these, it is claimed, are without question genuine moral defects in any meaningful human relationship. They are, moreover, defects that are capable of being eradicated once their cause is perceived and corrective action taken. The solution, so the argument does, is to "deprofessionalize" the professions; not do away with the professions entirely, but weaken or eliminate those features of professionalism that produce these kinds of defective, interpersonal relationships.

To decide whether this would be a good idea we must understand better what the proposal is and how the revisions might proceed. Because thinking somewhat along these lines has occurred in professions other than the law, *e.g.,* psychiatry, a brief look at what has been proposed there may help us to understand better what might be claimed in respect to the law.

I have in mind, for example, the view in psychiatry that begins by challenging the dominant conception of the patient as someone who is sick and in particular need of the professional, the psychiatrist, who is well. Such a conception, it is claimed, is often inadequate and often mistaken. Indeed, many cases of mental illness are not that at all; they are merely cases of different, but rational behavior. The alleged mental illness of the patient is a kind of myth, encouraged, if not created, by the professionals to assure and enhance their ability to function as professionals. So, on this view one thing that must occur is that the accepted professional concepts of mental illness and health must be revised.[4]

In addition, the language of psychiatry and mental illness is, it is claimed, needlessly technical and often vacuous. It serves no very useful communicative

---

[4] On this, and the points that follow, I am thinking in particular of the writings of Thomas Szasz, *e.g.,* T. S. Szasz, *The Myth of Mental Illness* (1974), and of R. D. Laing, *e.g.,* R. D. Laing and A. Esterson, *Sanity, Madness and the Family* (1964).

purpose, but its existence does of course help to maintain the distinctive status and power of the psychiatric profession. What is called for here is a simpler, far less technical language that permits more direct communication between the patient and the therapist.

Finally, and most significantly, the program calls for a concomitant replacement of the highly role-differentiated relationship between the therapist and the patient by a substantially less differentiated relationship of wholeness of interaction and equality. There should not, for instance, be mental hospitals in which the patients are clearly identified and distinguished from the staff and the professionals. Instead, therapeutic communities should be established in which all of the individuals in the community come to see themselves both as able to help the other members of the community and as able to be helped by them. In such a community, the distinctions between the professionals and the patients will be relatively minor and uninteresting. In such a community the relationship among the individuals, be they patients or professionals, will be capable of being more personal, intimate and complete—more undifferentiated by the accident of prior training or status.

Now, if this is a plausible proposal to make, it is possible that it is because of reasons connected with therapy rather than with the professions generally. But I do not think this is so. The general analysis and point of view is potentially generic; and certainly capable, I think, of being taken seriously in respect to the law as well as in respect to psychiatry, medicine, and education. If the critique is extravagant even when applied to psychiatry, as I think it is, I am more impressed by the truths to be extracted from it than I am by the exaggerations to be rejected. For I do think that professionals generally and lawyers in particular do, typically, enter into relationships with clients that are morally objectionable in virtue of the paternalistic and impersonal fashion in which the client is viewed and treated.

Thus it is, for example, fairly easy to see how a number of the features already delineated conspire to depersonalize the client in the eyes of the lawyer *qua* professional. To begin with, the lawyer's conception of self as a person with special competencies in a certain area naturally leads him or her to see the client in a partial way. The lawyer *qua* professional is, of necessity, only centrally interested in that part of the client that lies within his or her special competency. And this leads any professional including the lawyer to respond to the client as an object—as a thing to be altered, corrected, or otherwise assisted by the professional rather than as a person. At best the client is viewed from the perspective of the professional not as a whole person but as a segment or aspect of a person—an interesting kidney problem, a routine marijuana possession case, or another adolescent with an identity crisis.[5]

---

[5] This and other features are delineated from a somewhat different perspective in an essay by Erving Goffman. *See* "The Medical Model and Mental Hospitalization: Some Notes on the Vicissitudes of the Tinkering Trades" in E. Goffman, *Asylums* (1961), especially Parts V and VI of the essay.

Then, too, the fact already noted that the professions tend to have and to develop their own special languages has a lot to do with the depersonalization of the client. And this certainly holds for the lawyers. For the lawyer can and does talk to other lawyers but not to the client in the language of the profession. What is more, the lawyer goes out of his or her way to do so. It is satisfying. It is the exercise of power. Because the ability to communicate is one of the things that distinguishes persons from objects, the inability of the client to communicate with the lawyer in the lawyer's own tongue surely helps to make the client less than a person in the lawyer's eyes—and perhaps even in the eyes of the client.

The forces that operate to make the relationship a paternalistic one seem to be to be at least as powerful. If one is a member of a collection of individuals who have in common the fact that their intellects are highly trained, it is very easy to believe that one knows more than most people. If one is a member of a collection of individuals who are accorded high prestige by the society at large, it is equally easy to believe that one is better and knows better than most people. If there is, in fact, an area in which one does know things that the client doesn't know, it is extremely easy to believe that one knows generally what is best for the client. All this, too, surely holds for lawyers.

In addition there is the fact, also already noted, that the client often establishes a relationship with the lawyer because the client has a serious problem or concern which has rendered the client weak and vulnerable. This, too, surely increases the disposition to respond toward the client in a patronizing, paternalistic fashion. The client of necessity confers substantial power over his or her wellbeing upon the lawyer. Invested with all of this power both by the individual and the society, the lawyer *qua* professional responds to the client as though the client were an individual who needed to be looked after and controlled, and to have decisions made for him of her by the lawyer, with as little interference from the client as possible.

Now one can, I think, respond to the foregoing in a variety of ways. One could, to begin with, insist that the paternalistic and impersonal ways of behaving are the aberrant rather than the usual characteristics of the lawyer-client relationship. One could, therefore, argue that a minor adjustment in better legal education aimed at sensitizing prospective lawyers to the possibility of these abuses is all that is required to prevent them. Or, one could, to take the same tack described earlier, regard these features of the lawyer-client relationship as endemic but not as especially serious. One might have a view that, at least in moderation, relationships having these features are a very reasonable price to pay (if it is a price at all) for the very appreciable benefits of professionalism. The impersonality of a surgeon, for example, may make it easier rather than harder for him or for her to do a good job of operating successfully on a patient. The impersonality of a lawyer may make it easier rather than harder for him or for her to do a good job of representing a client. The paternalism of lawyers may be justified by the fact that they do in fact know better—at least within many areas of common concern to the parties involved—what is best for the client. And, it might even be claimed, clients want to be treated in this way.

But if these answers do not satisfy, if one believes that these are typical, if not systemic, features of the professional character of the lawyer-client relationship, and if one believes, as well, that these are morally objectionable features of that or any other relationship among persons, it does look as though one way to proceed is to "deprofessionalize" the law—to weaken, if not excise, those features of legal professionalism that tend to produce these kinds of interpersonal relationships.

The issue seems to me difficult just because I do think that there are important and distinctive competencies that are at the heart of the legal profession. If there were not, the solution would be simple. If there were no such competencies—if, that is, lawyers didn't really help people any more than (so it is sometimes claimed) therapists do—then no significant social goods would be furthered by the maintenance of the legal profession. But, as I have said, my own view is that there are special competencies and that they are valuable. This makes it harder to determine what to preserve and what to shed. The question, as I see it, is how to weaken the bad consequences of the role-differentiated lawyer-client relationship without destroying the good that lawyers do.

Without developing the claim at all adequately in terms of scope or detail, I want finally to suggest the direction this might take. Desirable change could be brought about in part by a sustained effort to simplify legal language and to make the legal processes less mysterious and more directly available to lay persons. The way the law works now, it is very hard for lay persons either to understand it or to evaluate or solve legal problems more on their own. But it is not at all clear that substantial revisions could not occur along these lines. Divorce, probate, and personal injury are only three fairly obvious areas where the lawyers' economic self-interest says a good deal more about resistance to change and simplification than does a consideration on the merits.

The more fundamental changes, though, would, I think, have to await an explicit effort to alter the ways in which lawyers are educated and acculturated to view themselves, their clients, and the relationships that ought to exist between them. It is, I believe, indicative of the state of legal education and of the profession that there has been to date extremely little self-conscious concern even with the possibility that these dimensions of the attorney-client relationship are worth examining—to say nothing of being capable of alteration. That awareness is, surely, the prerequisite to any serious assessment of the moral character of the attorney-client relationship as a relationship among adult human beings.

I do not know whether the typical lawyer-client relationship is as I have described it; nor do I know to what degree role-differentiation is the cause; nor do I even know very precisely what "deprofessionalization" would be like or whether it would on the whole be good or bad. I am convinced, however, that this, too, is a topic worth taking seriously and worth attending to more systematically than has been the case to date.

ETHICAL RESPONSIBILITIES OF ENGINEERS IN LARGE ORGANIZATIONS: THE PINTO CASE

RICHARD T. DE GEORGE

The myth that ethics has no place in engineering has been attacked, and at least in some corners of the engineering profession has been put to rest.[1] Another myth, however, is emerging to take its place—the myth of the engineer as moral hero. A litany of engineering saints is slowly taking form. The saints of the field are whistle blowers, especially those who have sacrificed all for their moral convictions. The zeal of some preachers, however, has gone too far, piling moral responsibility upon moral responsibility on the shoulders of the engineer. This emphasis, I believe, is misplaced. Though engineers are members of a profession that holds public safety paramount,[2] we cannot reasonably expect engineers to be willing to sacrifice their jobs each day for principle and to have a whistle ever by their sides ready to blow if their firm strays from what they perceive to be the morally right course of action. If this is too much to ask, however, what then is the actual ethical responsibility of engineers in a large organization?

I shall approach this question through a discussion of what has become known as the Pinto case, i.e., the trial that took place in Winamac, Indiana, and that was decided by a jury on March 16, 1980.

Reprinted from *Business and Professional Ethics Journal,* Vol. 1, No. 1 (1981) 1–14, with permission of the author. Copyright © 1981 by Richard T. De George.

[1] The body of literature on engineering ethics is now substantive and impressive. See *A Selected Annotated Bibliography of Professional Ethics and Social Responsibility in Engineering,* compiled by Robert F. Ladenson, James Choromokos, Ernest d'Anjou, Martin Pimsler, and Howard Rosen (Chicago: Center for the Study of Ethics in the Professions, Illinois Institute of Technology, 1980). A useful two-volume collection of readings and cases is also available: Robert J. Baum and Albert Flores, *Ethical Problems in Engineering,* 2nd ed.) Troy, N.Y.: Rensselaer Polytechnic Institute, Center for the Study of the Human Dimensions of Science and Technology, 1980). See also Robert J. Baum's *Ethics and Engineering Curricula* (Hastings-on-Hudson, N.Y.: Hastings Center, 1980).

[2] See, for example, the first canon of the 1974 Engineers Council for Professional Development Code, the first canon of the National Council of Engineering Examiners Code, and the draft (by A. Oldenquist and E. Slowter) of a "Code of Ethics for the Engineering Profession" (all reprinted in Baum and Flores, *Ethical Problems in Engineering.*)

In August 1978 near Goshen, Indiana, three girls died of burns in a 1973 Pinto that was rammed in traffic by a van. The rear-end collapsed "like an accordian,"[3] and the gas tank erupted in flames. It was not the first such accident with the Pinto. The Pinto was introduced in 1971 and its gas tank housing was not changed until the 1977 model. Between 1971 and 1978 about fifty suits were brought against Ford in connection with rear-end accidents in the Pinto.

What made the Winamac case different from the fifty others was the fact that the State prosecutor charged Ford with three (originally four, but one was dropped) counts of reckless homicide, a *criminal* offense, under a 1977 Indiana law that made it possible to bring such criminal charges against a corporation. The penalty, if found guilty, was a maximum fine of $10,000 for each count, for a total of $30,000. The case was closely watched, since it was the first time in recent history that a corporation was charged with this criminal offense. Ford spent almost a million dollars in its defense.

With the advantage of hindsight I believe the case raised the right issue at the wrong time.

The prosecution had to show that Ford was reckless in placing the gas tank where and how it did. In order to show this the prosecution had to prove that Ford consciously disregarded harm it might cause and the disregard, according to the statutory definition of "reckless," had to involve "substantial deviation from acceptable standards of conduct."[4]

The prosecution produced seven witnesses who testified that the Pinto was moving at speeds judged to be between 15 and 35 mph when it was hit. Harly Copp, once a high ranking Ford engineer, claimed that the Pinto did not have a balanced design and that for cost reasons the gas tank could withstand only a 20 mph impact without leaking and exploding. The prosecutor, Michael Cosentino, tried to introduce evidence that Ford knew the defects of the gas tank, that its executives knew that a $6.65 part would have made the car considerably safer, and that they decided against the change in order to increase their profits.

Federal safety standards for gas tanks were not introduced until 1977. Once introduced, the National Highway Traffic Safety Administration (NHTSA) claimed a safety defect existed in the gas tanks of Pintos produced from 1971 to 1976. It ordered that Ford recall 1.9 million Pintos. Ford contested the order. Then, without ever admitting that the fuel tank was unsafe, it "voluntarily" ordered a recall. It claimed the recall was not for safety but for "reputational" reasons.[5] Agreeing to a recall in June, its first proposed modifications failed the safety standards tests, and it added a second protective shield to meet safety standards. It did not send out recall notices until August 22. The accident in question took place on August 10. The prosecutor claimed

---

[3] Details of the incident presented in this paper are based on testimony at the trial. Accounts of the trial as well as background reports were carried by both the *New York Times* and the *Chicago Tribune*.

[4] *New York Times,* February 17, 1980, IV, p. 9.

[5] *New York Times,* February 21, 1980, p. A6. *Fortune,* September 11, 1978, p. 42.

that Ford knew its fuel tank was dangerous as early as 1971 and that it did not make any changes until the 1977 model. It also knew in June of 1978 that its fuel tank did not meet federal safety standards; yet it did nothing to warn owners of this fact. Hence, the prosecution contended, Ford was guilty of reckless homicide.

The defense was led by James F. Neal who had achieved national prominence in the Watergate hearings. He produced testimony from two witnesses who were crucial to the case. They were hospital attendants who had spoken with the driver of the Pinto at the hospital before she died. They claimed she had stated that she had just had her car filled with gas. She had been in a hurry and had left the gas station without replacing the cap on her gas tank. It fell off the top of her car as she drove down the highway. She noticed this and stopped to turn around to pick it up. While stopped, her car was hit by the van. The testimony indicated that the car was stopped. If the car was hit by a van going 50 mph, then the rupture of the gas tank was to be expected. If the cap was off the fuel tank, leakage would be more than otherwise. No small vehicle was made to withstand such impact. Hence, Ford claimed, there was no recklessness involved. Neal went on to produce films of tests that indicated that the amount of damage the Pinto suffered meant that the impact must have been caused by the van's going at least 50 mph. He further argued that the Pinto gas tank was at least as safe as the gas tanks on the 1973 American Motors Gremlin, the Chevrolet Vega, the Dodge Colt, and the Toyota Corolla, all of which suffered comparable damage when hit from the rear at 50 mph. Since no federal safety standards were in effect in 1973, Ford was not reckless if its safety standards were comparable to those of similar cars made by competitors; that standard represented the state of the art at that time, and it would be inappropriate to apply 1977 standards to a 1973 car.[6]

The jury deliberated for four days and finally came up with a verdict of not guilty. When the verdict was announced at a meeting of the Ford Board of Directors then taking place, the members broke out in a cheer.[7]

These are the facts of the case. I do not wish to second-guess the jury. Based on my reading of the case, I think they arrived at a proper decision, given the evidence. Nor do I wish to comment adversely on the judge's ruling that prevented the prosecution from introducing about 40% of his case because the evidence referred to 1971 and 1972 models of the Pinto and not the 1973 model.[8]

The issue of Ford's being guilty of acting recklessly can, I think, be made plausible, as I shall indicate shortly. But the successful strategy argued by the defense in this case hinged on the Pinto in question being hit by a van at 50 mph. At that speed, the defense successfully argued, the gas tank of any subcompact would rupture. Hence that accident did not show that the

    [6] *New York Times,* March 14, 1980, p. 1.
    [7] *Time,* March 24, 1980, p. 24.
    [8] *New York Times,* January 16, 1980, p. 16; February 7, 1980, p. 16.

Pinto was less safe than other subcompacts or that Ford acted recklessly. To show that would require an accident that took place at no more than 20 mph.

The contents of the Ford documents that Prosecutor Cosentino was not allowed to present in court were published in the *Chicago Tribune* on October 13, 1979. If they are accurate, they tend to show grounds for the charge of recklessness.

Ford had produced a safe gas tank mounted over the rear axle in its 1969 Capri in Europe. It tested that tank in the Capri. In its over-the-axle position, it withstood impacts of up to 30 mph. Mounted behind the axle, it was punctured by projecting bolts when hit from the rear at 20 mph. A $6.65 part would help make the tank safer. In its 1971 Pinto, Ford chose to place the gas tank behind the rear axle without the extra part. A Ford memo indicates that in this position the Pinto has more trunk space, and that production costs would be less than in the over-the-axle position. These considerations won out.[9]

The Pinto was first tested it seems in 1971, after the 1971 model was produced, for rear-end crash tolerance. It was found that the tank ruptured when hit from the rear at 20 mph. This should have been no surprise, since the Capri tank in that position had ruptured at 20 mph. A memo recommends that rather than making any changes Ford should wait until 1976 when the government was expected to introduce fuel tank standards. By delaying making any change, Ford could save $20.9 million, since the change would average about $10 per car.[10]

In the Winamac case Ford claimed correctly that there were no federal safety standards in 1973. But it defended itself against recklessness by claiming its car was comparable to other subcompacts at that time. All the defense showed, however, was that all the subcompacts were unsafe when hit at 50 mph. Since the other subcompacts were not forced to recall their cars in 1978, there is *prima facie* evidence that Ford's Pinto gas tank mounting was substandard. The Ford documents tend to show Ford knew the danger it was inflicting on Ford owners; yet it did nothing, for profit reasons. How short-sighted those reasons were is demonstrated by the fact that the Pinto thus far in litigation and recalls alone has cost Ford $50 million. Some forty suits are still to be settled. And these figures do not take into account the loss of sales due to bad publicity.

Given these facts, what are we to say about the Ford engineers? Where were they when all this was going on, and what is their responsibility for the Pinto? The answer, I suggest, is that they were where they were supposed to be, doing what they were supposed to be doing. They were performing tests, designing the Pinto, making reports. But do they have no moral responsibility for the products they design? What after all is the moral responsibility of engineers in a large corporation? By way of reply, let me emphasize that no

---

[9] *Chicago Tribune,* October 13, 1979, p. 1, and Section 2, p. 12.
[10] *Chicago Tribune,* October 13, 1979, p. 1; *New York Times,* October 14, 1979, p. 26.

engineer can morally do what is immoral. If commanded to do what he should not morally do, he must resist and refuse. But in the Ford Pinto situation no engineer was told to produce a gas tank that would explode and kill people. The engineers were not instructed to make an unsafe car. They were morally responsible for knowing the state of the art, including that connected with placing and mounting gas tanks. We can assume that the Ford engineers were cognizant of the state of the art in producing the model they did. When tests were made in 1970 and 1971, and a memo was written stating that a $6.65 modification could make the gas tank safer,[11] that was an engineering assessment. Whichever engineer proposed the modification and initiated the memo acted ethically in doing so. The next step, the administrative decision not to make the modification was, with hindsight, a poor one in almost every way. It ended up costing Ford a great deal more not to put in the part than it would have cost to put it in. Ford still claims today that its gas tank was as safe as the accepted standards of the industry at that time.[12] It must say so, otherwise the suits pending against it will skyrocket. That it was not as safe seems borne out by the fact that only the Pinto of all the subcompacts failed to pass the 30 mph rear impact NHTSA test.

But the question of wrongdoing or of malicious intent or of recklessness is not so easily solved. Suppose the ordinary person were told when buying a Pinto that if he paid an extra $6.65 he could increase the safety of the vehicle so that it could withstand a 30 mph rear-end impact rather than a 20 mph impact, and that the odds of suffering a rear-end impact of between 20 and 30 mph was 1 in 250,000. Would we call him or her reckless if he or she declined to pay the extra $6.65? I am not sure how to answer that question. Was it reckless of Ford to wish to save the $6.65 per car and increase the risk for the consumer? Here I am inclined to be clearer in my own mind. If I choose to take a risk to save $6.65, it is my risk and my $6.65. But if Ford saves the $6.65 and I take the risk, then I clearly lose. Does Ford have the right to do that without informing me, if the going standard of safety of subcompacts is safety in a rear-end collision up to 30 mph? I think not. I admit, however, that the case is not clear-cut, even if we add that during 1976 and 1977 Pintos suffered 13 fiery fatal rear-end collisions, more than double that of other U.S. comparable cars. The VW Rabbit and Toyota Corolla suffered none.[13]

Yet, if we are to morally fault anyone for the decision not to add the part, we would censure not the Ford engineers but the Ford executives, because it was not an engineering but an executive decision.

My reason for taking this view is that an engineer cannot be expected and cannot have the responsibility to second-guess managerial decisions. He is responsible for bringing the facts to the attention of those who need them to

[11] *New York Times,* February 4, 1980, p. 12.

[12] *New York Times,* June 10, 1978, p. 1; *Chicago Tribune,* October 13, 1979, p. 1, and Section 2, p. 12. The continuous claim has been that the Pinto poses "no serious hazards."

[13] *New York Times,* October 26, 1978, p. 103.

make decisions. But the input of engineers is only one of many factors that go to make up managerial decisions. During the trial, the defense called as a witness Francis Olsen, the assistant chief engineer in charge of design at Ford, who testified that he bought a 1973 Pinto for his eighteen-year-old daughter, kept it a year, and then traded it in for a 1974 Pinto which he kept two years.[14] His testimony and his actions were presented as an indication that the Ford engineers had confidence in the Pinto's safety. At least this one had enough confidence in it to give it to his daughter. Some engineers at Ford may have felt that the car could have been safer. But this is true of almost every automobile. Engineers in large firms have an ethical responsibility to do their jobs as best they can, to report their observations about safety and improvement of safety to management. But they do not have the obligation to insist that their perceptions or their standards be accepted. They are not paid to do that, they are not expected to do that, and they have no moral or ethical obligation to do that.

In addition to doing their jobs, engineers can plausibly be said to have an obligation of loyalty to their employers, and firms have a right to a certain amount of confidentiality concerning their internal operations. At the same time engineers are required by their professional ethical codes to hold the safety of the public paramount. Where these obligations conflict, the need for and justification of whistle blowing arises.[15] If we admit the obligations on both sides, I would suggest as a rule of thumb that engineers and other workers in a large corporation are morally *permitted* to go public with information about the safety of a product if the following conditions are met.

1. If the harm that will be done by the product to the public is serious and considerable;
2. If they make their concerns known to their superiors; and
3. If, getting no satisfaction from their immediate superiors, they exhaust the channels available within the corporation, including going to the board of directors.

If they still get no action, I believe they are morally *permitted* to make public their views; but they are not morally *obliged* to do so. Harly Copp, a former Ford executive and engineer, in fact did criticize the Pinto from the start and testified for the prosecution against Ford at the Winamac trial.[16] He left the company and voiced his criticism. The criticism was taken up by Ralph Nader and others. In the long run it led to the Winamac trial and probably helped in a number of other suits filed against Ford. Though I

[14] *New York Times,* February 20, 1980, p. A16.

[15] For a discussion of the conflict, see, Sissela Bok, "Whistleblowing and Professional Responsibility," *New York University Educational Quarterly,* pp. 2–10. For detailed case studies see, Ralph Nader, Peter J. Petkas, and Kate Blackwell, *Whistle Blowing* (New York: Grossman Publishers, 1972); Charles Peters and Taylor Branch, *Blowing the Whistle: Dissent in the Public Interest* (New York: Praeger Publishers, 1972); and Robert M. Anderson, Robert Perrucci, Dan E. Schendel, and Leon E. Trachtman, *Divided Loyalties: Whistle-Blowing at BART* (West Lafayette, Ind.: Purdue University, 1980).

[16] *New York Times,* February 4, 1980, p. 12.

admire Mr. Copp for his actions, assuming they were done from moral motives, I do not think such action was morally required, nor do I think the other engineers at Ford were morally deficient in not doing likewise.

For an engineer to have a moral *obligation* to bring his case for safety to the public, I think two other conditions have to be fulfilled, in addition to the three mentioned above.[17]

4. He must have documented evidence that would convince a reasonable, impartial observer that his view of the situation is correct and the company policy wrong.

Such evidence is obviously very difficult to obtain and produce. Such evidence, however, takes an engineer's concern out of the realm of the subjective and precludes that concern from being simply one person's opinion based on a limited point of view. Unless such evidence is available, there is little likelihood that the concerned engineer's view will win the day simply by public exposure. If the testimony of Francis Olsen is accurate, then even among the engineers at Ford there was disagreement about the safety of the Pinto.

5. There must be strong evidence that making the information public will in fact prevent the threatened serious harm.

This means both that going public the engineer should know what source (government, newspaper, columnist, TV reporter) will make use of his evidence and how it will be handled. He should also have good reason to believe that it will result in the kind of change or result that he believes is morally appropriate. None of this was the case in the Pinto situation. After much public discussion, five model years, and failure to pass national safety standards tests, Ford plausibly defends its original claim that the gas tank was acceptably safe. If there is little likelihood of his success, there is no moral obligation for the engineer to go public. For the harm he or she personally incurs is not offset by the good such action achieves.[18]

My first substantive conclusion is that Ford engineers had no moral *obligation* to do more than they did in this case.

My second claim is that though engineers in large organizations should

---

[17] The position I present here is developed more fully in my book *Business Ethics* (New York: Macmillan Publishing Co., 1982). It differs somewhat from the dominant view expressed in the existing literature in that I consider whistle blowing an extreme measure that is morally obligatory only if the stringent conditions set forth are satisfied. Cf. Kenneth D. Walters, "Your Employees' Right to Blow the Whistle," *Harvard Business Review* (July–August 1975).

[18] On the dangers incurred by whistle blowers, see Gene James, "Whistle-Blowing: Its Nature and Justification," *Philosophy in Context,* 10 (1980). pp. 99–117, which examines the legal context of whistle blowing; Peter Raven-Hansen, "Dos and Don'ts for Whistleblowers: Planning for Trouble," *Technology Review* (May 1980), pp. 34–44, which suggests how to blow the whistle; Helen Dudar, "The Price of Blowing the Whistle," *The New York Times Magazine,* 30 October, 1977, which examines the results for whistle blowers; David W. Ewing, "Canning Directions," *Harpers* (August 1979), pp. 17–22, which indicates "how the government rids itself of troublemakers" and how legislation protecting whistle blowers can be circumvented; and Report by the U.S. General Accounting Office, "The Office of the Special Counsel Can Improve Its Management of Whistleblower Cases," December 30, 1980 (FPCD-81-10).

have a say in setting safety standards and producing cost-benefit analyses, they need not have the last word. My reasons are two. First, while the degree of risk, e.g., in a car, is an engineering problem, the acceptability of risk is not. Second, an engineering cost-benefit analysis does not include all the factors appropriate in making a policy decision, either on the corporate or the social level. Safety is one factor in an engineering design. Yet clearly it is only one factor. A Mercedes-Benz 280 is presumably safer than a Ford Pinto. But the difference in price is considerable. To make a Pinto as safe as a Mercedes it would probably have to cost a comparable amount. In making cars as in making many other objects some balance has to be reached between safety and cost. The final decision on where to draw the balance is not only an engineering decision. It is also a managerial decision, and probably even more appropriately a social decision.

The difficulty of setting standards raises two pertinent issues. The first concerns federal safety standards. The second concerns cost-benefit analyses. The state of the art of engineering technology determines a floor below which no manufacturer should ethically go. Whether the Pinto fell below that floor, we have already seen, is a controverted question. If the cost of achieving greater safety is considerable—and I do not think $6.65 is considerable— there is a built-in temptation for a producer to skimp more than he should and more than he might like. The best way to remove that temptation is for there to be a national set of standards. Engineers can determine what the state of the art is, what is possible, and what the cost of producing safety is. A panel of informed people, not necessarily engineers, should decide what is acceptable risk and hence what acceptable minimum standards are. Both the minimum standards and the standards attained by a given car should be a matter of record that goes with each car. A safer car may well cost more. But unless a customer knows how much safety he is buying for his money, he may not know which car he wants to buy. This information, I believe, is information a car buyer is entitled to have.

In 1978, after the publicity that Ford received with the Pinto and the controversy surrounding it, the sales of Pintos fell dramatically. This was an indication that consumers preferred a safer car for comparable money, and they went to the competition. The state of Oregon took all its Pintos out of its fleet and sold them off. To the surprise of one dealer involved in selling turned-in Pintos, they went for between $1,000 and $1,800.[19] The conclusion we correctly draw is that there was a market for a car with a dubious safety record even though the price was much lower than for safer cars and lower than Ford's manufacturing price.

The second issue is the way cost-benefit analyses are produced and used. I have already mentioned one cost-benefit analysis used by Ford, namely, the projection that by not adding a part and by placing the gas tank in the rear the company could save $20.9 million. The projection, I noted, was grossly mistaken for it did not consider litigation, recalls, and bad publicity which

[19] *New York Times,* April 21, 1978, IV, p. 1, 18.

have already cost Ford over $50 million. A second type of cost-benefit analysis sometimes estimates the number and costs of suits that will have to be paid, adds to it fines, and deducts that total amount from the total saved by a particular practice. If the figure is positive, it is more profitable not to make a safety change than to make it.

A third type of cost-benefit analysis, which Ford and other auto companies produce, estimates the cost and benefits of specific changes in their automobiles. One study, for instance, deals with the cost-benefit analysis relating to fuel leakage associated with static rollover. The unit cost of the part is $11. If that is included in 12.5 million cars, the total cost is $137 million. That part will prevent 180 burn deaths, 180 serious burn injuries and 2100 burned vehicles. Assigning a cost of $200,000 per death, $67,000 per major injury, and $700 per vehicle, the benefit is $49.5 million. The cost-benefit ratio is slightly over 3-1.[20]

If this analysis is compared with a similar cost-benefit analysis for a rear-end collision, it is possible to see how much safety is achieved per dollar spent. This use is legitimate and helpful. But the procedure is open to very serious criticism if used not in a comparative but in an absolute manner.

The analysis ignores many factors, such as the human suffering of the victim and of his or her family. It equates human life to $200,000, which is based on average lost future wages. Any figure here is questionable, except for comparative purposes, in which case as long as the same figure is used it does not change the information as to relative benefit per dollar. The ratio, however, has no *absolute* meaning, and no decision can properly be based on the fact that the resulting ratio of cost to benefit in the above example is 3 to 1. Even more important, how can this figure or ratio be compared with the cost of styling? Should the $11 per unit to reduce death and injury from roll-over be weighed against a comparable $11 in rear-end collision or $11 in changed styling? Who decides how much more to put into safety and how much more to put into styling? What is the rationale for the decision?

In the past consumers have not been given an opportunity to vote on the matter. The automobile industry has decided what will sell and what will not, and has decided how much to put on safety. American car dealers have not typically put much emphasis on safety features in selling their cars. The assumption that American drivers are more interested in styling than safety is a decision that has been made for them, not by them. Engineers can and do play an important role in making cost-benefit analyses. They are better equipped than anyone else to figure risks and cost. But they are not better equipped to figure the acceptability of risk, or the amount that people should be willing to pay to eliminate such risk. Neither, however, are the managers of automobile corporations. The amount of acceptable risk is a public decision that can and should be made by representatives of the public or by the public itself.

Since cost-benefit analyses of the types I have mentioned are typical of

[20] See Mark Dowie, "Pinto Madness" *Mother Jones* (September-October 1977), pp. 24–28.

those used in the auto industry, and since they are inadequate ways of judging the safety a car should have, given the state of the art, it is clear that the automobile companies should not have the last word or the exclusive word in how much safety to provide. There must be national standards set and enforced. The National Highway Traffic Administration was established in 1966 to set standards. Thus far only two major standards have been established and implemented: the 1972 side impact standard and the 1977 gasoline tank safety standard. Rather than dictate standards, however, in which process it is subject to lobbying, it can mandate minimum standards and also require auto manufacturers to inform the public about the safety quotient of each car, just as it now requires each car to specify the miles per gallon it is capable of achieving. Such an approach would put the onus for the basic safety on the manufacturers, but it would also make additional safety a feature of consumer interest and competition.

Engineers in large corporations have an important role to play. That role, however, is not usually to set policy or to decide on the acceptability of risk. Their knowledge and expertise are important both to the companies for which they work and to the public. But they are not morally responsible for policies and decisions beyond their competence and control. Does this view, however, let engineers off the moral hook too easily?

To return briefly to the Pinto story once more, Ford wanted a subcompact to fend off the competition of Japanese imports. The order came down to produce a car of 2,000 pounds or less that would cost $2000 or less in time for the 1971 model. This allowed only 25 months instead of the usual 43 months for design and production of a new car.[21] The engineers were squeezed from the start. Perhaps this is why they did not test the gas tank for rear-end collision impact until the car was produced.

Should the engineers have refused the order to produce the car in 25 months? Should they have resigned, or leaked the story to the newspapers? Should they have refused to speed up their usual routine? Should they have complained to their professional society that they were being asked to do the impossible—if it were to be done right? I am not in a position to say what they should have done. But with the advantage of hindsight, I suggest we should ask not only what they should have done. We should especially ask what changes can be made to prevent engineers from being squeezed in this way in the future.

Engineering ethics should not take as its goal the producing of moral heroes. Rather it should consider what forces operate to encourage engineers to act as they feel they should not; what structural or other features of a large corporation squeeze them until their consciences hurt? Those features should then be examined, evaluated, and changes proposed and made. Lobbying by engineering organizations would be appropriate, and legislation should be passed if necessary. In general I tend to favor voluntary means where possible. But where that is utopian, then legislation is a necessary alternative.

[21] *Chicago Tribune,* October 13, 1979, Section 2, p. 12.

The need for whistle blowing in a firm indicates that a change is necessary. How can we preclude the necessity for blowing the whistle?

The Winamac Pinto case suggests some external and internal modifications. It was the first case to be tried under a 1977 Indiana law making it possible to try corporations as well as individuals for the criminal offenses of reckless homicide. In bringing the charges against Ford, Prosecutor Michael Cosentino acted courageously, even if it turned out to have been a poor case for such a precedent-setting trial. But the law concerning reckless homicide, for instance, which was the charge in question, had not been rewritten with the corporation in mind. The penalty, since corporations cannot go to jail, was the maximum fine of $10,000 per count—hardly a significant amount when contrasted with the 1977 income of Ford International which was $11.1 billion in revenues and $750 million in profits. What Mr. Cosentino did *not* do was file charges against individuals in the Ford Company who were responsible for the decisions he claimed were reckless. Had highly placed officials been charged, the message would have gotten through to management across the country that individuals cannot hide behind corporate shields in their decisions if they are indeed reckless, put too low a price on life and human suffering, and sacrifice it too cheaply for profits.

A bill was recently proposed in Congress requiring managers to disclose the existence of life-threatening defects to the appropriate Federal agency.[22] Failure to do so and attempts to conceal defects could result in fines of $50,000 or imprisonment for a minimum of two years, or both. The fine in corporate terms is negligible. But imprisonment for members of management is not.

Some argue that increased litigation for product liability is the way to get results in safety. Heavy damages yield quicker changes than criminal proceedings. Ford agreed to the Pinto recall shortly after a California jury awarded damages of $127.8 million after a youth was burned over 95 percent of his body. Later the sum was reduced, on appeal, to $6.3 million.[23] But the criminal proceedings make the litigation easier, which is why Ford spent $1,000,000 in its defense to avoid paying $30,000 in fines.[24] The possibility of going to jail for one's actions, however, should have a salutary effect. If someone, the president of a company in default of anyone else, were to be charged in criminal suit, presidents would soon know whom they can and should hold responsible below them. One of the difficulties in a large corporation is knowing who is responsible for particular decisions. If the president were held responsible, outside pressure would build to recognize the corporation so that responsibility was assigned and assumed.

If a corporation wishes to be moral or if society or engineers wish to apply pressure for organizational changes such that the corporation acts morally

[22] *New York Times,* March 16, 1980, IV, p. 20.
[23] *New York Times,* February 8, 1978, p. 8.
[24] *New York Times,* February 17, 1980, IV, p. 9; January 6, 1980, p. 24; *Time* (March 24, 1980), p. 24.

and responds to the moral conscience of engineers and others within the organization, then changes must be made. Unless those at the top set a moral tone, unless they insist on moral conduct, unless they punish immoral conduct and reward moral conduct, the corporation will function without considering the morality of questions and of corporate actions. It may by accident rather than by intent avoid immoral actions, though in the long run this is unlikely.

Ford's management was interested only in meeting federal standards and having these as low as possible. Individual federal standards should be both developed and enforced. Federal fines for violations should not be token but comparable to damages paid in civil suits and should be paid to all those suffering damage from violations.[25]

Independent engineers or engineering societies—if the latter are not co-opted by auto manufacturers—can play a significant role in supplying information on the state of the art and the level of technical feasibility available. They can also develop the safety index I suggested earlier, which would represent the relative and comparative safety of an automobile. Competition has worked successfully in many areas. Why not in the area of safety? Engineers who work for auto manufacturers will then have to make and report the results of standard tests such as the ability to withstand rear-end impact. If such information is required data for a safety index to be affixed to the windshield of each new car, engineers will not be squeezed by management in the area of safety.

The means by which engineers with ethical concerns can get a fair hearing without endangering their jobs or blowing the whistle must be made part of a corporation's organizational structure. An outside board member with primary responsibility for investigating and responding to such ethical concerns might be legally required. When this is joined with the legislation pending in Congress which I mentioned, the dynamics for ethics in the organization will be significantly improved. Another way of achieving a similar end is by providing an inspector general for all corporations with an annual net income of over $1 billion. An independent committee of an engineering association might be formed to investigate charges made by engineers concerning the safety of a product on which they are working;[26] a company that did not allow an appropriate investigation of employee charges would become subject

[25] *The Wall Street Journal,* August 7, 1980, p. 7, reported that the Ford Motor Company "agreed to pay a total of $22,500 to the families of three Indiana teen-age girls killed in the crash of a Ford Pinto nearly two years ago. . . . A Ford spokesman said the settlement was made without any admission of liability. He speculated that the relatively small settlement may have been influenced by certain Indiana laws which severely restrict the amount of damages victims or their families can recover in civil cases alleging wrongful death."

[26] A number of engineers have been arguing for a more active role by engineering societies in backing up individual engineers in their attempts to act responsibly. See, Edwin Layton, *Revolt of the Engineers* (Cleveland: Case Western Reserve, 1971); Stephen H. Unger, "Engineering Societies and the Responsible Engineer," *Annals of the New York Academy of Sciences,* 196 (1973), pp. 433–37 (reprinted in Baum and Flores, *Ethical Problems in Engineering,* pp. 56–59; and Robert Perrucci and Joe Gerstl, *Profession Without Community: Engineers in American Society* (New York: Random House, 1969).

to cover-up proceedings. Those in the engineering industry can suggest and work to implement other ideas. I have elsewhere outlined a set of ten such charges for the ethical corporation.[27]

In addition to asking how an engineer should respond to moral quandaries and dilemmas, and rather than asking how to educate or train engineers to be moral heroes, those in engineering ethics should ask how large organizations can be changed so that they do not squeeze engineers in moral dilemmas, place them in the position of facing moral quandaries, and make them feel that they must blow the whistle.

The time has come to go beyond sensitizing students to moral issues and solving and resolving the old, standard cases. The next and very important questions to be asked as we discuss each case is how organizational structures can be changed so that no engineer will ever again have to face *that* case.

Many of the issues of engineering ethics within a corporate setting concern the ethics of organizational structure, questions of public policy, and so questions that frequently are amenable to solution only on a scale larger than the individual—on the scale of organization and law. The ethical responsibilities of the engineer in a large organization have as much to do with the organization as with the engineer. They can be most fruitfully approached by considering from a moral point of view not only the individual engineer but the framework within which he or she works. We not only need moral people. Even more importantly we need moral structures and organizations. Only by paying more attention to these can we adequately resolve the questions of the ethical responsibility of engineers in large organizations.

[27] Richard T. De George, "Responding to the Mandate for Social Responsibility," *Guidelines for Business When Societal Demands Conflict* (Washington, D.C.: Council for Better Business Bureaus, 1978), pp. 60–80.

MEDICAL PATERNALISM

ALLEN E. BUCHANAN

I

Among the physicians in this country, the medical paternalist model appears to be a prevalent way of conceiving the physician-patient relationship. I contend that the practice of withholding the truth from patients or their

Reprinted from Rolf Sartorius (ed.), *Paternalism* (Minneapolis: The University of Minnesota Press, 1983), pp. 61–80, with permission of the publisher and the author. The article is a revised version of a piece with the same title originally published in *Philosophy & Public Affairs*, Vol. 7, No. 4 (1978) 371–390.

families, a particular form of medical paternalism, is not adequately supported by the arguments advanced to justify it. Further, I shall argue that the distinction between "ordinary" and "extraordinary" therapeutic measures both expresses and helps perpetuate the dominance of the medical paternalist model.

Paternalism is usually characterized as interference with a person's liberty of action, when the alleged justification for the interference is that it is for the good of the person whose liberty of action is thus restricted.[1] To focus exclusively on interference with liberty of *action,* however, is to construe paternalism too narrowly. If a government lies to the public or withholds information from it, and if the alleged justification of its policy is that it benefits the public itself, the policy may properly be called paternalistic.

On the one hand, there may be a direct connection between such a policy and actual interference with the citizen's freedom to act. In order to withhold information from the public, agents of the government may physically interfere with the freedom of the press to gather, print, or distribute the news. Or government officials may misinform the public in order to restrict its freedom to perform specific acts. The police, for example, may erect signs bearing the words "Detour: Maintenance Work Ahead" to route unsuspecting motorists around the wreckage of a truck carrying nerve gas. On the other hand, the connection between withholding of information and actual interference with freedom of action may be indirect at best. To interfere with the public's freedom of information the government need not actually interfere with any-one's freedom to act—it may simply not divulge certain information. With-holding information may preclude an *informed* decision, and it may interfere with attempts to reach an informed decision, without thereby interfering with a person's freedom to decide and to act on his decision. Even if I am deprived of information that I need to make an informed decision, I may still be free to decide and to act.

Granted the complexity of the relations between information and action, it seems plausible to expand the usual definition of paternalism as follows: Paternalism is interference with a person's freedom of action or freedom of information, or the deliberate dissemination of misinformation, when the alleged justification for interfering or misinforming is that it is for the good of the person who is interfered with or misinformed. The notion of freedom of information is, of course, unsatisfyingly vague, but the political examples sketched above, along with the medical examples to follow, will make it clearer.

A more serious difficulty with this expanded definition, however, is that it too fails to cover some cases of paternalism. It is sometimes possible to interfere with a person's decision-making by forcing information upon her, rather than by withholding it. For example, a physician might override a patient's request that she not be given certain information about her condition;

---

[1] See, for example, Gerald Dworkin, "Paternalism," in S. Gorovitz et al., *Moral Problem in Medicine* (Englewood Cliffs, N.J.: Prentice-Hall, 1976), p. 185.

the patient may wish to make a decision without taking certain information into account or she may wish not to be the one to make certain decisions at all. At least some cases in which a person's decision not to be given certain information is overridden (allegedly for that person's own good) are properly called paternalism.[2] To include these cases as well as those discussed earlier might broaden our definition even further:

> Paternalism is the interference with a person's freedom of action or freedom of information, or the dissemination of misinformation, or the overriding of a person's decision not to be given information, when this is allegedly done for the good of that person.

Somewhat more briefly, we might say that paternalism occurs whenever a person's opportunities for deciding or acting, or her decisions about the conditions under which she shall or shall not decide, are interfered with, allegedly for her own good.

Whether or not this third definition includes all and only cases of paternalism, it does seem to be an improvement on the earlier proposals and it appears to cover most of the paternalistic practices that occur in medicine. However, since the overwhelming majority of instances of paternalism in medicine seem to be cases of withholding information rather than of forcing it upon the patient, I shall concentrate on examining the former in this essay. We can now turn to a brief consideration of evidence for the claim that medical paternalism is a widespread phenomenon in our society.

II

The evidence for medical paternalism is both direct and indirect. The direct evidence consists of survey findings that systematically report physicians' practices concerning truth-telling and decision-making, and of articles and discussions in which physicians and other acknowledge or defend paternalistic medical practices. The indirect evidence is more subtle. One source of indirect evidence for the pervasiveness of medical paternalistic attitudes is the language we use to describe physician-patient interactions. Let us consider some of the direct evidence.

Although there are many ways of classifying cases of medical paternalism, two distinctions are especially important. We can distinguish between the cases in which the patient is legally competent and those in which the patient is legally incompetent, and between those cases in which the intended beneficiary of paternalism is the patient himself and those in which the intended beneficiary is the patient's guardian or one or more members of the patient's family. The first distinction classifies cases according to the *legal status of the patient,* the second according to the *object of paternalism.*

---

[2] Donald VanDeVeer makes this point in "The Contractual Argument for Withholding Medical Information," *Philosophy & Public Affairs,* 9, no. 2 (1980), p. 203.

A striking revelation of medical paternalism in dealings with legally competent adults is found in Donald Oken's essay, "What to Tell Cancer Patients: A Study of Medical Attitudes." [3] The chief conclusion of this study of internists, surgeons, and generalists is that "there is a strong and general tendency to withhold" from the patient the information that he has cancer. Almost ninety percent of the total group surveyed reported that their usual policy is not to tell the patient that he has cancer. Oken also notes that "no one reported a policy of informing every patient." Further, Oken reports that some physicians falsified diagnoses:

> Some physicians avoid even the slightest suggestion of neoplasia and quite specifically substitute another diagnosis. Almost everyone reported resorting to such falsification on at least a few occasions, most notably when the patient was in a far-advanced state of illness at the time he was seen.[4]

The physicians' justifications for withholding or falsifying diagnostic information were uniformly paternalistic. They assumed that if they told the patient he had cancer they would be depriving him of all hope and that the loss of hope would result in suicidal depression or at least in a serious worsening of the patient's condition.

A recent malpractice suit illustrates paternalistic withholding of information of a different sort. As in the Oken study, the object of paternalism was the patient and the patient was a legally competent adult. A bilateral thyroidectomy resulted in permanent paralysis of the patient's vocal cords. The patient's formerly healthy voice became frail and weak. The damage suit was based on the contention that by failing to tell the patient of the known risks to her voice, the physician had violated his duty to obtain informed consent for the operation. The physician's testimony is clearly paternalistic:

> In court the physician was asked, "You didn't inform her of any dangers or risks involved? Is that right?" Over his attorney's objections, the physician responded, "Not specifically . . . I feel that were I to point out all the complications—or even half the complications—many people would refuse to have anything done, and therefore would be much worse off.[5]

There is also considerable evidence of medical paternalism in the treatment of legally incompetent individuals through the withholding of information from the patients or their guardians or both.[6]

The law maintains that it is the parents who are primarily responsible for

---

[3] Donald Oken, "What to Tell Cancer Patients: A Study of Medical Attitudes," in Samuel Gorovitz et al., *Moral Problems in Medicine* (Englewood Gliffs, N.J.: Prentice-Hall, 1976), p. 112.

[4] *Ibid.,* p. 113.

[5] *Malpractice Digest* (St. Paul, Minn.: The St. Paul Property and Liability Insurance Company, July-August 1977), p. 6.

[6] It is interesting to note that, according to both the usual and the expanded characterization of paternalism stated earlier, only people who have certain physical and mental capacities can be objects of paternalism, since it is only when these capacities are present that it is correct to speak of interfering with those individuals' freedom of action, misinforming them, or withholding information from them.

decisions concerning the welfare of their minor children.[7] Nonetheless, physicians sometimes assume primary or even total responsibility for the most awesome and morally perplexing decisions affecting the welfare of children.

The inescapable need to make such decisions arises daily in neonate intensive-care units. The most dramatic decisions are whether to initiate or not initiate, or to continue or discontinue, life-sustaining therapy. Three broad types of cases have been frequently discussed in recent literature. First, there are infants who are in an asphyxiated condition at birth and can be resuscitated but may suffer irreversible brain damage if they survive. Second, there are infants with Down's syndrome (mongolism) who have potentially fatal but surgically correctable congenital cardiovascular or gastrointestinal defects. Third, there are infants with spina bifida, a congenital condition in which there is an opening in the spine and which may be complicated by paralysis and hydrocephaly. New surgical techniques make it possible to close the spine and drain the fluid from the brain, but a large percentage of the infants thus treated suffer varying degrees of permanent brain-damage and paralysis.

A. Shaw notes that some physicians undertake the responsibility for making decisions about life and death for defective newborns in order to relieve parents of the trauma and guilt of making a decision. He cites the following comment as an example of this position.

> At the end it is usually the doctor who has to decide the issue. It is . . . cruel to ask the parents whether they want their child to live or die . . . .[8]

We have already seen that the information which physicians withhold may be of at least two different sorts. In the cases studied by Oken, physicians withhold the diagnosis of cancer from their patients. In the thyroidectomy malpractice case the physician did not withhold the diagnosis but did withhold information about known risks of an operation. The growing literature on life or death decisions for defective neonates revelas more complex paternalistic practices. Some physicians routinely exclude parents from significant participation in decision-making either by not informing the parents that certain choices can or must be made, or by describing the child's condition and the therapeutic options in such a skeletal way as to preclude genuinely informed consent.

A case cited by Shaw is a clear example of a physician withholding from parents the information that there was a choice to be made.

> Baby A was referred to me at 22 hours of age with a diagnosis of esophageal atresia and tracheoesophageal fistula. The infant, the firstborn of a professsional couple in their early thirties, had obvious signs of mongolism, about which they were fully informed by the referring physician. After explaining the nature of the surgery to the distraught father, I offered him the operative consent. His pen hesitated briefly

[7] For a helpful summary, see J. A. Robertson and N. Fost, "Passive Euthanasia of Defective Newborn Infants: Legal Considerations," *The Journal of Pediatrics,* 88, no. 5 (1976), pp. 883–89.

[8] A. Shaw, "Dilemmas of 'Informed Consent' in Children," *The New England Journal of Medicine,* 289, no. 17 (1973), p. 886.

above the form and then as he signed, he muttered, "I have no choice, do I?" He didn't seem to expect an answer and I gave him none. The esophageal anomaly was corrected in routine fashion, and the infant was discharged to a state institution for the retarded without ever being seen again by either parent.[9]

The following description of practices in a neonate intensive-care unit at Yale Medical Center illustrates how parents may be excluded because of inadequate information about the child's condition or the character of various therapeutic options.

> Parents routinely signed permits for operations though rarely had they seen their children's defects or had the nature of various management plans and their respective prognoses clearly explained to them. Some physicians believed that parents were too upset to understand the nature of the problems and the options for care. Since they believed informed consent had no meaning in these circumstances, they either ignored the parents or simply told them that the child needed an operation on the back as the first step in correcting several defects. As a result, parents often felt completely left out while the activities of care proceeded at a brisk pace.[10]

Not every case in which a physician circumvents or overrides parental decision-making is a case of paternalism toward the parents. In ignoring the parents' primary legal responsibility for the child, the physician may not be attempting to shield the parents from the burdens of responsibility—he may simply be attempting to protect what he perceives to be the interests of the child.

These examples are presented, not as conclusive evidence for the claim that paternalistic practices of the sorts discussed above are widespread, but as illustrations of the practical relevance of the justifications for medical paternalism, which I shall now articulate and criticize.

III

In spite of the apparent pervasiveness of paternalistic practices in medicine, no systematic justification of them is available for scrutiny. Nonetheless, there appear to be at least three main arguments that advocates of paternalism could and sometimes do advance in justification of withholding information or misinforming patients or their families. Since withholding information seems to be more commonly practiced and advocated than outright falsification, I should consider the three arguments only as justifications of the former rather than the latter. Each of these arguments is sufficiently general to apply to each of the types of cases described above. For convenience we can label these three arguments (A) the Prevention of Harm Argument, (B) the Contractual Version of the Prevention of Harm Argument, and (C) the Argument from the Inability to Understand.

[9] *Ibid.,* p. 885.
[10] R. Duff and A. Campbell, "Moral and Ethical Dilemmas in the Special-Care Nursery," *The New England Journal of Medicine,* 289, no. 17, 1973, p. 893.

The Prevention of Harm Argument is disarmingly simple. It may be out-lined as follows:

1. The physician's duty—to which she is bound by the Oath of Hippoc-rates—is to prevent or at least to minimize harm to her patient.
2. Giving the patient information X will do great harm to him.
3. (Therefore) it is permissible for the physician to withhold information X from the patient.

Several things should be noted about this argument. First of all, the conclusion is much weaker than one would expect, granted the first premise which is that it is the physician's *duty* to prevent or minimize harm to the patient, not just that it is *permissible* for her to do so. However, since the weaker conclusion—that withholding information is permissible—seems more in-tuitively plausible than the stronger one, I shall concentrate on it.

Second, the argument as it stands is invalid. From the claims that (1) the physician's duty (or right) is to prevent or minimize harm and that (2) giving information X will do the patient great harm, it does not follow that (3) it is permissible for the physician to withhold information X from the patient. At least one other premise is needed: (2') giving information X will do greater harm to the patient on balance than withholding the information will.

The addition of (2') is no quibble. Once (2') is made explicit we begin to see the tremendous weight that this paternalistic argument places on the physician's power of judgment. She must not only determine that giving the information will do harm or even that it will do great harm. She must also make a complex comparative judgment: Will withholding the information result in less harm on balance than divulging it? Yet neither the physicians interviewed by Oken nor those discussed by Shaw even mention this com-parative judgment in their justifications for withholding information. They simply state that telling the truth will result in great harm to patients or their families. No mention was made of the need to compare this expected harm with harm that might result from withholding the information, and no rec-ognition of the difficulties involved in such a comparison was reported.

Consider two of the examples described above: the patient with terminal cancer and the thyroidectomy malpractice suit. In order to justify withholding the diagnosis of terminal cancer from the patient, the physician must not only determine that informing the patient would do great harm but that the harm would be greater on balance than whatever harm may result from withholding information. Since the notion of great harm is vague unless a context for comparison is supplied, we can concentrate on the physician's evidence for the judgment that the harm of informing is greater than the harm of withholding. Oken's study shows that the evidential basis for such comparative judgments was remarkably slender:

> It was the exception when a physician could report known examples of the unfa-vorable consequences of an approach which differed from his own. It was more common to get reports of instances in which different approaches had turned out

satisfactorily. Most of the instances in which unhappy results were reported to follow a differing policy turned out to be vague accounts from which no reliable inference could be drawn.

Oken then goes on to focus on the nature of the anticipated harm:

> It has been repeatedly asserted that disclosure is followed by fear and despondency which may progess into overt depressive illness or culminate in suicide. This was the opinion of the physicians in the present study. Quite representative was the surgeon who stated, "I would be afraid to tell and have the patient in a room with a window." When it comes to actually documenting the prevalence of such untoward reactions, it becomes difficult to find reliable evidence. Instances of depression and profound upsets came quickly to mind when the subject was raised, but no one could report more than a case or two, or a handful at most . . . . The same doctors could remember many instances in which the patient was told and seemed to do well.[11]

It is not simply that these judgments of harm are made on the basis of extremely scanty evidence. The problem goes much deeper than that. To say that physicians base such judgments on weak evidence is to overlook three important facts. First, the judgment that telling the truth would result in suicidal depression is an unqualified psychiatric generalization. So even if there were adequate evidence for this generalization or, more plausibly, for some highly qualified version of it, it is implausible to maintain that ordinary physicians are in a position to recognize and properly assess the evidence in a given case. Second, it is doubtful that psychiatric specialists are in possession of any such reliable generalization, even in qualified form. Third, the paternalistic physician is simply assuming that suicide is not a rational choice for the terminally ill patient.

If we attempt to apply the Prevention of Harm Argument to cases in which the patient's family or guardian is the object of paternalism, other difficulties become apparent. Consider cases of withholding information from the parents of a neonate with Down's syndrome or spina bifida. The most obvious difficulty is that premise (1) states only that the physician has a duty (or a right) to prevent or minimize harm to the patient, not to his family. If this argument is to serve as a justification of paternalism toward the infant patient's family, the advocate of paternalism must advance and support one or the other of two quite controversial premises. She must either add premise 1' or replace premise 1 with premise 1":

1'. X is a guardian or parent of patient Y and Y is the patient of physician Z, then X is also a patient of physician Z.
1". It is the duty of the physician to prevent or minimize harm to her patient and to the guardian or family of her patient.

Since both the law and common sense maintain that one does not become a patient simply by being related to a patient, it seems that the best strategy for the medical paternalist is to rely on 1" rather than on 1'.

---

[11] Oken, pp. 112, 113.

Reliance on 1″, however, only weakens the case for medical paternalism toward parents of defective neonates. For now the medical paternalist must show that she has adequate evidence of psychiatric predictions the complexity of which taxes the imagination. She must first determine all the relevant effects of telling the truth, not just on the parents themselves, but on siblings as well, since whatever anguish or guilt the parents will allegedly feel may have significant effects on their other children. Next she must ascertain the ways in which these siblings—both as individuals and as a peer group—will respond to the predicted anguish and guilt of their parents. Then the physician must determine how the siblings will respond to each other. Next she must consider the possible responses of the parents to the responses of the children. And, of course, once she has accomplished all this, the physician must look at the other side of the question. She must consider the possible harmful effects of withholding information from patients or of preventing them from taking an active part in decision-making. The conscientious paternalist must consider not only the burdens that the exercise of responsibility will allegedly place upon the parents, and indirectly upon their children, but also the burdens of guilt, self-doubt, and shame that may result from the parents' recognition that they have abdicated their responsibility.

In predicting whether telling the truth or withholding information will cause the least harm for the family as a whole, the physician must first make intrapersonal comparisons of harm and benefit for each member of the family, if that information is available. Then she must somehow combine these various intrapersonal net-harm judgments into an estimate of the total negative effect that divulging the information will have on the family as a whole. Then she must ask similar intrapersonal and interpersonal net-harm judgments about the results of *not* telling the truth. Finally she must compare these totals and determine which course of action will minimize harm to the family as a whole.

Although the problems of achieving defensible predictions of harm as a basis for paternalism are clearest in the case of defective neonates, they are in no way peculiar to those cases. Consider the case of a person with terminal cancer. To eliminate the complication of interpersonal net-harm comparisons, let us suppose that this person has no relatives and is himself legally competent. Suppose that the physician withholds information of the diagnosis because she believes that knowledge of the truth would be more harmful than withholding the truth. I have already indicated that even if we view this judgment of comparative harm as a purely clinical one—more specifically a clinical psychiatric judgment—it is difficult to see how the physician could be in a position to make it. But it is crucial to note that the concepts of harm and benefit appropriate to these deliberations are not exclusively clinical concepts, whether psychiatric or otherwise. In taking it upon herself to determine what will be most beneficial or least harmful to this patient, the physician is not simply making ill-founded medical judgments that might someday be confirmed by psychiatric research. She is making *moral* evaluations of the most basic and problematic kind.

The physician must determine whether it will be better for the patient to live his remaining days in the knowledge that his days are few or to live in ignorance of his fate. But again, this is a gross simplification: it assumes that the physician's attempt to deceive the patient will be successful. E. Kübler-Ross claims that in many, if not most, cases the terminally ill patient will guess or learn his fate whether the physician withholds the diagnosis from him or not.[12] Possible harm resulting from the patient's loss of confidence in the physician or from a state of uncertainty over his prospects must be taken into account.

Let us set aside this important complication and try to appreciate what factors would have to be taken into account in well-founded judgment that the remainder of a person's life would be better for that person if she did not know that she had a terminal illness than if she did.

Such a judgment would have to be founded on a profound knowledge of the most intimate details of the patient's life history, her characteristic ways of coping with personal crises, her personal and vocational commitments and aspirations, her feelings of obligation toward others, and her attitude toward the completeness or incompleteness of her experience. In a society in which the personal physician is an intimate friend who shares the experience of families under his care, it would be somewhat more plausible to claim that the physician might possess such knowledge. Under the present conditions of highly impersonal specialist medical practice it is quite a different matter.

Yet even if the physician could claim such intimate personal knowledge, this would not suffice. For he must not only predict, but also evaluate. On the basis of an intimate knowledge of the patient as a person, he must determine which outcome would be best for that person. It is crucial to emphasize that the question which the physician must pose and answer is whether ignorance or knowledge will make possible a life that is better *for the patient herself.* The physician must be careful not to confuse this question with the question of whether ignorance or knowledge would make for a better life for the physician if the physician were terminally ill. Nor must he confuse it with the question of whether the patient's life would be a *better life*—a life more valuable to others or to society—if it ended in ignorance rather than in truth. The question, rather, is whether it would be better *for the patient herself* to know or not to know her fate.

To judge that a certain ending of a life would be best for the person whose life it is, is to view that life as a unified process of development and to conclude that that ending is a fitting completion for that process. To consider a human life as a unified process of development, however, is to view it selectively. Certain events or patterns of conduct are singled out as especially significant or valuable. To ascertain the best completion of a person's life for that person, then, is to make the most fundamental judgments about the value of that person's activities, aspirations, and experiences.

[12] Elisabeth Kübler-Ross, excerpts from *Death and Dying,* quoted in *Moral Problems in Medicine,* p. 122.

It might be replied that we do make such value judgments when we decide to end the physiologic life of a permanently comatose individual. In such cases we do make value judgments, but they are not judgments of this sort. On the contrary, we believe that since this individual's experience has ended, her life-process is already completed.

When the decision to withhold information of impending death is understood for what it is, it is difficult to see how anyone could presume to make it. My conjecture is that physicians are tempted to make these decisions in part because of a failure to reflect upon the disparity between two quite different kinds of judgments about what will harm or benefit the patient. Judgments of the first sort are estimates of how a particular decision will affect the patient's health and fall within physicians' competence as highly trained medical experts. Judgments of the second sort are evaluations of another human being's life as a whole. There is nothing in their training that qualifies physicians to make judgments of the second sort. Further, once the complexity of these judgments is appreciated and once their evaluative character is understood, it is implausible to hold that the physician is in a better position to make them than the patient or her family. The failure to ask what sorts of harm/benefit judgments may properly be made by physicians in their capacities as physicians is a fundamental feature of medical paternalism.

There is a more sophisticated version of the attempt to justify withholding of information in order to minimize harm to the patient or her family. This is the Contract Version of the Prevention of Harm Argument. The idea is that the physician-patient relationship is contractual and that the terms of this contract are such that the patient authorizes the physician to minimize harm to the patient (or her family) by whatever means he, the physician, deems necessary. Thus if the physician believes that the best way to minimize harm to the patient is to withhold information from her, he may do so without thereby wronging the patient. To wrong the patient the physician would either have to do something he was not authorized to do or fail to do something it was his duty to do and which was in his power to do. But in withholding information from the patient he is doing just what he is authorized to do. So he does the patient no wrong.

This version is vulnerable to the same objections raised against the non-contractual Prevention of Harm Argument. The most serious of these is that in the cases of paternalism under discussion it is very doubtful that the physician will or even could possess the psychiatric and moral knowledge required for a well-founded judgment about what will be least harmful to the patient. In addition, the Contract Version is vulnerable to other objections. Consider the claim that the patient-physician relationship is a contract in which the patient authorizes the physician to prevent or minimize harm by whatever means the physician deems necessary, including the withholding of information. This claim could be interpreted in either of two ways: as a descriptive generalization about the way physicians and patients actually understand their relationship or as a normative claim about the way the physician-patient relationship should be viewed or may be viewed.

As a descriptive generalization it is certainly implausible: there are many people who do not believe they have authorized their physician to withhold the truth from them, and the legal doctrine of informed consent supports their view. Let us suppose for a moment that some people do believe their relationship to their physician includes such an authorization and that there is nothing morally wrong with such a contract so long as both parties entered into it voluntarily and in full knowledge of the terms of the agreement. The first thing to notice is that when the patient actually authorizes the withholding of information it appears that we no longer have a case of paternalism, since what is done with permission is no longer an *interference* of the sort that the definition of paternalism describes.[13]

But from the fact that withholding information with explicit authorization may be neither paternalistic nor wrong nothing follows about cases in which explicit authorization is lacking. The fact that some people authorize physicians to withhold information from them would not justify the physician in acting toward other patients as if they had done so. The physician can only justify withholding information from a particular patient if this sort of contract were entered into freely and in full knowledge by *this* patient.

The medical paternalist might reply that patients or their families often give verbal or linguistic clues that lead the physician to assume that there is authorization, even if it is not explicit. The physician should be careful, however, not to assume that a remark or a bit of behavior which indicates an inclination not to be told is reliable evidence that the person's strongest preference is that he or she should not be told. People often have conflicting inclinations, and when there is no explicit authorization the physician may often not be in a position to assess the relative strength of the patient's conflicting inclinations. But even when this is possible, it is still not enough, because an inclination, even a strong inclination, is not the same as an authorization. An authorization is a purposeful act of communication of a very special sort, an often highly ritualized or at least conventional expression of *resolve,* a determination of *will,* intended to create or waive obligations on the part of others. Granted that this is so, the physician should not confuse behavioral or linguistic evidence of the patient's or the family's inclination not to be told with an authorization not to tell. It appears, then, that the descriptive generalization—the claim that patients or their families authorize physicians to withhold information when they see fit—is implausible.

There is an equally serious difficulty with the normative claim that the physician-patient relationship should or may be viewed as including an authorization for physicians to withhold information whenever they see fit. Even the more extreme advocates of medical paternalism must agree that there are some limits to the contractual relationship between physician and patient. Hence the obligations of each party are conditional upon the other party's observing the limits of the contract. The law, the medical profession, and the general public usually recognize that there are such limits. The patient may

[13] VanDeVeer, pp. 201–2.

seek a second opinion, or she may terminate the relationship altogether. Moreover, it is acknowledged that to decide to do any of these things the patient may—indeed perhaps must—rely on her own judgment. If she is conscientious she will base such decisions on whether the physician is doing a reasonable job of rendering the services for which he was hired.

There are general constraints on how those services may be rendered. If the treatment is unreasonably slow, if the physician's technique is patently sloppy, or if he employs legally questionable methods, the patient may rightly conclude that the physician has not lived up to the implicit terms of the agreement and she may terminate the relationship. There are also more special constraints on the contract stemming from the special nature of the problem that led the patient to seek the physician's services. If you go to a physician for treatment of a skin condition, but he ignores that problem and sets about trying to convice you to have cosmetic nose surgery, you may rightly terminate the relationship. These general and special constraints are limits on the agreement from the patient's point of view.

Once it is admitted that there are any such terms—that the contract does have some limits and that the patient has the right to terminate the relationship if these limits are not observed by the physician—it must also be admitted that the patient should be in a position to discover whether those limits are being observed. But if the patient were to authorize the physician to withhold information, she might deprive herself of information relevant to determining whether the physician has observed the limits of the agreement.

I am not concerned with arguing that authorizing a physician to withhold information is logically incompatible with the contract being conditional. My point, rather, is that to make such an authorization would indicate either that (a) one did not view the contract as being conditional or that (b) one did not take seriously the possibility that the conditions of the contract might be violated or that (c) one simply did not care whether the conditions were violated. Since it is generally unreasonable to expect a patient to make an unconditional contract or to ignore the possibility that conditions of the contract will be violated, and since one typically does care whether these conditions are observed, it is generally unreasonable to authorize the physician to withhold information whenever he sees fit. And if it is generally unreasonable, then it is implausible to contend that simply because she has entered the relationship the patient may or should be viewed as having authorized the physician to withhold information whenever he sees fit. I conclude, then, that on both the descriptive and the normative interpretations, the Contract Version of the Prevention of Harm Argument is not much of an improvement over its simpler predecessor.

There is one paternalist argument in favor of withholding information that remains to be considered. This may be called the Argument from the Inability to Understand. The main premise is that the physician is justified in withholding information when the patient or his family is unable to understand the information. This argument is often used to justify paternalistic policies toward parents of defective infants in neonate intensive-care units. The idea is that either their lack of intelligence or their excited emotional condition prevents parents from giving informed consent because they are incapable of being adequately informed. In such cases, it is said, "the doctrine of informed consent does not apply."[14]

This argument is also vulnerable to several objections. First, it too relies upon dubious and extremely broad psychological generalizations—in this case, psychological generalizations about the cognitive powers of parents of defective neonates.

Second, and more important, it ignores the crucial question of the character of the institutional context in which parents find themselves. To the extent that paternalistic attitudes shape medical institutions, this bleak estimate of parental capacity for comprehension and rational decision-making tends to be a self-fulfilling prophecy. In an institution in which parents routinely sign operation permits without having even seen their newborn infants and without having the nature of the therapeutic options clearly explained to them, parents may indeed be incapable of understanding the little that they are told.

Third, it is a mistake to maintain that the legal duty to seek informed consent applies only when the physician can succeed in adequately informing parents. The doctor does not and cannot have a duty to make sure that all the information she conveys is understood by those to whom she conveys it. Her duty is to make a reasonable effort to be understood.[15]

Fourth, exactly why is it so important not to give parents information that they allegedly will not understand? If the reason is that a parental decision based on inadequate understanding will be a decision that is harmful to the *infant,* then the Argument from the Inability to Understand is not an argument for paternalism toward *parents.* If this argument is to provide a justification for withholding information from parents for *their* benefit, then the claim must be that their failure to understand will somehow be harmful to *them.* But why should this be so? If parents will not only fail to understand but become distressed because they realize that they do not understand, then the Argument from the Inability to Understand turns out not to be a new argument at all. Instead, it is just a restatement of the Prevention of Harm Argument examined above—and is vulnerable to the same objections. I conclude that none of the three justifications examined provide adequate support for the paternalistic practices under consideration. If adequate justification is to be found, advocates of medical paternalism must marshal more powerful arguments.

IV

So far I have examined several specific medical paternalistic practices and criticized some general arguments offered in their behalf. Medical paternalism,

---

[14] Duff and Campbell, p. 893.
[15] I would like to thank John Dolan for clarifying this point.

however, goes much deeper than the specific practices themselves. For this reason I have spoken of "the medical paternalist model," emphasizing that what is at issue is a paradigm, a way of conceiving the physician-patient relationship. Indirect evidence for the pervasiveness of this model is to be found in the very words we use to describe physicians, patients, and their interactions. One widely used distinction that expresses and helps perpetuate the paternalist model is the distinction between "ordinary" and "extraordinary" therapeutic measures.

Many physicians, theologians, ethicists, and judges have relied on this distinction since Pius XII employed it in an address on "The Prolongation of Life" in 1958. In reply to questions concerning conditions under which physicians may discontinue or refrain from initiating the use of artificial respiration devices, Pius first noted that physicians are duty-bound "to take the necessary treatment for the preservation of life and health." He then distinguished between "ordinary" and "extraordinary" means:

> But normally one is held to use only ordinary means—according to circumstances of persons, places, times, and culture—means that do not involve any grave burden for oneself or another.[16]

Although he is not entirely explicit about this, Pius assumes that it is the right of the physician to determine what will count as "ordinary" or "extraordinary" means in any particular case.

In the context of deciding when a highly trained specialist is to employ sophisticated life-support equipment, it is natural to assume that the distinction between "ordinary" and "extraordinary" means is a distinction between higher and lower degrees of technological sophistication. The Pope's unargued assumption that the medical specialist is to determine what counts as "ordinary" or "extraordinary" reinforces a technological interpretation of the distinction. After all, if the distinction is a technological one, then it is natural to assume that it is the physician who should determine its application since it is he who possesses the requisite technical expertise. In my discussions with physicians, nurses, and hospital administrators I have observed that they tend to treat the distinction as a technological one and to argue that since it is a technological distinction the physician is the one who should determine in any particular case whether a procedure would involve "ordinary" or "extraordinary" means.[17]

Notice, however, that even though Pius introduced the distinction in the context of the proper use of sophisticated technical devices and even though he assumed that it was to be applied by those who possess the technical skills to use such equipment, it is quite clear that the distinction he explicitly introduced is not itself a technological distinction. Recall that he defines

---

[16] Pius XII, "The Prolongation of Life." In Stanley Joel Reiser, Arthur J. Dyck, and William Curran, *Ethics in Medicine* (Cambridge, Mass.: MIT Press, 1977), pp. 501–4.

[17] These discussions occurred in the course of my work as a member of a committee that drafted ethical guidelines for Children's Hospital of Minneapolis.

"ordinary" means as those that "do not involve any grave burden for oneself or another." "Extraordinary" means, then, would be those that do involve a grave burden for oneself or for another.

If what counts as "extraordinary" measures depended only upon what would constitute a "grave burden" to the patient himself, it might be easier to preserve the illusion that the decision is an exercise of medical expertise. But once the evaluation of burdens is extended to the patient's family, it becomes obvious that the judgment that a certain therapy would be "extraordinary" is not a technological or even a clinical, but rather a *moral,* decision. And it is a moral decision regardless of whether the evaluation is made from the perspective of the patient's own values and preferences or from that of the physician.

Even if one is to evaluate only the burdens for the patient himself, however, it is implausible to maintain that the application of the distinction is an exercise of technological or clinical judgment. For as soon as we ask what would result in "grave burdens" for the patient, we are immediately confronted with the task of making moral distinctions and moral evaluations concerning the quality of the patient's life and his interests as a person.

Sometimes "extraordinary" means are defined somewhat more broadly as "those which, in the circumstances, would no longer serve any meaningful purpose." It should be obvious that the phrase "meaningful purpose," like the phrase "grave burdens," is not a medical one, but rather an evaluative term that summarizes an indefinite and unarticulated set of moral judgments. The judgments that lead an individual to conclude that continued treatment would serve no meaningful purpose usually include quite controversial moral judgments concerning the "quality" or "value" of the patient's life. For example, whether or not resuscitative efforts that will prolong a senile patient's life for a week or two "serve any meaningful purpose" cannot be ascertained simply through medical judgment. Nor will it do to say that whether any meaningful purpose would be served depends upon the "quality" of the life thus prolonged, and that judgments about the quality of life are the province of medical expertise.

First of all, it is a moral question, not a medical one, as to *which* notion of "quality of life," if any, is relevant to such decisions. "Quality of life" may be used in either a comparative or a non-comparative sense. In the former sense, quality-of-life judgments are interpersonal ranking judgments: the worth or value of one individual is compared with that of others according to some conception of social utility or in terms of the individual's "contribution to society." In the latter, non-comparative sense, a quality-of-life judgment is one in which we assess the value or quality of an individual's life to or for *that individual,* irrespective of how society or would-be calculators of social utility evaluate it relative to that of other individuals.

Second, even after the moral decision has been made to use one or the other of these radically different conceptions of quality of life, moral judgment is still required to determine what counts as an acceptable level of quality of life if we are to arrive at the conclusion that a certain treatment would or would not "serve any meaningful purpose," and hence count as "ordinary" or "extraordinary." Here, as with Pius's definition, the apparently simple distinction between "ordinary" and "extraordinary" measures masks moral perplexities; the widespread belief that it is a medical distinction and hence properly left to medical experts is clearly false.

When pressed for an explanation of how physicians actually apply the distinction between "ordinary" and "extraordinary" therapeutic measures, the director of a neonate intensive-care unit explained to me that what counts as "ordinary" or "extraordinary" differs in "different contexts." Surgical correction of a congenital gastrointestinal blockage in the case of an otherwise normal infant would be considered an "ordinary" measure. But the same operation on an infant with Down's syndrome would be considered "extraordinary".

I am not concerned here with criticizing the moral decision to refrain from aggressive surgical treatment of infants with Down's syndrome. My purpose in citing this example is simply to point out that this decision *is* a moral decision and that the use of the distinction between "ordinary" and "extraordinary" measures does nothing to help one make the decision. The use of the distinction does accomplish something though: it obscures the fact that the decision *is* a moral decision. Even worse, it is likely to lead one to mistake a very controversial moral decision for a value-free technological or clinical decision. More important, to even suggest that a complex moral judgment is a clinical or technological judgment is to prejudice the issue of *who* has the right to decide whether life-sustaining measures are to be initiated or continued. Once controversial moral decisions are misperceived as clinical or technological decisions, it becomes much easier for the medical paternalist to use the three arguments examined above to justify the withholding of information. Once it is conceded that her medical expertise gives the physician the right to make certain decisions, she can then argue that she may withhold information where this is necessary for the effective exercise of this right. By disguising complex moral judgments as medical judgments, then, the "ordinary/extraordinary" distinction reinforces medical paternalism.

V

It is plausible to contend that the strongest arguments against paternalism must be *rights-based* arguments. Such arguments, if successful, would show that paternalism is unjustified because it violates individuals' rights. The rights in question may be either of two sorts: general or special. General rights are said to accrue to persons independently of their participation in certain voluntary interactions and independently of their standing in certain special relationships to others. Among the general rights that some have sought to defend are the right to life and the right to liberty. Special rights are said to be generated by promises, by the making of contracts, and by voluntary participation in certain cooperative enterprises, or are said to be based on special relationships such as that of child to parent.

In contrast to rights-based attacks, there are strictly consequentialist criticisms of paternalism. My criticisms of the Prevention of Harm Argument and of the Argument from the Inability to Understand are of this type. In the former I attacked the paternalist's assumption that the physician, rather than the patients or their families, will typically, or even frequently, be in a position to judge what would be most harmful or beneficial to the patients or families in the cases in question. In the latter, I attacked the paternalist's generalizations about the cognitive deficiencies of patients and their families when faced with life or death decisions.

The Contractual Version of the Prevention of Harm Argument is not itself strictly consequentialist, but rather is an argument based on the premise that the physician-patient relationship is in fact or should be viewed as a contractual relationship that authorizes the physican to withhold information whenever he sees fit. But in my criticism of this argument, as in my criticisms of the two preceding paternalist arguments, I did not rely upon premises ascribing general or special rights to patients or their families and then argue that the paternalist violates those rights when he withholds information without explicit authorization.

There are good reasons for attempting to criticize paternalism without recourse to the rights arguments. The success of general rights-based critiques of paternalism depends ultimately upon whether a coherent theory of general rights can be articulated and given a rational foundation. If, as seems likely, the relevant general right is a right to liberty, there is the difficulty not only of justifying the claim that there is such a right, but also of specifying just what its content is. While it seems clear enough that a right to liberty, if it exists, is a limited right, the task of articulating its limits is an onerous one. Further, what counts as a violation of the right and what counts as a legitimate limitation of it must be distinguished in such a way that the question is not begged against paternalism.

On the other hand, one might attempt to base the critique of paternalism upon a special right to informed consent (or a special right to information of some kind). However, if we merely assume that patients enjoy a moral (as distinct from a legal) right of informed consent simply by virtue of the special nature of the physician-patient relationship, or if we merely assume that such a right is generated by the making of a contract between physician and patient, the medical paternalist—who has a different conception of the relationship or the contract—may again accuse us of begging the question.

It is for these reasons that I have so far eschewed talk about rights, whether general or special. But this strategy comes at a price. Insofar as my criticisms of the Prevention of Harm Argument and of the Argument from the Inability to Understand are strictly consequentialist, it might be thought that they are vulnerable to a strictly consequentialist rejoinder. Alan Goldman has offered the following paternalist rejoinder:

> You are quite right to point out that judgments about what would be most harmful or beneficial to the patient or her family are often extremely complex and difficult to make with accuracy. But what you say about the fallibility of the judgment that withholding information will be most beneficial to the patient or her family also applies to the judgment that divulging information will be less harmful. So here, as in all cases of medical judgment, the physician must rely upon her own judgment, while recognizing, of course, her fallibility. Similarly, the judgment that the patient or family will be able to understand the information if it is divulged is just as complex and difficult to make as the judgment that the information would not be understood. But here, too, since the physician's duty is to minimize harm, the best she can do is to estimate the consequences as accurately as she can and then either divulge or withhold information accordingly.[18]

It is here that the temptation to rely upon rights becomes almost irresistible. For claims of right are characteristically thought of as "trumping" considerations of welfare, whether it be the general welfare or the welfare of the right-holder himself. To take rights seriously is to refuse to allow valid rights-claims to be overridden by considerations of the personal or social utility that could be gained by overriding those claims.

According to a less rigorous and more plausible understanding of rights, to take rights seriously is to refuse to allow rights-claims to be overriden by appeals to social utility or the utility of the right-holder himself, except perhaps where the utility to be gained by overriding the right-claim would be *very great*. The difficulty with this weakened version, of course, is that the exception-clause threatens to render rights-claims impotent. For even if there are some cases in which the gain in utility would be so great as to justify overriding a valid right-claim, they will presumably be not only relatively infrequent but also difficult to identify (except perhaps in retrospect), granted human fallibility and the complexity of the judgments of harm and benefit in question. If this is so, it seems plausible to add the following epistemic requirement: to take rights seriously is to refuse to override valid rights-claims for the sake of utility, except when the utility to be gained is very great *and* when the prediction concerning the gain in utility enjoys a very high degree of certainty.

This epistemic condition is especially plausible in the medical context for two reasons. First, as we have already seen, the non-medical harm/benefit judgments in question are so enormously complex that reliable predictions of utility are very hard to come by. Second, because physicians are trained to reason consequentially about purely medical matters, and because they are highly motivated to act for the patient's welfare and tend to define their role in terms of maximizing benefit or avoiding harm, they are especially suscep-

---

[18] Alan Goldman discusses this paternalist rejoinder in *The Moral Foundation of Professional Ethics* (Totowa, N.J.: Roman and Littlefield, 1980), pp. 175–76.

tible to being overconfident in their consequentialist judgments. The evidence of paternalistic practices adduced earlier supports this hypothesis. If the rigorous notion of rights is accepted, rights-based arguments against the paternalist's practices examined above will always be decisive; but even in the less rigorous interpretation, rights-claims will, in virtually all the cases considered, block appeals to the patients' or families' welfare, because the epistemic condition will not be satisfied.

It would be a mistake, however, to conclude that the only fully effective reply to the paternalist must be rights-based. Insofar as the consequentialist rejoinder assumes that the harm/benefit judgments in question are simply medical judgments (judgments that the physician's medical expertise qualifies her to make) it again conflates judgments of medical expertise with complex and controversial moral and psychological judgments. From the fact that the physician must often make difficult medical judgments, even though she knows she is fallible, it does not follow that training as a physician qualifies her to make moral and psychological judgments. Even if a physician is often required to make highly problematic medical judgments and even if she is often in no worse a position to make the moral and psychological judgments in question than the patient or family, this is not sufficient to show that it is the physician who should make them.

But even more important, I think I have shown that in many, if not most, of the cases under consideration, especially under the impersonal conditions of highly specialized medical practice, the physician is *less* likely than the patient or family to be in a position to make even roughly accurate judgments of the sort required. Similarly, in criticizing the Argument from the Inability to Understand, I think I have shown both that physicians' judgments that patients and families are often unable to understand are based on inadequate evidence and that what evidence there is is largely an artifact of the same paternalistic practices which that evidence is supposed to justify. To put it differently, since the physician is advancing the claim that patients and their families typically or at least frequently cannot understand certain information and since, as I have argued, that information, if properly presented, is not technical, the burden of proof is on the physician to present evidence for her generalization about the cognitive deficiencies of patients and families in those situations. I have argued that this burden of proof has not been borne and that there is some reason to think it cannot be borne successfully. I conclude, therefore, that even when limited to strictly consequentialist considerations, my arguments are a serious challenge to most instances of medical paternalism and to the medical paternalist model, which assumes that paternalism toward patients and their families is frequently justified.

One can go beyond strictly consequentialist arguments without going all the way to rights-based arguments. Even without assuming that there is a *right* to informed consent, or a *right* to liberty, one can assume, quite plausibly, that there are valid moral principles of other sorts, including rules that forbid lying and other forms of deception and that require telling the truth at least where others' vital legitimate interests are affected. Although it may prove difficult to provide a sound theoretical underpinning for such principles, they are intuitively plausible and do seem to constitute an important part of our common moral code. If this is so, then it appears that anyone who abridges these principles incurs a burden of proof—he must show either that these rules are to be rejected outright or that the conduct in question constitutes a legitimate exception to the relevant rule. In either case, there is a moral *presumption* to be rebutted. Even though moral presumption against lying, or deception, or withholding information relevant to someone's decisions about his or her legitimate vital interests may not be as strong as the presumption entailed by a moral *right* to informed consent, it must be taken seriously if the moral principles in question are acknowledged as intuitively plausible elements of our shared morality. But if this is so, then the burden of rebutting the presumption lies squarely on the shoulders of the medical paternalist who would disregard those principles. The antipaternalist consequentialist arguments I offered earlier can therefore be reinterpreted as arguments to show that the presumption against the physician's lying or withholding information in the cases discussed has not been rebutted, and that this can be shown to be so without reliance upon rights, whether special or general.

The paternalist who accepts the moral rules in question might insist that although these principles are generally valid, they do not apply to the singular case of the physician-patient relationship. This reply, however, will not do, as my earlier arguments show. Presumably the claim that physician-patient relationship is such that the physician is not subject to the moral principles that generally apply to us all either rests upon the descriptive claim that the relationship *is,* or the normative claim that is *should* be, one in which the patient authorizes the physician to withhold information whenever he sees fit; or it rests upon the assumption that the physician typically or very frequently is in a better position to make certain very complex moral and psychological judgments than the patient or her family. I have argued both against the claim about the factual or normative character of the physician-patient relationship and against the assumption of the physician's qualifications for making the judgments in question.

If, however, it is admitted that patients and their families have a *right* to informed consent (or a right to active participation in decision-making that vitally affects their legitimate interests), my case against paternalism becomes correspondingly stronger, because of the greater strength of the presumption against withholding information which such a right implies. In sum, my arguments can be viewed in three different ways: (1) as strictly consequentialist arguments, (2) as arguments showing that the paternalist's consequentialist justifications for overriding the moral presumption against withholding information do not adequately rebut that presumption, or (3) as arguments showing that even if there are cases in which consequentialist considerations qualify or even outweigh the right to informed consent, such cases are much rarer and much more difficult to identify prospectively with any degree of certainty than the medical paternalist assumes.

VI

In this paper I have attempted to articulate and challenge some basic features of the medical paternalist model of the physician-patient relationship. I have also given an indication of the powerful influence this model exerts on medical practice and on ways of talking and thinking about medical treatment.

There are now signs that medical paternalism is beginning to be challenged from within the medical profession itself.[19] This, I believe, is all to the good. So far, however, challenges have been fragmentary and unsystematic. If they are to be theoretically and practically fruitful, they must be grounded in a systematic understanding of what medical paternalism is and in a critical examination of the justifications for medical paternalistic practices. The present paper is an attempt to begin the task of such a systematic critique.

[19] See, for example, A. Waldman, "Medical Ethics and the Hopelessly Ill Child," *The Journal of Pediatrics,* 88, no. 5 (1976), pp. 890–92.

SELECTED BIBLIOGRAPHY: PROFESSIONAL RESPONSIBILITY

Bayles, Michael D. *Professional Ethics*. Belmont, Calif.: Wadsworth Publishing Co., 1981.

Bowie, Norman E. (ed.). *Ethical Issues in Government*. Philadelphia: Temple University Press, 1981.

Braybrooke, David. *Ethics in the World of Business*. Totowa, N.J.: Rowman and Allanaheld, 1983.

DeGeorge, Richard T. *Business Ethics*. New York: Macmillan Publishing Co., 1982.

Freedman, Monroe H. *Lawyers' Ethics in an Adversary System*. New York: The Bobbs-Merrill Co., Inc., 1975.

Fried, Charles. "The Lawyer As Friend: The Moral Foundations of the Lawyer-Client Relation." *Yale Law Journal*, 85 (1976), 1060.

Goldman, Alan H. *The Moral Foundations of Professional Ethics*. Totowa, N.J.: Rowman and Allanheld, 1980.

Luban, David (ed.). *The Good Lawyer*. Totowa, N.J.: Rowman and Allanheld, 1983.

Muyskens, James L. *Moral Problems in Nursing*. Totowa, N.J.: Rowman and Allanheld, 1982.

Postema, Gerald. "Moral Responsibility in Professional Ethics." *New York University Law Review,* 55:1 (1980), 63.

Regan, Tom (ed.). *Just Business: New Introductory Essays in Business Ethics*. New York: Random House, 1984.

Robison, Wade H., Michael S. Pritchard, and **Joseph Ellin** (eds.). *Profits and Professions*. Clifton, N.J.: The Humana Press, 1983.

Snoeyenbos, Milton, Robert Almeder, and **James Humber** (eds.). *Business Ethics*. Buffalo, N.Y.: Prometheus Press, 1983.

Toulmin, Stephen. "The Meaning of Professionalism: Doctors' Ethics and Biomedical Science." In Engelhardt, H. Tristram Jr., and Daniel Callahan (eds.). *Knowledge, Value and Belief* (Vol. II, *The Foundations of Ethics and Its Relationship to Science*). Hastings-on-Hudson, N.Y.: The Hastings Center, 1977, p. 254.

Veatch, Robert M. *A Theory of Medical Ethics*. New York: Basic Books, 1981.

FIVE

War

THE KILLING OF THE INNOCENT

JEFFRIE G. MURPHY

After war has been begun, and during the whole period thereof up to the attainment of victory, it is just to visit upon the enemy all losses which may seem necessary either for obtaining satisfaction or for securing victory, provided that these losses do not involve intrinsic injury to innocent persons, which would be in itself an evil.

SUÁREZ, *The Three Theological Virtues*

> Fight on land and on sea
> All men want to be free
> If they don't, never mind
> We'll abolish all mankind
> PETER WEISS, *Marat / Sade*

Reprinted from *The Monist,* Vol. 57, No. 4 (1973) 527–550, with permission of the publisher and the author.

AUTHOR'S NOTE: Many people were kind enough to comment on this manuscript in various stages of its preparation, and I should like to take this opportunity to express my sincere appreciation for the help that they provided. In particular, I should like to thank the following: Lewis White Beck, Robert L. Holmes, Gareth Matthews, Ronald Milo, Richard Wasserstrom, Donald Wells, Peter Winch, and Anthony D. Woozley. I should also like to thank the members of my graduate seminar on war at the University of Arizona for stimulating discussion. Since I have perversely gone my own way on several points in spite of advice to the contrary, I alone am to be held responsible for any errors that remain. In setting a philosophical framework for a discussion of the problem of killing the innocent in war, I have been greatly influenced by Richard Wasserstrom's "On the Morality of War: A Preliminary Inquiry" in his useful collection of essays *War and Morality* (Belmont, Calif.: Wadsworth Publishing Co., 1970). I am presupposing that the reader is familiar with Miss G. E. M. Anscombe's two articles "Modern Moral Philosophy," *Philosophy,* 33, No. 124 (January 1958), and "War and Murder" (in the Waserstrom collection). I am also presupposing a familiarity with Jonathan Bennetts' "Whatever the Consequences," *Analysis,* 26, No. 3 (January 1966).

INTRODUCTION

Murder, some may suggest, is to be defined as the intentional and uncoerced killing of the innocent; and it is true by definition that murder is wrong. Yet wars, particularly modern wars, seem to require the killing of the innocent, e.g., through antimorale terror bombing. Therefore war (at least modern war) must be wrong.

The above line of argument has a certain plausibility and seems to lie behind much philosophical and theological discussion of such problems as the Just War and the nature of war crimes.[1] If accepted in full, it seems to entail the immorality of war (i.e., the position of pacifism) and the moral blameworthiness of those who participate in war (i.e., warmakers and un-coerced soldiers are all murderers). To avoid these consequences, some writers will challenge some part of the argument by maintaining (a) that there are no innocents in war or (b) that modern war does not in fact require the killing of the innocent or (c) that war involves the suspension of moral considerations and thus stands outside the domain of moral criticism entirely or (d) that contributing to the death of innocents is morally blameless so long as it is only foreseen but not intended by those involved in bringing it about (the Catholic principle of the Double Effect) or (e) that the prohibition against killing the innocent is only prima facie[2] and can be overridden by even more important moral requirements, e.g., the defense of freedom.

In this paper I want to come to terms with at least some of the important issues raised by the killing of innocents in time of war. The issues I shall focus on are the following:

1. What does it mean, in a context of war, to describe an individual as *innocent?*
2. Why is it morally wrong to kill individuals so described?
3. Is the moral wrongness merely prima facie (i.e., subject to being overridden by other, more weighty, moral considerations) or is it absolute?

I shall avoid making any final judgments on the morality of war (modern wars or otherwise) since such judgments would involve not just philosophical claims but also empirical claims, e.g., the claim that in fact modern wars cannot be waged so as to avoid the killing of the innocent. However, certain answers to the questions I shall explore will, when coupled with empirical

---

[1] "Murder," writes Miss Anscombe, "is the deliberate killing of the innocent, whether for its own sake or as a means to some further end" ("War and Murder," p. 45). Deliberate killing of the innocent (or noncombatants) is prohibited by the Just War Theory and is a crime in international law. A traditional account of the Catholic Just War Theory may be found in Chapter 35 of Austin Fagothey's *Right and Reason: Ethics in Theory and Practice* (St. Louis: C. V. Mosby Co., 1963). A useful sourcebook for inquiry into the nature of war crimes is the anthology *Crimes of War,* ed. by Richard A. Falk, Gabriel Kilko, and Robert Jay Lifton (New York: Random House, 1971).

[2] By "prima facie wrong" I mean "can be overridden by other moral requirements"—*not,* as a literal translation might suggest, "only apparently wrong."

premises, clearly have moral consequences. For example: *If* the killing of innocents is absolutely and not just prima facie immoral (a philosophical claim), and *if* modern wars necessarily involve the killing of innocents (an empirical claim), *then* war for modern times must be absolutely condemned, i.e., pacifism is the required moral posture for the twentieth century. I shall leave it to sociologists and military historians, however, to supply the correct factual premises.

I shall, then, mainly be concerned to seek answers to the above three questions. However, before launching into my discussion, I want to make one thing clear. Just because I am focusing upon the killing of innocents, it should not be thought that I am confident that it is right to kill the guilty and thus that it is *only* the killing of the innocent that stands in need of analysis and justification. I have no such confidence. I am starting with what any man who is not a moral imbecile must admit to be, at the very least, an obvious prima facie objection to indiscriminate war. In so doing, I do not mean to suggest that there may not be strong nonobvious objections to be made against discriminate war.

THE CONCEPT OF INNOCENCE

The notions of innocence and guilt seem most at home in a legal context and, somewhat less comfortably, in a moral context. Legally, a man is innocent if he is not guilty, i.e. if he has not engaged in conduct explicitly prohibited by rules of the criminal law. A man may be regarded as morally innocent if his actions do not result from a mental state (e.g., malice) or a character defect (e.g., negligence) which we regard as morally blameworthy. In any civilized system of criminal law, of course, there will be a close connection between legal guilt and innocence and moral guilt and innocence, e.g., murder in the criminal law has as one of its material or defining elements the blameworthy mental state *(mens rea)* of "malice aforethought." But this close connection does not show that the legal and moral concepts are not different. The existence of strict liability criminal statutes is sufficient to show that they are different. Under a strict liability statute, a man can be guilty of a criminal offense without having, at the time of his action, any blameworthy mental state or character defect, not even negligence.[3] However, the notion of strict *moral* responsibility makes little sense; for an inquiry into moral responsibility for the most part just is an inquiry into such matters as the agent's motives, intentions, beliefs, etc.[4] Also, the issue of legal responsibility

---

[3] For example: In the criminal offense of statutory rape, the defendant is strictly liable with respect to his knowledge of the age of a girl with whom he has had sexual relations, i.e., no matter how carefully he inquired into her age, no matter how reasonable (i.e., nonnegligent) his belief that she was of legal age of consent, he is liable if his belief is in fact mistaken. For a general discussion of such offenses, see Richard Wasserstrom's "Strict Liability in the Criminal Law," *Stanford Law Review,* 12 (July 1960).

[4] In discussion, Richard Wasserstrom has expressed scepticism concerning my claim that

is much more easily determinable than that of moral responsibility. For example: It is noncontroversial that negligence can make one legally responsible. Anyone who doubts this may simply be given a reading assignment in any number of penal codes.[5] But whether or not negligence is a mental state or a character defect for which one is *morally* responsible is a matter about which reasonable men can disagree. No reading assignment or simple inquiry into "the facts" will lay this worry to rest.[6]

Now our reasonably comfortable ability to operate with these concepts of guilt and innocence leaves us when we attempt to apply them to the context of war. Of course, the legal notions will have application in a limited number of cases, i.e., with respect to those who are legally war criminals under international law. But this will by no means illuminate the majority of cases. For example: Those who have written on the topic of protecting innocents in war would not want to regard the killing of an enemy soldier engaged in an attack against a fortified position as a case of killing the innocent. He is surely, in the right sense (whatever that is), among the guilty (or, at least, among the noninnocent) and is thus a fitting object for violent death. But he is in no sense *legally* guilty. There are no rules of international law prohibiting what he is doing; and, even if such rules were created, they would surely not involve the setting up of a random collection of soldiers from the other side to act as judges and executioners of this law. Thus the legal notions of guilt and innocence do not serve us well here.

What, then, about moral guilt or innocence? Even to make this suggestion plausible in the context of war, we surely have to attempt to narrow it down to moral innocence or guilt *of* the war or *of* something within the war—not just moral innocence of guilt *simpliciter.* That is, we surely do not want to say that if a bomb falls (say) on a man with a self-deceiving morally impure heart who is a civilian behind the lines that this is not, in the relevant sense, a case of killing an innocent. Similarly, I think it would be odd for us to want to say that if a soldier with a morally admirable character is killed in action that this is a case of killing an innocent and is to be condemned on those grounds. If we take this line, it would seem that national leaders should attempt to make some investigation of the motives and characters of both soldiers and civilians and kill the unjust among both classes and spare the

---

there is something unintelligible about the concept of strict moral responsibility. One could regard the *Old Testament* and *Oedipus Rex* as containing a strict liability conception of morality. Now I should be inclined to argue that the primitiveness of the *Old Testament* and of *Oedipus Rex* consists in these peoples not yet being able to draw a distinction between legality and morality. However, I am prepared to admit that it might be better to weaken my claim by maintaining simply that no *civilized* or *enlightened* morality would involve strict liability.

[5] In California criminal law, for example, vehicular manslaughter is defined as vehicular homicide "in the commission of an unlawful act, not amounting to felony, with gross negligence; or in the commission of a lawful act which might produce death, in an unlawful manner, and with gross negligence . . ." (*California Penal Code,* 192, 3, a).

[6] For an excellent discussion of moral and legal responsibility for negligence, see H. L. A. Hart's "Negligence, *Mens Rea* and Criminal Responsibility," in his *Punishment and Responsibility: Essays in the Philosophy of Law* (Oxford: Oxford University Press, 1963).

just. (Only babes in arms would be clearly protected.) Now this sort of judgment, typically thought to be reserved for God if for anyone, is surely a very disquieting thing if advocated for generals and other war leaders. Thus the notions of moral innocence and guilt *simpliciter* must be dropped in this context.

Suppose, then, we try to make use of the notions of moral innocence *of the war* or moral guilt *of the war* (or of something within the war). Even here we find serious problems. Consider the octogenarian civilian in Dresden who is an avid supporter of Hitler's war effort (pays taxes gladly, supports warmongering political rallies, etc.) and contrast his case with that of the poor, frightened, pacifist frontline soldier who is only where he is because of duress and who intends always to fire over the heads of the enemy. It seems reasonable to say that the former is much more morally guilty of the war than the latter; and yet most writers on the topic would regard killing the former, but not the latter, as a case of killing an innocent.

What all this suggests is that the classical worry about protecting the innocent is really a worry about protecting *noncombatants*. And thus the distinction between combatants and noncombatants is what needs to be illucidated. Frontline soldiers are clearly combatants; babes in arms clearly are not. And we know this without judging their respective moral and legal guilt or innocence. And thus the worry, then, is the following: Under what circumstances is an individual truly a combatant? Wars may be viewed as games (terrible ones of course) between enemies or opponents. Who, then, is an enemy or opponent?

One suggestion for defining a combatant might be the following: Only soldiers engaged in fighting are combatants. But this does not seem adequate. For if killing an enemy soldier is right, then it would also seem to be right to kill the man who *orders* him to the frontline. If anything, the case for killing (say) a general seems better, since the soldier is presumably simply acting in some sense as his agent, i.e., the general kills *through* him. Perhaps the way to put the point, then, is as follows: The enemy is represented by those who are *engaged in an attempt* to destroy you.[7] And thus all frontline combat soldiers (though not prisoners, or soldiers on leave, or wounded soldiers, or chaplains, or medics) are enemies and all who issue orders for destruction are enemies. Thus we might try the following: Combatants are those anywhere within the *chain of command or responsibility*—from bottom to top. If this is correct, then a carefully planned attack on the seat of government, intended to destroy those civilians (and only those) directing

---

[7] I say "engaged in an attempt" rather than "attempting" for the following reason: A mortar attack on an encampment of combat soldiers who happen to be sleeping is surely not a case of killing noncombatants even though persons who are asleep cannot be attempting anything. Sleeping persons can, however, be engaged in an attempt—just as sleeping persons can be accomplices in crime and parties to a criminal conspiracy. Being engaged in an attempt, unlike attempting, is not necessarily a full time job. I am grateful to Anthony Woozley for pointing this out to me.

the war effort, would not be a case of killing noncombatants or, in the relevant sense, innocents.

But what is a chain of command or responsibility? It would be wrong to regard it solely as a causal chain, though it is *at least* that. That is, the notion of responsibility has to be stronger than that expressed in the sentence "The slippery pavement was *responsible* for the accident." For to regard the chain here as solely causal in character would lead to the following consequence: If a combatant is understood solely as one who performs an action which is a causally necessary condition for the waging of war, then the following are going to be combatants: farmers, employees at a city water works, and anyone who pays taxes. Obviously a country cannot wage war if there is no food, no management of the basic affairs of its cities, and no money to pay for it. And of course the list of persons "responsible" for the war in this sense could be greatly extended. But if all these persons are in the class of combatants, then the rule "protect noncombatants" is going to amount to little more than "protect babies and the senile." But one would, I think, have more ambition for it than that, e.g., one would hope that such a rule would protect housewives even if it is true that they "help" the war effort by writing consoling letters to their soldier husbands and by feeding them and providing them with emotional and sexual relief when they are home on leave. Thus I think that it is wrong to regard the notion of chain here as merely causal in character.

What kind of chain, then, is it? Let us call it a *chain of agency*. What I mean by this is that the links of the chain (like the links between motives and actions) are held together logically and not merely causally, i.e., all held together, in this case, under the notion of who it is that is *engaged in an attempt* to destroy you. The farmer qua farmer is, like the general, performing actions which are causally necessary conditions for your destruction; but, unlike the general, he is not necessarily engaged in an attempt to destroy you. Perhaps the point can better be put in this way: The farmer's role bears a contingent connection to the war effort whereas the general's role bears a necessary connection to the war effort, i.e., his function, unlike the farmer's, is not logically separable from the waging of war. Or, following Thomas Nagel,[8] the point can perhaps be put in yet another way: The farmer is aiding the soldier qua human being whereas the general is aiding the soldier qua soldier or fighting man. And since your enemy is the soldier qua soldier, and not qua human being, we have grounds for letting the farmer off. If we think of a justified war as one of self-defense,[9] then we must ask the question "Who

[8] Thomas Nagel, "War and Massacre," *Philosophy and Public Affairs,* 2 (Winter 1972). In the same issue, Richard Brandt replies to Nagel in his "Utilitarianism and the Rules of War." I am grateful to Professors Nagel and Brandt for allowing me to read their articles prior to publication.

[9] For reasons of simplicity in later drawing upon important and instructive principles from the criminal law, I shall use the phrase "self-defense." (I shall later want to draw on the notion of *reasonable belief* in the law of self-defense.) However, what I really want to focus on is the concept of "defense" and not the concept of "self." For it seems to me that war can be justified, not just to defend oneself or one's nation, but also to defend others from threats that transcend

can be said to be *attacking* us such that we need to defend ourselves against him? Viewed in this way, the farmer seems an unlikely candidate for combat status.

This analysis does, of course, leave us with borderline cases. But, since there *are* borderline cases, this is a virtue of the analysis so long as it captures just the right ones. Consider workers in a munitions factory. Are they or are they not combatants? At least with certain munitions factories (making only bombs, say) it is certainly going to be odd to claim that their activities bear only a contingent connection to the war effort. What they make, unlike food, certainly supports the fighting man qua fighting man and not qua human being. Thus I should be inclined to say that they are properly to be regarded as combatants and thus properly subject to attack. But what about workers in munitions factories that only in part supply the war effort, e.g., they make rifles both for soldiers and for hunters? Or workers in nonmunitions factories that do make some war products, e.g., workers in companies, like Dow Chemical, which make both Saran Wrap and Napalm? Or workers in ball bearing factories or oil refineries, some of their product going to war machines and some not? Here, I submit, we do have genuine borderline cases. And with respect to these, what should we do? I should hope that reasonable men would accept that the burden of proof lies on those claiming that a particular group of persons are combatants and properly vulnerable. I should hope that men would accept, along with the famous principle in the criminal law, the principle "noncombatant until proven otherwise" and would attempt to look at the particular facts of each case as carefully and disinterestedly as possible. I say that I hope this, not that I expect it.

Who, then, is a combatant? I shall answer this question from the point of view of one who believes that the only legitimate defense for war is self-defense.[10] It is, in this context, important to remember that one may legitimately plead self-defense even if one's belief that one's life is being threatened is false. The only requirement is that the belief be *reasonable* given the evidence that is available. If a man comes to my door with a toy pistol and says, pointing the pistol at me, "Prepare to meet your Maker for your time has

---

nationality, e.g., genocide. If one wants to speak of self-defense even here, then it must be regarded as self-defense for the *human,* not just national, community. The phrase "self-defense" as it occurs in what follows should always be understood as carrying this qualification. And, of course, even clear cases of self-defense are not always necessarily justified. Given the morally debased character of Nazi Germany, it is by no means obvious that it acted rightly in trying to defend itself near the end of World War II (i.e., after it had ceased to be an aggressor).

[10] Remember that this carries the qualification stated in note 9. For a survey of the law of self-defense, the reader may consult any reliable treatise on the criminal law, e.g., pp. 883 ff. of Rollin M. Perkins's *Criminal Law* (Brooklyn, N.Y.: Foundation Press, 1957). The criminal law is a highly moralized institution, and it is useful (though by no means always definitive) for the moral philosopher in that it provides an accumulated and systematized body of reflection on vital moral matters of our culture. For my purposes, I shall in what follows focus upon the *reasonable belief* condition in the law of self-defense. Other aspects of the law of self-defense (e.g., the so-called "retreat requirement"), have, I think, interesting implications for war that I cannot pursue here.

come," I act in my self-defense if I kill him even if he was joking so long as my belief was reasonable, i.e., I had no way of knowing that the gun was a toy or that he was joking. Thus: combatants may be viewed as all those in the territory or allied territory of the enemy of whom it is reasonable to believe that they are engaged in an attempt to destroy you.

What about our Dresden octogenarian? Is he a combatant on this analysis? Since he does not act *on authority,* it is at least prima facie odd to regard him as part of a chain of command literally construed—the concept of command being most at home in a context of authority. He does not, of course, have much to do with the war effort; and so we might find his claim that he is "helping to defeat the Americans" quaint on purely factual grounds. And yet none of this prevents its being true that he can properly be said to be engaged in an *attempt* to destroy the enemy. For people can attempt even the impossible so long as they do not *know* it is impossible. Thus I am prepared to say of him that he is, in fact, engaged in an attempt to destroy the enemy. But I would still say that killing him would count as a case of killing a noncombatant for the following reason: that the concept of attempt here is to be applied, not from the agent's point of view, but from the point of view of the spectator who proposes to plead self-defense in defense of his acts of killing. Combatants are all those who may *reasonably* be regarded as engaged in an attempt to destroy you. This belief is reasonable (though false) in the case of the frontline soldier who plans always to shoot over the heads of the enemy and unreasonable (even if true) in the case of our octogenarian. It would be quite unreasonable to plan a bombing raid on a nonmilitary and nonindustrial city like Dresden and say, in defense of the raid, that you are just protecting yourself or your country from all those warmongering civilians who are attempting to destroy you. For making such a judgment imposes upon you a burden of proof which, given the circumstances of war, you could not satisfy. You probably could not get *any* evidence for your claim. You certainly could not get what the law calls a "preponderance of the evidence"— much less "proof beyond a reasonable doubt."

Combatants, then, are all those of whom it is reasonable to believe that they are engaged in an attempt at your destruction. Noncombatants are all those of whom it is not reasonable to believe this. Having the distinction, we must now inquire into its moral importance.

WHY IS IT WRONG TO KILL THE INNOCENT?

From what I have said so far, it should be obvious that this question cannot adequately be answered unless one specifies the sense of innocence that one has in mind. First, with respect to moral innocence, we can take babes in arms as paradigms. Here I should argue that no reasons can be given for why it is wrong to kill babies; neither are any reasons needed. If anything can be taken as a brute datum for moral philosophy, surely the principle "Do not kill innocent babies" is a very good candidate—much more plausible for an ethical primitive than, say, "promote your self-interest" or "maximize the general utility" (other candidates that have been offered for ethical primitives). The person who cannot just *see* that there is something evil about killing babies could not, I suspect, be made to see anything else about morality and thus could not understand any reasons that one might attempt to give. And any "ethical" theory which entailed that there is nothing wrong at all with killing babies would surely deserve to be rejected on the basis of this counterexample alone. Miss G. E. M. Anscombe puts the point in the following way:

> If someone really thinks, *in advance,* that it is open to question whether such an action as procuring the judicial execution of the innocent should be quite excluded from consideration—I do not want to argue with him; he shows a corrupt mind.[11]

Consider an example from literature: If a reader of Melville's *Billy Budd* cannot see why Captain Vere is deeply troubled because he has a legal obligation to execute Billy, a morally innocent (thought legally guilty) man, what would one *say* to him? What could one do except repeat, in a louder tone of voice perhaps, "But, don't you see, Billy is morally *innocent*"? What I am saying is that, though it is reasonable to expect ethical theories to correct some of our moral intuitions or pretheoretical convictions, we cannot reasonably expect these theories to correct *all* of them—since there is a class of such intuitions or convictions which makes ethical theory itself possible and testable.[12] Kant, I think, was perhaps one of the first to begin to see this when he argued that utilitarianism cannot be correct because it cannot account for the obvious wrongness of making slaves of people, punishing the innocent, etc.

Now with respect to legal innocence (when this does not, as it often does, overlap moral innocence) a set of reasons for not killing (or punishing) the innocent *can* be given. These reasons will be in terms of *utility* (it makes people insecure to live in a society which punishes them whether they obey the rules or not), *justice* (it is not fair to punish people who conform their conduct to the rules), and general observations about the *purposes* and *techniques* of the criminal law as a system of control through rules. As John Rawls has argued,[13] a system of criminal law can be viewed minimally as a price system for controlling conduct (i.e., the rules state a price that has to be paid for certain bits of behavior in the hope that most people will regard the price as too high to pay). And obviously this sort of system is going to work only if the price is generally charged when and only when the "commodity" (i.e., the behavior) is "purchased."

---

[11] "Modern Moral Philosophy," p. 17. For reasons I shall note later, Miss Anscombe weakens her point by adding the word *judicial.*

[12] See William H. Gass, "The Case of the Obliging Stranger," *Philosophical Review,* 66 (April 1957).

[13] John Rawls, "Two Concepts of Rules," *Philosophical Review,* 64 (January 1955).

When we move to war, however, difficulties begin to present themselves. We have seen that what people have had in mind when they have argued for the protection of innocents in war was neither clearly moral innocence nor clearly legal innocence. Rather it was *noncombatant* protection. But when we put the principle as "Do not kill noncombatants" we lose the background of moral and legal thinking which makes the principle seem plausible when formulated in terms of innocence.

Why, then, should we worry about killing noncombatants and think it wrong to do so—especially when we realize that among the noncombatants there will be some, at any rate, who are morally and/or legally guilty of various things and that among the combatants there will be those who are morally and/or legally innocent?

What I suggest is the following: If one believes (as I do) that the only even remotely plausible justification for war is self-defense, then one must in waging war confine one's hostility to those against whom one is defending oneself, i.e., those in the (both causal and logical) chain of command or responsibility or agency, all those who can reasonably be regarded as engaged in an attempt to destroy you. If one does not do this, then one cannot be said merely to be defending oneself. And insofar as one is not defending oneself, then one acts immorally in killing one's fellow human beings. The enemy can plausibly be expanded to include all those who are "criminal" accomplices—those who, in Judge Learned Hand's phrase, have a "stake in the venture." [14] But it cannot be expanded to include all those who, like farmers, merely perform actions causally necessary for the attack—just as in domestic law I cannot plead self-defense if I kill the one (e.g., the wife or mother) who feeds the man who is engaged in an attempt to kill me. [15]

In passing, I should note why I described my position as weakly as I did— namely, that self-defense is the only *remotely plausible* defense of war. I do this because, with respect to nations, the whole idea of self-defense is strongly in need of analysis. What, for example, is it for a state to die or to be threatened with death? Can nations, like individuals, fear death and act compulsively on the basis of that fear? And, insofar as the death of a state is not identical with the deaths of individual human beings, why is the death of a state a morally bad thing? Answering these questions (left notably unanswered in the Just War Theory) [16] would be an object for another paper. I mention them

[14] See, for example, *United States* v. *Falcone,* United States Court of Appeals, Second Circuit, 1940, 109 F.2d 579.

[15] Consider the case of the homicidal diabetic: He is chasing you through the woods of an enclosed game preserve, attempting to kill you for sport with a pistol. However, because of his medical condition, he must return to a cabin in the middle of the preserve every hour in order that his aged mother can give him an insulin shot. Without it, he will take ill or die and will thus be forced to abandon his attempt to kill you. Even if blocking that insulin shot seems your only hope, killing the mother in order to do it would be a very doubtful case of self-defense.

[16] Austin Fagothey, in his well-known statement of the Just War Theory cited previously, allows injury to national honor to count as a ground for a war of self-defense. I cite Fagothey's book because of its influence. It was, for example, appealed to by Justice Douglas in the 1971 *Gillette* case, a case where the defendant refused induction on the grounds of his belief that the Vietnam War is unjust (*Gillette* v. *United States,* 401 U.S. 437).

here to point up latent problems and to further explain my unwillingness, expressed earlier, to affirm that even the killing of the "guilty" (combatants) is morally justified. I am certainly inclined to suspect the Just War Theory's willingness to regard war as an activity giving rise to autonomous moral problems (i.e., problems solely about war and not reducible to ordinary moral problems) and thus to make moral capital out of suspect notions like "national honor" and "national interests" and "national self-defense." Though I am obviously inclined to regard the concept of self-defense as having an important application in the context of war, I am sceptical that the "self" to be legitimately defended must always be the nation or state. It is at least worth considering the possibility that the only moral problems arising in war are the oldest and most common and most important—namely, are human beings being hurt and killed, who are they, and why are they?

IS KILLING THE INNOCENT ABSOLUTELY IMMORAL?

That is, is killing the innocent a prima facie immorality that can be overridden by other, more weighty, moral requirements or is it absolutely immoral, i.e., incapable of being overridden by any other moral requirements? Miss Anscombe[17] holds that the prohibition against killing the innocent is absolute in this sense. And one would suspect that she would echo Kant's sentiments that we should do no injustice though the heavens fall. Unfortunately, she tends simply to assert her position rather than argue for it and so fails to come to terms with the worry that might bother anti-Kantians—namely, does it not matter upon whom the heavens fall? I agree with Miss Anscombe that no argument can be given to demonstrate that there is *something* wrong with killing babies, but it does not follow from this alone that this "something" is not capable of being overridden by another "something"—saving the lives of even more babies, perhaps.

Now in trying to come to grips with this issue, I propose to start with the case of killing babies as a clear example of killing creatures innocent in every possible sense. If a case can be made out that it is sometimes right to kill them, then I assume it will follow a fortiori that it is sometimes right to kill those who may be innocent in a less rich sense, e.g., merely noncombatant. Of course if it is *not* ever right to kill babies, this will not in itself show that it is not ever right to kill noncombatants; for it may be the special kind of innocence found in babies (but not necessarily in noncombatants) which protects them.

First of all, we need to ask ourselves the question "What is it deliberately to kill a baby?" I am certain that Miss Anscombe does not mean the following: that one deliberately kills a baby whenever one pursues a policy that one knows will result in the deaths of some babies. If anyone meant this, then that person would have to regard the construction of highways as absolutely

[17] "Modern Moral Philosophy."

immoral. For it is a statistical fact that on every completed highway a certain number of babies meet their deaths in accidents. Yet normally we do not regard this as a moral case against highways or as a moral proof that highway engineers are murderers. What is done is to weigh the social value of a highway against the knowledge that some deaths will occur and judge that the former outweighs the latter. (If we did not make this judgment, and if this judgment was not reasonable, then we *would* be acting immorally. For example: Suppose we let people blast with dynamite whenever and wherever they felt like it—conduct with little or no social value—in spite of our knowledge that this would result in many children dying.) Of course, situations comparable to the highway example arise in war. For example, consider the pinpoint bombing of a military installation in a war reasonably believed to be necessary and just coupled with the knowledge that bombs will occasionally go off target and that occasionally a wife, with baby in arms, may be visiting her husband on the base.

The natural way to interpret Miss Anscombe's view is as follows: One kills a baby deliberately either when one (a) brings about the death of a baby as one's final purpose or (b) brings about the death of a baby as a *means* to one's final purpose.[18] Since war is hardly to be regarded as motivated by fetishistic infanticide, it is (b) which is crucial. And (b) lets off the highway engineer. For the highway engineer, whom we do not want to regard as a murderer, will not be a murderer on (b). The deaths of babies in highway accidents are in no sense *means* to the socially useful goal of good transportation but are rather accidental byproducts. That is, highway transportation is not furthered by these deaths but is, if anything, hindered by them. And so it is unreasonable to suppose that highway engineers desire the deaths of babies because they want to use their deaths as a means to their goal of transportation. Similarly with the accidental deaths of babies resulting from a pinpoint bombing raid on a military installation.

But consider the following kind of case: One knows that one is fighting a war in defense of civilization itself. (It was not unreasonable to regard the war against Hitler in such terms.)[19] Suppose also that one knows that the only way (causally) to bring a power like Hitler's to a collapse is to undercut his support among the German people by achieving their total demoralization. Further suppose that one knows that the only way to do this is by the obliteration terror bombing of civilian centers (e.g., Dresden) so that, by killing many German babies among others, one can create a desire on the part of the German people to abandon the venture. I am not suggesting that we could ever in fact know these things (they might be false) or that we

---

[18] Another factor, relevant both to war and to the highway example, is the following: acting with the knowledge that deaths could be prevented by taking reasonable precautions and yet not taking those precautions. Such grossly negligent or reckless behavior, while perhaps not "deliberate" in the strict sense, is surely immoral in either context.

[19] See Michael Walzer, "World War II: Why Was This War Different?," *Philosophy and Public Affairs*, 1, No. 1 (Fall 1971).

should ever even let ourselves believe such things.[20] But my worry here is one of principle—namely, assuming the factual situation is as described, would it be wrong *on principle* to initiate a campaign of antimorale obliteration bombing? Here I take it that Miss Anscombe will say that, even in such circumstances, those making a decision to initiate such a campaign are murderers. For they will be deliberately killing the innocent as a means to their goal and that (no matter how good the goal) is absolutely wrong.

But why? Miss Anscombe fails to bring fully into the open a latent issue that is absolutely crucial here—namely, are we as morally responsible for our omissions (e.g., failing to save lives) as for our commissions (e.g., killing people)? Of course there are differences between the two expressions, but are they *morally relevant* differences? If our basic value here is the sanctity of life, or the sanctity of innocents, or the sanctity of babies, then—as Jonathan Bennett has pointed out[21]—it is hard to see their moral difference. For consider the following kind of case: Suppose we know that a victory by Hitler would mean the extermination of all or a great many non-Aryan babies. And further suppose that these babies far outnumber the German babies to be killed in an obliteration bombing campaign.[22] Now, given this knowledge, what would a man who really values the lives of babies do? Is the moral case to rest upon the different descriptions "killing babies" and "letting babies die"? If so, *why?* If the argument is that by not positively killing we will at least be preserving our own moral purity, then it is important to note that this argument, in addition to being rather selfish, is question-begging. For to assume that one remains morally pure if one does nothing is to beg the question of whether we are as responsible for omissive as for commissive conduct. If moral purity means never choosing anything which one will have to regard as in some sense wrong and regret for all one's days, then moral purity may be impossible in a complex world. Albert Camus based this theory of rebellion on this kind of claim—a theory which Howard Zinn summarizes as follows:

> Camus spoke in *The Rebel* of the absurdities in which we are trapped, where the very acts with which we seek to do good cannot escape the imperfections of the world we are trying to change. And so the rebel's "only virtue will lie in never yielding to the impulse to be engulfed in the shadows that surround him, and in obstinately dragging the chains of evil, with which he is bound, toward the good.[23]

The issue here is not over whether we should ever allow ourselves to be

---

[20] As the citizens of London and Hanoi have illustrated, for example, terror bombing has a tendency to backfire. Rather than demoralizing the enemy, it sometimes strengthens their courage and will to resist.

[21] Jonathan Bennett, "Whatever the Consequences," *Analysis,* 26, No. 3 (January 1966).

[22] I take it that, from a moral point of view, their being *German* babies is irrelevant. As Howard Zinn has argued, we should accept the principle that "all victims are created equal" (*Disobedience and Democracy: Nine Fallacies on Law and Order* [New York: Random House, 1968], p. 50).

[23] Ibid., p. 40.

persuaded by any argument that killing the innocent is *in fact* necessary; and I am certainly not suggesting that I find plausible such arguments as have actually been given in the past. For a practical maxim I am much in favor of the slogan. "Never trade a certain evil for a possible good." However, this does not solve the issue of principle. If the good (e.g., saving the lives of scores of babies) *is certain* and not just possible, is it anything more than dogmatism to assert that it would never be right to bring about this good through evil means? The maxim "Never trade a certain evil for a certain good" is by no means self-evidently true and, indeed, does not even seem plausible to many people. Thus I do not think that it has yet been shown that it is always absolutely wrong, whatever the consequences, to kill innocent babies. And thus it has not yet been shown that it is absolutely wrong to kill those innocent in a less rich sense of the term, i.e., noncombatants. Of course we may *feel* differently about actually killing innocents and simply letting innocents die; but I do not think that this phenomenological evidence in itself proves anything. Bomber pilots no doubt feel differently about dropping bombs on babies from thirty thousand feet than they would about shooting a baby face to face, but surely this does not show that the acts differ in moral quality.

Feelings do not prove anything in morality; but they sometimes *point* to something. And it is at least possible that we have not yet captured the worry which motivates the responses of people like Kant, Miss Anscombe, and those who want to defend some version of the doctrine of the Double Effect. If what they really value is the lives of babies and other innocents *simpliciter,* then—as Bennett argues—it does not seem that the distinction between "killing babies" and "letting babies die" will help them to save their principle. But perhaps this is to conceive their position too teleologically. That is, we have so far (with Bennett) been assuming that the person who says "never kill babies" says this because he sees the maxim as instrumental to *something else* that he values—namely, the lives of babies. But it is at least possible that he does not hold this principle to be instrumentally right (in which case he would be subject to Bennett's refutation) but intrinsically right, i.e. right in itself or from its very description. The problem is to explicate this notion of intrinsic rightness in such a way that it does not involve either of the two following pitfalls noted by Bennett:

(a) *Authoritarianism,* e.g., "God commands not killing babies."
(b) *Dogmatism,* e.g., "It is just absolutely wrong to kill babies; and, if you do not see this, you are just too corrupt to talk to."

Now the reason why (a) is a bad move is obvious—namely, it is an appeal to authority rather than reason and thus has no place in a philosophical discussion of moral questions. But (b) is more problematical. For I have said that I am willing to accept such a move if made in the name of there being *something* wrong with killing babies. Why will I not accept such a move in favor of its being *absolutely* wrong to kill babies?

Roughly, I should argue as follows: That there is something wrong with killing babies (i.e., that "*A* is a case of killing a baby" *must* count as a moral reason against *A*) explicates, in part, what may be called "the moral point of view." To be worried about moral issues just is, among other things, to be worried about killing innocents. But the judgment "Never kill babies under any circumstances" does not explicate the moral point of view but is, rather, a controversial moral judgment—or, if you prefer, explicates *a* moral point of view rather than *the* moral point of view. And so, to build *it* into the moral point of view is to beg a controversial question of moral substance—something which presumably metaethics should not do. Someone who said "I see nothing at all wrong with killing babies so let's bomb Dresden" would be an *a*moral monster—one with whom it would be senseless to conduct a moral argument. But one who sincerely said "Of course it is terrible to kill babies but I believe, to save more lives, we must regretfully do it in this case" is not such a monster. He is one with whom, if we think him wrong (*im*moral), we should hope to be able to argue.[24] Since, among war supporters, there are (one would hope) few of the former sort but many of the latter sort, being able to argue with and persuade the latter has some practical importance. It will hardly do simply to say to them "But I can just see the absolute wrongness of what you contemplate and, if you do not, I refuse to discuss the matter with you." We know, alas, what will then happen.

Now I am not going to pretend that I can give anything resembling a *proof* that it is absolutely wrong to kill the innocent (though not to allow them to die), but I hope at least to be able to elaborate a way of thinking which (a) does give some sense to such a prohibition and (b) cannot be condemned as simple dogmatism or authoritarianism, i.e., is a way of *thinking*.[25]

[24] One important metaethical inquiry that has been conducted in recent years concerns the nature of moral judgments and the moral point of view or "language game." The task here is to distinguish the moral from the *non*moral or *a*moral. Normative ethics, on the other hand, is concerned to distinguish the moral from the *im*moral. This is too large a dispute to enter here, but I can at least make my own commitments clear. Unlike the so-called "formalists" (e.g., R. M. Hare, *The Language of Morals* [Oxford: Oxford University Press, 1952]), I am inclined to believe that the moral point of view must be defined, in part, in terms of the *content* of the judgments it contains. Here I am siding, if I understand them correctly, with such writers as H. L. A. Hart (*The Concept of Law* [Oxford: Oxford University Press, 1961]), and G. J. Warnock (*The Object of Morality* [London: Methuen, 1971]). Someone who does not see that "*A* is a case of killing an innocent" is a relevant reason against doing *A*, does not understand what moral discourse is all about, what it is *necessarily* concerned with. And this is so no matter how much he is prepared to universalize and regard as overriding his own idiosyncratic imperatives. If this is true, then the gulf between metaethics and normative ethics is not quite as wide as many have supposed, since the relevance of certain substantive judgments is now going to be regarded as part of the *meaning* of morality as a point of view, language game, or form of life. There still is some gulf between metaethics and normative ethics, however, since I should argue that only the *relevance,* and not the *decisiveness,* of certain substantive judgments (e.g., do not kill the innocent) can be regarded as a defining feature of the moral point of view. Normative ethics, however, is primarily interested in which of the relevant moral considerations are, in certain circumstances, decisive. (I am grateful to Ronald Milo for discussing these matters with me. He is totally responsible for whatever clarity is to be found in my views.)

[25] Though I shall not explore it here, I think that the religious acceptance of the principle could be elaborated as a way of thinking and so distinguished from the authoritarianism and

The way of thinking I want to elaborate is one in which the notion of people's having *rights* plays a predominate role. (Kant's ethical theory, in broad outline, is one such way of thinking.) And an ethical outlook in which the notion of rights looms large will want to draw a distinction between the following two claims:

(1) Doing *A* to Jones would be to violate one of his rights.
(2) It would be bad to do *A* to Jones.

To use Kant's own examples:[26] If I have made a promise to Jones, he has a *right* to expect me to keep it, can properly regard me as having *wronged* him if I do not keep it, and could properly expect that others (the state) should *coerce* me into keeping it. Kant's opaque way of putting this is to say that keeping a promise is a *perfect* duty. A quite different situation is the following: If Jones is in distress (assuming I have not put him there) and I could help him out without extraordinary sacrifice, he would certainly want me to help him and I would be doing something bad if I did not help him. But he does not have a *right* to expect my help, is not *wronged* if I fail to help him, and it would be unreasonable to expect the state or anyone else to *coerce* me into helping him. Helping him is beneficence and (unlike justice) is a comparatively weak moral demand. Kant's opaque way of putting this is to say that the duty to help others in distress is *imperfect.*

When a man has a right, he has a claim against interference. Simply to refuse to be beneficent to him is not an invasion of his rights because it is not to interfere with him at all. When a person uses his freedom to invade the rights of others, he forfeits certain of his own rights and renders interference by others legitimate. (Kant calls this a moral title or authorization— *Befugnis*—to place "obstacles to obstacles to freedom.")[27] Thus if I have an imperfect duty to help others, I may interfere with those trying to harm those others because, by such an attempt, they have forfeited their right against interference. Here I have the imperfect duty; and, since those attacking have

---

dogmatism that Bennett so rightly condemns. The view I shall develop also has implications (though I shall not draw them out here) for the abortion issue. For more on this, see Philippa Foot's "Abortion and the Doctrine of the Double Effect," *Oxford Review* (1967). This has been reprinted in *Moral Problems: A Collection of Philosophical Essays,* ed. by James Rachels (New York: Harper and Row, 1971), and in my *An Introduction to Moral and Social Philosophy: Basic Readings in Theory and Practice* (Belmont, Calif.: Wadsworth Publishing Co., 1973). She sees the doctrine of the Double Effect as groping in a confused way toward an insight of moral importance: "There is worked into our moral system a distinction between what we owe people in the form of aid and what we owe them in the way of non-interference."

[26] These well-known examples are drawn from Kant's *Foundations of the Metaphysics of Morals,* trans. by Lewis White Beck (Indianapolis: Bobbs-Merrill Co., 1959), pp. 39 ff.; pp. 421 ff. of the Academy edition of Kant's works. Kant distinguishes perfect duties (duties of respect) and imperfect duties (duties of love) in many places. See, for example, *The Doctrine of Virtue,* trans. by Mary J. Gregor (New York: Harper and Row, 1964), pp. 134–35; p. 463 of the Academy edition.

[27] Kant, *Metaphysical Elements of Justice,* trans. by John Ladd (Indianapolis: Bobbs-Merrill Co., 1965), pp. 35 ff.; pp. 230 ff. of the Academy edition. See also pp. 94 ff. and 107–9 of my *Kant: The Philosophy of Right* (New York: St. Martin's Press, 1970).

by the attack forfeited certain of their rights, I violate no perfect duty in interfering with them. Thus there is no conflict here. However, if the only way I could save someone from harm would be by interfering with an innocent person (i.e., one who has not forfeited his rights by initiating attack against others) then I must not save the person, for this would be to violate a perfect duty. And, in cases of conflict, perfect duties override imperfect duties.

Suppose that Jones is being attacked by Smith. In such a case it is certainly true to say that Jones's *rights* to liberty, security, etc. are being threatened and that Smith, therefore, is acting wrongly and thereby forfeits his right to be left free from interference. Thus I would not be acting wrongly (i.e., against Smith's rights) if I attacked him to prevent his attack on Jones. Similarly, Jones would not be acting wrongly if he defended himself. However, it does not follow from any of this that I have a *duty* to help Jones or even that Jones has a *duty* to defend himself. Defense, though permissible, is not obligatory. This being so, it does not follow that Jones has a *right to be saved* by me. Thus, since it is far from obvious that Jones has a right to be saved even from an attack by the guilty, it is even more implausible to assert that he has a right to be saved if so doing would involve killing the innocent. (Consider the following: We are all, at this very moment, sitting and talking philosophy and are thus omitting to save the lives of countless people we might save throughout the world. Are we acting wrongly in so doing? If we are, is this because all these people have a *right* to be saved by us?)

Now what sort of a moral view could one hold that would make one accept the principle that perfect duties, resting on rights, override imperfect duties, not resting on rights? I think it is this: a view which makes primary the status of persons as free or choosing beings who, out of respect for that status, are to be regarded as having the right to be left alone to work out their own lives—for better or worse. This is a basic right that one has just because one is a person. Respecting it is what Kant calls respecting the dignity of humanity by not treating people as *means* only. Part of respecting them in this sense is not to use them as a means in one's calculations of what would be good for others. It is fine (indeed admirable) for a person to sacrifice himself for others by his own choice; but it is presumptuous (because lacking in respect for his choices) if *I* choose to sacrifice him. This is his business and not mine. I may only interfere with the person who, by his own evil actions, has forfeited his right against interference. Innocent persons by definition have not done this. And therefore it is absolutely wrong to sacrifice the innocent, though not to kill aggressors. On this view there is something terribly perverse in arguing, as many do, that a defense of freedom requires a sacrifice of those who in no way give their free consent to the sacrifice.[28]

---

[28] Someone (e.g., Jan Narveson in his "Pacifism: A Philosophical Analysis," *Ethics,* 75 [1965]) might say the following: If what you value are the *rights* of people, does this not entail (as a part of what it means to say that one values something) that you would recognize an obligation to take steps to secure those rights against interference? Perhaps. But "take steps" does not have to mean "do whatever is causally necessary." Such an obligation will presumably be limited by

Of course babies are not yet, in the full sense, free or choosing beings who clearly have rights. They are, perhaps, only potential or dispositional persons and enjoyers of rights. But if one accepts the maxim "Innocent until proven otherwise" they may be regarded as equally protected in the above way of thinking. For they certainly cannot be described in the only way which, on this view, makes harmful interference permissible—namely, described as having, through their own deliberate acts of aggression, forfeited their right to be left in peace.

Now this view that what is central in morality involves notions like rights, dignity, freedom, and choice (rather than notions like maximizing the general utility) cannot be proven. But it is a plausible view which may lie behind the maxim "Never kill the innocent" and is a view which would be sacrificed (at least greatly compromised) by the maxim "Kill the innocent to save the innocent." I am myself deeply sympathetic to this way of thinking and would make neither the compromise nor the sacrifice. But I cannot *prove* that one ought not make it. Neither, of course, can my teleological opponent prove his case either. For we lie here at the boundaries of moral discourse where candidates for ultimate principles conflict; and it is part of the logical character of an ultimate principle that it cannot be assessed by some yet higher ("more ultimate"?) principle.[29] You pays your money and you takes your choice. It is simply my hope that many people, if they could see clearly what price they have to pay (i.e. the kind of moral outlook they have to give up and what they have to put in its place) would make the choice against killing the innocent.

Consider the following example: Suppose that thousands of babies could be saved from a fatal infant disease if some few babies were taken by the state and given over to a team of medical researchers for a series of experiments which, though killing the babies, would yield a cure for the disease. In what way except degree (i.e., numbers of babies killed) does this situation differ from the rationale behind antimorale obliteration bombing raids, i.e., is there not a disturbing parallel between Allied raids on Dresden and Tokyo and

---

(a) what I can reasonably be expected to do or sacrifice and (b) my moral judgment about the permissibility of the *means* employed. It does seem perverse for a person to say "I value the rights of people above all else but I do not propose to do anything to secure those rights." However, it by no means seems to me equally perverse to say the following: "I deplore interferences with human rights above all else and I will do everything in my power to prevent such interferences—everything, of course, short of being guilty of such interferences myself."

[29] See Brian Barry, "Justice and the Common Good," *Analysis,* 21–22 (1960–61). Though the existentialists tend to overdo this sort of claim, there is truth in their claim that there are certain moral problems that are in principle *undecidable* by any rational decision procedure. Such cases are not perhaps as numerous as the existentialists would have us believe, but they do arise, e.g. when candidates for ultimate moral principles conflict. In such cases, we find it impossible to nail down with solid arguments those principles which matter to us the most. Perhaps this even deserves to be called "absurd." In his article "The Absurd" (*Journal of Philosophy,* 68, No. 20 [October 21, 1971]), Thomas Nagel suggests that absurdity in human life is found in "the collision between the seriousness with which we take our lives and the perpetual possibility of regarding everything about which we are serious as arbitrary, or open to doubt." It is here that talk about faith or commitment seems to have some life.

Nazi "medicine"? With respect to either suggestion, when we really think about it, do we not want to say with the poet James Dickey

> Holding onto another man's walls
> My hat should crawl on my head
> In streetcars, thinking of it,
> The fat on my body should pale.[30]

How can any such thing be in the interest of humanity when its practice would change the very meaning of "humanity" and prevent us from unpacking from it, as we now do, notions like rights, dignity, and respect? No matter how good the consequences, is there not some point in saying that we simply do not have the *right* to do it? For there is, I think, an insight of secular value in the religious observation that men are the "children of God." For this means, among other things, that other people do not *belong* to me. They are not *mine* to be manipulated as resources in my projects. It is hard to imagine all that we might lose if we abandoned this way of thinking about ourselves and others.

My appeal here, of course, is in a sense emotive. But this in my judgment is not an objection. Emotive appeals may rightly be condemned if they are masquerading as proofs. But here I am attempting to prove nothing but only to say—"Here, look, see what you are doing and what way of thinking your doing it involves you in." If one sees all this and still goes forth to do it anyway, we have transcended the bounds of what can be *said* in the matter.

What about noncombatants? Though they are not necessarily innocent in all the senses in which babies are, they clearly are innocent in the sense I have elaborated above—namely, they have not performed actions which forfeit their right to be free from execution (or, better: it is not *reasonable* for the enemy to believe this of them). Thus, in a very tentative conclusion, I suggest the following: I have not been able to prove that we should never kill noncombatants or innocents (I do not think this could be proven in any ordinary sense of proof); but I do think that I have elaborated a way of thinking which gives sense to the acceptance of such an absolute prohibition. Thus, against Bennett, I have at least shown that one can accept the principle "Never kill the innocent" without thereby necessarily being an authoritarian or a dogmatic moral fanatic.

[30] James Dickey, "The Firebombing," in *Poems* 1957–1967 (Middletown, Conn.: Wesleyan University Press, 1967), p. 185. Reprinted with the permission of the publisher.

CONVENTIONS AND THE MORALITY OF WAR

GEORGE I. MAVRODES

The point of this paper is to introduce a distinction into our thinking about warfare, and to explore the moral implications of this distinction. I shall make two major assumptions. First, I shall assume without discussion that under some circumstances and for some ends warfare is morally justified. These conditions I shall lump together under such terms as "justice" and "just cause," and say no more about them. I shall also assume that in warfare some means, including some killing, are morally justified. I sometimes call such means "proportionate," and in general I say rather little about them. These assumptions, incidentally, are common to all of the philosophers whom I criticize here.

The distinction which I introduce can be thought of either as dividing wars into two classes, or else as distinguishing wars from certain other international combats. I have no great preference for one of these ways of speaking over the other, but I shall generally adopt the latter alternative. I am particularly interested in the moral significance of this distinction, and I shall explore in some detail its bearing on one moral question associated with warfare, that of the intentional killing of noncombatants.

My paper has two main parts. In the first I examine three closely related treatments of this moral question: the arguments of Elizabeth Anscombe, John C. Ford, and Paul Ramsey. These treatments seem to ignore the distinction which I will propose. I argue that on their own terms, and without reference to that distinction, they must be counted as unsatisfactory.

In the second part of the paper I propose and explain my distinction. I then explore what I take to be some of its moral implications, especially with reference to the alleged immunity of noncombatants, and I argue that it supplies what was missing or defective in the treatments previously criticized.

I. THE IMMUNITY THEORISTS

A number of philosophers have held that a large portion of the population of warring nations have a special moral status. This is the *noncombatant* segment of the population, and they have a moral immunity from being intentionally killed. This view seems to have been especially congenial to philosophers who have tried to apply Christian ethics to the problems of warfare. Among the philosophers who have held this view are Elizabeth Anscombe, John C. Ford, and Paul Ramsey. I shall refer to this trio of thinkers as the *immunity theorists*.

Reprinted from *Philosophy & Public Affairs,* Vol. 4, No. 2 (1975) 117–131, with permission of the author and the publisher, Princeton University Press.

Perhaps we should indicate a little more in detail just what the immunity theorists appear to hold, specifying just what segment of the population is being discussed and just what their immunity consists in. The immunity theorists commonly admit that there is some difficulty in specifying exactly who are the noncombatants.[1] Roughly, they are those people who are not engaged in military operations and whose activity is not immediately and directly related to the war effort. Perhaps we could say that if a person is engaged only in the sort of activities which would be carried on even if the nation were not at war (or preparing for war) then that person is a noncombatant. So generally farmers, teachers, nurses, firemen, sales people, housewives, poets, children, etc. are noncombatants.[2] There are, of course, difficult cases, ranging from the high civilian official of the government to the truck driver (either military or civilian) who hauls vegetables toward the front lines. But despite the hard cases it is held that warring nations contain large numbers of readily identifiable people who are clearly noncombatants.

What of their immunity? The writers whom I consider here make use of the "principle of double-effect."[3] This involves dividing the consequences of an act (at least the foreseeable consequences) into two classes. Into the first class go those consequences which constitute the goal or purpose of the act, what the act is done for, and also those consequences which are means to those ends. Into the other class go those consequences which are neither the sought-after ends nor the means to those ends. So, for example, the bombing of a rail yard may have among its many consequences the following: the flow of supplies toward the front is disrupted, several locomotives are damaged, and a lot of smoke, dust, etc. is discharged into the air. The disruption of transport may well be the end sought by this action, and perhaps the damage to locomotives is sought as a means of disrupting transport. If so, these consequences belong in the first class, a class which I shall generally mark by using the words "intentional" or "intended." The smoke, on the other hand, though as surely foreseeable as the other effects, may be neither means nor end in this situation. It is a side-effect, and belongs in the second class (which I shall sometimes call "unintentional" or "unintended").

Now, the moral immunity of noncombatants consists, according to these writers, in the fact that their death can never, morally, be made the intended consequence of a military operation. Or to put it another way, any military operation which seeks the death of noncombatants either as an end or a means is immoral, regardless of the total good which it might accomplish.

The *unintended* death of noncombatants, on the other hand, is not absolutely forbidden. A military operation which will foreseeably result in such

[1] Elizabeth Anscombe, "War and Murder." In *War and Morality,* ed. Richard A. Wasserstrom (Belmont, Calif.: 1970), p. 52; John C. Ford, "The Morality of Obliteration Bombing," ibid., pp. 19–23; Paul Ramsey, *The Just War* (New York: 1968), pp. 157, 158.

[2] Ford gives a list of over 100 occupations whose practitioners he considers to be "almost without exception" noncombatants.

[3] Anscombe, pp. 46, 50, 51; Ford, pp. 26–28; Ramsey, pp. 347–58.

deaths, neither as means nor ends but as side effects, may be morally acceptable according to these writers. It will be morally acceptable if the good end which it may be expected to attain is of sufficient weight to overbalance the evil of these noncombatant deaths (as well as any other evils involved in it). This principle, sometimes called the principle of proportionality, apparently applies to foreseen but unintended noncombatant deaths in just the same way as it applies to the intended death of combatants, the destruction of resources, and so on. In all of these cases it is held to be immoral to cause many deaths, much pain, etc., in order to achieve minor goals. Here combatant and non-combatant stand on the same moral ground, and their deaths are weighed in the same balances. But when the slaying of noncombatants is envisioned as an end or, more commonly, as a means—perhaps in order to reduce the production of foodstuffs or to damage the morale of troops—then there is an unqualified judgment that the projected operation is flatly immoral. The intentional slaying of combatants, on the other hand, faces no such prohibition. This, then, is the place where the moral status of combatant and noncombatant differ sharply.

Now, if a scheme such as this is not to appear simply arbitrary it looks as though we must find some morally relevant basis for the distinction. It is perhaps worthwhile to notice that in this context the immunity of noncombatants cannot be supported by reference to the sanctity or value of human life, nor by reference to a duty not to kill our brothers, etc. For these authors recognize the moral permissibility, even perhaps the duty, of killing under certain circumstances. What must be sought is the ground of a distinction, and not merely a consideration against killing.

Such a ground, however, seems very hard to find, perhaps unexpectedly so. The crucial argument proposed by the immunity theorists turns on the notions of guilt and innocence. Anscombe, for example, says:

> Now, it is one of the most vehement and repeated teachings of the Judaeo-Christian tradition that the shedding of innocent blood is forbidden by the divine law. No man may be punished except for his own crime, and those "whose feet are swift to shed innocent blood" are always represented as God's enemies.[4]

Earlier on she says, "The principal wickedness which is a temptation to those engaged in warfare is the killing of the innocent,"[5] and she has titled one of the sections of her paper, "Innocence and the Right to Kill Intentionally." Clearly enough the notion of innocence plays a large role in her thinking on this topic. Just what that role is, or should be, will be considered shortly. Ford, in the article cited earlier, repeatedly couples the word "innocent" with "civilian" and "noncombatant." His clearest statement, however, is in another essay. There he says:

> Catholic teaching has been unanimous for long centuries in declaring that it is never permitted to kill directly noncombatants in wartime. Why? Because they are

---

[4] Anscombe, p. 49.
[5] Ibid., p. 44.

innocent. That is, they are innocent of the violent and destructive action of war, or of any close participation in the violent and destructive action of war. It is such participation *alone* that would make them legitimate targets of violent repression themselves.[6]

Here we have explicitly a promising candidate for the basis of the moral distinction between combatants and noncombatants. It is promising because innocence itself seems to be a moral property. Hence, if we could see that noncombatants were innocent while combatants were not it would be plausible to suppose that this fact made it morally proper to treat them in different ways.

If we are to succeed along this line of thought, then we must meet at least two conditions. First, we must find some one sense of "innocence" such that all noncombatants are innocent and all combatants are guilty. Second, this sense must be morally relevant, a point of the greatest importance. We are seeking to ground a moral distinction, and the facts to which we refer must therefore be morally relevant. The use of a morally tinged word, such as "innocent," does not of itself guarantee such relevance.

Well, is there a suitable sense for "innocent"? Ford said that noncombatants "are innocent of the violent and destructive action of war." Anscombe, writing of the people who can properly be attacked with deadly force, says, "What is required, for the people attacked to be noninnocent in the relevant sense, is that they themselves be engaged in an objectively unjust proceeding which the attacker has the right to make his concern; or—the commonest case—should be unjustly attacking him." On the other hand, she speaks of "people whose mere existence and activity supporting existence by growing crops, making clothes, etc.," might contribute to the war effort, and she says, "such people are innocent and it is murderous to attack them, or make them a target for an attack which he judges will help him towards victory."[7] These passages contain, I think, the best clues we have as to the sense of "innocent" in these authors.

It is probably evident enough that this sense of "innocent" is vague in a way parallel to the vagueness of "noncombatant." It will leave us with troublesome borderline cases. In itself, that does not seem to me a crucial defect. But perhaps it is a clue to an important failing. For I suspect that there is this parallel vagueness because "innocent" here is just a synonym for "noncombatant."

What can Ford mean by saying that some people are "innocent of the violent and destructive action of war" except that those people are not engaged in the violence of war? Must not Anscombe mean essentially the same thing when she says that the noninnocent are those who are themselves "engaged in an objectively unjust proceeding"? But we need not rely wholly on these rhetorical questions. Ramsey makes this point explicitly. He first distinguishes between close and remote cooperation in military operations, and then he

---

[6] John C. Ford, "The Hydrogen Bombing of Cities." *Morality and Modern Warfare,* ed. William J. Nagle (Baltimore: Helicon Press, 1960), p. 98.

[7] Anscombe, p. 45.

alludes to the distinction between the "guilty" and the "innocent." Of this distinction he says, "These are very misleading terms, since their meaning is exhaustively stated under the first contrast, and is reducible to degrees of actual participation in hostile force."[8] In this judgment Ramsey certainly seems to me to be right.

Now, we should notice carefully that a person may be an enthusiastic supporter of the unjust war and its unjust aims, he may give to it his voice and his vote, he may have done everything in his power to procure it when it was yet but a prospect, now that it is in progress he may contribute to it both his savings and the work which he knows best how to do, and he may avidly hope to share in the unjust gains which will follow if the war is successful. But such a person may clearly be a noncombatant, and (in the sense of the immunity theorists) unquestionably "innocent" of the war. On the other hand, a young man of limited mental ability and almost no education may be drafted, put into uniform, trained for a few weeks, and sent to the front as a replacement in a low-grade unit. He may have no understanding of what the war is about, and no heart for it. He might want nothing more than to go back to his town and the life he led before. But he is "engaged," carrying ammunition, perhaps, or stringing telephone wire or even banging away ineffectually with his rifle. He is without doubt a combatant, and "guilty," a fit subject for intentional slaughter. Is it not clear that "innocence," as used here, leaves out entirely all of the relevant moral considerations— that it has no moral content at all? Anscombe suggests that intentional killing during warfare should be construed on the model of punishing people for their crimes, and we must see to it, if we are to be moral, that we punish someone only for his own crime and not for someone else's. But if we construe the criminality involved in an unjust war in any reasonable moral sense then it must either be the case that many noncombatants are guilty of that criminality or else many combatants are innocent. In fact, it will probably be the case that *both* of these things are true. Only if we were to divest "crime" of its moral bearings could we make it fit the combatant/noncombatant distinction in modern wars.

The fact that both Anscombe and Ramsey[9] use the analogy of the criminal in discussing this topic suggests that there is an important fact about warfare which is easily overlooked. And that is that warfare, unlike ordinary criminal activity, is not an activity in which individuals engage qua individuals or as members of voluntary associations. They enter into war as members of nations. It is more proper to say that the nation is at war than that its soldiers are at war. This does not, of course, entail that individuals have no moral responsibility for their acts in war. But it does suggest that moral responsibility may not be distributed between combatant and noncombatant in the same way as between a criminal and his children. Many of the men who are soldiers,

---

[8] Ramsey, p. 153.
[9] Ibid., p. 144.

perhaps most of them, would not be engaged in military operations at all if they did not happen to be citizens of a warring nation. But noncombatants are citizens of warring nations in exactly the same sense as are soldiers. However these facts are to be analyzed they should warn us not to rely too heavily on the analogy with ordinary criminality.

We seem, then, to be caught in a dilemma. We can perhaps find some sense for notions such as *innocence* and *criminality* which will make them fit the distinction in which we are interested. But the price of doing so seems to be that of divesting these notions of the moral significance which they require if they are to justify the moral import of the distinction itself. In the ordinary senses, on the other hand, these notions do have the required moral bearings. But in their ordinary senses they do not fit the desired distinction. In neither way, therefore, can the argument from innocence be made to work, and the alleged moral immunity of noncombatants seems to be left as an arbitrary claim.

II. CONVENTION-DEPENDENT MORALITY

Despite the failure of these arguments I have recently come to think that there may be something of importance in this distinction after all, and even that it may have an important moral bearing. How might this be?

Imagine a statesman reflecting on the costliness of war, its cost in human life and human suffering. He observes that these costs are normally very high, sometimes staggering. Furthermore, he accepts the principle of proportionality. A consequence of this is that he sometimes envisions a just war for a just cause, but nevertheless decides not to prosecute that war even though he believes it could be won. For the cost of winning would be so high as to outweigh the good which would be attained. So he must sometimes let oppression flourish and injustice hold sway. And even in those wars which can be prosecuted the costs eat very seriously into the benefits.

Then he has an idea. Suppose—just suppose—that one could replace warfare with a less costly substitute. Suppose, for example, that one could introduce a convention—and actually get it accepted and followed by the nations—a convention which replaced warfare with single combat. Under this convention, when two nations arrived at an impasse which would otherwise have resulted in war they would instead choose, each of them, a single champion (doubtless a volunteer). These two men would then meet in mortal combat, and whoever won, killing his opponent or driving him from the field, would win for his nation. To that nation would then be ceded whatever territory, influence, or other prize would have been sought in the war, and the nation whose champion was defeated would lose correspondingly.

Suppose, too, that the statesman believes that if such a convention were to come into force his own nation could expect to win and lose such combats in about the same proportion as it could now expect to win and lose ordinary wars. The same types of questions would be settled by such combats as would otherwise be settled by war (though perhaps more questions would be submitted to combat than would be submitted to war), and approximately the same resolutions would be arrived at. The costs, however—human death and suffering—would be reduced by several orders of magnitude. Would that not be an attractive prospect? I think it would.

While the prospect may seem attractive it may also strike us as hopelessly utopian, hardly to be given a serious thought. There seems to be some evidence, however, that exactly this substitution was actually attempted in ancient times. Ancient literature contains at least two references to such attempts. One is in the Bible, I Samuel 17, the combat between David and Goliath. The other is in the *Iliad,* book 3, where it is proposed to settle the seige of Troy in the very beginning by single combat between Menelaus and Paris. It may be significant that neither of these attempts appears to have been successful. The single combats were followed by bloodier and more general fighting. Perhaps this substitute for warfare is too cheap; it cannot be made practical, and nations just will not consent in the end to abide by this convention. But consider, on the one hand, warfare which is limited only by the moral requirements that the ends sought should be just and that the means used should be proportionate, and, on the other hand, the convention of single combat as a substitute for warfare. Between these extremes there lie a vast number of other possible conventions which might be canvassed in the search for a less costly substitute for war. I suggest that the long struggle, in the western world at least, to limit military operations to "counter-forces" strategies, thus sparing civilian populations, is just such an attempt.

If I am right about this, then the moral aspects of the matter must be approached in a way rather different from that of the immunity theorists. Some, but not all, of their conclusions can be accepted, and somewhat different grounds must be given for them. These thinkers have construed the immunity of noncombatants as though it were a moral fact which was independent of any actual or envisioned convention or practice. And they have consequently sought to support this immunity by argument which makes no references to convention. I have already argued that their attempts were failures. What I suggest now is that all such attempts *must* be failures, for they mistake the sort of moral requirement which is under consideration. Let me try to make this clearer.

I find it plausible to suppose that I have a moral obligation to refrain from wantonly murdering my neighbors. And it also seems plausible to discuss this, perhaps in utilitarian terms, or in terms of the will of God, or of natural law, or in terms of a rock-bottom deontological requirement, but in any case without essential reference to the laws and customs of our nation. We might, indeed, easily imagine our laws and customs to be other than they are with respect to murder. But we would then judge the moral adequacy and value of such alternative laws and customs by reference to the moral obligation I have mentioned and not vice versa. On the other hand, I may also have a moral obligation to pay a property tax or to drive on the right side of the street. It does not seem plausible to suppose, however, that one can discuss these duties without immediately referring to our laws and customs. And it seems likely that different laws would have generated different moral duties, e.g. driving on the left. These latter are examples of "convention-dependent" moral obligations. More formally, I will say that a given moral obligation is convention-dependent if and only if (1) given that a certain convention, law, custom, etc., is actually in force one really does have an obligation to act in conformity with that convention, and (2) there is an alternative law, custom, etc. (or lack thereof) such that if that had been in force one would not have had the former obligation.

At this point, before developing the way in which it may apply to warfare, let me forestall some possible misunderstandings by a series of brief comments on this notion. I am not claiming, nor do I believe, that all laws, customs, etc., generate corresponding moral obligations. But some do. I am not denying that one may seek, and perhaps find, some more general moral law, perhaps independent of convention which explains why this convention generates the more specific obligation. I claim only that one cannot account for the specific obligation apart from the convention. Finally, I am not denying that one might have an obligation, perhaps independent of convention, to try to change a convention of this sort. For I think it possible that one might simultaneously have a moral obligation to conform to a certain convention and also a moral obligation to replace that convention, and thus to eliminate the first obligation.

Now, the core of my suggestion with respect to the immunity of noncombatants is this. The immunity of noncombatants is best thought of as a convention-dependent obligation related to a convention which substitutes for warfare a certain form of limited combat. How does this bear on some of the questions which we have been discussing?

To begin with, we might observe that the convention itself is presumably to be justified by its expectable results. (Perhaps we can refer to some moral rule to the effect that we should minimize social costs such as death and injury.) It seems plausible to suppose that the counter-forces convention, if followed, will reduce the pain and death involved in combat—will reduce it, that is, compared to unlimited warfare. There are surely other possible conventions which, if followed, would reduce those costs still more, e.g., the substitution of single combat. Single combat, however, is probably not a live contender because there is almost no chance that such a convention would actually be followed. It is possible, however, that there is some practical convention which is preferable to the present counter-forces convention. If so, the fact that it is preferable is a strong reason in favor of supposing that there is a moral obligation to promote its adoption.

It does not follow, however, that we now have a duty to act in conformity with this other possible convention. For the results of acting in conformity with a preferable convention which is not widely observed may be much worse than the results of acting in conformity with a less desirable convention which is widely observed. We might, for example, discover that a "left-hand" pattern of traffic flow would be preferable to the present system of "right-hand" rules, in that it would result in fewer accidents, etc. The difference might be so significant that we really would be morally derelict if we did not try to institute a change in our laws. We would be acquiescing in a very costly procedure when a more economical one was at hand. But it would be a disaster, and, I suspect, positively immoral, for a few of us to begin driving on the left before the convention was changed. In cases of convention-dependent obligations the question of what convention is actually in force is one of considerable moral import. That one is reminded to take this question seriously is one of the important differences between this approach and that of the immunity theorists.

Perhaps the counter-forces convention is not really operative now in a substantial way. I do not know. Doubtless, it suffered a severe blow in World War II, not least from British and American bombing strategies. Traffic rules are embedded in a broad, massive, comparatively stable social structure which makes their status comparatively resistant to erosion by infraction. Not so, however, for a convention of warfare. It has little status except in its actual observance, and depends greatly on the mutual trust of the belligerents; hence it is especially vulnerable to abrogation by a few contrary acts. Here arises a related difference with the immunity theorists. Taking the obligation to be convention-independent they reject argument based on the fact that "the enemy did it first," etc.[10] If the obligation were independent they would be correct in this. But for convention-dependent obligations, what one's opponent does, what "everyone is doing," etc., are facts of great moral importance. Such facts help to determine within what convention, if any, one is operating, and thus they help one to discover what his moral duties are.

If we were to decide that the counter-forces convention was dead at present, or, indeed, that no convention at all with respect to warfare was operative now, it would not follow that warfare was immoral. Nor, on the other hand, would it follow that warfare was beyond all moral rules, an area in which "anything goes." Instead, we would simply go back to warfare per se, limited only by independent moral requirements, such as those of justice and pro-portionality. That would, on the whole, probably be a more costly way of handling such problems. But if we live in a time when the preferable substitutes are not available, then we must either forgo the goods or bear the higher costs. If we had no traffic laws or customs, traffic would be even more dangerous and costly than it is now. Traveling, however, might still be justified, if the reason for traveling were sufficiently important.

In such a case, of course, there would be no obligation to drive on the right, or in any regular manner, nor would there be any benefit in it. Probably the best thing would be to drive in a completely ad hoc way, seeking the best maneuver in each situation as it arose. More generally, and ignoring for the

---

[10] For example, Ford, "The Morality of Obliteration Bombing," pp. 20, 33.

moment a final consideration which will be discussed below, there is no obligation and no benefit associated with the unilateral observance of a convention. If one's cause is unjust then one ought not to kill noncombatants. But that is because of the independent moral prohibition against prosecuting such a war at all, and has nothing to do with any special immunity of noncombatants. If one's cause is just, but the slaying of noncombatants will not advance it to any marked degree, then one ought not to slay them. But this is just the requirement of proportionality, and applies equally and in the same way to combatants. If one's cause is just and the slaying of noncombatants would advance it—if, in other words, one is not prevented by considerations of justice and proportionality—this is the crucial case. If one refrains unilaterally in this situation then he seems to choose the greater of two evils (or the lesser of two goods). By hypothesis, the good achieved, i.e. the lives spared, is not as weighty as the evil which he allows in damage to the prospects for justice or in the even more costly alternative measures, e.g. the slaying of a larger number of combatants, which he must undertake. Now, if the relevant convention were operative, then his refraining from counter-population strategies here would be related to this enemy's similar restraint, and indeed it would be related to the strategies which would be used in future wars. These larger considerations might well tip the balance in the other direction. But by hypothesis we are considering the case in which there is no such convention, and so these larger considerations do not arise. One acts unilaterally. In such a situation it certainly appears that one would have chosen the worse of the two alternatives. It is hard to suppose that one is morally obligated to do so.

I said above that we were ignoring for the moment one relevant consideration. It would not be ignored forever. I have already called attention to the fact that conventions of warfare are not, like traffic rules, embedded in a more massive social structure. This makes them especially precarious, as we have noted. But it also bears on the way in which they may be adopted. One such way, perhaps a rather important way, is for one party to the hostilities to signal his willingness to abide by such a convention by undertaking some unilateral restraint on his own part. If the opponent does not reciprocate, then the offer has failed and it goes no further. If the opponent does reciprocate, however, then the area of restraint may be broadened, and a kind of mutual respect and confidence may grow up between the belligerents. Each comes to rely on the other to keep the (perhaps unspoken) agreement, and therefore each is willing to forgo the immediate advantage which might accrue to him from breaking it. If this happens, then a new convention has begun its precarious life. This may be an event well worth seeking.

Not only may it be worth seeking, it may be worth paying something for it. For a significant increase in the likelihood that a worthwhile convention will be adopted it may be worth accepting an increased risk or a higher immediate cost in lives and suffering. So there may be some justification in unilateral restraint after all, even in the absence of a convention. But this justification is prospective and finite. It envisions the possibility that such a convention may arise in the future as a result of this restraint. Consequently, the justification should be proportioned to some judgment as to the likelihood of that event, and it should be reevaluated as future events unfold.

III. CONVENTION VS. MORALITY

I began by examining some attempts to defend a certain alleged moral rule of war, the immunity of noncombatants. These defenses have in common the fact that they construe this moral rule as independent of any human law, custom, etc. I then argued that these defenses fail because they leave a certain distinction without moral support, and yet the distinction is essential to the rule. Turning then to the task of construction rather than criticism, I suggested that the immunity of noncombatants is not an independent moral rule but rather a part of a convention which sets up a morally desirable alternative to war. I argued then that some conventions, including this one, generate special moral obligations which cannot be satisfactorily explained and defended without reference to the convention. And in the final pages I explored some of the special features of the obligation at hand and of the arguments which are relevant to it.

The distinction I have drawn is that between warfare per se on the one hand, and, on the other hand, international combats which are limited by convention and custom. But the point of the distinction is to clarify our thinking about the *morality* of such wars and combats. That is where its value must be tested.

MISSILES AND MORALS: A UTILITARIAN LOOK AT NUCLEAR DETERRENCE

DOUGLAS P. LACKEY

Though American foreign policy since 1945 has oscillated between conciliation and confrontation, American military policy at the strategic level has remained firmly tied to the notion of nuclear deterrence. After Hiroshima and Nagasaki, it was apparent that the effects of nuclear weapons were so terrible that their future use could never be condoned. But the threat to use nuclear weapons need not require their use, and such threats, in themselves,

Reprinted from *Philosophy & Public Affairs*, Vol. 11, No. 3 (1982) 189–231, with permission of the author and the publisher, Princeton University Press. (Only Parts I–VI of the original article are included.)

might prevent great evils. For those worried about Soviet expansion, a credible threat to use nuclear weapons might hold Soviet power in check. For those worried about future nuclear wars, the threat to use the bomb in retaliation might prevent nuclear wars from beginning. For an American public eager for demobilization, nuclear threats provided an appealing substitute for foot soldiering on foreign soil.[1] The stance of deterrence, of threat without use, appeared to both liberals and conservatives to command an overwhelming moral and prudential case. Small wonder, then, that after several abortive, perhaps deliberately abortive,[2] attempts at the internationalization of atomic weapons, the United States opted for unilateral development of nuclear weapons and delivery systems. Whatever residual qualms policy makers felt about the possession of nuclear arms were effectively silenced by the explosion of the first Soviet bomb in 1949. That the Soviets should possess nuclear weapons when the United States did not was politically unthinkable. Thirty-two years and ten thousand American nuclear weapons later, it still is.

Nevertheless it was arguable almost from the first that the case for deterrence was weaker than it seemed. The effectiveness of nuclear threats as a deterrent to Soviet aggression or Communist expansion was and remains barely credible. If the threat to use nuclear weapons did not prevent the subversion of Czechoslovakia, the blockade of Berlin, the collapse of Chiang Kai-shek, the fall of Dienbienphu, or the invasion of Hungary, all of which occurred before the Soviet Union could effectively deter an American nuclear strike with nuclear weapons and missiles of its own, how much less effective must nuclear threats have been towards deterring the Soviet invasion of Czechoslovakia in 1968 and the invasion of Afghanistan in 1979, and how little effect could such threats have as a deterrent to the much discussed but little expected invasion of West Germany by forces of the Warsaw pact?[3]

---

[1] In the sequence of these things, the idea of nuclear threats as a deterrent to nuclear war seems, oddly, to have come first. As early as 1946, Bernard Brodie wrote:

> The first and most vital step in any American security program for the age of atomic bombs is to take measures to guarantee to ourselves in case of attack the possibility of retaliation in kind. The writer in making this statement is not for the moment concerned about who will win the next war in which atomic bombs have been used. Thus far the chief purpose of our military establishment has been to win wars. From now on its chief purpose must be to avert them. It can have almost no other useful purpose (Bernard Brodie, ed., *The Absolute Weapon* [New York: Harcourt Brace, 1945], p. 76).

But the idea of nuclear retaliation as a deterrent to nonnuclear aggression followed soon after, and to this date the United States has persistently and repeatedly refused to announce a policy of "no first use."

[2] The case that the 1946 Baruch Plan for the internationalization of atomic weapons was deliberately designed to be nonnegotiable is persuasively made by Gregg Herken, *The Winning Weapon: The Atomic Bomb in the Cold War* (New York: Knopf, 1980). According to Herken the earlier Acheson-Lillienthal plan might have been negotiable.

[3] Nigel Calder in *Nuclear Nightmares: An Investigation into Possible Wars* (New York: Viking, 1980), p. 42 notes that the NATO concept of deterring a Warsaw pact invasion of West Germany with NATO nuclear retaliation assumes that NATO will not be deterred from this nuclear first strike by the thought of a massive Soviet second strike in return. Calder correctly observes that this is odd thinking, since the possibility of an American second strike is supposed to be the

Since there have been no uses of nuclear weapons in war since 1945, the case for nuclear threats as a deterrent to first uses of nuclear weapons seems a bit stronger. Nevertheless the role that nuclear deterrence has played in keeping the world free of nuclear war is a matter for debate. In the case of wars in progress, nuclear weapons have not been introduced in many cases because they cannot be effectively deployed relative to overall military objectives. The Israelis cannot use nuclear weapons on the Golan for fear of polluting the Kennerit; the Iraquis could not use them against Jerusalem without destroying the mosques they seek to liberate. The United States could not use nuclear weapons in South Vietnam without contaminating the countryside of our own allies; the Soviets could not use them against Prague and Budapest without destroying the industries they seek to exploit. As for the prevention through deterrence of large-scale nuclear war, it can be argued that every decrease in the chance of a nuclear first strike that results from fear of a retaliatory second strike is matched by an increase in the chance of a nuclear first strike that results from accident or mistake, human or mechanical failure; that every decrease in the chance that innocent millions will die from an undeterred first strike is matched by an increase in the chance that innocent millions will die from a nuclear second strike that cannot be stopped after initial deterrence has failed. To these dangers we should add the consideration that the American argument, "the United States must have the bomb if the Soviet Union has one," is replicable by every nation state, producing pressure for proliferation which in turn increases the chance of war, and the consideration that no degree of threat can deter a nuclear terrorist who prefers to be dead rather than blue, or red, or green, and who had built his bomb with the help of weapons technology developed by states that are sworn "to deterrence only." There is little, at least in a preliminary survey of the evidence, that supports the idea that the construction of nuclear weapons for the purpose of issuing nuclear threats has contributed to the prevention of nuclear wars since 1945, or will contribute towards preventing them in the future. Whatever the game theorists say, the common sense view that you cannot prevent wars by building bombs still has some weight.

The argument that nuclear deterrence can replace the war of soldiers on the ground with a war of threats in the air has also seen hard sledding since 1945. The need for retaining conventional forces has been apparent since the Berlin blockade, and the effect that reliance on nuclear deterrence has had on the quality of conventional forces is by now well known. It is no accident that the last successful American military operation (Inchon) precedes the

---

threat which deters a Soviet first strike. Apparently the tacticians believe that the thought of destruction of Russian cities will deter the Soviets in a way that the thought of the destruction of American cities will not deter NATO. Since this belief is very probably false, we have a paradox: either nuclear deterrence will deter nonnuclear aggression but not nuclear aggression, or it will deter nuclear aggression but not nonnuclear aggression. Thus deterrence in the European theater cannot simultaneously do the two jobs for which it was originally designed: deterring Soviet aggression, and deterring nuclear war.

development of ICBMs, and the increasing ineptitude of American conventional forces exhibited in the successively botched Son Tay, Mayaguez, and Iranian rescue attempts is too obvious to bear comment. There is no necessary connection between nuclear strength and conventional weakness, but in a world of limited resources the development of strategic forces has twisted military budgets in favor of high technology, and the result has been complicated guns that won't shoot and complicated planes that can't fly.[4] The idea that the nation's "first line" of defense consists of radar towers and missiles rather than men on the battlefield must inevitably weaken the morale of the Army and the Marines. However plausible it may have seemed to John Foster Dulles, there is little support now for the view that nuclear threats can substitute in any way for the painful sacrifices of conventional war.

The moral and prudential case for deterrence seems overcome by events. But there is a rejoinder to these criticisms that many find decisive: deterrence is bad, but disarmament is worse. Elected officials remember well that the only Presidential candidate since 1945 with a kind word for nuclear disarmament was humiliated in 1972 and voted out of the Senate in 1980. Fortunately moral philosophers do not stand for election and are free to examine all the options regardless of practical constraints. This is what I propose to do, with the important limitation that the moral systems I shall bring to bear upon the subject are all utilitarian systems. In normal circumstances one may have one's doubts about utilitarianism, but if nuclear war is among the results of policies under consideration, the gravity of the consequences carries all else before.

I. FOUR DECISION RULES

The agreeable utilitarian idea that the moral worth of acts and policies is to be measured in the value of their consequences has been troubled from the beginning by the problem that the consequences of policies are often uncertain. Suppose that Policy 1 will produce either *A* or *B,* that Policy 2 will produce either *C* or *D,* and that by some accepted standard of value *A* is better than *C* but *B* is worse than *D.* The rule that the best policy is the one with the best consequences will not tell us which policy to choose, and there is no consensus among utilitarian theorists as to how the general rule should be modified in order to generate the morally right choice. Nevertheless there are many ingenious suggestions about how to deal with choice under uncertainty, and in this essay we will deploy four different principles of choice: Minimax, Dominance, Disaster Avoidance, and Expected Value Maximization. Each principle will be used twice over, first, for the utilitarian calculation, which we will call the moral calculation; second, for a prudential calculation,

---

[4] The gun is the M-16 and the plane is the F-111. For the tragic history of the M-16 see James Fallows, *National Defense* (New York: Random House, 1981), chap. 4.

which will indicate, from the standpoint of the United States, what the prudential course of action might be.

Each prudential and moral calculation requires a standard of value, and in the essay the usual standard of value will be the satisfaction of preferences. In the utilitarian calculation, we will consider outcome *A* to be better than outcome *B* if the vast majority of persons in this and in several future generations would prefer *A* to *B*. In the prudential calculation, we will consider outcome *A* to be better than outcome *B* if the vast majority of Americans in this and in several future generations would prefer *A* to *B*. Given the subject matter of nuclear war, for many problems value can be equated with human lives, and outcome *A* can be considered better than outcome *B* if fewer people are killed by war in *A* than are killed by war in *B*. But considering that at least some Americans are on record as preferring being dead to being red, and since many Americans (I think) would prefer a small chance of nuclear attack to a very large chance of Soviet world domination, the equation of value with human lives cannot always be relied upon, especially in the prudential calculation.

In all four models of choice we confine our inquiry to just two nations— the United States and the Soviet Union. These are the primary protagonists in the nuclear drama, and we will argue in a later section that conclusions reached about the bilateral case can also be applied straightforwardly to the multilateral case. Furthermore, we will apply our four models of choice to just three strategies, *Superiority, Equivalence,* and *Nuclear Disarmament.* Though there are many strategies for nuclear armament, these three have been at the center of the strategic debate at least since the late 1950s:

S: Maintain second strike capacity; seek first strike capacity; threaten first and second strikes ("Superiority").

E: Maintain second strike capacity; do not seek first strike capacity; threaten second strikes only ("Equivalence").

ND: Do not seek to maintain second strike capacity ("Nuclear Disarmament").

In the statement of these strategies the terminology is standard: Nation *A* is presumed to have *first-strike capacity* against *B* if *A* can launch a nuclear attack on *B* without fear of suffering unacceptable damage from *B*'s subsequent counterstrike; nation *A* is said to have *second-strike capacity* against *B* if *A* is capable of inflicting unacceptable damage on *B* after having suffered a nuclear first strike by *B*.

Strategy *S* has been the favored strategy of hard-line anticommunists ever since the early 1950s. In its original form, as we find it in John Foster Dulles, the Superiority Strategy called for threats of American first strikes against Russian cities in retaliation for what American policy defined as Soviet acts of aggression. In its present form, as it is developed by Paul Nitze, Colin Gray, and others, the Superiority Strategy calls for threats, or implied threats, of American first strikes against Soviet military forces, combined with large-scale increases in American strategic arms.[5]

The Superiority Strategy, however, is not the exclusive property of doctrinaire anticommunists or hard-line "forward" strategists. Since aiming one's missiles at enemy missiles implies a desire to destroy those missiles before they are launched, that is, a desire to launch a first strike, all retargeting of American missiles from Soviet cities to Soviet missiles, up to and including President Carter's Directive 59 in the summer of 1980, imply partial endorsement of Strategy S.[6] Such "counterforce" as opposed to "countervalue" targetings are entailed by Strategy *S* even if they do not in fact bring first strike capacity; Strategy *S* as defined implies that the United States will *seek* first strike capacity, not that it will in fact obtain it. Strategy *S* advocates steps which will produce first strike capacity unless new countermeasures are developed by the Soviet Union to cancel them out.

Strategy *E,* the "equivalence" strategy, enshrines Robert McNamara's doctrine of Assured Destruction, and includes both massive retaliations against massive strikes and flexible responses against lesser strikes.[7] The possibility and permanence of Strategy *E* seemed assured by SALT I in 1972, since negotiated restrictions on the deployment of antiballistic missiles seemed to guarantee permanent second-strike capacity to both sides. Unfortunately, SALT I did not limit the development and deployment of MIRVs (multiple independently targeted reentry vehicles), and the deployment of MIRVs through the 1970s has led to cries on both sides that mutual second-strike capacity is dissolving and mutual first-strike capacity is emerging.[8]

Notice that although Strategy *E* permits bilateral arms control, it actually

[5] On "massive retaliation" see John Foster Dulles, Dept. of State Bulletin, 30, 791, 25 Jan. 1954. For Superiority policy in the 1960s see, for example, Barry Goldwater, *Why Not Victory?* (New York: McGraw-Hill, 1962), p. 162:

We must stop lying to ourselves and our friends about disarmament. We must stop advancing the cause of the Soviet Union by playing along with Communist inspired deception.

"Disarmament," for Goldwater, includes arms control, since he warns against the danger of "disarmament, or arms control, as the 87th Congress cutely puts it" (p. 99). For a recent interpretation of Superiority see Colin Gray and Keith Payne, "Victory Is Possible," *Foreign Policy,* 39 (Summer 1980), 14–27, and Colin Gray, "Nuclear Strategy: The Case for a Theory of Victory, *International Security,* 4 (Summer 1979), 54–87.

[6] The uproar caused by the announcement of Directive 59 on 25 July 1980 prompted administration defenders to make the discomfiting revelation that counterforce retargetings are regarded by the Defense Department as matters of course. See for example, Walter Slocombe, "The Countervailing Strategy," *International Security,* 5, no. 4 (Spring 1981).

[7] Robert McNamara, *The Essence of Security* (London: Hodder and Stoughton, 1968).

[8] The much discussed Soviet threat to American land-based missiles does not imply Soviet progress towards a first strike, given the invulnerability of American nuclear submarines. But the development of the American MIRV, combined with the vulnerability of Soviet missile submarines, most of which remain in port and all of which, apparently, can be tracked by American antisubmarine forces, *does* imply the development of *American* first-strike capacity. Under current conditions my estimate is that the United States can pursue strategy *E* only by abandoning some fraction of its antisubmarine surveillance. For a recent study of vulnerability of land-based missiles see Eliot Marshall, "A Question of Accuracy," *Science,* 11 (September 1982), 1230–31.

prohibits substantial reductions in nuclear arms. The delicate balance of mutual second-strike capacity becomes increasingly unstable as arms levels are lowered, and sooner or later, mutual disarmament brings a loss of second-strike capacity on one side and the emergence of first-strike capacity on the other, contrary to *E*.

Strategy *ND* calls for a unilateral halt in the development of American nuclear weapons and delivery systems, even if such a halt eventuates in Soviet first strike capacity. Strategy *ND* is a policy of *nuclear* disarmament; it does *not* call for the abandonment of conventional weapons and should not be equated with pacifism or confused with general and complete disarmament. In fact, increases in conventional weapons levels are compatible with Strategy *ND*.

II. MINIMAX

Considering the hundreds of billions of dollars the United States has spent on strategic weapons since 1945, it is remarkable how little anyone knows about what would happen should these weapons be used. In an unsettling account of the present state of national defense James Fallows writes:

> There has never been a nuclear war, and nobody knows what a nuclear war would mean. . . . No one knows how these weapons would perform if they were fired; whether they would hit the targets at which they are aimed; whether human society would be set back for decades, centuries as a result. . . . Most strategic arguments (are) disputes of faith rather than fact.[9]

Fallows's gloomy judgment is confirmed by a report presented to Congress in 1979 by the Office of Technology Assessment:

> The effects of nuclear war that cannot be calculated are at least as important as those for which calculations are attempted. Moreover even these very limited calculations are subject to large uncertainties . . . This is particularly true for indirect effects such as deaths resulting from injuries and the unavailability of medical care, or for economic damage resulting from disruptions and disorganization rather than direct disruption.[10]

Fallows and the OTA do not exaggerate. To date no Minuteman missile has been test-fired from an operational silo; no American ICBM has been properly tested on a North-South trajectory, and missile accuracy reports are a guessing game subject to vagaries of wind, gravitational anomaly, and fratricidal interference from other "friendly" missiles. On top of all this, the entire defense communications network and all electronic guidance systems

---

[9] Fallows, *National Defense,* pp. 139–40.
[10] "The Effects of Nuclear War," U.S. Congress, Office of Technology Assessment, 1979, p. 3.

may be disrupted by the electromagnetic pulses that emanate from thermonuclear blasts.[11]

Anyone who accepts such estimates of the depth of our ignorance about nuclear war will be encouraged to use a principle of choice that does not require knowledge of the probabilities that a given nuclear policy will produce a given result. Of such principles, perhaps the most widely used in both prudential and moral calculation is the Minimax Principle:

> Choose any policy the worst outcome of which is at least as good as the worst outcome of any other policy.

Let us do the Minimax moral calculation first. The worst outcome of both the Superiority Strategy and the Equivalence Strategy is a large scale thermonuclear exchange in which both sides launch as many of their missiles as possible. The worst outcome of the Nuclear Disarmament Strategy is a unilateral nuclear strike on the United States by the Soviet Union followed by whatever increases in Soviet power such a strike might bring. (I list a unilateral Soviet nuclear attack as an outcome of *ND* not because *ND* makes such attacks likely but because they are physically possible given *ND*. Minimax pays no heed to probabilities.) Since the vast majority of persons (especially Russian persons) in this and several future generations would prefer a one-sided attack on the United States to all-out nuclear war between the United States and the Soviet Union, the utilitarian Minimax Principle declares that the morally right policy is Nuclear Disarmament.

The prudential calculation is not so straightforward. Americans as a group will agree with people at large as to the worst outcome associated with each policy. But it is not so clear that Americans will agree that an outcome in which the Soviet Union attacks an unresponding United States is preferable to an outcome in which the Soviet Union attacks and the United States responds. A reasonable survey of prevailing American sentiments would probably report (a) that a substantial number of Americans would prefer one-sided destruction to two-sided destruction, even if the destroyed side happens to be the American side, on grounds that more lives are saved if only one side is destroyed, and (b) that a substantial number of Americans would prefer two-sided destruction to one-sided destruction, on the grounds that if the Soviet Union attacks the United States, the Soviet Union deserves to be punished. If these are the genuine American preferences, the Minimax Principle yields no verdict in the prudential case. For the record, we might also note that Minimax reasoning fails to distinguish, either morally or prudentially, between the Equivalence Strategy and the Superiority Strategy, since the same disaster is the worst outcome in either case.

---

[11] On the electromagnetic pulse or EMP, see Janet Raloff, "EMP: A Sleeping Dragon," *Science News,* 9 May 1981, pp. 300–302, and 16 May 1981, pp. 314–15.

III. DOMINANCE

Like Minimax, Dominance is a principle of choice under uncertainty which makes no reference to probabilities of outcomes:

> Choose a policy (if any) yielding results which cannot be improved, no matter what the opposition or nature may choose to do.

Obviously such policies are rarely found, but many writers feel that such a dominant strategy is available in the arena of nuclear choice. For simplicity, let us consider only the Equivalence Strategy and the Nuclear Disarmament Strategy, and let us assume that the only variable in the development is the Soviet choice between E and ND. Since each side has two options, there are four outcomes:

1. The United States arms; the Soviet Union disarms;
2. The United States and the Soviet Union both disarm;
3. The United States and the Soviet Union both arm; and
4. The United States disarms; the Soviet Union arms.

If we suppose (as most students of strategy do) that the vast majority of American people prefer these outcomes in the order in which they are presented, then prudentially the United States should remain armed, no matter what the Soviet Union does.[12] By the Dominance Principle, then, the United States should stick with Equivalence.

Since these ratings are made from the national point of view, the conclusion thus far is strictly prudential. The moral argument yields surprisingly different results. Presumably a large majority of people in the world prefer 2 to 1, that is, they prefer neither side having nuclear arms to one side having them. This suffices to show that Equivalence does not dominate from the moral point of view. Furthermore, if we assume that a large majority of people in the world, fearful of all-out nuclear war, prefer that the United States practice ND even if the Soviet Union does not, it is Nuclear Disarmament that dominates from the moral point of view.

We have the consistent but disagreeable result that, if we follow Dominance, prudence dictates one policy while morality dictates another. We could challenge this conclusion by making different assessments of preferences. But there are other grounds which might lead us to conclude that the real problem here is not the assessment of preferences but the Dominance Principle itself.

---

[12] Technically, it might be possible to develop a prudential case for nuclear disarmament as follows: (a) take all alleged preferences for two-sided destruction, (b) subtract from these all preferences based on the idea that a second strike against Russia is needed to deter their first strike; this idea is illicit since the preference poll in all cases assumes that the first strike has already occurred, and (c) subtract all preferences based on considerations of retributive justice on the grounds that these are political preferences rather than personal evaluations of the utility present in the situations judged. (For the distinction between political preferences and personal preferences see Ronald Dworkin, "What is Equality? Part 1: Equality of Welfare," *Philosophy & Public Affairs*, 10, no. 3 [Summer 1981], 197–98.) The residue of support for nuclear retaliation might be small enough for us to judge that the American people prudentially prefer disarmament.

IV. CONCEPTUAL PROBLEMS

Both the Minimax and the Dominance Principles are examples of game-theoretical strategic principles that treat each outcome as the result of equally permissible and equally possible moves in a gamelike situation. Rapoport, Green, and others in the past have criticized certain aspects of the game-theoretical approach;[13] its tendency, for example, to treat situations of nuclear strategy as zero sum games in which cooperation is impossible, rather than as constant sum games in which it can be prudent to cooperate. But the game-theoretical approach is inadequate in a way that cannot be remedied by shifting to broader principles and a wider range of games. In the standard logic of games each alternative is taken as given, and there is no room for calculating how the threat to make one move will influence the chance that another move is made, a consideration which is at the heart of the argument for deterrence. Consider the following argument, which proceeds on the basis of fixed alternatives: "The logical possibilities are that either the Soviets will attack or they will not attack. If they attack, there is no point in threatening to counterattack, since the whole point of the threat was to prevent the attack. If they do not attack, there is no point in threatening to counterattack, since there is no initial attack for the threat to deter: we conclude, therefore, nuclear threats are futile, or they are otiose." The notion that threats might diminish the chance of attack goes by the board. Perhaps we should dispense with deterrence, but the argument for dispensing with it cannot be this easy!

Even worse difficulties can be generated by combining information about outcomes with the dominance principle. Suppose that Americans prefer outcomes 1 through 4 as stated in the previous Section, and suppose that it is given information that (a) whenever the United States arms, the Soviet Union will arm, and that (b) whenever the United States disarms, the Soviet Union will disarm. Since Americans prefer mutual disarmament to mutual armament, the preferred strategy in the light of the given information is for the United States to disarm. But game-theoretical reasoning still insists that the preferred strategy is to remain armed. Even if the Soviets will disarm when the United States disarms, it remains true that they will either arm or disarm. If they arm, it is better for the United States to arm. If they disarm, it is better for the United States to arm. Therefore the United States should arm in any event. The result will be mutual armament, a situation worse than that which could confidently be achieved by the choice of disarmament. It is not possible here to review all the systems devised in recent years by game theorists attempting to cope with this problem. Suffice it to say that there is a consensus that something must be done but no consensus about what to

---

[13] For criticisms of the zero-sum approach to nuclear strategy see Anatol Rapoport, *Strategy and Conscience* (New York: Harper & Row, 1984); and Philip Green, *Deadly Logic* (Columbus: Ohio State University Press, 1966).

do, and the state of the field is sufficiently unsettled to warrant serious investigation of more information-sensitive decision principles.[14]

V. DISASTER AVOIDANCE

Let us suppose that one type of information that we *do* have about nuclear war is information pertaining to the ordering of the probabilities of the various outcomes. For example, most people would agree that the chance of nuclear war on the Superiority Strategy is greater than the chance of war on the Equivalence Strategy, though what quantitative probabilities are, in either case, is difficult to say. If this type of information is all the information we have, and if there are outcomes of parties identify as disastrous, the rational course of action. Gregory Kavka suggests, is dictated by what he calls the Disaster Avoidance Principle:

> When choosing between potential disasters under two dimensional uncertainty, it is rational to select the alternative that minimizes the probability of disaster occurrence.[15]

Kavka does not advance the Avoidance Principle as a solution for all problems of two dimensional uncertainty, but he recommends its use in situations in which nine special conditions are satisfied. Use of the Avoidance Principle is rational if and only if: (i) quantitative probabilities and utilities are unknown; (ii) conditional probabilities are known; (iii) all disastrous outcomes are extremely unacceptable; (iv) all disastrous outcomes are roughly the same order

---

[14] For approaches which attempt to break out of the static analyses which have prevailed since von Neumann and Morgenstern see Nigel Howard, *Paradoxes of Rationality* (Cambridge, Mass.: The MIT Press, 1971); Michael Taylor, *Anarchism and Cooperation* (New York: John Wiley & Sons, 1976); and Steven Brams and Donald Wittman, "Nonmyopic Equilibria in a 2×2 Games" (forthcoming). Howard, Taylor, and Brams and Wittman all note that the prudential argument for armament presented here for the United States will lead Soviet strategists to the same result, and thus individual prudence produces a collective result (mutual armament), which is less liked by each side than mutual disarmament. In sum, all these authors assume that nuclear arms races are Prisoners' Dilemmas. Howard's theory of metagames, Taylor's theory of supergames, and the Brams/Wittman theory of moves all try to show that a proper theory of games will establish that the mutually preferred solution is an equilibrium from which prudent players will not depart. I find it impossible to connect Howard's metagame equilibria with the psychology of the players; see, *contra* Howard John Harsanyi, "Communication," *American Political Science Review,* 68 (1974), 729–31, 1692–95. Taylor's supergame equilibria require repeated plays of the game, and for obvious reasons repeated plays of games involving nuclear war have little relation to reality. Furthermore, Taylor's equilibria require low discount rates, and in most thought about nuclear war, long run payoffs are highly discounted in favor of such short run results as political intimidation or war prevention. Bram's theory of moves is not affected by discount rates, but it provides no clue as to how to move to the cooperative solution when history has trapped players in a noncooperative equilibrium. A far better approach to escaping the Prisoners' Dilemma is to never enter it, and I have suggested ("Ethics and Nuclear Deterrence," in *Moral Problems,* 2d ed., ed. James Rachels [New York: Harper & Row, 1975], pp. 332–45) that nuclear arms races in particular are not Prisoners' Dilemmas if the payoffs are properly evaluated.

[15] Gregory Kavka, "Deterrence, Utility, and Rational Choice," *Theory and Decision,* 12 (1980), 50.

of magnitude; (v) the chooser regards the difference in utility between non-disastrous outcomes to be small compared to the difference between disastrous outcomes and nondisastrous outcomes; (vi) the choice is unique, that is, not one of a series of choices; (vii) the probabilities of the disasters are not thought to be insignificant; (viii) the probability of the greater disaster is not thought to be very large; and (ix) the probabilities of the disasters are not thought to be very close to equal.

Kavka argues that all nine of these conditions are satisfied by the problem of nuclear choice, and proceeds to apply the Disaster Avoidance Principle to the choice between Equivalence and Nuclear Disarmament. (He does not consider the Superiority Strategy.) Arguing that:

> We can be confident that the likelihood of Soviet domination if the U.S. disarms is greater than the likelihood of war if the U.S. practices deterrence,[16]

he concludes that the rational choice is the Equivalence Strategy. Since there is no place in the calculations for differences between the preferences of Americans and the preferences of all people, it follows from Kavka's reasoning that the Equivalence Strategy is the morally preferred choice—at least for utilitarians.

This is not the place for full theoretical analysis of Kavka's Avoidance Principle, which supplies a principle of rational choice to problems beset by what Daniel Ellsberg called "ambiguity," as opposed to "risk."[17] For our purposes, let us agree that the principle *does* represent a principle of rational choice *if* all nine of Kavka's qualifying conditions are satisfied. What is more at issue is whether the conditions are in fact satisfied in the case of nuclear choice and whether the principle has been properly applied to this particular problem.

Kavka's fourth condition is that "disastrous outcomes must be roughly of the same order of magnitude." Obviously if one outcome is hundreds of times more disastrous than the other, and the probabilities of the disasters are not known, minimax reasoning should prevail. Kavka argues that the disaster which might be produced by the Equivalence Strategy is nuclear war, and the disaster which might be produced by nuclear disarmament is Soviet domination. For Kavka these are disasters "roughly equal in magnitude," which shows that, for Kavka, "roughly equal" is very rough indeed. But it would be useless to belabor the comparison of nuclear war with Soviet domination, since in fact the comparison is irrelevant. The main catastrophe of the Equivalence Strategy is *all-out* nuclear war; the main catastrophe of Nuclear Disarmament is a *one-sided* nuclear war. Are *these* disasters roughly equal in magnitude?

Clearly a two-sided nuclear war would be rated by everyone as a "great disaster" and a one-sided nuclear war would be rated by everyone as a "great

---

[16] Ibid., p. 51.
[17] Daniel Ellsberg, "Risk Ambiguity, and the Savage Axioms," *Quarterly Journal of Economics,* 75 (1961), 643–69.

disaster." This might tempt us to conclude that these are disasters roughly equal in magnitude. Indeed, most people are not capable of discriminating finely between nuclear wars, a psychological fact that advocates of limited nuclear war are given to deplore. But let us suppose that 20,000,000 Americans will die in a one-sided nuclear war and that 60,000,000 Americans and 60,000,000 Russians will die in a two-sided nuclear war, figures which are not unreasonable and which reflect the fact that a Soviet first strike would be relatively smaller against an America practicing nuclear disarmament. If we shake the Strangelovian dizziness out of our heads, we can make a serious attempt to compare the magnitude of 20,000,000 deaths and 120,000,000 deaths. If we take the comparison to be *six to one,* we might agree with Kavka that the two disasters are "roughly equal in magnitude." But this is obviously not the proper way to make the comparison. We must ask whether X and Y should be rated roughly equal in magnitude given that X and Y are quite the same *except* that in Y there are 100,000,000 more deaths than in X. Certainly 100,000,000 dead as opposed to no dead at all is a matter of very great magnitude, and thus Kavka's assumption that there is no difference between the magnitude of the disaster produced by deterrence and the magnitude of the disaster produced by disarmament is false—even if it makes the disaster produced by disarmament much *greater* than he assumes it to be.

Even more disturbing than Kavka's claim that his nine conditions are satisfied is his final deduction of the result that disarmament is irrational. The major premise of this argument is the Avoidance Principle; the minor premise—a crucial step in the deduction—is the claim that the likelihood of disaster under disarmament is greater than the likelihood of disaster under deterrence. This empirical claim is presented as a proposition of which "we can be confident," but I feel no confidence whatsoever about it, and it is asserted without argument or evidence.[18] Not a single author who has discussed nuclear deterrence feels that the risk of nuclear war resulting from the practice of deterrence is negligible, and there are many—the whole staff of the *Bulletin of Atomic Scientists,* for example—who consider it to be substantial. In discussion of nuclear disarmament, there are many who feel that the Soviet Union might *attempt* nuclear blackmail if it gained first-strike capacity, but there are not many who are sure that such attempts at blackmail would succeed. The sole evidence which history provides on this subject is the sobering fact that the period of nuclear supremacy for the United States

---

[18] Kavka, "Deterrence," p. 45, writes, "This appears to be the way things stand with respect to expert opinion, as seen from the point of view of the United States. (See, e.g., Levine 1963, Herzog 1965, and Van Cleave 1973)." Unpaginated footnotes are a curse, and I cannot find passages in the books cited that defend Kavka's case. Levine and Herzog, throughout, seem to be leaning to the opposite view. Van Cleave is summarizing and takes no stand of his own. See Arthur Herzog, *The War-Peace Establishment* (New York: Harper & Row, 1965); Arthur Levine, *The Arms Debate* (Cambridge, Mass.: Harvard University Press, 1963); and Van Cleave's chapter in *American Defense Policy,* 3rd ed., ed. Richard Head and Ervin Bakke (Baltimore, MD: Johns Hopkins University Press, 1973).

was precisely the period of greatest communist expansion in the world (1945–49). One can only speculate that Kavka, like many authors who dismiss nuclear disarmament as unwise and impractical, has blurred together the effects of *nuclear* disarmament and the effects of *general and complete* disarmament.[19] As a result, he has illicitly upgraded the chance of Soviet domination resulting from the strategy of *nuclear* disarmament and begs the question in favor of Equivalence.

VI. EXPECTED VALUE

Perhaps the most natural of all responses to the problem of uncertainty is to discount the weight of consequences by whatever chance there is that they will not occur. To compute the "expected value" of a policy, then, we should consider each possible outcome of the policy, multiply the utility of that outcome by the probability that it will occur, and take the sum of all these products. In the area of nuclear strategy we cannot supply precise numbers for the probabilities of the outcomes, nor can we attempt to supply precise figures for the corresponding utilities. Nevertheless, we *do* have much more information about these subjects than the orderings of probabilities to which we were restricted in the Disaster Avoidance model, and what imprecision there is in our information can be respected by stating the information in the form of approximations. For example, we can classify the probability of outcomes as "negligible," "small but substantial," "fifty-fifty," "very likely," and "almost certain," and we can classify outcomes as "extremely bad," "bad," "neutral," and so forth. In considering the products of utilities and outcomes, we can neglect all outcomes of negligible probability, and all outcomes of small but substantial probability *except* those classified as extremely good or extremely bad. In many cases, use of such estimates will yield surprisingly definite results.

Now, what are the "outcomes" the probabilities of which we ought to consider? Given the traditionally assumed goals of deterrence, we should certainly consider the effects of each policy on the probability of nuclear war, the probability of Soviet nonnuclear aggression, and the probability of Soviet nuclear blackmail. As we have noted, in considering the probability of nuclear war, it is essential to distinguish the probability of a one-sided nuclear strike from the probability of all-out nuclear war. Among other outcomes, we will consider only the effects of nuclear strategies on military spending, since the impact of policies on spending can be determined with little controversy. Since we have four outcomes and three policies to consider, the probabilities can be represented on a three-by-four grid (see Table 1). Each probability assessment will be defended in turn.

---

[19] The speculation that Kavka has confused nuclear with general and complete disarmament is not idle. On page 44 he writes of "unilateral nuclear disarmament," but on pages 45 and 51, in the thick of the argument, he speaks only of "unilateral disarmament."

Table 1

	One-sided Strike *	All-out Nuclear War	Soviet Aggression	Very High Military Spending
Superiority	Fifty-fifty [a]	Fifty-fifty [b]	Small [c]	Certain [d]
Equivalence	Small [e]	Small [f]	Small [g]	Fifty-fifty [b]
Nuclear Disarmament	Small [i]	Zero [j]	Small [k]	Small [l]

* A "one-sided strike" is a first strike that may or may not be answered by a second strike. A comparison of the probability of one-sided strikes and two-sided strikes in a given row indicates that a first strike will lead to an all-out nuclear war.

Value of the Superiority Strategy

[a] Strategists disagree about the probability of Soviet or American first strike under the Superiority Strategy. All students of the subject rate it as having at least a small but substantial probability. I believe that it is more reasonable to rate the probability as fifty-fifty within a time frame of about fifty years, since (1) every real or presumed step towards first strike capacity by either side raises the chance of a preemptive first strike by the side falling behind; (2) the concentration on technological development prompted by the Superiority Strategy raises that chance of a technological breakthrough that might destabilize the balance of power; (3) the increasing technological complexity of weapons required by the Superiority Strategy raises the chance of a first strike as a result of accident or mistake; (4) the constant changes of weaponry required by the Superiority Strategy creates pressure for proliferation, either because obsolete weapons are constantly disposed of on the international arms market or because wealthy developing countries, dazzled by new weapons, make buys to keep up with appearances.

[b] Under Superiority, the chance of an American second strike—given a Soviet first strike—is practically the same as the chance of a Soviet first strike. Though it is always possible that the President or his survivor will not respond to a Soviet first strike, the military and technological systems installed under the Superiority Strategy are geared for belligerence. Accordingly the chance of an American failure to respond is negligible.

[c] Even in the face of the Superiority Strategy, the chance of Soviet nonnuclear aggression (an invasion of West Germany or Iran, for example) must be rated as small but not negligible. The prospect of an American first strike in response to a Soviet conventional attack may not be taken seriously by the Soviets, especially if Soviet military personnel think that they can deter any American first strike with the prospect of a massive Soviet second strike.

[d] The sums of money required to sustain the Superiority Strategy are

staggering. The Reagan administration's rejection of SALT and its apparent acceptance of the Superiority Strategy will produce an increase in the fraction of the American gross national product devoted to defense from five to six and one-half percent: an increase of over $150 billion per year over the Carter projections, which were largely keyed to the Equivalence Strategy.

Value of the Equivalence Strategy

[e] Most students of strategy agree that the chance of an American or Soviet first strike under the Equivalence Strategy is small but substantial. The peculiar pressures for a first strike listed under the Superiority Strategy are absent, but there is still the chance of a first strike through accident, mistake, human folly, or a suicidal leadership.

[f] Since the chance of a first strike is less under Equivalence than under Superiority, there is less chance of an all-out nuclear war under Equivalence than under Superiority. The chance of a first strike under Equivalence is small, and the chance of all-out war following a first strike is smaller still. Since the primary aim of the Equivalence Strategy is not to "defeat" the Soviet Union or to develop a first-strike capacity, but to deter a Soviet first strike, it may be obvious to the President or his survivor that once a Soviet first strike is actually launched, there is no point whatsoever in proceeding with an American second strike. If the chance that the President will fail to respond is substantial, the chance of an all-out war under Equivalence is considerably less than the chance of a first strike under Equivalence.[20] On the other hand, the credibility of the American deterrent to a first strike depends on the perception by Soviet planners that an American second strike is inevitable once a Soviet first strike is launched, and the President and his defense strategists may decide that the only convincing way to create this perception is to make the American second strike a *semi-automatic* response. Thus it might be difficult to stop an American second strike even if the

---

[20] The thought that an American President may lack the nerve to destroy civilization depresses the military mind. In stating the requirements of deterrence, General Maxwell Taylor writes, "So understood, deterrence depends essentially on an assured destruction capability, a strong communications net, and a strong President unlikely to flinch from his responsibility. . . . Such reflections emphasize the importance of the character and will of the President as a factor adding to the deterrent effect of our weapons. Since the attitude of the President will be strongly influenced by that of the people whom he represents, national character also participates in the effectiveness and stability of deterrence. . . . In addition to the moral [sic] qualities of the President and the nation there are a number of other factors which may stabilize or undermine deterrence" (Maxwell Taylor, *Precarious Security* [New York: W. W. Norton, 1976], pp. 68–69). On the other hand, some military figures, at least in their public statements, are entirely confident that the President will respond and launch the second strike. General George Seignious, former director of the joint staff of the Joint Chiefs of Staff, testified in 1979, "I find such a surrender scenario irresponsible—for it sends the wrong message to the Soviets. We have not built and maintained our strategic forces—at the cost of billions—in order to weaken their deterrent impact by telling the Russians and the world that we would back down—when, in fact, we would not" (quoted in Herbert Scoville, *MX: Prescription for Disaster* [Cambridge, Mass.: The MIT Press, 1981], p. 82).

President wished to forgo it. On balance, it seems reasonable to rate the chance of the second strike as greater than one-half the chance that the Soviet first strike will be launched. This would make the chance small but still substantial.

[g] Over the years two arguments have been proposed to show that Superiority provides a more effective deterrent against Soviet aggression than does Equivalence.

(1) The Superiority Strategy requires constant technological innovation, and technological innovation is an area in which the United States possesses a relative advantage. If the United States presses forward with strategic weapons development, the Soviet Union will be so exhausted from the strain of keeping up with the United States that it will have little money or energy left over for nonnuclear aggression. In the end, the strain such competition will exert on the Soviet economy might produce food riots like those in Poland in 1970, and might even bring down the Soviet socioeconomic system.

But since "the strain of keeping up" did not stop the Soviets from invading Hungary, Czechoslovakia, and Afghanistan, the level of expenditure needed to produce truly effective strain is unknown. Furthermore, the assumption of *relative* economic stress is undemonstrated: at least one economist who has seriously studied the subject has argued on various grounds that a unit of military spending by the United States disrupts the American economy far more than the equivalent military spending by the Soviet Union.[21]

(2) It is occasionally argued that the Soviets will take the possibility of an American second strike more seriously under the Superiority Strategy than under the Equivalence Strategy, since the Superiority Strategy gives the United States something closer to first-strike capacity and therefore something less to fear from a Soviet second strike.

But in the game of nuclear strategy one cannot "almost" have first strike capacity; one either has it or one doesn't. There is no reason to think that the Superiority Strategy will ever yield first-strike capacity, since the Soviet Union will feel forced to match the United States step for step. The Soviets know that the President will never be confident enough in American striking capacity to risk the survival of the United States on a nuclear response to Soviet nonnuclear aggression. Consequently, there is no reason to think that Superiority provides a better deterrent against Soviet aggression than does Equivalence. The chance of serious nonnuclear Soviet aggression under Equivalence is small.

[h] In the presence of serious efforts at arms control, expenditures for strategic weapons will be much less under Equivalence than under Superiority. If efforts at arms control fail, then expenditures will remain very high. The chance of very high expenditures under Equivalence would best be put at about fifty-fifty.

---

[21] See Seymour Melman, *Our Depleted Society* (New York: Holt, Rinehart & Winston, 1965), and *Pentagon Capitalism* (New York: McGraw-Hill, 1970).

Value of the Nuclear Disarmament Strategy

[i] Most strategists are agreed that the chance of a Soviet first strike under the Equivalence Strategy is small. I believe that the chance of a Soviet first strike is small even under the strategy of Nuclear Disarmament.

(1) Since under Nuclear Disarmament at most one side retains nuclear arms, the chance of nuclear war occurring by accident is reduced at least by one half, relative to the Equivalence Strategy. Since only half the technology is deployed, there is only half the chance of a mechanical malfunction leading to war.

(2) Since at most one side remains armed, there is considerably less chance under Nuclear Disarmament that a nuclear war will occur by mistake. The principal mistake that might cause a nuclear war is the mistake of erroneously thinking that the other side is about to launch a nuclear attack. Such mistakes create enormous pressure for the launching of preemptive strikes, in order to get one's weapons in the air before they are destroyed on the ground. There is no chance that this mistake can occur under Nuclear Disarmament. The side that remains armed (if any) need not fear that the other side will launch a nuclear attack. The side that chooses to disarm cannot be tempted to launch a preemptive strike no matter what it believes the other side is doing, since it has no weapons with which to launch the strike.

(3) Even the opponents of Nuclear Disarmament describe the main peril of nuclear disarmament as nuclear blackmail by the Soviet Union. Opponents of disarmament apparently feel that after nuclear disarmament, nuclear threats are far more probable than nuclear disasters.

(4) Though nuclear weapons are not inherently more destructive than other sorts of weapons, conceived or actual (the napalm rapids on Tokyo in March 1945 caused more deaths than Hiroshima or Nagasaki), nuclear weapons are universally *perceived* as different in kind from nonnuclear weapons. The diplomatic losses a nation would incur upon using even tactical nuclear weapons would be immense.

(5) A large scale nuclear attack by the Soviet Union against the United States might contaminate the American and Canadian Great Plains, a major source of Soviet grain imports. The Soviets could still turn to Argentina, but the price of grain after the attack would skyrocket, and no combination of Argentinean, Australian, or other grain sources could possibly compensate for American or Canadian losses.

(6) The Soviets will find it difficult to find actual military situations in which it will be practical to use atomic weapons against the United States, or against anyone else. Nuclear weapons proved superfluous in the Soviet invasions of Hungary and Czechoslovakia, and they do not seem to be practicable in Afghanistan, where the human costs of the Soviet attempt to regain control are high. If the Soviets did not use nuclear weapons against China between 1960 and 1964 in order to prevent the development of Chinese nuclear capacity, it is hardly likely that they could use them against a nonnuclear United States. Of course it is always *possible* that the Soviet Union might

launch a nuclear attack against a nonnuclear United States, perhaps as an escalatory step in a conventional conflict, but it is also *possible* that the Soviet Union will launch a nuclear attack on the United States *right now,* despite the present situation of Equivalence. The point is that there is no such thing as a guarantee against nuclear attack, but the probability of an actual attack is small under either strategy.

[j] The chance of all-out nuclear war under the Equivalence Strategy is slight, but the chance of all-out nuclear war under Nuclear Disarmament is zero. There cannot be a two-sided nuclear war if only one side possesses nuclear arms.

[k] In considering the threat of Soviet nonnuclear aggression under Nuclear Disarmament, we must consider Soviet nuclear threats—usually called "nuclear blackmail"—as well as possible uses of conventional arms by the Soviets.

(1) Suppose that the United States unilaterally gives up second-strike-capacity. What are the odds that the Soviet Union would attempt to influence American behavior through nuclear threats? Obviously, one's views about the chances for successful nuclear blackmail depends on one's views about the chances of a Soviet first strike against a nonnuclear United States. If the chances of a Soviet first strike are slight, then the chances of successful blackmail will also be slight. We have already argued on a variety of grounds that chances of a Soviet first strike under *ND* are small. I would suggest that the ability of the Soviet Union to manipulate a nonnuclear United States would be the same as the ability of the United States to manipulate the Soviet Union from 1945 to 1949, when strategic conditions were reversed. Anyone who reflects on events from 1945 to 1949 will conclude that nuclear threats have little effect on nations capable of acting with resolve.

There is always the chance that the Soviet Union will carry out its nuclear threats, but there is always the chance that the Soviet Union will carry out its threats even if the United States retains nuclear weapons. There is no device that provides a guarantee against nuclear blackmail. Consequently it cannot be argued that Equivalence provides a guarantee against blackmail that Nuclear Disarmament does not.

The foregoing dismissal of nuclear blackmail violates conventional strategic wisdom, which is concerned with nuclear blackmail almost to obsession. Numerous authors, for example, cite the swift fall of Japan after Hiroshima as evidence of the strategic usefulness of nuclear weapons and nuclear threats. The case of Japan is worth considering. Contrary to the canonical view certified by Secretary Stimson in his famous (and self-serving) *Harper's* article in 1947,[22] I believe that the bombings of Hiroshima and Nagasaki had almost no effect on events leading to the surrender of Japan. If so, the force of the

---

[22] Stimson's "The Decision to Use the Atomic Bomb" appeared in the February 1947 *Harper's Magazine,* pp. 97–107. Typical of Stimson's *post hoc ergo propter hoc* is:

We believed that our attacks struck cities which must certainly be important to the Japanese military leaders, both Army and Navy, and we waited for a result. We waited one day.

Japanese precedent, which still influences strategic thought, is greatly attenuated.

Obviously the bombings of Hiroshima and Nagasaki had no effect on the popular desire for peace in Japan, since the Japanese public did not know of the atomic bombings until the war was over. What is more surprising is that the bombings do not seem to have influenced either the Emperor or the military command in making the decision to sue for peace. The Emperor, as is now well known, had decided for peace as early as January 1945, and if he was set on peace in January, he did not need the bombings of August to make up his mind. The military, on the other hand, do not seem to have desired peace even after the bombs were dropped; the record shows that the military (a) correctly surmised that the United States had a small supply of these bombs, (b) debated improved antiaircraft measures to prevent any further bombs from being delivered, and (c) correctly inferred that bombs of this type could not be used to support a ground invasion, which they felt they could repulse with sufficient success to secure a conditional surrender. What tipped the political scales so that the Emperor could find his way to peace was not the bombing of Nagasaki on 9 August, but the Russian declaration of war on 8 August. Unaware of Stalin's commitment at Yalta to enter the war against Japan, the Japanese had hoped through the spring and summer of 1945 that the Soviets would mediate a negotiated settlement between the United States and Japan rather than send the Red Army into a new theater of war. When the Russians invaded Manchuria on 9 August, Premier Suzuki, according to reports, cried, "The game is over," and when the Emperor demanded surrender from the Council of Elders on 10 August, he never mentioned atomic bombs as the occasion of his demand for peace.[23] Little can be inferred from such evidence about the effectiveness of nuclear threats.

(2) The strategy of Nuclear Disarmament does not forbid uses of conventional arms in response to acts of aggression. Since there is no reason to believe that adoption of the strategy of Nuclear Disarmament by the United States will make acts of Soviet aggression any more palatable than they are at present, in all probability the American government under *ND* will appropriate funds for conventional arms sufficient to provide a deterrent to Soviet aggression roughly comparable to the deterrent provided by nuclear arms under *S* and *E*. This argument assumes that the deterrent effects of the

---

[23] For the Emperor's active attempts to obtain peace see Herbert Feis, *The Atomic Bomb and the End of World War II* (Princeton: Princeton University Press, 1966), p. 66. For the military response to the atomic bombings see Hanson Baldwin, *Great Mistakes of the War* (New York: Collins-Knowlton-Wing, 1950), pp. 87–107. For Suzuki's remark that "The game is over" see W. Craig, *The Fall of Japan* (New York: Dial, 1967), p. 107. One interesting suggestion about the special effectiveness of the atomic bomb against Japan is found in a remark made by General Marshall to David Lilienthal in 1947, "We didn't realize its value to give the Japanese such a shock that they could surrender without loss of face" (quoted in Feis, *The Atomic Bomb,* p. 6). Marshall's remark is prima facie reasonable, but I can find nothing in the documents on the Japanese side that supports it.

American strategic nuclear arsenal (whatever they are) can be obtained with a developed arsenal of modern conventional weapons. A review of the difficulties involved in the use of strategic nuclear weapons in concrete situations may convince the reader that conventional weapons can match the deterrent effect of nuclear weapons. Indeed, the whole development of "flexible response" systems during the McNamara era testifies to the widespread recognition that strategic nuclear weapons provide little leverage to nations who would seek to control the flow of world events.

[1] Since it is impossible to predict how much money must be spent on conventional forces in order to supply a deterrent equal to the present (nuclear) deterrent against Soviet nonnuclear aggression, it is possible that levels of military spending under *ND* will be greater than levels under *E*. But it is also possible that the levels of spending will be much less. The technical equipment needed to maintain *E* is fantastically expensive, but the labor costs of training and improving conventional forces can also be staggering. All things considered, it is still likely that spending will be less under *ND* than under *E*, especially if the draft is revived.

Comparison of Superiority and Equivalence

The chance of a Soviet first strike is greater under Superiority than under Equivalence, and the chance of all-out nuclear war is greater under Superiority than under Equivalence. The ability of Equivalence to deter Soviet nonnuclear aggression is equal to the ability of Superiority to deter such aggression, and the Equivalence strategy costs less. Thus Equivalence is preferable to Superiority from both the prudential and the moral point of view.

Comparison of Equivalence and Nuclear Disarmament

We have argued that Nuclear Disarmament and Equivalence are equal in their ability to deter Soviet nonnuclear aggression. In the category of military spending Nuclear Disarmament is preferable to Equivalence. In the category of "all-out war" *ND* is clearly superior to *E*, and in the category of "first strikes," *ND* seems to be about equal to *E*. Thus we have what seems to be a decisive prudential and moral argument in favor of Nuclear Disarmament: in every category, *ND* is either equal to or superior to *E*.

NUCLEAR DETERRENCE: SOME MORAL PERPLEXITIES

GREGORY S. KAVKA

Is it morally permissible for the United States to practice nuclear deterrence, given that doing so could eventuate in large-scale nuclear war, an unprecedented disaster for humanity?[1] This is a question not only of obvious moral (and political) importance, but also of great intellectual difficulty and complexity. I shall not attempt to answer it, but shall sort out and discuss some of the myriad of perplexities that must be dealt with before an answer can be found. Hopefully, a potentially fruitful way of looking at the moral problem of nuclear deterrence will emerge from this discussion.

To get our minds churning on the subject, let us consider a fictional situation[2] that parallels the nuclear balance of terror in certain key respects. Hearing from a usually reliable source that a certain rival is out to get you, you begin to carry a gun when you go out. While you are so armed, an elevator you are riding in stops, apparently stuck, between floors. Looking up from your newspaper, you discover that the other occupants are a group of young children and your rival, who has noticed you and seems to be drawing a weapon. You simultaneously draw your gun and a standoff quickly ensues, with each of you pointing a gun at the other. You realize that firing could break out at any time and kill or injure the children as well as yourself and your rival. Yet you are afraid your rival will shoot you if you drop your gun, nor do you trust him to keep an agreement to drop your guns simultaneously. In these circumstances, is it permissible for you to continue to point your gun at your rival? On the one hand, it appears clear that it is, since this reasonably seems necessary for self-defense. On the other hand, the act seems wrong because it seriously threatens the innocent youngsters with injury and death. Here we have a moral dilemma with no immediately evident solution.

Now if we take you and your rival to be the governments and armed forces of the two superpowers,[3] and the youngsters to be the rest of the population of these countries (and other countries that would suffer in a nuclear war), our elevator case can serve as a model of the nuclear balance of terror. The two situations possess many of the same morally relevant features and pose

Reprinted from Douglas MacLean (ed.), *The Security Gamble: Deterrence Dilemmas in the Nuclear Age* (Totowa, N.J.: Rowman and Allanheld, 1984) with permission of the author and the publisher.

[1] I focus on the morality of U.S. nuclear policies, but roughly the same analysis might apply to Soviet policies. Also, I only discuss the morality of nuclear deterrence, not the morality of actually waging nuclear war.

[2] Adapted from James Mills' novel *Report to the Commissioner* (New York: Pocket Books, 1973).

[3] Perhaps others belong in this group as well. Cf. sec. II below.

somewhat similar moral dilemmas. In fact, I propose viewing the moral problem of nuclear deterrence as, like the elevator case, essentially involving a tension between threatening innocent people and doing what appears necessary for self-defense.

This tension is best brought out by noting that the following three propositions form an inconsistent triad, i.e., they cannot all three be true, though each pair of them is consistent.

1. *Threat Principle:* It is impermissible to threaten, and impose risks of death upon, large numbers of innocent people.
2. *National Defense Principle:* It is permissible for a nation to do whatever it reasonably believes is necessary for national self-defense.
3. *Necessity Claim:* Practicing nuclear deterrence against the U.S.S.R. in a way that involves threatening, and imposing risks of death upon, a large number of innocent Soviet civilians is necessary for the self-defense of the U.S. and is reasonably believed to be so by U.S. leaders and citizens.

Two of these propositions are absolutist moral principles. The Threat Principle is prohibitive; it says acts of a certain sort are wrong in any circumstances. The National Defense Principle is permissive; it says acts of a particular kind are permissible in any circumstances. The Necessity Claim is an essentially factual[4] proposition that ascribes two properties to the practice of nuclear deterrence by the U.S. The first of these—that it threatens the innocent— renders the practice impermissible according to the Threat Principle. The second—that it is necessary for national defense—insures, by the National Defense Principle, that the practice is permissible. Hence the inconsistency, which is disturbing in view of the fact that each of the three propositions has a considerable degree of initial plausibility.

How should this inconsistency be resolved? Which of the three propositions should we reject? Considering them in turn, I shall suggest that none of the propositions is acceptable as it stands. Each must be modified and revised. Identifying the weaknesses of these propositions, and the nature of the modifications needed to correct them, suggests further areas of inquiry. And while it does not provide a direct solution to the moral problem of deterrence, it does shed some definite light on what the problem really is.

I. THREATS TO THE INNOCENT

In practicing nuclear deterrence, the U.S. *threatens* Soviet civilians in two senses: we declare that we will kill them if their leaders behave in certain ways, and we actually put them under some risk of death. That is, nuclear deterrence normally involves a *declarative threat* together with *risk imposition.*

---

[4] The question of whether the belief in question is reasonable might be regarded as normative, although not (directly) moral.

It is this combination, directed against large numbers of innocents, that is morally prohibited under all circumstances by the Threat Principle.

Is such an absolutist prohibition plausible? To answer this I propose considering the two elements separately, focusing on the declarative threat first. Let us ask then, "What is normally wrong with threats, aside from the actual risks they impose on those to whom they are addressed?" Four things come immediately to mind: threats may be counterproductive and encourage the wrongful conduct they attempt to deter, they may be effective in deterring permissible conduct (thus restricting the threatened party's rightful liberty), they may cause fear and anxiety, and their use may damage relations between the parties in question. Yet none of these seems to be the sort of consideration that would support an absolute prohibition. Furthermore, there is little reason to suppose that declarative threats should not be permitted when these features are largely absent. Suppose, for example, that a declarative threat will very probably be effective, is aimed at deterring clearly impermissible conduct, does not cause devastating anxiety (compared to alternative courses of action open to the threatener) because people are used to living with it, and does not destroy relations between the parties because threats of this kind are considered a normal element in those relations. It is doubtful that a declarative threat of this sort is wrong simply because it is a threat. Yet it is arguable that the declarative threat involved in nuclear deterrence is just of this kind.

But perhaps it is the specific nature of the nuclear threat, rather than simply its being a threat, which insures its wrongfulness. It has been frequently noted, for example, that the balance of terror holds each sides' civilian population hostage to the good behavior of its government. And at least one writer has suggested that nuclear deterrence is wrong because hostage taking is wrong.[5] But, if civilians are hostages to an adversary nation's nuclear weapons, they are hostages *in place,* who may go on with their normal activities without physical restriction. Hence, two of the usual objections to taking hostages do not apply: the violation of their personal integrity in seizing them, and the subsequent imposition of substantial limits on their liberty.[6] In view of this, it seems unlikely that nuclear deterrence must be wrong because, in a sense, it makes civilians hostages.

Does the *content* of the nuclear threat—to kill a large number of innocent people—render that threat impermissible under any circumstances? Suppose that we accept an absolute prohibition on killing the innocent and also accept the Wrongful Intentions Principle, which says that if an act is wrong, intending to perform it is also wrong. Since threats of nuclear retaliation (unless they are bluffs) involve the intention to kill innocent people, it follows that they are wrong.[7]

---

[5] See Douglas Lackey, "Ethics and Nuclear Deterrence." In James Rachels, ed., *Moral Problems,* 2nd ed. (New York: Harper and Row, 1975), pp. 343–44.

[6] This point is also made in Micheal Walzer, *Just and Unjust Wars* (New York: Basic Books, 1977), p. 271.

[7] According to Brian Hehir in his piece, "Moral Issues in Deterrence Policy" (in MacLean

This reasoning is valid, but unsound. As I have argued elsewhere,[8] the Wrongful Intentions Principle fails when applied to a conditional intention adopted solely to prevent the occurrence of the circumstances in which the intention would be acted upon. Thus, for example, if I know I can prevent you from thrashing me only by sincerely threatening to retaliate against your beloved and innocent brother, it may not be wrong for me to do so. Since the intentions behind the threats of those who practice nuclear deterrence are presumably of this sort, these threats are not necessarily wrong.

I conclude that the present absolutist form of the Threat Principle cannot be supported on the basis of the declarative threat element. But, if we focus instead on the imposition of risks, we again find little reason to adopt an absolutist principle of this type.[9] For it is generally recognized that if we evaluate policies in terms of the risks involved, we are must also consider and weigh up the benefits the policies bestow and the risks and benefits entailed by alternative policies. So our Threat Principle must assume some modified and nonabsolutist form such as:

(1') *Revised Threat Principle.* It is wrong to *disproportionately* threaten, and impose risks of death upon, large numbers of innocent people.

This revised principle is to be interpreted as requiring that threats to the innocent not be excessively harmful or risky, compared to available alternatives. But how, in principle, are we to determine whether relevant harms and risks are proportionate or excessive? The most natural initial suggestion is to apply a utilitarian standard and ask whether a policy of nuclear deterrence promotes worldwide human welfare better than would its abandonment. However, casting the problem in these terms confronts us with yet another dilemma. For while we cannot reliably estimate the precise numerical probabilities, most of us would endorse the following ordinal judgment: it is considerably more likely that the Soviets would attack and/or dominate the world by blackmail, if the U.S. practiced unilateral nuclear disarmament for a given period of time, than it is that continued U.S. nuclear deterrence (during the same period) would led to large-scale nuclear war. If we believe this, then the choice we face, in utilitarian terms, is essentially between a smaller risk of a graver disaster for humanity (i.e., nuclear war), and a greater risk of a smaller disaster for humanity (i.e., Soviet attack and/or domination).[10]

(ed.) *The Security Gamble: Deterrence Dilemmas in the Nuclear Age*) this argument still has considerable influence on Catholic thinking about the moral status of nuclear deterrence.

[8] "Some Paradoxes of Deterrence," *Journal of Philosophy,* 75 (June 1978), 285–302, especially sec. II. Compare, however, the rather different view expressed in David Gauthier's piece, "Deterrence, Maximization, and Rationality," also in the MacLean volume.

[9] If in (1), we read "threaten" purely in the risk imposition sense (ignoring the declarative element), the principle is obviously inadequate. For, in some situations, every alternative may involve a risk of death for large numbers of innocents.

[10] See my "Deterrence, Utility, and Rational Choice," *Theory and Decision,* 12 (March 1980), 41–60.

Perhaps we could avoid this utilitarian dilemma by assessing risks in another way. In any case, evaluation of the prohibitory Threat Principle leads toward viewing the moral problem of deterrence as a problem of risk assessment under uncertainty. Does a similar view emerge if we approach the problem from the perspective of the permissive National Defense Principle?

II. NATIONAL DEFENSE

What is the moral basis on which we posit the existence of a right of National Defense? For present purposes, I shall take it that such a right is derived from principles of individual self-defense in one of two ways. By analogy, with the reasoning being that a nation is like a person in morally significant respects, and therefore possesses a right of self-defense like that of a person. Or by composition, with the right of national defense consisting in an authorized government's exercising, in a coordinated fashion, the combined individual rights of self-defense of its citizens. In either case, we may assume that the right of national defense has the same limitations as the right of individual self-defense, unless there are specific differences between the situations of nations and individuals that either cancel or extend those limitations. Then we may use our knowledge of the individual right of self-defense to discover what limits, if any, govern the moral right of national defense.

Richard Wasserstrom, in his discussion of the morality of war, notes four restrictions on the individual legal right of self-defense—there must be an actual attack, the defender (unless on his own property) must have been unable to safely retreat, the force used must have been reasonably necessary, and the harm inflicted must be comparable to (or less than) that which would otherwise have been suffered by the defender.[11] Suppose that we agree that these are all limitations on the moral, as well as legal, right of individual self-defense. Are they also limits on the right of national defense?

With the exception of the use of force being reasonably necessary (a condition already reflected in the National Defense Principle), it is doubtful that they are. For the other three limitations seem justified only because individuals generally can appeal to public authorities to protect themselves and vindicate their rights. Temporary retreat and acceptance of limited harm and/or risk to oneself are morally acceptable if actual and potential assailants can be punished and deterred through the legal system. But there is no effective system of international criminal law to punish and deter aggressor states. If nations retreat as far as possible, or wait until the other side attacks, they may gravely weaken their chances of defending themselves successfully, with no hope of having their losses restored. Furthermore, if deterrence of aggression is to be effective in the absence of an international police force to mete

[11] Richard Wasserstrom, "On the Morality of War: A Preliminary Inquiry." In Wasserstrom, ed., *War and Morality* (Belmont, Calif.: Wadsworth Publishing Co., 1970), p. 89.

out punishments, successful defenders may have to inflict more than comparable harm on unsuccessful aggressors.[12] Hence, the legal limits on the right of individual self-defense do not point to any substantial limitations on the right of national defense, beyond those already contained in our National Defense Principle.

As Wasserstrom notes,[13] nations do not die in the same sense as people do. Does this imply any special restrictions on the right of national defense that might apply to nuclear deterrence? To answer this, we must first distinguish between two senses in which a nation can die. Its people can be physically annihilated (death $_1$), or the people can survive but lose their independence or have their basic institutions substantially and forcibly altered by outsiders (death $_2$). Now it is doubtful that nuclear deterrence is the only way a nation can prevent its death $_1$. It is highly likely, for example, that either superpower could safeguard the lives of (at least most of all) its citizens if it were willing to accept death $_2$ by simply surrendering to its rival.

However, consideration of the nature of the right of individual self-defense makes it plausible to suppose that nations have a strong right to defend themselves from death $_2$ as well as death $_1$. Suppose a gang goes around kidnapping people and then, without ever killing them, either (1) locks them up in secret prisons for life, or (2) blinds them and amputates their limbs, or (3) destroys their higher faculties by brain operations, or (4) brainwashes them so they come to love what they previously hated and hate what they previously loved. Clearly, whatever people are justified in doing to save themselves from murderers, they would be equally justified in doing to prevent being kidnapped by this gang. The implication of this is that the right of self-defense applies to the preservation of the central values of one's life as well as to biological survival. This suggests that a nation's right of self-defense applies to its central values (including its independence and the structure of its basic institutions), as well as the biological survival of its members— especially if, as seems likely, the central values of many of those members (and the survival of some of them) are inextricably bound up with the survival of the nation and its central values.[14] So even if nuclear deterrence were reasonably necessary only to protect our nation from death $_2$, it could still be sanctioned by a legitimate right of national defense.

We have yet, however, to consider the most important limit on the right of individual self-defense: restrictions on the risks or harms one may impose on other innocent parties in attempting to protect oneself. Suppose, for example, that mobsters credibly threaten to kill you unless you murder several innocent people. You may reasonably believe that doing these killings is necessary to save your life. It would be wrong, nonetheless, to do them. The same is true even in some cases in which the risk or harm you impose is

---

[12] Cf. Locke's *Second Treatise of Government,* sec. 8.

[13] Wasserstrom, "Morality of War," p. 90.

[14] This presupposes that the values in question are not extremely evil. Nazi Germany, for example, had no right to survive as a Nazi state.

decidedly less than the harm you are defending against. Thus, if you need a new kidney to survive, you have no right to kidnap an appropriate donor and have your surgeon friend transplant one of his kidneys into you.[15]

The lesson of the kidney case seems to be that one can, at most, actively impose substantially lesser risks or harms on other innocent people to protect oneself. Can this lesson be applied to national as well as individual self-defense? One might contend that it cannot be, appealing for support to the hallowed ought-implies-can principle. According to that principle, agents— including nations—can only be obligated to act in ways they are capable of acting. But, it may be suggested, nations are literally incapable of refraining from taking steps believed to be necessary for national defense, even if these impose horrible risks or harms on outside innocents. For any government that failed to undertake the requisite defensive actions (e.g., any government that abandoned nuclear deterrence) would be quickly ousted and replaced by a government willing to undertake them.

This argument that nations may permissibly do anything to protect themselves, because they can do no other, is interesting but unconvincing. In the first place, history shows that not all governments that fail to take available courses of action necessary for national defense fall when this becomes apparent. Thus, Chamberlain's appeasement of Hitler led to his downfall, but Stalin's did not lead to his. This example suggests restricting the argument to *democratic nations,* where the people clearly have the power to replace unsatisfactory leaders.[16]

But there are further difficulties with the argument. If democratic governments are incapable, because of popular pressure, of refraining from necessary defensive actions, democratic *nations* are not. For the nation includes the people, and if *they* allowed a government to forgo elements of defense to protect third parties, the government could do so. Hence, for the argument to establish that democratic *nations* are permitted to do whatever is necessary for defense, it must claim that people, or an effective majority of them, are collectively incapable of doing otherwise. But this would seem exceedingly difficult to establish, especially when—as in the case of nuclear deterrence— the acts thought necessary for defense themselves risk national and international destruction. No known principle of individual or group psychology indicates that an effective majority of an independent nation's people *must* prefer to risk their own deaths and those of countless other innocents to losing their political indpendence. They certainly may so prefer, but the argument in question succeeds only if the opposite preference is impossible.

Finally, suppose it were true that democratic nations, at least, could do no other than defend themselves, even at the cost of imposing serious harms or risks on innocent others. Can we appropriately apply the ought-implies-

[15] See Judith Jarvis Thomson, "A Defense of Abortion," *Philosophy and Public Affairs,* 1 (Fall 1971), 47–66.

[16] For an explanation of how a nation's people might lack the capacity to replace unsatisfactory leaders, see my "Rule by Fear," *Nous,* 17 (Nov. 1983), 601–620.

can principle to conclude such nations act permissibly in imposing these harms and risks? Comparisons with the case of individuals suggests not. Neither law nor morality allows people to kill other innocents in self-defense. Even when there is genuine irresistible compulsion derived from self-pre-servative instincts, this at most excuses the killing of innocent others or mitigates appropriate punishment;[17] it does not justify the killing. The same presumably holds true of the imposition of lesser, but still serious, harms (e.g., the theft of a kidney) and serious risks (e.g., tossing someone out of a crowded lifeboat when they have some reasonable chance of swimming to shore.) The "ought" in the moral rule "One ought not impose death, serious harms, or substantial risk thereof on innocent people" is apparently not strictly governed by the ought-implies-can principle. Hence, an unlimited right of national defense would not follow even from a nation's incapacity to refrain from taking whatever measures seem necessary for defense.

Suppose then we accept the limit on the right of national defense suggested by the kidney case: nations, like individuals, can at most impose substantially lesser risks or harms on other innocent parties to protect themselves. We might be tempted to conclude that nuclear deterrence is impermissible because it imposes on innocent Soviet civilians risks as great as those from which it protects us. Before, however, we jump to that conclusion, we must look more closely at the concept of "innocence."

III. INNOCENCE AND IMMUNITY

As used in such claims as "Nuclear deterrence is wrong because it imposes risks on innocent people" and "It is wrong to kill innocent people," the notion of innocence has two components. Those people described as innocent are asserted to be innocent *of doing* (or bringing about) certain things, in the sense of lacking moral responsibility for them. Also, a certain moral status is ascribed to these people: that of being immune from deliberately imposed harm or risk. Thus, this use of the concept of innocence contains within itself a substantive moral doctrine.

IMMUNITY THESIS. Persons have moral immunity, and it is impermissible to deliberately impose significant harms or risks on them, unless they are themselves morally responsible for creating relevant harms or dangers.[18]

The intended concept of moral responsibility may be explained as follows.

---

[17] See, e.g., the report on the *United States* v. *Holmes* lifeboat case, in Philip Davis, ed., *Moral Duty and Legal Responsibility* (New York: Appleton-Century-Crofts, 1966). pp. 102–18.

[18] The term "relevant" must be included because moral responsibility for one harm or danger does not render a person morally liable to just any harm or risk that might be imposed. There must be a rational connection between the two, such as the latter being (i) the recognized penalty for creating the former, or (ii) a way of alleviating the former. A more precise specification of the Immunity Thesis would spell this out in more detail and would introduce qualifications to take account of justified paternalism and consent of the victim.

An agent is morally responsible for certain harms or risks when two conditions hold. First, certain moral flaws or shortcomings of the agent are expressed in his acts (or omissions) and make a significant causal contribution to the existence of those harms or risks. Second, the agent possesses the general psychological capacities necessary for being responsible for one's actions. Now, applying punishment only to those who are morally responsible in this sense seems sensible. It insures that people are only punished for things over which they had some significant degree of control. And those punished can reasonably be said to merit punishment because their moral flaws have produced identifiable harms or dangers. However, the concept of immunity has a use in some contexts in which punishment is not what is at issue. In particular, the question of an agent's moral immunity may arise in a dangerous situation,[19] as one considers acting so as to redistribute risks among various parties. Our intuitions about certain situations of this kind imply that the Immunity Thesis is not universally valid.

Imagine that a powerful man, whom I know to hate me and to be insane, rushes me with a knife. I can stop him either by shooting him or by shooting a third party who would fall in his path and delay him long enough for me to escape. It is clear that the former alternative is morally preferable, even though neither the lunatic nor the bystander is morally responsible for the danger to my life. Note also the standard belief that, in war, you are justified in shooting at enemy soldiers because they pose a threat to you, your comrades, and your country. An enemy soldier may not be morally responsible, in the sense described above, for the threat he poses. (He may reasonably believe that he is obligated to fight for his country, or he may have been coerced into fighting by threats of death.) Yet his lack of moral responsibility would not impose on you the obligation to treat him as you would a civilian bystander. Finally, consider an example involving nuclear deterrence. Compare deterring country Y from attacking by threatening retaliation against its cities, with deterring it by threatening to retaliate against the cities of uninvolved nation Z. Most of us believe that, questions of effectiveness aside, there is a substantial moral difference between the two, with the latter practice being much more objectionable. Yet, the vast majority of citizens of Y, as well as the citizens of Z, probably lack individual moral responsibility for the danger that Y creates.

The correct explanation of our reactions to these cases seems to be this: Our moral beliefs about dangerous situations are complex enough to take account of the fact that there are various kinds of connections an individual may have to a given danger, and that these may hold in various combinations and degrees. We regard the kind of connection set out in the usual conception of moral responsibility as sufficient to annul the agent's immunity. But other "looser" connections—creating danger out of madness or belonging to a

---

[19] We may define a "dangerous situation" as one in which not everyone's life can be protected—i.e., in which any action (including inaction) will place (or leave) some people at significant risk of losing their lives.

group responsible for producing a harm—are also sometimes taken to weaken or annul that immunity.

It is not hard to understand why we thus subject the Immunity Thesis to qualification. The basic purpose of holding people liable for risks and harms is to protect people, by deterring and preventing dangerous and harmful acts. It is generally most efficient to control such acts by holding liable those morally responsible for them. Furthermore, so doing gives people the opportunity to avoid liability by refraining from performing dangerous or harmful acts. There are, however, conditions under which control of harmful behavior is attained much more efficiently if looser conditions of liability are used. When the penalties are not severe, and the efficiencies are relatively large, we are not greatly bothered by such loosening of liability conditions. When penalties are more serious, such as imprisonment, death, or risk of serious injury, we generally believe that tight standards of liability should be employed. Thus, we are less inclined to accept vicarious liability in criminal than in civil law. However, when there is a significant present danger, and control of that danger *requires* loosening the conditions of liability, our inclination is to regard some loosenings as justified. This does not mean that we break down all distinctions. We still hold that the uninvolved bystander retains his immunity. What happens is that we shift more agents with intermediate degrees of connection to the danger out of the immune category (where the bystander resides), into the nonimmune category (where the deliberate wrongdoer resides) or into an intermediate "semi-immune" category.

Our justification for doing so in the case of collective action by an organized group is evident. In cases of cooperative action involving large numbers of people, it would be silly to require for liability that an individual's contribution to the group act be significant and flow from a flaw in the individual's character. When large groups act, individual member's contributions are typically indirect and too small to have substantial impact. Furthermore, organizational decision procedures and group pressures can often funnel individually blameless inputs into an immoral group output. Hence, to require a significant causal contribution flowing from a character defect as a precondition of liability in such cases would be to let too many people (in some cases perhaps *everyone*) off the hook and largely lose the ability to influence group acts by deterrence. This is especially so when the group in question is a sovereign nation. For then, usually, outsiders can do little to punish key leaders who bear individual moral responsibility for the group's misbehavior, except by imposing military, economic, or political sanctions that affect the entire nation.

If we accept this limited defense of applying some notion of collective responsibility to citizens of nations, the argument against nuclear deterrence that was offered at the end of the last section fails. Soviet civilians typically lack full individual moral responsibility for the nuclear threat their government and military pose to us, but this does not render them fully immune to counterthreats from us. Like the mad attacker, they are partially responsible and hence partly liable. (As we are toward them; our mutual nuclear threats may even reciprocally justify each other.[20])

Taken together, considerations advanced in this section and the last suggest that a proper form of the National Defense Principle will be neither absolutely permissive nor absolutely prohibitory. It will not permit *anything* reasonably necessary for national defense, for there must be limits on what may be done to the innocent or partially innocent. But, as the adversary's civilian population lacks full immunity, it will not forbid imposing any substantial risks or harms on them. Perhaps, the principle should read as follows:

> (2') *Revised National Defense Principle:* It is permissible for a nation to do whatever it reasonably believes is necessary for national self-defense, provided such measures do not impose disproportionate risks or harms on other parties.

The key term in this principle is "disproportionate." The appropriate criteria of proportionality take into account not only the relative sizes of the various risks and the risks that would be produced by alternative courses of action, but also the "degree" of innocence or immunity of the threatened parties. Considerations advanced in this section indicate that risks imposed on guilty parties count for much less than those imposed on the partially innocent (e.g., those only collectively responsible), which in turn count for less than those imposed on purely innocent bystanders. Reading backward, we should also add this element to the interpretation of the term "disproportionately" in the Revised Threat Principle (1').[21] This renders our two revised principles of one mind. Both forbid imposing disproportionate risks or harms on others, but allow all proportionate measures necessary for national defense.

However, we now see that the moral problem of deterrence is more complex, in at least one important way, than the utilitarian dilemma sketched at the end of Section I. It involves assessing the degrees of responsibility and liability for military threats to others of the various parties and groups involved in the balance of terror, and appropriately integrating this information into one's (otherwise) utilitarian analysis of risks and benefits.[22] The difficulty of this

---

[20] Here two wrongs may make a right. See my "When Two Wrongs Make a Right: An Essay on Business Ethics," *Journal of Business Ethics,* 2 (1983), 61–66. Note, however, that this approach does not deal with the nuclear risks—due to fallout or off-target missiles—imposed by the superpowers on citizens of other countries. Analysis of this problem would involve consideration of the moral significance of alliances and of the distinctions between intended and unintended effects of actions, and direct and indirect imposition of risks.

[21] With the term "disproportionate" thus interpreted to take account of numbers, nature of the risks, alternatives, and degrees of innocence, we may reword and simplify the principle into the following. (1") *Final Threat Principle:* It is wrong to disproportionately threaten, and impose risks upon, other people. The Necessity Claim must also be revised, so that Soviet civilians are described as "partly innocent."

[22] One very crude way of doing it would be to choose very broad categories (e.g., military-government, civilians, populations of uninvolved neighboring nations that would be harmed in the event of nuclear war), and to assign to each a weighting-factor between zero (for the guilty or responsible) and one (for the purely innocent bystander), thought to represent the relative

task may make us wish to avoid it. We could surely do so if nuclear deterrence were unnecessary for national defense, but is it?

IV. IS DETERRENCE NECESSARY?

Is threatening Soviet civilians with nuclear retaliation necessary for the defense of the U.S., given the Soviets' possession of a vast nuclear arsenal? At least one recent writer has answered "no" on the grounds that conventional arms alone would suffice to deter the Soviets from attack or successful nuclear blackmail,[23] but I shall make the usual assumption that this is wrong.[24] A recent proposal of President Reagan's suggests a different basis for answering our question in the negative.[25] Deterrence by threat of nuclear retaliation might be replaced by an effective technological defense against nuclear missiles, a system of lasers, missiles, and/or particle beams that would destroy enemy missiles before they have reached their targets. Critics of this proposal have claimed that such a system would be enormously expensive, would not work well enough, would itself be vulnerable to attack, could be counteracted by the other side building more missiles, and might conceivably tempt the other side to strike before the system was completed. They are probably right about much of this. But, unless such systems are perfect (i.e., 100 percent reliable) shields, there is yet another powerful strategic and moral reason against building them: they provide increased incentives for each side selecting the other's cities instead of its missile bases as its primary targets.[26]

One side's possession of an effective defensive system makes the other side's missiles relatively less attractive targets—since they can probably be destroyed once fired, if necessary, they need not be attacked on the ground. This is starkly apparent in the simplest imaginary case in which each side has one missile, and one side has a defensive system providing a 90 percent probability of intercepting the other's missile if it is fired. If it lacked this defensive system, the side now possessing it would have to target the other side's missile as its own first-strike target. But now it may target the other's capital, relying on the defensive system to protect it against retaliation. Although the math-

---

degree of immunity of members of the group. These weights would then be incorporated into one's utilitarian analysis.

[23] Douglas Lackey, "Missiles and Morals: A Utilitarian Look at Nuclear Deterrence," *Philosophy and Public Affairs,* (Summer 1982), 189–231.

[24] I reply to Lackey in "Doubts About Unilateral Nuclear Disarmament," *Philosophy and Public Affairs,* 12 (Summer 1983), 255–60.

[25] See "Current Policy No. 472," United States Department of State (Washington, D.C.: March 1983).

[26] At current levels of offensive nuclear armaments, this may make little practical difference. For, as George Quester indicates in his contribution to this volume, there are now enough weapons to cover all sensible targets. But the problems discussed below might become practical at some future time if defensive systems were conjoined with substantial negotiated reductions in offensive systems.

ematics are more complicated, the same principle would seem to apply to cases involving more missiles.

What of the side that *lacks* a defensive system but faces an opponent with one? To insure being able to inflict enough retaliatory damage to deter a first strike by its defended opponent, it will be forced to target virtually all its missiles on its opponent's population centers. In the case of *both* sides having effective, but imperfect, defensive systems, these two effects reinforce one another. The other side's missiles are rendered relatively less attractive as first-strike targets by one's own possession of a missile defense. And one's opponent's cities are rendered even more attractive as targets of retaliation. So the cumulative protective effect for civilians of both sides having 90 percent effective antimissile defensive systems would be *much less* than that provided by a 90 percent reduction of missiles on both sides (with defenses foregone.) For the retargeting incentives with effective but imperfect defensive systems are such as to render population centers relatively more attractive as both first and second strike targets.

For this reason, as well as the others mentioned, I do not feel that technological defenses provide much hope of rendering nuclear deterrence entirely obsolete. It does not follow, however, that the answer to our question about whether threatening civilians with nuclear destruction is necessary for national defense is a simple "yes." For defense by deterrence is a matter of degree, or probability. Different nuclear policies may deter different possible moves by a nation's adversaries with various degrees of reliability. Whether a given nuclear policy is "necessary" for defense depends on what we seek to defend against and what probability of successful defense would satisfy us.

Nuclear deterrence policies vary along a number of dimensions. The one discussed above, targeting, has been frequently discussed in the literature. In particular, the issue of whether to target military bases and missiles, or cities, has been seen to have considerable moral, as well as strategic, significance.[27] I shall henceforth focus on a less noted and analyzed dimension, that of our willingness to retaliate if attacked with nuclear weapons.

Different imaginable policies reflect varying degrees of likely response, and willingness to respond, to nuclear attack. At one end of the spectrum is the construction of an *automatic retaliator* (such as the doomsday machine of "Dr. Strangelove") that we could not turn off even if we wanted to, once we had been attacked. Convincing our adversaries that we had such a system in operation would provide maximum credibility of response to nuclear attack. Moving down the ladder of likely response, we might have a semiautomatic retaliatory system, a sincere and declared intention to retaliate, no announced policy about the use of our nuclear arsenal, or a bluff posture—i.e., a public policy of retaliation conjoined with a private determination by our leaders

---

[27] See, e.g., Robert Gessert and J. Bryan Hehir, *The New Nuclear Debate* (New York: Council on Religion and International Affairs, 1976); and Arthur Lee Burns, *Ethics and Deterrence* (London: Institute for Strategic Studies, 1969), Adelphi Paper no. 69.

not to retaliate if the occasion should actually arise. Finally, at the very end of the scale, is the least-threatening posture possible short of dismantling our nuclear weapons—a public policy of *not retaliating* even if attacked.[28] To emphasize that deterrence is a matter of degree, and to trace some moral implications of this fact, let us look more closely at the two extremes along this dimension, the no-retaliation policy and the automatic retaliator.

Even a no-retaliation policy would probably have considerable deterrent value. The Soviets probably would not believe that we really did not now intend to retaliate and, if they did believe it, might with good reason fear that we would change our minds if actually attacked. In other words, there would probably be enough uncertainty about our response to provide us with a considerable degree of what McGeorge Bundy, in his contribution to the MacLean volume, calls "existential deterrence." Nonetheless, such a policy would probably make deterrence considerably less reliable than it is now. In any case, it would be a domestic political impossibility, for—irrespective of its strategic or moral merits and demerits—it would require the government to spend billions on weapons it was pledged not to use under any circumstances.

The no-retaliation policy would mainly seem attractive to moralists who wish to retain an element of deterrence, but believe that *intending* to retaliate against civilians under any circumstances is impermissible. Above, in Section I, I briefly summarized some reasons for rejecting this belief. It is worth noting, in addition, that a no-retaliation policy does not escape the main moral objection to the U.S. practicing nuclear deterrence—that it imposes serious risks on many Soviet civilians. For, as just mentioned, a no-retaliation policy might well be abandoned in the heat of battle. Furthermore, by decreasing the reliability of deterrence, such a policy might substantially raise the probability of Soviet nuclear attack. This could actually *increase* the net danger to Soviet civilians over that which they experience under present policies.[29]

What of the policy, on the other extreme, of building the automatic retaliator? Because of the dangers of mechanical breakdown and accidental war, and the problem of convincing an adversary that the system is nonrecallable, it is doubtful that this would ever, *in practice*, be a morally permissible alternative. But suppose we put these problems aside by stipulation, and imagined a mistake-proof and perfectly credible automatic retaliation system. Would there be any convincing moral objection to building such a system to obtain maximal deterrence?

---

[28] In addition to discussing this policy in my seminars some years ago, I have recently seen it discussed in an unpublished paper by James Sterba.

[29] That is, the probability of Soviet attack might increase more than the probability of U.S. retaliation to Soviet attack decreases. In that case, the probability of U.S. retaliation, which is the product of these two, would rise.

Some writers have suggested that it is wrong to create circumstances that one knows could lead uncontrollably to disaster.[30] In turning deterrence over to an autoretaliator, we certainly would be doing this. But the principle that always forbids doing this is too strong. We cannot prohibit all acts that could uncontrollably lead to grave moral wrongs. If we applied this principle on a smaller scale, we would be much too restricted in our actions. We would not parole criminals, because this could lead to more serious crimes being committed. We could not give a political speech for disarmament, because this could cause a riot. More to the point, in the case of nuclear deterrence, any course of action we adopt *could* lead, in a way we could no longer control, to nuclear holocaust. If we built an autoretaliator, a Soviet version of (fictional) General Jack Ripper could set it off. But it also could be, for all we know, that if we do not build it, the Soviets will eventually attack us. Choices of this sort must be evaluated in terms of how grave and how likely the various possible outcomes are, and what the alternatives are. We cannot proceed simply on the basis of what *could* happen.

There is also a positive argument that suggests it might be permissible, in principle, to build an autoretaliator. Imagine that the U.S. invents a radio device that 50 percent of the time is able to deflect Soviet ballistic missiles in flight and send them to preset targets. For purposes of deterrence, the U.S. programs Soviet cities instead of the oceans as targets and announces this openly. I think we would regard it as morally permissible to build and operate such a defensive system. (Just as we would regard it as permissible for you to use a bullet-deflecting shield against your rival in the elevator, if you had one, even if the deflected bullets might strike the children as well as your rival.) Yet the system seems like an autoretaliator in virtually all morally relevant respects. The primary purpose of each system is deterrence,[31] and each could be built to preclude our side striking first. Both insure the truth of the conditional statement, addressed to the Soviets, "If you attack us, your cities will be destroyed," and place control of the fate of both countries out of our hands and into that of our potential adversaries. There is this difference: in our latest scenario, the Soviets, if they attacked, would be destroyed by missiles they built themselves.[32] But is this a morally significant

---

[30] See, e.g., Walter Stein, "The Limits of Nuclear War: Is a Just Deterrence Strategy Possible." In James Finn, ed., *Peace, The Churches and the Bomb* (New York: Council on Religion and International Affairs, 1965), p. 83. Cf. Robert Nozick, *Anarchy, State, and Utopia* (New York: Basic Books, 1974), pp. 126–31.

[31] Being only 50 percent effective, it could not physically protect our cities from destruction in an all-out Soviet attack. Hence, warding off an actual attack would probably be only a secondary purpose. Note that, due to its relative lack of defensive effectiveness and its capacity to punish an attacker with his own missiles, the deflector system would not provide its possessor with the retargeting incentives associated with the purely defensive system discussed earlier in this section.

[32] They also *fire* the missiles themselves. But, in a sense, they also fire our missiles if they attack our autoretaliator.

difference? It does not seem so. After all, nuclear deterrence as now practiced would be no less problematic if we were pointing captured (or purchased) Soviet missiles at the U.S.S.R. I conclude that, in principle, an ideal automatic nuclear retaliator might be permissible to build, although I reemphasize that I am not thereby endorsing dangerous launch-on-warning strategies or other similar strategies in the circumstances we actually face.

Our analysis of the no-retaliation and automatic-retaliation policies illustrates that there is a variety of different nuclear deterrence policies, each with its own advantages, dangers, and moral characteristics. This reinforces the main conclusion that emerged from our consideration of the Threat and National Defense principles: no absolutist principle—either permissive or prohibitory—is going to provide us with an easy and satisfactory solution to the moral problems posed by nuclear deterrence. Our approach to these problems must be more complex, beginning with the development of ways of assessing, under uncertainty, the dangers and advantages, for all humanity, of the various alternative nuclear deterrence policies.

V. THE SHAPE OF THE PROBLEM

I have argued that a utilitarian balancing of risks and benefits, rather than a rigid application of absolutist principles, should be the starting point of a moral evaluation of nuclear deterrence. But a starting point is only that. There are nonutilitarian dimensions to our problem as well, only some of which have been hinted at above, and all of which require careful attention. We need to know more about such issues as collective responsibility and its role in diluting civilian immunity, the relevance of the fact that the nuclear threats that superpowers impose on one another are reciprocal, and the manner of creation of a right of national defense out of individual rights of self-defense. To deal with the risks imposed by the balance of terror on non-nuclear nations and their citizens, special moral analysis of indirect risks and unintended side effects is required. The moral significance of the *motives* of those who practice deterrence must also be considered; in particular, it is important to know which (if any) practitioners' motives must be purely defensive in order for a deterrent policy to be potentially morally permissible. Finally, there is the very special moral problem of how to take account of the risk of human extinction entailed by the practice of nuclear deterrence.[33]

In conclusion then, the unsolved utilitarian core of the moral problem of nuclear deterrence is itself surrounded by a number of complex and unresolved

---

[33] See, e.g., Jonathan Schell, *The Fate of the Earth* (New York: Avon Books, 1982), Part II; and Jefferson McMahan, "Nuclear Deterrence and Future Generations." In Avner Cohen and Steven Lee, eds., *Nuclear Weapons and the Future of Humanity* (Rowman and Allanheld, 1984), forthcoming.

moral issues. As a result, we possess only one fairly obvious moral imperative concerning the balance of terror—that we should seek increasingly to dissolve it through negotiations and mutual (eventually multilateral) disarmament.[34] The rest is a series of perplexities as stubborn and difficult as the plight of nervous armed rivals trapped together in a stalled elevator.

[34] Perhaps, as the National Conference of Catholic Bishops' Ad Hoc Committee on War and Peace suggests in "The Challenge of Peace: God's Promise and Our Response," (*Origins,* 12 [October 28, 1982], 316–17), the permissibility of our practicing nuclear deterrence is *conditional* on our obeying this moral imperative. Although the idea of conditional moral permissibility may sound a bit odd, it makes a good deal of sense when applied in contexts in which a significant danger or harm can be alleviated in the short run only by normally impermissible means, but may be alleviated over the long run by nonobjectionable means. In such contexts, the permissibility of taking and continuing the short run "objectionable" means is conditional upon pursuing the nonobjectionable means of solving the long-run problem. Thus, it is permissible for starving men to go on stealing bread only if they seek work, or government aid, or private aid, so as to eliminate the necessity of stealing. Similarly, if the social and economic costs to the local community of closing his polluting factory outweigh the health risks imposed by the pollution, a factory owner may keep his plant operating—but only so long as he pursues the available means of reducing or eliminating the pollution.

SELECTED BIBLIOGRAPHY: WAR

Cohen, Avner, and **Steven Lee** (eds.). *Nuclear Weapons and the Future of Humanity.* Totowa, N.J.: Rowman and Allanheld, 1984.

Cohen, Marshall, Thomas Nagel, and **Thomas Scanlon** (eds.). *War and Moral Responsibility.* Princeton, N.J.: Princeton University Press, 1973.

Gallie, W. B. *Philosophers of Peace and War.* Cambridge, England: Cambridge University Press, 1978.

Ginzberg, Robert T. (ed.). *The Critique of War.* Chicago: Henry Regnery Company, 1969.

Hardin, Russell. "Unilateral Versus Mutual Disarmament." *Philosophy & Public Affairs,* 12:3 (1983), 236.

Humanities and Society, 5:1, 2 (1982). (Issue on militarism and war)

Kavka, Gregory S. "Doubt About Mutual Disarmament." *Philosophy & Public Affairs,* 12:3 (1983), 255.

Lackey, Douglas P. "Disarmament Revisited: A Reply to Kavka and Hardin." *Philosophy & Public Affairs* 12:3 (1983), 261.

————. *Missiles and Morals: The Moral Foundations of Defense Policy.* Totowa, N.J.: Rowman and Allanheld, 1984.

Margolis, Joseph. "The Concepts of War & Peace." *Social Theory and Practice,* 6:2 (1980), 209.

Ryan, Cheyney C. "Self-Defense, Pacifism, and the Possibility of Killing." *Ethics,* 93:3 (1983), 508.

Wakim, Malham (ed.) *War, Morality and the Military Profession.* Boulder, Colo.: Westview Press, 1979.

Walzer, Michael. *Just and Unjust Wars.* New York: Basic Books, 1977.

Wasserstrom, Richard A. "Conduct and Responsibility in War." In Richard A. Wasserstrom, *Philosophy and Social Issues: Five Studies.* Notre Dame, Ind.: University of Notre Dame Press, 1980.

————. (ed.). *War and Morality.* Belmont, Calif.: Wadsworth Publishing Co., 1970.

SIX

Abortion

ROE v. *WADE*
410 U.S. 113, 93 S.Ct. 705 (1973)

[Editor's Note: One of the plaintiffs in this case was a pregnant single woman who sued under the fictitious name of Jane Roe to challenge the constitutionality of various Texas criminal statutes relating to abortion. The section of the Texas Penal Code under attack read as follows:

1. "Article 1191. Abortion

"If any person shall designedly administer to a pregnant woman or knowingly procure to be administered with her consent any drug or medicine, or shall use towards her any violence or means whatever externally or internally applied, and thereby procure an abortion, he shall be confined in the penitentiary not less than two not more than five years; if it be done without her consent, the punishment shall be doubled. By 'abortion' is meant that the life of the fetus or embryo shall be destroyed in the woman's womb or that a premature birth thereof be caused.

"Art. 1192. Furnishing the means

"Whoever furnishes the means for procuring an abortion knowing the purpose intended is guilty as an accomplice.

"Art. 1193. Attempt at abortion

"If the means used shall fail to produce an abortion, the offender is nevertheless guilty of an attempt to produce abortion, provided it be shown that such means were calculated to produce that result, and shall be fined not less than one hundred nor more than one thousand dollars.

"Art. 1194. Murder in producing abortion

"If the death of the mother is occasioned by an abortion so produced or by an attempt to effect the same it is murder.

"Art. 1196. By medical advice

"Nothing in this chapter applies to an abortion procured or attempted by medical advice for the purpose of saving the life of the mother."

In addition, Article 1195, not challenged in the lawsuit read:

"Art. 1195. Destroying unborn child

"Whoever shall during parturition of the mother destroy the vitality or life in a child in a state of being born and before actual birth, which child would otherwise have been born alive, shall be confined in the penitentiary for life or for not less than five years."

In her lawsuit Jane Roe asked the federal district court for a declaratory judgment that the statutes were unconstitutional and for an injunction against their enforcement. She claimed that she was unable to secure a safe abortion performed by a competent physician under clinical conditions because her life was not threatened by the pregnancy. She also claimed that she lacked the funds to travel to any other state where safe abortions for persons such as herself were legal.

What follows are portions of the majority opinion by Justice Blackmun, the concurring opinion of Justice Douglas, and the dissenting opinion of Justice White. The concurring opinion of Justice Stewart and the dissenting opinion of Justice Rehnquist have been omitted and the remaining footnotes have been renumbered.]

• • •

MR. JUSTICE BLACKMUN delivered the opinion of the Court.

Three reasons have been advanced to explain historically the enactment of criminal abortion laws in the 19th century and to justify their continued existence.

It has been argued occasionally that these laws were the product of a Victorian social concern to discourage illicit sexual conduct. Texas, however, does not advance this justification in the present case, and it appears that no court or commentator has taken the argument seriously. The appellants and *amici* contend, moreover, that this is not a proper state purpose at all and suggest that, if it were, the Texas statutes are overboard in protecting it since the law fails to distinguish between married and unwed mothers.

A second reason is concerned with abortion as a medical procedure. When most criminal abortion laws were first enacted, the procedure was a hazardous one for the woman.[1] This was particularly true prior to the development of antisepsis. Antiseptic techniques, of course, were based on discoveries by Lister, Pasteur, and others first announced in 1867, but were not generally accepted and employed until about the turn of the century. Abortion mortality was high. Even after 1900, and perhaps until as late as the development of antibiotics in the 1940s, standard modern techniques such as dilation and curettage were not nearly so safe as they are today. Thus it has been argued that a State's real concern in enacting a criminal abortion law was to protect the pregnant woman, that is, to restrain her from submitting to a procedure that placed her life in serious jeopardy.

Modern medical techniques have altered this situation. Appellants and various *amici* refer to medical data indicating that abortion in early pregnancy, that is, prior to the end of first trimester, although not without its risk, is now relatively safe. Mortality rates for women undergoing early abortions,

[1] See C. Haagensen and W. Lloyd, *A Hundred Years of Medicine,* 19 (1943).

where the procedure is legal, appear to be as low as or lower than the rates for normal childbirth.[2] Consequently, an interest of the State in protecting the woman from an inherently hazardous procedure, except when it would be equally dangerous for her to forgo it, has largely disappeared. Of course, important state interests in the area of health and medical standards do remain. The State has a legitimate interest in seeing to it that abortion, like any other medical procedure, is performed under circumstances that insure maximum safety for the patient. This interest obviously extends at least to the performing physician and his staff, to the facilities involved, to the availability of aftercare, and to adequate provision for any complication or emergency that might arise. The prevalence of high mortality rates at illegal "abortion mills" strengthens, rather than weakens, the State's interest in regulating the conditions under which abortions are performed. Moreover, the risk to the woman increases as her pregnancy continues. Thus the State retains a definite interest in protecting the woman's own health and safety when an abortion is proposed at a late stage of pregnancy.

The third reason is the State's interest—some phrase it in terms of duty—in protecting prenatal life. Some of the argument for this justification rests on the theory that a new human life is present from the moment of conception.[3] The State's interest and general obligation to protect life then extends, it is argued, to prenatal life. Only when the life of the pregnant mother herself is at stake, balanced against the life she carries within her, should the interest of the embryo or fetus not prevail. Logically, of course, a legitimate state inerest in this area need not stand or fall on acceptance of the belief that life begins at conception or at some other point prior to live birth. In assessing the State's interest, recognition may be given to the less rigid claim that as long as at least *potential* life is involved, the State may assert interests beyond the protection of the pregnant woman alone.

Parties challenging state abortion laws have sharply disputed in some courts the contention that a purpose of these laws, when enacted, was to protect prenatal life. Pointing to the absence of legislative history to support the contention, they claim that most state laws were designed solely to protect the woman. Because medical advances have lessened this concern, at least with respect to abortion in early pregnancy, they argue that with respect to such abortions the laws can no longer be justified by any state interest. There is some scholarly support for this view of original purpose. The few state

[2] Potts, "Postconception Control of Fertility," 8 *Int'l J. of G. & O.*, 957, 967 (1970) (England and Wales); "Abortion Mortality," 20 *Morbidity and Mortality*, 208, 209 (July 12, 1971) (U.S. Dept. of HEW, Public Health Service) (New York City); Tietze, "United States: Therapeutic Abortions, 1963–1968," 59 *Studies in Family Planning*, 5, 7 (1970); Tietze, "Mortality with Contraception and Induced Abortion," 45 *Studies in Family Planning* 6 (1969) (Japan, Czechoslovakia, Hungary); Tietze and Lehfeldt, "Legal Abortion in Eastern Europe," 175 *JAMA*, 1149, 1152 (April 1961). Other sources are discussed in Lader, 17–23 [L. Lader, *Abortion*, 1966].

[3] See Brief of Amicus National Right to Life Foundation; R. Drinan, "The Inviolability of the Right to Be Born," in *Abortion and the Law*, 107 (D. Smith ed. 1967); Louisell, "Abortion, The Practice of Medicine, and the Due Process of Law," 16, *UCLA L.Rev.*, 233 (1969); Noonan 1 [J. Noonan, ed. *The Morality of Abortion*, 1970].

courts called upon to interpret their laws in the nineteenth and early twentieth centuries did focus on the State's interest in protecting the woman's health rather than in preserving the embryo and fetus. Proponents of this view point out that in many States, including Texas, by statute or judicial interpretation, the pregnant woman herself could not be prosecuted for self-abortion or for cooperating in an abortion performed upon her by another. They claim that adoption of the "quickening" distinction through received common law and state statutes tacitly recognizes the greater health hazards inherent in late abortion and impliedly repudiates the theory that life begins at conception.

It is with these interests, and the weight to be attached to them, that this case is concerned.

The Constitution does not explicitly mention any right of privacy. In a line of decisions, however, going back perhaps as far as *Union Pacific R. Co.* v. *Botsford,* 141 U.S. 250, 251, 11 S.Ct. 1000, 1001, 35 L.Ed. 734 (1891), the Court has recognized that a right of personal privacy, or a guarantee of certain areas or zones of privacy, does exist under the Constitution. In varying contexts the Court or individual Justices have indeed found at least the roots of that right in the First Amendment . . .; in the Fourth and Fifth Amendments, . . . in the penumbras of the Bill of Rights, . . . in the Ninth Amendment, or in the concept of liberty guaranteed by the first section of the Fourteenth Amendment, . . . These decisions make it clear that only personal rights that can be deemed "fundamental" or "implicit in the concept of ordered liberty," . . . are included in this guarantee of personal privacy. They also make it clear that the right has some extension to activities relating to marriage, . . . procreation, . . . contraception, . . . family relationships, . . . and child rearing and education, ...

This right of privacy, whether it be founded in the Fourteenth Amendment's concept of personal liberty and restrictions upon state action, as we feel it is, or, as the District Court determined, in the Ninth Amendment's reservation of rights to the people, is broad enough to encompass a woman's decision whether or not to terminate her pregnancy. The detriment that the State would impose upon the pregnant woman by denying this choice altogether is apparent. Specific and direct harm medically diagnosable even in early pregnancy may be involved. Maternity, or additional offspring, may force upon the woman a distressful life and future. Psychological harm may be imminent. Mental and physical health may be taxed by child care. There is also the distress, for all concerned, associated with the unwanted child, and there is the problem of bringing a child into a family already unable, psychologically and otherwise, to care for it. In other cases, as in this one, the additional difficulties and continuing stigma of unwed motherhood may be involved. All these are factors the woman and her responsible physician necessarily will consider in consultation.

On the basis of elements such as these, appellants and some *amici* argue that the woman's right is absolute and that she is entitled to terminate her pregnancy at whatever time, in whatever way, and for whatever reason she alone chooses. With this we do not agree. Appellants' arguments that Texas either has no valid interest at all in regulating the abortion decision, or no interest strong enough to support any limitation upon the woman's sole determination, is unpersuasive. The Court's decisions recognizing a right of privacy also acknowledge that some state regulation in areas protected by that right is appropriate. As noted above, a state may properly assert important interests in safeguarding health, in maintaining medical standards, and in protecting potential life. At some point in pregnancy, these respective interests become sufficiently compelling to sustain regulation of the factors that govern the abortion decision. The privacy right involved, therefore, cannot be said to be absolute. In fact, it is not clear to us that the claim asserted by some *amici* that one has an unlimited right to do with one's body as one pleases bears a close relationship to the right of privacy previously articulated in the Court's decisions. The Court has refused to recognize an unlimited right of this kind in the past. *Jacobson* v. *Massachusetts,* 197 U.S. 11, 25 S.Ct. 358, 49 L.Ed. 643 (1905) (vaccination); *Buck* v. *Bell,* 274 U.S. 200, 47 S.Ct. 584, 71 L.Ed. 1000 (1927) (sterilization).

We therefore conclude that the right of personal privacy includes the abortion decision, but that this right is not unqualified and must be considered against important state interests in regulation.

We note that those federal and state courts that have recently considered abortion law challenges have reached the same conclusion. A majority, in addition to the District Court in the present case, have held state laws unconstitutional, at least in part, because of vagueness or because of over-breadth and abridgement of rights. . . .

Although the results are divided, most of these courts have agreed that the right of privacy, however based, is broad enough to cover the abortion decision; that the right, nonetheless, is not absolute and is subject to some limitations; and that at some point the state interests as to protection of health, medical standards, and prenatal life, become dominant. We agree with this approach.

Where certain "fundamental rights" are involved, the Court has held that regulation limiting these rights may be justified only by a "compelling state interest," . . . and that legislative enactments must be narrowly drawn to express only the legitimate state interests at stake. . . .

In the recent abortion cases, cited above, courts have recognized these principles. Those striking down state laws have generally scrutinized the State's interest in protecting health and potential life and have concluded that neither interest justified broad limitations on the reasons for which a physician and his pregnant patient might decide that she should have an abortion in the early stages of pregnancy. Courts sustaining state laws have held that the State's determinations to protect health or prenatal life are dominant and constitutionally justifiable.

The District Court held that the appellee failed to meet his burden of demonstrating that the Texas statute's infringement upon Roe's rights was necessary to support a compelling state interest, and that, although the defendant presented "several compelling justifications for state presence in the area of abortions," the statutes outstripped these justifications and swept "far beyond any areas of compelling state interest." . . . Appellant and appellee both contest that holding. Appellant, as has been indicated, claims an absolute right that bars any state imposition of criminal penalties in the area. Appellee argues that the State's determination to recognize and protect prenatal life from and after conception constitutes a compelling state interest. As noted above, we do not agree fully with either formulation.

A. The appellee and certain *amici* argue that the fetus is a "person" within the language and meaning of the Fourteenth Amendment. In support of this they outline at length and in detail the well-known facts of fetal development. If this suggestion of personhood is established, the appellant's case, of course, collapses, for the fetus' right to life is then guaranteed specifically by the Amendment. The appellant conceded as much on reargument. On the other hand, the appellee conceded on reargument that no case could be cited that holds that a fetus is a person within the meaning of the Fourteenth Amendment.

The Constitution does not define "person" in so many words. Section 1 of the Fourteenth Amendment contains three references to "person." The first, in defining "citizens," speaks of "persons born or naturalized in the United States." The word also appears both in the Due Process Clause and in the Equal Protection Clause. "Person is used in other places in the Constitution: in the listing of qualifications for representatives and senators, Art. I § 2, cl. 2, and § 3, cl. 3; in the Apportionment Clause, Art. I, § 2, cl. 3;[4] in the Migration and Importation provision, Art. I, § 9, cl. 1; in the Emolument Clause, Art. I, § 9, cl. 8; in the Electors provisions, Art. II, § 1, cl. 2, and the superseded cl. 3; in the provision outlining qualifications for the office of President, Art. II, § 1, cl. 5; in the Extradition provisions, Art. IV, § 2, cl. 2, and the superseded Fugitive Slave cl. 3; and in the Fifth, Twelfth, and Twenty-second Amendments as well as in §§ 2 and 3 of the Fourteenth Amendment. But in nearly all these instances, the use of the word is such that it has application only postnatally. None indicates with any assurance, that it has any possible pre-natal application.[5]

[4] We are not aware that in the taking of any census under this clause, a fetus has ever been counted.

[5] When Texas urges that a fetus is entitled to Fourteenth Amendment protection as a person, it faces a dilemma. Neither in Texas nor in any other State are all abortions prohibited. Despite broad proscription, an exception always exists. The exception contained in Art. 1196, for an abortion procured or attempted by medical advice for the purpose of saving the life of the mother, is typical. But if the fetus is a person who is not to be deprived of life without due process of law, and if the mother's condition is the sole determinant, does not the Texas exception appear to be out of line with the Amendment's command?

There are other inconsistencies between Fourteenth Amendment status and the typical abortion statute. It has already been pointed out, . . . that in Texas the woman is not a principal or an accomplice with respect to an abortion upon her. If the fetus is a person, why is the woman not a principal or an accomplice? Further, the penalty for criminal abortion specified by Art. 1195 is significantly less than the maximum penalty for murder prescribed by Art. 1257 of the Texas Penal Code. If the fetus is a person, may the penalties be different?

All this, together with our observation, *supra,* that throughout the major portion of the nineteenth century prevailing legal abortion practices were far freer than they are today, persuades us that the word "person," as used in the Fourteenth Amendment, does not include the unborn.[6] This is in accord with the results reached in those few cases where the issue has been squarely presented. . . . Indeed, our decision in *United States* v. *Vuitch,* 402 U.S. 62, 91, S.Ct. 1294, 20 L.Ed.2d 601 (1971), inferentially is to the same effect, for we there would not have indulged in statutory interpretation favorable to abortion in specified circumstances if the necessary consequence was the termination of life entitled to Fourteenth Amendment protection.

This conclusion, however, does not of itself fully answer the contentions raised by Texas, and we pass on to other considerations.

B. The pregnant woman cannot be isolated in her privacy. She carries an embryo and, later, a fetus, if one accepts the medical definitions of the developing young in the human uterus. See Dorland's *Illustrated Medical Dictionary,* 478–479, 547 (24th ed. 1965). The situation therefore is inherently different from marital intimacy, or bedroom possession of obscene material, or marriage, or procreation, or education, with which *Eisenstadt, Griswold, Stanley, Loving, Skinner, Pierce,* and *Meyer* were respectively concerned. As we have intimated above, it is reasonable and appropriate for a State to decide that at some point in time another interest, that of health of the mother or that of potential human life, becomes significantly involved. The woman's privacy is no longer sole and any right of privacy she possesses must be measured accordingly.

Texas urges that, apart from the Fourteenth Amendment, life begins at conception and is present throughout pregnancy, and that, therefore, the State has a compelling interest in protecting that life from and after conception. We need not resolve the difficult question of when life begins. When those trained in the respective disciplines of medicine, philosophy, and theology are unable to arrive at any consensus, the judiciary, at this point in the development of man's knowledge, is not in a position to speculate as to the answer.

It should be sufficient to note briefly the wide divergence of thinking on this most sensitive and difficult question. There has always been strong support for the view that life does not begin until live birth. This was the belief of the Stoics. It appears to be the predominant, though not the unanimous, attitude of the Jewish faith.[7] It may be taken to represent also the position of a large segment of the Protestant community, insofar as that can be ascertained; organized groups that have taken a formal position on the abor-

----

[6] Cf. the Wisconsin abortion statute, defining "unborn child" to mean "a human being from the time of conception until it is born alive," Wis.Stat. § 940.04(6) (1969), and the new Connecticut statute, Public Act No. 1, May 1972 Special Session, declaring it to be the public policy of the State and the legislative intent "to protect and preserve human life from the moment of conception."

[7] Lader 97–99; D. Feldman, *Birth Control in Jewish Law,* 251–294 (1968). For a stricter view, see I. Jakobovits, "Jewish Views on Abortion," in *Abortion and the Law,* 124 (D. Smith, ed. 1967).

tion issue have generally regarded abortion as a matter for the conscience of the individual and her family. As we have noted, the common law found greater significance in quickening. Physicians and their scientific colleagues have regarded that event with less interest and have tended to focus either upon conception or upon live birth or upon the interim point at which the fetus becomes "viable," that is, potentially able to live outside the mother's womb, albeit with artificial aid.[8] Viability is usually placed at about seven months (28 weeks) but may occur earlier, even at 24 weeks.[9] The Aristotelian theory of "mediate animation," that held sway throughout the Middle Ages and the Renaissance in Europe, continued to be official Roman Catholic dogma until the 19th century, despite opposition to this "ensoulment" theory from those in the Church who would recognize the existence of life from the moment of conception.[10] The latter is now, of course, the official belief of the Catholic Church. As one of the briefs *amicus* discloses, this is a view strongly held by many non-Catholics as well, and by many physicians. Substantial problems for precise definition of this view are posed, however, by new embryological data that purport to indicate that conception is a "process" over time, rather than an event, and by new medical techniques such as menstrual extraction, the "morning-after" pill, implantation of embryos, artificial insemination, and even artificial wombs.[11]

In areas other than criminal abortion the law has been reluctant to endorse any theory that life, as we recognize it, begins before live birth or to accord legal rights to the unborn except in narrowly defined situations and except when the rights are contingent upon live birth. For example, the traditional rule of tort law had denied recovery for prenatal injuries even though the child was born alive.[12] That rule has been changed in almost every jurisdiction. In most States recovery is said to be permitted only if the fetus was viable, or at least quick, when the injuries were sustained, though few courts have squarely so held. In a recent development, generally opposed by the commentators, some States permit the parents of a stillborn child to maintain an action for wrongful death because of prenatal injuries. Such an action, however, would appear to be one to vindicate the parents' interest and is thus consistent with the view that the fetus, at most, represents only the potentiality

[8] L. Hellman and J. Pritchard, *Williams Obstetrics,* 493 (14th ed. 1971); *Dorland's Illustrated Medical Dictionary,* 1689 (24th ed., 1965).

[9] Hellman and Pritchard, *supra,* n. 58, at 493.

[10] For discussions of the development of the Roman Catholic position, see D. Callahan, *Abortion: Law, Choice and Morality,* 409–47 (1970); Noonan 1.

[11] See D. Brodie, "The New Biology and the Prenatal Child," 9 *J.Fam. L.,* 391, 397 (1970); R. Gorney, "The New Biology and the Future of Man," 15 *UCLA L.Rev.,* 273 (1968); Note, "Criminal Law—Abortion—The Morning-After Pill and Other Pre-Implantation Birth-Control Methods and the Law," 46 *Ore.L.Rev.* 211 (1967); G. Taylor, *The Biological Time Bomb,* 32 (1968); A. Rosenfeld, *The Second Genesis,* 138–39 (1969); G. Smith, "Through a Test Tube Darkly: Artificial Insemination and the Law," 67 *Mich.L.Rev.,* 127 (1968); Note, Artificial Insemination and the Law, *U.Ill.L.F.,* 203 (1968).

[12] Prosser, *Handbook of the Law of Torts,* 335–38 (1971); 2 Harper and James, *The Law of Torts,* 1028–31 (1956); Note, 63 *Harv.L.Rev.,* 173 (1949).

of life. Similarly, unborn children have been recognized as acquiring rights or interests by way of inheritance or other devolution of property, and have been represented by guardians *ad litem.*[13] Perfection of the interests involved, again, has generally been contingent upon live birth. In short, the unborn have never been recognized in the law as persons in the whole sense.

In view of all this, we do not agree that, by adopting one theory of life, Texas may override the rights of the pregnant woman that are at stake. We repeat, however, that the State does have an important and legitimate interest in preserving and protecting the health of the pregnant woman, whether she be a resident of the State or a non-resident who seeks medical consultation and treatment there, and that it has still *another* important and legitimate interest in protecting the potentiality of human life. These interests are separate and distinct. Each grows in substantiality as the woman approaches term and, at a point during pregnancy, each becomes "compelling."

With respect to the State's important and legitimate interest in the health of the mother, the "compelling" point, in the light of present medical knowledge, is at approximately the end of the first trimester. This is so because of the now established medical fact, referred to above . . . that until the end of the first trimester mortality in abortion is less that mortality in normal childbirth. It follows that, from and after this point, a State may regulate the abortion procedure to the extent that the regulation reasonably relates to the preservation and protection of maternal health. Examples of permissible state regulation in this area are requirements as to the qualifications of the person who is to perform the abortion; as to the licensure of that person; as to the facility in which the procedure is to be performed, that is, whether it must be a hospital or may be a clinic or some other place of less-than-hospital status; as to the licensing of the facility; and the like.

This means, on the other hand, that, for the period of pregnancy prior to this "compelling" point, the attending physician, in consultation with his patient, is free to determine, without regulation by the State, that in his medical judgment the patient's pregnancy should be terminated. If that decision is reached, the judgment may be effectuated by an abortion free of interference by the State.

With respect to the State's important and legitimate interest in potential life, the "compelling" point is at viability. This is so because the fetus then presumably has the capability of meaningful life outside the mother's womb. State regulation protective of fetal life after viability thus has both logical and biological justifications. If the State is interested in protecting fetal life after viability, it may go so far as to proscribe abortion during that period except when it is necessary to preserve the life or health of the mother.

Measured against these standards, Art. 1196 of the Texas Penal Code, in restricting legal abortions to those "procured or attempted by medical advice

---

[13] D. Louisell, "Abortion, The Practice of Medicine, and the Due Process of Law," 16 *UCLA L.Rev.,* 233, 235–38 (1969); Note, 56 *Iowa L.Rev.,* 994, 999–1000 (1971); Note, "The Law and the Unborn Child," 46 *Notre Dame Law,* 349, 351–54 (1971).

for the purpose of saving the life of the mother," sweeps too broadly. The statute makes no distinction between abortions performed early in pregnancy and those performed later, and it limits to a single reason, "saving" the mother's life, the legal justification for the procedure. The statute, therefore, cannot survive the constitutional attack made upon it here.

This conclusion makes it unnecessary for us to conder the additional challenge to the Texas statute asserted on grounds of vagueness. . . .

• • •

MR. JUSTICE DOUGLAS, concurring. [MR. JUSTICE DOUGLAS' concurrence applied both to this case and to the companion case from Georgia, *Doe* v. *Bolton,* 410 U.S. 179.]

While I join the opinion of the court, I add a few words.

The questions presented in the present cases go far beyond the issues of vagueness, which we considered in *United States* v. *Vuitch,* 402 U.S. 62, 91 S.Ct. 1294, 28 L.Ed.2d 601. They involve the right of privacy, one aspect of which we considered in *Griswold* v. *Connecticut,* 381 U.S. 479, 484, 85 S.Ct. 1678, 1681, 14 L.Ed.2d 510, when we held that various guarantees in the Bill of Rights create zones of privacy.[1]

The *Griswold* case involved a law forbidding the use of contraceptives. We held that law as applied to married people unconstitutional:

We deal with a right of privacy older than the Bill of Rights—older than our political parties, older than our school system. Marriage is a coming together for better or for worse, hopefully enduring, and intimate to the degree of being sacred. *Id.,* 486, 85 S.Ct., 1682.

The District Court in *Doe* held that *Griswold* and related cases "establish a Constitutional right to privacy broad enough to encompass the right of a woman to terminate an unwanted pregnancy in its early stages, by obtaining an abortion." . . .

---

[1] There is no mention of privacy in our Bill of Rights but our decisions have recognized it as one of the fundamental values those amendments were designed to protect. The fountainhead case is *Boyd* v. *United States,* 116 U.S. 616, 6 S.Ct. 524, 29 L.Ed. 746, holding that a federal statute which authorized a court in tax cases to require a taxpayer to produce his records or to concede the Government's allegations offended the Fourth and Fifth Amendments. Justice Bradley, for the Court, found that the measure unduly intruded into the "sanctity of a man's home and the privacies of life." *Id.,* 630, 6 S.Ct., 532. Prior to *Boyd,* in *Kilbourn* v. *Thompson,* 103 U.S. 168, 195, 26 L.Ed. 377, Mr. Justice Miller held for the Court that neither House of Congress "possesses the general power of making inquiry into the private affairs of the citizen." Of *Kilbourn* Mr. Justice Field later said, "This case will stand for all time as a bulwark against the invasion of the right of the citizen to protection in his private affairs against the unlimited scrutiny of investigation by a congressional committee." In re Pacific Ry. Comm'n, C.C., 32 F.241, 253 (cited with approval in *Sinclair* v. *United States,* 279 U.S. 263, 293, 49 S.Ct. 268, 271, 73 L.Ed. 692). Mr Justice Harlan, also speaking for the Court, in *Interstate Commerce Comm'n* v. *Brimson,* 154 U.S. 447, 478, 14 S.Ct. 1125, 1134, 38 L.Ed. 1047, thought the same was true of administrative inquiries, saying the Constitution did not permit a "general power of making inquiry into the private affairs of the citizen." . . .

The Supreme Court of California expressed the same view in *People* v. *Belous,*[2] 71 Cal.2d 954, 963, 80 *Cal.Rptr.* 354, 458 P.2d 194.

The Ninth Amendment obviously does not create federally enforceable rights. It merely says, "The enumeration in the Constitution of certain rights, shall not be construed to deny or disparage others retained by the people." But a catalogue of these rights includes customary, traditional, and time-honored rights, amenities, privileges, and immunities that come within the sweep of "the Blessings of Liberty" mentioned in the preamble to the Constitution. Many of them in my view come within the meaning of the term "liberty" as used in the Fourteenth Amendment.

> *First is the autonomous control over the development and expression on one's intellect, interests, tastes, and personality.*

These are rights protected by the First Amendment and in my view they are absolute, permitting of no exceptions. . . . The Free Exercise Clause of the First Amendment is one facet of this constitutional right. The right to remain silent as respects one's own beliefs, . . . is protected by the First and the Fifth. The First Amendment grants the privacy of first-class mail, . . . All of these aspects of the right of privacy are "rights retained by the people" in the meaning of the Ninth Amendment.

> *Second is freedom of choice in the basic decisions of one's life respecting marriage, divorce, procreation, contraception, and the education and upbringing of children.*

These rights, unlike those protected by the First Amendment, are subject to some control by the police power. Thus the Fourth Amendment speaks only of "unreasonable searches and seizures" and of "probable cause." These rights are "fundamental" and we have held that in order to support legislative action the statute must be narrowly and precisely drawn and that a "compelling state interest" must be shown in support of the limitation. . . .

The liberty to marry a person of one's own choosing, . . . the right of procreation, . . . the liberty to direct the education of one's children, . . . and the privacy of the marital relation, . . . are in this category. Only last Term in *Eisenstadt* v. *Baird,* 405 U.S. 438, 92 S.Ct. 1029, 31 L.Ed.2d 349, another contraceptive case, we expanded the concept of *Griswold* by saying:

> It is true that in Griswold the right of privacy in question inhered in the marital relationship. Yet the marital couple is not an independent entity with a mind and heart of its own, but an association of two individuals each with a separate intellectual and emotional make up. If the right of privacy means anything, it is the right of the *individual,* married or single, to be free from unwarranted governmental intrusion into matters so fundamentally affecting a person as the decision whether to bear or beget a child.

---

[2] The California abortion statute, held unconstitutional in the *Belous* case, made it a crime to perform or help perform an abortion "unless the same is necessary to preserve [the mother's] life." . . .

This right of privacy was called by MR. JUSTICE BRANDEIS the right "to be let alone." *Olmstead* v. *United States,* 277 U.S. 438, 478, 48 S.Ct. 564, 572, 72 L.Ed. 944. That right includes the privilege of an individual to plan his own affairs, for "outside areas of plainly harmful conduct, every American is left to shape his own life as he thinks best, do what he pleases, go where he pleases." *Kent* v. *Dulles,* 357 U.S. 116, 126, 78 S.Ct. 1113, 1118, 2 L.Ed.2d 1204.

> *Third is the freedom to care for one's health and person, freedom from bodily restraint or compulsion, freedom to walk, stroll, or loaf.*

These rights, though fundamental, are likewise subject to regulation on a showing of "compelling state interest." We stated in *Papachristou* v. *City of Jacksonville,* 405 U.S. 156, 164, 92 S.Ct. 839, 844, 31 L.Ed.2d 110, that walking, strolling, and wandering "are historically part of the amenities of life, as we have known [them]." As stated in *Jacobson* v. *Massachusetts,* 197 U.S. 11, 29, 25 S.Ct. 358, 362, 49 L.Ed. 643:

> There is, of course, a sphere within which the individual may assert the supremacy of his own will and rightfully dispute the authority of any human government—especially of any free government existing under a written constitution, to interfere with the exercise of that will.

In *Union Pac. Ry. Co.* v. *Botsford,* 141 U.S. 250, 252, 11 S.Ct. 1000, 1001, 35 L.Ed. 734, the Court said,

> The inviolability of the person is as much invaded by a compulsory stripping and exposure as by a blow.

In *Terry* v. *Ohio,* 392 U.S. 1, 8–9, 88 Ct. 1868, 1873, 20 L.Ed.2d 889, the Court in speaking of the Fourth Amendment stated

> This inestimable right of personal security belongs as much to the citizen on the streets of our cities as to the [Governor] closeted in his study to dispose of his secret affairs.

Katz v. *United States,* 389 U.S. 347, 350, 88 S.Ct. 507, 510, 19 L.Ed.2d 576, emphasizes that the Fourth Amendment

> protects individual privacy against certain kinds of governmental intrusion.

In *Meyer* v. *Nebraska,* 262 U.S. 390, 399, 43 S.Ct. 625, 626, 67 L.Ed. 1042, the Court said:

> Without doubt, it [liberty] denotes not merely freedom from bodily restraint but also the right of the individual to contract, to engage in any of the common occupations of life, to acquire useful knowledge, to marry, establish a home and bring up children, to worship God according to the dictates of his own conscience, and generally to enjoy those privileges long recognized at common law as essential to the orderly pursuit of happiness by free men.

The Georgia statute is at war with the clear message of these cases—that a woman is free to make the basic decision whether to bear an unwanted child. Elaborate argument is hardly necessary to demonstrate that childbirth may deprive a woman of her preferred life style and force upon her a radically different and undesired future. For example, rejected applicants under the Georgia statute are required to endure the discomforts of pregnancy; to incur the pain, higher mortality rate, and aftereffects of childbirth; to abandon educational plans; to sustain loss of income; to forgo the satisfactions of careers; to tax further mental and physical health in providing childcare; and, in some cases, to bear the lifelong stigma of unwed motherhood, a badge which may haunt, if not deter, later legitimate family relationships.

Such a holding is, however, only the beginning of the problem. The State has interests to protect. Vaccinations to prevent epidemics are one example, as *Jacobson* holds. The Court held that compulsory sterilization of imbeciles afflicted with hereditary forms of insanity or imbecility is another. . . . Abortion affects another. While childbirth endangers the lives of some women, voluntary abortion at any time and place regardless of medical standards would impinge on a rightful concern of society. The woman's health is part of that concern; as is the life of the fetus after quickening. These concerns justify the State in treating the procedure as a medical one.

One difficulty is that this statute as construed and applied apparently does not give full sweep to the "psychological as well as physical well-being" of women patients which saved the concept "health" from being void for vagueness in *United States* v. *Vuitch, supra,* 402 U.S. at 72, 91 S.Ct. at 1299. But apart from that, Georgia's enactment has a constitutional infirmity because, as stated by the District Court, it "limits the number of reasons for which an abortion may be sought." I agree with the holding of the District Court, "This the State may not do, because such action unduly restricts a decision sheltered by the Constitutional right to privacy." . . .

The vicissitudes of life produce pregnancies which may be unwanted, or which may impair "health" in the broad *Vuitch* sense of the term, or which may imperil the life of the mother, or which in the full setting of the case may create such suffering, dislocations, misery, or tragedy as to make an early abortion the only civilized step to take. These hardships may be properly embraced in the "health" factor of the mother as appraised by a person of insight. Or they may be part of a broader medical judgment based on what is "appropriate" in a given case, though perhaps not "necessary" in a strict sense.

The "liberty" of the mother, though rooted as it is in the Constitution, may be qualified by the State for the reasons we have stated. But where fundamental personal rights and liberties are involved, the corrective legislation must be "narrowly drawn to prevent the supposed evil," . . . and not be dealt with in an "unlimited and indiscriminate" manner. . . . Unless regulatory measures are so confined and are addressed to the specific areas of compelling legislative concern, the police power would become the great leveller of constitutional rights and liberties.

There is no doubt that the State may require abortions to be performed by qualified medical personnel. The legitimate objective of preserving the mother's health clearly supports such laws. Their impact upon the woman's privacy is minimal. But the Georgia statute outlaws virtually all such operations—even in the earliest stages of pregnancy. In light of modern medical evidence suggesting that an early abortion is safer healthwise than childbirth itself,[3] it cannot be seriously urged that so comprehensive a ban is aimed at protecting the woman's health. Rather, this expansive proscription of all abortions along the temporal spectrum can rest only on a public goal of preserving both embryonic and fetal life.

The present statute has struck a balance between the woman and the State's interests wholly in favor of the latter. I am not prepared to hold that a State may equate, as Georgia has done, all phases of maturation preceding birth. We held in *Griswold* that the States may not preclude spouses from attempting to avoid the joinder of sperm and egg. If this is true, it is difficult to perceive any overriding public necessity which might attach precisely at the moment of conception. As MR. JUSTICE CLARK has said:[4]

> To say that life is present at conception is to give recognition to the potential, rather than the actual. The unfertilized egg has life, and if fertilized, it takes on human proportions. But the law deals in reality, not obscurity—the known rather than the unknown. When sperm meets egg, life may eventually form, but quite often it does not. The law does not deal in speculation. The phenomenon of life takes time to develop, and until it is actually present, it cannot be destroyed. Its interruption prior to formation would hardly be homicide, and as we have seen, society does not regard it as such. The rites of Baptism are not performed and death certificates are not required when a miscarriage occurs. No prosecutor has ever returned a murder indictment charging the taking of the life of a fetus.[5] This would not be the case if the fetus constituted human life.

In summary, the enactment is overbroad. It is not closely correlated to the aim of preserving pre-natal life. In fact, it permits its destruction in several cases, including pregnancies resulting from sex acts in which unmarried

---

[3] Many studies show that it is safer for a woman to have a medically induced abortion than to bear a child. In the first 11 months of operation of the New York abortion law, the mortality rate associated with such operations was six per 100,000 operations. "Abortion Mortality," 20 *Morbidity and Mortality,* 208, 209 (1971) (U.S. Department of Health, Education, and Welfare, Public Health Service). On the other hand, the maternal mortality rate associated with childbirths other than abortions was 18 per 100,000 live births. Tietze, "Mortality with Contraception and Induced Abortion," 45 *Studies in Family Planning,* 6, (1969). See also C. Tietze and H. Lehfeldt, "Legal Abortion in Eastern Europe," 175 *JAMA,* 1149, 1152 (1961); V. Kolblova, Legal Abortion in Czechoslovakia, 196 *JAMA,* 371 (1966); Mehland, "Combating Illegal Abortion in the Socialist Countries of Europe," 13 *World Med. J.,* 84 (1966).

[4] "Religion, Morality and Abortion: A Constitutional Appraisal," 2 *Loy.U. (L.A.) L.Rev.,* 1, 10 (1969).

[5] In *Keeler v. Superior Court of Amador County,* 2 Cal.3d 619, 87 *Cal.Rptr.* 481, 470 P.2d 617, the California Supreme Court held in 1970 that the California murder statute did not cover the killing of an unborn fetus, even though the fetus be "viable" and that it was beyond judicial power to extend the statute to the killing of an unborn. It held that the child must be "born alive before a charge of homicide can be sustained." 2 Cal.3d, at 639, 87 *Cal.Rptr.,* at 494, 470 P2d, at 630.

females are below the statutory age of consent. At the same time, however, the measure broadly proscribes aborting other pregnancies which may cause severe mental disorders. Additionally, the statute is overbroad because it equates the value of embryonic life immediately after conception with the worth of life immediately before birth.

Under the Georgia Act the mother's physician is not the sole judge as to whether the abortion should be performed. Two other licensed physicians must concur in his judgment. Moreover, the abortion must be performed in a licensed hospital; and the abortion must be approved in advance by a committee of the medical staff of that hospital.

Physicians, who speak to us in *Doe* through an *amicus* brief, complain of the Georgia Act's interference with their practice of their profession.

The right of privacy has no more conspicuous place than in the physician-patient relationship, unless it be in the priest-penitent relation.

It is one thing for a patient to agree that her physician may consult with another physician about her case. It is quite a different matter for the State compulsorily to impose on that physician-patient relationship another layer or, as in this case, still a third layer of physicians. The right of privacy—the right to care for one's health and person and to seek out a physician of one's own choice protected by the Fourteenth Amendment—becomes only a matter of theory not a reality, when a multiple physician approval system is mandated by the State.

The State licenses a physician. If he is derelict or faithless, the procedures available to punish him or to deprive him of his license are well known. He is entitled to procedural due process before professional disciplinary sanctions may be imposed. . . . Crucial here, however, is state-imposed control over the medical decision whether pregnancy should be interrupted. The good-faith decision of the patient's chosen physician is overridden and the final decision passed on to others in whose selection the patient has no part. This is a total destruction of the right of privacy between physician and patient and the intimacy of relation which that entails.

The right to seek advice on one's health and the right to place his reliance on the physician of his choice are basic to Fourteenth Amendment values. We deal with fundamental rights and liberties, which, as already noted, can be contained or controlled only by discretely drawn legislation that preserves the "liberty" and regulates only those phases of the problem of compelling legislative concern. The imposition by the State of group controls over the physician-patient relation is not made on any medical procedure apart from abortion, no matter how dangerous the medical step may be. The oversight imposed on the physician and patient in abortion cases denies them their "liberty," *viz.,* their right of privacy, without any compelling, discernible state interest.

Georgia has constitutional warrant in treating abortion as a medical problem. To protect the woman's right of privacy, however, the control must be through the physician of her choice and the standards set for his performance.

The protection of the fetus when it has acquired life is a legitimate concern of the State. Georgia's law makes no rational, discernible decision on that scores.[6] For under the Act the developmental stage of the fetus is irrelevant when pregnancy is the result of rape or when the fetus will very likely be born with a permanent defect or when a continuation of the pregnancy will endanger the life of the mother or permanently injure her health. When life is present is a question we do not try to resolve. While basically a question for medical experts, as stated by MR. JUSTICE CLARK,[7] it is, of course, caught up in matters of religion and morality.

In short, I agree with the Court that endangering the life of the woman or seriously and permanently injuring her health are standards too narrow for the right of privacy that are at stake.

I also agree that the superstructure of medical supervision which Georgia has erected violates the patient's right of privacy inherent in her choice of her own physician.

• • •

MR. JUSTICE WHITE, with whom MR. JUSTICE REHNQUIST joins, dissenting.

At the heart of the controversy in these cases are those recurring pregnancies that pose no danger whatsoever to the life or health of the mother but are nevertheless unwanted for any one or more of a variety of reasons—convenience, family planning, economics, dislike of children, the embarrassment of illegitimacy, etc. The common claim before us is that for any one of such reasons, or for no reason at all, and without asserting or claiming any threat to life or health, any woman is entitled to an abortion at her request if she is able to find a medical advisor willing to undertake the procedure.

The Court for the most part sustains this position: During the period prior to the time the fetus becomes viable, the Constitution of the United States values the convenience, whim or caprice of the putative mother more than the life or potential life of the fetus; the Constitution, therefore, guarantees the right to an abortion as against any state law or policy seeking to protect the fetus from an abortion not prompted by more compelling reasons of the mother.

With all due respect, I dissent. I find nothing in the language or history of the Constitution to support the Court's judgment. The Court simply fashions and announces a new constitutional right for pregnant mothers and, with scarcely any reason or authority for its action, invests that right with sufficient substance to override most existing state abortion statutes. The upshot is that the people and the legislatures of the 50 States are constitutionally disentitled

---

[6] See Rochat, Tyler, and Schoenbucher, "An Epidemiological Analysis of Abortion in Georgia," 61 *Am. J. of Public Health,* 541 (1971).

[7] Religion, Morality and Abortion: A Constitutional Appraisal," 2 *Loy. U. (L.A.) L.Rev.,* 1, 10 (1969).

to weigh the relative importance of the continued existence and development of the fetus on the one hand against a spectrum of possible impacts on the mother on the other hand. As an exercise of raw judicial power, the Court perhaps has authority to do what it does today; but in my view its judgment is an improvident and extravagant exercise of the power of judicial review which the Constitution extends to this Court.

The Court apparently values the convenience of the pregnant mother more than the continued existence and development of the life or potential life which she carries. Whether or not I might agree with that marshalling of values, I can in no event join the Court's judgment because I find no constitutional warrant for imposing such an order of priorities on the people and legislatures of the States. In a sensitive area such as this, involving as it does issues over which reasonable men may easily and heatedly differ, I cannot accept the Court's exercise of its clear power of choice by interposing a constitutional barrier to state efforts to protect human life and by investing mothers and doctors with the constitutionally protected right to exterminate it. This issue, for the most part, should be left with the people and to the political processes the people have devised to govern their affairs.

It is my view, therefore, that the Texas statute is not constitutionally infirm because it denies abortions to those who seek to serve only their convenience rather than to protect their life or health. Nor is this plaintiff, who claims no threat to her mental or physical health, entitled to assert the possible rights of those women whose pregnancy assertedly implicates their health. This, together with *United States v. Vuitch,* 402 U.S. 62, 91 S.Ct. 1294, 28 L.Ed.2d 601 (1971), dictates reversal of the judgment of the District Court.

Likewise, because Georgia may constitutionally forbid abortions to putative mothers who, like the plaintiff in this case, do not fall within the reach of § 26–1202(a) of its criminal code, I have no occasion, and the District Court had none, to consider the constitutionality of the procedural requirements of the Georgia statute as applied to those pregnancies posing substantial hazards to either life or health. I would reverse the judgment of the District Court in the Georgia case.

AN ALMOST ABSOLUTE VALUE IN HISTORY

JOHN T. NOONAN, JR.

• • •

The most fundamental question involved in the long history of thought on abortion is: How do you determine the humanity of a being? To phrase the question that way is to put in comprehensive humanistic terms what the theologians either dealt with as an explicitly theological question under the heading of "ensoulment" or dealt with implicitly in their treatment of abortion. The Christian position as it originated did not depend on a narrow theological or philosophical concept. It had no relation to theories of infant baptism.[1] It appealed to no special theory of instantaneous ensoulment. It took the world's view on ensoulment as that view changed from Aristotle to Zacchia. There was, indeed, theological influence affecting the theory of ensoulment finally adopted, and, of course, ensoulment itself was a theological concept, so that the position was always explained in theological terms. But the theological notion of ensoulment could easily be translated into humanistic language by substituting "human" for "rational soul"; the problem of knowing when a man is a man is common to theology and humanism.

If one steps outside the specific categories used by the theologians, the answer they gave can be analyzed as a refusal to discriminate among human beings on the basis of their varying potentialities. Once conceived, the being was recognized as man because he had man's potential. The criterion for humanity, thus, was simple and all-embracing: if you are conceived by human parents, you are human.

The strength of this position may be tested by a review of some of the other distinctions offered in the contemporary controversy over legalizing abortion. Perhaps the most popular distinction is in terms of viability. Before an age of so many months, the fetus is not viable, that is, it cannot be removed from the mother's womb and live apart from her. To that extent, the life of the fetus is absolutely dependent on the life of the mother. This dependence is made the basis of denying recognition to its humanity.

There are difficulties with this distinction. One is that the perfection of artificial incubation may make the fetus viable at any time: it may be removed

Reprinted from John T. Noonan, Jr. (ed.), *The Morality of Abortion: Legal and Historical Perspectives* (Cambridge, Mass.: Harvard University Press, 1970), pp. 51–59, with permission of the author and the publisher. Copyright © 1970 by the President and Fellows of Harvard College. (Only the concluding section, Part VI, is included, and the footnotes have been renumbered.)

[1] According to Glanville Williams (*The Sanctity of Life and The Criminal Law,* 193 (1957), "The historical reason for the Catholic objection to abortion is the same as for the Christian Church's historical opposition to infanticide: the horror of bringing about the death of an unbaptized child." This statement is made without any citation of evidence. As has been seen, desire to administer baptism could, in the Middle Ages, even be urged as a reason for procuring an abortion. It is highly regrettable that the American Law Institute was apparently misled by Williams' account and repeated after him the same baseless statement. See American Law Institutes, *Model Penal Code: Tentative Draft No. 9* (1959), p. 148, n. 12.

and artificially sustained. Experiments with animals already show that such a procedure is possible.[2] This hypothetical extreme case relates to an actual difficulty: there is considerable elasticity to the idea of viability. Mere length of life is not an exact measure. The viability of the fetus depends on the extent of its anatomical and functional development.[3] The weight and length of the fetus are better guides to the state of its development than age, but weight and length vary.[4] Moreover, different racial groups have different ages at which their fetuses are viable. Some evidence, for example, suggests that Negro fetuses mature more quickly than white fetuses.[5] If viability is the norm, the standard would vary with race and with many individual circumstances.

The most important objection to this approach is that dependence is not ended by viability. The fetus is still absolutely dependent on someone's care in order to continue existence; indeed a child of one or three or even five years of age is absolutely dependent on another's care for existence; uncared for, the other fetus or the younger child will die as surely as the early fetus detached from the mother. The unsubstantial lessening in dependence at viability does not seem to signify any special acquisition of humanity.

A second distinction has been attempted in terms of experience. A being who has had experience, has lived and suffered, who possesses memories, is more human than one who has not. Humanity depends on formation by experience. The fetus is thus "unformed" in the most basic human sense.[6]

This distinction is not serviceable for the embryo which is already experiencing and reacting. The embryo is responsive to touch after eight weeks[7] and at least at that point is experiencing. At an earlier stage the zygote is certainly alive and responding to its environment.[8] The distinction may also be challenged by the rare case where aphasia has erased adult memory: has it erased humanity? More fundamentally, this distinction leaves even the older fetus or the younger child to be treated as an unformed inhuman thing. Finally, it is not clear why experience as such confers humanity. It could be argued that certain central experiences such as loving or learning are necessary to make a man human. But then human beings who have failed to love or to learn might be excluded from the class called man.

A third distinction is made by appeal to the sentiments of adults. If a fetus dies, the grief of the parents is not the grief they would have for a living child. The fetus is an unnamed "it" till birth, and is not perceived as per-

[2] E.g., R. L. Brinster and J. L. Thomson, "Development of Eight-Cell Mouse Embryos in Vitro," 42, *Experimental Cell Research,* 308 (1966).

[3] J. Edgar Morison, *Fetal and Neonatal Pathology,* 99–100 (1963).

[4] Peter Gruenwald, "Growth of the Human Fetus," 94, *American Journal of Obstetrics and Gynecology,* 1112 (1966).

[5] Morison, *Fetal and Neonatal Pathology, supra* n. 3, at 101.

[6] This line of thought was advanced by some participants at the International Conference on Abortion sponsored by the Harvard Divinity School in cooperation with the Joseph P. Kennedy, Jr., Foundation in Washington, D.C., Sept. 8–10, 1967.

[7] Frank D. Allan, *Essentials of Human Embryology,* 165 (1960).

[8] Frederick J. Gottlieb, *Developmental Genetics,* 28 (1966).

sonality until at least the fourth month of existence when movements in the womb manifest a vigorous presence demanding joyful recognition by the parents.

Yet feeling is notoriously an unsure guide to the humanity of others. Many groups of humans have had difficulty in feeling that persons of another tongue, color, religion, sex, are as human as they. Apart from reactions to alien groups, we mourn the loss of a ten-year-old boy more than the loss of his one-day-old brother or his 90-year-old grandfather. The difference felt and the grief expressed vary with the potentialities extinguished, or the experience wiped out; they do not seem to point to any substantial difference in the humanity of baby, boy, or grandfather.

Distinctions are also made in terms of sensation by the parents. The embryo is felt within the womb only after about the fourth month.[9] The embryo is seen only at birth. What can be neither seen nor felt is different from what is tangible. If the fetus cannot be seen or touched at all, it cannot be perceived as man.

Yet experience shows that sight is even more untrustworthy than feeling in determining humanity. By sight, color became an appropriate index for saying who was a man, and the evil of racial discrimination was given foundation. Nor can touch provide the test; a being confined by sickness, "out of touch" with others, does not thereby seem to lose his humanity. To the extent that touch still has appeal as a criterion, it appears to be a survival of the old English idea of "quickening"—a possible mistranslation of the Latin *animatus* used in the canon law.[10] To that extent touch as a criterion seems to be dependent on the Aristotelian notion of ensoulment, and to fall when this notion is discarded.

Finally, a distinction is sought in social visibility. The fetus is not socially perceived as human. It cannot communicate with others. Thus, both subjectively and objectively, it is not a member of society. As moral rules are rules for the behavior of members of society to each other, they cannot be made for behavior toward what is not yet a member. Excluded from the society of men, the fetus is excluded from the humanity of men.[11]

By force of the argument from the consequences, this distinction is to be rejected. It is more subtle than that founded on an appeal to physical sensation, but it is equally dangerous in its implications. If humanity depends on social recognition, individuals or whole groups may be dehumanized by being denied any status in their society. Such a fate is fictionally portrayed in *1984* and has actually been the lot of many men in many societies. In the Roman empire, for example, condemnation to slavery meant the practical denial of

---

[9] Allan, *Essentials of Human Embryology, supra* n. 7, at 165.

[10] See David W. Louisell and John T. Noonan, Jr., "Constitutional Balance," in John T. Noonan, Jr. (ed.), *The Morality of Abortions*, (1970), 220–260.

[11] Another line of thought advanced at the Conference mentioned in n. 6. Thomas Aquinas gave an analogous reason against baptizing a fetus in the womb: "As long as it exists in the womb of the mother, it cannot be subject to the operation of the ministers of the Church as it is not known to men" (*In sententias Petri Lombardi,* 4.6 1.1.2).

most human rights; in the Chinese Communist world, landlords have been classified as enemies of the people and so treated as nonpersons by the state. Humanity does not depend on social recognition, though often the failure of society to recognize the prisoner, the alien, the heterodox as human has led to the destruction of human beings. Anyone conceived by a man and a woman is human. Recognition of this condition by society follows a real event in the objective order, however imperfect and halting the recognition. Any attempt to limit humanity to exclude some group runs the risk of furnishing authority and precedent for excluding other groups in the name of the consciousness or perception of the controlling group in society.

A philosopher may reject the appeal to the humanity of the fetus because he views "humanity" as a secular view of the soul and because he doubts the existence of anything real and objective which can be identified as humanity.[12] One answer to such a philosopher is to ask how he reasons about moral questions without supposing that there is a sense in which he and the others of whom he speaks are human. Whatever group is taken as the society which determines who may be killed is thereby taken as human. A second answer is to ask if he does not believe that there is a right and wrong way of deciding moral questions. If there is such a difference, experience may be appealed to: to decide who is human on the basis of the sentiment of a given society has led to consequences which rational men would characterize as monstrous.[13]

The rejection of the attempted distinctions based on viability and visibility, experience and feeling, may be buttressed by the following considerations: Moral judgments often rest on distinctions, but if the distinctions are not to appear arbitrary fiat, they should relate to some real difference in probabilities. There is a kind of continuity in all life, but the earlier stages of the elements of human life possess tiny probabilities of development. Consider for example, the spermatozoa in any normal ejaculate: There are about 200,000,000 in any single ejaculate, of which one has a chance of developing into a zygote[14] Consider the oocytes which may become ova: there are 100,000,000 to 1,000,000 oocytes in a female infant, of which a maximum of 390 are ovulated.[15] But once spermatozoon and ovum meet and the conceptus is formed, such studies as have been made show that roughly in only 20 percent of the

[12] Compare John O'Connor, "Humanity and Abortion," 12, *Natural Law Forum,* 128–30 (1968), with John T. Noonan, Jr. "Deciding Who Is Human," 12, *Natural Law Forum,* 134–38.

[13] A famous passage of Montesquieu reads:

"Ceux dont il s'agit sont noirs depuis les pieds jusqu'à la tête; et ils ont le nez si écrasé qu'il est presque impossible de les plaindre.

"On ne peut se mettre dans l'esprit que Dieu qui est un être très-sage, ait mis une âme, surtout une âme bonne, dans un corps tout noir.

"Il est si naturel de penser que c'est la couleur qui constitue l'essence de l'humanité, que les peuples d'Asie, qui font des eunuques, privent toujours les noirs du rapport qu'ils ont avec nous d'une façon plus marquée." *Montesquieu, De l'esprit des lois,* in *Oeuvres Complètes,* book 15, chap. 5 (Paris, 1843).

[14] J. S. Baxter, *Frazer's Manual of Embryology,* 5 (1963).

[15] Gregory Pincus, *The Control of Fertility,* 197 (1965).

cases will spontaneous abortion occur.[16] In other words, the chances are about 4 out of 5 that this new being will develop. At this stage in the life of the being there is a sharp shift in probabilities, an immense jump in potentialities. To make a distinction between the rights of spermatozoa and the rights of the fertilized ovum is to respond to an enormous shift in possibilities. For about twenty days after conception the egg may split to form twins or combine with another egg to form a chimera, but the probability of either event happening is very small.

It may be asked, What does a change in biological probabilities have to do with establishing humanity? The argument from probabilities is not aimed at establishing humanity but at establishing an objective discontinuity which may be taken into account in moral discourse. As life itself is a matter of probabilities, as most moral reasoning is an estimate of probabilities, so it seems in accord with the structure of reality and the nature of moral thought to found a moral judgment on the change in probabilities at conception. The appeal to probabilities is the most commonsensical of arguments, to a greater or smaller degree all of us base our actions on probabilities, and in morals, as in law, prudence and negligence are often measured by the account one has taken of the probabilities. If the chance is 200,000,000 to 1 that the movement in the bushes into which you shoot is a man's, I doubt if many persons would hold you careless in shooting; but if the chances are 4 out of 5 that the movement is a human being's, few would acquit you of blame. Would the argument be different if only one out of ten children conceived came to term? Of course this argument would be different. This argument is an appeal to probabilities that actually exist, not to any and all states of affairs which may be imagined.

The probabilities as they do exist do not show the humanity of the embryo in the sense of a demonstration in logic any more than the probabilities of the movement in the bush being a man demonstrate beyond all doubt that the being is a man. The appeal is a "buttressing" consideration, showing the plausibility of the standard adopted. The argument focuses on the decisional factor in any moral judgment and assumes that part of the business of a moralist is drawing lines. One evidence of the nonarbitrary character of the line drawn is the difference of probabilities on either side of it. If a spermatozoon is destroyed, one destroys a being which had a chance of far less than 1 in 200 million of developing into a reasoning being, possessed of the genetic code, a heart and other organs, and capable of pain. If a fetus is destroyed, one destroys a being already possessed of the genetic code, organs, and sensitivity to pain, and one which had an 80 percent chance of developing further into a baby outside the womb who, in time, would reason.

The positive argument for conception as the decisive moment of humanization is that at conception the new being receives the genetic code.[17] It is

---

[16] *Idem.* Apparently there is some small variation by region.

[17] Gottlieb, *Developmental Genetics, supra* n. 8, at 17.

this genetic information which determines his characteristics, which is the biological carrier of the possibility of human wisdom, which makes him a self-evolving being. A being with a human genetic code is man.

This review of current controversy over the humanity of the fetus emphasizes what a fundamental question the theologians resolved in asserting the inviolability of the fetus. To regard the fetus as possessed of equal rights with other humans was not, however, to decide every case where abortion might be employed. It did decide the case where the argument was that the fetus should be aborted for its own good. To say a being was human was to say it had a destiny to decide for itself which could not be taken from it by another man's decision. But human beings with equal rights often come in conflict with each other, and some decision must be made as whose claims are to prevail. Cases of conflict involving the fetus are different only in two respects: the total inability of the fetus to speak for itself and the fact that the right of the fetus regularly at stake is the right to life itself.

The approach taken by the theologians to these conflicts was articulated in terms of "direct" and "indirect." Again, to look at what they were doing from outside their categories, they may be said to have been drawing lines or "balancing values." "Direct" and "indirect" are spatial metaphors; "line-drawing" is another. "To weigh" or "to balance" values is a metaphor of a more complicated mathematical sort hinting at the process which goes on in moral judgments. All the metaphors suggest that, in the moral judgments made, comparisons were necessary, that no value completely controlled. The principle of double effect was no doctrine fallen from heaven, but a method of analysis appropriate where two relative values were being compared. In Catholic moral theology, as it developed, life even of the innocent was not taken as an absolute. Judgments on acts affecting life issued from a process of weighing. In the weighing, the fetus was always given a value greater than zero, always a value separate and independent from its parents. This valuation was crucial and fundamental in all Christian thought on the subject and marked it off from any approach which considered that only the parents' interests needed to be considered.

Even with the fetus weighed as human, one interest could be weighed as equal or superior: that of the mother in her own life. The casuists between 1450 and 1895 were willing to weigh this interest as superior. Since 1985, that interest was given decisive weight only in the two special cases of the cancerous uterus and the ectopic pregnancy. In both of these cases the fetus itself had little chance of survival even if the abortion were not performed. As the balance was once struck in favor of the mother whenever her life was endangered, it could be so struck again. The balance reached between 1895 and 1930 attempted prudentially and pastorally to forestall a multitude of exceptions for interests less than life.

The perception of the humanity of the fetus and the weighing of fetal rights against other human rights constituted the work of the moral analysts. But what spirit animated their abstract judgments? For the Christian community it was the injunction of Scripture to love your neighbor as yourself. The fetus as human was a neighbor; his life had parity with one's own. The commandment gave life to what otherwise would have been only rational calculation.

The commandment could be put in humanistic as well as theological terms: Do not injure your fellow man without reason. In these terms, once the humanity of the fetus is perceived, abortion is never right except in self-defense. When life must be taken to save life, reason alone cannot say that a mother must prefer a child's life to her own. With this exception, now of great rarity, abortion violates the rational humanist tenet of the equality of human lives.

For Christians the commandment to love had received a special imprint in that the exemplar proposed of love was the love of the Lord for his disciples. In the light given by this example, self-sacrifice carried to the point of death seemed in the extreme situations not without meaning. In the less extreme cases, preference for one's own interests to the life of another seemed to express cruelty or selfishness irreconcilable with the demands of love.

A DEFENSE OF ABORTION[1]

JUDITH JARVIS THOMSON

Most opposition to abortion relies on the premise that the fetus is a human being, a person, from the moment of conception. The premise is argued for, but, as I think, not well. Take, for example, the most common argument. We are asked to notice that the development of a human being from conception through birth into childhood is continuous; then it is said that to draw a line, to choose a point in this development and say "before this point the thing is not a person, after this point it is a person" is to make an arbitrary choice, a choice for which in the nature of things no good reason can be given. It is concluded that the fetus is, or anyway that we had better say it is, a person from the moment of conception. But this conclusion does not follow. Similar things might be said about the development of an acorn into an oak tree, and it does not follow that acorns are oak trees, or that we had better say they are. Arguments of this form are sometimes called "slippery slope arguments"—the phrase is perhaps self-explanatory—and it is dismaying that opponents of abortion rely on them so heavily and uncritically.

Reprinted from *Philosophy & Public Affairs,* Vol. 1, No. 1 (1971), 47–66, with permission of the author and the publisher, Princeton University Press.

[1] I am very much indebted to James Thomson for discussion, criticism, and many helpful suggestions.

I am inclined to agree, however, that the prospects for "drawing a line" in the development of the fetus look dim. I am inclined to think also that we shall probably have to agree that the fetus has already become a human person well before birth. Indeed, it comes as a surprise when one first learns how early in its life it begins to acquire human characteristics. By the tenth week, for example, it already has a face, arms and legs, fingers and toes; it has internal organs, and brain activity is detectable.[2] On the other hand, I think that the premise is false, that the fetus is not a person from the moment of conception. A newly fertilized ovum, a newly implanted clump of cells, is no more a person than an acorn is an oak tree. But I shall not discuss any of this. For it seems to me to be of great interest to ask what happens if, for the sake of argument, we allow the premise. How, precisely, are we supposed to get from there to the conclusion that abortion is morally impermissible? Opponents of abortion commonly spend most of their time establishing that the fetus is a person, and hardly any time explaining the step from there to the impermissibility of abortion. Perhaps they think the step too simple and obvious to require much comment. Or perhaps instead they are simply being economical in argument. Many of those who defend abortion rely on the premise that the fetus is not a person, but only a bit of tissue that will become a person at birth; and why pay out more arguments than you have to? Whatever the explanation, I suggest that the step they take is neither easy nor obvious, that it calls for closer examination than it is commonly given, and that when we do give it this closer examination we shall feel inclined to reject it.

I propose, then, that we grant that the fetus is a person from the moment of conception. How does the argument go from here? Something like this, I take it. Every person has a right to life. So the fetus has a right to life. No doubt the mother has a right to decide what shall happen in and to her body; everyone would grant that. But surely a person's right to life is stronger and more stringent than the mother's right to decide what happens in and to her body, and so outweighs it. So the fetus may not be killed; an abortion may not be performed.

It sounds plausible. But now let me ask you to imagine this. You wake up in the morning and find yourself back to back in bed with an unconscious violinist. A famous unconscious violinist. He has been found to have a fatal kidney ailment, and the Society of Music Lovers has canvassed all the available medical records and found that you alone have the right blood type to help. They have therefore kidnapped you, and last night the violinist's circulatory system was plugged into yours, so that your kidneys can be used to extract poisons from his blood as well as your own. The director of the hospital now tells you, "Look, we're sorry the Society of Music Lovers did this to you—

---

[2] Daniel Callahan, *Abortion: Law, Choice and Morality* (New York, 1970), p. 373. This book gives a fascinating survey of the available information on abortion. The Jewish tradition is surveyed in David M. Feldman, *Birth Control in Jewish Law* (New York, 1968), Part 5; the Catholic tradition in John T. Noonan, Jr., "An Almost Absolute Value in History." In *The Morality of Abortion,* ed. John T. Noonan, Jr. (Cambridge, Mass., 1970).

we would never have permitted it if we had known. But still, they did it, and the violinist now is plugged into you. To unplug you would be to kill him. But never mind, it's only for nine months. By then he will have recovered from his ailment, and can safely be unplugged from you." Is it morally incumbent on you to accede to this situation? No doubt it would be very nice of you if you did, a great kindness. But do you *have* to accede to it? What if it were not nine months, but nine years? Or longer still? What if the director of the hospital says, "Tough luck, I agree, but you've now got to stay in bed, with the violinist plugged into you, for the rest of your life. Because remember this. All persons have a right to life, and violinists are persons. Granted you have a right to decide what happens in and to your body, but a person's right to life outweighs your right to decide what happens in and to your body. So you cannot ever be unplugged from him." I imagine you would regard this as outrageous, which suggests that something really is wrong with that plausible-sounding argument I mentioned a moment ago.

In this case, of course, you were kidnapped; you didn't volunteer for the operation that plugged the violinist into your kidneys. Can those who oppose abortion on the ground I mentioned make an exception for a pregnancy due to rape? Certainly. They can say that persons have a right to life only if they didn't come into existence because of rape; or they can say that all persons have a right to life, but that some have less of a right to life than others, in particular, that those who came into existence because of rape have less. But these statements have a rather unpleasant sound. Surely the question of whether you have a right to life at all, or how much of it you have, shouldn't turn on the question of whether or not you are the product of a rape. And in fact the people who oppose abortion on the ground I mentioned do not make this distinction, and hence do not make an exception in case of rape.

Nor do they make an exception for a case in which the mother has to spend the nine months of her pregnancy in bed. They would agree that would be a great pity, and hard on the mother; but all the same, all persons have a right to life, the fetus is a person, and so on. I suspect, in fact, that they would not make an exception for a case in which, miraculously enough, the pregnancy went on for nine years, or even the rest of the mother's life.

Some won't even make an exception for a case in which continuation of the pregnancy is likely to shorten the mother's life; they regard abortion as impermissible even to save the mother's life. Such cases are nowadays very rare, and many opponents of abortion do not accept this extreme view. All the same, it is a good place to begin: a number of points of interest come out in respect to it.

1. Let us call the view that abortion is impermissible even to save the mother's life "the extreme view." I want to suggest first that it does not issue from the argument I mentioned earlier without the addition of some fairly powerful premises. Suppose a woman has become pregnant, and now learns that she has a cardiac condition such that she will die if she carries the baby to term. What may be done for her? The fetus, being a person, has a right

to life, but as the mother is a person too, so has she a right to life. Presumably they have an equal right to life. How is it supposed to come out that an abortion may not be performed? If mother and child have an equal right to life, shouldn't we perhaps flip a coin? Or should we add to the mother's right to life her right to decide what happens in and to her body, which everybody seems to be ready to grant—the sum of her rights now outweighing the fetus' right to life?

The most familiar argument here is the following. We are told that performing the abortion would be directly killing[3] the child, whereas doing nothing would not be killing the mother, but only letting her die. Moreover, in killing the child, one would be killing an innocent person, for the child has committed no crime, and is not aiming at his mother's death. And then there are a variety of ways in which this might be continued. (1) But as directly killing an innocent person is always and absolutely impermissible, an abortion may not be performed. Or, (2) as directly killing an innocent person is murder, and murder is always and absolutely impermissible, an abortion may not be performed.[4] Or, (3) as one's duty to refrain from directly killing an innocent person is more stringent than one's duty to keep a person from dying, an abortion may not be performed. Or, (4) if one's only options are directly killing an innocent person or letting a person die, one must prefer letting the person die, and thus an abortion may not be performed.[5]

Some people seem to have thought that these are not further premises which must be added if the conclusion is to be reached, but that they follow from the very fact that an innocent person has a right to life.[6] But this seems to me to be a mistake, and perhaps the simplest way to show this is to bring out that while we must certainly grant that innocent persons have a right to life, the theses in (1) through (4) are all false. Take (2), for example. If directly

---

[3] The term "direct" in the arguments I refer to is a technical one. Roughly, what is meant by *direct killing* is either killing as an end in itself, or killing as a means to some end, for example, the end of saving someone else's life. See note 6, below, for an example of its use.

[4] Cf. *Encyclical Letter of Pope Pius XI on Christian Marriage,* St. Paul Editions (Boston, nd), p. 32: "however much we may pity the mother whose health and even life is gravely imperiled in the performance of the duty allotted to her by nature, nevertheless what could ever be a sufficient reason for excusing in any way the direct murder of the innocent? This is precisely what we are dealing with here." Noonan (*The Morality of Abortion,* p. 43) reads this as follows: "What cause can ever avail to excuse in any way the direct killing of the innocent? For it is a question of that."

[5] The thesis in (4) is in an interesting way weaker than those in (1), (2), and (3): they rule out abortion even in cases in which both mother *and* child will die if the abortion is not performed. By contrast, one who held the view expressed in (4) could consistently say that one needn't prefer letting two persons die to killing one.

[6] Cf. the following passage from Pius XII, *Address to the Italian Catholic Society of Midwives:* "The baby in the maternal breast has the right to life immediately from God.—Hence there is no man, no human authority, no science, no medical, eugenic, social, economic or moral 'indication' which can establish or grant a valid juridical ground for a direct deliberate disposition of an innocent human life, that is a disposition which looks to its destruction either as an end or as a means to another end perhaps in itself not illicit.—The baby, still not born, is a man in the same degree and for the same reason as the mother" (quoted in Noonan, *The Morality of Abortion,* p. 45).

killing an innocent person is murder, and thus is impermissible, then the mother's directly killing the innocent person inside her is murder, and thus is impermissible. But it cannot seriously be thought to be murder if the mother performs an abortion on herself to save her life. It cannot seriously be said that she *must* refrain, that she *must* sit passively by and wait for her death. Let us look again at the case of you and the violinist. There you are, in bed with the violinist, and the director of the hospital says to you, "It's all most distressing, and I deeply sympathize, but you see this is putting an additional strain on your kidneys, and you'll be dead within the month. But you have to stay where you are all the same. Because unplugging you would be directly killing an innocent violinist, and that's murder, and that's impermissible." If anything in the world is true, it is that you do not commit murder, you do not do what is impermissible, if you reach around to your back and unplug yourself from that violinist to save your life.

The main focus of attention in writings on abortion has been on what a third party may or may not do in answer to a request from a woman for an abortion. This is in a way understandable. Things being as they are, there isn't much a woman can safely do to abort herself. So the question asked is what a third party may do, and what the mother may do, if it is mentioned at all, is deduced, almost as an afterthought, from what it is concluded that third parties may do. But it seems to me that to treat the matter in this way is to refuse to grant to the mother that very status of person which is so firmly insisted on for the fetus. For we cannot simply read off what a person may do from what a third party may do. Suppose you find yourself trapped in a tiny house with a growing child. I mean a very tiny house, and a rapidly growing child—you are already up against the wall of the house and in a few minutes you'll be crushed to death. The child on the other hand won't be crushed to death; if nothing is done to stop him from growing he'll be hurt, but in the end he'll simply burst open the house and walk out a free man. Now I could well understand it if a bystander were to say, "There's nothing we can do for you. We cannot choose between your life and his, we cannot be the ones to decide who is to live, we cannot intervene." But it cannot be concluded that you too can do nothing, that you cannot attack it to save your life. However innocent the child may be, you do not have to wait passively while it crushes you to death. Perhaps a pregnant woman is vaguely felt to have the status of house, to which we don't allow the right of self-defense. But if the woman houses the child, it should be remembered that she is a person who houses it.

I should perhaps stop to say explicitly that I am not claiming that people have a right to do anything whatever to save their lives. I think, rather, that there are drastic limits to the right of self-defense. If someone threatens you with death unless you torture someone else to death, I think you have not the right, even to save your life, to do so. But the case under consideration here is very different. In our case there are only two people involved, one whose life is threatened, and one who threatens it. Both are innocent: the one who is threatened is not threatened because of any fault, the one who threatens does not threaten because of any fault. For this reason we may feel that we bystanders cannot intervene. But the person threatened can.

In sum, a woman surely can defend her life against the threat to it posed by the unborn child, even if doing so involves its death. And this shows not merely that the theses in (1) through (4) are false; it shows also that the extreme view of abortion is false, and so we need not canvass any other possible ways of arriving at it from the argument I mentioned at the outset.

2. The extreme view could of course be weakened to say that while abortion is permissible to save the mother's life, it may not be performed by a third party, but only by the mother herself. But this cannot be right either. For what we have to keep in mind is that the mother and the unborn child are not like two tenants in a small house which has, by an unfortunate mistake, been rented to both: the mother *owns* the house. The fact that she does adds to the offensiveness of deducing that the mother can do nothing from the supposition that third parties can do nothing. But it does more than this: it casts a bright light on the supposition that third parties can do nothing. Certainly it lets us see that a third party who says "I cannot choose between you" is fooling himself if he thinks this is impartiality. If Jones has found and fastened on a certain coat, which he needs to keep him from freezing, but which Smith also needs to keep him from freezing, then it is not impartiality that says "I cannot choose between you" when Smith owns the coat. Women have said again and again "This body is *my* body!" and they have reason to feel angry, reason to feel that it has been like shouting into the wind. Smith, after all, is hardly likely to bless us if we say to him, "Of course it's your coat, anybody would grant that it is. But no one may choose between you and Jones who is to have it."

We should really ask what it is that says "no one may choose" in the face of the fact that the body that houses the child is the mother's body. It may be simply a failure to appreciate this fact. But it may be something more interesting, namely the sense that one has a right to refuse to lay hands on people, even where it would be just and fair to do so, even where justice seems to require that somebody do so. Thus justice might call for somebody to get Smith's coat back from Jones, and yet you have a right to refuse to be the one to lay hands on Jones, a right to refuse to do physical violence to him. This, I think, must be granted. But then what should be said is not "no one may choose," but only "*I* cannot choose," and indeed not even this, but "*I* will not *act*," leaving it open that somebody else can or should, and in particular that anyone in a position of authority, with the job of securing people's rights, both can and should. So this is no difficulty. I have not been arguing that any given third party must accede to the mother's request that he perform an abortion to save her life, but only that he may.

I suppose that in some views of human life the mother's body is only on loan to her, the loan not being one which gives her any prior claim to it. One who held this view might well think it impartiality to say "I cannot choose." But I shall simply ignore this possibility. My own view is that if a human being has any just, prior claim to anything at all, he has a just, prior claim to his own body. And perhaps this needn't be argued for here anyway, since, as I mentioned, the arguments against abortion we are looking at do grant that the woman has a right to decide what happens in and to her body.

But although they do grant it, I have tried to show that they do not take seriously what is done in granting it. I suggest the same thing will reappear even more clearly when we turn away from cases in which the mother's life is at stake, and attend, as I propose we now do, to the vastly more common cases in which a woman wants an abortion for some less weighty reason than preserving her own life.

3. Where the mother's life is not at stake, the argument I mentioned at the outset seems to have a much stronger pull. "Everyone has a right to life, so the unborn person has a right to life." And isn't the child's right to life weightier than anything other than the mother's own right to life, which she might put forward as ground for an abortion?

This argument treats the right to life as if it were unproblematic. It is not, and this seems to me to be precisely the source of the mistake.

For we should now, at long last, ask what it comes to, to have a right to life. In some views having a right to life includes having a right to be given at least the bare minimum one needs for continued life. But suppose that what in fact *is* the bare minimum a man needs for continued life is something he has no right at all to be given? If I am sick unto death, and the only thing that will save my life is the touch of Henry Fonda's cool hand on my fevered brow, then all the same, I have no right to be given the touch of Henry Fonda's cool hand on my fevered brow. It would be frightfully nice of him to fly in from the West Coast to provide it. It would be less nice, though no doubt well meant, if my friends flew out to the West Coast and carried Henry Fonda back with them. But I have no right at all against anybody that he should do this for me. Or again, to return to the story I told earlier, the fact that for continued life that violinist needs the continued use of your kidneys does not establish that he has a right to be given the continued use of your kidneys. He certainly has no right against you that *you* should give him continued use of your kidneys. For nobody has any right to use your kidneys unless you give him such a right; and nobody has the right against you that you shall give him this right—if you do allow him to go on using your kidneys, this is a kindness on your part, and not something he can claim from you as his due. Nor has he any right against anybody else that *they* should give him continued use of your kidneys. Certainly he had no right against the Society of Music Lovers that they should plug him into you in the first place. And if you now start to unplug yourself, having learned that you will otherwise have to spend nine years in bed with him, there is nobody in the world who must try to prevent you, in order to see to it that he is given something he has a right to be given.

Some people are rather stricter about the right to life. In their view, it does not include the right to be given anything, but amounts to, and only to, the right not to be killed by anybody. But here a related difficulty arises. If everybody is to refrain from killing that violinist, then everybody must refrain from doing a great many different sorts of things. Everybody must refrain from slitting his throat, everybody must refrain from shooting him—and everybody must refrain from unplugging you from him. But does he have a right against everybody that they shall refrain from unplugging you from him? To refrain from doing this is to allow him to continue to use your kidneys. It could be argued that he has a right against us that *we* should allow him to continue to use your kidneys. That is, while he had no right against us that we should give him the use of your kidneys, it might be argued that he anyway has a right against us that we shall not now intervene and deprive him of the use of your kidneys. I shall come back to third-party interventions later. But certainly the violinist has no right against you that *you* shall allow him to continue to use your kidneys. As I said, if you do allow him to use them, it is a kindness on your part, and not something you owe him.

The difficulty I point to here is not peculiar to the right to life. It reappears in connection with all the other natural rights; and it is something which an adequate account of rights must deal with. For present purposes it is enough just to draw attention to it. But I would stress that I am not arguing that people do not have a right to life—quite to the contrary, it seems to me that the primary control we must place on the acceptability of an account of rights is that it should turn out in that account to be a truth that all persons have a right to life. I am arguing only that having a right to life does not guarantee having either a right to be given the use of or a right to be allowed continued use of another person's body—even if one needs it for life itself. So the right to life will not serve the opponents of abortion in the very simple and clear way in which they seem to have thought it would.

4. There is another way to bring out the difficulty. In the most ordinary sort of case, to deprive someone of what he has a right to is to treat him unjustly. Suppose a boy and his small brother are jointly given a box of chocolates for Christmas. If the older boy takes the box and refuses to give his brother any of the chocolates, he is unjust to him, for the brother has been given a right to half of them. But suppose that, having learned that otherwise it means nine years in bed with that violinist, you unplug yourself from him. You surely are not being unjust to him, for you gave him no right to use your kidneys, and no one else can have given him any such right. But we have to notice that in unplugging yourself, you are killing him; and violinists, like everybody else, have a right to life, and thus in the view we are considering just now, the right not to be killed. So here you do what he supposedly has a right you shall not do, but you do not act unjustly to him in doing it.

The emendation which may be made at this point is this: the right to life consists not in the right not to be killed, but rather in the right not to be killed unjustly. This runs a risk of circularity, but never mind: it would enable us to square the fact that the violinist has a right to life with the fact that you do not act unjustly toward him in unplugging yourself, thereby killing him. For if you do not kill him unjustly, you do not violate his right to life, and so it is no wonder you do him no injustice.

But if this emendation is accepted, the gap in the argument against abortion stares us plainly in the face: it is by no means enough to show that the fetus is a person, and to remind us that all persons have a right to life—we need to be shown also that killing the fetus violates its right to life, i.e., that abortion is unjust killing. And is it?

I suppose we may take it as a datum that in a case of pregnancy due to rape the mother has not given the unborn person a right to the use of her body for food and shelter. Indeed, in what pregnancy could it be supposed that the mother has given the unborn person such a right? It is not as if there were unborn persons drifting about the world, to whom a woman who wants a child says "I invite you in."

But it might be argued that there are other ways one can have acquired a right to the use of another person's body than by having been invited to use it by that person. Suppose a woman voluntarily indulges in intercourse, knowing of the chance it will issue in pregnancy, and then she does become pregnant; is she not in part responsible for the presence, in fact the very existence, of the unborn person inside her? No doubt she did not invite it in. But doesn't her partial responsibility for its being there itself give it a right to the use of her body?[7] If so, then her aborting it would be more like the boy's taking away the chocolates, and less like your unplugging yourself from the violinist—doing so would be depriving it of what it does have a right to, and thus would be doing it an injustice.

And then, too, it might be asked whether or not she can kill it even to save her own life: If she voluntarily called it into existence, how can she now kill it, even in self-defense?

The first thing to be said about this is that it is something new. Opponents of abortion have been so concerned to make out the independence of the fetus, in order to establish that it has a right to life, just as its mother does, that they have tended to overlook the possible support they might gain from making out that the fetus is *dependent* on the mother, in order to establish that she has a special kind of responsibility for it, a responsibility that gives it rights against her which are not possessed by any independent person— such as an ailing violinist who is a stranger to her.

On the other hand, this argument would give the unborn person a right to its mother's body only if her pregnancy resulted from a voluntary act, undertaken in full knowledge of the chance a pregnancy might result from it. It would leave out entirely the unborn person whose existence is due to

[7] The need for a discussion of this argument was brought home to me by members of the Society for Ethical and Legal Philosophy, to whom this paper was originally presented.

rape. Pending the availability of some further argument, then, we would be left with the conclusion that unborn persons whose existence is due to rape have no right to the use of their mothers' bodies, and thus that aborting them is not depriving them of anything they have a right to and hence is not unjust killing.

And we should also notice that it is not at all plain that this argument really does go even as far as it purports to. For there are cases and cases, and the details make a difference. If the room is stuffy, and I therefore open a window to air it, and a burglar climbs in, it would be absurd to say, "Ah, now he can stay, she's given him a right to the use of her house—for she is partially responsible for his presence there, having voluntarily done what enabled him to get in, in full knowledge that there are such things as burglars, and that burglars burgle." It would be still more absurd to say this if I had had bars installed outside my windows, precisely to prevent burglars from getting in, and a burglar got in only because of a defect in the bars. It remains equally absurd if we imagine it is not a burglar who climbs in, but an innocent person who blunders or falls in. Again, suppose it were like this: people-seeds drift about in the air like pollen, and if you open your windows, one may drift in and take root in your carpets or upholstery. You don't want children, so you fix up your windows with fine mesh screens, the very best you can buy. As can happen, however, and on very, very rare occasions does happen, one of the screens is defective; and a seed drifts in and takes root. Does the person–plant who now develops have a right to the use of your house? Surely not—despite the fact that you voluntarily opened your windows, you knowingly kept carpets and upholstered furniture, and you knew that screens were sometimes defective. Someone may argue that you are responsible for its rooting, that it does have a right to your house, because after all you *could* have lived out your life with bare floors and furniture, or with sealed windows and doors. But this won't do—for by the same token anyone can avoid a pregnancy due to rape by having a hysterectomy, or anyway by never leaving home without a (reliable!) army.

It seems to me that the argument we are looking at can establish at most that there are *some* cases in which the unborn person has a right to the use of its mother's body, and therefore some cases in which abortion is unjust killing. There is room for much discussion and argument as to precisely which, if any. But I think we should sidestep this issue and leave it open, for at any rate the argument certainly does not establish that all abortion is unjust killing.

5. There is room for yet another argument here, however. We surely must all grant that there may be cases in which it would be morally indecent to detach a person from your body at the cost of his life. Suppose you learn that what the violinist needs is not nine years of your life, but only one hour: all you need do to save his life is to spend one hour in that bed with him. Suppose also that letting him use your kidneys for that one hour would not affect your health in the slightest. Admittedly you were kidnapped. Admit-

tedly you did not give anyone permission to plug him into you. Nevertheless it seems to me plain you *ought* to allow him to use your kidneys for that hour—it would be indecent to refuse.

Again, suppose pregnancy lasted only an hour, and constituted no threat to life or health. And suppose that a woman becomes pregnant as a result of rape. Admittedly she did not voluntarily do anything to bring about the existence of a child. Admittedly she did nothing at all which would give the unborn person a right to the use of her body. All the same it might well be said, as in the newly emended violinist story, that she ought to allow it to remain for that hour—that it would be indecent in her to refuse.

Now some people are inclined to use the term "right" in such a way that it follows from the fact that you ought to allow a person to use your body for the hour he needs, that he has a right to use your body for the hour he needs, even though he has not been given that right by any person or act. They may say that it follows also that if you refuse, you act unjustly toward him. This use of the term is perhaps so common that it cannot be called wrong; nevertheless it seems to me to be an unfortunate loosening of what we would do better to keep a tight rein on. Suppose that box of chocolates I mentioned earlier had not been given to both boys jointly, but was given only to the older boy. There he sits, stolidly eating his way through the box, his small brother watching enviously. Here we are likely to say "You ought not to be so mean. You ought to give your brother some of those chocolates." My own view is that it just does not follow from the truth of this that the brother has any right to any of the chocolates. If the boy refuses to give his brother any, he is greedy, stingy, callous—but not unjust. I suppose that the people I have in mind will say it does follow that the brother has a right to some of the chocolates, and thus that the boy does act unjustly if he refuses to give his brother any. But the effect of saying this is to obscure what we should keep distinct, namely the difference between the boy's refusal in this case and the boy's refusal in the earlier case, in which the box was given to both boys jointly, and in which the small brother thus had what was from any point of view clear title to half.

A further objection to so using the term "right" that from the fact that A ought to do a thing for B, it follows that B has a right against A that A do it for him, is that it is going to make the question of whether or not a man has a right to a thing turn on how easy it is to provide him with it; and this seems not merely unfortunate, but morally unacceptable. Take the case of Henry Fonda again. I said earlier that I had no right to the touch of his cool hand on my fevered brow, even though I needed it to save my life. I said it would be frightfully nice of him to fly in from the West Coast to provide me with it, but that I had no right against him that he should do so. But suppose he isn't on the West Coast. Suppose he has only to walk across the room, place a hand briefly on my brow—and lo, my life is saved. Then surely he ought to do it, it would be indecent to refuse. Is it to be said "Ah, well, it follows that in this case she has a right to the touch of his hand on her brow, and so it would be an injustice in him to refuse"? So that I have a right to it when it is easy for him to provide it, though no right when it's hard? It's rather a shocking idea that anyone's rights should fade away and disappear as it gets harder and harder to accord them to him.

So my own view is that even though you ought to let the violinist use your kidneys for the one hour he needs, we should not conclude that he has a right to do so—we would say that if you refuse, you are, like the boy who owns all the chocolates and will give none away, self-centered and callous, indecent in fact, but not unjust. And similarly, that even supposing a case in which a woman pregnant due to rape ought to allow the unborn person to use her body for the hour he needs, we should not conclude that he has a right to do so; we should conclude that she is self-centered, callous, indecent, but not unjust, if she refuses. The complaints are no less grave; they are just different. However, there is no need to insist on this point. If anyone does wish to deduce "he has a right" from "you ought," then all the same he must surely grant that there are cases in which it is not morally required of you that you allow that violinist to use your kidneys, and in which he does not have a right to use them, and in which you do not do him an injustice if you refuse. And so also for mother and unborn child. Except in such cases as the unborn person has a right to demand it—and we were leaving open the possibility that there may be such cases—nobody is morally *required* to make large sacrifices, of health, of all other interests and concerns, of all other duties and commitments, for nine years, or even for nine months, in order to keep another person alive.

6. We have in fact to distinguish between two kinds of Samaritan: the Good Samaritan and what we might call the Minimally Decent Samaritan. The story of the Good Samaritan, you will remember, goes like this:

> A certain man went down from Jerusalem to Jericho, and fell among thieves, which stripped him of his raiment, and wounded him, and departed, leaving him half dead.
>
> And by chance there came down a certain priest that way; and when he saw him, he passed by on the other side.
>
> And likewise a Levite, when he was at the place, came and looked on him, and passed by on the other side.
>
> But a certain Samaritan, as he journeyed, came where he was; and when he saw him he had compassion on him.
>
> And went to him, and bound up his wounds, pouring in oil and wine, and set him on his own beast, and brought him to an inn, and took care of him.
>
> And on the morrow, when he departed, he took out two pence, and gave them to the host, and said unto him, "Take care of him; and whatsoever thou spendest more, when I come again, I will repay thee."
>
> (LUKE 10:30–35)

The Good Samaritan went out of his way, at some cost to himself, to help one in need of it. We are not told what the options were, that is, whether or not the priest and the Levite could have helped by doing less than the Good

Samaritan did, but assuming they could have, then the fact they did nothing at all shows they were not even Minimally Decent Samaritans, not because they were not Samaritans, but because they were not even minimally decent.

These things are a matter of degree, of course, but there is a difference, and it comes out perhaps most clearly in the story of Kitty Genovese, who, as you will remember, was murdered while thirty-eight people watched or listened, and did nothing at all to help her. A Good Samaritan would have rushed out to give direct assistance against the murderer. Or perhaps we had better allow that it would have been a Splendid Samaritan who did this, on the ground that it would have involved a risk of death for himself. But the thirty-eight not only did not do this, they did not even trouble to pick up a phone to call the police. Minimally Decent Samaritanism would call for doing at least that, and their not having done it was monstrous.

After telling the story of the Good Samaritan, Jesus said "Go, and do thou likewise." Perhaps he meant that we are morally required to act as the Good Samaritan did. Perhaps he was urging people to do more than is morally required of them. At all events it seems plain that it was not morally required of any of the thirty-eight that he rush out to give direct assistance at the risk of his own life, and that it is not morally required of anyone that he give long stretches of his life — nine years or nine months — to sustaining the life of a person who has no special right (we were leaving open the possibility of this) to demand it.

Indeed, with one rather striking class of exceptions, no one in any country in the world is *legally* required to do anywhere near as much as this for anyone else. The class of exceptions is obvious. My main concern here is not the state of the law in respect to abortion, but it is worth drawing attention to the fact that in no state in this country is any man compelled by law to be even a Minimally Decent Samaritan to any person; there is no law under which charges could be brought against the thirty-eight who stood by while Kitty Genovese died. By contrast, in most states in this country women are compelled by law to be not merely Minimally Decent Samaritans, but Good Samaritans to unborn persons inside them. This doesn't by itself settle anything one way or the other, because it may well be argued that there should be laws in this country — as there are in many European countries — compelling at least Minimally Decent Samaritanism.[8] But it does show that there is a gross injustice in the existing state of the law. And it shows also that the groups currently working against liberalization of abortion laws, in fact working toward having it declared unconstitutional for a state to permit abortion, had better start working for the adoption of Good Samaritan laws generally, or earn the charge that they are acting in bad faith.

I should think, myself, that Minimally Decent Samaritan laws would be one thing, Good Samaritan laws quite another, and in fact highly improper.

---

[8] For a discussion of the difficulties involved, and a survey of the European experience with such laws, see *The Good Samaritan and the Law,* ed. James M. Ratcliffe (New York, 1966).

But we are not here concerned with the law. What we should ask is not whether anybody should be compelled by law to be a Good Samaritan, but whether we must accede to a situation in which somebody is being compelled — by nature, perhaps — to be a Good Samaritan. We have, in other words, to look now at third-party interventions. I have been arguing that no person is morally required to make large sacrifices to sustain the life of another who has no right to demand them, and this even where the sacrifices do not include life itself; we are not morally required to be Good Samaritans or anyway Very Good Samaritans to one another. But what if a man cannot extricate himself from such a situation? What if he appeals to us to extricate him? It seems to me plain that there are cases in which we can, cases in which a Good Samaritan would extricate him. There you are, you were kidnapped, and nine years in bed with that violinist lie ahead of you. You have your own life to lead. You are sorry, but you simply cannot see giving up so much of your life to the sustaining of his. You cannot extricate yourself, and ask us to do so. I should have thought that — in light of his having no right to the use of your body — it was obvious that we do not have to accede to your being forced to give up so much. We can do what you ask. There is no injustice to the violinist in our doing so.

7. Following the lead of the opponents of abortion, I have throughout been speaking of the fetus merely as a person, and what I have been asking is whether or not the argument we began with, which proceeds only from the fetus' being a person, really does establish its conclusion. I have argued that it does not.

But of course there are arguments and arguments, and it may be said that I have simply fastened on the wrong one. It may be said that what is important is not merely the fact that the fetus is a person, but that it is a person for whom the woman has a special kind of responsibility issuing from the fact that she is its mother. And it might be argued that all my analogies are therefore irrelevant — for you do not have that special kind of responsibility for that violinist, Henry Fonda does not have that special kind of responsibility for me. And our attention might be drawn to the fact that men and women both *are* compelled by law to provide support for their children.

I have in effect dealt (briefly) with this argument in section 4 above; but a (still briefer) recapitulation now may be in order. Surely we do not have any such "special responsibility" for a person unless we have assumed it, explicitly or implicitly. If a set of parents do not try to prevent pregnancy, do not obtain an abortion, and then at the time of birth of the child do not put it out for adoption, but rather take it home with them, then they have assumed responsibility for it, they have given it rights, and they cannot *now* withdraw support from it at the cost of its life because they now find it difficult to go on providing for it. But if they have taken all reasonable precautions against having a child, they do not simply by virtue of their biological relationship to the child who comes into existence have a special responsibility for it. They may wish to assume responsibility for it, or they may not wish to. And I am suggesting that if assuming responsibility for it would require large sacrifices, then they may refuse. A Good Samaritan would not refuse — or anyway, a Splendid Samaritan, if the sacrifices that had to be made were enormous. But then so would a Good Samaritan assume responsibility for that violinist; so would Henry Fonda, if he is a Good Samaritan, fly in from the West Coast and assume responsibility for me.

8. My argument will be found unsatisfactory on two counts by many of those who want to regard abortion as morally permissible. First, while I do argue that abortion is not impermissible, I do not argue that it is always permissible. There may well be cases in which carrying the child to term requires only Minimally Decent Samaritanism of the mother, and this is a standard we must not fall below. I am inclined to think it a merit of my account precisely that it does *not* give a general yes or a general no. It allows for and supports our sense that, for example, a sick and desperately frightened fourteen-year-old schoolgirl, pregnant due to rape, may *of course* choose abortion, and that any law which rules this out is an insane law. And it also allows for and supports our sense that in other cases resort to abortion is even positively indecent. It would be indecent in the woman to request an abortion, and indecent in a doctor to perform it, if she is in her seventh month, and wants the abortion just to avoid the nuisance of postponing a trip abroad. The very fact that the arguments I have been drawing attention to treat all cases of abortion, or even all cases of abortion in which the mother's life is not at stake, as morally on a par ought to have made them suspect at the outset.

Secondly, while I am arguing for the permissibility of abortion in some cases, I am not arguing for the right to secure the death of the unborn child. It is easy to confuse these two things in that up to a certain point in the life of the fetus it is not able to survive outside the mother's body; hence removing it from her body guarantees its death. But they are importantly different. I have argued that you are not morally required to spend nine months in bed, sustaining the life of that violinist; but to say this is by no means to say that if, when you unplug yourself, there is a miracle and he survives, you then have a right to turn round and slit his throat. You may detach yourself even if this costs him his life; you have no right to be guaranteed his death, by some other means, if unplugging yourself does not kill him. There are some people who will feel dissatisfied by this feature of my argument. A woman may be utterly devastated by the thought of a child, a bit of herself, put out for adoption and never seen or heard of again. She may therefore want not merely that the child be detached from her, but more, that it die. Some opponents of abortion are inclined to regard this as beneath contempt — thereby showing insensitivity to what is surely a powerful source of despair. All the same, I agree that the desire for the child's death is not one which anybody may gratify, should it turn out to be possible to detach the child alive.

At this place, however, it should be remembered that we have only been pretending throughout that the fetus is a human being from the moment of conception. A very early abortion is surely not the killing of a person, and so is not dealt with by anything I have said here.

ON THE MORAL AND LEGAL STATUS OF ABORTION

MARY ANNE WARREN

We will be concerned with both the moral status of abortion, which for our purposes we may define as the act which a woman performs in voluntarily terminating, or allowing another person to terminate, her pregnancy, and the legal status which is appropriate for this act. I will argue that, while it is not possible to produce a satisfactory defense of a woman's right to obtain an abortion without showing that a fetus is not a human being, in the morally relevant sense of that term, we ought not to conclude that the difficulties involved in determining whether or not a fetus is human make it impossible to produce any satisfactory solution to the problem of the moral status of abortion. For it is possible to show that, on the basis of intuitions which we may expect even the opponents of abortion to share, a fetus is not a person, and hence not the sort of entity to which it is proper to ascribe full moral rights.

Of course, while some philosophers would deny the possibility of any such proof,[1] others will deny that there is any need for it, since the moral permissibility of abortion appears to them to be too obvious to require proof. But the inadequacy of this attitude should be evident from the fact that both the friends and the foes of abortion consider their position to be morally self-evident. Because pro-abortionists have never adequately come to grips with the conceptual issues surrounding abortion, most if not all, of the arguments which they advance in opposition to laws restricting access to abortion fail to refute or even weaken the traditional antiabortion argument, i.e., that a fetus is a human being, and therefore abortion is murder.

These arguments are typically of one of two sorts. Either they point to the

Reprinted from *The Monist,* Vol. 57, No. 1 (January 1973), 43–61, with the permission of the publisher and the author. The "Postscript on Infanticide" by Mary Anne Warren was added especially for this volume.

[1] For example, Roger Wertheimer, who in "Understanding the Abortion Argument" (*Philosophy and Public Affairs,* 1, No. 1 [Fall 1971], 67–95), argues that the problem of the moral status of abortion is insoluble, in that the dispute over the status of the fetus is not a question of fact at all, but only a question of how one responds to the facts.

terrible side effects of the restrictive laws, e.g., the deaths due to illegal abortions, and the fact that it is poor women who suffer the most as a result of these laws, or else they state that to deny a woman access to abortion is to deprive her of her right to control her own body. Unfortunately, however, the fact that restricting access to abortion has tragic side effects does not, in itself, show that the restrictions are unjustified, since murder is wrong regardless of the consequences of prohibiting it; and the appeal to the right to control one's body, which is generally construed as a property right, is at best a rather feeble argument for the permissibility of abortion. Mere ownership does not give me the right to kill innocent people whom I find on my property, and indeed I am apt to be held responsible if such people injure themselves while on my property. It is equally unclear that I have any moral right to expel an innocent person from my property when I know that doing so will result in his death.

Furthermore, it is probably inappropriate to describe a woman's body as her property, since it seems natural to hold that a person is something distinct from her property, but not from her body. Even those who would object to the identification of a person with his body, or with the conjunction of his body and his mind, must admit that it would be very odd to describe, say, breaking a leg, as damaging one's property, and much more appropriate to describe it as injuring one*self.* Thus it is probably a mistake to argue that the right to obtain an abortion is in any way derived from the right to own and regulate property.

But however we wish to construe the right to abortion, we cannot hope to convince those who consider abortion a form of murder of the existence of any such right unless we are able to produce a clear and convincing refutation of the traditional antiabortion argument, and this has not, to my knowledge, been done. With respect to the two most vital issues which that argument involves, i.e., the humanity of the fetus and its implication for the moral status of abortion, confusion has prevailed on both sides of the dispute.

Thus, both proabortionists and antiabortionists have tended to abstract the question of whether abortion is wrong to that of whether it is wrong to destroy a fetus, just as though the rights of another person were not necessarily involved. This mistaken abstraction has led to the almost universal assumption that if a fetus is a human being, with a right to life, then it follows immediately that abortion is wrong (except perhaps when necessary to save the woman's life), and that it ought to be prohibited. It has also been generally assumed that unless the question about the status of the fetus is answered, the moral status of abortion cannot possibly be determined.

Two recent papers, one by B. A. Brody,[2] and one by Judith Thomson,[3] have attempted to settle the question of whether abortion ought to be pro-

---

[2] B. A. Brody, "Abortion and the Law," *The Journal of Philosophy,* 68, No. 12 (June 17, 1971), 357–69.

[3] Judith Thomson, "A Defense of Abortion," *Philosophy and Public Affairs,* 1, No. 1 (Fall 1971), 47–66.

hibited apart from the question of whether or not the fetus is human. Brody examines the possibility that the following two statements are compatible: (1) that abortion is the taking of innocent human life, and therefore wrong; and (2) that nevertheless it ought not to be prohibited by law, at least under the present circumstances.[4] Not surprisingly, Brody finds it impossible to reconcile these two statements, since, as he rightly argues, none of the unfortunate side effects of the prohibition of abortion is bad enough to justify legalizing the *wrongful* taking of human life. He is mistaken, however, in concluding that the incompatibility of (1) and (2), in itself, shows that "the legal problem about abortion cannot be resolved independently of the status of the fetus problem" (p. 369).

What Brody fails to realize is that (1) embodies the questionable assumption that if a fetus is a human being, then of course abortion is morally wrong, and that an attack on *this* assumption is more promising, as a way of reconciling the humanity of the fetus with the claim that laws prohibiting abortion are unjustified, than is an attack on the assumption that if abortion is the wrongful killing of innocent human beings then it ought to be prohibited. He thus overlooks the possibility that a fetus may have a right to life and abortion still be morally permissible, in that the right of a woman to terminate an unwanted pregnancy might override the right of the fetus to be kept alive. The immorality of abortion is no more demonstrated by the humanity of the fetus, in itself, than the immorality of killing in self-defense is demonstrated by the fact that the assailant is a human being. Neither is it demonstrated by the *innocence* of the fetus, since there may be situations in which the killing of innocent human beings is justified.

It is perhaps not surprising that Brody fails to spot this assumption, since it has been accepted with little or no argument by nearly everyone who has written on the morality of abortion. John Noonan is correct in saying that "the fundamental question in the long history of abortion is, How do you determine the humanity of a being?"[5] He summarizes his own antiabortion argument, which is a version of the official position of the Catholic Church, as follows:

> . . . it is wrong to kill humans, however poor, weak, defenseless, and lacking in opportunity to develop their potential they may be. It is therefore morally wrong to kill Biafrans. Similarly, it is morally wrong to kill embryos.[6]

Noonan bases his claim that fetuses are human upon what he calls the theologians' criterion of humanity: that whoever is conceived of human beings is human. But although he argues at length for the appropriateness of this criterion, he never questions the assumption that if a fetus is human then abortion is wrong for exactly the same reason that murder is wrong.

---

[4] I have abbreviated these statements somewhat, but not in a way which affects the argument.
[5] John Noonan, "Abortion and the Catholic Church: A Summary History," *Natural Law Forum*, 12 (1967), 125.
[6] John Noonan, "Deciding Who Is Human," *Natural Law Forum*, 13 (1968), 134.

Judith Thomson is, in fact, the only writer I am aware of who has seriously questioned this assumption; she has argued that, even if we grant the anti-abortionist his claim that a fetus is a humen being, with the same right to life as any other human being, we can still demonstrate that, in at least some and perhaps most cases, a woman is under no moral obligation to complete an unwanted pregnancy.[7] Her argument is worth examining, since if it holds up it may enable us to establish the moral permissibility of abortion without becoming involved in problems about what entitles an entity to be considered human, and accorded full moral rights. To be able to do this would be a great gain in the power and simplicity of the proabortion position, since, although I will argue that these problems can be solved at least as decisively as can any other moral problem, we should certainly be pleased to be able to avoid having to solve them as part of the justification of abortion.

On the other hand, even if Thomson's argument does not hold up, her insight, i.e., that it requires *argument* to show that if fetuses are human then abortion is properly classified as murder, is an extremely valuable one. The assumption she attacks is particularly invidious, for it amounts to the decision that it is appropriate, in deciding the moral status of abortion, to leave the rights of the pregnant woman out of consideration entirely, except possibly when her life is threatened. Obviously, this will not do; determining what moral rights, if any, a fetus possesses is only the first step in determining the moral status of abortion. Step two, which is at least equally essential, is finding a just solution to the conflict between whatever rights the fetus may have, and the rights of the woman who is unwillingly pregnant. While the historical error has been to pay far too little attention to the second step, Ms. Thomson's suggestion is that if we look at the second step first we may find that a woman has a right to obtain an abortion *regardless* of what rights the fetus has.

Our own inquiry will also have two stages. In Section I, we will consider whether or not it is possible to establish that abortion is morally permissible even on the assumption that a fetus is an entity with a full-fledged right to life. I will argue that in fact this cannot be established, at least not with the conclusiveness which is essential to our hopes of convincing those who are skeptical about the morality of abortion, and that we therefore cannot avoid dealing with the question of whether or not a fetus really does have the same right to life as a (more fully developed) human being.

In Section II, I will propose an answer to this question, namely, that a fetus cannot be considered a member of the moral community, the set of beings with full and equal moral rights, for the simple reason that it is not a person, and that it is personhood, and not genetic humanity, i.e., humanity as defined by Noonan, which is the basis for membership in this community. I will argue that a fetus, whatever its stage of development, satisfies none of the basic criteria of personhood, and is not even enough *like* a person to be

---

[7] "A Defense of Abortion."

accorded even some of the same rights on the basis of this resemblance. Nor, as we will see, is a fetus's *potential* personhood a threat to the morality of abortion, since, whatever the rights of potential people may be, they are invariably overridden in any conflict with the moral rights of actual people.

I

We turn now to Professor Thomson's case for the claim that even if a fetus has full moral rights, abortion is still morally permissible, at least sometimes, and for some reasons other than to save the woman's life. Her argument is based upon a clever, but I think faulty, analogy. She asks us to picture ourselves waking up one day, in bed with a famous violinist. Imagine that you have been kidnapped, and your bloodstream hooked up to that of the violinist, who happens to have an ailment which will certainly kill him unless he is permitted to share your kidneys for a period of nine months. No one else can save him, since you alone have the right type of blood. He will be unconscious all that time, and you will have to stay in bed with him, but after the nine months are over he may be unplugged, completely cured, that is provided that you have cooperated.

Now then, she continues, what are your obligations in this situation? The antiabortionist, if he is consistent, will have to say that you are obligated to stay in bed with the violinist: for all people have a right to life, and violinists are people, and therefore it would be murder for you to disconnect yourself from him and let him die (p. 49). But this is outrageous, and so there must be something wrong with the same argument when it is applied to abortion. It would certainly be commendable of you to agree to save the violinist, but it is absurd to suggest that your refusal to do so would be murder. His right to life does not obligate you to do whatever is required to keep him alive; nor does it justify anyone else in forcing you to do so. A law which required you to say in bed with the violinist would clearly be an unjust law, since it is no proper function of the law to force unwilling people to make huge sacrifices for the sake of other people toward whom they have no such prior obligation.

Thomson concludes that, if this analogy is an apt one, then we can grant the antiabortionist his claim that a fetus is a human being, and still hold that it is at least sometimes the case that a pregnant woman has the right to refuse to be a Good Samaritan towards the fetus, i.e., to obtain an abortion. For there is a great gap between the claim that x has a right to life, and the claim that y is obligated to do whatever is necessary to keep x alive, let alone that he ought to be forced to do so. It is y's duty to keep x alive only if he has somehow contracted a *special* obligation to do so; and a woman who is unwillingly pregnant, e.g., who was raped, has done nothing which obligates her to make the enormous sacrifice which is necessary to preserve the conceptus.

This argument is initially quite plausible, and in the extreme case of pregnancy due to rape it is probably conclusive. Difficulties arise, however, when we try to specify more exactly the range of cases in which abortion is clearly justifiable even on the assumption that the fetus is human. Professor Thomson considers it a virtue of her argument that it does not enable us to conclude that abortion is *always* permissible. It would, she says, be "indecent" for a woman in her seventh month to obtain an abortion just to avoid having to postpone a trip to Europe. On the other hand, her argument enables us to see that "a sick and desperately frightened schoolgirl pregnant due to rape may *of course* choose abortion, and that any law which rules this out is an insane law" (p. 65). So far, so good; but what are we to say about the woman who becomes pregnant not through rape but as a result of her own carelessness, or because of contraceptive failure, or who gets pregnant intentionally and then changes her mind about wanting a child? With respect to such cases, the violinist analogy is of much less use to the defender of the woman's right to obtain an abortion.

Indeed, the choice of a pregnancy due to rape, as an example of a case in which abortion is permissible even if a fetus is considered a human being, is extremely significant; for it is only in the case of pregnancy due to rape that the woman's situation is adequately analogous to the violinist case for our intuitions about the latter to transfer convincingly. The crucial difference between a pregnancy due to rape and the *normal* case of an unwanted pregnancy is that in the normal case we cannot claim that the woman is in no way responsible for her predicament; she could have remained chaste, or taken her pills more faithfully, or abstained on dangerous days, and so on. If, on the other hand, you are kidnapped by strangers, and hooked up to a strange violinist, then you are free of any shred of responsibility for the situation, on the basis of which it could be argued that you are obligated to keep the violinist alive. Only when her pregnancy is due to rape is a woman clearly just as nonresponsible.[8]

Consequently, there is room for the antiabortionist to argue that in the normal case of unwanted pregnancy a woman has, by her own actions, assumed responsibility for the fetus. For if x behaves in a way which he could have avoided, and which he knows involves, let us say, a 1 percent chance of bringing into existence a human being, with a right to life, and does so knowing that if this should happen then that human being will perish unless x does certain things to keep him alive, then it is by no means clear that when it does happen x is free of any obligation to what he knew in advance would be required to keep that human being alive.

[8] We may safely ignore the fact that she might have avoided getting raped, e.g., by carrying a gun, since by similar means you might likewise have avoided getting kidnapped, and in neither case does the victim's failure to take all possible precautions against a highly unlikely event (as opposed to reasonable precautions against a rather likely event) mean that he is morally responsible for what happens.

The plausibility of such an argument is enough to show that the Thomson analogy can provide a clear and persuasive defense of a woman's right to obtain an abortion only with respect to those cases in which the woman is in no way responsible for her pregnancy, e.g., where it is due to rape. In all other cases, we would almost certainly conclude that it was necessary to look carefully at the particular circumstances in order to determine the extent of the woman's responsibility, and hence the extent of her obligation. This is an extremely unsatisfactory outcome, from the viewpoint of the opponents of restrictive abortion laws, most of whom are convinced that a woman has a right to obtain an abortion regardless of how and why she got pregnant.

Of course a supporter of the violinist analogy might point out that it is absurd to suggest that forgetting her pill one day might be sufficient to obligate a woman to complete an unwanted pregnancy. And indeed it *is* absurd to suggest this. As we will see, the moral right to obtain an abortion is not in the least dependent upon the extent to which the woman is responsible for her pregnancy. But unfortunately, once we allow the assumption that a fetus has full moral rights, we cannot avoid taking this absurd suggestion seriously. Perhaps we can make this point more clear by altering the violinist story just enough to make it more analogous to a normal unwanted pregnancy and less to a pregnancy due to rape, and then seeing whether it is still obvious that you are not obligated to stay in bed with the fellow.

Suppose, then, that violinists are peculiarly prone to the sort of illness the only cure for which is the use of someone else's bloodstream for nine months, and that because of this there has been formed a society of music lovers who agree that whenever a violinist is stricken they will draw lots and the loser will, by some means, be made the one and only person capable of saving him. Now then, would you be obligated to cooperate in curing the violinist if you had voluntarily joined this society, knowing the possible consequences, and then your name had been drawn and you had been kidnapped? Admittedly, you did not promise ahead of time that you would, but you did deliberately place yourself in a position in which it might happen that a human life would be lost if you did not. Surely this is at least a prima facie reason for supposing that you have an obligation to stay in bed with the violinist. Suppose that you had gotten your name drawn deliberately; surely *that* would be quite a strong reason for thinking that you had such an obligation.

It might be suggested that there is one important disanalogy between the modified violinist case and the case of an unwanted pregnancy, which makes the woman's responsibility significantly less, namely, the fact that the fetus *comes into existence* as the result of the woman's actions. This fact might give her a right to refuse to keep it alive, whereas she would not have had this right had it existed previously, independently, and then as a result of her actions become dependent upon her for its survival.

My own intuition, however, is that x has no more right to bring into existence, either deliberately or as a foreseeable result of actions he could have avoided, a being with full moral rights *(y),* and then refuse to do what he knew beforehand would be required to keep that being alive, than he has to enter into an agreement with an existing person, whereby he may be called upon to save that person's life, and then refuse to do so when so called upon. Thus, *x*'s responsibility for *y*'s existence does not seem to lessen his obligation to keep *y* alive, if he is also responsible for *y*'s being in a situation in which only he can save him.

Whether or not this intuition is entirely correct, it brings us back once again to the conclusion that once we allow the assumption that a fetus has full moral rights it becomes an extremely complex and difficult question whether and when abortion is justifiable. Thus the Thomson analogy cannot help us produce a clear and persuasive proof of the moral permissibility of abortion. Nor will the opponents of the restrictive laws thank us for anything less; for their conviction (for the most part) is that abortion is obviously *not* a morally serious and extremely unfortunate, even though sometimes justified act, comparable to killing in self-defense or to letting the violinist die, but rather is closer to being a morally neutral act, like cutting one's hair.

The basis of this conviction, I believe, is the realization that a fetus is not a person, and thus does not have a full-fledged right to life. Perhaps the reason why this claim has been so inadequately defended is that it seems self-evident to those who accept it. And so it is, insofar as it follows from what I take to be perfectly obvious claims about the nature of personhood, and about the proper grounds for ascribing moral rights, claims which ought, indeed, to be obvious to both the friends and foes of abortion. Nevertheless, it is worth examining these claims, and showing how they demonstrate the moral innocuousness of abortion, since this apparently has not been adequately done before.

II

The question which we must answer in order to produce a satisfactory solution to the problem of the moral status of abortion is this: How are we to define the moral community, the set of beings with full and equal moral rights, such that we can decide whether a human fetus is a member of this community or not? What sort of entity, exactly, has the inalienable rights to life, liberty, and the pursuit of happiness? Jefferson attributed these rights to all *men,* and it may or may not be fair to suggest that he intended to attribute them *only* to men. Perhaps he ought to have attributed them to all human beings. If so, then we arrive, first, at Noonan's problem of defining what makes a being human, and, second, at the equally vital question which Noonan does not consider, namely, What reason is there for identifying the moral community with the set of all human beings, in whatever way we have chosen to define that term?

1. On the Definition of "Human"

One reason why this vital second question is so frequently overlooked in the debate over the moral status of abortion is that the term "human" has two distinct, but not often distinguished, senses. This fact results in a slide of meaning, which serves to conceal the fallaciousness of the traditional argument that since (1) it is wrong to kill innocent human beings, and (2) fetuses are innocent human beings, then (3) it is wrong to kill fetuses. For if "human" is used in the same sense in both (1) and (2) then, whichever of the two senses is meant, one of these premises is question-begging. And if it is used in two different senses then of course the conclusion doesn't follow.

Thus, (1) is a self-evident moral truth,[9] and avoids begging the question about abortion, only if "human being" is used to mean something like "a full-fledged member of the moral community." (It may or may not also be meant to refer exclusively to members of the species *Homo sapiens.*) We may call this the *moral* sense of "human." It is not to be confused with what we will call the *genetic* sense, i.e., the sense in which *any* member of the species is a human being, and no member of any other species could be. If (1) is acceptable only if the moral sense is intended, (2) is non-question-begging only if what is intended is the genetic sense.

In "Deciding Who Is Human," Noonan argues for the classification of fetuses with human beings by pointing to the presence of the full genetic code, and the potential capacity for rational thought (p. 135). It is clear that what he needs to show, for his version of the traditional argument to be valid, is that fetuses are human in the moral sense, the sense in which it is analytically true that all human beings have full moral rights. But, in the absence of any argument showing that whatever is genetically human is also morally human, and he gives none, nothing more than genetic humanity can be demonstrated by the presence of the human genetic code. And, as we will see, the *potential* capacity for rational thought can at most show that an entity has the potential for *becoming* human in the moral sense.

2. Defining the Moral Community

Can it be established that genetic humanity is sufficient for moral humanity? I think that there are very good reasons for not defining the moral community in this way. I would like to suggest an alternative way of defining the moral community, which I will argue for only to the extent of explaining why it is, or should be, self-evident. The suggestion is simply that the moral community consists of all and only *people,* rather than all and only human beings;[10]

---

[9] Of course, the principle that it is (always) wrong to kill innocent human beings is in need of many modifications, e.g., that it may be permissible to do so to save a greater number of other innocent human beings, but we may safely ignore these complications here.

[10] From here on, we will use "human" to mean genetically human, since the moral sense seems closely connected to, and perhaps derived from, the assumption that genetic humanity is sufficient for membership in the moral community.

and probably the best way of demonstrating its self-evidence is by considering the concept of personhood, to see what sorts of entity are and are not persons, and what the decision that a being is or is not a person implies about its moral rights.

What characteristics entitle an entity to be considered a person? This is obviously not the place to attempt a complete analysis of the concept of personhood, but we do not need such a fully adequate analysis just to determine whether and why a fetus is or isn't a person. All we need is a rough and approximate list of the most basic criteria of personhood, and some idea of which, or how many, of these an entity must satisfy in order to properly be considered a person.

In searching for such criteria, it is useful to look beyond the set of people with whom we are acquainted, and ask how we would decide whether a totally alien being was a person or not. (For we have no right to assume that genetic humanity is necessary for personhood.) Imagine a space traveler who lands on an unknown planet and encounters a race of beings utterly unlike any he has ever seen or heard of. If he wants to be sure of behaving morally toward these beings, he has to somehow decide whether they are people, and hence have full moral rights, or whether they are the sort of thing which he need not feel guilty about treating as, for example, a source of food.

How should he go about making this decision? If he has some anthropological background, he might look for such things as religion, art, and the manufacturing of tools, weapons, or shelters, since these factors have been used to distinguish our human from our prehuman ancestors, in what seems to be closer to the moral than the genetic sense of "human." And no doubt he would be right to consider the presence of such factors as good evidence that the alien beings were people, and morally human. It would, however, be overly anthropocentric of him to take the absence of these things as adequate evidence that they were not, since we can imagine people who have progressed beyond, or evolved without ever developing, these cultural characteristics.

I suggest that the traits which are most central to the concept of personhood, or humanity in the moral sense, are, very roughly, the following:

1. consciousness (of objects and events external and/or internal to the being), and in particular the capacity to feel pain;
2. reasoning (the *developed* capacity to solve new and relatively complex problems);
3. self-motivated activity (activity which is relatively independent of either genetic or direct external control);
4. the capacity to communicate, by whatever means, messages of an indefinite variety of types, that is, not just with an indefinite number of possible contents, but on indefinitely many possible topics;
5. the presence of self-concepts, and self-awareness, either individual or racial, or both.

Admittedly, there are apt to be a great many problems involved in formulating precise definitions of these criteria, let alone in developing universally valid behavioral criteria for deciding when they apply. But I will assume that both we and our explorer know approximately what (1)–(5) mean, and that he is also able to determine whether or not they apply. How, then, should he use his findings to decide whether or not the alien beings are people? We needn't suppose that an entity must have *all* of these attributes to be properly considered a person; (1) and (2) alone may well be sufficient for personhood, and quite probably (1)–(3) are sufficient. Neither do we need to insist that any one of these criteria is *necessary* for personhood, although once again (1) and (2) look like fairly good candidates for necessary conditions, as does (3), if "activity" is construed so as to include the activity of reasoning.

All we need to claim, to demonstrate that a fetus is not a person, is that any being which satifies *none* of (1)–(5) is certainly not a person. I consider this claim to be so obvious that I think anyone who denied it, and claimed that a being which satisfied none of (1)–(5) was a person all the same, would thereby demonstrate that he had no notion at all of what a person is—perhaps because he had confused the concept of a person with that of genetic humanity. If the opponents of abortion were to deny the appropriateness of these five criteria, I do not know what further arguments would convince them. We would probably have to admit that our conceptual schemes were indeed irreconcilably different, and that our dispute could not be settled objectively.

I do not expect this to happen, however, since I think that the concept of a person is one which is very nearly universal (to people), and that it is common to both proabortionists and antiabortionists, even though neither group has fully realized the relevance of this concept to the resolution of their dispute. Furthermore, I think that on reflection even the antiabortionists ought to agree not only that (1)–(5) are central to the concept of personhood, but also that it is a part of this concept that all and only people have full moral rights. The concept of a person is in part a moral concept; once we have admitted that *x* is a person we have recognized, even if we have not agreed to respect, *x*'s right to be treated as a member of the moral community. It is true that the claim that *x* is a *human being* is more commonly voiced as part of an appeal to treat *x* decently than is the claim that *x* is a person, but this is either because "human being" is here used in the sense which implies personhood, or because the genetic and moral senses of "human" have been confused.

Now if (1)–(5) are indeed the primary criteria of personhood, then it is clear that genetic humanity is neither necessary nor sufficient for establishing that an entity is a person. Some human beings are not people, and there may well be people who are not human beings. A man or woman whose consciousness has been permanently obliterated but who remains alive is a human being which is no longer a person; defective human beings, with no appreciable mental capacity, are not and presumably never will be people; and a fetus is a human being which is not yet a person, and which therefore cannot coherently be said to have full moral rights. Citizens of the next century should be prepared to recognize highly advanced, self-aware robots or computers, should such be developed, and intelligent inhabitants of other worlds, should such be found, as people in the fullest sense, and to respect their moral rights. But to ascribe full moral rights to an entity which is not a person is as absurd as to ascribe moral obligations and responsibilities to such an entity.

3. Fetal Development and the Right to Life

Two problems arise in the application of these suggestions for the definition of the moral community to the determination of the precise moral status of a human fetus. Given that the paradigm example of a person is a normal adult human being, then (1) How like this paradigm, in particular how far advanced since conception, does a human being need to be before it begins to have a right to life by virtue, not of being fully a person as of yet, but of being *like* a person? and (2) To what extent, if any, does the fact that a fetus has the *potential* for becoming a person endow it with some of the same rights? Each of these questions requires some comment.

In answering the first question, we need not attempt a detailed consideration of the moral rights of organisms which are not developed enough, aware enough, intelligent enough, etc., to be considered people, but which resemble people in some respects. It does seem reasonable to suggest that the more like a person, in the relevant respects, a being is, the stronger is the case for regarding it as having a right to life, and indeed the stronger its right to life is. Thus we ought to take seriously the suggestion that, insofar as "the human individual develops biologically in a continuous fashion . . . the rights of a human person might develop in the same way." [11] But we must keep in mind that the attributes which are relevant in determining whether or not an entity is enough like a person to be regarded as having some of the same moral rights are no different from those which are relevant to determining whether or not it is fully a person—i.e., are no different from (1)–(5)—and that being genetically human, or having recognizably human facial and other physical features, or detectable brain activity, or the capacity to survive outside the uterus, are simply not among these relevant attributes.

Thus it is clear that even though a seven- or eight-month fetus has features which make it apt to arouse in us almost the same powerful protective instinct as is commonly aroused by a small infant, nevertheless it is not significantly more personlike than is a very small embryo. It is *somewhat* more personlike; it can apparently feel and respond to pain, and it may even have a rudimentary form of consciousness, insofar as its brain is quite active. Nevertheless, it seems safe to say that it is not fully conscious, in the way that an infant of a few months is, and that it cannot reason, or communicate messages of

[11] Thomas L. Hayes, "A Biological View," *Commonweal,* 85 (March 17, 1967), 677–78; quoted by Daniel Callahan, in *Abortion, Law, Choice, and Morality* (London: Macmillan & Co., 1970).

indefinitely many sorts, does not engage in self-motivated activity, and has no self-awareness. Thus, in the *relevant* respects, a fetus, even a fully developed one, is considerably less personlike than is the average mature mammal, indeed the average fish. And I think that a rational person must conclude that if the right to life of a fetus is to be based upon its resemblance to a person, then it cannot be said to have any more right to life than, let us say, a newborn guppy (which also seems to be capable of feeling pain), and that a right of that magnitude could never override a woman's right to obtain an abortion, at any stage of her pregnancy.

There may, of course, be other arguments in favor of placing legal limits upon the stage of pregnancy in which an abortion may be performed. Given the relative safety of the new techniques of artificially inducing labor during the third trimester, the danger to the woman's life or health is no longer such an argument. Neither is the fact that people tend to respond to the thought of abortion in the later stages of pregnancy with emotional repulsion, since mere emotional responses cannot take the place of moral reasoning in determining what ought to be permitted. Nor, finally, is the frequently heard argument that legalizing abortion, especially late in the pregnancy, may erode the level of respect for human life, leading, perhaps, to an increase in unjustified euthanasia and other crimes. For this threat, if it is a threat, can be better met by educating people to the kinds of moral distinctions which we are making here than by limiting access to abortion (which limitation may, in its disregard for the rights of women, be just as damaging to the level of respect for human rights).

Thus, since the fact that even a fully developed fetus is not person-like enough to have any significant right to life on the basis of its person-likeness shows that no legal restrictions upon the stage of pregnancy in which an abortion may be performed can be justified on the grounds that we should protect the rights of the older fetus; and since there is no other apparent justification for such restrictions, we may conclude that they are entirely unjustified. Whether or not it would be *indecent* (whatever that means) for a woman in her seventh month to obtain an abortion just to avoid having to postpone a trip to Europe, it would not, in itself, be *immoral,* and therefore it ought to be permitted.

4. Potential Personhood and the Right to Life

We have seen that a fetus does not resemble a person in any way which can support the claim that it has even some of the same rights. But what about its *potential,* the fact that if nurtured and allowed to develop naturally it will very probably become a person? Doesn't that alone give it at least some right to life? It is hard to deny that the fact that an entity is a potential person is a strong prima facie reason for not destroying it; but we need not conclude from this that a potential person has a right to life, by virtue of that potential. It may be that our feeling that it is better, other things being equal, not to destroy a potential person is better explained by the fact that potential people are still (felt to be) an invaluable resource, not to be lightly squandered. Surely, if every speck of dust were a potential person, we would be much less apt to conclude that every potential person has a right to become actual.

Still, we do not need to insist that a potential person has no right to life whatever. There may well be something immoral, and not just imprudent, about wantonly destroying potential people, when doing so isn't necessary to protect anyone's rights. But even if a potential person does have some prima facie right to life, such a right could not possibly outweigh the right of a woman to obtain an abortion, since the rights of any actual person invariably outweigh those of any potential person, whenever the two conflict. Since this may not be immediately obvious in the case of a human fetus, let us look at another case.

Suppose that our space explorer falls into the hands of an alien culture, whose scientists decide to create a few hundred thousand or more human beings, by breaking his body into its component cells, and using these to create fully developed human beings, with, of course, his genetic code. We may imagine that each of these newly created men will have all of the original man's abilities, skills, knowledge, and so on, and also have an individual self-concept, in short that each of them will be a bona fide (though hardly unique) person. Imagine that the whole project will take only seconds, and that its chances of success are extremely high, and that our explorer knows all of this, and also knows that these people will be treated fairly. I maintain that in such a situation he would have every right to escape if he could, and thus to deprive all of these potential people of their potential lives; for his right to life outweighs all of theirs together, in spite of the fact that they are all genetically human, all innocent, and all have a very high probability of becoming people very soon, if only he refrains from acting.

Indeed, I think he would have a right to escape even if it were not his life which the alien scientists planned to take, but only a year of his freedom, or, indeed, only a day. Nor would he be obligated to stay if he had gotten captured (thus bringing all these people-potentials into existence) because of his own carelessness, or even if he had done so deliberately, knowing the consequences. Regardless of how he got captured, he is not morally obligated to remain in captivity for *any* period of time for the sake of permitting any number of potential people to come into actuality, so great is the margin by which one actual person's right to liberty outweighs whatever right to life even a hundred thousand potential people have. And it seems reasonable to conclude that the rights of a woman will outweigh by a similar margin whatever right to life a fetus may have by virtue of its potential personhood.

Thus, neither a fetus's resemblance to a person, nor its potential for becoming a person provides any basis whatever for the claim that it has any significant right to life. Consequently, a woman's right to protect her health, happiness, freedom, and even her life,[12] by terminating an unwanted pregnancy, will always override whatever right to life it may be appropriate to ascribe to a fetus, even a fully developed one. And thus, in the absence of any overwhelming social need for every possible child, the laws which restrict the right to obtain an abortion, or limit the period of pregnancy during which an abortion may be performed, are a wholly unjustified violation of a woman's most basic moral and constitutional rights.[13]

POSTSCRIPT ON INFANTICIDE

Since the publication of this article, many people have written to point out that my argument appears to justify not only abortion, but infanticide as well. For a new-born infant is not significantly more person-like than an advanced fetus, and consequently it would seem that if the destruction of the latter is permissible so too must be that of the former. Inasmuch as most people, regardless of how they feel about the morality of abortion, consider infanticide a form of murder, this might appear to represent a serious flaw in my argument.

Now, if I am right in holding that it is only people who have a full-fledged right to life, and who can be murdered, and if the criteria of personhood are as I have described them, then it obviously follows that killing a new-born infant isn't murder. It does *not* follow, however, that infanticide is permissible, for two reasons. In the first place, it would be wrong, at least in this country and in this period of history, and other things being equal, to kill a new-born infant, because even if its parents do not want it and would not suffer from its destruction, there are other people who would like to have it, and would, in all probability, be deprived of a great deal of pleasure by its destruction. Thus, infanticide is wrong for reasons analogous to those which make it wrong to wantonly destroy natural resources, or great works of art.

Secondly, most people, at least in this country, value infants, and would much prefer that they be preserved, even if foster parents are not immediately available. Most of us would rather be taxed to support orphanages than allow unwanted infants to be destroyed. So long as there are people who want an infant preserved, and who are willing and able to provide the means of caring for it, under reasonably humane conditions, it is, *ceteris parabis,* wrong to destroy it.

But, it might be replied, if this argument shows that infanticide is wrong, at least at this time and in this country, doesn't it also show that abortion

---

[12] That is, insofar as the death rate, for the woman, is higher for childbirth than for early abortion.

[13] My thanks to the following people, who were kind enough to read and criticize an earlier version of this paper: Herbert Gold, Gene Glass, Anne Lauterbach, Judith Thomson, Mary Mothersill, and Timothy Binkley.

is wrong? After all, many people value fetuses, are disturbed by their destruction, and would much prefer that they be preserved, even at some cost to themselves. Furthermore, as a potential source of pleasure to some foster family, a fetus is just as valuable as an infant. There is, however, a crucial difference between the two cases: so long as the fetus is unborn, its preservation, contrary to the wishes of the pregnant woman, violates her rights to freedom, happiness, and self-determination. Her rights override the rights of those who would like the fetus preserved, just as if someone's life or limb is threatened by a wild animal, his right to protect himself by destroying the animal overrides the rights of those who would prefer that the animal not be harmed.

The minute the infant is born, however, its preservation no longer violates any of its mother's rights, even if she wants it destroyed, because she is free to put it up for adoption. Consequently, while the moment of birth does not mark any sharp discontinuity in the degree to which an infant possesses the right to life, it does mark the end of its mother's right to determine its fate. Indeed, if abortion could be performed without killing the fetus, she would never possess the right to have the fetus destroyed, for the same reasons that she has no right to have an infant destroyed.

On the other hand, it follows from my argument that when an unwanted or defective infant is born into a society which cannot afford and/or is not willing to care for it, then its destruction is permissible. This conclusion will, no doubt, strike many people as heartless and immoral; but remember that the very existence of people who feel this way, and who are willing and able to provide care for unwanted infants, is reason enough to conclude that they should be preserved.

ABORTION AND THE CONCEPT OF A PERSON

JANE ENGLISH

The abortion debate rages on. Yet the two most popular positions seem to be clearly mistaken. Conservatives maintain that a human life begins at conception and that therefore abortion must be wrong because it is murder. But not all killings of humans are murders. Most notably, self-defense may justify even the killing of an innocent person.

Liberals, on the other hand, are just as mistaken in their argument that since a fetus does not become a person until birth, a woman may do whatever

Reprinted from the *Canadian Journal of Philosophy,* Vol. 5, No. 2 (October 1975), with permission of the publisher.

she pleases in and to her own body. First, you cannot do as you please with your own body if it affects other people adversely.[1] Second, if a fetus is not a person, that does not imply that you can do to it anything you wish. Animals, for example, are not persons, yet to kill or torture them for no reason at all is wrong.

At the center of the storm has been the issue of just when it is between ovulation and adulthood that a person appears on the scene. Conservatives draw the line at conception, liberals at birth. In this paper I first examine our concept of a person and conclude that no single criterion can capture the concept of a person and no sharp line can be drawn. Next I argue that if a fetus is a person, abortion is still justifiable in many cases; and if a fetus is not a person, killing it is still wrong in many cases. To a large extent, these two solutions are in agreement. I conclude that our concept of a person cannot and need not bear the weight that the abortion controversy has thrust upon it. The several factions in the abortion argument have drawn battle lines around various proposed criteria for determining what is and what is not a person. For example, Mary Anne Warren[2] lists five features (capacities for reasoning, self-awareness, complex communication, etc.) as her criteria for personhood and argues for the permissibility of abortion because a fetus falls outside this concept. Baruch Brody[3] uses brain waves. Michael Tooley[4] picks having-a-concept-of-self as his criterion and concludes that infanticide and abortion are justifiable, while the killing of adult animals is not. On the other side, Paul Ramsey[5] claims a certain gene structure is the defining characteristic. John Noonan[6] prefers conceived-of-humans and presents counterexamples to various other candidate criteria. For instance, he argues against viability as the criterion because the newborn and infirm would then be nonpersons, since they cannot live without the aid of others. He rejects any criterion that calls upon the sorts of sentiments a being can evoke in adults on the grounds that this would allow us to exclude other races as nonpersons if we could just view them sufficiently unsentimentally.

These approaches are typical: foes of abortion propose sufficient conditions for personhood which fetuses satisfy, while friends of abortion counter with necessary conditions for personhood which fetuses lack. But these both presuppose that the concept of a person can be captured in a strait jacket of necessary and/or sufficient conditions.[7] Rather, "person" is a cluster of

[1] We also have paternalistic laws which keep us from harming our own bodies even when no one else is affected. Ironically, anti-abortion laws were originally designed to protect pregnant women from a dangerous but tempting procedure.

[2] Mary Anne Warren, "On the Moral and Legal Status of Abortion," *Monist,* 57 (1973).

[3] Baruch Brody, "Fetal Humanity and the Theory of Essentialism." In Robert Baker and Frederick Elliston (eds.), *Philosophy and Sex* (Buffalo, N.Y., 1975).

[4] Michael Tooley, "Abortion and Infanticide," *Philosophy and Public Affairs,* 2 (1971).

[5] Paul Ramsey, "The Morality of Abortion." In James Rachels (ed), *Moral Problems* (New York, 1971).

[6] John Noonan, "Abortion and the Catholic Church: A Summary History," *Natural Law Forum,* 12 (1967), pp. 125–31.

[7] Wittgenstein has argued against the possibility of so capturing the concept of a game, *Philosophical Investigations* (New York, 1958), § 66–71.

features, of which rationality, having a self concept and being conceived of humans are only part.

What is typical of persons? Within our concept of a person we include, first, certain biological factors: descended from humans, having a certain genetic makeup, having a head, hands, arms, eyes, capable of locomotion, breathing, eating, sleeping. There are psychological factors: sentience, perception, having a concept of self and of one's own interests and desires, the ability to use tools, the ability to use language or symbol systems, the ability to joke, to be angry, to doubt. There are rationality factors: the ability to reason and draw conclusions, the ability to generalize and to learn from past experience, the ability to sacrifice present interests for greater gains in the future. There are social factors: the ability to work in groups and respond to peer pressures, the ability to recognize and consider as valuable the interests of others, seeing oneself as one among "other minds," the ability to sympathize, encourage, love, the ability to evoke from others the responses of sympathy, encouragement, love, the ability to work with others for mutual advantage. Then there are legal factors: being subject to the law and protected by it, having the ability to sue and enter contracts, being counted in the census, having a name and citizenship, the ability to own property, inherit, and so forth.

Now the point is not that this list is incomplete, or that you can find counter-instances to each of its points. People typically exhibit rationality, for instance, but someone who was irrational would not thereby fail to qualify as a person. On the other hand, something could exhibit the majority of these features and still fail to be a person, as an advanced robot might. There is no single core of necessary and sufficient features which we can draw upon with the assurance that they constitute what really makes a person; there are only features that are more or less typical.

This is not to say that no necessary or sufficient conditions can be given. Being alive is a necessary condition for being a person, and being a U.S. Senator is sufficient. But rather than falling inside a sufficient condition or outside a necessary one, a fetus lies in the penumbra region where our concept of a person is not so simple. For this reason I think a conclusive answer to the question whether a fetus is a person is unattainable.

Here we might note a family of simple fallacies that proceed by stating a necessary condition for personhood and showing that a fetus has that characteristic. This is a form of the fallacy of affirming the consequent. For example, some have mistakenly reasoned from the premise that a fetus is human (after all, it is a human fetus rather than, say, a canine fetus), to the conclusion that it is *a* human. Adding an equivocation on "being," we get the fallacious argument that since a fetus is something both living and human, it is a human being.

Nonetheless, it does seem clear that a fetus has very few of the above family of characteristics, whereas a newborn baby exhibits a much larger proportion of them—and a two-year-old has even more. Note that one traditional anti-abortion argument has centered on pointing out the many ways in which a fetus resembles a baby. They emphasize its development ("It already has ten fingers . . .") without mentioning its dissimilarities to adults (it still has gills and a tail). They also try to evoke the sort of sympathy on our part that we only feel toward other persons ("Never to laugh . . . or feel the sunshine?"). This all seems to be a relevant way to argue, since its purpose is to persuade us that a fetus satisfies so many of the important features on the list that it ought to be treated as a person. Also note that a fetus near the time of birth satisfies many more of these factors than a fetus in the early months of development. This could provide reason for making distinctions among the different stages of pregnancy, as the U.S. Supreme Court has done.[8]

Historically, the time at which a person has been said to come into existence has varied widely. Muslims date personhood from fourteen days after conception. Some medievals followed Aristotle in placing ensoulment at forty days after conception for a male fetus and eighty days for a female fetus.[9] In European common law since the seventeenth century, abortion was considered the killing of a person only after quickening, the time when a pregnant woman first feels the fetus move on its own. Nor is this variety of opinions surprising. Biologically, a human being develops gradually. We shouldn't expect there to be any specific time or sharp dividing point when a person appears on the scene.

For these reasons I believe our concept of a person is not sharp or decisive enough to bear the weight of a solution to the abortion controversy. To use it to solve that problem is to clarify *obscurum per obscurius.*

II

Next let us consider what follows if a fetus is a person after all. Judith Jarvis Thomson's landmark article, "A Defense of Abortion,"[10] correctly points out that some additional argumentation is needed at this point in the conservative argument to bridge the gap between the premise that a fetus is an innocent person and the conclusion that killing it is always wrong. To arrive at this conclusion, we would need the additional premise that killing an innocent person is always wrong. But killing an innocent person is sometimes permissible, most notably in self defense. Some examples may help draw out our intuitions or ordinary judgments about self defense.

Suppose a mad scientist, for instance, hypnotized innocent people to jump

---

[8] Not because the fetus is partly a person and so has some of the rights of persons, but rather because of the rights of person-like non-persons. This I discuss in part III below.

[9] Aristotle himself was concerned, however, with the different question of when the soul takes form. For historical data, see Jimmye Kimmey, "How the Abortion Laws Happened," *Ms.,* 1 (April 1973), pp. 48ff, and John Noonan, *loc. cit.*

[10] J. J. Thomson, "A Defense of Abortion," *Philosophy and Public Affairs,* 1 (1971).

out of the bushes and attack innocent passers-by with knives. If you are so attacked, we agree you have a right to kill the attacker in self defense, if killing him is the only way to protect your life or to save yourself from serious injury. It does not seem to matter here that the attacker is not malicious but himself an innocent pawn, for your killing of him is not done in a spirit of retribution but only in self-defense.

How severe an injury may you inflict in self-defense? In part this depends upon the severity of the injury to be avoided: you may not shoot someone merely to avoid having your clothes torn. This might lead one to the mistaken conclusion that the defense may only equal the threatened injury in severity; that to avoid death you may kill, but to avoid a black eye you may only inflict a black eye or the equivalent. Rather, our laws and customs seem to say that you may create an injury somewhat, but not enormously, greater than the injury to be avoided. To fend off an attack whose outcome would be as serious as rape, a severe beating or the loss of a finger, you may shoot; to avoid having your clothes torn, you may blacken an eye.

Aside from this, the injury you may inflict should only be the minimum necessary to deter or incapacitate the attacker. Even if you know he intends to kill you, you are not justified in shooting him if you could equally well save yourself by the simple expedient of running away. Self-defense is for the purpose of avoiding harms rather than equalizing harms.

Some cases of pregnancy present a parallel situation. Though the fetus is itself innocent, it may pose a threat to the pregnant woman's well-being, life prospects or health, mental or physical. If the pregnancy presents a slight threat to her interests, it seems self defense cannot justify abortion. But if the threat is on a par with a serious beating or the loss of a finger, she may kill the fetus that poses such a threat, even if it is an innocent person. If a lesser harm to the fetus could have the same defensive effect, killing it would not be justified. It is unfortunate that the only way to free the woman from the pregnancy entails the death of the fetus (except in very late stages of pregnancy). Thus a self-defense model supports Thomson's point that the woman has a right only to be freed from the fetus, not a right to demand its death.[11]

The self-defense model is most helpful when we take the pregnant woman's point of view. In the pre-Thomson literature, abortion is often framed as a question for a third party: do you, a doctor, have a right to choose between the life of the woman and that of the fetus? Some have claimed that if you were a passer-by who witnessed a struggle between the innocent hypnotized attacker and his equally innocent victim, you would have no reason to kill either in defense of the other. They have concluded that the self-defense model implies that a woman may attempt to abort herself, but that a doctor should not assist her. I think the position of the third party is somewhat more complex. We do feel some inclination to intervene on behalf of the victim

[11] *Ibid.,*

rather than the attacker, other things equal. But if both parties are innocent, other factors come into consideration. You would rush to the aid of your husband whether he was attacker or attackee. If a hypnotized famous violinist were attacking a skid row bum, we would try to save the individual who is of more value to society. These considerations would tend to support abortion in some cases.

But suppose you are a frail senor citizen who wishes to avoid being knifed by one of these innocent hypnotics, so you have hired a bodyguard to accompany you. If you are attacked, it is clear we believe that the bodyguard, acting as your agent, has a right to kill the attacker to save you from a serious beating. Your rights of self defense are transferred to your agent. I suggest that we should similarly view the doctor as the pregnant woman's agent in carrying out a defense she is physically incapable of accomplishing herself.

Thanks to modern technology, the cases are rare in which a pregnancy poses as clear a threat to a woman's bodily health as an attacker brandishing a switchblade. How does self defense fare when more subtle, complex and long-range harms are involved?

To consider a somewhat fanciful example, suppose you are a highly trained surgeon when you are kidnapped by the hypnotic attacker. He says he does not intend to harm you but to take you back to the mad scientist who, it turns out, plans to hypnotize you to have a permanent mental block against all your knowledge of medicine. This would automatically destroy your career which would in turn have a serious adverse impact on your family, your personal relationships and your happiness. It seems to me that if the only way you can avoid this outcome is to shoot the innocent attacker, you are justified in so doing. You are defending yourself from a drastic injury to your life prospects. I think it is no exaggeration to claim that unwanted pregnancies (most obviously among teenagers) often have such adverse lifelong consequences as the surgeon's loss of livelihood.

Several parallels arise between various views on abortion and the self defense model. Let's suppose further that these hypnotized attackers only operate at night, so that it is well known that they can be avoided completely by the considerable inconvenience of never leaving your house after dark. One view is that since you could stay home at night, therefore if you go out and are selected by one of these hypnotized people, you have no right to defend yourself. This parallels the view that abstinence is the only acceptable way to avoid pregnancy. Others might hold that you ought to take along some defense such as Mace which will deter the hypnotized person without killing him, but that if this defense fails, you are obliged to submit to the resulting injury, no matter how severe it is. This parallels the view that contraception is all right but abortion is always wrong, even in cases of contraceptive failure.

A third view is that you may kill the hypnotized person only if he will actually kill you, but not if he will only injure you. This is like the position that abortion is permissible only if it is required to save a woman's life. Finally we have the view that it is all right to kill the attacker, even if only to avoid a very slight inconvenience to yourself and even if you knowingly walked down the very street where all these incidents have been taking place without taking along any Mace or protective escort. If we assume that a fetus is a person, this is the analogue of the view that abortion is always justifiable, "on demand."

The self-defense model allows us to see an important difference that exists between abortion and infanticide, even if a fetus is a person from conception. Many have argued that the only way to justify abortion without justifying infanticide would be to find some characteristic of personhood that is acquired at birth. Michael Tooley, for one, claims infanticide is justifiable because the really significant characteristics of person are acquired some time after birth. But all such approaches look to characteristics of the developing human and ignore the relation between the fetus and the woman. What if, after birth, the presence of an infant or the need to support it posed a grave threat to the woman's sanity or life prospects? She could escape this threat by the simple expedient of running away. So a solution that does not entail the death of the infant is available. Before birth, such solutions are not available because of the biological dependence of the fetus on the woman. Birth is the crucial point not because of any characteristics the fetus gains, but because after birth the woman can defend herself by a means less drastic than killing the infant. Hence self-defense can be used to justify abortion without necessarily thereby justifying infanticide.

III

On the other hand, supposing a fetus is not after all a person, would abortion always be morally permissible? Some opponents of abortion seem worried that if a fetus is not a full-fledged person, then we are justified in treating it in any way at all. However, this does not follow. Nonpersons do get some consideration in our moral code, though of course they do not have the same rights as persons have (and in general they do not have moral responsibilities), and though their interests may be overridden by the interests of persons. Still, we cannot just treat them in any way at all.

Treatment of animals is a case in point. It is wrong to torture dogs for fun or to kill wild birds for no reason at all. It is wrong Period, even though dogs and birds do not have the same rights persons do. However, few people think it is wrong to use dogs as experimental animals, causing them considerable suffering in some cases, provided that the resulting research will probably bring discoveries of great benefit to people. And most of us think it all right to kill birds for food or to protect our crops. People's rights are different from the consideration we give to animals, then, for it is wrong to experiment on people, even if others might later benefit a great deal as a result of their suffering. You might volunteer to be a subject, but this would be supererogatory; you certainly have a right to refuse to be a medical guinea pig.

But how do we decide what you may or may not do to nonpersons? This is a difficult problem, one for which I believe no adequate account exists. You do not want to say, for instance, that torturing dogs is all right whenever the sum of its effects on people is good—when it doesn't warp the sensibilities of the torturer so much that he mistreats people. If that were the case, it would be all right to torture dogs if you did it in private, or if the torturer lived on a desert island or died soon afterward, so that his actions had no effect on people. This is an inadequate account, because whatever moral consideration animals get, it has to be indefeasible, too. It will have to be a general proscription of certain actions, not merely a weighing of the impact on people on a case-by-case basis.

Rather, we need to distinguish two levels on which consequences of actions can be taken into account in moral reasoning. The traditional objections to Utilitarianism focus on the fact that it operates solely on the first level, taking all the consequences into account in particular cases only. Thus Utilitarianism is open to "desert island" and "lifeboat" counterexamples because these cases are rigged to make the consequences of actions severely limited.

Rawls' theory could be described as a teleological sort of theory, but with teleology operating on a higher level.[12] In choosing the principles to regulate society from the original position, his hypothetical choosers make their decision on the basis of the total consequences of various systems. Furthermore, they are constrained to choose a general set of rules which people can readily learn and apply. An ethical theory must operate by generating a set of sympathies and attitudes toward others which reinforces the functioning of that set of moral principles. Our prohibition against killing people operates by means of certain moral sentiments including sympathy, compassion and guilt. But if these attitudes are to form a coherent set, they carry us further: we tend to perform supererogatory actions, and we tend to feel similar compassion toward person-like nonpersons.

It is crucial that psychological facts play a role here. Our psychological constitution makes it the case that for our ethical theory to work, it must prohibit certain treatment of nonpersons which are significantly person-like. If our moral rules allowed people to treat some person-like nonpersons in ways we do not want people to be treated, this would undermine the system of sympathies and attitudes that makes the ethical system work. For this reason, we would choose in the original position to make mistreatment of some sorts of animals wrong in general (not just wrong in the cases with public impact), even though animals are not themselves parties in the original position. Thus it makes sense that it is those animals whose appearance and behavior are most like those of people that get the most consideration in our moral scheme.

It is because of "coherence of attitudes," I think, that the similarity of a fetus to a baby is very significant. A fetus one week before birth is so much

---

[12] John Rawls, *A Theory of Justice* (Cambridge, Mass., 1971), § 3–4.

like a newborn baby in our psychological space that we cannot allow any cavalier treatment of the former while expecting full sympathy and nurturative support for the latter. Thus, I think that anti-abortion forces are indeed giving their strongest arguments when they point to the similarities between a fetus and a baby, and when they try to evoke our emotional attachment to and sympathy for the fetus. An early horror story from New York about nurses who were expected to alternate between caring for six-week premature infants and disposing of viable 24-week aborted fetuses is just that—a horror story. These beings are so much alike that no one can be asked to draw a distinction and treat them so very differently.

Remember, however, that in the early weeks after conception, a fetus is very much unlike a person. It is hard to develop these feelings for a set of genes which doesn't yet have a head, hands, beating heart, response to touch or the ability to move by itself. Thus it seems to me that the alleged "slippery slope" between conception and birth is not so very slippery. In the early stages of pregnancy, abortion can hardly be compared to murder for psychological reasons, but in the latest stages it is psychologically akin to murder.

Another source of similarity is the bodily continuity between fetus and adult. Bodies play a surprisingly central role in our attitudes toward persons. One has only to think of the philosophical literature on how far physical identity suffices for personal identity or Wittgenstein's remark that the best picture of the human soul is the human body. Even after death, when all agree the body is no longer a person, we still observe elaborate customs of respect for the human body; like people who torture dogs, necrophiliacs are not to be trusted with people.[13] So it is appropriate that we show respect to a fetus as the body continuous with the body of a person. This is a degree of resemblance to persons that animals cannot rival.

Michael Tooley also utilizes a parallel with animals. He claims that it is always permissible to drown newborn kittens and draws conclusions about infanticide.[14] But it is only permissible to drown kittens when their survival would cause some hardship. Perhaps it would be a burden to feed and house six more cats or to find other homes for them. The alternative of letting them starve produces even more suffering than the drowning. Since the kittens get their rights second-hand, so to speak, *via* the need for coherence in our attitudes, their interests are often overridden by the interest of full-fledged persons. But if their survival would be no inconvenience to people at all, then it is wrong to drown them, *contra* Tooley.

Tooley's conclusions about abortion are wrong for the same reason. Even if a fetus is not a person, abortion is not always permissible, because of the resemblance of a fetus to a person. I agree with Thomson that it would be wrong for a woman who is seven months pregnant to have an abortion just to avoid having to postpone a trip to Europe. In the early months of pregnancy

---

[13] On the other hand, if they can be trusted with people, then our moral customs are mistaken. It all depends on the facts of psychology.

[14] *Op. cit.*

when the fetus hardly resembles a baby at all, then, abortion is permissible whenever it is in the interests of the pregnant woman or her family. The reasons would only need to outweigh the pain and inconvenience of the abortion itself. In the middle months, when the fetus comes to resemble a person, abortion would be justifiable only when the continuation of the pregnancy or the birth of the child would cause harms—physical, psychological, economic or social—to the woman. In the late months of pregnancy, even on our current assumption that a fetus is not a person, abortion seems to be wrong except to save a woman from significant injury or death.

The Supreme Court has recognized similar gradations in the alleged slippery slope stretching between conception and birth. To this point, the present paper has been a discussion of the moral status of abortion only, not its legal status. In view of the great physical, financial and sometimes psychological costs of abortion, perhaps the legal arrangement most compatible with the proposed moral solution would be the absence of restrictions, that is, so-called abortion "on demand."

So I conclude, first, that application of our concept of a person will not suffice to settle the abortion issue. After all, the biological development of a human being is gradual. Second, whether a fetus is a person or not, abortion is justifiable early in pregnancy to avoid modest harms and seldom justifiable late in pregnancy except to avoid significant injury or death.[15]

[15] I am deeply indebted to Larry Crocker and Arthur Kuflik for their constructive comments.

SELECTED BIBLIOGRAPHY: ABORTION

Brody, Baruch. *Abortion and the Sanctity of Human Life.* Cambridge, Mass.: The MIT Press, 1975.

Callahan, Daniel. *Abortion: Law, Choice and Morality.* New York: Macmillan Publishing Co., 1970.

Cohen, Marshall, Thomas Nagel, and **Thomas Scanlon** (eds.). *The Rights and Wrongs of Abortion.* Princeton, N.J.: Princeton University Press, 1974.

Devine, Philip. *The Ethics of Homicide.* Ithaca, N.Y.: Cornell University Press, 1978.

Feinberg, Joel (ed.). *The Problem of Abortion* (2d ed.). Belmont, Calif.: Wadsworth Publishing Co., 1983.

Foot, Philippa. "The Problem of Abortion and the Doctrine of Double Effect." *Oxford Review,* 5 (1967).

Grisez, Germain. *Abortion: The Myths, the Realities, and the Arguments.* New York: Corpus Books, 1970.

Humber, James M. "Abortion: The Avoidable Moral Dilemma." *Journal of Value Inquiry,* 9 (1975), 282.

Jaggar, Alison. "Abortion and a Woman's Right to Decide." *Philosophical Forum,* 5 (1973–74), 347.

Sumner, L. W. *Abortion and Moral Theory.* Princeton, N.J.: Princeton University Press, 1981.

Werner, Richard. "Abortion: The Ontological and Moral Status of the Unborn." *Social Theory and Practice,* 3:4 (1974), 201.

Zaitchik, Alan. "Viability and the Morality of Abortion." *Philosophy & Public Affairs,* 10:1 (1981), 18.

SEVEN

Humans and the Nonhuman Environment

ETHICAL VEGETARIANISM AND COMMERCIAL ANIMAL FARMING

TOM REGAN

1. INTRODUCTION

Time was when a few words in passing usually were enough to exhaust philosophical interest in the moral status of animals other than human beings. "Lawless beasts," writes Plato. "Of the order of sticks and stones," opines the nineteenth century Jesuit W. D. Ritchie. True, there are notable exceptions, at least as far back as Pythagoras, who advocate vegetarianism on ethical grounds—Cicero, Epicurus, Herodotus, Horace, Ovid, Plutarch, Seneca, Virgil, hardly a group of "animal crazies"! By and large, however, a few words would do nicely, thank you, or, when one's corpus took on grave

Reprinted with permission of the author.

AUTHOR'S NOTE: This essay was prepared for distribution at a multidisciplinary conference at the University of Florida on the topic, Agriculture, Change and Human Values. It is published in the *Proceedings* of that Conference and is published here with the permission of the Humanities and Agriculture Program, University of Florida, 243 Arts and Sciences Building, Gainesville, Florida 32611.

proportions, a few paragraphs or pages. Thus we find Kant, for example, by all accounts one of the most influential philosophers in the history of ideas, devoting almost two full pages to the question of our duties to animals, while St. Thomas Aquinas, easily the most important philosopher-theologian in the Catholic tradition, bequeaths perhaps ten pages to the topic at hand.

Times change. Today an even modest bibliography listing titles of the past decade's work on the moral status of animals would easily equal the length of Kant's and Aquinas' treatments combined, a quantitative symbol of the changes that have taken place, and continue to take place, in philosophy's attempts to rouse slumbering prejudices lodged in the anthropocentrism of western thought.

With relatively few speaking to the contrary (St. Francis always comes to mind in this context), theists and humanists, rowdy bedfellows in most quarters, have gotten along amicably when questions were raised about the moral center of the terrestrial universe: *Human* interests form the center of that universe. Let the theist look hopefully beyond the harsh edge of bodily death, let the humanist denounce, in Freud's terms, this "infantile view of the world," at least the two could agree that the moral universe revolves around us humans—our desires, our needs, our goals, our preferences, our love for one another. The intense dialectic now characterizing philosophy's assaults on the traditions of humanism and theism, are assaults aimed not only at the traditional account of the moral status of animals but at the foundation of our moral dealings with the natural environment, with Nature generally— these assaults should not be viewed as local skirmishes between obscure academicians, each bent on occupying a deserted fortress. At issue are the validity of alternative visions of the scheme of things and our place in it. The growing philosophical debate over our treatment of animals and the environment is both a symptom and a cause of a culture's attempt to come to critical terms with its past as it attempts to shape its future.

At present there are three major challenges being raised against moral anthropocentrism. The first is the one issued by *utilitarians:* the second, by proponents of *moral rights;* and the third, emanates from the camp of those who advocate what we shall term a *holistic ethic.* This essay offers brief summaries of each position with special reference to how their advocates answer two questions: (a) Is vegetarianism required on ethical grounds?, and (b) Judged ethically, what should we say, and what should we do about, commercial animal agriculture? To ask whether vegetarianism is required on ethical grounds is to ask whether there are reasons other than those that relate to one's own welfare (for example, other than those that relate to one's own health or financial well-being) that call for leading a vegetarian way of life. As for the expression "commercial animal agriculture," that should be taken to apply to the practice of raising animals to be sold for food. The ethics of other practices that involve killing animals (for example, hunting, the use of animals in science, "the family farm" where the animals raised and killed and eaten by the people who raise them, etc.) will not be considered, except in passing, not because the ethics of these practices should not demand our close attention but because space and time preclude our giving them this attention here. Time and space also preclude anything approaching 'complete' assessments of the three views to be discussed. None can be proven right or wrong in a few swift strokes. Even so, it will be clear where my own sympathies lie.

2. TRADITIONAL MORAL ANTHROPOCENTRISM

Aquinas and Kant speak for the anthropocentric tradition. That tradition does not issue a blank check when it comes to the treatment of animals. Morally, we are enjoined to be kind to animals and, on the other side of the coin, not to be cruel to them. But we are not enjoined to be the one and prohibited from being the other because we owe such treatment to *animals themselves*—not, that is, because we have any duties *directly* to nonhumans; rather, it is because of *human* interests that we have these duties regarding animals. "So far as animals are concerned," writes Kant, "we have no direct duties. . . . Our duties to animals are merely indirect duties to mankind." In the case of cruelty, we are not to be cruel to animals because treating them cruelly will develop a habit of cruelty, and a habit of cruelty, once it has taken up lodging in our breast, will in time include human beings among its victims. "[H]e who is cruel to animals becomes hard also in his dealings with men." And *that* is why cruelty to animals is wrong. As for kindness, "[t]ender feelings towards dumb animals develop humane feelings toward mankind."[1] And *that* is why we have a duty to be kind to animals.

So reasons Kant. Aquinas, predictably, adds theistic considerations, but the main story line is the same. Witness the following passage from his *Summa Contra Gentiles.*

> Hereby is refuted the error of those who said it is sinful for a man to kill dumb animals: for by divine providence they are intended for man's use in the natural order. Hence it is no wrong for man to make use of them, either by killing, or in any other way whatever. . . . And if any passages of Holy Writ seem to forbid us to be cruel to dumb animals, for instance to kill a bird with its young: this is either to remove men's thoughts from being cruel to other men, and lest through being cruel to animals one becomes cruel to human beings: or because injury to an animal leads to the temporal hurt of man, either of the doer of the deed, or of another: or on account of some (religious) signification: thus the Apostle expounds the prohibition against *muzzling the ox that treadeth the corn.*[2]

[1] Immanuel Kant, "Duties to Animals and Spirits," in his *Lectures on Ethics,* trans. Louis Infield (New York: Harper and Row, 1963) pp. 239–41. Collected in *Animal Rights and Human Obligations,* Tom Regan and Peter Singer, eds. (Englewood Cliffs, N.J.: Prentice-Hall Inc., 1976) pp. 122–23.

[2] St. Thomas Aquinas, *Summa Contra Gentiles,* literally translated by the English Dominican Fathers (Benzinger Books, 1928), Third Book, Part II, Chap. C XII. Collected in *Animal Rights and Human Obligations, op. cit.,* pp. 58–9.

To borrow a phrase from the twentieth century English philosopher Sir W. D. Ross, our treatment of animals, both for Kant and Aquinas, is "a practice ground for moral virtue." The *moral game* is played between human players or, on the theistic view, human players plus God. The way we treat animals is a sort of moral warmup, character calisthentics, as it were, for the moral game in which animals themselves play no part.

3. THE UTILITARIAN CHALLENGE

The first fairly recent spark of revolt against moral anthropocentrism comes, as do other recent protests against institutionalized prejudice, from the pens of the nineteenth century utilitarians, most notably Jeremy Bentham and John Stuart Mill. These utilitarians, who count the balance of pleasure over pain for all sentient creatures as the yardstick of moral right and wrong, and who reject out of hand Descartes' famous teaching that animals are "nature's machines," lacking any trace of conscious awareness—these utilitarians recognize the direct moral significance of the pleasures and pains of animals. In an oft-quoted passage, Bentham enfranchises animals within the utilitarian moral community by declaring that "[t]he question is not, 'Can they talk?', or 'Can they reason?', but, 'Can they suffer?' "[3] And Mill stakes the credibility of utilitarianism itself on its implications for the moral status and treatment of animals, writing that "[w]e" (that is, those who subscribe to utilitarianism) "are perfectly willing to stake the whole question on this one issue. Granted that any practice causes more pain to animals than it gives pleasure to man: is that practice moral or immoral? And if, exactly in proportion as human beings raise their heads out of the slough of selfishness, they do not with one voice answer 'immoral' let the morality of the principle of utility be forever condemned."[4] The duties we have regarding animals, then, are duties we have *directly to them,* not indirect duties to humanity. For utilitarians, animals are themselves involved in the moral game.

Viewed against this historical backdrop, the position of the contemporary Australian moral philosopher, Peter Singer, can be seen to be an extension of the attack on the tradition of moral anthropocentrism initiated by his utilitarian forebearers. For though this sometimes goes unnoticed by friend and foe alike, Singer, whose book *Animal Liberation* is unquestionably the most influential work to date on the topic of the ethics of our treatment of animals, *is* a utilitarian.[5] That view requires, he believes, observance of the equality of interests principle. This principle requires that, before we decide

[3] Jeremy Bentham, *The Principles of Morals and Legislation* (1789: many editions), Chapter XVII, Section 1. Collected in *Animal Rights and Human Obligations, op. cit.,* pp. 129–30.

[4] John Stuart Mill, "Whewell on Moral Philosophy," in Mill's *Collected Works,* Vol. X, pp. 185–87. Collected in *Animal Rights and Human Obligations, op. cit.,* pp. 131–32.

[5] Peter Singer, *Animal Liberation* (New York: Avon Books, 1975). By far the best factual account of factory farming is J. Mason and Peter Singer, *Animal Factories* (New York: Collier Books, 1982).

what to do, we consider the interests (that is, the preferences) of all those who are likely to be affected by what we do *and* weigh equal interests equally. We must not, that is, refuse to consider the interests of some of those who will be affected by what we do because, say, they are Catholic, or female, or black. *Everyone's* interests must be considered. And we must not discount the importance of comparable interests because they are the interests of, say, a Catholic, woman, or black. Everyone's interests must be weighed *equitably.* Of course, to ignore or discount the importance of a woman's interests *because she is a woman* is the very paradigm of the moral prejudice we call sexism, just as to ignore or discount the importance of the interests of blacks (or Native Americans, Chicanos, etc.) are paradigmatic forms of racism. It remained for Singer to argue, which he does with great vigor, passion, and skill, that a similar moral prejudice lies at the heart of moral anthropocentrism, a prejudices which Singer, borrowing a term first coined by the English author and animal activist Richard Ryder, denominates *speciesism.*[6] Like Bentham and Mill before him, Singer, the utilitarian, *denies* that we are to treat animals well in the name of the betterment of humanity, *denies* that we are to do this because this will help us discharge our duties to our fellow humans, *denies* that acting dutifully toward animals is a moral warm-up for the real moral game played between humans, or, as theists would add, between humans-and-humans-and-God. *We owe it to those animals who have interests to take their interests into account, just as we also owe it to them to count their interests equitably.* Our duties regarding animals are, in these respects, *direct* duties we have to them, not indirect duties to humanity. To think otherwise is to give sorry testimony to the prejudice of speciesism Singer is intent upon unmasking.

4. FARMING TODAY

Singer believes that the utilitarian case for ethical vegetarianism is strengthened when we inform ourselves of the changes taking place in commercial animal farming today. In increasing numbers, animals are being brought in off the land and raised indoors, in unnatural, crowded conditions—raised "intensively," to use the jargon of the animal industry, in structures that look for all the world like factories. Indeed, it is now common practice to refer to such commercial ventures as *factory farms.* The inhabitants of these 'farms' are kept in cages, or stalls, or pens, or closely-confined in other ways, living out their abbreviated lives in a technologically created and sustained environment: automated feeding, automated watering, automated light cycles, automated waste removal, automated what-not. And the crowding: as many as 9 hens in cages that measure 18 by 24 inches; veal calves confined to 22

---

[6] Richard Ryder, "Experiments on Animals," in *Animals, Men and Morals,* ed. S. and R. Godlovitch and J. Harris (New York: Taplinger, 1972). Collected in *Animal Rights and Human Obligations, op. cit.,* pp. 33–47.

inch wide stalls; hogs similarly confined, sometimes in tiers of cages, two, three, four rows high. Could any impartial, morally sensitive person view what goes on in a factory farm with benign approval? Certainly many of the basic interests of the animals are simply ignored or undervalued, Singer claims, because they do not compute economically. Their interest in physical freedom or in associating with members of their own species, these interests routinely go by the board. And for what? So that we humans can dine on steaks and chops, drum sticks and roasts, food that is simply inessential for our own physical well-being. Add to this sorry tale of speciesism on today's farm the enormous waste that characterizes the animal industry, waste to the tune of six or seven pounds of vegetable protein to produce a pound of animal protein in the case of beef cattle, for example; and add to the accumulated waste of nutritious food the chronic need for just such food throughout the countries of the Third World, whose populations characteristically are malnourished at best and literally starving to death at worst—add all these factors together and we have, Singer believes, the basis for the utilitarian's answers to our two questions. In response to the question, "Is vegetarianism required on ethical grounds?", the Singer-type utilitarian replies affirmatively. For it is not for self-interested reasons that Singer calls us to vegetarianism (though such reasons, including a concern for one's health, are not irrelevant). It is for ethical reasons that we are to take up a vegetarian way of life. And as for our second question, the one that asks what we should think and do about commercial animal farming, Singer's utilitarian argument prescribes, he thinks, that we should think ill of today's factory farms and act to bring about significant humane improvements by refusing to purchase their products. Ethically considered, we ought to become vegetarians.

5. THE CHALLENGE TO UTILITARIANISM

Singer, then, is the leading contemporary representative of the utilitarian critique of the anthropocentric heritage bequeathed to us by humanism and theism. How should we assess his critique? Our answer requires answering two related questions. First, "How adequate is the general utilitarian position Singer advocates?" and second, "How adequate is Singer's application of this general position to the particular case of commercial animal agriculture and, allied with this, the case for ethical vegetarianism?" A brief response to each question, beginning with the second, will have to suffice. Consider Singer's claim that each of us has a duty to become a vegetarian. How can this alleged duty be defended on *utilitarian* grounds? Well, on this view, we know, the act I *ought* to perform, the act I have a *duty* to do, is the one that will bring about the best consequences for all those affected by the outcome, which, for Singer, means the act that will bring about the optimal balance of preference satisfaction over preference frustration. But it is naive in the extreme to suppose that, were *I* individually henceforth to abstain from eating meat and assiduously lead a vegetarian existence, it is naive in the extreme to suppose that this will improve the lot of a single animal. Commercial animal farming simply does not work in this way. It does not, that is, fine-tune its production to such a high degree that it responds to the decisions of each individual consumer. So, no, the individual's abstention from meat will not make the slightest dent, will not effect the smallest change in commercial animal agriculture. No one, therefore, Singer included, can ground *the individual's* ethical obligation to be vegetarian on the effects *the individual's* acts will have on the welfare of animals.

Similar remarks apply to the other presumed beneficiaries of the individual's conversion to vegetarianism. The starving, malnourished masses of the Third World will not receive the food they need if I would but stop eating animals. For it is, again, naive in the extreme to suppose that the dietary decisions and acts of any given *individual* will make the slightest difference to the quality of life for any inhabitant in the Third World. Even were it true, which it is not (and it is not true because commercial animal agriculture is not *so* fine-tuned in this respect either), that a given amount of protein-rich grain *would not be fed to animals* if I abstained from eating meat, it simply would not follow that this grain *would find its way to any needy human being*. To suppose otherwise is to credit one's individual acts and decisions with a kind of god-like omnipotence that a robust sense of reality cannot tolerate. Thus, since the type of utilitarianism Singer advocates prescribes that we decide what our ethical duties are by asking what will be the consequences of our acts, and since there is no realistic reason to believe that the consequences of my abstaining from meat will make any difference whatsoever to the quality of life of commercially raised farm animals or the needy people of the Third World, the alleged duties to become a vegetarian and to oppose commercial animal agriculture lack the kind of backing a utilitarian like Singer requires.

Here one might attempt to defend Singer by arguing that it is the total or sum of the consequences of *many* people becoming vegetarians, not just the results of each individual's decisons, that will spare some animals the rigors of factory farms and save some humans from malnutrition or starvation. Two replies to this attempted defense may be briefly noted. First, this defense at most gives *a sketch of a possible* reply; it does not give a finished one. As a utilitarian, Singer must show that the consequences for everyone involved would be better if a number of people became vegetarians than if they did not. But to show this, Singer must provide a thorough run-down of what the consequences would be, or would be in all probability, if we abstained from eating meat, *or* ate less of it, *or* ate none at all. And this is no easy task. Would the grains not fed to animals even be grown if the animal industry's requirements for them were reduced or eliminated? Would there be an economically viable market for corn, oats, and other grains if we become vegetarians? Would farmers have the necessary economic incentive to produce enough grain to feed the world's hungry human beings? Who knows? In particular, does Singer know? One looks in vain to find the necessary empirical backing for an answer here. Or consider: Suppose the grain is available. From a utilitarian point of view, would it be best (that is, would we be acting to produce the best consequences) if we made this grain available to the present generation of the world's malnourished? Or would it be better in the long run to refuse to aid these people at this point in time? After all, if we assist them now, will they not simply reproduce? And won't their additional numbers make the problem of famine for the next generation even more tragic? Who knows what the correct answers to these questions are? Who knows what is even "most likely" to be true? It is not unfair to a utilitarian such as Singer to mark the depths of our ignorance in these matters. And neither is it unfair to emphasize how our ignorance stands in the way of his attempt to ground the obligatoriness of vegetarianism on utilitarian considerations. If we simply do not know what the consequences of our becoming vegetarians would be, or are most likely to be, and if we simply do not know whether the consequences that would result would be, or are most likely to be, better than those that would obtain if we did not become vegetarians, then we simply lack any semblance of a utilitarian justification for the obligation to become vegetarians or for mounting a frontal assault on commercial animal agriculture. The decision to lead a vegetarian way of life and, by doing so, to lodge a moral complaint against commercial animal agriculture, viewed from the perspective of Singer's utilitarianism, must be diagnosed as at best symbolic gestures.

Aside from these matters, what can be said about the adequacy of utilitarianism in general? That is a question raised earlier to which we must now direct our attention. There is a vast literature critical of utilitarian theory, and it will obviously not be possible to survey it here. Here let us note just one difficulty. Utilitarianism, at least as understood by Singer, implies that whether *I* am doing what I ought to do is crucially dependent on what *other* people do. For example, although the consequences of *my* abstaining from eating meat are too modest to make any difference to how animals are raised or whether grains are made available to needy people, if enough *other* people join me in a vegetarian way of life we could collectively bring about changes in the number of animals raised, how they are raised, what use is made of grain, etc. The situation, in other words, is as follows: If enough people join me so that the consequences of what we do *collectively* makes some impact, then what I do might be right, whereas if too few people join me, with the result that the consequences of what we do fails to make any difference to how animals are raised, etc., then I am *not* doing what is right.

To make the morality of an individual's acts depend on how others behave is a highly unsatisfactory consequence for any moral theory. When people refuse to support racist or sexist practices (for example, in employment or education), they do what is right, but their doing what is right does not depend on how many *other* people join them. The number of people who join them determines how many people do or support what is right, *not* what is right in the first place. Utilitarianism, because it makes *what is right* dependent in many cases on how many people act in a certain way, puts the moral cart before the horse. What we want is a theory that illuminates moral right and wrong independently of how many people act in this or that way. And that is precisely what utilitarianism, at least in the form advocated by Singer, fails to give us. For all its promise as an attack on the anthropocentric traditions of humanism and theism, for all its insistence on the direct relevance of the interests of animals, and despite the radical sounding claims made by utilitarians in criticism of current practices on the farm and in the laboratory, utilitarianism proves to be more ethical shadow than substance. If we look beyond the rhetoric and examine the arguments, utilitarianism might not change these practices as much as it would fortify them.[7]

6. THE RIGHTS VIEW

An alternative to the utilitarian attack on anthropocentrism is what we shall call *the rights view.*[8] Those who accept this view holds that (1) certain individuals have certain moral rights, (2) these individuals have these rights independently of considerations about the value of the consequences of treating them in one way or another, and (3) the duty the individual has to respect the rights of others does not depend on how many other people act in ways that respect these rights. The first point distinguishes proponents of the rights view from, among others, those utilitarians like Bentham and Singer who deny that individuals have moral rights; the second distinguishes advocates of the rights view from, among others, those utilitarians such as Mill who hold that individuals have moral rights if, and only if, the general welfare would be promoted by saying and acting as if they do; and the third point distinguishes those who champion the rights view from, among others, any advocate of utilitarianism who holds that my duty to act in certain ways depends on how many other people act in these ways. According to the rights view, certain individuals have moral rights, and my duty to act in ways that respect such an individual's (*A*'s) rights is a duty I have directly to *A*, a duty I have to *A* that is not grounded in considerations about the value of consequences for all those affected by the outcome, and a duty I have to *A* whatever else others might do to *A*. *Those who advocate animal rights, understanding this idea after the fashion of the rights view, believe that some of those individuals who have moral rights, and thus some of those to whom we have duties of the type just described, are animals.*

---

[7] These criticisms of utilitarianism are developed at greater length in my *The Case For Animal Rights* (Berkeley: University of California. London: Routledge and Kegan Paul, 1983).

[8] The rights view is developed at length in *The Case For Animal Rights, ibid.*

7. GROUNDS FOR THE RIGHTS VIEW

To proclaim "the moral rights of Man" sounds good but is notoriously difficult to defend. Bentham, who writes more forcefully to support what he rejects than to establish what he accepts, dismisses rights other than legal rights as "nonsense upon stilts." So we will not settle the thorny question about human rights in an essay's reading or writing. And, it goes without saying, the moral rights of animals must remain even less established. Were Bentham in his grave—(in fact he remains above ground, encased in glass in an anteroom in University College, London, where he is dutifully brought to dinner each year on the occasion of his birthday)—he would most certainly roll over at the mere mention of *animal* rights! Still, something needs to be said about the rational grounds for the rights view.

An important (but not the only possible) argument in this regard takes the following form: Unless we recognize that certain individuals have moral rights, we will be left holding moral principles that sanction morally reprehensible conduct. Thus, in order to avoid holding principles that allow such conduct, we must recognize that certain individuals have moral rights. The following discussion of utilitarianism is an example of this general line of argument.

Utilitarians cut from the same cloth as Bentham would have us judge moral right and wrong by appeal to the consequences of what we do. Well, suppose aged Aunt Bertha's heirs could have a lot more pleasure than she is likely to have in her declining years if she were to die. But suppose that neither nature nor Aunt Bertha will cooperate: She simply refuses to die as expeditiously as, gauged by the interest of her heirs, is desirable. Why not speed-up the tempo of her demise? The reply given by Bentham-type utilitarians shows how far they are willing to twist our moral intuitions to save their theory. If we were to kill Aunt Bertha, especially if we took pains to do so painlessly, then, these utilitarians submit, we would do no wrong to Aunt Bertha. However, if *other* people found out about what we did, they would quite naturally grow more anxious, more insecure about their own safety and mortality; and these mental states (anxiety, insecurity, and the like) are painful. Thus, so we are told, killing Aunt Bertha is wrong (if it is) because of the painful consequences for others!

Except for those already committed to a Bentham-style utilitarianism, few are likely to find this account satisfactory. Its shortcomings are all the more evident when we note that *if* others did not find out about our dastardly deed (and so were not made more anxious and insecure by their knowledge of what we did), and *if* we have a sufficiently undeveloped conscience not to be terribly troubled by what we did, and *if* we do not get caught, and *if* we have a jolly good time with Aunt Bertha's inheritance, a much better time, in fact, than we would have had if we had waited for nature to run its course—if we assume all this, then Bentham-style utilitarianism implies that we did nothing wrong in killing Aunt Bertha and, indeed, acted as we morally ought to have acted. People who, in the face of this kind of objection, remain

Bentham-type utilitarians, may hold a consistent position. But one pays a price for a "foolish consistency." The spectacle of people "defending their theory to the last" in spite of its grave implications must, to put it mildly, take one's moral breath away.

There are, of course, many ethical theories in addition to utilitarianism, and many versions of utilitarianism in addition to the one associated with Bentham. So even if the sketch of an argument against Bentham's utilitarianism proves successful, the rights view would not thereby "win" in its competition with other theories. But the foregoing does succeed in giving a representative sample of one argument deployed by those who accept the rights view: If you deny moral rights, as Bentham does, then the principles you put in their place, which, in Bentham's case, is the principle of utility, will sanction morally reprehensible conduct (for example, the murder of Aunt Bertha). If those who affirm and defend the rights view could show this, given *any* initially plausible theory that denies moral rights, and if they could crystalize and defend the methodology on which this argument depends, then they would have a powerful reason for their position.

8. THE VALUE OF THE INDIVIDUAL

The rights view aspires to satisfy our intellect, not merely our appetite for rhetoric, and so it is obliged to provide a theoretical home for moral rights. Part, but by no means the whole, of this home is furnished by the rights views' theory of value. Unlike utilitarian theories (for example, value hedonism), the rights view recognizes *the value of individuals,* not just the value of their mental states (for example, their pleasures). Following custom, let us call these latter sorts of value "intrinsic values"; and let us introduce the term "inherent value" for the type of value attributed to individuals. Then the notion of inherent value can be explained as follows. First, the inherent value of an individual who has such value is not the same as, is not reducible to, and is incommensurate with the intrinsic value of that individual's, or of any combination of individuals', mental states. The inherent value of an individual, in other words, is not equal to any sum of intrinsic values (for example, any sum of pleasures). Second, all individuals who have inherent value have it equally. Inherent value, that is, does not come in degrees; some who have it do not have it more or less than others. One either has it or one does not, and all who have it have it to the same extent. It is, one might say, a categorical concept. Third, the possession of inherent value by individuals does not depend on their utility relative to the interests of others, which, if it were true, would imply that some individuals have such value to a greater degree than do others, because some (for example, surgeons) have greater utility than do others (for example, bank thieves). Fourth, and relatedly, individuals cannot acquire or lose such value by anything they do. And fifth, and finally, the inherent value of individuals does not depend on what or how others think or feel about them. The loved and admired are neither more nor less inherently valuable than the despised and forsaken.

Now, the rights view claims that any individual who has inherent value is due treatment that respects this value (has, that is, a *moral right* to such treatment), and though not everything can be said here about what such respect comes to, at least this much should be clear: We fail to treat individuals with the respect they are due whenever we assume that how we treat them can be defended *merely* by asking about the value of the mental states such treatment produces for those affected by the outcome. This must fail to show appropriate respect since it is tantamont to treating these individuals as if they lacked inherent value—as if, that is, we treat them as we ought whenever we can justify our treatment of them *merely* on the grounds that it promotes the interests other individuals have in obtaining preferred mental states (for example, pleasure). Since individuals who have inherent value have a kind of value that is not reducible to their utility relative to the interests of others, we are not to treat them merely as a means to bringing about the best consequences. We ought not, then, kill Aunt Bertha, given the rights view, even if doing so brought about "the best" consequences. That would be to treat her with a lack of appropriate respect, something she has a moral right to. To kill her for these reasons would be to violate her rights.

9. WHICH INDIVIDUALS HAVE INHERENT VALUE?

Even assuming the rights view could succeed in providing a coherent, rationally persuasive theoretical framework for "the rights of Man," further argument would be necessary to illuminate and justify the rights of animals. That argument, not surprisingly, will be long and torturous. At least we can be certain of two things, however. First, it must include considerations about the criteria of right possession; and, second, it will have to include an explanation and defense of how animals meet these criteria. A few remarks about each of these two points will have to suffice.

Persons[9] are the possessors of moral rights, and though most human beings are persons, not all are. And some persons are not human beings. Persons are individuals who have a cluster of actual (not merely potential or former) abilities. These include awareness of their environment, desires and preferences, goals and purposes, feelings and emotions, beliefs and memories, a sense of the future and of their own identity. Most adult humans have these abilities and so are persons. But some (the irreversibly comatose, for example) lack them and so are not persons. Human fetuses and infants also are not persons, given this analysis, and so have no moral rights (which is not to say that we may therefore do anything to them that we have a mind to; there

---

[9] I use the familiar idea of 'person' here because it is helpful. I do not use it in *The Case For Animal Rights*. I do not believe anything of substance turns on its use or nonuse.

are moral constraints on what we may do in addition to those constraints that involve respect for the moral rights of others—but this is a long story. . . !)

As for nonhumans who are persons, the most famous candidate is God as conceived, for example, by Christians. When believers speak of "the blessed Trinity, three persons in one," they don't mean "three human beings in one." Extraterrestrials are another obvious candidate, at least as they crop up in standard science fiction. The extraterrestrials in Ray Bradbury's *Martian Chronicles,* for example, are persons, in the sense explained, but they assuredly are not human beings. But, of course, the most important candidates for our purposes are animals. And they are successful candidates if they perceive and remember, believe and desire, have feelings and emotions, and, in general, actually possess the other abilities mentioned earlier.

Those who affirm and defend the rights of animals believe that some animals actually possess these abilities. Of course, there are some who will deny this. All animals, they will say, lack all, or most, or at least some of the abilities that make an individual a person. In a fuller discussion of the rights view, these worries would receive the respectful airing they deserve. It must suffice here to say that the case for animal rights involves the two matters mentioned and explained—first, considerations about the criteria of right possession (or, alternatively, personhood), and, second, considerations that show that some animals satisfy these criteria. Those who would squelch the undertaking before it gets started by claiming that "it's *obvious* that animals cannot be persons!" offer no serious objection; instead, they give sorry expression to the very speciesist prejudice those who affirm and defend the rights of animals seek to overcome.

10. LINE DRAWING

To concede that some animals are persons and so have moral rights is not to settle the question, *"Which* animals are persons?" "Where do we draw the line?" it will be asked; indeed, it must be asked. The correct answer seems to be: We do not know with certainty. Perhaps there is no exact line to be drawn in this case, anymore than there is an exact line to be drawn in other cases (for example, "Exactly how tall do you have to be to be tall?", "Exactly how old must you be before you are old?"). What we must ask is where in the animal kingdom we find individuals who are *most like* paradigmatic persons—that is, most like us, both behaviorally and physiologically. The greater the similarity in these respects, the stronger the case for believing that these animals have *a mental life similar to our own* (including memory and emotion, for example), a case that is strengthened given the major thrust of evolutionary theory. So, while it remains a matter of uncertainty *exactly* where we are to draw this line, it is implausible to deny that adult mammalian animals have the abilities in question (just as, analogously, it would be implausible to deny that 88-year-old Aunt Bertha is old because we don't know exactly how old someone must be before they are old). To get this far in the argument for animal rights is not to finish the story, but it is to give a rough outline of a major chapter in it.

11. THE INHERENT VALUE OF ANIMALS

Moral rights, as explained earlier, (7, above), need a theoretical home, and the rights view provides this by its use of the notion of inherent value. Not surprisingly, therefore, the rights view affirms this value in the case of those animals who are persons; not to do so would be to slide back into the prejudice of speciesism. Moreover, because all who possess this value possess it equally, the rights view makes no distinction between the inherent value human persons possess as distinct from that possessed by those persons who are animals. And just as *our* inherent value as persons does not depend on our utility relative to the interests of others, or on how much we are liked or admired, or on anything we do or fail to do, the same must be true in the case of animals who, as persons, have the same inherent value we do.

To regard animals in the way advocated by the rights view makes a truly profound difference to our understanding of what, morally speaking, we may do to them, as well as how, morally speaking, we can defend what we do. Those animals who have inherent value have a moral right to respectful treatment, a right we fail to respect whenever we attempt to justify what we do to them by appeal to "the best consequences". What these animals are due, in other words, is the same respectful treatment we are. We must never treat them in this or that way merely because, we claim, doing so is necessary to bring about "the best consequences" for all affected by the outcome.

The rights view therefore calls for the total dissolution of commercial animal agriculture as we know it. Not merely 'modern' intensive rearing methods must cease. For though the harm visited upon animals raised in these circumstances is real enough and is morally to be condemned, its removal would not eliminate the basic wrong its presence compounds. The *basic* wrong is that animals raised for commercial profit are viewed and treated in ways that fail to show respect for their moral right to respectful treatment. *They* are not (though of course they may be treated as if they are) "commodities," "economic units," "investments," "a renewable resource," etc. They are, like us, persons and so, like us, are owed treatment that accords with their right to be treated with respect, a respect we fail to show when we end their life before doing so can be defended on the grounds of mercy. Since animals are routinely killed on grounds other than mercy in the course of commercial animal agriculture, that human enterprise violates the rights of animals.

Unlike the utilitarian approach to ethical vegetarianism, the rights view's basis does not require that we know what the consequences of our individual or collective abstention from meat will be. The moral imperatives to treat farm animals with respect and to refuse to support those who fail to do so do no rest on calculations about consequences. And unlike a Singer-type utilitarianism, the rights view does not imply that the individual's duty to become a vegetarian depends on how many other people join the ranks. *Each individual* has the duty to treat others with the respect they are due independently of how many others do so, and each has a similar duty to refrain in principle from supporting practices that fail to show proper respect. Of course, anyone who accepts the rights view must profoundly wish that others *will* act similarly, with the result that commercial animal agriculture, from vast agribusiness operations to the traditional family farm, will go the way of the slave trade—will, that is, cease to exist. But the *individual's* duty to cease to support those who violate the rights of animals does not depend on humanity in general doing so as well.

The rights views is, one might say, a 'radical' position, calling, as it does, for the total abolition of a culturally accepted institution—viz., commercial animal farming. The way to "clean up" this institution is not by giving animals bigger cages, cleaner stalls, a place to roost, thus and so much hay, etc. When an institution is grounded in injustice, because it fails to respect the rights of those involved, there is no room for internal house cleaning. Morality will not be satisfied with anything less than its total abolition. And that, for the reasons given, is the rights view's verdict regarding commercial animal agriculture.

12. HOLISM

The 'radical' implications of the rights view suggest how far some philosophers have moved from the anthropocentric traditions of theism and humanism. But, like the utilitarian attacks on this tradition, one should note that the rights view seeks to make its case by working within the major ethical categories of this tradition. For example, hedonistic utilitarians do not deny the moral relevance of human pleasures and pain, so important to our humanist forbears; rather, they accept this and seek to extend our moral horizons to include the moral relevance of the pleasures and pains of animals. And the rights view does not deny the distinctive moral importance of the individual, a central article of belief in theistic thought; rather, it accepts this moral datum and seeks to widen the class of individuals who are to be thought of in this way to include many animals.

Because both the positions discussed in the preceding pages work with major ethical categories handed down to us by our predecessors, some influential thinkers argue that these positions are, despite all appearances, in the hip pocket, so to speak, of the *Weltanschauung* they aspire to overturn. What is needed, these thinkers contend or imply, is not a broader interpretation of traditional categories (for example, the category of 'the rights of the individual'); rather, what is required is the overthrow of these categories. Only then will we have a new vision, one that liberates us from the last vestiges of anthropocentrism.

13. "THE LAND ETHIC"

Among those whose thought moves in this direction, none is more influential than Aldo Leopold.[10] *Very* roughly, Leopold can be seen as rejecting the 'atomism' dear to the hearts of those who build their moral thinking on "the value (or rights) of the individual." What has ultimate value is not the individual but the collective, not the "part" but the "whole," where by "the whole" is meant the entire biosphere: the *totality* of the things and systems in the natural order. Acts are right, Leopold claims, if they tend to promote the integrity, beauty, diversity, and harmony of the biosphere; they are wrong if they tend contrariwise. As for individuals, be they humans or animals, they are merely "members of the biotic team," having neither more nor less value in themselves than any other member—having, that is, *no* value "in themselves." What good individuals have, so far as this is computable at all, is instrumental only: They are good to the extent that they promote the "welfare," so to speak, of the biosphere. For a Leopoldian, the rights view rests on the fictional view that individuals have a kind of value they in fact lack.

Traditional utilitarianism, not just the rights view, goes by the board, given Leopold's vision. To extend our moral concern to the experiences of animals (for example, their pleasures and pains) is not to overcome the prejudices indigenous to anthropocentrism. One who does this is still in the grip of these prejudices, supposing that mental states that matter to humans must be the yardstick of what matters morally. Utilitarians are people who escape from one prejudice (speciesism) only to embrace another (what we might call "sentientism," the view that mental states allied with or reducible to pleasure and pain are what matter morally). "Animal liberation" is not "nature liberation." In order to forge an ethic that liberates us from our anthropocentric tradition, we must develop a holistic understanding of things, a molecular, rather than an atomistic, vision of the scheme of things and our place in it. "The land" must be viewed as meriting our moral concern. Water, soil, plants, rocks—inanimate, not just animate, existence must be seen to be morally considerable. All are "members" of the same team—the "biotic team."

14. HOLISM AND ETHICAL VEGETARIANISM

The holism Leopold advocates has interesting implications regarding how we should approach the issue of ethical vegetarianism. Appeals to the rights of animals, of course, are ruled out from the start. Based, as they are, on ideas about the independent value of the individual, such appeals are the voice of

---

[10] Aldo Leopold, *A Sand Country Almanac* (New York: Oxford University Press, 1949). For additional criticism and suggested readings, see William Aiken, "Ethical Issues in Agriculture," in Tom Regan, ed., *Earthbound: New Introductory Essays in Environmental Ethics* (New York: Random House (paper); Philadelphia: Temple University Press (cloth) 1983) pp. 268–70.

anthropocentrism past. That ghost can be exorcised once and for all only if we see the illusoriness of the atomistic view of the individual, *any* individual, as having an independent value, dignity, sanctity, etc. Standard versions of utilitarianism, restricted as they are to sentient creation, are similarly out of place. The "moral community" is comprised of all that inhabits the biosphere, not just some select portion of it, and there is no guarantee that what optimizes the balance of, say, pleasure over pain for sentient creation would be the right thing to do, when gauged by what promotes the "welfare" of the biosphere as a whole. If we are to approach the question of ethical vegetarianism with a clear head, therefore, we should refuse the guidance of both the rights view and utilitarianism.

Holism implies that the case for or against ethical vegetarianism must be decided by asking how certain practices involving animals promote or diminish the integrity, diversity, beauty, and harmony of the biosphere. This will be no easy task. Utilitarianism, as was noted earlier, (4, above), encounters a very serious problem, when it faces the difficulty of saying what the consequences will be, or are most likely to be, if we do one thing rather than another. And this problem arises for utilitarians despite the fact that they restrict their calculations just to the effects on sentient creation. How much more difficult it must be, then, to calculate the consequences for *the biosphere!* There is some danger that "the Land Ethic" will not be able to get off the ground.

Let us assume, however, that this challenge could be met. Then it seems quite likely that the land ethic might judge some practices involving animals morally right, others wrong. For example, raising cattle on nonarable pastures might promote the biosphere's "welfare," whereas destroying a delicately balanced ecosystem in order to construct a factory farm, or allowing chemicals used in animal agriculture to pollute a stream or pond, might be roundly condemned as "unhealthy" for the biosphere. Holism, in short, presumably would decide the ethics of animal agriculture on a case by case basis. When a given commercial undertaking meets the principles of the land ethic, it is right, and we are free to support it by purchasing its wares. When a given commercial undertaking fails to meet the appropriate principles, it is wrong, and we ought not to help it along by buying its products. So far as the matter of the pain, stress, and deprivations that might be caused farm animals in a commercial endeavor that promotes the "welfare" of the biosphere, these "mental states" simply do not compute, and to be morally troubled by such concerns is unwittingly to slip back into the misplaced atomistic concern for the individual holism aspires to redirect.

15. HOLISM AS ENVIRONMENTAL FASCISM

Few will be easily won over to this "new vision" of things. Like political fascism, where "the good of the State" supersedes "the good of the individual," what holism gives us is a fascist understanding of the environment. Rare species of wild grasses doubtless contribute more to the diversity of the biosphere than do the citizens of Cleveland. But are we therefore morally obliged to "save the wild grasses" at the expense of the life or welfare of these people? If holism is to hold its ground, it must acknowledge that it has this implication, and, in acknowledging this it must acknowledge further that its theoretical boat will come to grief on the shoals of our considered moral beliefs. Of course, those who are determined to awaken us to holism's virtues may be expected to reply that they are out to *reform* our moral vision, to *change* it, and so should not be expected to provide us with a theory that conforms with our "moral intuitions"—intuitions which, they are likely to add, are but another layer of our uncritical acceptance of our anthropocentric traditions and the ethnocentrism with which they are so intimately allied.

Well, perhaps this is so. Everything depends on the arguments given to support these bold pronouncements. What those arguments come to, or even if they come, must be considered elsewhere.[11] Here it must suffice to note that people who remain sympathetic to notions like "the rights of Man" and "the value of the individual" will not find environmental fascism congenial. And that is a crucial point, given the debate over ethical vegetarianism and commercial animal agriculture. For one cannot consistently defend meat eating or commercial animal agriculture by appeal to the principles of "the Land Ethic," on the one hand, and, on the other, appeal to principles involving human rights and the value of the individual to defend one's convictions about how human beings should be treated. Environmental fascism and *any* form of a rights theory are like oil and water; they don't mix.

16. SUMMARY

Two related questions have occupied our attention throughout: (1) Is vegetarianism required on moral grounds?, and (2) Judged ethically, what should we say, and what should we do about, commercial animal agriculture? Three different ways to approach these questions have been characterized: utilitarianism, the rights view, and holism. Of the three, the rights view is the most 'radical'; it calls for the total abolition of commercial animal agriculture and argues that, as individuals, we have an obligation to cease eating meat, including the meat produced by the animal industry, independently of how many other people do so and independently of the actual consequences our individual abstention have on this industry. Since this industry routinely violates the rights of farm animals, those who support it, not just those who run and profit from it, have "dirty hands."

Some utilitarians evidently seek the same answers offered by the rights view, but their arguments are radically different. Since what we ought to do

---

[11] See *The Case For Animal Rights, op. cit.,* Chapter 5.

depends on the consequences, and since our individual abstention from meat eating would not make a whit of difference to any individual animal, it seems we cannot have an obligation to be vegetarians, judged on utilitarian grounds. If, in reply, we are told that it is the consequences of *many* people becoming vegetarians, not just those that flow from the individual's abstention, that grounds the obligation to be vegetarian, utilitarians are, so to speak, out of the frying pan but into the fire. First, we do not know what the consequences will be (for example, for the economy, the starving masses of the third world, or even farm animals) if many people became vegetarians, and, second, it distorts our very notion of the duties of the individual to suppose that these duties depend on how many other people act in similar ways. So no, these utilitarians do not succeed in showing *either* that we have an obligation to be vegetarians *or* that commercial animal agriculture is morally to be condemned. These utilitarians may want the conclusions the rights view reaches, but, paradoxically, their utilitarianism stands in the way of getting them.

Holism (the kind of theory we find in Aldo Leopold's work, for example) was the third view considered. So long as we have reason to believe that this or that commercial endeavor in farm animals is not contrary to the beauty, harmony, diversity, and integrity of the biosphere, we have no reason to condemn its operation nor any reason to refuse to consume its products. If, however, particular commercial ventures are destructive of these qualities of the biosphere, we ought to bring them to a halt, and one way of helping to do this is to cease to buy their products. Holism, in short, answers our two questions, one might say, with an unequivocal "Yes and no." Very serious questions remain, however, concerning how we can know what, according to holism, we must know, before we can say that a given act or practice is right or wrong. Can we really presume to know the consequences of our acts "for the biosphere"? Moreover, holism implies that individuals are of no consequence apart from their role as "members of the biotic team," a fascist view of the individual that would in principle allow mass destruction of the members of a plentiful species (for example, Homo sapiens) in order to preserve the last remaining members of another (for example, a rare wild flower), all in the name of preserving "the diversity" of the biosphere. Few will find holism intuitively congenial, and none can rely on it to answer our two questions and, in mid-stride, invoke "the rights of Man" to defend a privileged moral status for human beings. At least none can consistently do this.

Despite their noteworthy differences, the three views we have examined speak with one voice on the matter of the tradition of anthropocentrism bequeathed to us by humanism and theism. That tradition is morally bankrupt. On that the three are agreed. And on this, it seems, we may all agree as well. That being so, and while conceding that the foregoing does not "prove" its merits, it can be no objection to the rights view's answers to our two questions to protest that they are at odds with our moral traditions. To be at odds with these traditions is devoutly to be wished.

Nor is it an objection to the rights view to claim that because it proclaims the rights of animals, it must be unmindful of "the rights of Man" or insensitive to the beauty or integrity of the environment. The rights view does not deny "the rights of Man"; it only refuses to be species-bound in its vision of inherent value and moral rights. No principle it upholds opposes making grains not fed to animals available to needy humans, as commercial animal agriculture winds down. It simply insists that *these* real or imaginary consequences of the dissolution of commercial animal agriculture are not the reason why we ought to seek to dissolve it. As for the natural environment, one can only wonder what more one could do to insure that its integrity and beauty are promoted or retained, than to act in ways that show respect to animals, including wild animals. In respecting the rights of this "part" of the biosphere, will not the "welfare of the whole" be promoted?

17. CONCLUSION

Theories are one thing; our practices quite another. And so it may seem that all this talk about rights and duties, utility and preferences, the biosphere and anthropocentrism—all this comes to naught. People are people, and they will do what they are used to doing, what they like to do. History gives the lie to this lazy acquiescence in the face of custom and convenience. Were it true, whites would still own blacks, women would still lack the vote, and people could still be put to death for sodomy. Times and customs change, and one (but by no means not the only) force for change are the ideas that trickle down over time into the language and thought of a culture. The language of "animal rights" is in the air, and the thought behind those words is taking root. What not too long ago could be laughed out of court now elicits serious concern. Mill says it well: "All great movements go through three states: ridicule, discussion, adoption." The movement for animal rights is beyond the stage of ridicule. For those persuaded of its truth, it is an irresistable force. Commercial animal agriculture is the movable object.

MORAL RIGHTS AND ANIMALS

H. J. McCLOSKEY

IMPORTANCE OF THIS INQUIRY

The issue of what constitutes morally proper treatment of and concern for animals and animal welfare *vis-à-vis* human beings and their well-beings, is obviously of the greatest practical as well as of considerable theoretical importance. To be mistaken here, to advocate and to encourage others as well as one's self to act on the basis of mistaken views, be they views which favour animals wrongly at the expense of humans or humans wrongly at the expense of animals, is to be, and to foster conduct which morally may be, gravely wrong. The kind of view to be arrived at here must affect moral priorities in a very basic way. Error therefore is to be avoided. Yet there are few areas in ethics which present greater, more difficult, conceptual and normative problems. Certainty is impossible; at best we can hope for rationally based belief.[1]

The issue of whether or not nonhuman animals, all or only some, may and do possess rights relates in an important way to the question of the morally proper treatment of and concern for animals and their well-being *vis-à-vis* human beings and their well-beings. The nature of the duties human persons have in respect of animals will be significantly influenced by the nature of the rights, if any, that animals possess. There are good reasons for believing that it is via the claim that animals possess rights that the strongest kind of case, both for improved treatment and for greater concern at a higher level, is to be made out. This is partly because rights are seen prima facie at least as giving rise to duties in others, to important, comprehensive duties of active assistance to, protection of, the possessor of the right, partly because rights are seen to be constraints, if not absolute constraints, constraints of a very stringent character on what it is permissible to do and refrain from doing in respect of the possessor of the right. The possession of moral rights by animals would both impose important duties and seriously limit the moral freedom of human persons.

However, the moral considerations in favour of better treatment of and concern for animals based on the contention that they possess moral rights are not alternative to, but rather they are such that they may be reinforced and supplemented by other ethical considerations which in no way rest on the view that animals possess rights. Typically, the claim that animals possess

Reprinted from *Inquiry,* Vol. 22, Nos. 1–2 (1979) 23–54, with permission of the author and the publisher, Universitetsforlaget, Oslo, Norway.

[1] I am much indebted to Dr. Jan Srzednicki of the University of Melbourne for reading a draft of this paper, and making a number of important critical and constructive comments concerning it.

rights is seen as adding to and strengthening other important considerations. Thus, even if it could be shown that animals do not possess rights and are incapable of possessing rights, many other kinds of considerations would need to be explored to determine what constitutes morally proper treatment of animals. Thus, whether or not they accept the principle of hedonistic utilitarianism, most people today recognize that animal pain and suffering, even if not animal pleasure and happiness, are factors of which account is to be taken in our moral deliberations, and which, if fully and adequately noted, would lead to different, improved treatment of many animals. Acceptance of the principle of hedonistic utilitarianism, with its insistence on the duty to promote pleasure equally with that of eliminating pain, would lead to an even more drastic rethinking of how morally we ought to treat animals, if it were to be applied on the basis of a proper understanding of the relevant facts. P. Singer's discussion in *Animal Liberation* is illuminating in this connection, and this even though there is scope for interpretation concerning the details of the utilitarian calculus.[2] Acceptance of the hedonistic principle as simply one among a number of principles in an ethical pluralism of the kind developed by Richard Price, W. D. Ross and others, would also lead to considerable modification of conventional moral theory and practice. Another possible approach towards a rethinking of the proper moral treatment of animals is via a more careful thinking out of ideal utilitarianism in terms of the kinds of things G. E. Moore and other ideal utilitarians have acknowledged to be intrinsic goods. Implications in respect of the treatment of animals seem there not to have been worked out in full. Again, it may be possible to argue for a rethinking of conventional morality as it bears on the treatment of animals by way of a more basic, radical rethinking of ideal utilitarianism, by attributing intrinsic value to life, animal life, sentient life, conscious life, self-conscious life. P. Singer and others seem currently to be exploring this kind of radical rethinking of ideal utilitarianism.[3] Clearly, whether or not animals possess rights, ethically important conclusions concerning how they ought to be treated would follow if claims that life, sentient life, conscious life, self-conscious life, possessed instrinsic value, could be sustained. Utilitarianism does not provide the only possible avenue to a rethinking of morality in this area, although it is true that it is via utilitarianism that such rethinking is so commonly approached. Other approaches are possible, although they seem as yet not seriously to have been explored. Thus just as it might be argued that it is intrinsically wrong to take innocent human life (whether or not it possesses intrinsic value), so it may be argued that it is intrinsically wrong to take innocent animal life. (Conservationists and preservationists seem often implicitly although not explicitly to adopt such a position in respect of exterminating species; and there is an increasing movement towards acceptance of such a principle, at least as a prima facie one in the condemnation

---

[2] *Animal Liberation,* (New York: Random House, 1975).
[3] See P. Singer, "Animals and the Value of Life." In Tom Regan (ed.), *Matters of Life and Death* (New York: Random House, 1979).

as immoral of the vandalism called hunting and of the arbitrary killing of unwanted pets at holiday seasons, and the like.) If such a principle could be shown to be a sound one, it would bear very importantly on how we ought to treat animals.

Thus, to show that animals do not possess rights and cannot be bearers of rights, is still to leave open a good many questions concerning what are our moral obligations in respect to animals. Nonetheless, to establish that animals, some or all, can and do possess rights, is to establish something positive and important, although, as will be argued in Section III, it is to establish something much less important and the implications of which are far less clear, than advocates of the view that animals possess rights have suggested is the case.

I. CONCEPTUAL ISSUES: THE CONCEPT OF A MORAL RIGHT

Possible Bearers of Moral Rights

Often those who claim that animals possess rights do not mean what they claim—they simply misuse the language of rights to express their belief that we have important, stringent, commonly neglected duties in respect of animals.[4] Others who appear to wish to maintain that animals possess moral rights, seem on closer scrutiny really to wish simply to argue that animals ought to be accorded legal rights, legal rights to life, freedom from avoidable suffering, and the like. This discussion is not concerned to examine views such as these. Rather it is directed at examining the claim that in the strict, literal sense of the term "moral rights", animals can be and are possessors of moral rights. To assess this claim the concept of a moral right needs first to be elucidated.

1. The Concept of a Moral Right

Moral rights are distinct from privileges, legitimate claims on others, duties owed by others to us, powers, liberties, or the like, that we ought to possess, or which ought to be accorded us. Rights are entitlements to do, enjoy, have, have done, such that where there are no other relevant moral factors to be taken into account, when we do, enjoy, have, demand that to which we have a right, morally we need offer no further justification to others, other than that we possess a right, the ground of which can be indicated. Moral rights thus have two aspects. They are entitlements which confer moral liberties on their possessors to do, demand, enjoy, etc.; and they are entitlements which

---

[4] The UNESCO proposed charter of animal rights would seem to be no more than this, a very misleading way of drawing attention of duties in respect of animals; it may also be a demand that legal rights be accorded to animals.

impose moral constraints on others, to abstain from interference, to do, to assist, etc.

Moral rights are distinguished from legal rights, rights as members of voluntary associations, churches, clubs, trade and professional associations, and from rights as participants in games. We may lack the moral right to do that which we have a legal or other institutional right to do. The moral rights are the important rights in that they override other rights. Lack of a moral right to do what we have legal or other rights to do renders them morally null and void. The characterization of a right as a moral right is therefore an important, positive characterization. It is to mark out that the right is based on moral considerations or grounds, and that morally it is an entitlement that is to be respected, both by its possessor and by others. It morally opens avenues for its possessor, and closes avenues for others, commonly imposing on them duties of abstaining from interference, and of protecting and aiding the possessor of the right in his enjoyment of his right. To claim that a right is a moral right is to claim something about the entitlements of the possessor, not simply concerning the duties of others. It is to say that morally he is acting as he is entitled when he acts, takes, enjoys, demands what he has a moral right to do, take, etc. The first-person question, "Have I the right to . . . ?" is important with all kinds of rights. With moral rights, it is central and basic. We can have no moral right unless we are at least prima facie entitled to do, demand, etc., that to which we have a right.

Basic moral rights are possessed by their possessors independently of other beings. My moral right to moral autonomy and integrity springs from my nature and being; it depends on no one else, and is conferred by no one else. However, certain moral rights may be conferred on us by others who possess the moral right to do so. I may confer on another the right to the use of my property. Some would argue that parents may confer not simply the legal but the moral right on their children who are minors, to marry. What is important in respect of accorded rights, and what limits the kinds and numbers of moral rights that may be accorded, by contrast with the basic, intrinsic rights, is the fact that for a right to be accorded there must be a person possessed of the moral right and power to accord the right. Once the right is accorded it comes to be possessed by the being to whom it is accorded, as long as it is accorded. By contrast, all institutional rights, legal and other, are accorded; none is intrinsic to the possessor.

It is commonplace to speak of rights as being possessed. Yet, when one reflects on what it is that is being expressed by talk of moral rights as being possessed, it is less clear what we mean than our ready use of such language might suggest. One use of the word "possess" is to refer to attributes that people have or possess—blue eyes, blond hair. People have rights; yet they are not attributes nor are they a kind of capacity, power or ability. A right is an entitlement that is ours, that we own, that belongs to us. To deny us the enjoyment of our rights is to deny us what is ours. Legally, to own something is to have legal rights in respect of it. Morally to own something is morally to have rights in respect of it, rights of control, use, or the like. The ownership of a moral right cannot be that, a moral right to a moral right, *ad infinitum*. This suggests that rights must be owned, possessed in a distinct sense again. The elucidation of that sense, however, presents problems.

Rights and duties, whilst obviously connected, are clearly distinct. There is no simple correlativity of rights and duties. Duties in respect of X need imply no rights in X—e.g., duties of charity in respect of X. Rights possessed by X need not imply any duties in others, for example rights to moral autonomy and integrity of the terrorist. One may have a moral right to follow one's erroneous conscience, yet others may have no duty, prima facie or other, to refrain from preventing one from so acting. The lack of correlativity of duties and rights is of obvious importance in the context of discussion of the rights of animals. To show that animals possess moral rights, moral rights against persons, it is not sufficient to establish that persons have duties in respect of animals.

Perhaps the most important feature of talk about moral rights, and that which most distinguishes such talk from talk about duties, is the reference to exercising, claiming, forgoing, yielding up one's rights. Whilst there may be rights which morally we may not be able to give up, which we continue to possess irrespective of whether we consent to forgo them, and which morally we must exercise, the concept of a moral right is such that there is no logical incompatibility between possessing a moral right and being able to waive it, yield it up, surrender it, or hold it but to choose, temporarily or for life, not to exercise it. The notion of exercising, acting on the basis of our rights, is central to rights. If the possessor of the right cannot himself exercise it, really to be a right it must admit in principle of being claimed and exercised on his behalf by some other person or persons.

These various features of the concept of a moral right are relevant to who or what can be a bearer of a moral right.

2. Possible Bearers of Rights

The problem as to the kind of being to which it is possible meaningfully to ascribe rights has no parallel with other moral concepts. There are no serious problems in respect of such moral concepts as ought, duty, right, and good.

(a) Considerations based on the concept of a right: The concepts most nearly related to that of a right would seem to be those of duty and obligation. These concepts relate to action, and to those capable of action. The agent who has a duty, who is under a moral obligation, must be capable of doing what he is obliged to do; he must be capable of acting. By contrast, this, at first sight at least, would seem not necessarily to be the case in respect of rights. To possess a right, it would seem not to be necessary actually to be able to act in ways relevant to the right. We seem meaningfully to ascribe rights to those who have suffered strokes and are in comas. First appearances may, however, be misleading here. Thus whilst it is true that, besides the rights which are entitlements which we may ourselves exercise by doing, demanding, requiring, there are also entitlements simply to enjoy, receive, have done, nevertheless the notion of accepting, not exercising, waiving the latter kind of right has meaning and import. Further, where the right relates to action, and where the possessor of the right is incapable of action, whilst the ascription of the right then typically has as its major import implications about how others ought to act, these obligations are not the essence of the right, but things that follow from it. Thus, possession of a right by X who is incapable of action of any kind, may create duties and rights in others to goods, services, liberties, removal of obstacles and impediments, and the like; yet there remains that essential core of the right, by virtue of which it can be exercised, not exercised, waived, forgone. These relate to actions by or on behalf of the possessor of the right.

That the duties are distinct and follow from the right is evident from the fact that were there no other beings capable of duties, and even where the possessor of the right himself had no specific duties, the ascription of a right such as a right to take his own life, would be meaningful and important. Indeed, the ascription of a right to a person at that time subject to no duties, temporarily incapable of action, where there are no other free agents with duties in respect of him, is meaningful. However, it is meaningful only on the basis of the possibility of action at some future time.

This suggests that the reason there seems to be a kinship between the concepts of duty and obligation on the one hand, and of a right on the other, lies not in there being some sort of correlativity of rights and duties, but in both deriving meaning and content from the possibility of action—in the case of duty, in the person subject to the duty, in the case of rights, in the possessor of the right or in someone who, by virtue of the right, has duties to act or refrain from acting in certain ways in respect of the possessor of the right, where his duties are coloured by how the possessor of the right would will to exercise or not exercise his right, in so far as this can be determined or inferred. In brief: The basic thought in the ascription of moral rights is that there be the possibility or potentiality of action. This suggests that the paradigm possessor of a right is an actor or potential actor, one who can act by doing what he is entitled to do, or act by demanding, claiming, requiring, what he is entitled to demand, claim, require. Where there is no possibility of action, potentially or actually, in the being towards whom duties are held, and where the being is not a member of a kind which is normally capable of action, we withhold talk of rights, and confine ourselves to talk of duties. Relevant here is the fact that the core use of talk about rights is first-person rights talk, talk in terms of possession, exercise, demanding recognition of them. Whilst for pragmatic, political reasons, including reasons of justice, it is often important to appeal to the rights of other people, the primary issue with rights as with duties, is the first-person one, "To what do I have a moral right?", "How shall I exercise my right?", "Shall I insist on my rights, or shall I forgo them in the interests of the common good, charity, harmony or the like?" Where the possessor of the right is himself incapable of exercising, claiming, demanding his right, the ascription of the right is fully meaningful only on the basis of an hypothesis that it can be exercised, claimed, demanded, in a real and meaningful way, on his behalf, as he would exercise, claim, demand, or waive it, were he to be capable of such action. More will be said later in explanation and justification of this contention.

(b) Considerations arising from paradigm possible possessors of rights: Philosophers have commonly ascribed rights to God (implicitly rather than explicitly) and to free rational, morally autonomous agents. There seems to be nothing paradoxical in so ascribing rights. Thus Locke sought to derive the rights he attributed to men from rights possessed by God.[5] This is most evident in his discussion of the right to life. Other philosophers have simply argued from the assumption that normal adult human beings can possess rights, since they have the relevant capacities in respect of exercising, claiming, yielding rights, and in respect of the content of the rights claimed, rights such as those to life, liberty, private property, moral autonomy and integrity. The puzzle cases have been and are human "monsters", human "vegetables", and infants. These are seen to be puzzle cases because, when we think of God and normal adult human beings as paradigm cases of possible possessors of rights, we are thinking of them as capable of being morally entitled to act, to make demands for goods, benefits, services, and to receive or decline such. It is because they are actors, and more, moral actors, capable of acting according to what they are entitled to do, and capable of refraining from doing what they are not entitled to do, that we believe that we can meaningfully ascribe them rights. It is true that in ascribing some rights we seem to be asserting entitlements to goods and services independently of any capacity for action by the possessor of the right; yet even there there is the implication in respect of action, that the right could have been waived, not exercised, had its possessor been capable of this. Further, if the only rights this kind of being could ever possess were rights of this kind, where he could exercise no judgment in respect to them, we should be reluctant to speak of such beings as possessing rights and as being capable of possessing rights. It is *qua* moral agent, possessed of a capacity to be morally self-determining, that we attribute the basic rights, the ascription of which gives some meaning and import to the ascription of these other kinds of rights in the puzzle cases.

That it is the capacity for moral autonomy, for moral self-direction and self-determination, that is basic to the possibility of possessing a right is confirmed by the fact that if we imagine the existence of any other kind of being, be it an angel, a purely spiritual being, a Martian, a whale, a dolphin, or the like, whether or not it be thought to possess sentience, capacity for feeling, for pain and pleasure, or the like, we should meaningfully ascribe rights to them if we believed them to be possessed of a capacity for moral

---

[5] Locke, *Second Treatise of Civil Government,* ch. II, esp. sect. 7.

self-determination, for moral autonomy. What is commonly overlooked in this connection by those who argue that other factors such as sentience, capacity for pleasure and pain, and the like, are basic to the possession of rights, is the fact that a being may be lacking in various of these capacities, and yet be a paradigm case of a possessor of rights. Thus it is commonly denied that God is capable of experiencing pain (and pleasure), yet this seems irrelevant to whether or not He has the capacity to possess rights, for example the right to inflict pointless suffering. Some human beings lack the capacity to experience pain. That too is irrelevant to whether they can be possessors of rights. Those that lack the capacity to experience pain commonly possess a capacity for pleasure, but were that not so, it too would be irrelevant. This is because it is capacity for action, moral action, that is basic to the ascription of rights.

There are problems in respect of potential persons, the very young, on the one hand, and on the other hand ex-persons, the brain-damaged, the extremely senile, the nonpersons, those born with damaged or undeveloped brains and who have no potentiality to become persons. When speaking uncritically, unreflectively, we ascribe the possibility of possession of rights, and even the possession of rights to all such human beings. When we so ascribe rights, I suggest we are doing something akin to what we are doing when we describe a cat as a quadruped, knowing that some cats are born with more and others with fewer than four legs. *Qua* cat, an animal, even this animal born with only three legs, is naturally a quadruped. *Qua* human being, where human beings naturally and normally become persons, human beings are possessors of rights. However, if we are to speak with strict accuracy, we must deny rights and the possibility of possession of rights to ex-persons, nonpersons who have no potentiality to become persons. Potential persons, infants who will come to be persons, possessed of rational, moral wills, such that they will be able to exercise their rights, are differently placed. Here everything turns on the importance that is to be attached to potentiality and the grounds for attaching this importance. Whatever criteria are indicated as the relevant criteria for the capacity to possess rights, this problem will arise, although it will be more acute, less easy to resolve in terms of some criteria than of others. Considerations to be outlined in (c) below bring out how reference to the capacity for rational, moral self-determination, moral autonomy, makes the ascribing of rights to potential persons more reasonable than ascribing them to those who potentially possess other attributes claimed to be the basis for being a bearer of rights.

(c) Attributes which have been claimed to be relevant to the capacity to be a bearer of a right: Few if any would wish to deny that mere things, inanimate objects, stones, mountains, paintings, buildings, and the like, cannot be possessors of rights. Yet we may have very comparable duties in respect of things to those we have towards some of those persons who possess rights of recipience. Thus we may have duties to protect, care for, preserve, a valued, valuable inanimate object, just as we may have a duty to protect the life of a possessor of a right to life. The duties may be exactly parallel, yet we resist the move to speak of the inanimate object of the duties as a possessor of rights. Here it may be argued that this is because the duties are not duties to the inanimate object, they are not duties accepted *for the sake of* that object, but rather that ultimately they are duties to possessors of rights, to human persons. Against this, whilst it is true that such duties are often explained in terms of the rights of and duties to human beings, this is not necessary, either normatively or conceptually, for the ascription of such duties to be meaningful. An ideal utilitarian may argue for the duty to preserve a beautiful painting, mountain, or the like, without any reference to their appreciation by human beings. We could meaningfully accept that we have the duty to make serious financial sacrifices to preserve a work of art, a desert region or other inanimate object, for its own sake and not for the sake of future human beings. Yet, when so explained, the duty is clearly distinct from a right in the inanimate object. This is because for us to accept the object of the duties as being a possessor of a right, the duty must be seen to derive from the right. Mere things may be the objects of duties; they may even give rise to duties, as ideal utilitarians have claimed. However, they cannot be bearers of rights which give rise to duties. This is because they cannot exercise rights, nor have them exercised for them.

The distinction between inanimate and animate things is an important one for many purposes. In the sphere of rights, it seems to be of little importance. Certainly, few, even among those who wish to argue that animals, some or all, may be bearers of rights, wish to argue that mere capacity for life is all that is necessary for something to be a bearer of rights. Again, the reason for this seems to be that mere life does not necessarily carry with it any suggestion of a capacity for action. It is nonetheless important to note what is being claimed and conceded when it is acknowledged that plants cannot be bearers of rights. We can have duties in respect of plants, to care for and protect them as ends in themselves, to refrain from pointless mutilation of them. We can ascribe them value for their own sakes, and act to benefit them for their own sakes, at the expense of human goods. In an extended sense of "interests" we can speak of the interests of a plant, such that a command, "In my absence so act as to protect the interests of this tree," would be an intelligible one. Pruning is seen to be contrary to the interests of certain kinds of plants, the application of certain fertilizers to be in their interests, and so on. Plants respond to stimuli, to light, heat, etc. Animal-eating plants do so in a more obvious way than do some other plants, so much so that some may wish to speak of them as being stimulated to "act," in some very extended analogous sense of "act." The distinction between plants and animals is not a sharp one, but is such that any one who sought to argue that all animals possessed or could possess rights, would encounter problems in justifying not extending the claim to encompass plants as well. The reason for the reluctance to ascribe rights to plants lies in the fact that they are seen to be things, incapable of action, lacking selves, wills, identities as beings.

This brings us to a consideration of animals and the features of animals which have been claimed to be relevant and adequate grounds for the ascription of rights. Features which are said to mark off animals, or animals that can be bearers of rights, from plants and mere things, include sentience, consciousness, capacity for pleasure and pain, capacity to have desires, capacity to have interests, self-consciousness, rationality in some fuller sense or senses, such as a capacity to conceptualize, construct a language, communicate with others, engage in acts of creativity, be able to make moral judgments and act on the basis of them.

Sentience: *The Concise Oxford Dictionary* explains that sentient means "having the power of sense-perception." More commonly, sentience is interpreted as the capacity for feeling. Perception and capacity to experience feelings are clearly distinct. A being may perceive that X is red, but be incapable of any feeling reaction of any kind. A being may experience feelings but be devoid of the capacity to perceive, the feelings resulting entirely from internal causes. We therefore need to consider separately the claims of sentience as sense perception and as the capacity for feelings.

Sense-perception covers a whole range of things from a capacity to respond to a stimulus, as with such plants as animal-eating ones, to sense-perception as we know it in man, where it involves not simply a response to outside stimuli but a cognitive apprehension of an outside reality as such. Mere capacity to respond to stimuli seems irrelevant to the question of capacity to be a bearer of rights. So too with the capacity to experience sensations as of redness, heat, hardness. In so far as these involve consciousness—it is not clear that they must do so—they may best be considered when considering the claims of consciousness. Perception in the sense of a full cognitive awareness of an outside reality as such would seem to involve not simply consciousness but self-consciousness, awareness of an awareness of sensation as providing knowledge of a non-self to the self. It may best be discussed when considering the claims of self-consciousness.

Sentience understood as the capacity for feeling, including feelings such as those of pleasure and pain, heat and cold (where not necessarily related to perception of external reality), and the like, seems again to have little relevance to the capacity to be a bearer of rights. This is evident if we consider a being that is sentient only in this sense of sentience, having no capacity for sense-perception. There might well be duties concerning it, arising out of its capacity to feel, but they would be independent of whether or not the being possessed rights. Such a being might be said to have interests by virtue of its capacity to experience feelings, depending on how the concept of interests is construed. If desires are essential for interests, then, since the capacity for experiencing feelings is distinct from the capacity to desire, they would lack interests. If the feelings had no relation to pleasure and pain, it is unlikely that we should wish to attribute interests to such sentient beings, other than in the extended sense of "interests" in which plants might be said to have interests.

The capacity to experience pleasure and pain seems to have greater moral significance than the mere capacity to experience feelings of other kinds. However, again, apart from the fact that this capacity might be a ground for ascribing interests, and interests be a ground for ascribing a capacity for possessing rights, the moral significance of the capacity to experience pleasure and pain seems to relate only to duties, not to the capacity to be a bearer of rights. Again, all that need be considered here is the animal which possesses this one capacity.

Importance has been attributed to consciousness, both as a source of value, and as relating to the capacity to be a bearer of rights. Yet it is hard to see its relevance to either. Consciousness may be consciousness of sensation, feeling, perception, mere thoughts. A being may be conscious of another being's existence, without being capable of any feelings in the sense of pleasure or pain, and without any awareness of itself as a self. It is hard to see how mere consciousness of this kind, a consciousness of shape, color, size, and the like, can be of relevance here. So too with mere consciousness of feelings. At best only certain kinds of conscious beings can possess value, be bearers of rights. This brings us to a consideration of special capacities attributed to certain beings possessed of consciousness.

The capacity to have desires has been advanced by some as a candidate for a criterion which marks off those who may be possible bearers of rights. A number of issues need to be distinguished here. One relates to what is involved in the capacity to have a desire. R. G. Frey has argued, with some cogency, that to desire, as distinct from having a need, is to have a belief that one lacks that which is desired, and hence, that to be capable of desiring, a being must be capable of belief.[6] This in turn suggests that for a being to have a capacity to desire, it must have a large number of rational capacities, and, in a real sense, be a rational animal. It must be able to conceptualize, hold beliefs, be self-conscious and not simply conscious, conscious of itself as believing that it lacks that which is desired. When we speak of animals as having desires, we commonly do not use the word "desire" in this strict sense which marks off needs and desires. Indeed, we are rarely if ever in a position to know that these conditions of desiring are met in the cases of animals. A second point of importance is that the mere capacity to desire as such, rather than as an aspect of rationality, seems to have little to do with being a bearer of rights. It is *qua* rational activity that desiring seems to have serious claims to consideration as a relevant criterion. This is confirmed by the fact that it is desired as an intellectual activity that is relevant, not as some sort of animal drive or appetite. A purely intellectual being such as God, a Kantian being with a holy will, or the like, is capable of desiring in the intellectual sense; it is incapable of appetitive desires. If capacity to desire is seen to be a necessary and sufficient condition for being a bearer of rights, it must be construed intellectually, otherwise such paradigm cases of possessors of rights would be excluded as not meeting the criterion. A third issue raised by desires and

---

[6] R. G. Frey, "Russell and the Essence of Desire", forthcoming in *Philosophy*.

the capacity to desire, if this account of desire is correct, is that of whether
rationality, in the respects that desiring involves rationality, is a relevant
ground for possession of rights. Much here will depend on how the details
are to be filled out. If there is no capacity for alternative action other than
along the lines directed by the desire, and if there is no way of marking off
belief and desire from what occurs in computers which are programmed to
develop "beliefs" as means to achieving goals, the rational capacities seem
to have little moral significance. It is because the notions of belief and desire
carry with them the suggestion of self-activity and self-determination that
they appear to be morally relevant. Yet they do not necessarily involve either
self-activity or self-determination.

Quite a number of philosophers including myself have argued that the
capacity to have interests, or the having of interests, is all that is necessary
for a being to be capable of being a bearer of rights.[7] The thought here has
been that rights which cannot be claimed directly by their possessor, involve
the possibility of representation by a proxy; that were it not in principle
possible for either the possessor of the rights or a proxy to claim the rights,
it is not meaningful to ascribe either rights or the possibility of possessing
rights. From this kind of basis, attempts have been made to argue that beings
capable of sense-perception, feelings, feelings of pleasure and pain, of desires,
are capable of possessing interests, and indeed, do possess interests. Much of
the debate has turned on whether only human beings, or even only some
human beings, may possess interests.

I now believe my arguments here to have been mistaken, misconceived,
and misdirected in quite a number of ways. First, I wish to concede that the
concept of interests is a much looser one than I previously suggested. The
original usage of the expression "interests" may well have been, and its present
paradigm use may still be, such as to relate interests to persons, where a
person's interests relate to his good as that person as a physical and spiritual
being. His good, and hence his interests, are distinct from his well-being, and
are determined by many factors including his physical and mental well-being,
the roles he has adopted and identified with himself, and his rational aspirations and ideals. We may distinguish what is in a man's interests from what
is dictated by his welfare, from what he desires, what he desires most, from
what will give him most pleasure and least pain, and so on. Thus, with human
persons there is no equation of feelings, maximizing certain feelings, satisfying
desires, or the like, with the realization of their interests. Whatever its original
range of application, the concept of interests is no longer restricted to human
interests. We also speak of interests in the strict sense of interests in respect
of corporate bodies, states, churches, business corporations, voluntary asso-

---

[7] See my "Rights," *Philosophical Quarterly,* Vol. 15 (1965). Also relevant are T. Regan,
"McCloskey on Why Animals Cannot Have Rights," *Philosophical Quarterly,* Vol. 26 (1976);
R. G. Frey, "Interests and Animal Rights," *Philosophical Quarterly,* Vol. 27 (1977); and J.
Feinberg, "The Rights of Animals and Unborn Generations." In W. Blackstone (ed.), *Philosophy
and Environmental Crisis* (Athens: University of Georgia Press, 1974).

ciations such as sporting clubs, where various of these contrasts do not arise, and where the interests of the organization relate to its good which may be distinct from the good of all the present members of the organization. It could well be in the interests of a state or a multinational corporation that it thwart the interests of all its present members. Some organizations see and act on this kind of basis, withholding funds as reserves which could well be paid on dividends, to secure future growth, where the interests of the organization are seen to lie in expansion and longevity. We seem now to be prepared to extend the range of application of the expression "interests" even further, and to speak of the interests of a thing where it is a living thing possessed of a good which can be affected by its actions or by human actions. Certainly, if it is legitimate to speak of the interests of ICI, where these are distinct from those of its share-holders and employees, it is hard to see why we should resist the extension of talk about interests to animals and plants. They possess goods which can be affected by what they "do" or what is done to them. Further, provided we are clear as to what we are speaking of when we speak of interests, no philosophical point of substance would seem to turn on the range of application of the concept of interests. If I am right in this, then the questions of whether desires, capacity to feel pleasure or pain, are essential or sufficient for the having of interests, are nonquestions. Relevant here is the fact that the attempt to restrict the range of application of the concept of interests, and to write more and more into the concept, simply obscures the solution to our problem concerning the necessary conditions for being a bearer of rights. This is evident from J. Feinberg's account of why plants cannot have interests, and of all that must be written into that concept to establish this. Feinberg writes:

> Yet trees are not mere things like rocks. They grow and develop according to the laws of their own nature. Aristotle and Aquinas both took trees to have their own "natural ends." Why then do I deny them the status of beings with interests of their own? The reason is that an interest, however the concept is finally to be analyzed, presupposes at least rudimentary cognitive equipment. Interests are compounded out of *desires* and *aims,* both of which presuppose something like *belief,* or cognitive awareness.[8]

A second respect in which I believe my earlier position to have been mistaken is in linking interests and the having of interests, with the having of the capacity to be a bearer of rights. I know of no convincing argument to this effect. L. Nelson who, in his *System of Ethics,* from a very different standpoint had developed the same view, seems to offer only the flimsiest of arguments, definitional fiats rather than genuine arguments.[9] Thus he writes:

> According to the principle of personal dignity, every being that has interests, in other words, every person, has a claim to respect for his interests. This claim is

---

[8] Op. cit., p. 52.
[9] L. Nelson, *System of Ethics,* trans. by N. Guterman (New Haven: Yale University Press, 1956).

the person's right. Thus every person is a subject of rights; for he is, by definition, a subject of interests.[10]

To subsume a being under the concept of person, it is sufficient that this being be capable of experiencing pleasure and pain: for pleasure and pain designate those interests of which we are conscious independently of any judgment, and which do not necessarily operate as impulses of the will. Any being that can feel pleasure or pain is therefore a subject of rights, and has dignity in the sense defined above.[11]

J. Feinberg seeks to offer a serious argument by reference to his analysis of the concept of interests as one involving conative and cognitive life (see the passage quoted above concerning why plants cannot be possessors of interests), and in terms of animals, some at least, as possessors of interests and those attributes on which the possession of interests rest, and hence being the kinds of things that can be recipients of goods for *their*—not our—sakes. Here Feinberg writes:

> Now ... a crucial principle ... namely, that the sorts of beings who *can* have rights are precisely those who have (or can have) interests. I have come to this tentative conclusion for two reasons: (1) because a right holder must be capable of being represented and it is impossible to represent a being that has no interests, and (2) because a right holder must be capable of being a beneficiary in his own person, and a being without interests is a being that is incapable of being harmed or benefitted, having no good or "sake" of its own. Thus, a being without interests has no "behalf" to act in, and no "sake" to act for.[12]

A number of objections may be urged to such an argument. The claim made in (2) has already been contested and rejected in the discussion of things and plants. The claim in (1) will be argued against in the next paragraph on the grounds that representation of rights is something very different from representation of interests. More generally, this general argument simply transfers the problem that Feinberg and others pose in terms of interests, to that of determining whether animals have desires, aims, beliefs, and the other relevant capacities necessary for them to be bearers of rights. And of course, argument will still be needed for accepting the possession of such capacities as a ground for attributing rights.

A third respect in which I wish to modify my view about rights and interests relates to the consideration that interests can be represented. I argued, and I believe, rightly, that it is possible to represent a being in respect of its interests, although the practical difficulties in the way of doing so are very considerable. However, in principle, we can seek to make informed judgments about what constitute the interests of a being, whether it be a person, a child, an animal, or a plant. This fact alone, that the interests of plants can be judged, protected, fostered, by a representative itself suggests that nothing of importance concerning rights follows from the possibility of there being representatives of the interests of non-humans. However, there is a more basic,

---

[10] Ibid., p. 99.
[11] Ibid., p. 100.
[12] Op. cit., p. 51.

positive objection to any attempt to argue that those who are capable of possessing interests are capable of possessing rights. The important objection lies in the fact that rights and interests are completely distinct things. A possessor of rights may wish to exercise his rights contrary to his interests. It may be in a person's interests to deprive him of the opportunity to exercise his moral rights. A person may, on moral grounds, wish to exercise his rights contrary to his interests. He may lack the moral right to pursue his interests—this is so when his interests involve evil actions and ends, as with the racist leader, the professional criminal, and the like. It is the paternalist who seeks to protect the individual's interests, where he deems the individual not to be the best judge or guardian of his own interests. The *laissez-faire* liberal opposes paternalism in favour of securing the individual in the enjoyment of his rights, albeit at the expense of his enjoyment of his interests. The criteria as to success in representing a person in the exercising of his rights are very different from those relating to interests. Indeed, there are moral as well as practical problems in determining what is the morally proper way to represent one who cannot communicate his wishes in respect of the exercise of his rights. Thus, that interests may be represented tells us nothing about whether or not rights can be represented. There are very considerable problems involved in representing a person in respect of their interests—the mistakes of well-meaning paternalists are only too well known. With rights, what has to be determined and represented by the representative is something much more difficult to determine. It is how the possessor of the rights who cannot express his wishes—who may not even be conscious or have wishes—would wish to exercise his rights, indeed, whether or not he would wish to claim his rights. This involves reading his mind, his moral mind, not simply determining what is for his good. Where there is no mind or will, actually or potentially, to be read, there can be no representation of rights nor of the exercising or waiving of moral rights.

Rights are moral rights. How they are to be exercised involves moral issues. A person representing another who cannot communicate his wishes must make moral judgments on that person's behalf about how to exercise his rights. By contrast, a judgment about what action or actions are dictated by a person's interests typically raises no moral question although in special cases it may do so. Pursuit of interests may involve doing what is gravely immoral, what one lacks the right to do. The view that has been canvassed by R. M. Hare, P. Singer, and others that interests *qua* interests ought to be respected, and respected equally, rests on a completely uncritical appraisal of what is involved in interests and their pursuit.

A final point concerning rights and interests that is worth noting here is that we are fully aware that organizations may have interests *qua* organizations, but deny that the organizations *qua* organizations can have moral rights. It is officials of the organization who have or lack moral rights to act on behalf of the organizations. The organization itself cannot have moral rights; this is because, as an organization, it is incapable of moral judgment, moral decision, moral action. What holds of organizations seems equally to hold of plants, all lower animals, and indeed of all animals which are incapable of moral judgment which allows them morally to determine whether to exercise their rights and how, or whether to waive them.

Consciousness and self-consciousness have each been claimed to be a sufficient condition for the ascription of rights. What has already been said makes it clear enough that mere consciousness establishes nothing. Only certain kinds of consciousness have any sort of claims to serious consideration. That their claims are unsound becomes evident if one considers what might be expected to be the stronger case of self-consciousness.

Here again, if we consider self-consciousness as such and not special kinds of self-consciousness, there seems to be little to suggest that self-consciousness has special claims. Consider self-consciousness which consists simply in the capacity to be aware of one's self as thinking or sensing, perceiving red objects, imagining them, but without the capacity to feel pleasure or pain, and without the capacity to act, choose, decide, make valuations, moral decisions, and the like. Mere self-awareness seems to be of little importance. It is the *kind* of being that is self-aware that is of importance. This leads on to a consideration of the claims of rationality, and of what is involved in rationality, and of the kind or kinds of rationality that are relevant to the possession of rights.

Consciousness and self-consciousness are aspects of rationality. Ability to conceptualize is another capacity relating to reason. Capacity to choose, decide, to act on the basis of conscious decisions, are other rational activities. The capacities morally to evaluate and to act on the basis of these moral evaluations are two further rational capacities.

There are problems in ascribing rights to beings possessed of rational capacities, even of highly developed, higher rational capacities, capacities to conceptualize, communicate, and the like, if this falls short of a capacity to act and to decide to act on the basis of a moral evaluation of the alternative possible actions. This is evident from a consideration of the paradigm cases of possessors of rights, free moral agents. In accepting and exercising their rights, they must call upon their moral capacities, make moral judgments and act within the limits of their moral entitlements. What is true and important about the argument from representation and interests, where the possessor of rights is one who cannot speak for himself and who can only exercise rights via a representative or proxy, is that possession of rights, involves the possibility of representation, moral representation, not representation of interests. Mere rationality without the rational capacity for moral judgments is not enough, since it is the moral will that must be represented. It is not what is in a rational being's interests, nor what a rational being wills, but what he wills within the limits of his moral rights, that the representative must seek to represent. The capacity for moral deliberation and decision is a crucial factor. Just as one may lack a right to what is in one's interests, so one may lack a right to that which one rationally wills. Thus there are two things involved in representing a possessor of rights in respect of his rights. The one relates to the area bounded by the rights possessed. The other relates to what is willed as being within these moral boundaries. Just as a legal representative representing a person in the exercise of his legal rights must first determine what are that person's legal rights, what their bounds are, and then and only then what he wills to do within these boundaries, so too in respect of moral rights. Supporting this argument is the fact that where representation is in principle impossible in respect of either legal or moral rights, the ascription of rights to one who can in no way himself claim his rights, is meaningless. Consider here the conferring of property rights by the state on someone who is permanently, irreversibly in a coma, where the conferring of the property rights is linked with a denial of all legal rights to others legally to represent that person or otherwise act to protect, secure the property rights on his behalf. We should say that the conferring of such property rights was a sham, a mockery, and not a reality. So too in respect of moral rights where no significant meaning can be given to moral representation of the so-called possessor of the right, the human being in an irreversible coma, the being without a moral will, potentially or actually, the being which lacks the capacity to formulate moral concepts and hence to make moral judgments, potentially or actually.

This leaves us with seeming problems in respect of infants, the permanently insane, the psychopath, and the irreversibly brain damaged. I suggest that there is no problem in respect of the latter. They lack the capacity to be bearers of rights. With most who are declared to be insane, there is limited sanity and a real moral capacity, such that they may be real possessors of rights. Further, it is seldom that we can say with confidence that there is not potentiality for sanity and moral autonomy. The psychopath constitutes a worrying case. If it could be known with certainty that there is no potentiality for moral autonomy, then the logic of the above argument would dictate the conclusion pressed on other grounds by A. I. Melden.[13] With infants the problem is that of potentiality. It is one which arises in respect of most candidates for acceptable criteria for being a bearer of rights. I suggest that it is meaningful to ascribe rights here on the basis of what would be/will be the moral will of the being who is now an infant.

As regards animals, the position is clear. If an animal has the relevant moral capacities, actually or potentially, then it can be a possessor of rights. The evidence available to date about the rational capacities of animals is far from complete, but to date it appears to be decidedly unfavourable to the view that any animals possess the relevant moral capacities. Thus, whilst research on chimpanzees, monkeys, and many other animals, reveals a significant degree of rationality which provides an important ground for justified moral demands that they be better treated than they now are, the degree and kind of rationality fall far short of that necessary for moral judgment and moral self-determination. Although there is limited evidence in respect of

---

[13] A. I. Melden, *Rights and Persons* (Blackwell, Oxford: 1977), esp. Ch. VI.

certain animals of a capacity for seeming "self-sacrificing," "disinterested," "benevolent" actions in limited, somewhat arbitrary areas, there is no real evidence of a capacity to make moral judgments, morally to discriminate when self-sacrifice, gratitude, loyalty, benevolence is morally appropriate, and more relevantly, to assess their moral rights and to exercise them within their moral limits. However, further research on animals such as whales and dolphins, although seemingly not in respect of monkeys, apes, chimpanzees, may yet reveal that man is not the only animal capable of being a bearer of rights. It may for this reason be morally appropriate for us meanwhile to act towards the former animals *as if* they are possessors of rights.

II. NORMATIVE QUESTIONS: THE RIGHTS ANIMALS MIGHT POSSESS IF THEY COULD POSSESS RIGHTS

If animals were to be capable of possessing rights, what rights would they possess? For all the concern by animal rightists about the rights of animals, relatively little has been written concerning this normative question; what has been written is not impressive. Thus, rather than follow the unsatisfactory discussions in this area where so often it is assumed that successfully to show that animals, some or all, can possess rights, is to show that they do possess the rights to life and to freedom from suffering, or that, because some unsatisfactory arguments for certain human rights seem to admit of restatement in respect of animals, that animals and humans are on all fours in respect of these rights—I shall proceed in a more positive way by looking at how arguments concerning human rights proceed, first examining their general patterns, and then briefly noting particular arguments for particular rights. This discussion will reveal that the establishing of the existence of moral rights is a subtle, complex matter, that the arguments available in respect of human rights do not establish either that all humans possess the same rights, or that where they do possess the same rights, they possess them equally. Further it will be evident that most of the important arguments relating to human rights, rights such as those to life, liberty, self-development, private property, privacy, and the like, are not transferable to animals.

1. The Kinds of Considerations Urged in Support of Human Rights

If the considerations urged in support of human rights are examined, it will be found that the more important are:

(a) A persistent claim more common in the eighteenth century than today, has been that certain rights are self-evidently so. It is an appeal which I suggest is appropriate in respect of certain basic rights, if "self-evident" is understood correctly, as by W. D. Ross in the context of his discussion of our knowledge of the principles of prima facie obligation. Rights such as the rights to life as persons, to moral autonomy and integrity, to respect as persons, appear to be rights which are self-evident, and in respect of which, argument other than that directed at clarification of what is involved in acknowledging the moral right is neither necessary nor possible. No animal right appears to be a self-evident right. The facts which make the right to life of persons a self-evident right do not hold of animals.

(b) Theistic arguments that seek to derive human rights from God's right— for example, Locke's argument for man's right to life—have figured prominently in discussions of human rights. Such arguments are equally possible in respect of animal rights but seem not to have been forthcoming. On the contrary, orthodox Christianity denies that God confers rights on animals, whilst those Eastern religions which prescribe respect for animals seem not to do simply *qua* animals. In any case, there are problems in the way of theistic arguments for rights, making as they do, the existence of human moral rights depend on the existence of God, and explaining them as accorded and not as intrinsic rights. Few moral philosophers today would be happy to accept the view that there can be no rational grounds for belief in the existence of human moral rights if God does not exist, or cannot be known to exist.

(c) Many arguments that have been urged in support of specific human rights, for example J. S. Mill's arguments for the right to liberty in *Liberty,* proceed by reference to the claim that certain things, knowledge, rationality, rational belief, self-development, right living, moral responsibility, pleasure and happiness (interests), are intrinsically good. The precise details of such arguments are hard to fill in, and seem to vary from writer to writer. Some writers, including Mill on one possible interpretation, seem to assume that we have a right to what is intrinsically good, or at least, a right to access to what is intrinsically good. A more likely interpretation of Mill's argument is that unless rights to access to these goods are accorded to civilized adult human beings, these persons will be unable to enjoy these goods, that these goods will be lost to mankind, and hence, that moral and legal rights must be accorded to civilized adults.

These are important arguments. The first version either rests on a claim that we have as a self-evident right, a right to these goods, or to access to them, or it is incomplete and requires filling out by reference to an argument in support of this more basic right. It is significant that the argument is seen to establish not that all human beings possess rights such as the right to liberty, equally, but only that some humans, mature, civilized adults possess that right, and then not always, that is, not equally. If the basic right to goods or to access to them could be shown also to hold of animals, this argument would have a limited application in respect of them. It would be limited in two ways. Most, but not all of the goods upon which it rests, are goods not available to animals. Secondly, the considerations which tell against ascribing various rights on this basis to children, the insane, the weak, and the gullible, would in a large measure also hold in respect of animals. Their exercise of such rights would more often lead to evils than to goods. However, this would not always be so, for example, in respect of pleasure and freedom from pain. Where captivity leads to pointless suffering, or where an animal such as a chimpanzee is harmlessly and with pleasure collecting and eating bananas and other food, to interfere with its liberty would be to deprive it of pleasure, even to cause it pain. Relevant here is J. Rachels's discussion.[14] However, as is evident from the Millian argument, only very limited rights, rights of only some few animals, could be argued for along these lines.

The second version of the argument, that which Mill probably intended to urge, would seem to be a telling argument for according legal rights, and for social rights, if meaning can be given to the latter concept. It is less evidently sound as an argument for moral rights. Typically moral rights are possessed intrinsically rather than accorded by someone else, other than in the case of property rights where moral rights may be transferred. Nonetheless, it is true that a moral authority, God or the state in so far as it is or may be a moral authority, could accord moral rights, but the circumstances in which this could occur must be very special ones. The same limitations hold in respect of the kinds of goods on which the argument rests, and concerning those with the capacity and judgment successfully to seek and realize these goods if accorded the relevant rights.

As noted earlier, those who claim that animals possess rights often mean simply that animals ought to be accorded legal and/or social rights. If this is what they mean, they would do well to state their position more accurately. They would then see that this Millian argument might well provide qualified—very qualified—support for their position.

The real worry about these arguments, whether they be arguments for human or animal rights, is that the version which seeks to establish what would be genuinely moral rights rests on a claim that we have a basic moral right to goods or to access to goods, when it is far from clear that we possess such a right, whilst the other version avoids this very questionable assumption by arguing only for accorded rights, where the only plausible meaning that can be given to the accorded rights is as legal or social, but not as moral rights.

(d) Many arguments for rights proceed by deriving rights from duties, from duties in others, or duties in the being claimed to possess the right.

Rights as based in duties in others: Certain rights and duties—most evidently, contractual rights and duties between specific persons—are correlative in the sense that the duty of X to Y, confers a right in Y against X, and vice versa. Indeed, the promise or contract which creates the right and duty, may well be said to create both in the one act such that it is the promise which is the source of both, rather than the duty the source of the right, or the right, the duty. Such rights as contractual rights are obviously one kind of special case. Duties of justice are also of this kind. Consider here rights and duties which derive from merit, desert, possession of a relevant attribute.

[14] See J. Rachels, "Do Animals Have a Right to Liberty?" in T. Regan and P. Singer (eds.), *Animals and Human Obligations* (Englewood Cliffs, N.J.: Prentice-Hall, 1976).

Here rights and duties may also be correlative, although they need not always be such since the duties need not be to determinate persons but to groups of persons, etc. There are other cases in which duties to determinate persons, for example, duties of parents to their children, are commonly thought to create correlative rights in the children. However, again, as with the case of promising, I suggest a closer examination of the case reveals that a strong case for the children being said to have a correlative right can be developed only by establishing that the duty and right spring from the same source. Otherwise we can simply, although usefully, speak *as if* the children have rights against their parents by virtue of their parents' duties, but strictly this will not be the case. This is confirmed by cases of duties of charity to specific persons. No matter how specific these duties are, the person who is the object of the duty of charity has no real right against the person subject to the duty to help him. A case to the contrary can be made out only if the right and the duty are to be derived from some common base.

What then of more general duties towards others—towards other human beings in general, or towards conscious beings, sentient beings, or the like? I suggest that rights do not follow from such duties. At best we can talk as if rights are conferred by the duties, but often this will be seriously misleading. Further it would involve a very drastic revision of our ordinary conception of a right. This is important in the context of animal rights, as it would be along these lines that the most plausible avenue of argument for animal rights could otherwise have been developed. Clearly we have a duty not to inflict pointless suffering on sentient beings, nonhuman and human. We have a duty not to destroy beautiful objects and beings. And so on. The former duty would confer certain rights to freedom from suffering on all animals capable of suffering and the latter duty would confer certain rights to life and freedom from mutilation on some members of the animal kingdom, many carnivores, birds, etc., although in the case of the former, possibly at the expense of a right to freedom, if there were the correlativity of duties and rights that is being denied here. Vexed questions would of course have arisen on this view concerning beauty and which animals possessed rights on this count. Similarly, were there such a correlativity, and had men the duty not to exterminate or let die endangered species, the members of such species would have possessed the right to life on that count.

Since not all duties create correlative rights, the most relevant arguments here when considering animal rights might seem to be those that relate to the duties which do involve correlative rights. Yet here too there appear to be problems. The rights which rest on promises and contracts and the duties created by them cannot arise in respect of animals. Animals cannot make promises, and we cannot make promises to animals. The duties of justice are the other important kinds of duties that carry with them correlative rights. Here it is commonly assumed that the duties of justice relate only to humans, and that therefore the relevant correlative rights can hold only of humans. However, if one considers the accounts that have been given of justice, the rendering to each what is due, treating equals equally, unequals unequally in the relevant respects, discriminating only on the basis of a relevant difference, there seems no reason in the nature of justice itself why its principles could not be extended, if there were no other grounds for rejecting such an extension. I suggest that the reason the principles are not so applied is because the notion of a right held by the object of the duty of justice is so basic and intrinsic to the whole concept of justice, that where the object of the duty is apprehended as one who is incapable of rights, it is seen therefore to be incapable of being an object of a duty of justice. Since here we are proceeding on the hypothesis that animals could possess rights, it would follow that they could be the objects of duties of justice, and hence possess the rights that are correlative with these duties. The substantial question would then become that of determining what duties of justice could hold in respect of animals.

The key to justice is the treating of equals equally, discriminating only on the basis of a relevant difference. Some, such as P. Singer and others, who see animals as coming under the orbit of justice, see as the basic duty of justice that of respecting all interests, whatever their nature and content, equally, the relevant equality being equality in being possessors of interests. There are obvious objections to treating interests as a relevant basis for treatment—some interests are evil, and ought to be overridden, thwarted, morally ignored. It is what makes up the content of interests that is relevant to justice. This varies from person to person, being to being. I suggest that a serious approach to animal rights via justice would involve examining why, when, and in what ways, considerations such as desert, merit, well-being, levels of well-being, needs properly understood, wishes, desires, are relevant considerations in respect of justice in the treatment of human beings, and then considering whether these considerations apply as dictates of justice in respect of animals. Much is made in discussions of justice of the claims based on needs. If the concept of need is used as a normative concept, its use prejudges the normative question, and the relevant task would be that of determining what ought to be called needs. If the concept is used as a non-normative one, then it will be evident that the needs of humans—and seemingly the same sort of thing will hold of other beings—should be taken into account not because they are needs, but because they are needs of a certain kind of being, human beings; and where the neglect to satisfy them leads to certain kinds of evil results.[15] Justice does not dictate that all needs of all human beings be satisfied. Needs *qua* needs carry no moral weight—otherwise plant needs, the needs of lower animals, and the like, morally would have to be taken into account. Similarly in respect of well-being and levels of well-being. The kind and quality of well-being are of importance, not well-being in the abstract. Thus the unravelling of what justice would dictate in respect of animals is a very subtle, complex, difficult enterprise. However, whilst many considerations of justice, merit, desert, and the like, will not apply to

[15] See my "Human Needs, Rights and Political Values", *American Philosophical Quarterly*, Vol. 13 (1976).

animals, some relevant considerations will apply such that some rights of justice may be derived from the relevant duties, if the other basic difficulty about the possibility of possessing rights could be overcome.

Rights as based on duties of the possessor of the right: Many arguments for human rights proceed from the fact that human beings are moral agents with moral duties. Thus, whilst the Thomistic theory of natural law derives both rights and duties from man's natural (and supernatural) end, many exponents of natural rights theories seem to argue for specific natural rights from the duty man has to attain his natural (and supernatural) end, and from his right to carry out that duty. Such arguments are among the more straightforward, important arguments for human moral rights. They obviously are not available in respect of animals.

(e) It is also argued that rights spring from man's capacity to be a moral agent, a moral person. A basic, self-evident right, and one which carries with it many far-reaching, derivative rights, is the right to be a moral being. This right does not spring from any duty such as a duty to be a moral being; the mere capacity to be a moral agent self-evidently confers the right to be such. From this right flow many other rights, including the rights to life, to moral liberty, self-development, to care for one's offspring and generally to carry out the duties one has as a person and as a unique person. This is one of the most powerful arguments for human rights. It is not available in respect of animals.

As is evident from the discussion in (c) many arguments for rights which are commonly seen as being basic rights are in fact arguments from some more basic right such as the right to access to intrinsic goods, the right to be a moral being, the right to be self-developing, the right to life. In so far as these basic rights can appertain only to free agents, to persons, to that extent the arguments from them can hold only of free agents.

It is important to note that the above considerations upon which claims about human rights are based do not seek to establish that all human beings possess the same rights, nor that, where they do possess the same rights, they possess them equally. They imply that different people may have different rights, and that men may have different rights to different degrees or under different conditions, and that not all the rights possessed by men need be possessed by them all their lives. The same kinds of qualifications would carry over in respect of any rights animals may be shown to possess in terms of such considerations.

2. Human Rights and Their Possible Relevance to Animals and Animal Rights

Rights commonly claimed in respect of human beings include the rights to life and health; the rights to moral and physical integrity; the right to happiness and to freedom from suffering; the right to liberty; the right to self-development; the right to private property; marriage and family rights;

rights to knowledge, true and rational belief; the right to education; the right to privacy.

Various of these rights cannot apply to animals. This is so in respect of the rights to moral integrity, self-development, knowledge, true and rational belief, and to education as it is understood by those who stress that right, because of the lack of the relevant capacities. There are some problems on this count in respect of the rights to private property, to marry, to have and care for one's offspring. However, important aspects of these rights, for example, with private property rights, rights of use if not of control and disposal, are possible for animals. Various of the arguments urged in support of these rights in respect of humans—from the right to life, etc., if such rights hold of animals—appear to be transferable, although notwithstanding Rachels's ingenious although utterly unconvincing discussion, not Locke's very unsatisfactory labour argument for private property.[16] (That whole argument depends on the concept of the person, of the labour as labour of a rational, planning being, which knows what it is doing. We think of human activity as capable of creating rights because and in so far as it is rationally directed towards planned goals. Mere human activity seems not even prima facie to create rights. Even less that of animals, parasites, predators, and the like. Further, the argument assumes the absence of prior ownership. It assumes a right of the first labourer unrestrictedly to appropriate that on which he labours, albeit that his labour is only a small element of what he appropriates. These assumptions have never been satisfactorily dealt with. They become even more difficult to handle if the animal kingdom is to be included in the group of labourers. Is anything in the world free of pre-ownership? Can any meaningful application be given to the labour theory in the contemporary world given existing ownership and pre-ownership by humans and animals?)

Our earlier discussion brought out the limited nature of the arguments available in support of an animal right to liberty. Animals are incapable of positive liberty. The Kantian arguments for a right to liberty from respect for autonomy, especially moral autonomy do not apply to animals. And, as already noted, the utilitarian arguments apply only with great qualifications in respect of human beings, and with vastly more qualifications in respect of animals, and then only in respect of a right to negative liberty, a right to limited freedom from interference for certain animals. The same utilitarian considerations may give other animals a right to be confined and protected. Even greater qualifications would seem to hold in respect of the right to privacy. The arguments relevant to the human right—which I myself deny to be a basic human right—most likely to be transferable to animals are those from there being a need, from happiness via the need, and those from the enjoyment of privacy as essential for security from evils and harm. Obviously, as bird-watchers and animal-watchers generally so commonly claim, few if any animals are harmed by unobtrusive, secret invasions of their privacy.

The human rights of most obvious relevance to those concerned with

---

[16] *Op. cit.*, p. 208.

animals and animal rights are the rights to life and to freedom from suffering. These are the least discussed and least argued of all human rights. The rights to freedom from suffering is implicitly covered by the utilitarian arguments discussed in (c) above. The same sorts of qualifications which hold in respect of humans would hold of animals, but more so. And the basic difficulties encountered by the kinds of arguments for rights noted there remain. The less unsatisfactory arguments for the right to life of humans proceed by reference not to life in the abstract, but to the kind and quality of life of which human beings are capable. They point to features of human life and existence that are not shared with animals. Different arguments are necessary in respect of animals. If it could be shown that animal life—some or all— has intrinsic value, an attempt to establish animal rights to life could be made in terms of the utilitarian arguments. However, as is evident from P. Singer's thoughtful, careful discussion, there are difficulties in the way of plausibly attributing intrinsic value to animal life.[17]

3. Specifically Animal Rights

Would there be specifically animal rights, tiger rights, pelican rights, tapeworm rights, if animals were to be capable of possessing rights? I suggest that any specifically animal rights are likely only to arise from special needs of the different animals, where these are needs that ought to be respected. Thus carnivores, needing to kill other animals in order to live, might be claimed to have the right to kill these other animals, whereas their vegetarian victims may lack the right to kill other animals except in self-defence, but have the right to eat grass, leaves, or the like, provided they leave enough for other animals. Problems which arise from pursuing this line of thought may best be discussed in Section III.

III. RESPECTING RIGHTS, ANIMAL AND HUMAN

The arguments and considerations on which rights are grounded are such as to imply two things about rights, whether they be animal or human. The one is that no right is always an absolute right—some are prima facie rights, always rights but not always absolute rights, some are conditional rights, only rights under certain conditions, and even then possibly only prima facie and not necessarily absolute rights. The other implication is that rights are not possessed by all members of a species *qua* member of a species, but *qua* possessor of relevant attributes. This means that different beings may possess different rights, and the rights they possess they may possess to different degrees. It is evident from the discussion in Section II that if animals were to be capable of possessing rights, rights to life, freedom from suffering,

---

[17] "Animals and the Value of Life," loc. cit.

liberty, and the like, they would possess rights to different degrees, from one another, and with respect to human possessors of rights.

Further, rights clash with one another. We are familiar with this in the human situation, and seek to resolve these clashes by weighing up the conflicting rights in terms of their various stringencies, when it is impossible to find some way of avoiding the conflict. There are conflicts within particular rights, between the claims of the right to life of different individuals, and between the claims of different rights, to life, liberty, property, moral integrity. It is impossible to set out priority rules for resolving such conflicts. They are to be resolved only by reference to the relative stringencies of the rights involved; and this is to be determined by reference to the ground of the right, and the basis on which the individuals concerned come to possess the rights. In many cases, the conflicts seem rationally to be irresoluble. Consider here the right to life as a right of recipience, and the clashes over conflicting needs for help. The problems posed by clashes of human rights then are immense. However, we are clear about our goal. Our goal is that of the maximum satisfaction of or respect for rights, taking into account the relative stringencies of rights.

If it were to be shown that animals possess moral rights, the problems posed by clashes of rights would become vastly more difficult. Besides the clashes within human rights, and between human and animal rights, we should be faced with clashes between animals rights. Since animals are incapable of engaging in the relevant moral deliberations and acting to resolve the conflicts, it would be left to man to act to resolve them. Can he satisfactorily do this? Indeed, are there possible moral solutions of such conflicts? Consider here the rights to life, health, freedom from suffering. Today, because of the reasons discussed earlier in this paper, it would generally be agreed that these rights are rights of recipience. The considerations bearing on this would seem to hold, if rights apply at all, in respect of the rights of at least certain animals. The human person faced with the conflict between the rights of carnivores and predators, of disease-causing, debilitating parasites, and like animals, on the one hand, and their victims on the other, would have to weigh the rights to life, health, freedom from suffering of the aggressors, against the rights to life, health, freedom from suffering of the victims. Is this possible? Is a meaningful solution possible? Indeed, is it possible meaningfully to speak of the rights to life of the victims—rights which normally are seen to carry with them a right to self-defence and to be defended by others in whose care they are—and at the same time speak of the aggressor's right to kill? Surely the human guardian of animal rights would be faced with logically incompatible demands, a demand that he protect the threatened animal to safeguard its right to life as a right of recipience, and, at the same time, to prevent interferences with the aggressor's right to kill—and to life—where it too is a right of recipience. It is not simply that there can be no priority rules, nor that the weighing up of the conflicting rights is extremely difficult, but that there is a logical incompatibility in the claims made by the rights. The possessor of a right to life has a right not to be let die, and not simply not to be killed. Yet this involves killing or allowing to be killed another possessor of an equally stringent right to life. So too with the rights to health and to freedom from suffering. This problem would not be a remote, rare one. If our domestic pets, cats and dogs, cannot lead healthy, happy lives on vegetarian diets, we should be confronted with this problem immediately it were established that they possess these rights. I suggest therefore that there would not simply be vastly difficult practical problems and calculations to be faced in determining what constituted the maximum morally right satisfaction of rights. There would also be the theoretical problem of whether acceptance of the kinds of rights that are likely to be ascribed to animals is compatible with the maximum satisfaction of rights' remaining a meaningful, logically coherent goal.

PRESERVATION

JOHN PASSMORE

By "preservation" I mean the attempt to maintain in their present condition such areas of the earth's surface as do not yet bear the obvious marks of man's handiwork and to protect from the risk of extinction those species of living beings which man has not yet destroyed. The word is often used rather more widely, as when we speak of "preserving" buildings or villages, stretches of urbanized landscape like Tuscany, cities like Venice. For my present purposes, however, I shall exclude from consideration the preservation of artifacts; the case for preserving them overlaps, but does not coincide, with the case for preserving what human beings have not created. As we have seen, it is generally agreed that works of art ought not to be destroyed; there is no such agreement that it is wrong to destroy wildernesses or undomesticated species. Should there be? This is the first issue we have to consider. We have seriously to ask ourselves whether it constitutes a genuine problem that at an ever-increasing rate men are converting wildernesses into tamed landscape—into farms, towns, suburbs, tourist resorts—and destroying the plants and animals which once shared the earth with him. Does it really matter that the moa no longer stalks the New Zealand plain? Does it really matter that tourist resorts have been set up in the remotest corners of New Caledonia? In his "Song of the Redwood Tree" Walt Whitman asserts that the redwood

Reprinted from John Passmore, *Man's Responsibility for Nature*, Second Edition (New York: Scribner's, 1974; London: Duckworth, 1980) pp. 101–126, with permission of the author and the publishers. (Chapter 5, "Preservation," is included here.)

tree must "abdicate" his forest-kingship so that man can "build a grander future." What, if anything, is wrong with this attitude?

There are two different ways of trying to answer these questions; we can think of wildernesses and of species as having either a purely instrumental or an intrinsic value. On the first view, wildernesses and species ought to be preserved only if, and in so far as, they are useful to man. On the second view, they ought to be preserved even if their continued existence were demonstrably harmful to human interests. As it is sometimes put, they have a "right to exist." The first view can easily be incorporated within the traditional Graeco-Christian picture of the world, the second view presents greater difficulties.

"Usefulness" need not be narrowly interpreted: wildernesses and species, it might be argued, are valuable not only as economic resources, actual and potential, but as providing opportunities for the pursuit of science, for recreation and retreat, as sources of moral renewal and aesthetic delight. Let us look at each of these in turn. Take first the economic value of wildernesses and wild species. Biologists have now demonstrated that wet-lands, mangrove swamps, are not infertile appendages to the shore, fit candidates for draining and levelling, but hospitable providers of food and lodging for the young of economically valuable fish. This is only one illustration of the manner in which the preservation of a wilderness can be economically profitable. Somewhat less directly, by studying the behavior of trees and plants in wild conditions, biologists can hope to discover why the yield gradually falls off under cultivation; the wilderness acts as a norm.

Something similar is true of wild species, whether plant or animal. Cultivated plants and animals have been bred for special purposes; they are liable, in consequence of their breeding, to diseases which could in principle entirely wipe them out. Men need a reservoir of wild species, with their greater genetic diversity, to protect them against this eventuality. Species once destroyed cannot be replaced: to destroy a species is a peculiarly irreversible act, which may well have quite calamitous long-term ecological consequences. To attempt totally to wipe out dangerous species of viruses and bacteria, even, might encourage the emergence of still more dangerous mutants. A species often turns out to be unexpectedly useful, a tropical plant to contain pharmacologically valuable substances. There are good economic and biological arguments, then, essentially conservationist in character, for thinking much more carefully than we ordinarily do—obsessed as we are with the "conquest", and "development", the "perfecting" of nature—about the total effects of transforming a patch of wild country, whether swamp or mountain, or acting in a way which may lead to the extinction of species. No doubt, the human race has survived without apparent harm the disappearance of the moa and the dinosaur, the transformation of Europe into a tamed landscape. But a purely economic argument will suffice to establish at least a prima facie case against the clearing of wildernesses, the destruction of species.

To turn now to the scientific value of wildernesses. I have already drawn attention to the utility of biological investigations in nature reserves. But biological inquiry has a value in itself as a form of human enterprise, quite apart from its utility. We should not think it right to destroy a scientist's laboratory; for the same good reason we should try to preserve areas in which the biologist—or the geologist—can work, even when his investigations have no immediate practical value. There is then, taking together the economic and the scientific value of biological inquiry, a strong case for setting up what in South Africa are known as "Strict Nature Reserves" which only scientists would be permitted to enter—reserves differing in their rock-structure, climate, flora, fauna, and big enough to permit those large animals to roam whose role in the preservation of eco-systems is so often vital.

Then there is the need for recreation. Recreations are not all, of course, of equal value. Few of us, nowadays, would be impressed by the argument that cocks ought to be preserved since otherwise cockfighting will die out. The case of hunting is more difficult. In the nineteenth century, "preservation" meant in fact the preservation of game—the cutting off of rivers and moors and woodland from public access so that landed proprietors and their friends could enjoy the sport of hunting. The enthusiasm for killing, purely for sport, is a form of enjoyment the West sometimes carries to the point of mania, whether it be the small bird or the elephant which is the victim. (The explorer Speke, to take only one instance, counted any day a loss on which he did not have unfamiliar game to shoot.) In such Eastern books of moral instruction as the Chinese *Concerning Rewards and Punishments* (Kan Yin Pien) hunting is, in contrast, condemned as wholly perverse. There is something more than a little odd, certainly, about the view that wild species ought to be preserved in their wild conditions because some men enjoy killing them. For my part, I should agree with Plutarch that "sport should be joyful and between playmates who are merry on both sides."[1] And I am unable to persuade myself that the kangaroo enjoys being hunted. (On purely preservationist grounds, herds may have to be culled; that is a different matter.)

Yet even for so ardent a preservationist as Aldo Leopold hunting obviously meant a great deal: in his eyes, "public wilderness areas are, first of all, a means of perpetuating, in sport form, the more virile and primitive skills in pioneering travel and subsistence."[2] For most of his long history, man has been a hunter; we should not lightly assume, whatever our personal distaste for hunting, that he can now set that legacy aside. But at best the recreational value of hunting will justify the preservation of only a relatively few species of animals and those plants that give them sustenance. At worst, as Leopold himself fully recognises, it leads to the destruction of those species which limit the success of hunting, the acclimatisation of species which are destructive of wildernesses, and the opening up of hunting grounds, in a manner which destroys their original character, to make them more accessible to hunters.

---

[1] Plutarch: "Whether land or sea animals are cleverer." In *Moralia,* 12, 964–65, trans. W. Helmbold, Loeb Classical Library, p. 353.
[2] *Sand County Almanac,* p. 269.

Something the same is true of other, morally less dubious, forms of recreation. "Even the purest of nature lovers," it has been pointed out, "has
physical weight and boots on his feet." Assured of his total innocence, he
can yet destroy the sparse grass of mountain heights or so firm the trails that
trees and shrubs can no longer survive around them.[3] In search of a wilderness,
he by his very presence converts it into a man-made landscape. It was for
long supposed that in National Parks the interests of the hunter, the tourist,
the biologist, could all be reconciled. In *The Earth as Modified by Human
Action* Marsh had set out thus attractively his policy for national parks:

> It is desirable that some large and easily accessible region of American soil should
> remain, as far as possible, in its primitive condition, at once a museum for the
> instruction of the student, a garden for the recreation of the lover of nature, and
> an asylum where indigenous tree . . . plant . . . beast, may dwell and perpetuate their
> kind.[4]

But we have now discovered that neither a museum nor an asylum can be
at the same time a "garden for recreation."

The seeker after recreation does not for the most part want wildernesses
in the strict sense of that word. His conception of wilderness "subsumes the
existence of picnic tables, wells, toilets, washrooms, and the like."[5] What he
is looking for are pleasant surroundings in which to enjoy forms of recreation
which are not available to him in cities. The decision to open up the National
Parks by building roads into them has been described as "one of the great
statesman-like acts of American history."[6] But it was a decision to put
recreation first, the preservation of wildernesses second—and therefore nowhere. For a wilderness opened up to all comers is rapidly converted into a
tamed and as often as not a degraded landscape.

Garrett Hardin has suggested that wildernesses should be specially reserved
for the use of those who are fit enough to enjoy a sojourn in untouched
wildernesses. "A wilderness that can be entered only by a few of the most
physically fit," he has argued, "will act as an incentive to myriads more to
improve their physical condition."[7] As it stands, however, this is a paradoxical
policy: if the myriads were in fact to improve their condition they would be
able to enter the wildernesses and the whole object of the exercise would be
subverted. That is why Hardin is obliged to suggest that this restrictive policy
should be supplemented by a lottery.

The general principle that so far as possible forms of enjoyment should be
preserved, provided only that they are not morally objectionable, is a sound

---

[3] See F. Fraser Darling and N. D. Eichhorn, "Man and Nature in the National Parks." In
W. Anderson (ed.), *Politics and Environment*, p. 221.

[4] This is the title under which G. P. Marsh published the second edition of his *Man and
Nature* (New York, 1874). The quotation is from p. 327.

[5] David Lowenthal, "Daniel Boone is Dead." In A. Meyer (ed.), *Encountering the Environment*
(New York, 1971), p. 52.

[6] R. L. Means, "The New Conservation," in ibid., p. 2.

[7] Garrett Hardin, "The Economics of Wilderness," reprinted from *Natural History* (1969).
In C. E. Johnson (ed.), *Eco-Crisis* (New York, 1970), p. 176.

one. But the real problem is that there are in this case conflicting interests: what Hardin is in fact proposing is that people who do not fit into a very limited category—physically fit lottery-winners—should not be permitted to enter wildernesses. And it is not *obviously* apparent why they should be kept out: there is not the same obvious value in preserving wildernesses for a very limited class of recreationists as there is in preserving them for scientific or for economic reasons. Hardin's view that the state will thus encourage physical fitness is more than dubious; the existence of such wildernesses as the Antarctic, with admittance restricted to a selected few of the physically fit, has certainly done less for physical fitness than the opening up of civilised walks through the Swiss mountains. Taken in all the arguments, on purely recreational grounds, for preserving wildernesses as distinct from public parks is by no means a strong one—at least in those areas of the world where there is a pressing need for recreational facilities.

What about the need for solitude? Do men need places where they can be totally alone? John Stuart Mill's argument for preserving wildernesses rested in large part on this assumption that "it is not good for man to be kept perforce . . . in the presence of his species." "A world from which solitude is extirpated, he continues, "is a very poor ideal."[8] The enjoyment of solitude is, however, something of a paradox. A peculiarly human enjoyment, it yet depends, for its very existence, on the absence of human beings. It is the enjoyment, one might even say, of human absence. The virtues of solitude are by no means universally recognized. The inhabitants of a crowded camping ground and the solitary walker over the mountain look at one another with incomprehension, distaste, and even fear. That is why the searcher after solitude is often resented, and the preservation of wildernesses—as distinct from "opening them up to tourists"—condemned as the attempt of a misanthropic few to limit the enjoyment of the gregarious many. "A conservationist [preservationist]," Galbraith has ironically remarked, "is a man who concerns himself with the beauties of nature in roughly inverse proportion to the number of people who can enjoy them."[9] Or as the point has been more savagely put: he wishes "to keep nature locked up as a private preserve, to be enjoyed only by those with a great deal of money or free time."[10]

The arguments of preservationists on this point are sometimes more than a little disingenuous. Not long ago the government of Tasmania decided to flood a lake in a remote part of that island as an element in a hydro-electric scheme. As part of their case, in many respects a strong one, against that decision, the preservationists argued that "man has a need to know himself," and that this self-knowledge he can achieve through adventures with nature in the country around Lake Pedder. "Its appeal," the argument admits "is specific and selective. It is not for everyman's taste but for those who would

[8] *Principles of Political Economy* (London, 1848), bk. 4, ch. 6, 2.

[9] J. K. Galbraith, "How Much Should a Country Consume?." In H. Jarrett (ed.), *Perspectives on Conservation* (Baltimore, 1958), p. 92.

[10] R. L. Means, "The New Conservation." In A. Meyer (ed.), *Encountering the Environment,* p. 2.

make the effort to know themselves. *In this sense it is everyman's opportunity.*"[11] There could scarcely be a better example of the illicit use, in such arguments, of the general concept of "Man." Instead of saying frankly, and being content with this, that a very small percentage of the population obtains not only enjoyment but a special sort of spiritual refreshment out of Lake Pedder, the pretence is that somehow Lake Pedder is, in the last resort, for everyman, in spite of the fact that "its appeal" is—and this puts the matter mildly—"specific and selective." Such sophistry cannot in the end do preservationism any good, even if it is easy to understand the political motives which lie behind it.

The mere fact that, like the enjoyment of poetry, the enjoyment of solitude or private meditation is a minority enjoyment does nothing to suggest, of course, that there is no virtue in trying to ensure its continuance. Human beings differ greatly in their sources of enjoyment, minorities have their rights; the preservation of these rights is what democracy is about. But the special consideration that the enjoyment of solitary wildernesses may only be possible at the cost of greatly restricting the recreation of others raises problems not only about its political feasibility but even about its moral desirability—unless a case can be made out for its being a form of enjoyment of such value and importance that other forms of enjoyment ought to be sacrificed to it, that just as none but biologists should be allowed into strict Nature Reserves so other wildernesses should be reserved as places of recreation for the meditative solitary-loving few. (Lotteries for mystics?)

This is a claim often made: it is strongly suggested in the Lake Pedder manifesto. Arguing in support of the view that Niagara Falls ought to be preserved from industrial development, Charles Eliot Norton described the falls as "one of those works of Nature which is fitted to elevate and refine the character and to quicken the true sense of the relations of man with that Nature of which he is a part."[12] What force is there in this claim? Some force, I think. Nature, on this scale, helps to preserve men from *hubris,* to make them conscious that things go in their own way, indifferent to man and man's concerns: it encourages a kind of humility which has in it nothing of servility.

It helps to free men, too, from the bondage of Philistinism. "We city-dwellers," as Brecht's Herr Keuner puts it, "get dazed from never seeing anything but use-objects; . . . trees, at any rate for me, have something independent about them outside myself."[13] Even more is this true of waterfalls and mountain crags, of the life of animals and birds in a wilderness, of the desert and the swamp. Here, if anywhere, we escape from the "What's in it for me?" attitude so characteristic of our society.

Yet doubts remain. "Any protracted, genuine association with nature," so

[11] Lake Pedder Action Committee, *Lake Pedder* (Adelaide, 1972), p. 35 (my italics).
[12] C. E. Norton, *Letters,* II, 95 n., as cited in Hans Huth, *Nature and the American* (Berkeley, 1957), p. 173.
[13] Bertolt Brecht, *Tales from the Calendar,* trans. Y. E. Kapp (London, 1961), p. 110.

a writer in the *Yale Review* once argued, "means a reversion to a state of brutal savagery.[14] This objection cannot be lightly dismissed. Thoreau tells us—and Garrett Hardin quotes the passage with approval—that what men learn in the wilderness is "that Nature is so rife with life that myriads can afford to be sacrificed and suffered to prey on one another; that tender organisations can be so serenely squashed out of existence like pulp."[15] Is this the sort of moral lesson which we need to learn from nature? It is a lesson, certainly, that more than a few inhabitants of the wilderness carry away from it and apply to human life.

Herder had qualms of a rather different sort. "It appears," he writes, "among what people the imagination is most highly strained: among those namely, who love solitude, and inhabit the wild regions of nature, deserts, rocks, the stormy shores of the sea, the feet of volcanoes, or other moving and astonishing scenes."[16] And this highly strained imagination, he goes on to argue, has been the source of fanatical religions, of superstitious terrors.

It would appear, then, that the moral advantages of wilderness experiences are by no means indisputable; quite the contrary. I have suggested, and many of us will know from our own experience, that there is refreshment as well as enjoyment to be found in wandering through wild country. (Not only recreation but *re*creation; it renews one's sense of proportion.) But it is not at all clear that to sustain this experience the wild country needs to be a wilderness in the full sense of the word: were it, for example, to be purged of flies I, for one, would not find the refreshment diminished. It is much easier to state a case for the preservation of humanised wildernesses as places of recreation than for the preservation of wildernesses proper.

Finally, let us look briefly at the aesthetic value of wildernesses. For the Graeco-Roman tradition enjoyable "scenery" meant the olive grove, the cultivated field, the orchard, the carefully disposed villa or temple. Mountains and wildernesses were crude, unformed, inhuman, unperfected, not worth the attention of a cultivated man. The gods might make their home on mountain tops or, like Jahweh, hand down from the heights their decrees. But mountains were no place for ordinary men and women; they were dangerous, frightening, with wild animals still a serious threat. Man allowed himself the luxury of admiring them only when he was no longer intimidated by their ferocities. And only after the success of his farming ensured that he had enough to eat did he enjoy the spectacle of wasteland.

The typical classical attitude is still expressed in Charles Cotton's seventeenth-century poem, *The Wonders of the Peak* (1681). Here is his description of the Derbyshire Peak country:

A country so deformed, the traveller
Would sware those parts Nature's pudenda were.

[14] T. K. Whipple, "Aucassin in the Sierras," *Yale Review*, New Series, 16 (July 1927), p. 714, quoted in P. J. Schmitt, *Back to Nature* (New York, 1969), p. 176.

[15] In C. E. Johnson (ed.), *Eco-Crisis*, p. 175.

[16] J. G. von Herder, *Reflections on the Philosophy of the History of Mankind* (trans. T. O. Churchill, London: 1800), bk. 8, ch. 2, sect. 3.

Shameful, unfit for the eyes of man, so that coach-blinds should be kept
drawn as it was traversed—that is a characteristic classical description of
the wildernesses which in the nineteenth-century men were so extravagantly
to admire.[17]

There have always been occasional exceptions, of course: that atypical Basil
the Great raised Gregory of Nazianzus' eyebrows by praising the wild country
in which his monastery was set. Gregory's response is typical. "All that has
escaped the rocks," he wrote in remonstration, "is full of gullies, and whatever
is not a gully is a thicket of thorns; and whatever is above the thorns is
precipice."[18] It would not do to praise that unreformed wilderness which
symbolised man's sin, a reminder of his woeful state. Eden knew no thickets,
or gullies, or precipices; on Milton's account, indeed, they are what now
make Eden inaccessible to man. When the hermit went into the wilderness
it was not in order to enjoy it but to remove himself from all sources of
worldly enjoyment: to be wholly alone with a God who was not of this world.
He went there, too, to fight with the demons who inhabited the wilderness.
"By no means satisfied," as John Cassian expressed their attitude in the fifth
century, "with that victory whereby they had trodden under foot the hidden
snares of the devil (while still living among men), they were eager to fight
with the devils in open conflict, and a straightforward battle, and so feared
not to penetrate the vast recesses of the desert." If in the wilderness they
hoped to find perfection, this was only by first conquering, in God's name,
its diabolic inhabitants. Through the desert to paradise—that was the motto
for anchorite and for mystic. But only because the wilderness was the last
foe which had to be conquered.[19]

It might be supposed that wild nature, as coming directly from the hands
of God, ought, rather than civilisation, to be enjoyed. Christian theologians,
indeed, had difficulties on this point. On the one side they felt it incumbent
upon them, like the psalmist, to praise the handiwork of God; on the other
side, they condemned the world as a corruption of God's original intent. Only
the heavens were still pure, untouched by Adam's sin, which, so Luther
argued, cursed not only the soil he was to work but the whole earth, innocent
though it was. "We must speak of the whole of Nature since its corruption,"
he wrote, "as an entirely altered face of things—a face which Nature has
assumed, first, by means of sin, and secondly by the awful effects of the
universal deluge."[20] The world, so it was commonly argued, must once have
been a perfect sphere; the irregularities of its surface—mountains, wilder-

[17] Cotton is quoted in Edward Malins, *English Landscaping and Literature* (London, 1966),
p. 8. On this theme in general see Marjorie Nicholson, *Mountain Gloom and Mountain Glory*
(Cornell, 1959).

[18] See D. S. Wallace-Hadrill, *The Greek Patristic View of Nature* (Manchester, 1968), pp. 87–
91.

[19] The quotation is from John Cassian, *Colloquia* (III), xviii, 6, and xix, 5. On this complex
question see especially G. H. Williams, *Wilderness and Paradise in Christian Thought* (New
York, 1962), esp. p. 41.

[20] See "Luther on the Creation." In J. N. Lenker (ed.), *Martin Luther: Precious and Sacred
Writings* (Minneapolis, 1903), vol. 1, pp. 64–5.

nesses—are not God's creation but the effects of sin. Indeed, not only the earth but the "rude and ragged moon" are, in Thomas Burnet's words, "the image or picture of a great ruin, and have the true aspect of a world lying in its rubbish."[21] To enjoy the wilderness, on this interpretation of the situation, is to indulge in a wholly perverted taste.

Until relatively recently, indeed, to call a place a wilderness was unmistakably to load it with abuse. Gerard Manley Hopkins' "Long live the weeds and the wilderness yet"[22] would have seemed an absolute paradox to the first New England settlers who saw their new country as "a hideous and desolate wilderness, full of wild beasts and wild men."[23] Here is Tertullian, roused for once to enthusiasm: "All places are now accessible, all are well known, all open to commerce; most pleasant farms have obliterated all traces of what were once dreary and dangerous wastes; cultivated fields have subdued forests; flocks and herds have expelled wild beasts; sandy deserts are sown; rocks are planted; marshes are drained; and where once were hardly solitary cottages, there are now large cities. No longer are [savage] islands dreaded, nor their rocky shores feared; everywhere are houses, and inhabitants, and settled government, and civilized life."[24] Eighteenth- and nineteenth-century romanticism, with its nature-mysticism, was responsible for a transvaluation of values. God and nature were identified; and the enjoyment of nature was thereby elevated to its highest point, at the hands of such American transcendentalists as Dwight, into a religion. And on the whole that attitude of mind has persisted into the twentieth century. It is thought desirable for a house to have "a view," rather than an enclosed garden prospect—most desirably a view of a landscape in which the hand of man is not blatantly obvious.* That it will persist into the twenty-first century, however, can certainly not be taken for granted.

It is a very considerable presumption, indeed, that our descendants will

[21] Thomas Burner, *The Sacred Theory of the Earth*, bk. 1, ch. 9.

[22] The quotation from Hopkins is in "Inversnaid," *Poems of Gerard Manley Hopkins*, ed. R. Bridges (London, 1918).

[23] The views of the New England settlers are as summed up by Nathaniel Morton, keeper of the records for the Plymouth Colony; quoted in S. L. Udall, *The Quiet Crisis* (New York, 1963), p. 13.

[24] Tertullian: *De Anima*, In A. Roberts and J. Donaldson (eds.), *The Writings of Tertullian*, vol. 2, p. 481; Ante-Nicene Christian Library, vol. 15.

* It is worth remembering, however, that when that notorious nature-fancier William Wordsworth wrote his famous line: "Earth has not anything to show more fair," what he was describing was not a Lake District mountain, dale or stream but the view of London from Westminster Bridge. And if looking at that view nowadays we can only sadly reflect with an older poet:

> Quid non mortalia pectora cogis
> Auri sacra fames!

Wordsworth's lines still come naturally into our minds as we look at the Tuscan landscape or the view of Florence from the Piazzale Michelangelo. In the United States the beauties of the wilderness have been highly esteemed, but the townscape and the rural countryside largely ignored. What the West now needs, it is by no means absurd to argue, is a revival of the classical feeling for town and rural landscape much more than the Romantic passion for wilderness. Compare David Lowenthal on "The American scene," in *Geographical Review*, **58**, 1 (January 1968), pp. 61–88.

continue to admire wildernesses aesthetically, just as it is a considerable
assumption that they will continue to enjoy solitude. Neither attitude of mind
is at all universal; it is not in the least like assuming that they will continue
to enjoy, most of them, eating or drinking or making love. This consideration,
echoing a now familiar difficulty, may serve to underline what will already
be obvious; the argument for preservation, as I have so far presented it, is a
special case of the argument for conservation. We ought, I have so far
maintained, to preserve wildernesses because they may turn out to be useful
and because they may afford recreational pleasures, scientific opportunities
and aesthetic delight, to our successors. The first of these considerations, our
argument has suggested, is a powerful one, the others less powerful in so far
as they rest on the presumption that our descendants will still delight in what
now delights only some of us and did not delight our predecessors. On the
other side, they do not call upon us entirely to sacrifice present enjoyments
for the future; we, anyhow, can find pleasure in biological inquiry, in wil-
derness-recreations—even if most of us prefer the tamed to the true wilderness—and in the sight and smell and sound of wild animals, plants and birds.

The real difficulty arises, of course, out of the fact that there can be clashes
of interests. These raise very sharply the question of "rights." We have already
drawn attention to the clash of interest between the wilderness-lover and the
ordinary vacationist. This conflict can be construed economically as a conflict
over the best use of scarce resources. More obviously, there can be sharp
conflicts between the tourist *industry* and the preservationist as also—an old
battle this—between the preservationist and the miner. None of the arguments
I have so far advanced is strong enough to permit the conclusion that in
every such case, where a species or a wilderness is seriously threatened, the
victory ought to go, on moral grounds, to the preservationist. In a particular
case the interests of the tourist industry, mining, farming may be involved
to such a degree that their spokesmen will certainly have the political, and
may even have the moral, advantage. That is one reason why the arguments
I have so far advanced would not be considered adequate by the more
uncompromising preservationists.

Sometimes, indeed, such arguments are dismissed out of hand as, in a broad
sense of that word, essentially economic. "I am not greatly moved," writes
Fraser Darling, "when I hear supporters of the national park and nature
reserve movement argue that living things have educational value, that the
beauties of nature give pleasure to humanity, that they are of scientific
value . . . and that we cannot afford to lose them." And this is because, he
tells us, 'the essential attitude [in such arguments] is not far in advance of
that of the timber merchant', i.e., it still determines what ought, or ought
not, to be allowed to survive in what are substantially economic terms, by
reference to human needs.[25]

It is at this point, indeed, that the cry grows loudest for a new morality,

[25] F. Fraser Darling, "Man's Responsibility for the Environment." In F. J. Ebling (ed.):
Biology and Ethics, Symposia of the Insitute of Biology, no. 18 (London, 1969), p. 119.

a new religion, which would transform man's attitude to nature, which would lead him to believe that it is *intrinsically* wrong to destroy a species, cut down a tree, clear a wilderness. As I have already suggested, these demands strike one, at a certain level, as merely ridiculous. One is reminded, indeed, of the exchange between Glendower and Hotspur in *Henry IV Pt. I* (III.i.53):

Glendower: I can call spirits from the vasty deep.

Hotspur: Why so can I, or so can any man,
            But will they come when you do call for them?

A morality, a religion, is not, as I have already argued, the sort of thing one can simply conjure up. It can only grow out of existing attitudes of mind, as an extension or development of them, just because, unlike a speculative hypothesis, it is pointless unless it actually governs man's conduct. But it may be true that in fact men's attitudes are already changing, that the "new morality" would be a natural outcome of a change that is already in process, which can now be hastened by exhortation or argument. That possibility we should at least explore.

We shall look first at one change that has already taken place. Men now commonly recognise that they ought not unnecessarily to inflict pain on animals. This means that they recognise at least one point at which their relationships with nature are governed by moral principles. This has not always been so. By looking at what happened in this case we may hope to learn something of the grounds that already exist in the Western tradition for a more radical reassessment of man's relationship with nature.

In the Old Testament, men and animals have a common principle of life (*Nebesh*); as we have already seen, God is represented as caring for animals just as he does for men. At least one of the Talmudic teachers argued that "the avoidance of suffering of dumb animals is a Biblical law."[26] But in Christian thinking, as we have also seen, Paul's rhetorical question "doth God take care for oxen?" was for long decisive.[27] The Stoic teaching, with which Paul concurs, that the Universe exists only for the sake of its rational members carried with it the conclusion that between men and animals—to say nothing of plants—there was no sort of moral or legal tie. Augustine lent his immense authority to this doctrine. "Christ himself," he writes, "shows that to refrain from the killing of animals and the destroying of plants is the height of superstition, for, *judging that there are no common rights between us and the beasts and trees,* he sent the devils into a herd of swine and with a curse withered the tree on which he found no fruit." "Surely," Augustine continues, "the swine had not sinned, nor had the tree."[28] Jesus, that is, was not punishing the swine when he sent devils into them, or *blaming*

[26] *Babylonian Talmud,* Seder Mo'ed, vol. 1, trans. I. Epstein (London, 1938), 128*b*, ch. 18, p. 640.
[27] Compare on this theme Edward Westermarck, *Christianity and Morals* (London, 1939), ch. 19.
[28] Augustine, *The Catholic and Manichaean Ways of Life,* trans. D. A. Gallagher and I. J. Gallagher (Boston, 1966), ch. 17, p. 102.

the barren tree. If he had sent the devils into a bystander or cursed a woman for being barren, we could only have concluded that they had sinned; otherwise Jesus's action would be morally indefensible. But he was trying to show us, according to Augustine, that we need not govern our behavior towards animals by the moral rules which govern our behaviour towards men. That is why he deliberately transferred the devils to swine instead of destroying them, as he could easily have done.

So for centuries it came to be standard Christian teaching that men could do what they liked with animals, that their behaviour towards them need not be governed by any moral considerations whatsoever. There were, of course, occasional exceptions. Francis of Assisi is the most famous example of a Christian nature-lover, calling upon birds as his sisters in an Umbria still not entirely Christianised out of nature worship. (Modern ecologists not uncommonly proclaim him their patron saint.) But his case is anything but a clear one. Biographies by English animal-lovers, often Protestant, naturally stress his fellowship with nature; Roman Catholic biographers, in contrast, are intent on establishing his orthodoxy. They write with scorn of those who see in Francis a sentimental nature-lover, only by an accident of time ineligible for the Presidency of the Royal Society for the Prevention of Cruelty to Animals. Nor is there any hope of settling such controversies by returning to primary sources; those sources were for the most part deliberately designed to create a particular image of Francis, the image varying from chronicler to chronicler. On the face of it, however, his attitude to nature is reminiscent of the psalmist's or of that old English hymn which tells us, in a somewhat unfortunate metaphor, that "even the worm bends his knee to God."

Only once, however, does the question of callousness arise in the biographies of Francis written by his friends or near-contemporaries and then it does so rather disconcertingly. One of the brethren, taken ill, told Francis' disciple Jonathan that he had a longing for pigs' trotters. "In great fervour of spirit," Jonathan cut the trotters off a living pig. Francis rebuked him, but with no reference whatsoever to his callousness. He urged him, only, to apologise to the owner of the pig for having damaged his property.

In any case, Francis had little or no influence. The Franciscan philosophers accepted the traditional Aristotelian-Stoic view of the relationship between man and animals. Pius IX refused to sanction the setting up of a Society for the Prevention of Cruelty to Animals in Rome, on the ground that it would suggest that men had duties to the animal kingdom. In so far as cruelty to animals was wrong, this was only because, so it was argued by Aquinas, by Kant, and by a multitude of lesser thinkers, it might induce a callousness towards *human* suffering. There was nothing wrong with cruelty to animals *in itself.*

These conclusions were supposed to follow automatically from the fact that animals could not reason and therefore had no rights. But there was an alternative argument, more fundamental, on which some of the Stoics particularly insisted. Human life, they contended, would become quite impossible if men thought of themselves as governed in their relationships with animals by moral considerations. It would then be quite wrong to kill animals for food, to harness them for work in the fields, to use them as beasts of burden. And that would mean the collapse of civilisation—"we shall be living the life of beasts once we give up the use of beasts." [29] In other words, only by supposing themselves to be quite free from all moral considerations in their relationship with nature can human beings, according to the Stoics, justify their civilising of it.

In the long run, these considerations did not prevail. It is now generally agreed by moral philosophers, and has been for a century or more, that it is wrong to treat animals in such a way as to inflict on them unnecessary pain— even if the range of this principle is still disputed, how it applies, for example, to vivisection. Interestingly enough, too, moral philosophers now take it to be *obvious* that cruelty to animals is morally wrong. Such otherwise so different moral philosophers as Schopenhauer, Mill, Laird, Rashdall, Leonard Nelson all maintain that their predecessors must have been blinded by what Rashdall, himself a Dean, called "prejudices of theological origin." [30]

This, then, is one case in which men have experienced a change of heart; they have come, in the very long run, to accept certain moral limitations on their dealings with nature. As we have already suggested, however, this limitation has not been carried in the West very far—not, except for a relatively few, to the conclusion that it is wrong to kill animals but only to the belief that it is wrong so to act as to cause animals quite *unnecessary* suffering, suffering, that is, which is not essential for the satisfaction of fundamental human needs.

And what is the theoretical foundation of this new moral attitude? This is important, if we are to decide what the likelihood is that it might be extended to the preservation of species. In part, perhaps, a growing recognition— certainly extensible—that men and animals are more alike than Augustinian Christians were prepared to concede. The Augustinian view reached its apogee in the seventeenth century when, as we have already pointed out, Descartes and Malebranche were capable of arguing that animals not only could not reason but could not even feel.* Such sceptical thinkers as Montaigne and

[29] The argument is cited in Plutarch, "The cleverness of animals," *Moralia,* 964, p. 347.

[30] See Arthur Schopenhauer, *On the Basis of Morality,* trans. E. F. J. Payne (Indianapolis, 1965), pt. 2, sect. 8, p. 96, and pt. 3, sects. 19, 7, pp. 175–82; J. S. Mill, *Principles of Political Economy,* bk. 5, ch. 11, §9; John Laird; *A Study in Moral Theory* (London, 1926), pp. 296, 302; Hastings Rashdall, *The Theory of Good and Evil* (London, 1907), vol. 1, pp. 213–15; Leonard Nelson, *System of Ethics,* trans. N. Guterman (New Haven, 1956), p. 136.

* Only within a theodicy does the question: "Why do animals suffer?" so much as arise. But in the West that question rather than "How can we reduce animal suffering?" was, for centuries, the problem of problems. It engendered fantastically elaborate solutions. So the Chevalier Ramsay suggests that the less guilty of the fallen angels were shut up in animal bodies and made men's slaves. They tempted man to fall, and as a consequence were still further degraded, losing the remnants of reason and the power of speech with which their own fall had still left them. Their sufferings as animals are at once a punishment and a means through which they might be purified and thus regain their former state. See D. P. Walker, *The Ancient Theology* (London, 1972), pp. 254–5. Ramsay's fantasy was constructed well after Descartes wrote; it suggests the

Hume, in contrast, insisted at once on the resemblance between men and animals and the need to treat them humanely. In his *Apology for Raimon Sebond* Montaigne argued that it is absurdly presumptuous for men to set themselves up above the animals; in his "Essay on Cruelty" he drew the conclusion that "we have a general duty to be humane, not only to such animals as possess life, *but even to trees and plants.*" [31] Hume, intent on arguing that human and non-human intelligence worked in the same general way, did not go so far as Montaigne in his moral conclusions. But at least he laid it down, in relation to animals, that "we should be bound by the laws of humanity to give gentle usage to those creatures." [32] Both Hume and Montaigne, it is necessary to observe, accept the Stoic principle that we are not called upon, and cannot be called upon, to act *justly* towards animals. But what Hume calls "the cautious, jealous virtue of justice" is not, both he and Montaigne rightly argue, in this case the relevant one. And it is not incompatible with the preservation of civilisation, far from it, to extend humane feelings, as distinct from justice, to the animal kingdom.

This was the approach that won the day. "The French have already discovered," Bentham wrote, "that the blackness of the skin is no reason why a human being should be abandoned without redress to the caprice of a tormentor. It may come one day to be recognised, that the number of the legs . . . or the termination of the *os sacrum* are reasons equally insufficient for abandoning a sensitive being to the same fate." [33] Observe the characteristic transition from slave to animal; humane feelings towards animals arose as a development of humane feelings towards man in general—whether slaves, or criminals, or the insane. Bentham's Utilitarianism looks not to the rationality of the agent or the patient, in the Stoic manner, but to the effect of the agent's actions on all sentient beings. The pains of animals, because they do not include the pains of anticipation, might be less than the pains felt by man, but that is no reason for not taking them into account. The question is neither, so Bentham argues, "can they reason?" nor "can they talk?" but "can they suffer?" Basically, that is, cruelty to animals was condemned on humanitarian grounds. Just for that reason, only those animals whose suffering is most humanlike were brought under the protection of the law: the "lower" living things, such as insects, were not protected. Ants could still be killed by poisoning or by pouring hot water on their nests without fear of legal consequences or moral reprobation.

---

extremes into which any alternative hypothesis led the justifiers of God's ways. Malebranche is quite explicit that for purely theological reasons, it is necessary to deny that animals can suffer, since all suffering is the result of Adam's sin and the animals do not descend from Adam. This is another point at which Christianity has encouraged an exploitative attitude to nature.

[31] Montaigne, *Oeuvres Complètes* (Paris, 1925), vol. 3, p. 246 (my italics).

[32] Hume, *Enquiry Concerning the Principles of Morals,* ed. L. A. Selby-Bigge, sect. 3, pt. 1, §152, §145.

[33] Jeremy Bentham, *Introduction to the Principles of Morals and Legislation,* written 1780, published 1789, ed. J. H. Burns and H. L. A. Hart (London, 1970), ch. 17, §4, note *b.* In some other editions the chapter number is 19.

In general, then, the argument was that the deliberate infliction of pain on animals whose sufferings were obvious was a morally bad form of conduct. And it was not, in general, thought necessary to carry the argument beyond that point. But there were a few more intransigent exceptions; some of the advocates of anti-cruelty legislation argued not only that animals had feelings but that they had rights, thus setting themselves wholly at odds with the Stoic-Augustinian tradition. In 1792 the Platonist Thomas Taylor published a work entitled *A Vindication of the Rights of Brutes.* (It consists in large part of quotations from a neo-Platonic work, Prophyry's *Concerning Abstinence.*) His purpose was ironic. His title page bears the epigraph *Quid Rides?;* his work as a whole is intended as a *reductio ad absurdum* of Thomas Paine's *The Rights of Man* and Mary Wollstonecraft's just published *A Vindication of the Rights of Woman,* the latter work echoed in his title. Here, he is saying, are the conclusions to which you are driven if once you allow, with Paine, that even the least rational of men—or what is worse, with Wollstonecraft, that even women—have rights. Before you know where you are you will be treating animals as having rights.

And this prophecy was to be fulfilled in, for example, H. S. Salt's *Animals' Rights.*[34] In defence of the view that animals have rights Salt argues that they are protected by law. If that argument suffices, however, then we should have to conclude that not only animals but trees and plants and even rocks and landscapes can have rights; for they, too, can be protected by law—and not only, as Salt concedes, as *property.* Salt's view misconceives the nature of the change that has taken place in Western moral thought. What has happened over the last century and a half in the West is not that animals have been given, by law and public opinion, more power, more freedom, or anything else which might be accounted as a right. We are still perfectly free to kill them, if it suits us to do so. Rather, men have lost rights; they no longer have the same power over animals, that can no longer treat them as they choose. This is characteristic of a moral change; it follows from the fact that, in Hart's words, "moral rules impose obligations and withdraw certain areas of conduct from the free option of the individual to do as he likes."[35] But that men have lost rights over them does nothing to convert animals into bearers of rights, any more than we give rights to a river by withdrawing somebody's right to pollute it.*

[34] First published in London in 1892. The revised edition (1922) attempts to reply to Ritchie's criticisms—referred to below—but not, in my judgment, successfully.

[35] H. L. A. Hare, *The Concept of Law* (Oxford, 1961), p. 7.

* In his *A System of Ethics,* Leonard Nelson argues that to establish that we have duties to animals, it is only necessary to establish—what is, he says, obviously true—that they have *interests,* which he takes immediately to entail that they have rights. It is not, however, clear to me in what sense animals have interests. If all that is meant is that unless certain things are done for them they will die, that they have *needs,* this is also true of plants. The crucial difference between plants and animals is that animals are sentient, that they suffer if those needs are not satisfied. And to justify the view that we ought not to treat them in certain ways nothing more is needed. Having interests does not entail having rights, unless "interests" is interpreted in a sense in which animals do *not* have interests—as a person may, for example, have an interest in an estate.

Disputing Salt's conclusions, D. G. Ritchie has argued, in my view correctly, that animals cannot have rights since they "are not members of human
society." [36] We sometimes now meet with the suggestion, however, that animals
do in fact form, with men, a single community, and so can properly be said
to have rights. Indeed, Aldo Leopold has gone further than this: "When we
see land as a community to which we belong," he writes, 'we may begin to
use it with love and respect." [37] (As a final absurdity, it is worth noting,
Thomas Taylor's *Vindication of the Rights of Brutes* had looked forward to
a time when "even the most contemptible clod of earth" would be thought
of as having rights. He was better as a prophet than as an ironist.) Ecologically,
no doubt, men form a community with plants, animals, soil, in the sense that
a particular life-cycle will involve all four of them. But if it is essential to a
community that the members of it have common interests and recognise
mutual obligations then men, plants, animals and soil do *not* form a community. Bacteria and men do not recognize mutual obligations nor do they
have common interests. In the only sense in which belonging to a community
generates ethical obligation, they do not belong to the same community. To
suggest, then, as Fraser Darling does, that animals, plants, landscapes have
a "right to exist," is to create confusion. The idea of "rights" is simply not
applicable to what is nonhuman.†

We have already suggested, however, that the condemnation of cruelty to
animals does not depend on the presumption that men and animals—let
alone men, animals, plants, soil—form a single moral community. It has
been a movement of sensibility, a movement based on the growing recognition
that not only a positive delight in suffering—so much moralists have always
admitted—but even callousness, an insensibility to suffering, is a moral defect
in a human being. It is one thing to say that it is wrong to treat animals
cruelly, quite another to say that animals have rights.

The principle that we ought not unnecessarily to cause animals to suffer
does not carry us far, no doubt, as part of a case for preservation. It does

---

[36] D. G. Ritchie, *Natural Rights* (London, 1894), p. 107.
[37] Foreword to *Sand County Almanac,* p. xviii.
† This is one of the many points at which I am troubled by the apparent dogmatism of my
observations. There are some contexts in which the concept of rights is straightforward, as when
someone says of a professor that he has a right to take a sabbatical and means no more than
that he has a contract which lays this down. In other contexts it is relatively straightforward
as in such remarks as: "Schoolteachers have a right to take a sabbatical" when this means that
schoolteachers *ought* to have the right which a professor *actually* has, a judgment which might
be supported by arguing that a schoolteacher has the same need as a professor for long periods
during which he can think, read, travel, gain fresh intellectual contacts. But in other cases, as
when someone says that "every man has the right to live," it becomes very difficult to know
what he is claiming unless something like this: it is morally wrong for one man to take away
the life or the livelihood of another. And that last utterance, or so I have suggested, is not in
fact equivalent to "every man has a right to live." The supposition that "it is morally wrong to
treat *x* in the manner *y*" entails "*x* has a right not to be treated in the manner *y*" initiates the
sort of confusion which culminates in utterances like "insects have a right to live." That is what
I have substantially argued. But I am only too conscious of the fact that many would wish to
challenge my assumption that the proper starting point for a theory of rights is the use of the
word in legal contexts.

not permit of extension, although Montaigne tried so to extend it, to animals, plants, soils, which either do not suffer or do not suffer in ways which impress themselves on the consciousness of human beings. Nor does it exclude, oddly enough, the *killing* of animals. Indeed, in many ways its position in our moral code is somewhat paradoxical.[38] Its importance for us, however, is that, first, it represents a case in which Western men have come to believe that their dealings with nature can properly be subjected to moral approval or condemnation; secondly, that it is a change which grew out of certain "seeds" in Western thought—in particular, the humanitarian "seed." The question now is whether we can construct a case for preservation by finding other such "seeds," without having to fall back on such certainly non-Western principles as that "nature is sacred."

There is, it might be said, such a "seed" in the Old Testament. In Genesis (7:15) Jahweh is represented as telling Noah to take with him into the Ark "two and two of all flesh, wherein is the breath of life"—not only the "clean," it will be observed, but even the "unclean." And this shows God's concern, so it has been argued, for the preservation of animal species.* What potency has this seed? Certainly its prevalence explains why scientists were for so long reluctant to believe that fossils could be relics of species and varieties now extinct. The world, so it was thought, had been created as a perfect and complete system—a great chain of being—in which everything had a place. The destruction of a species would be the disruption of a system. The botanist John Ray, writing at the beginning of the eighteenth century, points out that if the fossil evidence were taken at its face value, "it would follow that many species of shell-fish are lost out of the world." But this, he says, "philosophers hitherto have been unwilling to admit, esteeming the destruction of any one species as dismembering of the Universe, and rendering it imperfect; whereas they think the Divine Providence is especially concerned to secure and preserve the works of the creation"—a doctrine lent support, he says, by the fact that Providence "was so careful to lodge all land-animals in the ark at the time of the general deluge."[39] (As late as 1836, in Büchner's *Woyzeck,* the travelling artisan announces his intention of making "a hole in nature" by destroying all fleas.)

One is sometimes reminded of this "great chain of being" by the "ecological niches" now such favourites with preservationists. The traditional doctrine no doubt reflected in part, as well as metaphysico-theological prepossessions,

---

[38] Compare Roslind Godlovitch; "Animals and Morals," *Philosophy,* 46: 175 (January 1971), pp. 23–33, revised in S. and R. Godlovitch and John Harris (eds.), *Animals, Men and Morals* (London, 1971). But Godlovitch is mainly concerned with the much stronger principle that we ought to *prevent* animal suffering.

* Aquinas specifically argues that in the case of every species except man God cares nothing for the benefit of the individual but does watch over the species as a whole. So, without any disrespect to God's intention, man can do as he will with individual animals and plants—they form no part of God's concern. God will ensure that man's treatment of individuals does not destroy the species as a whole. See Aquinas, *Summa Contra Gentiles,* chs. CXII–III.

[39] John Ray, *Three Physico-Theological Discourses* (London, 1703). Quoted from the third edition (1713), p. 149, in A. O. Lovejoy, *The Great Chain of Being* (Harvard, 1948), pp. 243, 365.

a recognition of the interdependence of species, crudely expressed in Swift's familiar lines:

> So, naturalists observe, a flea
> Hath smaller fleas that on him prey;
> And these have smaller fleas to bite 'em
> And so proceed *ad infinitum*.

Everything—plants as well as animals—lives in a particular kind of region, a region which contains both its prey and its predators, opportunities and limitations. To destroy a predator is to increase the opportunities for other predators, or to make less confined the numbers of its prey. It leaves open, that is, an "ecological niche."

It is no longer possible to suppose, however, that "Nature" or "Providence" so arranges matters that a region will never be transformed, except as a result of human interference, in such a way as to reduce the opportunities of a species to a point at which it will disappear. In the present mood of disillusionment with humanity, man the hunter, rather than the ice ages, is now often blamed for the extinction of the large species which once roamed the earth.[40] Perhaps some, at least, of these allegations will in fact turn out to be correct. Certainly, too, over the last few centuries, human beings have managed to destroy species at an unprecedented rate and are continuing to do so. The fact still remains that gradual or catastrophic changes in the biosphere of completely nonhuman origin have produced, and may well in the future produce, destruction as notable as, if less rapid than, any men can bring about. Man is not the only agency which destroys species. There is no ground for asserting that "Providence" or "Nature" always ensures the preservation of species—even if this were a satisfactory route to the conclusion that men ought to follow its example.

In search of a more viable "seed," one might turn to Aquinas' principle of diversity. "Although an angel, considered absolutely," writes Aquinas, "is better than a stone, nevertheless two natures are better than one only; and therefore a Universe containing angels and other things is better than one containing angels only."[41] If this be so, then to destroy a species is always to diminish the value of the Universe by reducing the number of natures it contains. But this is a very hard doctrine to sustain. It means that even if I could wipe out mosquitoes merely by raising my right hand, and even if by so acting I ran no ecological risks, I should be wrong to do so, merely because I should be decreasing the number of species in the Universe. Is it so obvious that a Universe consisting of human beings and a cobra is better than a Universe consisting of men alone? Should St. Patrick be condemned if, indeed,

---

[40] See especially P. S. Martin and H. E. Wright (eds.), *Pleistocene Extinctions: The Search for a Cause,* Proceedings of the 7th Congress of the International Association for Quaternary Research (New Haven, 1967), vol. 6; in *Nature* (1967), 215: 5097, pp. 212–13, and in *Natural History* (January 1968), pp. 73–5 the controversy is continued by L. S. B. Leakey and P. S. Martin.

[41] Quoted in A. O. Lovejoy, *The Great Chain of Being,* p. 77.

he drove the snakes out of Ireland? And if to drive them out of Ireland is worthy of praise, should it not be equally praiseworthy to drive them out of the world? (Leaving aside, as I am doing for the sake of argument, any possible ecological side effects.)

Yet there is something to be said for Aquinas' praise of diversity, and so far a case for preservation. We are faced at this point, no doubt, with a fundamental conflict of attitudes. There are those, like Thomas Burnet, for whom every sort of diversity is intolerable, for whom the earth as a uniform sphere would be an infinitely more desirable place than our own dear warty world, a monoculture is more attractive than a diversified landscape, a grid-iron city of glass cubes more "perfect" than one which exhibits a diversity of styles and shapes. Metaphysicians—Fichte and Teilhard de Chardin will serve as examples—have not uncommonly sung the praises of uniformity. "The multitude of beings," Teilhard once wrote, "is a terrible affliction." He was confident that the world could not remain for ever "a huge and disparate thing, just about as coherent . . . as the surface of a rough sea." [42] There are others for whom diversity is everything, and any kind of uniformity demonstrates a failure of imagination, the deadening of creativity. Yet, metaphysical enthusiasts like Teilhard de Chardin apart, few, I think, would wish to argue that it is always better either to reduce, or to increase, diversity. For the reduction of diversity finally issues in a pure Being which is indistinguishable from nothingness, the multiplication of diversity in a world so diversified as to be wholly unmanageable.

The acclimatisation societies which flourished in the nineteenth century were enthusiasts for diversity. They sought, in every country in which they operated, to acclimatise as wide a variety as possible of exotic animals and plants. To introduce a new species was, in their eyes, a major triumph. It would now generally be agreed that this policy was a mistaken and to some degree a disastrous one; acclimatised plants and animals have provoked many an ecological calamity, as the landscape both of Australia and of New Zealand still bears witness. It is not a good thing to attempt to introduce the maximum diversity into every individual ecological system: to do so may seriously diminish the prosperity of other members of the system. Man is himself perhaps the most striking example of an acclimatised invader, and an established ecosystem can be greatly weakened by his presence. But goats or rabbits or deer or prickly pear can be scarcely less destructive. For all their intrinsic attractiveness, they can impoverish, aesthetically as well as economically, the system into which they are introduced. A countryside is not necessarily improved in appearance by the introduction of exotic trees. Wordsworth long ago condemned the introduction of the larch into the English Lake district, for all that it adds so much to the beauty of the Dolomites, and the exotic pine forests add a drab note to the Australian landscape.

[42] *Le Milieu Mystique* (1917) quoted in Henri de Lubac, *The Religion of Teilhard de Chardin*, trans. R. Hague (London, 1967), p. 13. Compare John Passmore, *The Perfectibility of Man*, pp. 23 ff.

This kind of diversity, then, the preservationist is almost certain to oppose. Indeed, he is likely to be if anything too rigorously puritanical in his attitude— for there can be no real doubt that, for example, such introduced trees as the elm and oak have worked wonders for the landscape of Great Britain, as has the eucalypt in California or the casuarina in Egypt. If preservation is taken to imply that no landscape should ever be modified from its original form by the introduction of exotic plants and animals then it has not, in my judgment, a leg to stand on. The introduction of such species, indeed, may be the only thing that can save a countryside from destruction or restore its fertility.

There are, then, two principles which seem to be untenable: the first, that it is always better to increase the diversity of an ecosystem; the second, that it is never better to do so. All that can be properly said is that in modifying the degree of diversity there are always inherent dangers, biological dangers, and there is also the real risk of destroying the "character" of a landscape, the complex set of relationships which constitute its attractiveness.

This is certainly so when diversity is reduced by the destruction of species, the rooting out of hedgerows, the bulldozing of bushland, for the sake of monoculture, whether of barley or of pine. No doubt, as we have suggested, there are those to whom the tidy rows of pine are, economics apart, infinitely superior to the untidiness of a snow-gum forest, an unbroken expanse of uniform crops to the uneven irregularities characteristic of mixed farming. But Mill, scarcely an opponent of economic development, wrote with distaste of such a monocultured world, and many of us would share his feelings. "Nor is there much satisfaction in contemplating the world with nothing left to the spontaneous activity of nature; with every rood of land brought into cultivation which is capable of producing food for human beings; every flowery waste or natural pasture ploughed up, all quadrupeds or birds which are not domesticated for man's use exterminated as his rivals for food, every hedgerow or superfluous tree rooted out, and scarcely a place left where a wild shrub or flower could grow without being eradicated in the name of improved agriculture."[43] There are now good biological arguments, too, against extensive monocultures, arguments which draw attention to their vulnerability to disease and climatic calamity,[44] to their long-run effects on the soil, to the degree to which they have to be constantly maintained by infusions of insecticides and fertilisers which at once increase their cost and represent a danger to the wider region in which they are established, as the insecticides and fertilisers drain into rivers and thence into lakes and sea.[*]

---

[43] J. S. Mill, *Principles of Political Economy,* bk. 4, ch. 6, par. 2.

[44] Compare C. S. Elton, *The Ecology of Invasions* (London, 1958), pp. 145–53.

[*] It is customary to rebuke the European farmer for inefficiency, on the ground that his crop each year is relatively light in proportion to the size of his farm, or that it demands a heavy expenditure of labour. But in many cases a farmer of this sort has been farming the same ground for some hundreds of years. His "inefficiency" appears in a different light if we think of the production of his land over the centuries. Annual production is not the best test of efficiency—whether what is in question is a farm or a professor.

What we can properly conclude, I think, is that the onus is on anyone who seeks to modify an ecosystem's degree of diversity and that he has to produce a far more elaborate and complex argument than has ordinarily been supposed. This principle does not apply only to biological systems, but also, for example, to social and political "anomalies." The maxim that "the more uniform, the better" is usually defended by very short-sighted arguments. But this is not to say that it is always wrong to reduce, or always right to increase, the diversity of social institutions or biological systems. So there is no general argument from a principle of diversity to preservationist conclusions.

There is one other very broad principle which, were it acceptable, would certainly permit the conclusion that a species ought never to be destroyed. For it asserts that men ought, in general, to "reverence life." And this principle may be interpreted as forbidding the destruction not only of species but of any individual animal. (Indeed, in Theravada Buddhism the monk, and even the layman so far as he is able, "does no harm to seeds or plants.")[45] In its extremer forms, this principle has never been firmly established in the West. The poet Cowper, no doubt, would not include amongst his friends "the man who needlessly sets foot upon a worm."[46] Yet even Cowper was no vegetarian: and he would not condemn a man for setting foot on a worm were the worm destructive. This, in general, is as far as the West has been prepared to go. It is to the East, and in particular to the Jains, that we should have to turn for more far-reaching moral precepts. "Tolerate living beings, do not kill them, though they eat your flesh and blood." The Jains, indeed, took as their ideal a man who would direct his life by the objective of never killing any living thing, even by accident. "This is the quintessence of wisdom: not to kill anything."[47]

Nowhere in the traditional religions of the West is the killing of living things made so central a point. But in our own century the ideal of "reverence for life" has been emphasised by Albert Schweitzer to a degree previously unprecedented; he makes it central to his ethics. Like the Jains, too, he refuses to draw the characteristic Western distinction between "higher" (valuable) and "lower" (valueless) forms of life. "Who among us knows," he asks, "what significance any other kind of life has in itself, and as a part of the Universe?" There is no "category of worthless life"—life which human beings are free to destroy. To a man who is truly ethical, on Schweitzer's view, every life is sacred. No doubt such a "truly ethical" man has sometimes to sacrifice one living being to save another—to kill germs, for example, in order to save a human life. "But all through this series of decisions," according to Schweitzer, "he is conscious of acting on subjective grounds and arbitrarily, and knows that he bears the responsibility for the life which is sacrificed."[48] He will not,

---

[45] From *Dīgha Nikāya,* 1.4 ff., in W. T. de Bary (ed.), *The Buddhist Tradition* (New York, 1969), p. 34.

[46] Cowper, *The Task* (1785), bk. 6, 11. 562–3.

[47] The quotations are from the basic texts of the Jain scriptures in William Gerber, *The Mind of India* (New York, 1967), pp. 73, 80.

[48] Albert Schweitzer, *My Life and Thought,* trans. C. T. Campion (London, 1933), p. 271.

without a sense of guilt, pluck a leaf from a tree or pull a flower or trample on an insect: he will think of himself as having a "responsibility without limit towards all that lives."[49]

It is illuminating to observe Karl Barth's reaction to Schweitzer. Writing in the Calvinist tradition, Barth firmly asserts that ethical behaviour has to be defined through man's relationship to God, not through his relationship to living things. Each man, Barth tells us, is addressed by God as a member of a fellowship of men and through a particular book, God's word, the Bible. We can speculate, he allows, about the possibility that there are divine commands which apply to living beings in general, and not only to man. But we do not know of any such command, nor is it deducible from what we do know about animal and vegetable life. In the typical Christian manner, Barth insists, then, on the uniqueness of man, as the only living being to whom it is known that God addressed himself. To that extent his critique of Schweitzer would reinforce the opinion of those who see in the Christian tradition a principal obstacle to the emergence in the West of a less destructive attitude to nature.

Yet Barth is not wholly unsympathetic to Schweitzer's practical conclusions. Christianity, he admits, has failed to ask itself "how are we to treat the strange life of beasts and plants which is all around us." Schweitzer, as Barth reads him, is protesting against our "astonishing indifference and thoughtlessness in this matter."[50] He agrees with Schweitzer thus far: man has a secondary, although not a primary, responsibility to animal and vegetative life. Like the Jews, Barth insists that animals and plants do not belong to man but to God. At the same time, man, for Barth, takes precedence over them and is entitled to make use of them, by divine decree. When he harvests, he does not destroy but makes sensible use of superfluity. He is entitled to domesticate animals, but he ought to treat them in a considerate, friendly way.

But what about the *killing* of animals? Here Barth is less traditional; man must not kill, he argues, without divine authorisation. "He is already on his way to homicide if he sins in the killing of animals, if he murders an animal." Notice that Barth does not hesitate to speak of "murder" in connection with man's dealings with animals. Man "murders" when he kills except, as God has permitted him to do, in order to live. But vegetarianism Barth nevertheless condemns as "wanton anticipation of . . . existence in the new aeon for which we hope"; inevitably, he says, it is plagued by inconsistencies, sentimentality, fanaticism.[51] To kill for food is proper, in this interim life in which men now live.

What conclusions are we to draw from this controversy? It is in the first place evident, I should say, that the Jainist principle never to act in a way

---

[49] Albert Schweitzer, *Civilisation and Ethics* (1923), trans. C. T. Campion, 3rd ed. (London, 1946), p. 244.

[50] Karl Barth, *Church Dogmatics,* vol. 3; *The Doctrine of Creation,* ed. G. W. Bromiley and T. F. Torrance (Edinburgh, 1961), pt. 4, p. 350.

[51] Ibid., p. 355.

which could possibly result in the death of a living thing—so that the Jain priest walks on a path only at a time when the risk is minimal that he will inadvertently kill small insects—is far too strong. This is the more obvious now that we are aware of the minute living organisms which everywhere surround us. In breathing, in drinking, in eating, in excreting, we kill. We kill by remaining alive.

Nor should we hesitate about giving precedence to human beings. Schweitzer did so in fact, as Barth pointed out, when he became a doctor. Such precedence does not depend on peculiarly Christian teachings about divine revelation or a sacrificial God. If we prefer to save the life of a fellow-man rather than of the organism responsible for yellow-fever—an organism, no doubt, of considerable interest and beauty—it is because he has potentialities the yellow-fever organism lacks, potentialities for evil, admittedly, but also for good. That is why we may well be hesitant about preserving the life of those who lack such potentialities—although we may also be hesitant about allocating to any particular person the decision whether they have, or lack, them. The yellow-fever organism cannot love, or exhibit courage, or create ideas or works of art. It does not suffer as human beings suffer, or live in fear of death. Humanistic and compassionate considerations lead us to the same conclusion.

Yet, like the principle of diversity, the idea of "reverence for life" can serve perhaps as a guiding principle, with "seeds" in the reverence for *human* life characteristic of the Western tradition—in its theory, if by no means always in its practice. And, if I read the signs aright, a shift in sensibility is taking place at this point not unlike the shift in sensibility which has already taken place in relation to cruelty to animals. It does not imply that the living thing has to be treated as "sacred," as an object of worship or a source of occult powers. The new "reverence" for life is rather the sort of reverence one feels for a great building, a great work of art.

So far we can link it with another, more explicitly Western, tradition that it is wrong unnecessarily to destroy—a principle embodied in the concept of "vandalism." Admittedly, the principle that it is wrong unnecessarily to destroy has not been, to my knowledge, much emphasised by Western moralists. But one certainly finds it in the Jewish tradition, which bases itself on a passage in Deuteronomy (XX: 19–20) forbidding, even in time of war, the destruction of trees which might bear fruit, but interprets it widely. "Thou shalt not destroy" was indeed converted by Rabbinical commentators into a general moral principle.[52] The eighteenth-century philosopher, Baumgarten, writing in that same tradition, condemns in a forthright manner what he calls "the spirit of destruction" or "the habitual delight in the death of things" and urges that a man possessed by it be shunned.[53] One could at least go this far: the moral onus is on anyone who destroys. This is particularly so when, as in the case of species, the destruction is irreversible. We commonly speak,

[52] See the *Babylonian Talmud*, vol. 1, Shabbath 129*a*, ch. xviii, p. 644.
[53] A. G. Baumgarten, *Ethica Philosophica* (Halle, 1763), §398.

indeed, of "wanton" destruction where no defence of the destruction can be offered.

How far have we got, then, in our defence of preservationism on moral grounds? We looked first of all at those defences of preservationism which are primarily conservationist in spirit—which emphasise the usefulness of wildernesses and species as sources of genetic diversity, of scientific understanding, of moral renewal, of recreational enjoyment, of aesthetic pleasure. The first of these arguments, we suggested, is a strong one; the others, like so many conservationist arguments, depend on the presumption that our successors will continue to delight in certain rather special forms of activity which have been by no means universally characteristic of human society.

But they are none of them "knock-down" arguments; they all allow that economic considerations, in a broad sense of that phrase, might under certain circumstances outweigh the case for preservation. Scientific discoveries—for example, a method of constructing "seed-banks" so that species could always be reconstituted—or changes in tastes, could wholly undermine them. So we looked for ways of arguing that the destruction of species and wildernesses was *intrinsically* wrong. We saw that in at least one case Western men have generally come to accept a limitation on their dealings with nature; they now commonly disapprove of those ways of treating animals which involve the inflicting on them of "unnecessary" pain. And this is because, I suggested, they have come to feel that in this case men and animals—or certain animals—so resemble one another that it is inconsistent to condemn the infliction of unnecessary pain on human beings but not to condemn its infliction on animals.

With this case in mind, we then looked for possible sources, in the Western tradition, of a more general change in moral attitudes in a preservationist direction. It would not do, we said, to argue that "God" or "Nature" obviously wishes to preserve species or wildernesses; many species have been destroyed, many wildernesses transformed by nonhuman processes. As for the view that we ought always to preserve the maximum diversity, we suggested that Western society has been divided on this point, but that we can perhaps go this far: the existing degree of diversity in an ecosystem ought not to be modified without careful consideration. The ideal of reverence for life we accepted in so far as there is a tradition in the West of hostility to vandalism, and it is very natural to extend it to the destruction of nature as well as to works of art or forms of property. The man who cuts his name on a redwood is being a vandal, just as much as the man who scratches his initials on the portico of Wells Cathedral.

If we now ask about the political feasibility of action to preserve wildernesses and species we are asking about the strength of the arguments and the feelings I have been describing, in conflict with political pressures from a multitude of interests—miners, land developers, the tourist trade—to transform wildernesses in a way that is destructive of species or to wipe them out more directly as an obstacle to development. In conflict, too, with the pressure exerted by those other Western traditions that it is man's task either to conquer nature, or to transform it—to turn the world into the sort of garden in which there are no thorns, no thistles, no destructive insects or animals. Nobody needs to be told that the outcome of any such conflict is uncertain.[54] No doubt, if nature were conceived of as sacred and any modification of it as sacrilegious, the outcome would be less uncertain (unless, in the manner I shall later describe, the mystical attitude to nature found expression as the belief that nature can and will repair itself). If, to carry the same point further, it came to be regarded as morally wicked ever, under any circumstances, to destroy so much as an individual animal or plant, let alone a species, then the preservationist could certainly feel more confident of victory.

But this would be at a very great cost to civilisation. For my part, I agree, in the long run, with the Stoics: if men were ever to decide that they ought to treat plants, animals, landscapes precisely as if they were *persons,* if they were to think of them as forming with man a moral community in a strict sense, that would make it impossible to civilise the world—or, one might add, to act at all or even to continue living.[55] The Jain priest can walk abroad only because there are other, less spiritual, men to work in the fields by day and sweep the paths for him by night. I simply do not believe that in every dispute between preservationist and miner, the preservationist ought always to win—however much one may dislike the havoc miners have created on the landscape. Of course, as in the case of pollution, one again has to admit that miners and commercial interests are often in a position to exercise a degree of influence, whether over politicians or over media, with which the preservationist cannot compete, that preservationists will lose battles they ought to win, which they would win were the issues fairly represented and fairly fought out. But in this case, too, it would be quite wrong to conclude that the preservationist will never be successful, at least in countries affluent enough to forego immediate material gains in the interest of amenity.

I have tried to show that the preservationist can appeal not only to practical consequences but to established moral principles and to changing sensibilities, which he can hope to modify in a preservationist direction. This appeal will often be, has often been, successful. The scientist and the technologist can help, not only by drawing attention to the unintended consequences of destruction, but also by finding new means of mining, new means of restoring land, new methods of coping with those predators which are particularly damaging to human interests. A wider change in attitudes can help, too— less emphasis on consumer goods, a greater appreciation of the value of contemplation, of quiet enjoyment, of simply *looking* at the world around us, as itself an object of absorbing interest, not as an instrument or a resource. The Romantic Rebels of the sixties insisted on this point. Whether what was

[54] For a case-study description of five such conflicts see Roy Gregory, *The Price of Amenity* (London, 1971).

[55] See also on this theme R. D. Guthrie, "Ethics and Non-Human Organisms", *Perspectives in Biology and Medicine* (Autumn, 1967), pp. 52–62.

valuable in their rebellion can be absorbed into our society, without their drug-mysticism, without their violence, without their rejection of the responsibilities inherent in love, remains to be seen.

THE LIBERATION OF NATURE?*

JOHN RODMAN

Domestic races of animals and cultivated races of plants often exhibit an abnormal character as compared with natural species; for they have been modified not for their own benefit, but for that of man.[1]

DARWIN

1. ACTS AND EXPLANATIONS

Every reviewer brings to a book some personal solicitude, and I shall make mine explicit at the outset. I have wondered what it meant (as if it were possibly some symbolic turning point in history) when John Lilly opened the tank and freed the dolphins to return to the sea. And I have sometimes wondered why I spent a year out of my life struggling to save a 100-acre stretch of rather unremarkable southern California coastal sage and chaparral from being turned into a golf course. It is not the particular idiosyncratic motivations that interest me, but the principles implicit in the actions and what their implications are.

Christopher Stone has shrewdly remarked that people who justify their efforts to save wilderness or protect endangered species in the homocentric language of Resource Conservation or Survival Ecology often sound as if they are rationalizing, as if they "want to say something less egoistic and

Reprinted from *Inquiry,* Vol. 20, No. 1 (1977) 83–118, with permission of the author and the publisher, Universitetsforlaget, Oslo, Norway. (Only Parts 1–7 and the concluding section, Part 11, are reprinted here. A number of footnotes have been omitted and some have been renumbered.)

* [A review article of] Christopher Stone, *Should Trees Have Standing?: Toward Legal Rights for Natural Objects,* spec. rev. ed. (New York: Avon Books, 1975), $1.50 (paper). Peter Singer, *Animal Liberation: A New Ethics for Our Treatment of Animals* (New York: New York Review and Random House, 1975), $10.00 (hardcover).

I am grateful for criticisms and suggestions made by James Bogen, John Cobb, Philippe Cohen, Robert Epstein, Joan Hartmann, William Leiss, Lindsay Moore, Paul Shepard, and Sharon Snowiss, as well as by the authors under review, who were kind enough to comment on an earlier version of this paper. I should also like to express my appreciation to the National Audubon Society for funding the Conference on the Rights of Nonhuman Nature held at Pitzer College, Claremont, California, 18–20 April 1974, out of which parts of this paper have belatedly grown.

[1] *The Variation of Plants and Animals under Domestication* (1868) 2nd ed. (New York: Appleton, 1897), Vol. 1, p. 4.

more emphatic but the prevailing and sanctioned modes of explanation in our society—our rhetorics of motive—are not quite ready for it."[2] I confess that I sometimes have a similar impression of the logical gymnastics of moral and legal philosophers, who sound as if they want to say something less moralistic, less reasonable, more expressive of their total sensibility, but are afraid of seeming subjective, sentimental, or something that's somehow not quite respectable.

Peter Singer, for example, is a moral philosopher who hopes to lead us, not by "sentimental appeals for sympathy" but by vigorous moral reasoning, to make "a mental switch" in our "attitudes and practices towards a very large group of beings: members of species other than our own."[3] Those species are other sentient animals, whose suffering Singer believes we have an obligation to diminish. This could be relevant to Lilly's case, since the dolphins had begun to signify their unhappiness with the boredom of captivity by swimming at full speed head-on into the side of the tank so as to kill themselves.[4] But Singer's approach is not very germane to my case, since I perceived "my" area in terms of sage, scrub oak, and cactus, only later becoming aware of the plight of the dusky-footed woodrats.

On reflection, I find it as odd to think that the plants have value only for the happiness of the dusky-footed woodrats as to think that the dusky-footed woodrats have value only for the happiness of humans. As for the human pleasures and pains at stake, I suppose I could offset the joys of golfers and the financial benefit to the educational institution owning the land by invoking the intense, enduring, sophisticated, and life-enhancing pleasure that future generations of jaded urbanites and suburbanites might experience in contemplating the subtle and intricate beauty of somewhat messed-up arid ecosystems. But that wouldn't be honest (even if it were a true picture): not only would I be loading the equation with my notion of what people *really* need, but I'm too skeptical to be moved to action on the basis of so improbable a fantasy, especially when I'm not even sure of its relevance. Sorry, ladies and gentlemen: no sublime vistas from mountain peak or valley floor, no majestic redwoods connecting earth with sky, no voice of God (or even of John Muir) murmuring through a waterfall, no endangered species (yet), no ecological uniqueness here (except in the sense that every place is unique), not even a landscape still in virgin condition. What's in it for us anyhow?

---

[2] Stone, op. cit., p. 93. For a recent example, see Paul Watson's account of direct actions taken by members of the Greenpeace Foundation to obstruct the annual Newfoundland seal hunt. We are asked to believe that someone who risks physical injury and public ridicule in order to protect baby seals with his body—and who can write that "Baby seals are all around us, beautiful beyond expectation, each a personification of new born perfection. Chubby little bundles of soft white fur, large tear-filled ebony eyes and a cry practically indistinguishable from its human counter-part"—is acting from a sense of responsibility not to bequeath an unbalanced ecosystem to human posterity (*Greenpeace Chronicles,* Vol. 2, No. 2 [Spring/Summer 1976], 6–7; a slightly different version appeared in *Defenders* [June 1976], 140–5).

[3] Singer, op. cit., p. xi.

[4] See Sam Keen, "A Conversation with John Lilly," *Psychology Today* (December 1971), p. 77. For background see John C. Lilly, M.D., *Lilly on Dolphins* New York: Doubleday, 1975), which incorporates *Man and Dolphin, The Mind of the Dolphin,* and several papers.

Christopher Stone, a law professor sensitive to the gropings of contemporary consciousness towards something more than the workaday platitudes of common sense, aims to help us crystallize a "radical new conception of man's relationship to the rest of nature." More specifically, he argues that it is "not unthinkable" for us to regard "natural objects" such as trees, streams, wilderness areas, and even "the natural environment as a whole" as having "rights," and for groups of humans to assume the role of "guardians" or "trustees" to act in defense of those rights.[5] That comes closer to home, for some notion of "right" is certainly involved. Yet it was more that Lilly had reached the point of feeling that he "had *no right*" to keep wild, sentient, and highly-intelligent beings "in a concentration camp" even for the most high minded scientific purposes.[6] And I felt that a group of academic administrators and "trustees" [*sic!*] had *no right* simply to exterminate the native flora and fauna as if they didn't exist or didn't count (the Environmental Impact Report didn't even mention them), especially in order to replace them with something frivolous and ecologically inappropriate.

But what does having "no right" to do something mean in a case where the absence of a right to do it makes doing it wrong? What is violated? Must we suppose some human obligation of a "trusteeship" sort that is owed to God not to exploit His Creation, or that is owed to Our Own Posterity not to spoil their "environment"? Or must we suppose that at least some nonhuman beings have rights that we are obligated to respect and perhaps even to protect? Arguments can be advanced for all three positions, and the positions are not mutually exclusive; but it is partly dissatisfaction with the first two—a dissatisfaction grounded in an awareness of questions too often begged (the existence of God, the interpretation of "dominion," the ground of our duties to Posterity, the inadequacy of species self-interest to account for our sense of the wrongness of certain acts against nonhuman nature) and in the uneasy suspicion that we are rationalizing—that has brought so many people to the third position. Yet if the argument that certain kinds of nonhuman beings have rights has the advantage of being direct, it also presents us with its own cluster of difficult questions. What sorts of moral and/or legal rights do dolphins have (or ought dolphins to be "given")? As individuals or as a species? And by virtue of what characteristics? If the case for dolphins' rights depends on the "special nature" of cetacea (large brain size, high level of intelligence, compassionate behavior, etc.) and/or upon their "intolerable

[5] Stone, op. cit., pp. 101, 25 ff., 41 ff. At this point I state Stone's thesis in a rather more general (less legalistic) form than Stone himself does. I shall turn to the more legalistic version below.

[6] Keen, op. cit., emphasis added. As late as 1974 Lilly was still unwilling to interpret his release of the dolphins in terms of respecting the rights of dolphins (remarks recorded at the Conference on the Rights of Nonhuman Nature, Claremont, California, 18–20 April 1974). But he has recently begun to argue (citing Stone) that cetacea in general should be "*given* individual rights under state/national/international human laws" (John C. Lilly, "The Rights of Whales", *Greenpeace Chronicles,* op. cit., pp. 1, 10, emphasis added).

Lilly has not, to my knowledge, retroactively interpreted his own action in terms of respecting some right that cetacea already had, however.

situation" (the threat of extinction),[7] then it will probably not extend to laboratory rats or to coastal sage. If, on the other hand, sage has a right to go on living in its natural habitat, what does not? Under what conditions could such a right be justifiably infringed, if any? (My God, should we give "America" back to the "Indians" . . . or the sumac?)

Did Lilly and/or I act out an obligation to respect or protect the rights of dolphins and of sage? The very question is phrased from inside the moral/legal paradigm of entities, rights, and obligations that Singer and Stone share. That paradigm leaves out, or relegates to obscurity, an important part of experience which I think we can bring into focus (but not fully articulate) by exploring the notion of "liberation." I shall move gradually into that exploration in the course of discharging my obligation to give Singer's and Stone's books their due.

2. CONVERGENCE: THEORY AND PRACTICE

Singer's *Animal Liberation* is the most comprehensive work yet to emerge from the contemporary renascence and radicalization of the humane movement.[8] Arguing from "basic moral principles that we all accept" (that pain

[7] Lilly, "The Rights of Whales," loc. cit.

[8] Singer's book is an expansion of his essay on "Animal Liberation" published as a review of Stanley and Roslind Godlovich and John Harris (eds.), *Animals, Men, and Morals: An Enquiry into the Maltreatment of Non-humans,* (New York: Taplinger, 1972; Grove, New York n. d.) in *The New York Review of Books,* 5 (April 1973), and reprinted in *The National Observer,* **28** (April 1973), as well as of his article, "All Animals Are Equal," *Philosophic Exchange,* Vol. 1, No. 5 (Summer 1974). Two sections of Singer's book are reprinted in Tom Regan and Peter Singer (eds.), *Animal Rights and Human Obligations* (Englewood Cliffs, N.J.: Prentice-Hall, 1976).

See note 16 below for a partial list of other "philosophers whose writings have injected a new vigor into the movement" (the phrase is from Nicholas Wade, "Animal Rights: NIH Cat Sex Study Brings Grief to New York Museum," *Science,* Vol. 194 [8 October 1976], p. 162). A satisfactory history of the humane movement remains to be written, but I hazard the generalization that the movement became respectable and relatively ineffectual during the twentieth century after securing some of its objectives (anti-cruelty laws, humane transportation and slaughter laws, etc.), making its compromise with Science on the "vivisection" issue, and settling down to policing the local leash laws and maintaining shelters for stray cats and dogs—only to have this *status quo* upset by the great upsurge of government-funded scientific research following World War II and the passage in some states of laws authorizing research institutions to requisition unclaimed pound animals for experimental purposes. At least in the United States, this Counterrevolution of Science broke the previously established truce and provoked a veritable Reformation of the humane movement—a splintering into many factions and a continual radicalization of some of the smaller groups.

On top of this, Ruth Harrison's well-publicized exposé of intensive factory farming methods (*Animal Machines* [London: Stuart, 1964], serialized in *The Observer*) prompted the British government to appoint a committee of inquiry (the Brambell Committee, which reported in December 1965). The contemporary renascence of vegetarianism seems to stem partly from disapproval of factory farming but probably more from the health food/nutrition movement. While one now encounters "ecological" arguments for vegetarianism (e. g., Singer, op. cit., pp. xiv, 178 ff., 246), this is normally an ancillary argument used by people who became vegetarians for health or humane reasons. Meanwhile, ethological studies and film documentaries on animals in the wild began to make zoos seem like prisons for producing unnatural behavior and brought into sharper focus the longstanding paradox that experimental scientists regard certain nonhuman

is evil and we all have an obligation to minimize it, and that all interests should be given "equal consideration"), Singer examines in detail two major contemporary institutions, factory farming and the use of nonhuman animals in laboratory experimentation, and concludes that the massive suffering inflicted upon nonhuman animals is both unnecessary and uncompensated by the relatively trivial benefits to humankind. He concludes that we ought to become vegetarians and ought to curtail drastically the amount of laboratory experimentation on animals. He is under no illusion that such basic changes can be accomplished by the usual political processes (whose results are typified by the U.S. Animal Welfare Act, which requires that lab animals be provided "humane" conditions of transportation, housing, food, handling, etc., but leaves them totally unprotected "during actual research or experimentation by a research facility as determined by such research facility"); and he accepts that humans working for "animal liberation" will have to use boycotts (vegetarianism is depicted primarily as a type of "economic boycott") and selective civil disobedience. The strength of Singer's book lies in its combination of logical argument, moral indignation, and empirical evidence; in the author's willingness to take a clear position and not only defend it but seek the reader's conversion and enlistment in a campaign to change society; and in his confrontation of the dilemmas involved in undertaking a basic change of lifestyle. After reading *Animal Liberation* a reader is apt to feel that the pertinent question is not "Should I become a vegetarian?", but "Do I have any good reason for not becoming a vegetarian?" The weakness of this "new testament of the animal rights movement"[9] lies in the limitation of its horizon to the late eighteenth and early nineteenth century Utilitarian humane movement, its failure to live up to its own noble declaration that "Philosophy ought to question the basic assumptions of the age," and its tendency to utilize the contemporary rhetoric of "liberation" without fully comprehending what liberation might involve.[10]

---

species as sufficiently like *Homo sapiens* to make experimentation on them seem worthwhile, yet sufficiently unlike *Homo sapiens* (in ways difficult to state within the framework of the scientific worldview) to make those experiments morally permissible. Finally, there is evidence of some "spillover" from the atmosphere of the Civil Rights movement to Women's Liberation and from there to the Animal Rights movement (see, e.g., Valida Davila, "Declaration of the Rights of Animals," *Everywoman,* Issue 31 [April 1972]). I shall discuss this last topic further in Sect. 8 (The Liberation Analogy).

[9] The phrase is from Nicholas Wade, p. 165. Wade's article provides an interesting preliminary case study in the relation of theory to practice. The "chief architect" of the recent demonstrations and publicity protesting animal experimentation carried on at the American Museum of Natural History is a high school teacher and journalist who attended a course given by Peter Singer at New York University in 1974.

[10] Singer, op. cit., p. 264 (cf. p. x); more generally, see Preface and Chs. 1 and 6. I should make it clear that I am not going to deal with Singer's book on the level of evaluating the accuracy of his accounts of factory farming (Ch. III) or laboratory research (Ch. II). I think Singer's book is generally accurate, cogent within its own framework, and persuasive in many of its contentions. This review discussion will focus on the underlying frame of reference and mode of argument.

Stone's *Should Trees Have Standing?* contains, if not the first, then at least the most sweeping statement that I have seen of the increasingly popular view that Nature (not just animals) has, or should be given, rights.[11] Stone's

[11] While the notion that "animals" had certain kinds of rights has been familiar since the late eighteenth century, the tacit restriction to "higher animals" made it a dramatic moment at Grand Canyon in 1896 when John Muir stopped Gifford Pinchot from killing a tarantula on the ground that "it had as much right there as we did" (Gifford Pinchot, *Breaking New Ground* [New York: Harcourt Brace] 1947, p. 103). And the tacit restriction of rights to domesticated animals was so deeply ingrained that Joan McIntyre, writing in 1970, assumed that people would find "outrageous" and even "incomprehensible" her contention that "wildlife has its own intrinsic right to be: to exist in the world, to pursue its own destiny and follow the path of its own evolution," and that legislation should aim at "achieving a Bill of Rights for all wild creatures, everywhere" (in Garrett DeBell [ed.], *The Voter's Guide to Environmental Politics* [New York: Friends of the Earth and Ballantine 1970], pp. 84, 76). It is apparent from the context of the essay that "wildlife" meant wild *animals* for Ms. McIntyre, though it is not clear why.

The claim that nonanimal entities such as trees, stones, streams, landscapes, and ecosystems should be regarded as having rights is quite recent. The very assumption that rights are something that human beings have and can "extend" or "give" to nonhumans separates the contemporary notion of nonhuman rights from the ancient rites whereby humans gave the nonhuman realm its due, and from the Roman lawyers' conception of a Natural Right *(jus naturae)* shared at least in theory by "all animals."

In reviewing recent discussions of the human/nature relationship in terms of "rights," it is useful to distinguish four positions.

(1) There is the thesis that "all men" or the citizens of some nation-state have a moral right, and ought to have a legal right, to "wilderness," "an environment free of pollution and contamination" or "an environment capable of sustaining life and promoting happiness." In this version, it is still humans that have rights; the scope of human rights is merely widened to incorporate unconventional referents. See, e. g., Robert Marshall, "The Wilderness as a Minority Right," *Service Bulletin,* U.S. Forest Service, Vol. 12, No. 35 (27 August 1928), pp. 5–6; William O. Douglas, *A Wilderness Bill of Rights,* (Boston: Little Brown, 1965); Paul Ehrlich, *The Population Bomb* (1968), (New York: Ballantine, 1971), p. 171; "Initiative Measure to Be Submitted Directly to the Electors... An Amendment to Article 1 of the Constitution of California, relating to pollution," 1969; House of Representatives Joint Resolution 54, introduced 3 January 1969; Senate Joint Resolution 169, introduced 19 January 1970; Roderick Nash, "The Santa Barbara Declaration of Environmental Rights," Santa Barbara, California, January 1970; etc.

(2) The intermediate position is that human beings have "no right" to do certain things to nonhumans: for example, "Man must realize... that he does not have the moral right to exterminate any animal or plant species" (Jean Dorst, *Before Nature Dies,* trans. by C. D. Sherman, [Boston: 1970] Houghton Mifflin, pp. 323–4). See also Aldo Leopold, *A Sand County Almanac* (1949) (New York: Ballantine, 1970), p. 247 and *passim;* John A. Livingston. *One Cosmic Instant,* (Boston: Houghton Mifflin, 1973), pp. 223 ff.

(3) The third position focuses on some general notion such as "the land ethic" (Leopold, loc. cit.) or ecological "democracy" (see Lynn White, "The Historical Roots of Our Ecologic Crisis," *Science,* Vol. 155, 10 [March 1967], also Gary Snyder's essays in *The Center Magazine* [August 1970], and *The New York Times,* 12 January 1972), which implies or mentions in passing the notion of nonhuman rights but does not explicate it or make it central. Thus one can find a passage in Leopold to the effect that a land ethic affirms of soils, waters, plants, and animals "their right to continued existence, and, at least in spots, their continued existence in a natural state" (p. 240); but Leopold's basic approach was so much in terms of "the integrity, stability, and beauty [as well as the "health"] of the biotic community" as a whole (p. 262) that he did not develop the theme of rights as such.

(4) The fourth position focuses on the notion of nonhuman rights as central and attempts to develop the implications of such a notion. To my knowledge, the pioneering essay was written by Clarence Morris, "The Rights and Duties of Beasts and Trees: A Law Teacher's Essay for Landscape Architects," *Journal of Legal Education,* Vol. 17 (1964–65). Morris argued for "affirmatively creating nature's legal rights" by way of conservation and protection laws that

brief for "extending legal rights to natural objects" proceeds by indirection, suggestion, and the double-negative technique, so as gradually to build up a presumption that it is "not unthinkable" that the doctrine of judicial standing could be broadened so as to allow the Sierra Club and similar organizations or environmentally concerned individuals to bring suit for injunctions and damages on behalf of the rights of "natural objects" themselves (rather than having to establish a presumption of injury to the interests of their human members). The charm of Stone's essay lies in its stimulating blend of an almost Humean skepticism about common-sense certitudes, a perceptive awareness of the extent to which legal systems already operate with metaphors and fictions, an audacious willingness to risk trying to influence a case under adjudication, and a venturesome interest in "trying to imagine what a future

---

would "confer primary legal rights on nature—rights that can be enforced in the courts by nature's next friends, that can be furthered in legislatures by nature's lobbyists, that can be advocated in forums of public opinion by nature's vicar." The upshot would be to put "a burden of proof on those who propose to disturb nature" (pp. 189–90).

During 1970 I discovered that John B. Cobb, Jr., and I were each developing the theme of nonhuman rights independently. See Cobb's paper, "The Population Explosion and the Rights of the Subhuman World" (presented April 1970; published in *IDOC International,* North American edition, New York, 12 September 1970), and his subsequent "Ecology, Ethics, and Theology" (in Herman Daly [ed.], *Toward a Steady-State Economy* [San Francisco: Freeman, 1973]). My own efforts from that period—"Liberalism and the Ecological Crisis" (a paper presented at the annual meeting of the Western Political Science Association, April 1970) and "Political Theory and the Ecological Crisis" (a paper presented at the annual meeting of the American Political Science Association, September 1970)—remained unpublished, mainly because of unresolved feelings of ambivalence which will become apparent (and, I trust, clarified) in the course of this review article.

After 1970 the idea of the rights of nature was articulated with increasing frequency and on quite varied levels of discourse. See, e.g., Earl Finbar Murphy's article, "Has Nature Any Right to Life?" (22 *Hastings Law Journal,* 467, 1971), and the unexpected paragraph in President Nixon's third annual environmental message to Congress (9 February 1972) attributing to "wild places and wild things" "a higher right to exist—not granted them by man and not his to take away." The immediate impact of Stone's "Should Trees Have Standing?" first published as an article in the Spring 1972 issue of the *Southern California Law Review,* and the popularization of its central thesis in Mr. Justice Douglas's much-quoted and often-reprinted dissent in the case of *Sierra Club* v. *Morton* (405 U.S. 727, 19 April 1972), suddenly brought to popular attention an idea that had been increasingly "in the air."

Stone's article was republished without change in book form (under the same title) by William Kaufmann, Los Altos, California 1974, together with a Preface by Garrett Hardin and the opinions of the Supreme Court in *Sierra Club* v. *Morton.* The Avon edition (same title) cited above is an inexpensive popular edition that retains Hardin's Preface unchanged, omits the opinions of the Court, and features a revised version of Stone's essay. The main changes in the essay are: the incorporation of a few footnotes into the text, the omission of most footnotes (including some of the most interesting material in the original essay), the addition of passages commenting on the opinions of the Court in *Sierra Club* v. *Morton* (pp. 48 ff.) and some cases since 1972 (pp. 64, 110 ff.), the expansion of some passages and the omission of others, and a shift of tone to the effect that what was very recently "unthinkable" is now on the verge of occurring. Where the text is the same or similar, I cite the Avon edition, which is now more generally available; when there is a change that I consider important, I cite both editions. When no edition is specified, reference is to the Avon edition.

I should stipulate that I do not intend to deal with Stone's book on the level of legal tactics— that is, whether it is to the advantage of the Sierra Club and other environmentalist groups (the Wildlife Management Institute?!) to claim standing as "trustees" of forests and rivers, rather than as representatives of the interests of their members or as representatives of the general public. The notion that a forest itself has interests, rights, and "standing in its own right"

consciousness might look like." [12] Its effect is to leave the reader wondering, not whether some different conception of the human/nature relationship than the conventional modern one is needed, but which of the alternative models implicit in Stone's own essay, or what other model not contained in his essay, would be the most appropriate. The weakness lies in the author's unwillingness to take responsibility for the suggestions he makes and to risk trying to persuade us that what is "not unthinkable" should actually be thought, in his failure to confront the implicit tension between a rights model and an ecological model of nature, and in his apparent failure to see that his ultimate vision of the human/nature relationship is probably incompatible with a legal system that operates in terms of objects, interests, property rights, compensable damages, and National Forests.

On the surface, these two books seem to come out of different traditions, to have two different objectives, to represent two different currents of con-

---

certainly affects the burden of proof. The possibility of going to court for a restraining order on behalf of the sage and the dusky-footed woodrat could have been a useful weapon in my effort to preserve the local coastal sage. This essay, however, is concerned with the more underlying, long-run implications of Stone's argument and of the whole rights approach, which make me wonder whether the tactical gain would be worth the ultimate cost.

I have elsewhere tried to place the idea of nonhuman rights in the context of the evolving modern Liberal "philosophy of right" (see my article, "What Is Living and What Is Dead in the Political Philosophy of T. H. Green," *Western Political Quarterly,* Vol. XXVI, No. 3 [September 1973]; my book review in *Political Theory,* Vol. 4, No. 2 [May 1976], 242 ff.; and my epilogue to the Nozick symposium in *Western Political Quarterly,* Vol. XXIX, No. 2 [June 1976]). In "The Nature of Right and the Right of Nature" (a paper presented at the Conference on the Rights of Nonhuman Nature, April 1974) I attempted to set the idea of nonhuman rights in the longer-run context of Western thought. In "The Dolphin Papers" (*North American Review,* Vol. 259, No. 1 [Spring 1974]) I tried to suggest the kind of lines that a more radical approach might take.

[12] For Stone's own statement of purpose in writing the essay (to exemplify for his students how law evolves by adapting to changing modes of consciousness and, secondarily, to try to affect the outcome of *Sierra Club* v. *Morton*), see Stone, op. cit., pp. 8–11.

The legal context needed for a full understanding of Stone's essay can be summarized as follows. The Sierra Club was appealing to the U.S. Supreme Court the dismissal of its suit to restrain Morton, then Secretary of the Interior, from allowing a road and a power line to be built through the Sequoia National Park to make possible the development of a $35 million recreational complex (ski facilities, motels, restaurants, etc.) by Walt Disney Enterprises, Inc., in the Mineral King Valley, which lies in the adjacent Sequoia National Forest administered by the U.S. Forest Service under the Department of Agriculture. (The situation is complicated enough without Stone confusingly calling Mineral King a "park" [p. 9], incorrectly treating the Forest Service as under the Department of Interior [pp. 48, 59], and discussing the Department of the Interior as if it were the only department whose role as "a sort of guardian of the public lands" was in question [pp. 58 f.].) The suit alleged various grounds for the restraining order, but the difficult issue was that of the Sierra Club's "standing" in the case. The Club claimed standing as a "representative of the public," but the Court affirmed by a 4–3 vote (two new members not participating) the ruling of the Court of Appeals that the Sierra Club lacked standing because of its failure to show that its members would suffer any injury (economic, esthetic, recreational, or whatever) if the development proceeded. Mr. Justice Douglas, dissenting, adopted Stone's line, observing that the case would have been more aptly titled *Mineral King* v. *Morton.* Two other dissenting justices made reference to Douglas's opinion in ways that implied possible sympathy with the Stone position. The Sierra Club subsequently amended its complaint along the lines suggested by the Court majority opinion, rather than along the lines suggested by Stone. Since then several unrelated suits have been filed naming rivers and a town common as plaintiffs, but none has reached the Supreme Court.

temporary thought, and even to express incompatible points of view. Singer argues from essentially Benthamite premises and is primarily concerned to reduce the suffering of domesticated animals, while Stone argues in terms of rights and seems concerned to save the remnants of wilderness. Their difference on the priority of reducing the suffering of domesticated animals *vs.* protecting wilderness and wildlife is mirrored in their disagreement as to whether or not it is meaningful to speak of trees, stones, streams, or anything other than sentient animals as having rights.

Yet I think the similarities are more important than the differences. Singer, for all his feeling that "environmentalists have been more concerned with wildlife and endangered species than with animals in general," thinks there is a similarity involved in treating "whales as giant vessels filled with oil and blubber" and in treating "pigs as machine for converting grains to flesh." [13] And Stone's argument (that legal rights should be extended to trees and streams) borrows and adapts the basic approach of the humane movement in an effort to provide a moral/legal rationale for wilderness preservation. Singer proposes what he considers radical changes in order to diminish the suffering of domesticated animals, but he does not challenge domestication itself. Similarly, Stone is concerned to ward off the Walt Disney stage of "development," but seems to presuppose a continuation of the policy of confining and managing wilderness and wildlife in National Forests, National Parks, Wildlife Refuges, etc. Finally, there is no real incompatibility between Singer's Utilitarian approach and Stone's focus on rights, since rights of a non-absolute sort are easily derivable from the principle of utility (and have been so derived by Bentham, Mill, Singer, *et al.*), and since Stone does not regard rights as absolute prohibitions but as claims to be balanced against one another, even if some have a preferred status. [14] Readers who regard rights and duties as strictly correlative and cannot conceive of beings that possess rights but not duties will find Singer unacceptable, and readers who are convinced that morality entails some absolute prohibitions that are not susceptible to cost/benefit analysis will judge Singer and Stone to be partners in error. [15] The disagreement between Singer and Stone as to where to draw the boundary of rights is a disagreement within the framework of a shared method that I shall call The Method of Argument from Human Analogy and Anomaly. It is a method that produces a peculiarly double message for philosophic criticism to disentangle.

[13] Singer, op. cit., pp. 272, 25.

[14] Ibid., pp. 264 ff.; Stone, op. cit., pp. 27, 76–86.

[15] For the view that rights and duties are strictly correlative, and that nonhumans cannot have rights because they cannot have duties, see D. G. Ritchie. *Natural Rights* (London: Allen & Unwin, 1894). For a depiction of rights as absolute "side constraints" that can never justifiably be violated, and for an argument that nonhuman animals have such rights, see Robert Nozick, *Anarchy, State, and Utopia* (New York: Basic Books, 1974). Ch. 3, esp. pp. 35 ff. For an eloquent but confusing statement of the case for the "absolutely forbidden," see Stuart Hampshire, *Morality and Pessimism* (Cambridge: Cambridge University Press, 1972); reprinted in *The New York Review of Books,* Vol. XIX, Nos. 11–12 (25 January 1973). For an application of the Hampshire thesis in the form of "taboos which are universal," see Jerome Neu, "What Is Wrong with Incest?," *Inquiry,* Vol. 19, No. 1 (Spring 1976).

Singer's and Stone's books not only vibrate with an eagerness to change the world they are understanding; they reflect in the form of theory a convergence occurring in the world of practice of which they seem not to be fully aware. Segments of the humane movement, originally preoccupied with the sufferings of individual domesticated animals, have gradually become concerned about the sufferings of wild animals caused by humans (e.g., in the trapping of predators) and even about the accelerated rate of species extinction. The wilderness and wildlife preservation movement, which arose later and wholly separately, evolving out of the prudential rhetoric of sustained-yield timber and game conservation on the one hand and out of the reverential rhetoric of sublime and beautiful scenery-appreciation on the other, has now passed into the rhetoric of Survival Ecology in the silent knowledge that all these rhetorics are inadequate to articulate the enduring intuition that sustains the movement. In this situation, preservationists drift towards theories of nonhuman rights spawned by the evolving humane movement. The present transitional eclectic stage of both theory and practice is symbolized by the dual appeal of "Save the Whales" advertisements placed by the Animal Welfare Institute during the last several years, now repeated in the dual appeal contained in mailings of the Whale Protection Fund of the Center for Environmental Education: the whaling industry is inhumane, barbaric, cruel, inflicting agony on sentient beings; the whaling industry is dangerously close to bringing about the extinction of whole species of ocean mammals. Thus the Humane Society of the United States joins with the Sierra Club to co-sponsor a boycott of Japanese and Soviet products to help "save the whales." So far the convergence is limited to *"animal* welfare," and even that notion has not been systematically articulated. If Singer's and Stone's arguments seem to converge and each to convey a double message, this is not an isolated intellectual phenomenon but an ambiguity reflecting the imperfect convergence of two major social movements. The issue at stake is not merely the adequacy of Singer's logic or of Stone's imagination, but whether or not a revitalized and radicalized humane movement has any real niche in the ecological revolution, and whether the wilderness and wildlife preservation movement, by adapting the moral/legal theory of "rights," may sell its soul, its roots in mythic and ritual experience, to get easier judicial standing.

3. THE ARGUMENT FOR ANIMAL RIGHTS

Consistency of some sort is usually thought to be an essential part of what we mean by acting morally or being moral. When a philosopher feels he has no other ground to stand on, he can always take some platitude and explore the implications that would follow from being consistent about it. Thus, *if* we assume that there are certain human rights (e.g., to life and to just treatment), the philosopher can ask us on what basis we ascribe such rights to humans.[16] If we reply in terms of some quality or capacity that has traditionally been invoked to distinguish human beings from nonhumans (e.g., rationality) the philosopher will then call our attention to certain anomalies: e.g., infants, lunatics, the mentally retarded, and the senile. Since we are unwilling to say that it is all right to kill or torture these unfortunates, we seem to assume that they have certain rights. While we can regard the infant as a potentially rational adult, and can assume that the lunatic may someday recover his sanity, "the imbecile has been something of an embarrassment to moral philosophers."[17] There seems no way to avoid admitting that we regard severely mentally retarded persons as having certain kinds of rights even though they may not be "rational" in any operational sense.

At this point we seem to have a choice. Either we must say that (a) rights are ascribed on the basis of normal species characteristics, and anomalies will be treated as if they were not anomalies[18] (why?—in the interest of taxonomical economy?), or else we must say that (b) rights are ascribed on the basis of some broader criterion, such as sentience (the capacity for enjoying

[16] The argument outlined in this paragraph of the review discussion attempts to state the common denominator logic of many advocates of the rights of animals from the eighteenth century on. I do *not* deal with the earlier Pythagorean case against killing and eating animals, with the theological debate as to whether "brute beasts" have souls or not (and if so, what kind of souls), or with the argument between those who have claimed (with Montaigne and Hume) "that brute beasts reason," feel, choose, etc., and those who (like Descartes) have claimed that beasts are unthinking, nonsentient "machines."

The argument that I sketch emerged in the late eighteenth century, often still mixed with other arguments (such as that beasts had souls or that "man's dominion" should be construed as a "moral trust"), but had become reasonably distinct in the writings of Bentham and J. S. Mill. It was forcefully stated by H. S. Salt, *Animals' Rights* (New York and London: Macmillan, 1894); was revised by Leonard Nelson, *A System of Ethics* (written in the 1920s, trans. by N. Guterman, [New Haven: Yale University Press, 1956]); and has been given contemporary restatement by Singer, loc. cit. (esp. Chs. 1 and 6); Tom Regan, "The Moral Basis of Vegetarianism" (*Canadian Journal of Philosophy*, Vol. V. No. 2 [October 1975]); Joel Feinberg, "The Rights of Animals and Unborn Generations" (a paper presented in 1971, published in revised form in Wm. T. Blackstone [ed.], *Philosophy & Environmental Crisis*, [Athens: University of Georgia Press, 1974]; and "Human Duties and Animal Rights" (in Richard K. Morris [ed.], *Of Man, Animals, and Morals*, copyright held by the Humane Society of the United States, Washington, D.C., not yet published); Kai Nielsen, "Persons, Morals, and the Animal Kingdom" (in ibid.); Brigid Brophy, "In Pursuit of a Fantasy" (in *Animals, Men, and Morals*, cited in note 8, above); Roslind Godlovitch, "Animals and Morals" (in ibid.); and James Rachels, "Do Animals Have a Right to Liberty?" (in *Animal Rights and Human Obligations*, cited in note 8, above). For a watered-down, popularized version of the same argument, see the 15-page pamphlet, "Save the Animals," published by Friends of Animals, Inc., New York 1974.

A number of the writings listed in this note are reprinted or excerpted in *Animal Rights and Human Obligations*, which provides an excellent collection of materials ranging from the Bible and Aristotle through Descartes and Bentham to contemporary philosophers. I can fault it only for neglecting the Pythagorean/Empedoclean case against meat-eating and for slighting the extent to which the modern humane mentality, although having its perennial dimension, was a special product of the late eighteenth century manifested in a host of now-obscure writers (e.g., Humphrey Primatt, John Lawrence, Thomas Young) and bearing still now the imprint of that period.

As will become apparent, I regard Stone's general approach, though not focused upon or limited to animals, and though stressing legal rather than moral rights, as essentially similar.

[17] S. I. Benn, "Egalitarianism and Equal Consideration of Interests." In *Nomos IX: Equality* New York: Atherton, 1967), p. 70.

[18] Ibid., pp. 69–71.

pleasure and suffering pain) or conative life (the experience of desire and aversion). In the latter case there can be no ground for denying that (certain) nonhuman beings have (certain) rights, since the evidence suggests that horses, dogs, deer, mice, etc., suffer pain and enjoy pleasure, desire some things and flee from others. The question, as Bentham said pithily, is not whether they can reason or talk but whether they can suffer.[19] Recent philosophers are inclined to insert between sentience and rights the mediating term "interests," and it is increasingly assumed to be obvious that such animals as are sentient have interests and are thereby the kinds of beings capable of having rights (assuming that there are rights at all).[20]

Although Singer draws far more radical conclusions for conduct and policy than most humane reformers have done, his theoretical position is orthodox. He limits sentience, and therefore interests, and therefore rights, to animals. (The line, he suggests, should probably be drawn somewhere between shrimps and oysters.) There is, he says, "no reliable evidence that plants are capable of feeling pleasure or pain" (since experiments suggesting that they do have not been successfully replicated by the same scientific establishment that studies nature by torturing animals); and it would be nonsense to treat a stone as if it had rights, "because it cannot suffer," and "Nothing that we can do to it could possibly make any difference to its welfare." In fact, it is unthinkable (in terms of his version of the paradigm of Natural Selection) that species lacking locomotion could have evolved sentience, since it wouldn't serve any function for an entity to feel pain if it couldn't get out of the way.[21] While Singer does not discuss ecosystems, we can assume that he would extend rights to dusky-footed woodrats but not to sage or cactus. And the woodrats themselves would presumably have rights as individuals but not as a species.[22] The moral atomism that focuses on individual animals and their

[19] *The Principles of Morals and Legislation,* Ch. XVII [Ch. XIX in the Bowring ed.], Sect. 4, Note b.

[20] Examples are provided by Nelson, Feinberg, Singer, Regan, etc. For a weaker version of the argument sketched in this paragraph, eliminate the claim that sentient nonhuman animals have rights but retain the claim that humans have duties not to kill sentient nonhuman animals unnecessarily, not to treat them cruelly, etc. just as humans have duties towards the mentally retarded (whether the latter have rights or not).

[21] Singer, op. cit., pp. 9, 12 ff., 262 ff. The *a priori* argument from this particular version of the theory of Natural Selection is quite widespread among contemporary scientists, illustrating Kuhn's view of the power of "paradigms" to direct (and limit) our notion of what constitutes a problem or even a possibility. Actually, the close association of affective life with movement (construed as locomotion) with animals goes back to Aristotle's *De Anima.* Cf. Darwin's *The Movements and Habits of Climbing Plants* (1875), *The Power of Movement in Plants* (1880), *Autobiography* (in Stanley Edgar Hyman [ed.], *Darwin Today* [New York: Viking, 1963], p. 398), and the "reminiscences" of Darwin's son (whom Darwin had play a bassoon close to a plant to see if it would vibrate in response), in *The Autobiography of Charles Darwin and Selected Letters,* ed. by Francis Darwin (New York: Dover, 1958), p. 101.

For a more thoughtful examination of the continuities and discontinuities among the forms of organic life, see Hans Jonas, *The Phenomenon of Life: Toward a Philosophical Biology* (New York: Dell., 1968).

[22] This is explicit in Feinberg, "Human Duties and Animal Rights": "The name of a species . . . is the name of a mere collection of entities with certain defining characteristics in common." If we have a duty to preserve other species from extinction, Feinberg argues that it

subjective experiences does not seem well adapted to coping with ecological systems.

At the risk of seeming to deal with Singer's position somewhat as Dr. Johnson dealt with Bishop Berkeley's philosophy, I confess that I need only to stand in the midst of a clear-cut forest, a strip-mined hillside, a defoliated jungle, or a dammed canyon to feel uneasy with assumptions that could yield the conclusion that no human action can make any difference to the welfare of anything but sentient animals. I am agnostic as to whether or not plants, rocks, and rivers have subjective experience, and I am not sure that it really matters. I strongly suspect that the same basic principles are manifested in quite diverse forms—e.g., in damming a wild river and repressing an animal instinct (whether human or nonhuman), in clear-cutting a forest and bombing a city, in Dachau and a university research laboratory, in censoring an idea, liquidating a religious or racial group, and exterminating a species of flora or fauna.

It puzzles Singer that Bentham, working from essentially the same premises (pain is evil and ought to be minimized, and "every one to count as one"), justified meat-eating on the ground that the nonhuman animals suffered very little while the benefit to humans was very great. Bentham ought to have been more sensitive to the sufferings of farm animals, even before the battery henhouse and the Porcine Stress Syndrome, Singer believes.[23] But the location of value in the subjective experience of sentient entities allows for no small amount of subjectivity in our moral appraisals, since our judgments about the inner experience of others is either inferential, utilizing our criteria of evidence (the presence of a nervous system, the exhibition of what we recognize as pain-behavior, etc.), or sympathetic, depending upon our imaginative/emotional capacity to identify with others' sufferings, to put ourselves in their place.

Singer, like most philosophers and statesmen of the humane movement, represents himself as a stern moralist who disdains the "sentimentality" of little old ladies who fondle pet poodles and write animal shelters into their wills while eating ham sandwiches and wearing cosmetics that were tested on rabbits. He is "not appeased" by the U.S. Defense Department's offer to use rats instead of beagles to test poisonous gases.[24] Yet sentimentality, in the sense of our tendency to feel for "chubby little bundles of soft white fur" with "tear-filled eyes" and humanoid cries (see note 2, above), and not for tarantulas, is not so easily exorcised. Utilitarianism and the humane movement emerged together out of the eighteenth-century redefinition of moral action as—not that which was in accordance with the will of God, in accordance with Nature, or even in accordance with human reason—but that which was in accordance with human "moral sentiments". Through the admittedly di-

---

cannot be derived from any right possessed by those species and must be entailed by "the requirements of our unique station as rational custodians of the planet."

[23] Singer, op. cit., pp. 229 ff.

[24] Ibid., Preface and pp. 270 ff.

verse literature of the "theory of moral sentiments" (Shaftesbury, Hutcheson, Hume, Adam Smith, Rousseau, Lord Kames, *et al.*) there runs the central metaphoric pattern of the disinterested and benevolent spectator who sympathizes with the sufferings of the characters in a tragic stageplay, and whose judgments of approbation and disapprobation of actions and actors are made possible by his capacity for putting himself in the victim's place. The humane movement arose during the transition from traditional to modern urban/ industrial society, when horses were used to pull overloaded cabs through the city streets, and humans were being subjected to the harsh and frightening rigors of the mine, the factory, and the urban slum—in short, during a time when sensitive members of the upper classes began to be able to put themselves in the place not only of victimized humans but also of horses, cattle, dogs, etc., and to imagine what they must feel like when overloaded, driven hard, cooped up, starved, forced to fight one another, or led to slaughter.

That Singer can take up the cause of feedlot cattle and laboratory rats is not so much an indication that he is moral while the poodle-lover is sentimental, as that the poodle-lover is fixated at a particular stage in the evolution of the humane sensibility and is now an anachronism, while Singer's sensibility has kept up both with the changing effects of technology on domesticated animals and with the changing human condition insofar as that condition is reflected in the mirror of domesticated nature. As René Dubos has perceptively noted, the probable upshot of human overpopulation of the planet is the elimination of wilderness and wildlife, an increasing reliance on technology, and a growing regulation of human social life to the point where:

> there may emerge by selection a stock of human beings suited genetically to accept as a matter of course a regimented and sheltered way of life in a teeming and polluted world, from which all wilderness and fantasy of nature will have disappeared. *The domesticated farm animal and the laboratory rodent on a controlled regimen in a controlled environment will then become true models for the study of man.*[25]

In the end, Singer achieves "an expansion of our moral horizons" just far enough to include most animals, with special attention to those categories of animals most appropriate for defining the human condition in the years ahead. The rest of nature is left in a state of thinghood, having no intrinsic worth, acquiring instrumental value only as resources for the well-being of an elite of sentient beings. Homocentrist rationalism has widened out into a kind of zoöcentrist sentientism. Singer's characterization of the Brambell Report seems apt for his own book: "an enlightened and humane form of speciesism, but . . . still speciesism nevertheless."[26] We have here not a revolution in ethics but something analogous to the Reform Bill of 1832, when the British aristocracy extended selected rights to the upper middle class. The problem of the cosmic observer persists. If it would seem arbitrary to a visitor from Mars to find one species claiming a monopoly of intrinsic value by virtue of its

---

[25] Rene Dubos, *Man Adapting* (New Haven: Yale University Press, 1965), p. 313. my emphasis.
[26] Singer, op. cit., p. 151.

allegedly exclusive possession of reason, free will, soul, or some other occult quality, would it not seem almost as arbitrary to find that same species claiming a monopoly of intrinsic value for itself and those species most resembling it (e.g., in type of nervous system and behavior) by virtue of their common and allegedly exclusive possession of sentience? And would not the arbitrariness seem overwhelming if it were then discoverred that the populations of nonhuman species who were most prominent in this "humane" coalition were what Darwin aptly called "domestic productions"; that is, beings produced by the human manipulation of nonhuman animal gene pools for human purposes? [27]

4. EXTENDING RIGHTS TO "NATURAL OBJECTS"

How does Stone cross the boundary established by the humane movement's extension (and delimitation) of rights to sentient animals? Partly by arguments from a developmental view of law: "each successive extension of rights to some new entity [e.g., slaves, women, children, aliens, human foetuses] has been, theretofore, a bit unthinkable." Partly by the use of legal analogy: the Anglo-American legal system already grants rights of one sort or another to corporations, municipalities, ships, and some animals.[28] If we point out that slaves, women, children, and aliens are all human beings, that human foetuses are potential human beings, and that corporations and municipalities are associations of human beings, we are left with ships and (some) animals. Stone chooses not to make much of animals—perhaps because he does not want to get trapped within the traditional limitations of the humane movement.[29] But ships (human artifacts) do not seem a very promising base from which to extend rights to natural entities. Stone uses all these examples merely to point out that legal systems already accord rights to entities that are not wholly reducible to individual human beings, so that it would not be much more "unthinkable" for the law to "personify" trees and streams than for it

---

[27] A colleague objects that whether or not my hypothetical Martian would find these claims of earthlings arbitrary or not would depend on what kind of moral theory the Martian came equipped with. But my purpose is simply to invoke the notion of an impartial cosmic observer who sees the earth in all its diversity and is not limited by our species-specific perspective. It was somewhat in the spirit of my Martian observer that Xenophanes remarked long ago that "If oxen or lions had hands which enabled them to draw and paint pictures as men do, they would portray their gods as having bodies like their own: horses would portray them as horses, and oxen as oxen" (Philip Wheelwright [ed.], *The Presocratics* [New York: Odyssey, 1966], p. 33, DK 15). Of course, Xenophanes assumed that horses and oxen had gods, just as my colleague assumes that Martians have moral theories.

[28] Stone, op. cit. pp. 17–26.

[29] The original edition of Stone's essay contains mention of "animals (some of which already have rights in some senses)" and explicitly contrasts the homocentric approach of resource "conservationists" with the approach of "humane societies," but warns that "In this article I essentially limit myself to a discussion of nonanimal but natural objects" (notes 26 and 45, in Kaufmann edition). Stone's hypothetical case of the rare, temperature-sensitive sea urchin and his brief reference to "the pain and suffering of animals and other sentient objects" occur in both editions (Kaufmann edition, pp. 30–32; Avon edition, pp. 70–72).

to "personify" corporations and ships. Stone is a kind of legal existentialist/
pragmatist with no fixed ontology: legal systems *create* persons, property,
and rights, and can do pretty much what they please—hence the language
of "giving," "granting," and "extending" rights predominates over the language of "recognizing" or "acknowledging" rights.

Stone's underlying skepticism is reflected in his inconsistent use of the term
"natural object." At times he speaks of extending legal rights to natural
objects as if there were nothing strange in the notion of an object having a
right. At other times he puts "natural objects" in quotation marks or even
speaks of "so-called natural objects," so as to indicate that there may be more
possibilities than ordinary language and the vocabulary of the law have
considered. Indeed, Stone claims in effect that natural objects are really
subjects in that they have "needs (wants)" and "interests" and can communicate these to human beings pretty clearly. For example, Stone says it is
safe to assume that the smog-endangered stand of pines "wants" the smog
stopped.[30] Moreover, Stone raises the possibility that subjectivity in the sense
of sentience and/or consciousness may be present in all natural entities,
vegetable as well as animal, and even "latent" in molecules and atoms. Aside
from citing several reports of experiments in plant perception, Stone presents
no evidence or arguments for the universality of subjectivity.[31] It appears as
an alternative way of looking at the world, an ontology that would be appropriate if we were to extend rights to all natural entities. A reader (like
MR. JUSTICE DOUGLAS) passionately concerned to defend wilderness, or (like
Professor Garritt Hardin) deeply worried about impending eco-catastrophe,
can applaud Stone's proposal to extend rights to natural entities as a useful
weapon in the warfare of environmental litigation or a catchy idea in the
campaign for consciousness raising, without paying much attention to Stone's
metaphysics.[32] Indeed, Stone has made it easy for them by introducing the
postulate of universal subjectivity so indirectly and diffidently that he does
not commit himself to its defense: it is an idea "not easy to dismiss," a view

[30] Stone, op. cit., pp. 56 ff.
[31] Ibid., pp. 72, 105–8. The citations occur in note 93 of the Kaufmann edition omitted in
the Avon edition. The lengthy quotation from astrologer Dane Rudhyar's *Directives for a New
Life* (Ecology Center Press, 1971) that takes up most of pages 106–8 states a point of view but
does not provide an argument or evidence. While this quotation is introduced by a statement
of Stone's about our need for a new "myth" that can comprehend what we feel as well as think
about the rest of nature, it is clear that the type of myth that he thinks we need is one "that
can fit our growing body of knowledge of geophysics, biology and the cosmos" (p. 105). That
is to say, the myth is to be "scientific" or at least compatible with contemporary science.
    For a more thorough statement of the case for subjectivity as a widespread, if not universal,
characteristic, see the writings of Alfred North Whitehead, Charles Hartshorne, John B. Cobb,
Jr., and Charles Birch. A different version is developed by Hans Jonas, *The Phenomenon of
Life*.
[32] In Douglas's version, Stone's "natural objects" reappear as "inanimate objects," making
the notion of nonhuman rights seem even stranger (see Douglas's dissenting opinion, reprinted
in Stone, Kaufmann edition, pp. 73–84). While Hardin's Preface to Stone's book is highly
laudatory and expresses no reservations, Hardin elsewhere is explicit that he regards the legal
rights of natural objects as a useful fiction that makes the "rationalist" in him nervous (Hardin,
"The Rational Foundation for Conservation," *North American Review,* Vol. 259, No. 4 [Winter
1974], 16).

that we "may" come to hold.[33] And the concession of legal rights to ships, corporations, and states does not seem to presuppose that they are conscious or sentient entities. Yet without some such postulate it is unclear what entitles an entity to rights. Either natural "objects" are really subjects with their own natures and needs, or else Stone's whole essay is an exercise in arbitrary legal "creation," a forced attempt to graft a new ethics and legal theory onto the stock of the old Cartesian/Kantian ontology that dichotomizes (human) subjects from (nonhuman) objects. Some such postulate as universal consciousness is therefore necessary if the notion of rights for trees is not to seem a rootless fancy. But it is suspicious when a new ontology suddenly appears upon the scene to support a moral/legal theory that is presented as desirable for practical reasons. Stone seems to assume a commitment to Saving Nature which he neither justifies nor really explores. Perhaps it is as obvious to him that we should Save Nature as it is to Singer that we should Minimize Suffering.

At the risk of attributing greater consistency to Stone than his text may support, we can say that on the whole Stone and Singer follow a similar pattern: they pick a quality that is conceded to be normally possessed by humans; they make it the basis for the capacity for rights; then they find it writ large beyond the human pale. Singer picks sentience and stops with (most) animals. Stone picks consciousness as well as sentience and suggests that it may well be present in all natural "objects." Of course, there is a pecking order in this moral barnyard. Singer is explicit that the equal consideration of interests does not necessarily mean equal treatment; after all, different types of animals have different needs. Since "normal adult humans" are, in most situations, more sensitive to suffering than nonhuman animals are, if we had to choose we should inflict pain on the "animal". And since "normal adult humans" are blessed also with "self-awareness, intelligence, the capacity for meaningful relations with others, and so on," their lives are more worth saving than the lives of nonhumans.[34] "All Animals Are Equal", reads the title of Singer's first chapter, but some are more equal than others.

Stone is at least certain that "to say that the environment should have rights is not to say it should have . . . the same body of rights as human beings have. Nor is it to say that every thing in the environment should have the same rights as every other thing in the environment.[35] What this means in practice is not wholly clear, but Stone's postulate of universal "consciousness," combined with the suggestion that the function of the human species within the overall earth-organism is that of "mentalization," of bringing to self-consciousness in man the "planetary consciousness" that is only latent in other forms of life, combined with the human species' control of the legal system, may imply that nonhumans are properly subject to "Guardians" in

---

[33] Stone, op. cit., pp. 72, 105.

[34] Singer, op. cit., pp. 3, 17–24. Notice that the ecological value of a species (in terms of its function within the biosphere) is not for Singer a criterion of worth.

[35] Stone, op. cit., p. 27.

an almost Platonic sense.[36] (Our hypothetical visitor from Mars, interpreting the earth-organism ecologically, might wonder if bacteria did not perform a more important function by facilitating the decay of organic matter than humans do by mentalizing the cosmos—especially since mentalization seems so easily diverted into the production of ideologies that freeze process into rigid structures, turn the food chain into a caste system, and undermine natural limits and inhibitions by developing fanatical doctrines of interspeciesific imperialism and intraspeciesific "genocide."[37]

5. THE DOUBLE MESSAGE

I have suggested that the process of "extending" rights to nonhumans conveys a double message. On the one hand, nonhumans are elevated to the human level by virtue of their sentience and/or consciousness; they now have (some) rights. On the other hand, nonhumans are by the same process degraded to the status of inferior human beings, species-anomalies: imbeciles, the senile, "human vegetables"—moral half-breeds having rights without obligations (Singer), "legal incompetents" needing humans to interpret and represent their interests in a perpetual guardian/ward relationship (Stone).[38]

Is this, then, the new enlightenment—to see nonhuman animals as imbeciles, wilderness as a human vegetable? As a general characterization of nonhuman nature it seems patronizing and perverse. It is not so much that natural entities are degraded by being represented in human legal actions, or by not having us attribute to them moral obligations. They are degraded rather by our failure to respect them for having their own existence, their own character and potentialities, their own forms of excellence, their own integrity, their own grandeur—and by our tendency to relate to them either by reducing them to the status of instruments for our own ends or by "giving" them rights by assimilating them to the status of inferior human beings. It is perhaps analogous to regarding women as defective men who lack penises, or humans as defective sea mammals who lack sonar capability and have to be rescued by dolphins. With some allowances for terminology, Henry Beston's meditation on birds communicates something of the perspective from which the representation of nonhumans as imbeciles and human vegetables can be seen to be degrading:

---

[36] Ibid., pp. 105–8. Stone incorporates the earth-organism model of Rudhyar apparently without realizing that it provides, in effect, an alternative to his own model of a universe made up of entities having rights. The component parts of an organism have functions, and while functions *can* be translated into the language of rights and obligations it is only in a secondary and weak sense.

[37] On the dangers of the human proclivity for abstract thinking, see Livingston, pp. 181 ff., and Joseph W. Meeker, *The Comedy of Survival: Essays in Literary Ecology* (New York: Scribner's 1974), pp. 160 ff.

[38] "One ought, I think, to handle the legal problems of natural objects as one does the problems of legal incompetents" (Singer, op. cit., p. 41, using the example of human senility).

Remote from universal nature, and living by complicated artifice, man in civilization surveys the creature through the glass of his knowledge and sees thereby a feather magnified and the whole image in distortion. We patronize them for their incompleteness, for their tragic fate of having taken form so far below ourselves. And therein we err, and greatly err. For the animal shall not be measured by man. In a world older and more complete than ours they move finished and complete, gifted with extensions of the senses we have lost or never attained, living by voices we shall never hear. They are not brethren, they are not underlings; they are other nations, caught with ourselves in the net of life and time, fellow prisoners of the splendor and travail of the earth.[39]

"Other nations," however apparently anthropocentric the metaphor, echoes Black Elk's invocation of "all the nations that have roots or legs or wings" and the accompanying sense of kinship (based on common descent) with, and respect for the otherness of, nonhuman forms of life.[40]

And yet we can see the appropriateness of the Singer/Stone vision of nature as consisting of inferior human beings. Singer's subject-matter consists of the humanized, degraded, dependent, infantilized, domesticated animals bred for farm and lab. And Stone, for all his apparent concern for wilderness, is limited theoretically by having adopted the humane movement's basic approach (attributing rights to nonhuman entities by virtue of humanoid qualities) and practically by the fact that he is defending not so much wilderness as a section of a human creation called a National Forest which is already under the "multiple use" management of the Department of Agriculture and is simply threatened with further "development." Stone professes himself uncertain whether the mountain is "concerned about whether the pines stand or fall," but he is pretty sure that he knows "when my lawn wants (needs) water."[41] The difference in degree of certainty is not, as Stone suggests, merely a function of the size of the entity, but also a function of the difference between domestication and wilderness. The caricature of nature in terms of retarded persons and human vegetables (lawns?) tells us something about the stage that has been reached in the course of man's long domestication of nature and the concomitant domestication of human thought patterns.

6. ETHICS AND INTERSPECIES IMPERIALISM

Why do our "new ethics" seem so old, and our exercises in exploring the "unthinkable" so tame? Because the attempt to produce a "new ethics" by the process of "extension" perpetuates the basic presuppositions of the conventional modern paradigm, however much it fiddles with the boundaries.

---

[39] Henry Beston, *The Outermost House* [1928] (New York: Ballantine, 1971), pp. 19 f.
[40] *Black Elk Speaks, Being the Life Story of a Holy Man of the Oglala Sioux* as told through John G. Neihardt (1932), (New York: Pocket Books, 1973), pp. 1–2, 8, 35, 43, 54, 130, 139 ff., and *passim*.
[41] Stone, op. cit., pp. 56 ff.

The call for a "new ethics" to guide the human/nature relationship has grown increasingly insistent in the last decade, stemming from such varied sources as "the ecological crisis", the changing impression that ethology has wrought in our conceptions of "man" and "beast," and the widespread yearning revealed in the popular reception of studies of plant perception and interspecies animal communication.

But what would a "new ethics" involve, and how might it be arrived at? Many writers on "the environmental crisis", including some who seem to think they are propounding a new ethics, simply reaffirm the conventional homocentric goals of human survival, human civilization, the quality of [human] life, etc. while advocating more ecologically sophisticated means for securing those goals.[42] Others see homocentrism itself as at least one root of the crisis, and, whether it is or not, it certainly appears to be an increasingly arbitrary perspective in an age when the ecological imagination can shift reference points within the system and imagine the world to some extent from the standpoint of "the muskrat and its environment."[43] Efforts to purge our traditions of the homocentric perspective by reinterpreting the Judeo-Christian mandate of "man's dominion" in terms of enlightened "stewardship" rather than a license to dominate and exploit are doubtless therapeutic, but they reshuffle the elements of a tradition in accordance with criteria of ecologically "better" and "worse" that have been brought to the task. And so we come to Hans Jonas's sober statement:

> Only an ethic which is grounded in the breadth of being, not merely in the singularity or oddness of man, can have significance in the scheme of things. . . . an ethic no longer founded on divine authority must be founded on a principle discoverable in the nature of things. . .[44]

For all the classical overtones of "the nature of things," this is a radical statement by virtue of its discarding two of the major props of traditional moral philosophy—the reliance upon divine authority, and the even more basic reliance upon human *areté* (the assumed coincidence of species-specific peculiarity with goodness). From Plato and Aristotle through Augustine and Aquinas to Mill, Marx, and Sartre, it has been assumed that human beings ought to maximize their species-specific differentia (formulated variously in terms of rationality, spirituality, self-consciousness, freedom, speech, symbolic activity, creativity, etc.) rather than the capacities shared with other species. This axiom is now reduced to absurdity by the fact that it seems equally plausible to say (on the basis of comparative ethology) that man's uniqueness (if there is any) lies in his tendency to interspecies imperialism or in his lack

---

[42] E.g., Garrett Hardin, "The Tragedy of the Commons" *Science,* Vol. 162, 13 December 1968, pp. 1243–48, and *Exploring New Ethics for Survival: The Voyage of the Spaceship Beagle* (New York: Viking, 1972); (Baltimore: Penguin, 1973)

[43] I think that the cultivation of this capacity is one of the functions served by Aldo Leopold's *A Sand County Almanac.*

[44] *The Phenomenon of Life,* p. 284.

of effective inhibition against intraspeciesific aggression. So the question of Aristotle's *Ethics*—"what is the good for man?"—appears to presuppose a more fundamental question: what is the good for that larger whole (life? nature?) of which humanity is a part, and which is a part of humanity?

But between a felt need to transcend a homocentric ethics and an ability to discover an ontologically-grounded moral order in "the phenomenon of life" or "the nature of things" there lie three serious obstacles. First, there is the powerful prohibition of modern culture against confusing "is" and "ought," "fact" and "value," the "natural" with the "moral"—in short, the taboo against committing "the naturalistic fallacy." Thanks to this, the quest for an ethics is reduced to prattle about "values" taken in abstraction from the "facts" of experience; the notion of an ethics as an organic ethos, a way of life, remains lost to us. Second, we have become self-conscious about the apparent circularity involved in projecting models upon nature and then selectively applying them back again to society, lest we find that we have done with Ecology what the Social Darwinists did with Natural Selection. In our very notion of "projection" we implicitly reaffirm the dogma of two unrelated realms, nature and society, that are and must be kept distinct. Finally, we are uneasily aware that there is some truth to the contention that we cannot "return to nature" or even invoke "nature" as an absolute standard by which to criticize social practices, since nature itself is now seen to be historical, meaning that (a) nature is not static but in process, (b) the process of becoming is not obviously teleological, (c) we encounter nature as it has already been transformed by human impact, and (d) we tend to perceive nature through cultural lenses. It is, I suspect, partly in order to avoid these formidable obstacles (and partly for lack of an obvious alternative starting point) that we try to transcend homocentrism by *building up* a larger moral order through the *extension* of "basic moral principles which we [humans] all accept."

From the amnesiac perspective of modern culture, we then presume to be able to envisage the course of human evolution in terms of an ever-progressive widening of the sphere of moral concern from the individual ego to the family, to the clan, to the village, to the city, to the nation, to humanity ("regardless of race, creed, color, sex, or national origin"), and thence to "the lower animals," perhaps now to "the land" and all its inhabitants, culminating in "the rights of rocks."[45] The fact that this model is abstractly unhistorical, leaving out of account the historical priority of animistic and totemic societies, the tradition of Pythagoras and Empedocles, the Roman and Thomistic conception of the *jus naturae* as "that which nature has taught all animals," and the historical modernity of individualism, does not seem to lessen its appeal.

---

[45] Fragments or versions of this model can be found in Bentham, J. S. Mill, Lecky's *History of European Morals*, Darwin's *Descent of Man*, Leopold's *Sand County Almanac*, the opening pages of Stone, and Roderick Nash, "The Significance of the Arrangement of the Deck Chairs on the Titanic" (in *Not Man Apart*, mid-October 1975, pp. 7–9).

That appeal lies, I suggest, in the model's accidental association with the notion of Evolution (accidental in that while Darwin held it, it is in no way entailed by the theory that species evolve by natural selection, sexual selection, etc.), in its bold simplicity and optimism, in its apparent avoidance of the various modern "fallacies" that we fear to commit because we have not thought our way through or around them, and, above all, in the fact that the progressive extension model of ethics, which holding out the promise of transcending the homocentric perspective of modern culture, subtly fulfills and legitimizes the basic project of modernity—the total conquest of nature by man. Instead of discovering a larger normative order within which we and our species-specific moral and legal systems have a niche, limits, and responsibilities, we construct a transhuman moral/legal order by extending selected principles of modern human morality (individuals have rights, pain is bad, all interests should be equally considered, etc.) to encompass all or part of nonhuman nature.

Faced with such questions as whether nonhumans have obligations to us as well as rights against us, whether wolves have a right to prey upon deer, whether deer have a right to be selectively culled by wolves for their inter-generational genetic well-being, and whether wolves have an obligation to service deer populations in this way or else forfeit their right to prey on them, most "humanitarians" suddenly reverse direction and take refuge in a distinction between humans and nonhumans. Humans, it seems, are the only beings that can make moral choices and therefore the only beings to whom it makes sense to attribute moral obligations.[46] One criterion for attributing rights, another for attributing obligations—this is, of course, how we end up with a right to life for "human vegetables." But alleged agreement on an anomaly seems a weak ground upon which to base a case for separate criteria. The ancient Greeks, after all, practiced infanticide on anomalies such as physically deformed or mentally retarded children; and current controversies over whether a human foetus has a right to life, and whether a person reduced to the condition of a "human vegetable" has a right to death that supersedes the right/duty to life, cast some doubt on the degree of consensus prevailing with regard to human anomalies.

Stone did not shrink (at least in the original edition of his essay) from taking the logic of personifying natural entities all the way (which may be to a *reductio ad absurdum*): if natural entities are to be given legal rights they should perhaps have legal liabilities as well, so that we could sue a river for damages to human life and property following a flood (assuming, pre-

---

[46] See, e.g., Singer, op. cit., pp. 250 ff.; Regan, op. cit., p. 196; Brophy, op. cit., p. 130; Rachels, op. cit., p. 223; Feinberg, "Human Duties and Animal Rights," John Harris, "Killing for Food," in *Animals, Men and Morals,* pp. 104 ff.; and John Plamenatz, *Consent, Freedom, and Political Obligation,* 2nd ed., (Oxford: Oxford University Press, 1968), p. 83. Cf. Barry Lopez, "Wolf Kill" (*Harper's* [August 1976], 25–27), who suggests that the killing of a moose by a wolf involves a ritual "conversation" and that "The killing is by natural agreement," a result of a kind of "choice" on both sides.

sumably, that we could not pin responsibility upon the Bureau of Reclamation or the Corps of Engineers).[47] In ancient law, after all, oxen and trees could be held liable for damage done to human life and property; and the late Middle Ages and early modern times saw so many prosecutions of pigs for murder, rats for crop damage, cows for buggery, etc. that the advocate Chassenèe, who had defended the rats of Burgundy, wrote a treatise on the procedural rights of beasts accused of violating human laws.[48] "Perhaps," Stone conjectures,

> the liability of nonhuman matter [*sic!*] is, in the history of things, part of a paranoid, defensive phase in man's development; as humans become more abundant, both from the point of material wealth and internally, they may be willing to allow an advance to the stage where nonhuman matter [*sic!*] has rights.[49]

But if the evolution of legal doctrines is to be interpreted in the light of human psychopathology, and if the legal liability of natural entities expressed human paranoia and defensiveness, what state of mind may we suppose to be expressed in the notion of giving rights to natural objects—a total loss of ego-boundaries perhaps, occurring as human offensiveness nears the point of triumph, annihilating the otherness of nonhuman nature, and thereby making impossible any way of defining either humanity or nature?

7. TOWARDS THE ABOLITION OF DOMESTICATION?

The question is whether contemporary philosophers accompany the advance of technological society the way missionaries once accompanied the march of conquistadors, assimilating the conquered to the culture of the conquerers and ameliorating (making more 'humane') the harshness of the yoke, or whether they criticize the process of conquest in the interest of liberation. But on what ground would they have standing to make such a critique (or is "ground" any longer an appropriate image, now that nature has become historical)? On the basis of what I have said so far, it appears that both Singer and Stone play ambiguous roles and convey double messages. In their effort to expand or moral horizons so as to protect nonhuman nature, they extend human principles of morality and legality to interspecies relations and deal with nonhumans as inferior humans. Yet each book also contains elements that point in another direction than the humanization of nature.

While Singer's stated objective is to reduce as much as possible the suffering inflicted upon domesticated farm and lab animals, it is significant that the implementation of his proposals would go a long way towards abolishing the

---

[47] Stone, Kaufmann edition, p. 34 and note 98; omitted in Avon edition.
[48] O. W. Holmes, Jr., *The Common Law* (Boston: Little, Brown, 1881), Ch. 1; Plato, *Laws* 873–4; *The Old Testament,* Exodus 21:28. E. P. Evans, *The Criminal Prosecution and Capital Punishment of Animals* (London: Heinemann, 1906).
[49] Stone, Kaufmann edition, note 98.

very existence of domesticated animals. If universal vegetarianism came to pass, farm animals would become superfluous and could be allowed to wither away (probably with the aid of sterilization).[50] If laboratory experimentation on animals were greatly reduced, the dwindling of the market for rats, guinea pigs, etc. would be followed by a dwindling of their supply, since the breeding and supplying of them is an industry carried on for profit. Although Singer only mentions in passing the practice of "farming minks, foxes, and other animals for their fur"[51] I shall assume that a case could be made for abolishing this practice on grounds more or less analogous to the grounds for abolishing factory farming for food. From his brief mention of zoos, circuses, and rodeos, we can also safely assume that Singer would wish to phase out these institutions, since they involve "capturing," "imprisoning," and "tormenting" animals.[52] This leaves, I believe, one large category of domesticated animals: pets.

In some countries (for example, the United States) the pet population is growing faster than the human population. Humane societies, their 'shelters' overrun with abandoned pets, have taken on the new function of promoting spaying and neutering in order to achieve "zero pet population growth." A careful analysis needs to be made of the curious combination of material affluence and psychological impoverishment that underlies the "pet population explosion." If nothing else, it would be cruel to human beings to propose abolishing pets (or any other kind of neurotic adaptation) before we had diagnosed the "needs" which we use pets to try to satisfy.

But why abolish pets? Surely it is one thing to say that dogs should not be cruelly confined in too-small pens, even to argue that many species of dogs now used merely as pets were bred to hunt, retrieve, track, and otherwise be physically active in ways and to a degree that is increasingly incompatible with the living conditions of urban civilization; another thing to propose abolishing pet animals altogether.

But consider the way Singer discusses factory farming. Following the line taken by W. H. Thorpe, his emphasis falls repeatedly on the suffering systematically produced by:

conditions which completely suppress all or nearly all the *natural, instinctive urges and behavior patterns* characteristic of actions appropriate to the high degree of social organization *as found in the ancestral wild species and which have been little, if at all, bred out in the process of domestication.*[53]

---

[50] Singer stresses mainly that animals now raised for food need not be born in the first place, but he also appears to envisage some "herds of cattle and pigs . . . on large reservations, rather like our wildlife refuges" (pp. 253 ff.). This is apparently a "humane" alternative to the cruelty of sending domesticated animals back to the wild (see also Harris, pp. 104, 109). Sterilization would make both these alternatives unnecessary.

[51] Ibid., p. 25.

[52] Ibid.

[53] Singer, op. cit., p. 142, quoting from Thorpe's appendix to the Brambell Report; my emphasis.

Thus, animals who have never themselves known 'natural conditions' are still genetically programmed to move around, groom themselves, suck, care for their young, establish a social order, play, have sensory stimulation, etc. "Suffering"—and the gamut of "vices" and illnesses ranging from cannibalism among chickens to anemia and ulcers among calves—is thus a measure of the frustration of natural needs by the imposition of the "unnatural conditions" of factory farming.

Now, suppose it were possible to resolve this contradiction between natural needs and unnatural conditions by quickly and painlessly developing through selective breeding a new generation of farm animals that had no instinctive needs that the conditions of factory farming would frustrate; assume, in fact, that the new generation of farm animals would be perfectly adapted to the battery henhouse, the calf stall, the feedlot, etc. Would there be anything wrong with this way of resolving the problem of suffering?

It may be objected that we would still be killing animals needlessly, even if painlessly, and that this violates their right to life without justification (since we can get our protein directly from vegetables).[54] So let me limit the hypothetical case to the hen who is an egg-producer. Not being frustrated by her environment, she suffers none of the strain characteristic of battery hens today and therefore lives to a ripe old age. In short, let us bracket off the question of the morality of killing animals for food and stick to Singer's main line of argument: that suffering should be diminished. What, if anything, would be wrong with abolishing suffering through genetic engineering? And, if we feel that there is something wrong with it, can that "something" be accounted for within the Utilitarian calculus?

I suspect that most of the force of the case against factory farming stems not from the depiction of the pathos of animal suffering, but from variations on the central metaphor of "animal machines." Echoing, whether consciously or not, Marx's indictment of nineteenth-century capitalist industrialism for treating human workers as if they were "machines," Harrison and Singer continually reiterate that "animals are treated like machines" in practice, that the hen is even conceptualized in poultry industry publications as "an egg-producing machine," that "the sow is being turned into a living reproduction machine," etc.[55] Our indignation arises out of our sense of the inappropriateness, the perversity, the "unnaturalness" of treating animals as if they were machines when (Descartes' view to the contrary) there is ample evidence (including all the signs of suffering and "unnatural" behavior) that they are not. But now suppose that we can breed animals that behave *as if* they were

---

[54] Regan, op. cit., p. 204, makes this objection to the proposal that we "desensitize animals so that they don't feel any pain, even in the most barbarous surroundings" (cf. Singer, op. cit., p. 24). Whether and under what circumstances killing (as distinct from causing suffering) is wrong within the framework of utilitarian ethics is, of course, a much-argued issue. See, e.g., R. Stephen Talmage, "Utilitarianism and the Morality of Killing," *Philosophy,* Vol. XLVII, No. 179 (January 1972).

[55] Singer, op. cit., ch. III, esp. pp. 98, 108, 125; Harrison, *Animal Machines, passim.*

machines and seem quite content in the conditions of factory farming. I do not believe that this would fully satisfy us, however much it might suffice by Utilitarian criteria. The plight of "animal machines" on "factory farms" arouses us not so much because we disapprove of unnecessary suffering or pain (though, other things being equal, we tend to do so), but because we react indignantly to the spectacle of external mechanical conditions being imposed upon natural entities that have their own internal structures, needs, and potentialities. We feel that such an imposition is oppressive, that it censors all but one potentiality, reducing multi-faceted beings to a kind of economic "one-dimensionality," the unnaturalness of which is shown by the appearance of all kinds of unintended side-effects of an abnormal or neurotic character. Solving the problem by engineering away the needs that are frustrated by the conditions of oppression seems like cheating; it is wrong not because it is painful but because it is—well, "unnatural." We experience the same kind of resistance to the idea of engineering away the sources of human social discontent by genetic manipulation, brain surgery, electric shock treatments, or intensive drug therapy.

But the situation is more complicated. While Thorpe and Singer stress the genetic continuity between wild boars and domestic pigs, other writers emphasize the extent to which domestication has produced more variation at the expense of obscuring the basic types in which genetic diversity is grounded, has made animals less intelligent, less alert, less physically strong, more dependent, more infantile.[56] We may agree with Thorpe and Singer that *even* the instincts of domesticated animals are cruelly frustrated by the conditions of factory farming. But we need not on that account mistake a cow for the wild ancestor from which it has degenerated. Not only are the conditions of factory farming unnatural and cruel when judged by the needs of farm animals, domesticated farm animals are themselves unnatural and debased when judged by the standards of their wild ancestors and their wild brethren. If we should eliminate the conditions imposed by factory farming because they are unnatural, I suggest that we should go a step further and eliminate domesticated animals themselves because they are unnatural. Singer's reforms would, in effect, take a giant stride towards the realization of that objective. The major remaining obstacle would be the institution of the pet, the abolition of which would probably be difficult to justify on purely Utilitarian grounds and might necessitate our thinking more explicitly in terms of the liberation of nonhuman nature in general from the homocentric teleologies that we have imposed upon it—the liberation of nature from the status of human resource, human product, human caricature.[57]

---

[56] See Darwin, *Variation,* loc. cit.: Shepard, op. cit. ch. 1; Meeker, op. cit. pp. 122 ff., 151 ff.

[57] My view of the domestication of nonhuman animals clearly presupposes that it is a fundamentally coercive and exploitative institution. This view is not refuted by anyone's current feelings of having become the servant of his own cats. (The ironic dialectic of master and slave and the role reversals that it can involve have been analyzed from Hegel's *Phenomenology* to

The tragedy—or comedy—of the pet phenomenon lies in the frustration of the deeply felt human need to relate to the Other by the infantilizing and humanizing effects of domestication which negate the very Otherness with which we seek contact. Hence there is much truth in the claim that (non-human) pets function as substitutes for (human) children, (human) friends, (human) lovers, and (human) psychotherapists. But this is a poor substitute, both for real humans and, even more, for the kind of interspecies communication and communion among free and equal beings dreamed of from Plato to John Lilly.[58]

• • •

11. ECOLOGICAL RESISTANCE

Why did John Lilly let dolphins go? Why has the Greenpeace Foundation obstructed the Soviet whaling fleet? Why did I make a crusade out of saving some local coastal sage and chaparral from becoming another golf course? Why did Stone choose to devise a way of defending Mineral King in order to demonstrate "what a future consciousness might look like"? Why does Singer advocate, in effect, the abolition of domesticated farm and lab animals?

Joseph Losey's film "The Servant.") Nor is it refuted by imagining how much better off certain animals are in the servitude or captivity that they have become habituated to than they would be if we simply turned them loose to fend for themselves. Most domestication is exploitative at its foundation, whether the specific human purpose was originally an (human) economic or a (human) religious one. (For a statement of the case for the religious origins of the domestication of cattle, see Erich Isaac, "On the Domestication of Cattle," *Science,* Vol. 137 [1962], 195–204). The major difference is that domestication occurring originally for religious purposes is even less defensible now, since the symbolization involved has withered away. In cases of possible "self-domestication" or at least cooperation in a mutual process (e.g., by dogs), the relationship becomes exploitative when humans begin to manipulate canine gene pools to "improve the breed," i.e., for purposes of (human) esthetics, (human) sport, and/or (human) profit.

[58] For some inadvertent insights into the person/pet symbiosis, see Boris Levinson, *Pet-Oriented Child Psychotherapy* Springfield, Il.: Thomas, 1969). Cf. Plato, *Statesman,* 272b-c; *Lilly on Dolphins,* loc. cit. Paul Shepard suggests that "The social-psychological needs of the human individual to know and to participate, to be linked in some way to the 'other', to the reality of true wild species. . ." could be served by the formation of "human associations devoted to each species of animal" which would study the animal, monitor its status, and engage in "the political work necessary for the protection of each club's particular totem species" (Shepard, op. cit., pp. 266 ff.). Examples of such associations already in existence include Friends of the Sea Otter, the Committee for the Preservation of the Tule Elk, the Human/Dolphin Foundation, and the Desert Tortoise Council. I possess a membership card proclaiming that "John Rodman is a colleague of Project JONAH and responsible for the protection and understanding of all species of Cetacea." I do not, however, find that this satisfies my "social-psychological needs" to know and be linked to the Other in a participatory way. Jonah at least penetrated the belly of the whale.

It would be foolhardy to try to answer with a simple formula. We are, as Stone suggests, at a curious point in time when actions tend to be rationalized in obsolete or otherwise inappropriate terms. Unlike the Pythagoreans, we lack a suitable myth that comprehends and integrates our feelings and perceptions, articulates our intuitions, allows our actions ritual status, and makes us intelligible to ourselves in terms of an alignment with a larger order of things.[59] Camus's portrait of Sisyphus, continually pushing the rock up the mountain only to have it roll down again, is a *tour de force* that we can admire but not imitate for long. "Absurdity," after all, may characterize the relationship between human effort and the universe only in cases where man has chosen to work against rather than with the course of Nature (symbolized here by the force of gravity).[60]

Instead of trying to fabricate a mythology out of the materials of contemporary biology, let us instead pay attention to the patterns of metaphor already present in the language of those who protest the exploitation and liquidation of nonhuman nature. Lilly, Singer, and others are prone to invoke analogies with Nazi concentration camps, the Nürnberg trials, etc., as if our treatment of nonhuman nature involved acts that were crimes whether they violated established human law or not. The function of the Nazi analogy, I assume, is that it associates the extermination of a species with the attempted "liquidation" of a people, experimentation on "subhuman" animals in the name of Science with experimentation on humans classified as "subhuman" in the name of Science, crimes against Humanity with crimes against Nature, one group of "war crimes" with another, while carrying connotations of that which is unqualifiedly evil, wrong, atrocious, abominable, and absolutely forbidden. It is comforting to think of the Nazi experience as a pathological deviation from the course of modern history, but I suggest that it is rather a caricature of the ethos of modernity, that it takes to their logical conclusion two powerful themes in modern society—the ontological and moral dualism and the crusade to replace divesity with monoculture. It is not always realized that Hitler's conceptualization of Jews as subhuman animals went hand-in-hand with his vision of man's relation to nonhuman nature as a war of conquest culminating in the enslavement or liquidation of all competing forms of life down to the level of micro-organisms.

> The struggle against the great beasts is ended, but it is being inexorably carried on against the tiny creatures—against bacteria and bacilli. There is no . . . reconciliation on this score: it is either you or I, life or death, either extermination or servitude.[61]

---

[59] See my comment, "The Other Side of Ecology in Ancient Greece", *Inquiry,* Vol. 19, No. 1 (Spring, 1976).

[60] Cf. Albert Camus, *The Myth of Sisyphus* (1942) (New York: Vintage, 1959), pp. 88–91.

[61] Adolf Hitler, speech in München, 2 April 1927, reported in *Völkischer Beobachter,* 5 April 1927.

Hitler's view is merely an extreme version of the modern but pre-ecological "germ theory of disease," [62] and it is closely related to the widespread tendency to classify nonhuman animals into "good" ones and "bad" ones and to demand policies of "predator control"—a euphemism for the liquidation of wolves, coyotes, etc. In this kind of mentality there is no appreciation of diversity, no perception of "others" as having a right to exist, a niche to fill, a role to play. The insane vision of an Aryan Europe purged of Jewish influence is intimately bound up with the equally insane vision of a humanized planet on which all other species have been either enslaved or liquidated.

The key to the myth that I see emerging is the principle of metaphoric mirroring in accordance with which certain archetypal patterns—such as the struggle to defend diversity against the juggernaut of monoculture—are seen to be operative in several spheres, e.g., on a biological, a social, and a psychological level. Within this frame of reference, acts of ecological resistance do not stem so much from calculations of enlightened self-interest (whether of the individual, the group, or the species), or from a conscientious sense of moral or legal obligation to see that justice is done to others, as from a felt need to resist the repression, censorship, or liquidation of potentialities that lie within both human and nonhuman nature, and to liberate suppressed potentialities from the yoke of domestication and threatened extinction. From this perspective it matters little whether the primary victims are cooperatively organizing their own resistance. That pattern is carried over from the analogy of human liberation movements; it seems inapplicable in the case of most nonhuman animals and totally irrelevant in the case of, say, a wild river that is being dammed by the Bureau of Reclamation. The point is that the natural flow of the river is interrupted, diverted, distorted by the dam; the river struggles against the dam like an instinct struggles against an inhibition or a social movement struggles against a restrictive institution. The threat perceived by the human "Friends of the River" who try to prevent the dam's being built in the first place (or by "the monkey wrench gang" who blow up the dam after it has been constructed) is the threat of wildness being tamed, of a natural process interrupted and distorted, of the "individuality" of a natural being made to conform to an artificial pattern imposed upon it, of repression in the most general sense. [63] The threat to the river is no less a threat to the river for being also a threat to social and psychic diversity. In its broadest signification, the proposed dam is a threat to the very nature of

---

[62] On the view that virulence lies "solely within the microbes themselves" vs. the "ecological" view that microbes are an integral part of our environment (and our own bodies), so that the issue is not how to eliminate them but how to maintain a healthy equilibrium with them, see René Dubos, "Second Thoughts on the Germ Theory," *Scientific American,* Vol. 192 (May 1955), reprinted in *The Subversive Science,* loc. cit.

[63] Friends of the River is a California-based organization that opposes further extension of the dam-and-reservoir monoculture onto the wild rivers that are left. For a semi-fictional treatment of more violent (because more desperate) actions, see Edward Abbey's novel, *The Monkey Wrench Gang* (Philadelphia: Lippincott, 1975).

things. The resistance of a single person to that threat has thus a multidimensional depth of meaning impossible to translate into the language of mere self-interest or mere justice.

Let me offer for contemplation an exemplary character from the ecological resistance movement. My choice may seem surprising at first, for John Stuart Mill may seem anachronistic or irrelevant. But my Mill is not so much the encyclopedic philosopher whose *Logic* and *Political Economy* became standard Victorian textbooks, or even the Utilitarian who remained true to Bentham's inclusion of sentient animals within the sphere of morals and legislation, but the lesser-known mountain climber, "botanizer," and "lover of Nature" who indignantly protested the Royal Horticultural Society's contest for the two best herbaria collected in each county in England as an event that would make 1864 the last year that many already-rare species of wild flora would exist.[64] It was this same Mill who, as political/social theorist, so eloquently defended human "individuality" and "diversity" against the growing social pressures for conformity in belief and conduct,[65] the same Mill who authored the classic feminist tract of the nineteenth century, not only championing women's right to participate in public life but diagnosing the patriarchal family as the major agency of sexual stereotyping.[66] Finally, it was this same Mill who, as autobiographer, recorded for posterity the classic case study of a sensitive person trained to operate as an analytic thinking machine who "died" and was "reborn" through rediscovering the capacity for feeling, intuition, imagination, the enjoyment of poetry and natural beauty, the ability to cry and to contemplate—without losing the capacity for rational analysis or practical action.[67]

It would not, I think, violate the spirit of the term to speak of Mill as having displayed an "ecological" sensibility.[68] His views of psyche, polity, and cosmos all have a common structure. Diversity and richness of potentiality are natural conditions endangered by oppressive monoculture on all levels, and each level is a metaphor of the others. Thus Mill's feminism expressed itself both in the liberation of his own "feminine" side and in his attack upon

---

[64] See Mill's letter of 26 January 1864, published in the *Gardener's Chronicle and Agricultural Gazette,* printed by Anna J. Mill under the misleading title, "J.S.M., Conservationist" (*The Mill Newsletter,* Vol. X, No. 1 Winter 1975, 2 ff.). For the memorials of protest signed by prominent botanists and submitted by Mill to the Council of the Royal Horticultural Society, see Mill, *Later Letters* (*Collected Works,* Vol. XV, University of Toronto Press 1972, p. 937). Since neither Mill's *Autobiography* nor Michael St. John Packe's biography (*The Life of John Stuart Mill,* [London: Secker & Warburg, 1954]) contains more than occasional mention of Mill's passionate "botanizing" expeditions, the best source is Mill's correspondence. The characterization of Mill as a "lover of Nature" and an "enthusiastic lover of the pursuit [of botany]" comes from the obituary of Mill published in the *Gardeners' Chronicle,* 17 May 1873 (quoted by Anna Mill, p. 2).

[65] Mill, *On Liberty* (1859), esp. ch. III, "Of Individuality."

[66] Mill, *The Subjection of Women* (1869). See especially the Crofts Classics edition (Arlington Heights, Ill.: AHM, 1976), with an introductory essay by Sue Mansfield.

[67] Mill, *Autobiography,* Ch. V, "A Crisis in My Mental History."

[68] On "ecology" as a "perspective" rather than a "science," see Paul Shepard's Introduction to *The Subversive Science,* loc. cit.

the subjection of women as a social group. His defense of human individuality was expressed in the contrast between "a machine to be built after a model, and set to do exactly the work prescribed for it" and 'a tree, which requires to grow and develop itself on all sides, according to the tendency of the inward forces which make it a living thing.' [69]

Mill's prophetic vision of a steady-state society, limited in population and devoting itself more to cultural than to economic growth, emerged out of his nightmare anticipation of what could occur if "the unlimited increase of wealth and population" should continue to the point where we would be left to inhabit "a world from which solitude has been extirpated," a world:

> with nothing left to the spontaneous activity of nature; with every rood of land brought into cultivation, which is capable of growing food for human beings; every flowery waste or natural pasture ploughed up, all quadrupeds or birds which are not domesticated for man's use exterminated as his rivals for food, every hedgerow or superfluous tree rooted out, and scarcely a place left where a wild shrub or flower could grow without being eradicated as a weed in the name of improved agriculture. [70]

Such a world, Mill suggests, is "not good for man" (not to mention for the flora and the other fauna). But what does it mean to say that a totally humanized world would diminish us as human beings, to imply that we need nonhuman nature, that we draw sustenance from it, commune with it, find inspiration in its example? Does it not indirectly affirm the intrinsic value of the nonhuman realm, or at least suggest that common principles, common values, animate both it and us and that their loss in either realm is a loss of value?

Exactly what is so frightening about the prospective death of Nature? Three possible answers occur. One is suggested by Mill's metaphoric representation of human beings as trees: what happens when trees become uprooted? In René Dubos's version:

> Man is still of the earth, earthy, notwithstanding all the technological and medical advances that superficially seem to dissociate him from his evolutionary past. As

---

[69] *On Liberty,* Ch. III. See also Mill's critique of the "hothouse" mode of socialization that distorted the growth of the natural tendencies of women (*The Subjection of Women,* ch. 1). I do not mean to suggest that Mill was fully aware of the pattern that I have sketched, or that there were no discordant notes. A completion of this portrait will have to deal with Mill's essay on "Nature," which critiques the "argument from nature" in moral philosophy and is, at least on the surface, inconsistent with the pattern that I have outlined.

For some contemporary examples of writers who have perceived the same principles operating in different realms of the ecology of experience, see Joseph W. Meeker, "Mother Earth and Women's Lib" (*Journal of Environmental Education,* Summer 1974) and John E. Cantlon, "The Stability of Natural Populations and Their Sensitivity to Technology" (in *Diversity and Stability in Ecological Systems,* Brookhaven Symposia in Biology, No. 22, 1969, especially the "censorship" metaphor on p. 201).

[70] J. S. Mill, *Principles of Political Economy* (1848 and later), "Of the Stationary State" (*Collected Works,* Vol. III, [Toronto: University of Toronto Press, 1965], pp. 752–57, especially p. 756.

happened to Anteus of the Greek legend, his strength will probably wane if he loses contact with the biological ground from which he emerged and which still feeds him, physically and emotionally.[71]

The second possibility is that external nature, for all its historicity in the perspective of geologic and evolutionary time, provides a "regulative idea" of an ultimate and eternal reality against which we measure the ephemeral, the superficial, and the false. Thus political societies have always tended to articulate their structure as reflecting that of the cosmic order: this is as true for modern Newtonian constitutions as for archaic theocracies. On the level of exceptional individuals, we see throughout recorded history the ritual pattern of a withdrawal from society to the solitude of wilderness in order to "get into another space" and make contact with a different order of time, to transcend the demands of workaday and family life, the timeclock, expectations of respectability, and even the moral/legal consciousness, in order to "take one's bearings" and discover who one really is and what one really needs to do, and then to return to society.[72] In this respect Nature lies "beyond good and evil," which is why the attempt to bring it within the framework of the moral/legal consciousness is ultimately so perverse.

The third possibility is simply that the very otherness of nature, together with the diversity characteristic of natural ecosystems, provides for us an objective model of alternative possibilities and potentialities within the human psyche and human society, and that the loss or suppression of natural diversity "out there" tends to provoke in us an anxiety as if we felt increasingly trapped in a particular condition and could envision no alternatives.

These three possibilities connect in the notion of human nature as grounded in an order of biological diversity that is increasingly threatened by monoculture, so that every potentiality seems an endangered species, and every extinction of a species seems an impoverishment of human life. The struggle for the liberation of nature, both human and nonhuman, from the threat of totalitarian monoculture or one-dimensionality goes on at all levels. To that extent, as Singer senses, there are many "liberation" movements and they are ultimately all allies, for the same principles are at stake in every sphere. Hence, action on any one level bears a symbolic as well as a literal meaning, and it is likely that only some intuitive awareness that one's actions have symbolic depth—that defending diversity in one situation affirms a general principle applicable in many realms—can sustain the struggle for liberation in a world where the outcome seems so doubtful. In that respect I believe Singer's excessive preoccupation with the effects of action and his dismissal of the "*merely* symbolic" dimension of conduct to be a mistake.[73] In the

[71] Dubos, op. cit., p. 279.

[72] Thoreau's *Walden,* especially the chapter entitled "Economy," makes this pattern pretty explicit. Cf. Leo Marx, "Pastoral Ideals and City Troubles" (in *The Fitness of Man's Environment: Smithsonian Annual II,* Washington, D.C. 1968).

[73] Singer, op. cit., pp. 173 ff.; emphasis added.

present situation, it is often necessary to act when the chance of having much effect seems negligible or nonexistent. I doubt that even many practicing vegetarians are sustained in their faith and their ritual by calculating how much animal suffering they are preventing by their personal abstention from meat-eating, or by the effect of their example on others. Kohlberg's young son held out for six months because he felt that killing animals to eat them was "bad," not because he thought his abstention would significantly reduce suffering or save lives. In certain situations, acting or refusing to act is a matter of preserving one's own integrity, in the dual sense of the harmony within one's personality and the harmony between oneself and the larger order of things.

To depict an action in terms of "liberation," to depict it in terms of resisting oppression, and to depict it in terms of preserving integrity express different aspects (and sometimes stages) of the same phenomenon. The nonhuman world is full of what Mill called "inward forces," potentialities striving to actualize themselves; we can ally ourselves with those tendencies and resist the efforts of other human beings to obstruct them. In doing so we can speak (with Leopold) of the integrity of natural ecosystems, more familiarly of the integrity of the personality, and without any violence or mystery of the alignment of these two dimensions of experience as also involving a kind of integrity.

"Nature, too, awaits the revolution!", writes Marcuse, stressing the "receptive" capacity to "see things *in their own right,*" as having their own character and direction independent of us.[74] Given the history of homocentric imperialism the emphasis is a valid one. Yet a fully ecological sensibility knows with Carl Sandburg that:

> There is an eagle in me and a mockingbird . . . and the eagle flies among the Rocky Mountains of my dreams and fights among the Sierra crags of what I want . . . and the mockingbird warbles in the underbrush of my Chattanoogas of hope, gushes over the blue Ozark foothills of my wishes—And I got the eagle and the mockingbird from the wilderness.[75]

The "receptive" capacity by itself does not lead to action. Action is made possible by the recognition that, beyond the perception of otherness lies the perception of psyche, polity, and cosmos as metaphors of one another, and that the ancient dictum to "live according to Nature" now translates into Thoreau's maxim, "Let your life be a counter friction to stop the machine."[76]

[74] Marcuse, op. cit., p. 74.
[75] "Wilderness," in *The Complete Poems of Carl Sandburg* (New York: Harcourt Brace Jovanovich, 1970), p. 100.
[76] Thoreau, "Civil Disobedience" (1848). In Owen Thomas (ed.). *Walden and Civil Disobedience* (New York: Norton, 1966), p. 231.

SELECTED BIBLIOGRAPHY:
HUMANS AND THE NONHUMAN ENVIRONMENT

Blackstone, William T. (ed.). *Philosophy and Environmental Crisis.* Athens, Georgia: The University of Georgia Press, 1974.

Clarke, Ronald O., and Peter C. List (eds.). *Environmental Spectrum.* New York: D. Van Nostrand Company, 1974.

Goodpaster, Kenneth. "On Being Morally Considerable." *The Journal of Philosophy,* 75:6 (1978), 308.

———— and K. M. Sayne (eds.). *Ethics and Problems of the 21st Century.* Notre Dame, Indiana: University of Notre Dame Press, 1979.

Margolis, Joseph. "Animals Have No Rights and Are Not the Equal of Humans." *Philosophic Exchange,* 1:5 (1974), 119.

Narveson, Jan. "Animal Rights." *Canadian Journal of Philosophy,* VII: 1 (1977), 161.

Regan, Tom, and Peter Singer (eds.). *Animal Rights and Human Obligations.* Englewood Cliffs, N.J.: Prentice-Hall, Inc., 1976.

————. *And All That Dwell Therein: Essays on Animals Rights and Environmental Ethics.* Berkeley and Los Angeles: University of California Press, 1982.

————. *The Case for Animal Rights.* Berkeley and Los Angeles: University of California Press, 1983.

Rolston, H. "Is There an Ecological Ethic?" *Ethics,* 85:2 (1975), 93.

Sagoff, Mark. "On Preserving the Natural Environment." *Yale Law Journal,* 84 (1974), 205.

————. "Do We Need a Land Use Ethic?" *Environmental Ethics,* 3:4 (1981), 293.

Scherer, Donald, and Thomas Attig (eds.). *Ethics and the Environment.* Englewood Cliffs, N.J.: Prentice-Hall, Inc., 1983.

Singer, Peter. *Animal Liberation.* New York: New York Review Press, 1975.

Stone, Christopher. "Should Trees Have Standing? Toward Legal Rights for Natural Objects." *Southern California Law Review,* 45 (1972), 450.

Taylor, Paul W. "The Ethics of Respect for Nature." *Environmental Ethics,* 3:3 (1981), 197.